Full Circle

Full Circle

Ellen MacArthur

MICHAEL JOSEPH
an imprint of
PENGUIN BOOKS

MICHAEL JOSEPH

Published by the Penguin Group
Penguin Books Ltd, 80 Strand, London WC2R ORL, England
Penguin Group (USA) Inc., 375 Hudson Street, New York, New York 10014, USA
Penguin Group (Canada), 90 Eglinton Avenue East, Suite 700, Toronto, Ontario, Canada M4P 2Y3
(a division of Pearson Penguin Canada Inc.)
Penguin Ireland, 25 St Stephen's Green, Dublin 2, Ireland (a division of Penguin Books Ltd)
Penguin Group (Australia), 250 Camberwell Road, Camberwell, Victoria 3124, Australia
(a division of Pearson Australia Group Pty Ltd)
Penguin Books India Pvt Ltd, 11 Community Centre, Panchsheel Park, New Delhi – 110 017, India
Penguin Group (NZ), 67 Apollo Drive, Rosedale, North Shore 0632, New Zealand
(a division of Pearson New Zealand Ltd)
Penguin Books (South Africa) (Pty) Ltd, 24 Sturdee Avenue, Rosebank, Johannesburg 2196, South Africa

Penguin Books Ltd, Registered Offices: 80 Strand, London WC2R ORL, England

www.penguin.com

First published 2010

1

Copyright © Ellen MacArthur, 2010

The moral right of the author has been asserted

Printed in Great Britain by Clays Ltd, St Ives plc

A CIP catalogue record for this book is available from the British Library

Hardback edition ISBN: 978–0–718–14863–8
Trade paperback edition ISBN: 978–0–718–15757–9

www.greenpenguin.co.uk

Mixed Sources
Product group from well-managed
forests and other controlled sources
www.fsc.org Cert no. SA-COC-1592
© 1996 Forest Stewardship Council
FSC

Penguin Books is committed to a sustainable future
for our business, our readers and our planet.
The book in your hands is made from paper
certified by the Forest Stewardship Council.

'If you want to build a ship, don't drum up people together to collect wood and don't assign them tasks and work, but rather teach them to long for the endless immensity of the sea.'

Antoine de Saint-Exupéry

Contents

All line drawings are by the author; all photos are from the author's collection or Offshore Challenges unless stated otherwise.

First inset

1. Me with my Great Granddad.
2. With my brothers, Lewis and Fergus.
3. My Mum, older brother Lewis, Grandpa and Gran, younger brother Fergus and, at the front, me and Mac.
4. The grid that I made to mark off every penny I saved towards buying my first boat.
5. *Threpn'y bit.*
6. On board *Iduna*, aged eighteen, ready to set sail on my first big adventure – a solo trip around Britain.
7. The Vendée Globe, 2000. (Jacques Vapillon)
8. A shot taken moments after leaving Kingfisher. (Michel Birot)
9. During the Route du Rhum in 2002. (Jacques Vapillon)
10. In Guadeloupe at the finish of the Route du Rhum 2002. (Marie-Pierre Tricart)
11 and 12. Two images demonstrating the fragility of multihulls. (Gilles Martin-Raget)
13, 14 and 15. The capsize of *Foncia* during the Challenge Mondial Assistance, 2003. (Yvan Zedda)
16. *Kingfisher II*. (Jacques Vapillon)

17. The fantastic crew of *Kingfisher II*. (DPPI)
18. The makeshift mast, which allowed us to sail for Australia.
19. The Southern Ocean.
20 and 21. Photos taken during the build process of Mobi.

Second inset

22. Sailing Mobi for the first time. (Thierry Martinez)
23. Passing Cape Horn on the training sail with Loik and Mark.
24. Managing resources on board Mobi. (Billy Black / DPPI)
25 and 26. Setting off from New York on the West–East crossing.
(Billy Black / DPPI)
27. A life of lists!
28 and 29. Two images of the kit that I would take with me on the
solo attempt.
30. Looking out of the window in Falmouth towards the dock and
the boat, before setting off.
31. We're off … (Thierry Martinez)
32, 33, 34 and 35. Snapshots taken during the Round the World
Voyage, from fixing generators to building snowmen.
36, 37, 38 and 39. Images of exhaustion during the record attempt.
40. A visit from HMS *Gloucester*. (Royal Navy)
41. A Tornado flies above Mobi as we pass the Falklands. (1435
Squadron RAF)
42. A satellite image showing both Mobi (the orange dot) and the
remnants of the sun's light, setting in the west.
43. Reunited with Mum and Dad at the finish. (Liot Vapillon / DPPI)
44. On the podium at Falmouth. (Carlo Borlenghi / SEA and SEE /
DPPI)

Third inset

45. Keroman submarine base.
46. An abandoned fishing vessel, the *Victor Pleven*.
47. The ship's graveyard in Kerhervy on the Blavet river.
48. Mobi sits in front of the Shanghai skyline.
49 and 50. South Georgia.

51. Grytviken, a derelict whaling station established in 1904.

52. Grytviken in the 1960s. (Dave Wheeler)

53. Photograph of Solveig Jacobsen on the Grytviken flensing plan, taken by Magistrate Edward Binnie in 1916.

54, 55, 56, 57, 58, 59, 60 and 61. Images taken from our time on Bird Island.

62, 63 and 64. The exciting but demanding challenge of building a home.

65 and 66. Floss.

67, 68, 69, 70, 71 and 72. Images from our canal adventure.

Fourth inset

73. The annual Round the Island Race, 2007. (Rick Tomlinson)

74. IDEC, the boat in which Francis Joyon beat my record. (Jean Marie Liot)

75. With Francis at the finish of his record attempt (Thierry Martinez)

76 and 77. With Greg Homann on board 'Foxy Lady' on the Archipelago Raid. (Thierry Martinez)

78, 79, 80, 81, 82 and 83. Sailing with the Ellen MacArthur Trust. (Gleber Rodriguez; On Edition; Ellen MacArthur Trust; Maxine Duggins)

84. From an early age I can remember visiting farm sales in Derbyshire with my Dad.

85. With Eamonn, working the dogs.

86. Floss and 'Norm'.

87, 88, 89 and 90. My journey towards setting up the Ellen MacArthur Foundation has led to many unique and interesting experiences. (Steve Thearle; Renault)

91. A graph showing the increasing gap between the amount of oil we use and the amount which has been discovered. (Richard Crookes)

92. A diagram showing the difference between a linear and a circular economy. (Richard Crookes)

93 and 94. The house finally taking shape.

95. My Nan, on her graduation day. (*Derby Evening Telegraph*)

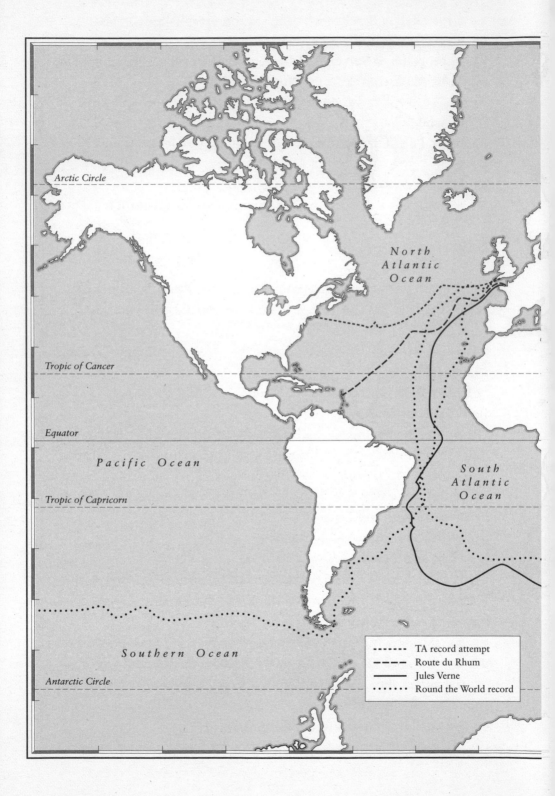

Arctic Circle

North
Atlantic
Ocean

Tropic of Cancer

Equator

Pacific Ocean

South
Atlantic
Ocean

Tropic of Capricorn

Southern Ocean

Antarctic Circle

- - - - - TA record attempt
- - - Route du Rhum
——— Jules Verne
· · · · · Round the World record

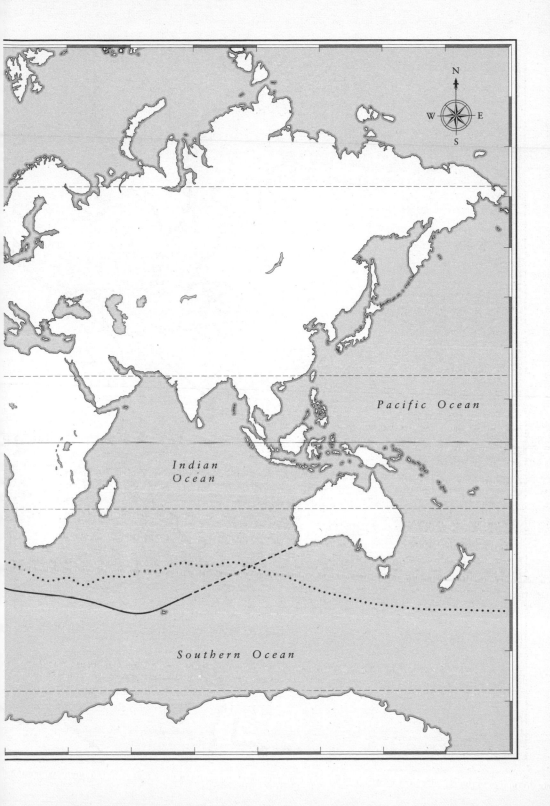

Pacific Ocean

Indian
Ocean

Southern Ocean

We travelled down to the dock very early on the morning of the start: in part to avoid the traffic, which inevitably builds up quickly, but also as I wanted to savour the atmosphere before the pontoons were smothered with people. The sea was flat as we drove along the beach, and the grey of the sky blended with the watery horizon to appear even more mystical and immense than I remembered. My mind was alive, flashing so many images back to me, like travelling through a gallery of time. The shapes of buildings on our right were the silhouettes which had marked my first ever landfall following an ocean crossing, and on our left was the beach on which I had swum in the days after as I dreamt of circling the globe. The *Nouch Sud*, the buoy marking the finish line of the Vendée Globe, floated silently in the distance, while the sea, quiet and flat, awaited the presence of twenty-six boats and their skippers who were about to make it their home. Even as the town uttered its first sounds of waking, there was a distinct air of nervous tension, and I could feel its familiar fingers rummaging around uncomfortably inside me once more.

Down on the pontoons, the skippers were feeling the pressure. Saying goodbyes, knowing that even if all went well it would be the last time they would hold their children and loved ones for three months, was almost too much for some. The looks on their faces said it all for me. In their eyes I could see those who had already made their farewells and were focused solely on the race and others still clinging on with the very ends of their fingertips, savouring every hug, smile and glance until the comfort of the land could be with them no more. Before the race had even begun they were holding back the tears as they dealt with the harsh reality that they were the cause of the unmaskable pain on the faces of those close to them together with the realization that their last moments of complete rest had passed until next year.

There were hundreds of thousands of people in Les Sables d'Olonne, and the atmosphere was electric. The air felt every bit as charged as it had in November 2000 when I was there with *Kingfisher* – I felt astonished that eight years had passed since then. Now, being older, I understood the event for what it really was and I was both intrigued and humbled to witness the excitement of the crowds and their reactions when they recognized one of the sailors.

Emotion, hope and silence were what I felt on the pontoons that morning. Not one person was raising their voice; no one was laughing. Hoards of people, all speaking in whispers as if at a wake. Only the isolated sessions of cheering stirred the atmosphere as each boat finally untied from the dock to leave.

Those who had never competed in the Vendée before were about to experience something truly remarkable; the journey down the mile-long channel, lined with crowds of people all willing them on with their adventure. Families, the old and the young, waving banners and cheering for each of the boats as they felt the 'finality' of their heading out to sea, to head to the bottom of the earth and back, solo, non-stop. There are few sights like it in the world. It's perhaps akin to the feeling in a football stadium – except that these sailors would soon be alone and a far cry away from the cheers of their fans. The contrast between that journey down the channel and their first night alone could not be more stark.

I looked out into the watery distance where the boats were all waiting to start; it was still grey and calm, and the sky and the sea seemed to merge as one. As I stared out the cluster of craft I could see began to blur as my eyes welled with tears . . . and time, just for a few minutes, seemed to stand utterly and totally still.

In that moment of emotion my heart knew why I wasn't going,

and as it was my heart which had sent me out there in the first place I put my faith in believing it. Perhaps it's like loving someone so much but knowing that you simply can't live with them any more – I don't know; but as I stood there watching the boats slip away I knew that the impossible had happened. My racing years were over.

Though I still felt as much in love with the sea as ever, something inside me had grown to eclipse that passion. I had experienced something three years before which made me see the world in a different light and, having seen that, I could not go on as before.

For me there was a much bigger race out there, and I had already crossed the start line . . .

Chapter One

I remember vividly how difficult I had found it leaving *Kingfisher* in February 2001. As I climbed over her guardrails, it felt like having a part of me I no longer knew how to live without torn out of me. It was not the fact that I had spent three months alone, but ironically the fact that I was stepping from the safety of her deck into an unfamiliar new world where hundreds of thousands of people were chanting my name. It was as if the second I stepped off her I had reached my destination, and there I was, standing uncomfortably at a junction, having no idea which path was next. The world around me was more turbulent and unpredictable than the wildest seas I had encountered deep in the Southern Ocean, and just when I expected to be caught by the strong, familiar arms of life, nothing happened.

Every minute of the Vendée had been a day in a dream. I had treasured every sunset, storm, high and low as if it was the last moment of my life. Though it had been a rollercoaster of emotions with the highs higher than you could ever imagine, and lows to match, I knew exactly why I was doing it. I had spent ninety-four incredible days at sea and had been in my element. I was twenty-four and I'd come second in the most high-profile solo ocean race in the world. But despite this, the moment which should have been pure elation as I crossed the finish line was shadowed in fear. There were two fears: the realization that the normality I craved, and had left behind on that same dock some three months before, was simply not there any longer; and the fear brought by the end of something, the end of a dream which had paved the path of my life in every conceivable way until that moment.

When I was a child my dreams hadn't been about crossing a finish line, or standing before a cheering crowd; they had always been about simply being out on the water. Ever since the age of four I'd dreamt of being at sea, and as I had grown up my dreams had grown with me. Sailing *Cabaret*, my Auntie Thea's boat, had been my first experience. My elder brother, Lewis, and I loved it so much that, bizarrely for a family from landlocked Derbyshire, our annual family exodus became sailing on the south coast. Nan (Mum's Mum, who was in her late sixties) came too, and when my younger brother, Fergus, and Mac the dog came along that made seven of us and a dog on board a boat that was essentially designed for four!

As we hoisted our sails, just simple triangles of fabric, I was riddled with a restless excitement. For the first time in my life I felt a boat come alive: the wind filled our sails, and we began to move through the water. Though I was experiencing this through the eyes of a child, I knew that, for the first time in my life, somehow, I had touched freedom. Dependent on nothing but the elements, I was convinced we could sail for ever, and to a country child used to running free in the fields 'for ever' felt like the biggest field imaginable. Almost endless, the ocean held more excitement and adventure than I could cram into my tiny head, and as each year passed I read everything I could get my hands on to learn more about it.

As its powerful lure began to eclipse my rural life, I realized the only way to overcome my frustration was to channel my savings into buying a boat. From the age of eight, I saved every penny I could, and by the time I had control of my dinner money, I was saving all but the 4p I spent on beans and 4p I spent on mash (with free gravy!) in my clear blue money box Blu-tacked firmly to my radiator. Hand-drawn on a piece of paper above was a grid containing 100 squares, and each time I reached a pound, I would drop the coins in and cross one off. When I'd saved £100 I took a celebratory trip to the building society, though much to the horror of the cashier, as all those coins took a lot of counting!

I named my first boat *Threpn'y bit*, but I was soon to realize that years' more saving were needed if I was to be able to afford to put her in a sailing club by the water. Even so, many happy hours were spent sitting in the garden, dreaming of the adventures we would one day have together.

But despite sailing taking over my world, what was around me in Derbyshire was quite different. Our home was a smallholding, with the sound of chickens and ducks outside as opposed to the sound of waves breaking on a shore. At school, too, sailing was a remote concept, and not even I could see then how a life at sea could ever materialize. Loving animals, and being surrounded by them from an early age, I felt drawn towards the idea of being a vet. I spent a week doing work experience at a practice near by and loved it; it seemed like a fulfilling career. Being around animals, particularly on the farms, was hard work, but it appealed hugely to me. Spending time with the farmers and being out in the countryside suited me far more than being stuck in any office, and for three years I spent virtually every Saturday there, helping out to gain experience.

Veterinary Science is one of the hardest university courses to get into, and, as my school had advised me not to bother applying, I'd decided to work my socks off to prove them wrong. However, despite my determination the situation was taken out of my control as I was struck down with glandular fever just a few months before my A-Level exams. It was a real blow; however, ironically it turned out to be one of the biggest turning points in my life. Though with my illness one door closed, another, previously hidden, opened. At 2 a.m. one morning there was a sailing programme on the TV, and, after borrowing my Nan's video recorder to tape it, I was able, despite my horizontal state, to watch images of people racing round the world. I remember vividly the opening sequence of images, with boats, sailors and the ocean, and in one split second I made the irrevocable decision that sailing was to become my future.

I knew I had no choice but to follow my heart, and before I had even finished taking my A-Level exams I had spread my wings and was gone. I began by teaching courses at a nautical school in Hull. The Humber was a wide, windswept, tidal river, but I loved it.

At eighteen I found myself working with the guys from the barges, tugs and workboats, as well as with people who wished to learn to sail and navigate. In my enthusiasm I had dived in the deep end and I grew up quickly. I was teaching a mixture of disciplines such as the splicing of tug tow lines as thick as my leg, identifying lights on ships at night and how the wind and tides worked. Some of my students were three times my age, but I put all I had into the teaching, and as we worked together with a great level of two-way banter I soon became one of them. During the courses we'd all go to the pub at lunchtime, and I especially relished the chance to chat with the guys from the barges and hear both sobering and amusing stories of their fathers and grandfathers who had all worked on the river. I felt at home with them, and they were real people. Their trade was one of the few still going on the river, as the fishing fleet Hull was once so famous for was now reduced to a few faded photographs and memories. I realized then just how much I enjoyed people's company – something that would make my subsequent journey more challenging.

In the spring of 1995, just weeks after my unexpected win of the Young Sailor of the Year award for passing my Yachtmaster qualification aged eighteen, I decided to embark on my first solo journey. It was not long after buying my third boat, *Iduna*, that I hatched a plan to sail round Britain. It was a huge challenge for me, and the feeling I had, aged eighteen, as I sailed out of those lock gates at Hull Marina was one of the most powerful ever. Behind me on the dock was the past; my two brothers, Mum and Dad, and many of my friends waving goodbye, and beyond me was the future, the wide expanse of the river Humber leading out to sea. I felt suspended in time between the past which was slowly slipping from view behind me on the dockside and the future which lay ahead. Just waiting to unfold.

I had never sailed solo before; nor had I spent more than a few hours sailing the tiny *Iduna*. I was nervous, but excited. Everything surrounding me felt new. Spending four and a half months in my own company was a totally alien experience for me, but the journey gave me confidence, both in myself and in my sailing ability. It also introduced me to the wider world outside Derbyshire and Hull. I talked to people, learnt from people, and saw more of the UK than

I had in my previous eighteen years. I relished the challenge and loved the experience of sailing at night, seeing new places and managing my little world of the boat. I explored, found tiny anchorages, frightened myself. Everything about the journey fascinated me, and every decision, repair or manoeuvre was part of a huge puzzle that I was relishing the opportunity to solve. I returned, not as the shy girl who had left, but as a young woman who was learning how to handle being alone, how to deal with fatigue and stress, and how to make life-and-death decisions.

It was an indication of what was to come. Before I had finished my Round Britain I was already setting my sights on the next challenge, and the following year, on my twentieth birthday, I left Boston, USA, to sail two-handed across the Atlantic. Things were changing in my life more quickly than I could keep up with, and each breath and step I took was a progression towards my ultimate goal. Now firmly etched in my mind, the goal of sailing round the world for the first time felt possible, and part of this was due to a chance meeting with a man called Mark Turner.

Mark worked in the marine industry and appeared to know everyone. He had decided his next sailing challenge would be the Mini-Transat, a race I too was keen on, and in January 1997 – eight months before the start – Mark and I formed a partnership which was to become instrumental in everything I achieved on the water. Offshore Challenges, our company, was to become the vehicle through which my career unfolded.

My enthusiasm and Mark's communication skills created a powerful partnership. After we made it, elated, to the finish of the Mini Transat, Mark decided to step back from sailing and take on the role of managing our project on land. Our shared goal was to find the funding for a competitive entry into the Vendée Globe, and to do this we almost had to achieve the impossible. We had nothing bar enthusiasm and the most intense ambition to share our project with the world, but that was enough to persuade Kingfisher plc to sponsor the twenty-two-year-old girl who stuck by her word.

Life at that time was on a knife edge. Mark had resigned from his job as marketing director for a marine company, and I was living in a Portakabin in a boatyard on £10 a week for food. Many things played a part in that dream coming true, but none touched me more than the unexpected but poignant gift I had been unknowingly left by my Nan. I used this to pay the entrance fee for the Route du Rhum, a race which we would use to demonstrate to Kingfisher that I could handle a race around the world. Though in a boat we chartered at the last minute, I won my class. Kingfisher were convinced, and five months later we announced our project to build a boat for the Vendée Globe. Though people would later say to me, 'Kingfisher were so lucky to sponsor you,' I would always reply that it wasn't luck. They took a gamble – a huge gamble to sponsor a young sailor with virtually no track record. They had believed in us, and it paid off.

The hills and valleys of Derbyshire had been replaced by the Southern Ocean's rolling waves, and the girl who'd saved her school dinner money for a boat in her landlocked years was about to become the skipper of a newly designed 60 foot boat. I couldn't believe it was my life as I sat there in the design meetings in total disbelief as we brought to life the most beautiful boat I could imagine. But she was not just any boat; she was called *Kingfisher*, and I was going to race her round the world.

Kingfisher was an IMOCA 60, a 4x4 of the ocean. They are powerful and awe-inspiring boats and designed primarily to be sailed solo round the world skippered by the world's best single-handed sailors. Just four months after her launch in Auckland, and after sailing her half-way round the world, I competed in my first race, the Europe 1 NEW MANSTAR race. The pressure was immense as I crossed the start line in Plymouth. I was twenty-three and racing to the USA in my first professional competition, and for the full two weeks at sea I was really nervous. But it culminated in success way beyond anyone's expectations. In just five years I'd gone from sailing solo for the first time in my life to winning my first race against the best single-handed sailors in the world.

Our second race, the Vendée Globe, began just five months later. It was this race which finished in Les Sables d'Olonne in February 2001. I finished second, and as a result, the race brought me into the public eye and changed my life for ever.

I had thought at the time that my wish to stay on board *Kingfisher* at the finish was solely because I loved the sea so much and was happy out there in a way that I had never found elsewhere in my life, but with hindsight I realize that a great part of the fear and emotion of leaving her was that I was leaving her safety. *Kingfisher* was the most incredible boat I could ever have wished to have sailed, and I felt like the luckiest person in the world to be able to call myself her skipper. In the year leading up to the Vendée I had spent more time on her than I had on land, and she had become my home. Life out there was different too, as, though you have no control of the elements, you are totally in control of the boat on which you sail. Many decisions may dictate success, failure or even, in extreme situations, life or death; but they are your decisions and yours alone. You hold the key to dealing with every single thing that happens to you out there, but on land, trying to satisfy requests coming in from all over the world, life could not have been more different.

Within minutes of stepping on the dock a particular photograph was taken of me. It was in black and white, and I'm holding my hands up before my face at the request of the photographer. Despite having finished second in the Vendée I was not smiling as I stood there in my worn old waterproofs, gently biting my bottom lip, my hair tousled and short from where I cut it myself ten days before the finish and the precious selection of good luck charms I'd been given around my neck. When I look into my own eyes in that photo now I see a frightened and vulnerable girl. I may have won the hearts of those who had given me such incredible strength and support, but I had lost my anonymity, and like so many things in life, you don't realize just how precious it is until you've lost it. In that tumultuous time in my life the one thing I craved was normality – and that was the last thing I could possibly have had.

Few people understood what I was going through that year, not even many who were close to me, and as I always gave my all in public, everyone around me thought that the Ellen they knew was fine. But I wasn't fine, far from it. Inside, I felt as if I was trapped at the base of a waterfall, held under water and, whilst trying not to panic, I was desperately struggling to find which way was up.

In effect 2001 taught me what really matters in life. It taught me how to be strong, and most importantly it taught me just how important having values was. I knew who my friends were, and when people I'd never spoken to before claimed to have known me from old, I knew the score. I remember people saying to me that they remembered me living in my little boat, or in the tiny Portakabin I rented in Hamble, but I knew the people who were friendly to me back then, and I could count them on one hand. I would be polite, but felt that it might have been nice if they'd said the briefest hello back then.

Life was a mixture of emotions, as some unbelievable things happened, such as receiving an MBE and even having a mountain named after me, but alongside the opportunities I found myself picking my way through a minefield of pitfalls. I was being pulled in every direction possible. Amidst all of this mayhem the one thing which gave me control of my life back was getting out to sea again. There I felt not only at home, but safe. Thankfully my own compass had pulled me back to where I could be me again . . . and that was doing exactly what I did best: getting out there on the water. This helped my relationship with Mark and Offshore Challenges too, as it gave me the space to reflect on my own future and rise above our challenges dealing with life on land.

After a brief trip to Scotland with Mum and Dad, which gave me the time to write down my thoughts, I met with Mark to discuss the future. It was a pivotal moment, as rather than shying away from the downsides of our success, I faced them head-on and decided to take control of my life again with a mammoth five-year plan.

My first goal was to sail *Kingfisher* again in the 2002 Route du Rhum. Next was the Jules Verne, a crewed round-the-world record attempt with the aim of being the fastest crew round the world ever. My third ambition, the most important to me, which I didn't make public at the time, was a solo attempt on the round-the-world record. Since being in the Southern Ocean on the Vendée I'd been both enchanted by and drawn to its seductive beauty, and I knew I had to return there. To break either the Jules Verne record or the solo record I would need to sail a multihull, and bar a couple of crewed races in them I had very little experience. I had already agreed to sail the Transat Jacques Vabre two-handed transatlantic race at the end of the year with my good friend Alain Gautier on his 60 foot trimaran *Foncia*. I knew this was an essential part of learning how to control these highly strung beasts.

Multihulls are very different from monohulls. Despite their gigantic structures they are lighter and faster than the equivalent length of monohull like *Kingfisher*. The biggest difference is that multis use floats or hulls to keep themselves the right way up, whereas *Kingfisher* had a huge 3 ton lump of lead 4.5 metres beneath the water to do the same. If a huge wave or the wind pushes a monohull over, then the keel will ultimately pull the boat back the right way up, like a pendulum. A multi has stabilizers, if you like, which make them very stable, until the point where they are pushed that little bit too far, when they can literally cartwheel through the air. Trimarans and catamarans both have much in common, both seemingly flying through the air, high above the water. They are fast and elegant but they can be flipped on to their backs in seconds as they capsize. They are actually more stable upside down than the right way up, which does not fill you with confidence when you are about to take one deep into the Southern Ocean, where waves can be as high as five- or six-storey buildings.

I wanted to sail in the south with a crewed multi first, to work out how likely it was that I'd kill myself down there. To make the decision harder, at the time there appeared to be no individual who had ever made it round the world non-stop in a multi, though several had tried. In fact, only a handful of boats had even made it round fully crewed, so for me the Jules Verne would be a decisive journey and would influence one of the most important decisions of my life: solo or not? If I decided 'yes', it would take the danger I had previously experienced at sea to a new level. Sailing solo in the Southern Ocean on a multi was nothing short of madness.

Chapter Two

The Route du Rhum had been a real eye-opener to me when I'd raced it for the first time back in 1998, and now, in 2002, I was to compete again. It was to be my final race with *Kingfisher*, and I was looking forward to being reunited for one last adventure. It would be the first time solo for me since the finish of the Vendée almost two years before.

Run every four years from St Malo in France to Guadeloupe in the Caribbean, the Rhum is a 3,540 mile race which starts in November. Though the destination sounds warm and inviting, the start is the absolute opposite. Freezing gales and storms are usually on order for the first week, and in the 1998 race I had worn my survival suit continuously for ten days. The weather reports then building up to the start were horrendous, and in the race I saw 65 knots, which, at force 12, is as high as the Beaufort scale goes! I remember looking at the weather charts before the start in the house that we'd rented as a team. I was incredibly nervous, which was not helped by the fact that one of the low-pressure systems heading across the Atlantic had 'BOMB' written next to it, which I did not take as a good sign!

The 50 foot boat that I'd sailed the first time had been chartered at the last minute, and, though she was a good boat, she was not my boat; I had managed to get her across the Atlantic, but it had been an incredibly hard physical struggle. This time, though, it was different: four years had passed, and I was sailing my beloved

Kingfisher. Though she was 10 feet bigger, I knew her inside out and back to front. In fact, I would go as far as saying she felt like an extension of me. Everything about her was wonderful, from her shape to the way she handled a storm. Plus, after sailing 75,000 miles in each other's company, we had a deal: I looked after her, and she looked after me. Together we made a very strong team.

When we had won the first race we had ever competed in together I am sure that many said that it was beginner's luck. It was even suggested by one competitor that I'd cheated. Then, five months later, I started the Vendée and finished second. Perhaps even then some felt I'd been lucky. Whatever their view, though, there was a real feeling that the skipper of *Kingfisher* for the Route du Rhum in 2002 was no longer the girl from Derbyshire who'd competed in the Vendée Globe. Now I was seen as a serious contender; and in racing terms it was my coming of age.

When we arrived in St Malo I was more relaxed than I'd ever been for a race before. We got on really well as a team that year: no matter if things went right or wrong, we always had a laugh about it. Humorous banter was something we had in truckloads, and I was in a good place mentally. It was the characters in the team such as Jonny, Charlie and Nobbers who made it feel so special. I had known Charlie for years, and, though Jonny and Nobbers had joined the team more recently, we all gelled extremely well. Though he had worked in sailing for years, one of Jonny's previous jobs was as a nightclub DJ, and he was capable of defusing any difficult situation with his wicked sense of humour. They chose to nickname me 'Miss', in the sense of a schoolteacher, which was quite amusing, and *Kingfisher* became the 'Mighty Fish'. We spent a good deal of time together over that year, and going out for a drink with the guys in those first evenings in St Malo was the perfect antidote to pre-race nerves. All in all, the guys brought out a relaxed and cheeky Ellen, and that state of mind certainly helped me psychologically in the build-up to the start. I also felt physically much more prepared. In 2002 I had begun training in earnest, and this time had a real fitness plan in place.

St Malo was bedlam before the race. Almost a million people

visited the boats and flocked into the area for the race start itself. I have no idea where that number of people could stay, as hotels must have been at bursting point. Vast numbers of people all with different-coloured jackets looked like hundreds and thousands on a cake as they thronged along the barriers, sometimes five or ten deep. The 2002 Rhum was the biggest since its inception back in 1978, with the docks crammed full with fifty-nine race boats and a staggering fleet of eighteen 60 foot multihulls. They looked spectacular as they lined the docks, each of them pretty much as wide as they were long. I knew many of the multihull skippers too, having raced the year before and earlier that year with my good friend Alain Gautier on *Foncia*, and always against the other boats in that fleet. There was my old rival Michel Desjoyeaux there, the only sailor ever to finish ahead of *Kingfisher* and me in a solo race. But this time he was racing in the 60 foot multis rather than the 60 foot monohulls, so we were no longer direct competitors. The monohulls' start was on Saturday 9 November, and the multis' was the following day, as they are much faster boats, and staggering the starts would mean they'd finish in Guadeloupe closer to the monos.

My greatest rivals in the seventeen-boat IMOCA 60 foot fleet, the largest of the monohull classes, were Roland Jourdain (nick-named Bilou) from France, Mike Golding from the UK and Jean-Pierre Dick, also from France. It felt reassuring to me that I had already raced against Bilou and Mike in the Vendée and that I no longer felt like the new kid on the block. Though being one of the race favourites put a lot of extra pressure on, I was not alone, as a sailor from our team, Nick Moloney, a great guy, friend and character in the sailing world, was also racing as part of the Offshore Challenges sailing team. He was racing in Class 2 monos, as I had in 1998. His previous solo race had been the Mini Transat, two years before. In fact we had got to know Nick as he had raced in my old Mini, *Le Poisson*.

The team had helped here a great deal with my confidence, however, and I was comforted by the fact I knew *Kingfisher* was faster than she had been in the Vendée. We had modified her a great deal over the previous winter, managing to lose 300 kg. We had swapped her steel rigging for a lighter material, which allowed us to change her keel bulb for a smaller one, and I was very much hoping that this would help us out.

In order not to spend all of the ten days before the start keeping a low profile and dodging the crowds, I headed off to stay in a barn for a few days. It belonged to Mark's mum, and though small was perfectly formed! It was an ancient stone building in an orchard; half was a tiny stone house with one room downstairs and one up, then next door in the 'real barn' part was the toilet and shower. There was no heating, just a huge open fire, but the place was magical and such a tranquil contrast to the bustle of St Malo.

My partner, Ian, had also come to join me. We'd been together about three years, and he had been through many race starts before. He understood the pressures. Since the Vendée I had never stopped: I had been continually travelling, attending meetings or sailing, so it was great to spend some quality time together at the barn. We cooked on the huge fire and chatted, and I spent the evenings looking at the weather charts, sorting out what clothes I'd have on board with me and packing the vitamin supplements I would take every day. It reminded me of the countryside in Derbyshire, and I felt at home there. It was the perfect place to relax in; the weather outside was crisp and sunny, and the cold mornings, with the orchard covered in the most beautiful haze, were very special.

On the day of the start I felt awful. The weather forecast was very bad for the first week of the race, and the wind was absolutely howling as I woke before daybreak and dressed in my thermals. Mornings of starts are always unpleasant: you are saying goodbye to one world and entering another, and you inevitably feel quite detached from what is going on around you. I felt sick inside with nerves and was seriously concerned about getting *Kingfisher* safely out and to the start line. There are many rocks surrounding the entrance to St Malo, and the conditions that day were challenging. The forecast was for gusts of 30–35 knots, and for the night, gusts of 35–40.

Ian and I drove down to the marina, where we said goodbye. He was the best person to have around during those stressful moments: he was incredibly supportive and knew just what to do. I felt a mixture of emotions at that moment. Leaving the safety of land and the warmth of a car for the unpredictable ocean is not always easy, but I also wanted to get on with the race and get the worrying and stressful start over and done with. I was a sailor who liked to be in a clear piece of ocean to make clear decisions. Close racing with many other boats had never been my thing. I was very, very nervous. I leant over and kissed Ian, shedding a couple of tears on his shoulder. Then, knowing it was time to go, I took a deep breath and wiped my eyes.

'Right, better go to work,' I said. And with that, I was gone . . .

I had decided that having Ian on board while getting the boat to the start line was not the right thing to do any more, as it's a stressful time, and, though he would never wish to be a distraction, I knew that ultimately that would be unavoidable. Mark wasn't on board either, as he had decided to be with Nick Moloney. The wind was still honking as I pulled my waterproof trousers and jacket on. It was 9 a.m., six hours to the start, and I was keener than ever to get settled into my new home. So many things were going through my head: what was the battery voltage, were the spinnakers all packed properly, what sails would the others have up for the start . . . The race boats have no engines, and as we were towed out through the channel I looked again at the weather; the forecast for two days' time was force 8–9 with a wave height of 6–8 metres. Luckily we would be out of the English Channel and in the Atlantic Ocean by then. Surrounding us on all sides were hundreds of boats: all shapes and sizes of spectator boats, the teams' support boats and the forty-one monohulls about to begin the race.

I don't know where the six hours went, because, before we knew it, it was time for the guys to get off. They were allowed to stay on board by race rules until four minutes before the start, and stay on they did! We had quickly realized that the conditions were so rough out there getting off would be difficult. Finally, with almost exactly four minutes to go, we got the rib close enough for the guys to jump. So energetic was their departure that they actually ended up diving into it, and it was a real miracle that they all made it.

Four minutes later, and despite our hurried disembarkation of the guys, *Kingfisher* was the first boat to cross the start line. Starts have never been my strong point, so I was both relieved and glad to be away cleanly and with good speed. My heart was racing; and, though nervous, I felt ecstatic I was back at sea with the Mighty Fish.

The mist cleared as we passed Cap Fréhel, which was wonderful for the thousands of people who were perched on and clinging to the rocks to catch a glimpse of the sailors heading off for the Atlantic. Despite the weather the turnout was once again staggering, and I can't explain just how encouraging it was to hear the spectators' cheers. I was second around the buoy, our final turning mark off the French coast: Bilou had beaten me, but I was not concerned so early in the race. Then, totally unexpected, our first hitch. *Kingfisher* suddenly careered off course. Even so early on in the race I knew it was happening, you become so tuned into the boat that you feel it instantly.

'Shit, shit, shit,' I cursed as I leapt across the cockpit to grab the helm. This was not good news.

I switched from one autopilot to the next; luckily we'd built a system capable of doing that easily. It put me on edge, though; we only had two pilots, so having a problem with one of them in the first hours was pretty worrying.

Not long after we rounded the buoy it began to get dark. The sky was still grey and nasty, and the weather deteriorating. The first night was a blur: I can't have had more than an hour's sleep, in short naps of ten or so minutes in the cockpit: as we were still in the English Channel I had to keep a constant eye out for ships. The nights were long in November, and out at sea on a cold, wet, rough night, you knew it. However, the good news was that, despite slipping into second place for the 0300 position report, we were up in first for the 0700.

With the forecast we had I was extremely cautious not to damage *Kingfisher* during the strong and unstable winds. Seb Josse, one of the French skippers, had been dismasted at the start, and it was a stark reminder that even in a tried and tested 60 footer, which had finished sixth in the Vendée Globe, things could go very wrong. The first night had been pretty horrible wind-wise, but the second day decided to give us hours of changeable and frustrating wind which was either too little or too much, knocking the boat flat on her side. Sailing upwind makes it harder too, as the wind is cold and energy-zapping as it races towards you across the deck. Raindrops become needles which assault your eyes when they are carried helplessly by a strengthening wind: you feel each one piercing your eyeballs as you squint ahead into the distance on the lookout for ships or fishing boats. It's really stressful in the Channel when you are ship-spotting and -dodging. As there is no one else on board to keep watch, it's down to you, and, though we have radar detectors which sound alarms when ships pop up over the horizon, there can't be many moments in the Channel where there aren't any alarms. Sailing close behind a huge ship to avoid it always keeps you on your toes . . . It's weird out there to know that there are other people so close: you can often see lights in the accommodation block lit up appearing to cut out the cold as people occupy their cabins. The huge stern light a big ship carries is very powerful, and if you pass close it can light up your world. You smell the exhaust fumes from the engine of this gigantic steel structure and you feel very small in your tiny sailing boat. Then there is the moment when the wind disappears – only for a few seconds, but the sails often flap, and the boat lurches to windward as the sails no longer balance the keel. As result I dropped back a few miles.

My tactic in the first days was to not break *Kingfisher*. The old adage of 'you have to finish to win' could never have been more important than in a race that starts in the winter gales. I had still not been able to solve the autopilot problem, which was a huge worry gnawing away at me. At this stage I had lost the lead and I tried to make sense of the weather by talking to Jean-Yves and Meeno, my weather routers. Tacking *Kingfisher* at the right time was crucial with all these shifting winds and weather fronts around. It sounds a bit obvious, but you cannot sail a sailing boat directly into the wind. About forty-five degrees off either side is what you can get on a 60 footer in any kind of seaway, so working out which side of the wind was the closest to the route was pretty essential. Tacking is also not as simple as pushing the tiller over in a dinghy and swapping sides. In a 60 footer you have to shift every item in the boat from one side to the other; from your food to the spares and sails in the forepeak, and then empty tons of water-ballast from one side, before filling the other. At the same time you are constantly thrown around in the dark, damp forepeak: it must be what it feels like in a washing machine!

Our second night at sea was more stable, but the wind was stronger. It was a force 7, and the waves were beginning to build. That evening the sea showed us its splendour as we went through the first of many fronts, with clear blue skies on the other side followed by a beautiful starlit night. I was in third; 23 miles behind the leader, Bilou, in *Sill*. Connecting to the internet for weather files and communication was getting harder, as the antennae could not cope with the sea conditions, and I realized that, if it was challenging now, it was going to get a whole lot worse.

It was not only the monohull fleet that was struggling, though. Our second night at sea was the first for the multis. One of the huge 60 foot tris had already capsized in the gusty squalls by the coast, and, frighteningly, another, *Bonduelle*, had sailed straight into him at full pelt. Little did we know it then, but this incident was the first of many in this race, which were to ultimately lead to the demise of the ORMA 60 foot trimaran class.

During the day conditions worsened. The bad weather was moving in. I had positioned myself further north and west than the other boats, which, though it did not help my ranking too much, had placed me as close to the weather front heading to us as possible. The idea was to head for the front; then, when the wind changed on the other side of it, you could head off at great speed on the course which you were after. The centre of the depression was sitting off Ireland, and none of us could predict when the front would come our way. However, by the fourth day of the race I had crossed it, and that night was horrendous, with aggressive and confused seas, and a wind gusting from 20 to 45 knots. Despite a night of wrestling with sails and anguish over when to tack, I had lost ground and was 24.8 miles behind Bilou and 10.3 behind Mike. With weather as changeable as we had it was impossible to know if our tactics would work. Being further north could have equally been a blessing or a failure.

We pressed on. The wind increased, and I began to feel more and more as if I was in a battle for survival rather than a race. All through the next day we pushed, the wind coming round, and the waves beginning to batter us harder and harder. I said on a phone call to Mark back at our office in Cowes: 'These are break-boat conditions, and the worrying thing is that it's only going to get worse.' I was pleased, though, to see how *Kingfisher* was dealing with the weather we were being dealt out there. She is a sturdy little lass with a big heart and a lot of guts, and her true colours were showing through. Solid water was now crashing over the deck, making her literally tons and tons heavier. Her cockpit would take ages to drain; it was even too deep for my wellies! Occasionally we got the chance to see the sun, though, and I remember a brief moment where the noise and violence of all around us melted into insignificance when we saw the golden sunrise, like a moody painting, bringing to life the 30 knots of spray.

Wave height was now up to 10 metres, and the worrying part was that the waves were hitting the side of *Kingfisher* very hard. They were not only breaking against the boat but also over her, and on numerous occasions I had to duck beneath her cuddy to dodge a wall of foamy water. Equipment needed to be tied down, as it was regularly thrown off the chart table, and our little cabin felt like a survival capsule. I had seen huge waves before, but this had a different element to it. This time the distance from the peak of one wave to the next was less, making the sides of the waves very steep. The water was white too, really white; it was like looking out across a frozen landscape. If the radar alarm went off, spotting other ships out there was a nightmare: the waves were so large that you could only actually see them for a few seconds every minute, when both of you happened to be on the crest of a wave. The biggest difference was that we were sailing across the waves, not away from them as you generally do in the Southern Ocean, and this meant that not only was *Kingfisher* being 'punched' by every wave, but, if I was on deck, I was too! I was used to hearing water rush beneath *Kingfisher*'s hull, but less used to hearing the waves slam into us, followed by deafening torrents of water surging over her deck, as if we were beneath the Niagara Falls.

I was just stepping into the cockpit, masked and hooded up in an effort to protect my eyes from the driving spray, when a wave lifted us high into the air and hit our rudder like a bullet. Suddenly *Kingfisher* bore away, and I leapt across her cockpit to grab the helm. Nothing happened; we continued bearing away. Not only were we sailing in the wrong direction, but, if we were forced into a crash gybe in these conditions, it would have been lethal. I pushed her tillers harder still, then suddenly realized that she sailed straight only when her rudders were totally skewed over on one side. Something serious had happened, and, as I calmed her heading down, I feared her rudders had been badly damaged. From one second to the next we had gone from all fine and under control to worrying whether I could even remain in the race. I dropped her mainsail, darting between the helm and the main halyard. All I could think of was 'Solve it fast!'

Somehow, despite having an ineffective steering system, I managed to 'heave to' and park *Kingfisher*. Huge lumps of ocean were still being thrown at her, but her hull had ceased charging through the waves. I went below, I could hardly stand, her motion was horrendous and more unpredictable than when we'd been flying along. I scrambled through the hatches in her black, cold interior. I checked the systems often, so I was well acquainted with the route. The moment I saw the rudder stock I realized what had happened. The huge nut on the shaft had slipped, and her tiller system, which was linked by bars to her rudder system, had been forced to the point of slipping round inside the centre of the quadrant. I searched in the tool kit for the spanner to tighten the nut. It wasn't there. *Damn it!* I raced back on deck and hauled the tillers as hard as I could. In my heart I was pretending to have the strength of an Atlantic wave, but

I couldn't do it. I tried again, bracing my feet against the centre console, waiting for the lull between the waves so I could put the most effort in. It worked, and the rudders centred. Not quite square, though: it was impossible to get them quite square, but the more I did it, the looser the stock would become. I did my best, trying to peer over her stern to find the best alignment. Her rudder reference unit was damaged too, which was essential for her to steer on the autopilot. I then sabotaged one to fix the other, recalibrated it, which frightened the life out of me, as it needed the tiller to be pushed all the way one way, then all the way the other. We were slewing round the ocean like a drunk. I hoisted the mainsail, which was easier said than done, as I had to feed the battens inside the lazy jacks, but, that done, we were back in business. I lay back in my cuddy seat and sighed with pure relief. Just another day in the office!

Day five was upon us, and I hadn't managed once to boil the kettle – the only way to have a hot meal. All I had been eating was snacks. It had been so challenging, and I was sure that everyone in the fleet was just as exhausted. Wind speeds overnight had been gusty and unpredictable, which made conditions quite treacherous, and hearing the reports coming from the rest of the fleet was sobering. There had been eighteen 60 foot multis at the start. After the initial two pulling out early on in the race, one more had pulled out after seeing the carnage. But things had gone from bad to worse. Francis Joyon on *Eure et Loire* had capsized, as had Yvan Bourgnon on *Rexona Men*. Yvan, with whom I'd raced three years before, had not even had any sails up. He was literally thrown over by an 80 knot gust hitting his mast. *Bayer* had decided not to continue after seeking shelter off the French coast, and, though *Belgacom* had restarted after repairs, she had quickly abandoned after hitting a channel marker while leaving the port. *Gitana* had sustained mast damage; Michel Desjoyeaux on *Géant* had pulled in for his third time in Porto Santos, Madeira; and Marc Guillemot on *Biscuits La Trinitaine* had been forced to stop in the Azores. *Sodebo* had pulled out of the race into Portugal, and *Sopra*, the fourth boat to capsize, had fallen victim to this same weather system which had left Loik Peyron having to abandon *Fuji Film* after his starboard hull had flown up in the air and sheared off. How the ocean could make a 60 foot racing boat appear to be made of paper was sobering for us all to see: *Fuji Film* had been torn apart by the waves smashing into her floats. Her sister ship, *Sergio Tacchini*, skippered by Karine Fauconnier, was near by and was also smashed to pieces. My good friend Alain pulled out after breaking a forward beam. He had also snapped the cruciate ligaments in his knee, though it seemed like an absolute miracle that no one had been seriously hurt.

It had been a multihull massacre out there, and it made all the skippers in the race feel uneasy. But it wasn't just the 60 foot tris; our fleet was hit too. *Virbac*, lying in fourth, had been dismasted, and Dominic Wavre had torn his headsail and decided to abandon too. I had survived, though there was certainly some worry back in Cowes when my emergency beacon went off by accident after being submerged by water in the cockpit. Mark had repeatedly tried to call the boat's satellite phone, but I was on deck, removing water by the bucketload from the mainsail to prevent it from tearing. Though they could see from the polling system that *Kingfisher* was racing along, I knew that they would be worried I'd fallen off. They were mightily relieved when I returned to the cabin and answered the phone – not being able to reach a sailor when they are at sea sparks off all sorts of worries.

I didn't lose my sense of humour through all this, though, as on one phone call, after vividly describing just how bad the sea state was, I continued to say, 'And I've got a wet arse . . . and it's never nice having a wet arse. It's a little bit too wet for comfort.'

My nearest rival had been Mike, with Bilou in the lead further south, but things were changing. That afternoon Mike moved into the lead, and it transpired that Bilou had ripped his mainsail in winds that had reached over 70 knots, causing damage so serious he was going to have to make a pit stop. I felt sad that there would be one boat fewer in our group, and that Bilou, for now at least, was out of the running. I was sure that Mike and I would miss him. I heard the news when I called the office: 'Really? Oh no. Poor Bilou. It sounded much worse further south. I'm sure he'll be back with us, though . . . The wind is really kicking in . . . 40 knots. Jeeze 42 . . . 43 . . . 44 . . . 46 . . . 48 . . . 52 . . . gotta go . . . will call you back.'

Later on I called back.

'Have you seen a position report?' I asked. Long pause.

'Yep. You're in the lead,' came Mark's reply.

'I am?'

'Yes, by three miles,' followed by an even longer pause.

'Nice work!' I replied excitedly, too tired to think of anything more appropriate to say in response.

'Sorry, I thought you would have known that,' Mark said.

'Does everyone in the office know?' I asked.

'We sure do,' said Mark. 'We live by the position reports.'

It was reassuring to know that there were others watching from afar what we were up to. We were now in the lead, for the first time in four days, and I was now going to do my level best to hang on to it!

PRESS RELEASE
Date: 14/11/2002

RHUM: KINGFISHER LEADING - SILL RIPS MAINSAIL HEADS TO MADEIRA . . .

As gale force winds hit the UK spare a thought for the RHUM skippers trying to survive these storms. KINGFISHER holds on to a 9.5 mile margin over Mike Golding (ECOVER). Yesterday KINGFISHER was 60 miles north of ECOVER - this morning this distance is reduced to just 17 miles as ELLEN moved south during the night to try to avoid huge seas building over a shallow shelf in the Atlantic.

I knew that night the storm would begin to abate, and I wanted to prepare myself for it. I rested as much as I reasonably could between the squalls and prepared myself to give my all. I knew that it was a very good time to take miles out of my competitors and push hard. It's exhausting making all those sail changes very quickly, but it's all too easy to kid yourself that it's worth waiting that extra hour before changing up a gear to stay on the pace.

My tactic worked, and we had a very active night. The wind

dropped from 55 to 25 knots over a matter of hours, and, though it was dark and I was exhausted, I dashed about the boat, determined and focused in my work, knowing that now was the time. The following morning's position report came through. We had increased the lead from 3 miles to 17.1. Yippee! Now the challenge was to not get sucked into the Azores high-pressure system which sat ahead. From this moment on the race would be a downwind sleigh ride, and as I knew Mike's boat was theoretically better downwind, I would have to sail *Kingfisher* as I never had before. Though I didn't realize at the time, this was the beginning of a 2,500 mile match race between Mike Golding and me.

It was hard to believe that we had only made it one-third of the way across the Atlantic. I was really chuffed to have gone up into the lead, but I was acutely aware that there was still a long way to go. A reminder of just how easily it could all be over was finding that the leeward runner pin, essential for holding the mast up on port tack, had almost worked itself loose enough to fall into the sea, and I knew why: it had been removed in St Malo to attach the race-banner to the side of *Kingfisher*. Though it sounds insignificant, if that had come out, and I'd gybed *Kingfisher*, we would have been dismasted.

The following day Mike went into the lead, predominantly because I slowed to deal with a whole host of issues on *Kingfisher*. Not only did we have something caught round the rudder, which meant we had to stop for an hour, but we also had some challenging windless conditions. I spoke to the team: 'All I can do right now is sail *Kingfisher* as fast as I possibly can between here and the finish line, try and make every tactical decision as best as I can and sleep as best as I can. And then, if I do all of that, then I guess the best man wins, don't they?'

I had seen Mike that morning: a tiny sail, almost a dot on the horizon. He was the first yacht I'd seen since the day after the start. With the problems I was having on board, he sailed straight past me. It was weird thinking of Mike's little world on board, wondering how he'd coped with the conditions, but it was also frustrating to have lost the lead. With his speed downwind I decided that

I should do something different tactically, so I hoisted the spinnaker and spent the rest of the day, running into the evening, staying lower and keeping further south. I managed to get a 40 mile latitude difference from him. That night was incredible: sailing gently along with the spinnaker, watching all the signs for where the centre of the high was, following wind shift and barometer, and checking and checking the weather charts to understand where the high was moving. The feeling of calm in the air brought with it a heart-stopping silence, and just like in a fairytale*Kingfisher* and I were sailing straight towards a beautiful full moon. Despite the import-ance of the decision about when to gybe, that night I felt clear headed. I really believed that we were on the right track, having taken the more southern option, and I felt confident the decision would come naturally. The risk of getting it wrong was that we'd end up stuck in the centre of the high with no wind; the good thing about getting it right would be that we'd make the most of the wind direction, sail as close as possible to the right direction and be the first boat to come out of the high, touching the new, stronger winds and setting off on the motorway to Guadeloupe! I slept a lot that night; in fact, it was a good, recuperative sleep. I woke to gybe, but found the benefits of being in a stable airflow with no huge black trade-wind clouds to sit on us, stealing our wind or knocking us flat (as they do both), quite liberating. It was a clear night, and I also had a funny feeling that it was the last chance I'd have to rest properly before hitting the powerful trades.

Date: 16/11/2002 (Day 7)
at last my first real e-mail from kingfisher . . . i have actually dreampt over the past half hour - which - for waht feels like a first in this race, shows that i have at least - to some extent slept . . .

    finaly here conditions have stabilised. though on the whole we got away with the storm very lightly, we have both lost stelleite antennaa's - water damaged - and i have to say nearly wahed away . . . as the solid water poounded over kingfisher, i would just close my eyes to see hwat remained. i lived in my oilskins, harnessed to the boat at all times. i felt like i was learning to walk again, crawling along her side decks - for that tortuous journey to see that the staysail was well trimmed, and that the next 50 knot squall was not going to see it's leech torn to shreds. typing here looking up it's incredible to see the masses of canvass - as waht we had up just 48 hours ago was a more shadow of this grand display. tiny traingles of canvass clinging onto an incredibly feeble like mast - seen only through a mask . . .

it feels wonderful to remove my wellies, and to be abel to go into the cockpit without getting instantl:y soaked - oh how things change. i remeber sitting in the gale - holding tight onto the chart table edge - just thiniking 'that in 36 hours we'll be sailing with our spiunnaker up.' i guess it's therse things which keep you going, toghether with the mesmorising beauty of the ferrocious waves, foaming crests and seas so large and rolling you could have built villages in their valleys.

one of the most long lasting impressions for me was seeing a pod of dolphins jump out of a mountainside of a sawave, seeing that for them it was probaby just another day in the office.

right now the sea i smuch flatter, butsleep is till light. i have been pushing hard to try to take miles from mike, nd a string of problems yesterday did not help . . . our 16 milo load was wiped away, as i saw him as i steered kingifsher back on course after sailing backwards to remove something from her rudder, and do some fine - tune rig adjustments . . . but that's life - you gain some, you lose some. as is it here and type i have seen the latest positiong reports. once again i have lost miles, sitting in a cloudy area of sky for an ohour or so . . . our time will come.

it is the most wonderful feeling to be sailing alone

on kingfisher once more . . . it is pure joy to be out
here, and though there are stressful moments - as
always - i am one very, very happy person to be out here
doing this . . .

here's to the next e-mail from beneath the stars . . .
in fact, that reminds me of a story . . . a man in skye,
standing staring over the ocean was once asked 'how far
can you see?' he replied 'on a really clear night . . .
you may even see the stars . . .'

From here until the finish Mike and I would fight a real duel,
a gybing match, and it was taking a lot out of both of us. I made it
23 miles ahead, and then, twenty-four hours later, that lead was
back down to just 1.8. Mike then retook the lead, only to see me
pull it back by 26. Mike then retook 20 from me, before I retook 15.
The course to Guadeloupe meant changing angle repeatedly, and
with each move came a difference in positions. I knew that he was
giving his all, as was I. Mike said in a video conference: 'I can't see
her allowing me any opportunity to take too much rest.' He followed
this by laughing. I was pretty sure that he wasn't going to let me
rest much either!

The difficult conditions meant spending hours and hours hand-
steering, as there was too much sail, and too much wind for the
autopilot to cope. I loved it, though; we were belting along, the
adrenalin was flowing, and I was feeling alive! With conditions now
warmer, I was sitting on *Kingfisher*'s side deck beneath the stars in
a T-shirt and thermal trousers and even put on a CD, which helped
me to stay awake and energized as we blasted along. I was really
enjoying this race. I loved being out there again with *Kingfisher*,
and it brought back so many wonderful memories of the Vendée
Globe. Being out on deck at night is such a special feeling – seeing
the moon come up gently over the horizon, huge and red, with its
reflection on the water changing from pink to silver as it rises. Predictable to the second, it seems to be surfacing from another world,
and you can't help but think back to the past, when sailors learnt to
navigate using it. On a night with a full moon it's bright enough to

read a book on deck and see everything around you. I missed this on land. I missed the connection that you have with life itself, the rhythms of the natural world, and that feeling that you are seeing something special. Sailing at night is like peeking through a forgotten window to a timeless world beyond, which you have temporarily misplaced. There is no reason on earth that we cannot still see this beauty on land, but due to so many distractions we so rarely do.

BANG!

The large spinnaker we were sailing with exploded before my eyes. This was the beginning of a heart-pounding and physically exhausting hour's work to get what I could of the torn sail back into its sock. Three hundred square metres of tracing-paper-thin fabric were billowing uncontrollably above me in the gusty wind. I worked quickly, changing to the smaller, stronger spinnaker. Not wanting to lose precious miles to Mike, I was in overdrive. That night we saw 29 knots of wind, which, as I was hand-steering, we could take without wiping out, but it was pretty stressful reacting to every wind shift and gust, and I was desperately hoping the wind would not get any stronger. Not knowing if I could actually get the spinnaker down to gybe was a big worry.

It's one of the most dangerous manoeuvres on a solo race boat, standing up on the foredeck, trying to pull the sock down over a sail which is whipping from side to side with a mind of its own 80 feet above your head. You hope that the wind moderates and that you will be able to leave the helm at some stage, but that night the wind was so strong I ended up hand-steering for four hours solid. The wind was too strong for the autopilot to control the boat as it was dragged across the ocean by its spinnaker, which in strong wind became an uncontrollable monster. It was a mesmerizing experience, a little like the buzz of being on a fairground ride, but here you could not get off until the wind subsided, and even then you were still powering through the ocean. I was wired with adrenalin and knew that any lapse in concentration could lead to a huge wipe-out, damaged sails or even a broken mast. The stars were peeking from behind the clouds, and the moon was bright above us, now almost full. *Kingfisher*'s white decks were lit up as clearly as the foamy white wash each side of her stern as we slid over the surface of the water. Though happy that night, and smiling inside, I was beginning to wonder if I'd ever be able to move away from the helm! As dawn crept in, however, the wind moderated, allowing the chance for a little recuperation, a pee and something to eat and drink.

18/11/2002 (Race day 9)
ELLEN LOG
  2350 GMT stressed ELLEN: . . . Full on here - three
times I've had to literally dash into the cockpit and
grab the helm to stop the boat gybing; we have really
marginal conditions. Sailing at 15-16 knots in 20-23
knots of breeze with small spinnaker up pretty fast down
direct line - close to the edge. Winds varying about
17-23 knots - one minute 17 knots next minute 23 knots -
wonder if I should put reef in (mainsail). Might help
but I'll slow down loads . . . can't do that . . .
  0300GMT ecstatic ELLEN: . . . Positions just come
through - distance to go 1557.1 1st Ellen MacArthur,
2nd Mr Golding 1578.7 miles to go - awesome! 21.6 miles
ahead - how cool is that. Really stressful night hand-
steered loads again with full mainsail and kite up -
it's started to die off a bit, bit easier. It's been
blowing 20 knots for last hour so we're all right. Good
news . . .
  0700 GMT ELLEN: . . . Bit stressed and very nervous,
basically, but that's fine, pretty normal, I think!
Winds 20-25 knots just had hour with 28-30 knots. Big
breeze for this spinnaker - couldn't get the thing down
if I tried in any case! Only thing to do was to hang on
so going very fast at the moment doing 18 knots over the
ground and going to be gybing in about half an hour I
think.

Early in the morning, with a miraculous drop in wind, we managed to gybe, but later that day we had our mother of all technical problems.

Date 19/11/2002 (Race day 10)
RHUM: JUST 1 MILE BETWEEN KINGFISHER AND ECOVER AT
0700 - GYBING CHESS GAME TAKES ITS TOLL ...
 ELLEN LOG FROM NETMEETING THIS MORNING AT 1000
 ... Yesterday was quite a big day in that basically
the lashing at the top of the mast that holds the
gennaker halyard at the top had chafed through so I
ended up in a situation where I couldn't keep the big
sails up without risking the halyard; so I had to climb
up the mast to re-lash it in again - it's the single-
handers worst nightmare to go to the top of the rig
especially when you only have 32 miles lead over the
next guy and you know you're going to lose some of that.
And I think as a result of that - delaying gybing and
sailing quite north in the night I've lost quite a lot
of miles to him - I'm only 1 mile ahead of Mike right
now. It seems that every time we gain miles we always
seem to lose them due to some problem. It's been a
little frustrating - we should be further ahead than
we are.
 Going up the rig is not not easy procedure at all ...
Basically, you have to free-climb with your own hands
all the way to the top which is obviously quite tiring.
Particularly, when mast is waving about in the sky. In
order to climb the mast I had to take down spinnaker
which was hanging on by the rest of its halyard - I was
pretty tired when I set off up the rig in first case. You
clip on at your waist and clip on to halyard and start
to climb. You use your hands to grab whatever you can in
order to get to the top of the rig and you're climbing
with tools and the halyard you're going to re-lash. But
the worst is getting back down because when you come

back down you have to actually undo the jumar and slide
back down and clip on again - that's pretty dicey
operation because you need your spare hand to hold on
to the rig to try to stop yourself getting bashed
against it . . .

Have a few bruises and a few marks on my neck from the
strap I had around my neck to hold the jumar. The worst
thing is your hands - they are like death . . . I can see
the blood vessels through my skin and they are very,
very sore. I ache all over from that climb but it's
done now, spinnaker back up - wonderful feeling.

Next 24 hours and really next 3 days will be broad
reaching, downwind conditions in the Trade Winds heading
straight for Guadeloupe. I think speed-wise Mike and I
are pretty evenly matched - it's going to be a really
tough race to the finish. I think the positions will
change every single position report and its going to
take a lot out of us . . .

I pushed hard that day before what was yet another challenging
night. During the daytime the trade winds were steady and quite
calm, but they showed a different personality at night with their
black gremlin clouds. The following morning I had been unable to
get to the computer, so on a quick call to the office I learnt of Mike's
problems. He had managed to get his spinnaker wrapped around his
forestay. If wrapped tightly it can be almost impossible to untangle,
requiring an ascent of the stay and a lot of work with a sharp knife
to cut it off. Slip, and you could even end up cutting the rope holding you up, the cable holding the mast up or yourself. In those
conditions it would be pretty hideous. I really felt for Mike. I also
learnt that I'd accrued a 26 mile lead, and even though that increased
to 71 miles later that day, the numbers paled into insignificance. I
couldn't help but think of Mike being beaten about trying to sort
his problem.

Then came the next piece of news. *Technomarine*, the leading
boat of the four multis still left in the race, had capsized. This hit

me hard, as just the day before I had been thinking about Steve Ravussin, the Swiss skipper, and how well he had done to survive the storm and make it into the lead. Steve is such a great character, and I really wanted him to do well. I had a soft spot for his boat too, as the previous year I had raced her all season under the name of *Foncia* with Alain Gautier. She held many fond memories for me, and I thought back to twelve months before, when Alain and I had sailed two-handed across the Atlantic in a fantastic race in which we were pipped to first place on the final night.

Steve had not activated his distress beacon, and the race control had not asked either Mike or me to stop, but his upturned boat was going to be right on our track, only 734 miles from Guadeloupe. As I approached the area where Steve was I stayed on deck. I was within a mile of him, but I never managed to spot him.

With Steve's news there was something else which suddenly became clear. *Kingfisher* was not only winning the monohull class, but was also ahead of the remaining three multis, the leader of which was none other than Michel Desjoyeaux, the very man who had beaten me in the Vendée!

The remaining two days passed quickly. *Kingfisher* and I were heading straight for Guadeloupe and managed to keep a pretty constant lead on Mike of about 70 miles. We had 60 miles to sail once we reached the island, as there was an extra way point to round before the finish line. Although Mike was 70 miles behind, all it needed was for me to be becalmed for five hours and he would be right there with me. It's really not over till it's over.

The sailing was fast and we were averaging 15 knots at the front of the fleet. We changed sails, to the code E, then the gennaker, then finally the genoa. As we were closing on the island there would be more sail changes. Steadily, I told myself, take one step at a time, don't screw things up now. The remaining miles were a blur of anxiety, bar a few key moments which I remember very clearly: sitting on the foredeck with a hand-held radio talking to a chopper who had flown out to see me was pretty cool. That was the first visit from anyone from the 'finish' side of the Atlantic, and, though the race was far from over, it was a great feeling. I was holding well ahead of Mike, and knowing that there was some wind at the finish was very reassuring. Finally, seeing the shore team in the rib was just fantastic, as a tiny dot on the horizon turned into the friendly faces that I knew so well.

We had just 60 miles to sail, right past the harbour, around the buoy at Basse Terre and then back to the finish line just off the harbour. It still didn't feel like a done deal, though; only on the final approach to the finish line did I actually accept that I was going to win the race. When the gun fired I felt the most powerful surge of happiness and emotion. Around us were hundreds of boats, and the welcome was incredible. It was 2245 at night (local time) on 23 November, and was a Friday night in Guadeloupe, which probably accounted for so many people being out! Flares were being let off left, right and centre, and as Mark, Jonny and Nobbers jumped on board I hugged them one by one. We had done it, together we had done it. My favourite cameraman jumped on: Erik, the man with the biggest smile and the biggest heart in the world. The air seemed alight with the most incredible feeling of happiness.

I was astounded that I was actually the first boat in, as since the inception of the race back in 1978 a monohull had never been the first boat across the finish line. Multihulls are much faster than monohulls and would under normal circumstances have beaten us by days. In the previous edition the winning multi, *Primagaz*, crossed the line six days before the winning 60 foot mono, *Aquitaine Innovations*. Not only this, but we'd had a fast race. *Kingfisher* and I had managed to knock 2 days and 6 hours off the existing monohull record as we finished in 13 days, 13 hours, 31 minutes and 47 seconds. All this made for an even more incredible finish.

You could feel the excitement in the air as thousands of people crammed into the square next to the dock where *Kingfisher* was safely moored at the end of her journey. A small rib came to collect us from the pontoon and take us to the dockside, where the media were waiting. It felt strange to leave her safety for the unpredictable world on land, and that sensation was intensified by the knowledge that this race was the last that *Kingfisher* and I were ever going to do alone.

As the rib closed in on the dock I was shocked to find the media had been put in pens behind railings and with an almost uncontrollable sense of urgency they seemed to be clambering over each other to attract my attention, ravenous for my story. I knew most of the journalists quite well and found it disturbing to see them all enclosed like caged animals. There was one 'pen' for the photographers, one for TV, one for radio and one for written press.

In a way, though, it was preparation for what was to come. The atmosphere the other side of those railings was like nothing I had ever experienced before or since. It hadn't really registered what was going on. But, as I was escorted through a parting in the railings, the scale of what I was at the centre of hit me. We were walking down a corridor formed between two sets of barriers, and gradually I realized that through the sea of noise I was being taken to a stage in the centre of a huge square. It was deafening. A sea of faces chanting my name, the sound growing in intensity and magnitude as I became visible to the crowds. It all felt quite surreal as I walked along barefoot in the still, moist Caribbean air. The excitement seemed to teeter on the edge of control. Ironically, I felt more vulnerable there than I ever had at sea.

I was continually grinning; with a huge wide smile to share with everyone around me. I waved to right and left, trying to look everyone in the eyes to show my appreciation. Faces, arms, legs and bodies were pressing against the barriers. Around me were four men, all in clean white pressed shirts with motifs. I assumed they were probably police, as was the man on my right who looked rather sinister in a black T-shirt and cap and who I swear had a gun in his right hand. Everyone was shouting, crying, yelling, reaching out to touch me, and every possible direction I could look in was filled with faces, mainly female, and all seeming to display the most incredible emotion.

I was glad to see Erik, the cameraman, right in front of me, but moments later, despite being guided backwards, he was knocked to the ground in the commotion. Though I didn't panic I felt adrenalin; all I could think about was making sure he was OK. I reached down to help him up; all he was worried about was his camera. I'd never seen anything faze Erik before, but that night when I looked into his eyes he seemed worried and tense. I carried on walking, but with Erik filming backwards again I spent most of my time trying to watch for anything on which he might trip. I was glad of the distraction; I was trying to appear natural when there was nothing natural about the moment at all.

As I climbed on to the stage, the crowd's noise erupted, and the tone could only be described as euphoric. It was one of the most intense moments of my life.

Chapter Three

My return from Guadeloupe marked the beginning of the next phase of my five-year plan: taking a large multihull into the Southern Ocean. Our goal was to be quite simply the fastest crew around the world on a sailing boat, and the experience would lead to my decision as to whether I could take on the whole journey alone. I had never sailed such a big boat before, let alone skippered one; and on top of everything it was a multihull. At the time of our announcement at the London Boat Show just one year earlier the record was held by Frenchman Olivier de Kersauson on the trimaran *Sport Elec*; it stood at 71 days, 14 hours, 22 minutes and 8 seconds. Out of eleven previous attempts made on the record, only four had been successful.

During 2002 we had spent a great deal of time finding a boat, and also a team who were experienced enough to take on the record. Finding a suitable boat was not as easy as it sounded. We had known from the outset that we would not be building a new Maxi cat, and there were few to choose from second hand. We settled on *Orange*, which just two months after our announcement in London had left, skippered by another Frenchman, Bruno Peyron, on a successful attempt to break Olivier's record. They smashed it, slicing almost a week off, taking it down to 64 days, 8 hours, 37 minutes and 24 seconds, and though the boat was bigger, at 108 feet compared to *Sport Elec*'s 90, the bar for us was undoubtedly raised much higher.

Kingfisher II, as we renamed *Orange*, felt a world apart from

Kingfisher. When we first sailed we needed eleven of us winching to get the huge mainsail up, and even then it was a very slow process. She felt more like a ship than a yacht, and it was truly awe-inspiring to feel her power.

She was a different animal from the monohulls I was more used to, closer to the multis of the Route du Rhum, illustrated by the fact that shortly before we took her over she was dismasted in the Mediterranean. Not only was it a huge knock to us, but it showed just how fragile a 2 ton mast could be. Luckily the bare tube of a spare mast was in existence, but it was not in any way completed, and, to put the scale of the task into perspective, her wing mast stood just under 40 metres tall and was big enough to fit three people up it at the same time. We had a real challenge on our hands to get her ready.

I had decided to go with a team structure which had three very strong watchleaders who were all effectively capable of running the boat. Outside the main watch system of twelve core crew was myself, skipper/navigator, and our media person, Andrew Preece (nickname Jack), whose job it was to document our adventure. All in all, they were some of the world's best sailors, and I couldn't wait to get out there with them. Their experience of these boats was essential to our project. The physical loads are immense, and the sheer scale of them is hard to get your head around. The winches were gigantic, the mast cables huge – almost an inch across – and the ropes thicker! Despite being a carbon-fibre multihull like a 60 foot tri, she handled quite differently. Though just under twice their length, she was four times heavier, weighing in at 22 tons!

On 15 January 2003 *Kingfisher II* officially went on standby for her Jules Verne record. She was ready, packed and sorted for her journey, and was sitting in her starting blocks. Personally I was relieved at this stage: I had hardly had a second to breathe between the end of the Rhum and this moment. But rest was short-lived as just eight days later, on Thursday 23 January, our standby mode switched to amber, the crew returned to Lorient. Four days later we were off . . .

*

We had 100 miles to sail before we were at the start line of the Jules Verne, which was lucky considering the fact that we had our first problem before we even reached it. We were storming along in the Channel, with some pretty feisty winds, when we noticed, just an hour or so from the line, that there was some black staining on the mast, marking damage to her mast track. This was unexpected and really did not mark a good start to our record. It forced us to head to the shelter of UK shores to make repairs.

The early setback left me feeling very nervous about the Jules Verne, and, though I did feel that we were ready when we crossed the start line, I wished that there had been time in the schedule to be together as a team and bond more strongly. I had great relationships with some of the guys, but I had wished to know at least half of them better before the off. I had never skippered such a large crew before, and there was a lot about this trip that was new to me. As we crossed the line in the early hours of the following morning with *KF2* ready to rock and roll, we saw almost 60 knots of wind, a fraction under 70 mph: motorway speed, and strong enough to take your breath away. In the nav station I was talking on the radio to 'Claude Breton, the Frenchman with the all-important stopwatch' in the lighthouse at Ushant, and Kevin McMeel, our medic and assistant navigator, was next to me, counting down the start to the guys on deck through our speaker system. Jack was also there filming, laughing with excitement as we crossed the line, as Kev said, 'This is what I live for . . . the start!' Then, as he counted down from ten to one, Jack said, 'Ladies and gentlemen, we are now floating in space . . . Welcome to the Jules Verne.'

On deck, on the other hand, it was a more serious story, as at the start line there were always strong currents that create a nasty sea. The motion was violent as her two massive hulls careered along at speeds of up to 37 knots through the waves, which, as they hit us, damaged both of our communication domes. It was a windy but very fast start, and everyone was over the moon to finally be off on our adventure.

Our watch system was a rotation of standby watch, on watch and then off watch. Each lasted four hours and was designed so that only four people need be up on deck for the full period, and there could be a back-up watch always ready to help with a sail change or manoeuvre as they were all kitted up and ready at a moment's notice. The standby watch also had the role of preparing the freeze-dried food, and food time was the watch change. The off watch however was really off, and each crew member had eight hours to sleep in a bunk per day, bar the time it took them to eat and get their kit on and off. It's amazing how life can be so different at sea, even more so when the crew quarters were split between two hulls with 50 feet and nothing but a large exposed piece of net between them. There were four bunks in each hull – two up and two down – and a passage next to them barely wide enough to squeeze two people through together.

Adding an additional element of pressure, nineteen days before we had left, another boat, *Geronimo*, had crossed the start line. The skipper was none other than Olivier de Kersauson, the former record holder. *Geronimo* was 111 feet long, a fraction bigger than ours. As we crossed the start line he was sailing into the Southern Ocean, and on passing the Equator he was already almost one and a half days up on Bruno Peyron's record-breaking voyage in *Orange*. Each day we were not only comparing our progress to *Orange*'s position, but were also looking very closely at where *Geronimo* had been too.

Though we had made the most of the wind to give us a slingshot south, with waves pelting *KF2* and her crew like fire hydrants it wasn't the easiest bit of sailing. Nonetheless, it was great to be out there finally. On board there was a great atmosphere, and our little world began to function like a ship, with the watches rotating like clockwork.

The dangers of these big cats are numerous. The faster you sail the faster the water hits you. The biggest risk by far is being washed overboard by the waves, and when they are flying at you at up to 35 mph it hurts. I remembered in the training when crew member Damian Foxall and I were standing next to each other by the boom and, even though we were travelling slowly, a wave washed up and hit the soles of our feet through the nets. We were both holding on, which was lucky, as within a fraction of a second we found ourselves flailing out sideways like flags from the boom. It felt like the ground had come up to hit you, and I couldn't help but think that, with a wave travelling a little faster, it would have been damn near impossible to hold on. It also really hurt the soles of your feet, and made you realize that it would be very easy to break your ankles that way too. Capsize is also a huge risk, and when one of the hulls on a 22 ton catamaran lifts clear of the water you totally involuntarily hold your breath. Just because the boat is bigger doesn't mean that it's more or less likely to capsize. When the waves in the Southern Ocean are 60 feet tall, a 108 foot catamaran looks like a beach cat. It's not so bad when you are on deck, as you are in control, but down below, when the constant sound of rushing water beneath you stops and you find your hull airborne, you can't help but wonder if the guys have a problem, or if all's OK. Sleeping when that's happening is nigh on impossible.

It had been a cold start to our record attempt, but conditions eased as we sped southward. These boats really were very fast, and it seemed that we were approaching the latitude of the Canaries before we could blink! Life was improving: the temperature was rising, boat speed was good, and morale was sky high. Inside the cabin I was down to just one layer of thermals, and with the water temp at 22 degrees life was becoming more civilized than it had been over the previous days. We were soon flying along and catching up quickly on *Orange*'s record. As we approached the Equator, the temperature inside the boat rose further still, but here I began to feel tense and worried as I could see the weather charts were not looking promising. Though for the first time since we crossed the start line we were ahead of *Orange*'s record, they showed a zone just a few hundred miles before us which could really slow us down. Frankly speaking, the South Atlantic was looking terrible, with no established weather system to sail round, and it worried the hell out of me.

We crossed the Equator at 0121 and 59 seconds on the morning of 7 February, day nine. We were only nine minutes behind *Orange*'s record. Unfortunately we were nearly two days behind *Geronimo*, but we had to console ourselves that they hadn't yet broken the record and we still had the whole Southern Ocean, where we were sure our boat was faster, to make up our time deficit. We had light airs after the doldrums, which lasted for two days, but the mood was raised when we had our traditional equatorial crossing ceremony for those on board who had not previously crossed, and Jack and Kevin were summoned on deck for King Neptune's initiation!

In my opinion they got off lightly, but there was no lack of amusement to be shared by the rest of the crew. They were summoned on deck and taken to the martingale, where Ronny and I tied them up with sail ties. Seeing the two guys standing there in their shorts was nothing short of hilarious, as their white torsos were asking for the application of the sloppy brown liquid we'd been preparing for days. Everyone was out and on deck and smiling: Jason Carrington with the camera taking pictures, and Damian Foxall with a worrying look in his eye as he began to apply the 'mixture' to the pair of them. Anthony Merrington was dressed as Neptune, with a hat made of freeze-dried bags, a beard of netting and a beautiful blue sash more commonly known as a safety line! More amusingly, he had a toilet plunger with which to try to feed the poor victims with a mixture that was enough to make anyone vomit. Just why it's important that it's foul I don't know, and although I had not been party to its making, I was aware that it had in it a few dead flying fish, some oily engine water and a substantial amount of leftover freeze-dried meal, mainly beef dill, which was everyone's least favourite meal. Not surprisingly both Jack and Kev spat out the concoction instantly, and the boys (and I of course) got great pleasure from watching the remainder of the mixture be either flung at the guys or, as the *pièce de resistance*, poured down the back of their pants until it dribbled down their legs. Nice.

Of course, the whole event was caught on film, but for me the funniest part was when Youngster surfaced, having removed his King Neptune disguise, and said, 'Andrew, I just missed the action. What was that all about? I just came from downstairs, and all of a sudden you're looking filthy. Did you have an accident?'

Andrew paused, and with a wry smile on his face replied, 'The beef dill just went straight through me.'

Life on deck may have felt steady, but life in the nav station was the opposite. I was seriously worried about the non-existence of the high-pressure system in the South Atlantic and was talking to the guys about the situation ahead. It helped hugely to share thoughts on what lay ahead, which was a very different scenario to that of the Vendée, where every decision is yours and yours alone, and there is no weather router on land to discuss things with either! Hervé Jan was the watch leader with the greatest number of equatorial crossings; he'd crossed the Equator about twenty-five times and could never remember the South Atlantic high being so messy. Ultimately we had no idea what the right option was, but with the winds at those speeds we were not going to go anywhere very quickly.

Spirits were up and down with the wind, and, though from time to time we had enough breeze to get *KF2* up to 20 knots, those periods were more than often short-lived. I wrote in my log:

```
Again we find ourselves in an unavoidable situation as
the wind gods cast a shadow over our world ...
```

That week was tough for me, and a few hours' sleep in twenty-four was not uncommon. I had been worrying about the performance data, feeding it up to the guys, and was concerned that I was not spending enough time on deck with them, talking about thoughts and strategy. There did not seem enough hours in the day to achieve everything, and even with a flat boat and very little wind it was a massive challenge. It was here that I realized that I could have done things differently on board. I had chosen to be the person who would skipper the boat and be the navigator, but it was proving difficult, and, as I am someone who likes to do everything well, it was causing me issues. But I was absolutely relishing being at sea, as was clear from my log:

```
As I sit here and type it is 5.30 in the morning.
The moon set about an hour or so ago, after lighting
up the horizon like it was the only path to take in
the world.
```

And, despite my own personal journey of trying to manage all that was going on around me, life was not all stress as many events on board raised a smile, especially Andrew's loss of one of his two precious pairs of pants overboard! We had one period when we hardly had any wind at all, and our boat speed dropped to 3 to 4 knots. The boys were quite chuffed that we hadn't seen the two doughnuts though – 0.0 on the speed readout – but just sitting in the water was quite unnatural for her, like a racehorse frozen mid-stride.

It was Neal McDonald's watch just before sunset. There was little wind, less than 15 knots, and the sea was as flat and quiet as it had ever been. It was approaching 2100 hours, and the sun was beginning to set, highlighting a dark line of cloud in the distance, which seemed to close on us very quickly. I called Meeno, our weather router, for our evening update, explaining all that I could see. Then, incredibly within that one phone call, we were sailing in 25 knots of wind with a really lively sea. I was amazed at how quickly things can just change unpredictably like that. We were suddenly crashing through the waves, making typing virtually impossible.

As Guillermo Altadill left his watch to hand over to Neal, he looked into the distance, seeing the clouds approach. 'Welcome to the gates of hell,' he proclaimed and promptly retired below to his bunk.

Within the crew there was a real feeling of unfinished business, and though there was an air of apprehension, we were all feeling that we just wanted to get on with it. Our first twenty-four-hour run of good wind was day sixteen; a week since we'd last had decent breeze. The daily log from the office read:

SPEED NOT LOVE - 567 MILES IN 24 HOURS!

It was our best yet, and it was 14 February, Valentine's Day. Since we had left we had not managed to cover that distance in twenty-four hours, and at an average speed of 23.6 knots we were absolutely smoking! Everyone was happy to be charging ahead again, and their determination to sail *KF2* fast led to us clawing back seventeen hours on *Orange*'s record.

Though Valentine's Day is not particularly important or really useful at sea, it did however briefly make me think of home. For the first time at sea I had felt quite distanced from Ian. On the Vendée he had been with me every day, but here it felt different. I had thought that perhaps it was due to the fact that I was with a crew and not alone at sea, but it was a strange feeling, and one which was to be the first indicator of what was to come a few months later.

We had arrived, and the timeless gatekeeper to the Southern Ocean had welcomed us. We had barely crossed the thirtieth parallel before we saw our first albatross. Hervé told me that the French call it the 'smoky gull', and I cursed myself for having come down here once again without having learnt more about the various species. The Southern Ocean is a fascinating place – full of life, much more so in fact than the South Atlantic. Though I hated to say it, we'd had bad luck in the Atlantic – the weather had been awful, and what made it even worse was that the Atlantic was the only ocean we had to sail through twice in this record attempt.

Almost on cue, as we approached the fortieth parallel, we sailed into the front of our first Southern Ocean low. The sky was grey, there were storm petrels fluttering over the water's surface, and the water temperature was losing a degree every watch change.

Each mile we speed south now is a plus. Each mile takes us closer and closer to the south, the indescribable south which can be filled with as much beauty and wildness that rotates around such vast contrasts. The most beautiful sunset can be followed by a day so black that it seems lit up by the minute flash of colour around the albatross' eyes.

I knew that the following month would have me constantly on my toes, watching every satellite picture coming in, monitoring every change in sea temperature, but I loved it. It's a 'real' and completely 'living' place to sail, with the waves bigger, the sky greyer, but at least I knew I would no longer be sitting in the nav station in a pool of sweat and that above all we could be getting on with it!

```
Last night kind of summed it all up really; there was a
full moon beaming out over KINGFISHER2, it was almost
as if the deck was floodlit by the heavens. As I wrote
the night's tactics out I didn't even need a torch.
```

The weather was once again showing how out of character it was choosing to be. Our first low was strengthening quickly behind us much more aggressively than predicted, and the sea was building fast to remind us. Making decisions on board was once again extremely difficult, and things were pretty full-on. We were doing 31 knots as I called the office, and said, 'As I'm speaking, 32, 33 ... 35.6 ... !'

I felt like we were playing the escapee as we powered along ahead of the cold front of the approaching low. Our boat speed was fast, averaging 26 knots for hours on end, and *KF2* was getting a bit of a hammering, with the beams at the back being pummelled by the waves. This led to some pretty serious delamination of the carbon on the port side under our back beam. Effectively this is the first stage of a boat falling apart, and like a fracture which spreads it had to be brought under control. In the Route du Rhum this fatal failure had led to the abandoning of boats, and now, deep in the Southern Ocean, the stakes were much, much higher. We patched it and held it together with numerous bolts and glue, but it certainly wasn't going to fix itself out there. We would need to be careful.

We were catching up with *Orange* by the day, despite the fact that we'd headed a long way north to avoid the worst of the sea state. By day nineteen we were just 1.5 hours behind the record, and, despite the temperature dropping, spirits were very high!

Sitting in my chilly nav station, I was beginning to worry again, as the low which we had been catapulted along by was now stalling, and we were set to have to sail through a high-pressure ridge. This tour seemed to go from one extreme to the other, and even amongst the boys there seemed to be some surprise at just what was being thrown at us.

KEVIN MCMEEL: I have not often seen seas like this.
They are majestic mountains of water which gradually
overtake us as they roll unimpeded by any land mass in
their journey eastward. The sun glints through the tops
of them highlighting the green in the blue just before
they turn a foamy white.

In contrast with this incredible beauty, he wrote:

They occasionally come aboard to remind me what it is
like to be hit with a sheet of plywood and dragged to
the end of your tether unless some solid object
intervenes.

Life on deck was not always easy, and things were uncomfortable down below. Wet people in dripping wet gear were regularly up and down the corridor to the nav station, and the boat was constantly humid thanks to the steaming bodies, and the floor was constantly wet. But spirits remained high as, all being well, that night we were due to overtake our invisible *Orange*.

For the first time since our eighth day at sea we would be ahead of the record, but just when you think all is well it often isn't, and in the middle of the night there was an almighty jerk, followed by a crunching sound, as if the starboard hull had hit a wall. I think that it sounded worse below, but I definitely felt the rudder, which was just a few metres from my nav station, hit something. It reminded me of the Vendée, when I ran into a submerged container just weeks from the finish, and it was a sickening noise. This time, though, we weren't at 10 knots, but over 20.

Heart pounding in my chest, I ran through the boat, almost expecting to see water gushing through the hull, and my head was running through our numerous safety drills. I was blinded by the head-torches of the guys in the corridor running through the boat to check too. We studied every compartment one by one, the dagger-boards and the rudders; and thankfully everything was dry bar a little water in the rudder compartment.

49

'The noise was pretty ******* loud where I was,' I said to the guys as we huddled round the rudder stock. There was some damage where it came through the bottom of the hull into the boat, and a little water was seeping in, but it wasn't bad, and the rudder seemed to still work fine. 'I've been unfortunate to hit things before, and it sounded like there was a lot of damage to me. On a scale of one to ten, that was up there.'

I was confused, as with the force of the impact I would have expected there to have been no rudder at all! The daggerboard moved up and down and seemed fine, so after a bit of laminating on the rudder stock by Jason, we were back on track. That was until the following afternoon, when after more investigation we discovered that we had ripped the bottom of the daggerboard clean off! So the evening after our collision turned into an evening of repairs. It needed eight of the crew to get the board out of its socket, and we were all pretty surprised we hadn't realized that the board was so damaged. The repair was entirely possible but frustrating, and though we couldn't return the board to its former glory, having had had 2 metres ripped off it, we did turn it upside down so at least the damage wouldn't get worse.

Unfortunately, our four-hour delay meant we failed to cross the high-pressure ridge and tap into the north-westerly breeze we'd hoped for. This in turn meant we had to find new favourable wind to overtake *Orange*, and a dive south was what was needed. Though I joked to Andrew that 'You've always talked about wanting to take photos of icebergs – so just for you we're going to hang a right,' there was definitely an air of trepidation on board as we did so.

We were now past the Cape of Good Hope and were very aware that *Geronimo* was soon to leave the Southern Ocean, giving us over 7,000 miles of uncluttered racetrack. The good part was that Olivier had rounded with only one and a half days' lead on the record, though their reasons for slowing were likely to affect us too. They had been forced north in the Pacific Ocean, as there were some potent storms and a lot of ice there, in an area which in three weeks' time we would be sailing through too.

I lay in my tiny bunk above the nav station with the constant drone of the water rushing past *KF2*'s hull. Above me was the white paint of the inside of her back beam, and an awful lot of condensation. Each breath seemed to bring with it a drip on to my already damp sleeping bag. I was feeling the pressure of being skipper on such a full-on adventure and as I lay there I began to think. We were about to plunge south now that we had missed our more favourable winds, and, though we could always gybe again to the north to get out of there, we all knew we were heading towards the ice fields. It was here that I had missed an iceberg by just 20 feet in the Vendée Globe just two years before, and a shiver went down my spine as I thought back to the moment I saw it. As I had dragged a cloth over *Kingfisher*'s window to wipe off the condensation I saw a wall of ice the other side of it. Then, though, I was on my own; all that was at stake was me. Back then there were no wives and children involved . . .

In the high-pressure ridge progress was slow, and our speed was reasonable but not as fast as it would have been if we'd been in the wonderful flow of north-westerly winds we could see just ahead of us on the wind charts. However, our slightly slower progress was put to the back of our minds momentarily as we sailed past Marion Island, and I was lucky enough to have a clear view of it for the second time in my life. The first had been in the Vendée Globe, and it was just as I'd remembered it, with green slopes, intense life and the most incredible number of birds flying over it.

The predicted weather for the following few days was more wind, and, as Neal put it, we were about to get our first 'real kicking'. I called the office, and my words in the conference call were: 'It's going to come in hard and strong tomorrow.'

To match the fall in sea temperature the barometer began to plummet, and the wind turned on to the nose from the north-east at 30 knots. It indicated the arrival of the low which would swing the wind round to the north-west and give us a more favourable angle. Wind on the nose in the south was pretty hard going, though the alternative was to slide south and get closer to the 65–70 knot winds near the low's centre. Another low was heading south from Madagascar and had been altering the normal westerlies of the south. Heading upwind in those seas, it was actually impossible to sleep in my bunk at all, as *KF2* was 'scissoring', and the motion was not dissimilar to a cake walk at the fair.

When the wind came round, it began to increase, and with it so did our speed, and so with the aim of riding the front for as long as possible we pushed hard with the storm spinnaker. The sea was of good size and building, and we had managed finally to get ahead of *Orange*'s record. The guys were stoked, as we felt like we'd hit the conveyor belt to take us to Cape Horn. The twelve-hour lead we now had was not to be sniffed at, and we were not even at the half-way stage! That day held some of the best Southern Ocean memories I have, with huge waves like mountains rolling steadily, confidently and unstoppably behind us. Though *KF2* was 108 feet long, she appeared tiny as she surfed down the waves. We had been spoilt with the clear-blue skies of the high-pressure ridge, and despite our lumpy upwind part we had managed to maintain a reasonable pace. That night, though, on Hervé's watch, we knew the front was upon us when the wind shot up to 50 knots in what seemed like an instant.

In seconds the standby watch was on deck and attempting to wind down the spinnaker. The most likely outcome was the spinnaker exploding, and getting it down was going to be a real struggle. The sail was thrashing about in the air like a tethered racehorse trying to break free, and the noise, let alone the motion, of it was deafening. Hervé, the man you'd want at the helm in a crisis, managed to steer her deep enough to drop the huge piece of canvas behind the mainsail, but unfortunately the titanium pulley on the halyard hit the mainsail, resulting in a tear in it. As the wind increased and we continued to surf down the waves, Hendo and Ronny spent hours up the mast fixing it, each held in position with a series of ropes like a spider's web. Their figures looked tiny suspended up the rig, and the job took several hours, starting before dusk and continuing into the darkness. When the two returned to the deck they were inseparable and joked that they were like a 'couple'.

If we had known then just what would happen that night, though, we probably wouldn't have bothered. Just hours later I called the office: 'This is the call I was hoping never to have to make . . . we've been dismasted.'

At 2222 on 23 February I was jolted forwards on the chart-table seat whilst discussing weather with Meeno. Jolts forward happen quite often in these boats as we fire down waves, but this was different: this was a gut-wrenching, ear-piercing, crunching and snapping sound. My instinct said that we'd stopped dead, having hit an iceberg. I had never experienced a dismasting before, and certainly not at 20 knots. I dropped the phone and hurled myself towards the companionway, looking round my feet as I went to see if there was water coming on board from anywhere; I could see nothing. As I reached the hatch all became clear. With a feeling of nausea I realized that the huge mast, which had powered us ahead of the record over the past twenty-four days, had been snapped like a matchstick and was lying sprawled across the deck, part of it submerged in the ocean.

On deck it looked like chaos, but Neal, who was on watch at the time, had done a great job of tasking the guys to cut the rigging free as soon as humanly possible. Leaving the mast attached could have sunk us. My first reaction was 'Is everyone OK?' and once I was satisfied that was the case I joined the race to cut the mast free from the boat as it pummelled into our hull. The waves were still huge, and walking around on the net was a challenge with the boat's unpredictable drunken motion. We had to be careful – some of the wires put in place to prevent us falling over the side were gone. There was rope, carbon, sails and rigging everywhere, and we tried to pull in as much of the rope as we could. The deck was alive with head-torches, illuminating the boat in the darkness; in fact I'm not sure that the whole crew of fourteen had actually been on deck together since the start. Everyone was busy. Earlier that evening, after we'd repaired the sail, I'd ripped my hand open, and even the bandage over my freshly sewn stitches seemed totally irrelevant with all that was going on around us. Like the others I was pulling ropes in. Precious ropes that we would need to get us home.

Once we were sure that the mast was free and the boat would come to no immediate danger, we huddled together as a team. The Kerguelen Islands we had now passed were only 100 miles away, but they were against the wind and had no facilities; our best option was to head north to Australia.

Adding to our problems, there was another storm brewing to the west. We were sitting there like a wounded bird, unable to fly, and more vulnerable than we had been at any stage in the trip. Not only that, but we were below the Antarctic convergence in iceberg territory; and whereas we had a staggering 2,200 miles to sail to Perth, Australia, only 900 miles separated us from the Antarctic peninsular and 420 from the pack ice surrounding it. We couldn't have found a more isolated piece of ocean to be drifting in. Not only was there a risk of being blown helplessly towards the icecap, a big storm now, at the wrong time, would mean a battering that could rip the boat apart. Speed had been our saviour before, and now we'd totally and utterly lost that.

Everyone was in shock but soon went into automatic pilot, and the energy which was left was thrown into the challenging task of getting KF2 moving again and out of this dangerous zone. What followed was one of the most impressive engineering feats I've ever witnessed as the guys set about raising the boom to become our new, much-shortened mast and jury rig.

After our dismasting, for the first time on this trip, the tears came. But they came with a feeling of frustration and anger. So much work, energy and commitment had gone into the project: each fitting sealed, each lashing tied, each circuit board checked . . . and now here we were cutting away parts of her over the side. It felt so destructive, and so final. But at the same time I felt pride. I was proud of the strength of the crew, proud of their commitment and humour, proud of their smiles and proud of the way that they had handled their frustration too. Although we were all disappointed, we had shifted our focus on getting ourselves moving again.

We were on the other side of the world, but my head was in London, Paris and Europe. *Come on, Ellen, it's your job – just keep it together, take a deep breath, don't close your eyes, just deal with it. Soon you can sleep.* I had been up through most of the darkness doing interviews which seemed to take for ever; especially as I was tired, really tired. You know that you're really exhausted when you wake with the phone still in your hand an hour later having no recollection of the last words you spoke in an interview. It was just over twenty-four hours since we had been dismasted. Once again I dozed off . . .

I woke, my head brimming over with images, remembering those moments before dawn when *Kingfisher II* sat lifeless, mastless and, painfully, just sticking to the waves. I pulled myself together then remembered feeling watched over for some strange reason; then it came to me: our silent friends. The albatross were watching us, coming closer than ever, even flying feet away from us in an inspection of their new visitor. Not many people come down here, so we may have been the first boat they had ever seen. I had never seen them so close before, so inquisitive. On my three trips to the Southern Ocean I had never seen an albatross flap its wings, not once. Now at least I had the time to appreciate their beauty.

What had frustrated me almost as much as our loss of the record was that I felt that I never really got into the trip. I was just beginning to feel more comfortable in my role on board; beginning to see life existing in abundance outside the nav station, finding the time to have a laugh with the guys, to try to stop worrying about the navigation and spending time on deck every so often. I was beginning to understand personalities and feel more at ease with people's characters and differences out there.

The sun came up this morning and it was 0100 GMT. I'm not really sure which time zone I'm in or where I belong right now. Just a few days ago, I belonged on KINGFISHER2 on a mission to break the Jules Verne record. I know now I still belong here but in a very different sense.

Though our Jules Verne is all but a cluster of vivid memories, we now have a new challenge, to sail our monster catamaran to Australia, which at 2000 miles from us is going to be no mean feat. That's further than most people would cruise in years ... We are still deep-south and conditions are still pretty cold. Somehow, summer in Australia seems a long, long way away.

It's both a blessing and a punishment to be sailing for another two weeks. Now for good or for bad we have that luxury of time to think about what has happened to us, and to realize what an incredible thing we were doing which ended so abruptly for us. Whether we fester in despair, or think positively to the future that has still to come through.

My role becomes crystal clear now. The skipper's role is one of motivation - whether at 30 knots or 3 knots. Whether winning or losing, whether hurting or rejoicing - on reflection, therefore, my challenge is far from over.

Come on guys, it may be a wee way off, but Australia here we come! ...

It's a hard realization that things go wrong - but a very real realization. Life is without purpose, right now. However; we go on though ... and there are new challenges out there, many of which I am sure I have never even dreamt about yet - many I am sure not even related to sailing ...

So here's to getting to Australia - here's to the next challenges, I hope you'll be able to live those with us too ... whatever that may be.

Thanks a million,

Ex

In usual *KF2* fashion the lads all rallied, and before you knew it we had backgammon sets, chess sets, draught sets and even a pack of home-made cards to play with! Tool handles, winch handles, safety cards, and even the backs of cupboard doors were used creatively for simple entertainment. Even when the winds were not in our favour we laughed and joked and enjoyed our time together.

Just before our arrival in Fremantle, Australia, I wrote my final log:

There is more time to see the water change, as now
sailing at 8 rather than 18 knots things happen more
slowly. These 2000 miles could have been covered in
4 days at the speeds we were sailing in the south, now
we've been at it for almost two weeks.

A couple of hours after sunset the sky to the south
began to glow. The colour was a cross between a bright
shimmering white and a flame yellow. The light shot what
looked like thousands of kilometres up in to the sky,
but not in a static way; as this light was moving,
almost dancing the most gentle dance as it rose up to
the atmosphere. We had been looking at the Aurora
Australis, an incredible phenomenon created by the
earth's magnetic field. The power of nature out here
knows no bounds - we are so lucky to live on an earth
so full of treasure.

There had barely been a day on board when I didn't think of being out at sea, alone on a multi; I even had drawings for the new boat secretly stashed beneath my bunk. The Jules Verne record for me really had been part of the process to decide whether or not to build the trimaran, and, rather than deter me, our experience made me want to do it more than ever. That feeling of new focus following disappointment cleared my head incredibly – and my last communication from the boat was a very positive one. I couldn't wait to get back down in the Southern Ocean. All being well, I'd be down there the following winter in a brand new boat.

But could we actually build a boat strong enough to take the south, small enough to be sailed solo by one person and big enough not to be capsized by 60 foot seas? The hard part was that the Jules Verne had showed me just what formidable machines multihulls are in the south. I had sailed *Foncia* a great deal, but you would never take her to the Southern Ocean: you would be flicked over by the huge waves and capsized in the first storm. As I'd seen in the Route du Rhum, the danger of solo multihulls was all too real. But I was enchanted by the irresistible challenge of the project. There had been a seed in my mind, and nothing could stop it from growing. Perhaps it was my innate stubbornness, or the overpowering draw of the oceans, but every time I thought about the project I was smiling inside.

Chapter Four

Things all happened quickly after the Jules Verne. I returned to the UK just a few days after we arrived in Fremantle, then got stuck straight in to the design meetings for the trimaran, which we started to build just four weeks later.

I was lucky too to be able to call the man who I believe is the most experienced multihull designer in the world my friend, so when we'd begun discussing a new boat design the summer before the Jules Verne there was no hesitation whatsoever about who to work with: British boat designer Nigel Irens. I had learnt a huge amount in the Jules Verne and was keen that the tri was as large as we felt one person could possibly sail. At the time we couldn't envisage a boat larger than 75 feet, and even for that I had to push hard, as Nigel was sure initially that 70 feet would be the optimum size. It was a dilemma between a boat too big to be sailed solo and a boat big enough to survive for a month in the storms of the south.

Time passed quickly on our return from Fremantle, and only eight weeks later I was back out on the water with *Foncia*, as a race called the Challenge Mondial Assistance was waiting. As well as being an important race in its own right, it was part of the training for Alain and me for the Transat Jacques Vabre at the end of the year, which had come along again, and ultimately for my round-the-world voyage. I felt confident as we carried out final preparations on *Foncia*, despite the fact that she, like so many of the 60 foot tris, had spent the winter undergoing repairs after the disastrous Rhum. There had been eighteen boats in the Rhum, and now in this race there were just twelve, with many of the boats fresh out of the boatyard. The course would take us down the Atlantic coast, into the Mediterranean and then round the tip of Italy to finish up in Rimini.

The crew was almost identical to the one we'd won with in the same race two years previously; we had Alain, Loik Gallon, Nicolas Bérenger and Philippe Peché (Pe-Peche). My job on board was the navigating, and I would sit outside the watch system. We loaded up our gear – our navigational charts and data, sleeping bags, food and spares. Alain, being French, was not so keen on freeze-dried, so he brought eggs and bacon on board, and there was a dry cured leg of ham too! It was great to be back on *Foncia*, and, though the boat had changed, the giggles were the same.

The start was blustery as we tacked out through the English Channel against a strong westerly wind. Spirits were high, and, though we were near the back of the fleet at the start, we were up to fifth place, just over 20 miles behind the leader, by the second night. We had set off into a low-pressure system, which was taking its toll on the fleet. There had been a lot of problems on the first and second days. *Sodebo*, skippered by Thomas Coville, pulled into La Trinité to repair their forestay, after fearing that they would lose their mast; *Gitana* had to repair a batten; *Bonduelle* had their mainsail down for eight hours to repair battens; and *Belgacom* broke their gennaker halyard twice then scheduled a stop in Spain.

On *Foncia* we'd decided to stay to the north and try to catch the front early in order to keep away from the worst of the conditions off the tip of the Brittany peninsula, where the tides are strong. It was always nerve-racking taking a decision as to where we should sail, so when the front went through and our wind switched to the north, allowing us to finally head south under clear skies and with a northerly breeze, we were relieved and happy. Life was good on board, *Foncia* was sailing blisteringly well, and we were right up in the leading pack without any serious technical problems. The new *Foncia* had curved foils, which gave her lift at high speeds, and the spume of water which would spin off her floats was mesmerizing. I felt really excited about our own race later that year.

Our watch system was roughly three hours on and three hours off, and life on board was beginning to settle into a routine. On the second morning of the race, being out of the front, we celebrated by having eggs and bacon, or *'oeuf – bacon'*, as Alain would say.

By late afternoon Alain was steering, and it was time for the watch change at 1800. I was just finishing a final mouthful of food before stepping out all kitted up to join Pe-Peche and Nico on their watch. We were laughing and joking in the galley about something which I can no longer remember and feeling happy with our speed at well over 20 knots . . .

Suddenly, after what sounded like a sharp tapping noise, *Foncia*'s feel changed. She was slewing to the right unnaturally, and, though my instinct was to get to the cockpit and release the gennaker sheet, it was impossible, as the floor began to tilt, and we were all thrown forwards with surprising force. The sudden unfamiliar and aggressive deceleration led to the realization that in seconds your whole world would turn upside down and go dark.

The next thing I knew was that Loik came flying past me as he jumped in, feet first, through the cabin hatchway. We were all hanging on to whatever we could grab, as our inverted cabin instantly became a darkened world into which water was flooding through the open hatchway in torrents. We smacked into each other, falling through the air into a pile of bodies and gear. It was disorientating, but you react on adrenalin-fuelled instinct. The only thing on my mind was to find Alain. He was outside, and there was a danger he was now trapped under the nets beneath the water. We always carry a knife on us when we are sailing a multihull in case we get trapped, and now I had mine in my hand as I scrambled out of the starboard escape hatch on to the upturned nets to find one of my best friends. Nico was out of the port one. I ran around, forcing my legs through the deep blue water, staring into it, desperately trying to catch a glimpse of Alain. If he were trapped there, he would be unable to breathe. I could see shapes, sails, ropes, sail bags all hanging, floating lifelessly, moving eerily and rhythmically with every wave which rolled beneath us. As the sea heaved up and down, my heart was racing in my chest. I felt the most overwhelming urgency, which I can only describe as the most total focus I have ever felt before or since in my life. I felt as if I was counting my heartbeats, trying to slow them down in a stupid attempt to win more time.

Desperate, but trying to remain calm, I tried to glance across to see if Nico had found him on the other side of the boat, but all I could see was a huge white inverted hull lying helpless in the water, blocking me from the other side. I did one more tour of the net – nothing, there was nothing.

I ran back to the hatch. Loik and Pe-Peche were there.

'*Alain – tu as Alain?*' I called as I neared the window. I looked into Pe-Peche's eyes, trying to read what had happened in the fractions of a second before he answered me.

'*Il est avec Nico.*' Nico had him, but was he alive? Was he breathing? Was he injured?

'*Et ça va?*' I replied.

'*Oui.*'

My heart sang in elation. He was OK. I felt like I could draw breath for the first time in what must have been only sixty seconds but what felt like an hour. That moment was the most scared I have ever been at sea, and it wasn't for my own safety. Alain had clung to the back of the boat as he felt her go over, and, when the mast hit and we were at ninety degrees, he'd managed to keep his grip, so he had his bearings for getting out.

Once under water he had managed to swim down deeper, under the guard wires, then surface for air, not letting go of the boat. The tri was upside down and helpless, if he'd lost the boat there would have been little we could have done to go and pick him up. There was something else that was lucky too, if you can call it that. As Alain had gone up on watch three hours earlier, I had offered to zip up his drysuit. For some reason, perhaps because the temperature was warmer, he had instead pulled a jacket over his drysuit to let it vent. Perhaps I'm wrong, but I don't believe that Alain would have stood a chance of swimming a metre and a half under water to get under the guard wires had the zip been sealed and his suit full of air.

It was hard enough avoiding the miles of rope waving in the water threatening to wrap round your ankle, but he managed to swim down, and, as it was filled with water, it allowed his passage.

I had already visualized what happens when a tri capsizes – what I'd do if I were on the helm, and how I'd try and survive. I had thought about how it must feel to have the boat rear up beneath you, and to look down at the sea, over 50 feet below you, just before she inverts totally and the sea approaches you like a train. The whole capsize cannot have taken more than five seconds – five seconds from laughing with the guys in the galley to fearing for someone's life.

Once we had alerted the team to our predicament and let them know that we were all safe, Alain changed into dry clothes, and we began what was to be forty-eight hours in *Foncia* upside down. We set about taking watches on the hull, with powerful torches and flares handy to alert anyone in the area of our presence. It's surprising just how vulnerable you feel sitting on a boat with no means of propulsion out in an ocean. Her inverted main hull was extremely smooth and slippery, and in order to climb up on to it we rigged a series of stirrups which were attached to the propeller. It must have been 10 feet up to the high point near the escape hatch, but from there we had a much better view. Being further south, the water was warmer, so despite the fact that we'd be out there at night, it shouldn't be too cold. Inside the boat felt odd. Everything was upside down – lockers, pockets, windows, electronics. Our floor was the ceiling, and in foot-deep water floated all our belongings: sleeping bags, food, eggs, batteries, socks, charts, computers . . . everything awash. We didn't really sleep much, as the bunks were all the wrong way up, but there was an area which was under the cockpit on which it was flat enough to lie down. It didn't really matter where we were, though: in our survival suits, even if we sat in the water on the cabin floor, we stayed dry.

It's remarkable what emotions you can go through while racing on a boat. You put your life in your crew members' hands totally, with a level of trust that you rarely get to experience in everyday life. Sometimes a glance says it all, and there are times when fear, pleasure and relief are shared intensely. Though our race, the boat and our objective had all fallen apart, there was a strange feeling of jubilation on board. We were all there, together and in one piece, and in a funny way everything else seemed irrelevant.

During the long nights which followed the capsize I thought a lot about what had happened. Alain was fine, but even in the years that I had been sailing competitively there had been many people who had lost their lives. Gerry Roufs was lost at sea in the 1996 Vendée Globe when his boat capsized; Nicolas Florin died when he was swept from *La Trinitaine* in the Round Europe in 1999; and Paul Vatine was lost at sea when his trimaran capsized in the Transat Jacques Vabre, also in 1999, during a huge storm. I was in that race in 1999: everyone was aware what had happened and no one who competed in the race will ever forget the news that Paul hadn't made it back on board. He was steering like Alain, and a quote from him a few months before he left rang round in my head: 'I don't want to die at sea, I want to live on land.'

On board *Foncia* we had not set off our EPIRB as a signal of distress, as we did not consider ourselves in need of rescue; but instead the team back on land in Lorient organized for a huge ocean-going tug to come out from Lisbon. Twenty-four hours later, it arrived, and we realized time had passed quickly as we'd chatted, watched out over the ocean and tidied the boat.

It was staggering to see the size of the tug. More suited to moving cargo ships weighing hundreds of thousands of tons than a trimaran at 5 tons, it dwarfed us. There was a crew on the tug as well as a diver, who had the job of jumping into the water, connecting the tow line and liberating parts of the rigging so that we could be towed without accruing further damage. It was a very dangerous job, and we were all aware of it. It would mean being under the water with a huge sea running, risking getting tangled by the mass of root-like ropes or having your cylinder knocked from your back by the heaving, unpredictable structure of a stranded trimaran. As the diver jumped from the tug, the huge blue superstructure towered above him, making his figure look tiny. It seemed to take for ever for him to reach us, and Nico went forward to help him on board with his heavy gear. He introduced himself as Luis, and we began a lengthy process of explaining what we needed him to do beneath the boat. It was quite tricky conveying exactly what to do to someone who spoke only basic English and had never seen the boat before. Finally he dived, and each time he went under we all held our breath, watching his bubbles beneath the water and sighing with relief when he surfaced. He must have been with us for well over an hour before the job was done, and we decided he should stay with us on *Foncia*, as it was too dangerous to try and clamber back on board the tug. He was running short of air in his tank, and the sea was still too rough.

As we set off with the tow we quickly realized that we couldn't go above 2 knots without risking further damage to *Foncia*; therefore our limp to Lisbon was going to take over twenty-four hours. Bearing in mind the length of the journey, we decided to get Luis into some dry clothes. I went up under the floor to root through everyone's bags to see what I could find that was actually dry. I remember feeling happy for him that it was only day two when we'd capsized, so most things in there were relatively clean! I beckoned for him to join me, then indicated to him that he could pick things that fitted. He seemed grateful. I felt slightly uncomfortable so, struggling to find something simple to understand, I asked him, 'Do you have children?'

'No – no children, no wife.' He turned to me and smiled. 'Just a great big dog.'

From that moment on we got along famously, and it was an early sign that we would spend a great deal of time together . . .

There were two incidents that month which would have a real impact on my life. One was meeting Luis, and the other was meeting my new boat for the first time in Australia. Eager to catch a glimpse of her in her early stages of build and just two weeks after the capsize I was on a plane to see her. With the summer on its way it was a stark reminder that we had to get our skates on, not only to build the new trimaran, but to sail her home before the Southern Ocean winter kicked in a few months after Christmas.

Oli Allard, who joined us shortly before the Jules Verne, had moved down to Sydney to be our full-time project manager there. He would liaise with Nigel, BoatSpeed (the boat builders), Albert (a nickname for Neil Graham, who had joined Offshore Challenges as technical director) and me. The first of many journeys which I made from Sydney airport to Gosford, which was about an hour and a half north up the coast, passed quickly. I was fascinated by the dense green bush and the stunning forest-lined creeks we were passing, but at the same time I was very keen to get to the yard to see the boat for the first time. Despite the fact it was winter, it was still hot when the sun shone, but the heat of the day disappeared behind us as we drew shut the heavy metal door of the boatyard where *B&Q Castorama*, our new trimaran, was being built. I eagerly walked in and was immediately taken aback. I drew a short breath and stood in awe at what I saw before me: she looked huge! Though I'd seen a few pictures that Oli had taken of her moulds taking shape, nothing could have prepared me for the first time I saw her form and scale. I felt like I was living a dream that couldn't possibly be my life. I smiled from ear to ear and felt like pinching myself to see if it really was all real. She was the most beautiful trimaran I had ever seen.

BoatSpeed were the most dedicated group of people I could have imagined working with. Albert had chosen the yard during our Jules Verne attempt, and he could not have done a better job. The guys who built her were brilliant, and the yard sang with skill and pride. The stakes were high with this one. One mistake in her build process could lead to disaster at sea, but here I felt in safe hands. It was going to be six long but exciting months before I could spend all my time with her, so I organized over the coming summer to visit her as often as I could. Progress was important too: as our plan was to deliver her home by sea we needed to set off from the southern hemisphere not long after Christmas, before the weather window was closed by storms.

I was desperate to spend a little time alone with her. Perhaps it's not as important for every solo sailor, but for me having a strong bond with my boat was fundamental. At the end of the day, just before Oli and I headed home to our rented house, I stayed round the yard for a few minutes, just to spend my first bit of time with her. Everyone had left, it was dark in the yard and almost eerie as the usual activities of the day had ended. My footsteps echoed on the concrete floor as I slowly moved around, gazing up in total wonder at her, not daring to let myself believe that in a year's time I was going to sail her solo round the world.

It was when I was standing near the bow of her main hull, with her grey and black topsides towering above me, that it came to me: everything about her said 'whale'. It was then that I nicknamed her. 'Hello, Mobi,' I whispered. Feeling a strange feeling of security in being with her I said, 'I'm going to look after you, girl.' I turned away, not letting myself look back and spoil the moment. I wanted that thought to stay with me for my whole flight home.

I was well aware that even just in delivering Mobi back from Sydney I was going to need to be as strong as I could be. In 2003 I ramped up my fitness training to another level, and, though I saw him rarely, I worked hard for Matt Scott, a fitness trainer from London. I had joined a gym just outside Cowes, and whenever I was home I would be there for at least two hours a day. Early starts and long, long sessions on the aerobic machines became the norm. Keeping my heart rate around 150 for well over an hour at a time left me soaked with sweat, but I needed it, and when I lifted the weights I would give it all I could, knowing that in a few months' time those extra kilos lifted could mean the difference between life and death. On the multihulls my respect for the sea had been heightened still, as I had felt all too well the power of the waves as they crossed through the nets as if they weren't there, carrying everything effortlessly along with them. I could feel myself getting stronger and I was pleased. As the summer progressed, I was up to thirteen chin-ups and could pull down well over my weight on the lat pull-down machine. Training was a means to an end, and I was longing for that end to be the finish line with a record.

My sailing for 2003 was varied, from America's Cup boats in San Francisco Bay to *Foncia*, but following our capsize my next real session on the water was sailing Formula 8 catamaran dinghies with team mate Nick Moloney over six days and five nights out in the Swedish archipelago, orienteering on water around the thousands of islands there in a race called the 'Archipelago Raid'. However, we were struck by bad luck, as in the early hours of the second morning of the race I impaled my leg on a knife which, unknown to me, was concealed in a bag. Within six hours we were forced to make the decision to pull out, as I had internal bleeding. I was sad not to finish the race. Even after our few days there I was mesmerized by the sheer beauty of the archipelago. It was like an undiscovered world and took me right back to *Swallows and Amazons* and the islands and adventures that had so captivated me as a child.

After another trip to Sydney came a host of sponsor presentations all over Europe for Kingfisher and a busy and action-packed Cowes Week in the UK, then it was back on the water for our first Grand Prix on *Foncia*. Immediately following that was the Trophée Clairfontaine in La Trinité, a relatively small French regatta against the best of the best in one-design 23 foot catamarans. As in the Archipelago Raid it pushed me out of my comfort zone, but it was great fun, and taught me a lot. I was sailing with Nico and Pe-Peche from *Foncia*, and it was to be my third time at this event. I was not only thinking of my round-the-world when it came to training: months later I'd be racing the Atlantic with Alain in the Transat Jacques Vabre, leaving from Le Havre in France and heading over to Salvador in Brazil. I was feeling positive, and the team spirit was just great, until all that was blown out of the water . . .

On the morning of the second day of training I was followed by a photographer and then stopped by a UK journalist who tried to question me about my personal life. One minute I was walking down the dockside looking at the wind direction in the port where we were about to race and the next I was feeling sick and angry. It was not only me that was targeted either. Luis, the diver from Portugal, had been tracked down and asked about any relationship we might have, as had my previous partner, Ian. I felt awful. I cared hugely for both of them and felt distressed that they had to deal with this.

The following day the paper came out with a full-page article with the headline 'Ellen splits with boyfriend and falls for hunky diver who saved her life', which wasn't true either. Luis hadn't saved our lives, but he had played a pretty important role in getting us home. It was true that Ian and I were no longer together, but we were still very good friends, and it hurt me deeply to hear that he had journalists camped outside his house. The press attention shook me profoundly, and, as I was over in France, it was totally unexpected. It was a horrible situation, and our results for the remainder of the event were atrocious.

An e-mail sent to Lou Newlands, who was not only a good friend but was responsible for our media relations, summed up my feelings:

```
All fairly disappointing, and it makes me feel quite
sick really.
   I hate this shit - I hate it so much, and sometimes,
just sometimes it makes you want to jack in any
relationship, and any life you have and emigrate
to South ******* Georgia where you might have a
chance in hell of being left alone.
```

Chapter Five

If I ever needed a leveller to remind me what really mattered in life then I had one. I'm not sure that I could ever imagine meeting more inspirational young people than those who I have met through the Ellen MacArthur Trust. Not only are they the epitome of courage but they display positivity in the most contagious and fun-loving way imaginable. Having been forced to face their own mortality at a young age, they somehow manage to convert that fear they must feel into energy for life.

When I first set foot on board boats with young people suffering from cancer I was really nervous. I had never in my life worked with young people, let alone those who were recovering from a serious illness. They were all French too, which did not make things easier, but I needn't have worried! Not only were the young people easy to get along with, but they put me to shame with their enthusiasm, sense of humour and absolutely unwavering passion for life. That day's sailing in the year 2000, just a few months before the Vendée Globe start, was going to have a long-lasting effect on me.

After solo races there are always many comments like 'You're so brave and it must have been so difficult,' but each time it was said something jarred inside me. Yes, it was difficult, I admit that, and yes, at times, I guess, particularly before the start, you look long and hard at your own mortality. But there is an important point to make: it was *my* choice to be out there in the first place, risking my life. But those young people are going through something harder than most of us could imagine with smiles on their faces and yet it's not their choice. I find that humbling.

I can never put myself in their position, having come through my childhood without anything worse than glandular fever, but I have tried to imagine what it might be like for them. You're fourteen years old and, like everyone else in your year, you're trying to work out what GCSEs you'd like to take. You're probably saving up for CDs, or clothes, even a boat if you're me, or perhaps something you've seen that you've set your heart on. You are probably just becoming aware of the fact that you will have to choose what you'd like to do in life, and you're just organizing where you're going to go on work experience. Your body is beginning to change, and you are in the middle of finding out your identity; perhaps you are just starting to notice the opposite sex. One day you have an ache in your leg, or a headache, or you are lacking in energy. You go to the doctor, never imagining that there can be something serious wrong. You are sent to hospital for further tests, and you begin to worry a bit about what it could be. And then, BANG, like having your feet taken from under you . . . you're told you've got cancer.

Suddenly everything changes, and the new milestones in your life become hospital trips, each round of chemotherapy ending, then finally feeling better again. You're frightened, you probably cry a lot, and you're worried because you've heard of cancer, as one of your grandparents possibly died of it. Your parents seem strong for you and tell you that everything will be all right, but you can see in their eyes that they are scared too. At the same time what seems like an endless phase of the unknown begins, as the cancer takes away any control that you ever had over your life. Your world is reduced to an inward-looking bubble, and the whole dynamic of your family changes as their focus is to get you better. Friends and relatives are always asking how you are and wanting your news, not daring to say to you what they have been up to. You begin to miss school, but then that's probably not so bad, as your friends at school don't know what to say when you become sick from the chemo-therapy and you begin to look different. You begin fighting, fighting

71

with all the energy you have. You fight when you don't think that you can fight any more, until your treatment finishes . . .

Then, when you return to school you are likely to have missed six months, sometimes years. Your priorities have been quite different from other young people's. Some of the friends you make in hospital may not have made it, and you will have had to grow up way faster than your friends. Whilst you crave the normality of getting on with life, you have had to cope with something which is so much more important than any exam. But you have to focus once again on learning, and you're not only behind at school, but you're worrying about getting through your five-year remission period, after which you are given the all-clear.

How the hell does a fourteen-year-old deal with that?

The thing that proves itself again and again after this horrific process is that young people lose their confidence. They have been 'out of the system' and they have not been through the same experiences as other young people. They are 'different' and have been treated 'differently' and in many cases they are quite probably still quite scared. So when we set up our own charity in the UK, The Ellen MacArthur Trust (EMT), unbeknown to us it was that 'confidence' issue that we were going to try to help with. We would take young people in recovery from cancer and leukaemia sailing in the same way that the French charity 'A Chacun Son Cap' continued to do, and our objective was to try to have as much fun as we could on the way! It had been Mark's suggestion to set up a charity in the UK. Having seen how passionate I had been about the French charity, he felt that channelling our energy into something that we really knew made a difference would be the right thing, especially as the special environment that ACSC created did not exist in the UK.

The first Trust trips were in the summer of 2003 during the build of our trimaran in Australia, and when the young people arrived for their first adventure I felt a strange mixture of excitement and apprehension. I knew that some of the young people were still quite poorly, and I also worried whether in the UK we could achieve that same atmosphere and laughter that we'd had in France.

Martin Noyle was not only our skipper but also our first trust manager, and I'm not sure I've ever met anyone who was better at getting on with young people than him. Being on their wavelength, he just slotted in on the boat but with a quiet authority that worked beautifully.

When the first group arrived we were worried. There were some tears as the young people said goodbye to their parents, which made you wonder if you were doing the right thing. It was in those harsh moments that you realize that in some cases these young people have virtually not left their parents' sight through their treatment – so heading off on a trip which would last for a few days must have been painful for all. Eman, Samantha and Katie all climbed on to the boat with ease, but Maxine, who was by far the most ill of the four of them, arrived in a wheelchair and looked so frail as she rose to her feet with the help of two sticks before we helped her on to the boat. She was understandably upset and looked thin and frail; she was clearly still undergoing treatment. I was aware of their medical forms and knew that she had Ewing's sarcoma, which in Maxine's case was a cancer of the spine. Not until a few days later did I realize that she'd had two complete vertebrae removed, and after her operation had had to learn to walk again.

Those days were just fantastic, and though I wasn't there for every moment of every day I very much wished I had been. The girls got on famously, and the chat and atmosphere were wonderful. The weather was warm, and the sailing was perfect. Kim, our nurse, was the perfect crew and was just wonderful with everyone.

The thing that startled me most about that trip was the change in the young people. From arriving on the boat afraid and worried, they had become a family. Each of them knew better than any of us adults just what the others had been through, and the speed at which they gelled was astonishing. Everyone quickly got into the rhythm of the boat, and washing up, making sandwiches and chatting late into the night became the norm. Within hours the boat felt like home for the girls; their cabins were as untidy as their bedrooms. We had water-balloon fights, made iced biscuits and covered ourselves with face paint. I'm not sure that I'd ever heard so much

giggling in all my life, and that was just from us adults on board –
we were all having so much fun. What we had on the boat was
probably the closest to normality that the girls had experienced in
months if not years. They were doing normal things, which did not
involve hospital tests or treatments – and for a few days they had
been able to forget their worries.

The final day of the trip arrived all too soon, and there was a
deflated feeling when the boat returned to Southampton, as no one
wanted the magic to end. Everyone had come out of themselves
and gained confidence, but the biggest change came from Maxine.
During the course of the four days she had gone from being a frail
girl in a wheelchair to a bubbly ten-year-old who had decided she
no longer needed even her sticks. When her mum arrived to collect
her she ran down the pontoon.

In that second everything that the Trust stood for became crystal
clear.

At the end of that trip we received a host of letters thanking us
for the fun that had been had. Maxine and her Mum, Sue, both sent
one, and Maxine enclosed a photograph she'd taken of herself on
the trip in her letter. She was wearing a white cap and smiling with
the widest, happiest smile you can imagine. Reading it brought
tears to my eyes, and that photo embodied everything you could
ever need to know about inspiration. Sue's letter read:

It has never been the cancer that has worried me but the depression that
came with it. She had lost her self confidence and had a very low self
esteem, but the Ellen MacArthur Trust has changed all that. From the
minute I picked her up she hasn't stopped smiling, she has talked non stop
about her trip, she is singing and dancing and walking tall. She was able to
have fun and relax for the first time in years. Of all the medicines she had,
this one – the trip – was the one that made her better!

It was all the proof that we could have ever needed to tell us that
the Trust could really change lives and that it was doing the right
thing. I felt privileged to have touched that magic in some way, to
have witnessed the benefits and to have been lucky enough to

spend time around these incredible young people. It was in that moment that I realized just what good the Trust could do and that from its small beginnings it should do its level best to give as many young people as possible the chance to experience this.

But that year my link to cancer was not just through the Trust.

Erik was special. He'd always called me Ellie and with his twinkle in his eye and cheeky grin he could get away with anything. He'd hug you so hard when he met you that you could never doubt that he meant it, and with his Swedish charm he had a special place in my heart. Erik was the cameraman we had worked with the longest, and I'd become especially close to him when we'd sailed across the Atlantic together on a delivery trip in *Kingfisher*. He was not only hugely talented, but he had a wonderful way of defusing a situation of stress, or making you smile when he knew that you were nervous. He'd ask me to autograph his lens, just to get the shot he was after and never ever stopped until he had it. It would always be Erik that had the lens just inches from your face. For five years he had been there at every race start and finish I'd competed in and as a result had got to see the nerves as well as the elation. When I left for the Vendée he put down his camera and hugged me hard, before breaking down on my shoulder and sobbing into my ear. He really cared, and that day he showed just how scared he was for me. We all loved him dearly.

The day I discovered he had cancer it was like being knocked down by a bus. My first reaction was to think that he could beat it, because he's a fighter and always looked so healthy, but quickly we realized it was so far progressed it was terminal. It seemed so unfair. Everyone hoped that a miracle would happen . . . but it didn't.

I was in Australia at the time of his funeral and totally devastated not to be able to be there in Sweden; I was so upset that I didn't sleep well for days. And when I did I woke with that sick feeling inside that something was really wrong. From Australia I spoke to Richard, who was with him shortly before he died, and what he told me had tears streaming down my face. Erik had a two-year-old copy of *Yachting World* titled 'Ellen' by his bedside, with a picture of *Kingfisher* and me on the cover . . .

I wrote a note to be passed on to his wife, Brit, at the funeral, but it didn't even begin to compensate for all that he had given us. The last time I'd seen him was in Perth, when he filmed us arriving after our disastrous Jules Verne, and we'd stayed behind together after lunch to have a long chat. Erik was one of the few people I could really talk to, and about anything. He really was someone I felt really understood me.

He died at just fifty-four years old, exactly one year to the day after he filmed me at the finish of the Route du Rhum.

Chapter Six

My final race of the year before leaving for Australia was a multi-hull race, the Transat Jacques Vabre. Alain and I had gone off together in our boat, *Foncia*, in October to sail 1,000 miles to qualify for the race and we were feeling happy with the way she was sailing. This was the second time that I had raced to Salvador with Alain, and we were looking forward to getting stuck in. Luis came over from Portugal to sail on the boat he'd only previously seen upside down, and also help me prepare before the off. The start of the Route du Rhum had been just twelve months earlier, but the aftermath of what happened was still fresh in all our minds. When the weather for the start day was forecast to be very gusty, the race organizers were understandably cautious, and the result was that the start for the multihulls was delayed by four days to 5 November.

Despite the better conditions, it was not long before we had a problem: on the second day we heard a shattering bang. With a sinking feeling we both realized that the noise had been the main halyard breaking. The most likely reason was that the repairs in the mast we'd had to make earlier in the year was chafing on the rope. Why that hadn't presented itself earlier we had no idea, but these things sometimes come up and bite you, and with the year we'd had we'd spent a lot less time on the water than we'd hoped. More problems occurred for us when the wind in the front which we had to pass increased from 25 to 40 knots, tearing the trinquete as we endeavoured to furl it. As we'd been able to sail with the mainsail at the position of second reef or less we had been able to carry on racing, but with no trinquete and a long sail upwind the other side of the doldrums we decided that we had no option but to stop. We chose Porto Santo, one of the islands in the archipelago of Madeira, and were not alone in our need for repairs. Despite getting back up to speed we never did make it back to the front of the fleet and ended up with a disappointing result of ninth place, but at least we'd made it!

Once we had safely tied up *Foncia*, the first thing I did was head straight for an internet connection so that I could log on and see the latest webcam pictures of Mobi. Whether it was by chance or not, I wasn't sure, but as I logged on, there she was in all her glory. She was about to be moved down the coast to a huge empty dockside building at the Glebe in the centre of Sydney. To complete the manoeuvre we needed four lorries: one for her floats, one for her main hull, and two with a beam on each. On the edge of my seat I could see two of her newly painted floats after they'd been lowered on to one of the lorries. I was so excited, and simply itching to get out there, but I didn't have long to wait: I'd be with her in ten days' time.

However, in the midst of all this excitement we received a piece of news that would add yet another layer of pressure to our record attempt, and this time a really significant one. A few days after our arrival a man called Francis Joyon set off to attempt to break the same solo round-the-world record we were after. He had bought the boat *Sport Elec*, now renamed *IDEC*, which had broken the crewed non-stop round-the-world record six years before. Now Francis was attempting to sail her solo to break the ninety-three-day solo record. At the time I'm not sure anyone thought it was possible to sail a 90 foot boat around the world on your own, especially one designed to be sailed with a crew, but Francis Joyon was a special man.

The 28th of November was the last time I was due to be on UK soil until spring the following year. Our plan was to sail Mobi from Sydney to Auckland, then either home or, if I was happy with the boat, to make the most of the final leg home by stopping in New York and having a crack at the solo transatlantic record attempt as a tester. We would arrive in New York at the end of April if all went well and would spend a couple of months waiting for the right weather before returning to the UK for the end of June at the latest, record or not.

The team was coming together in Sydney. Loik, with whom I'd sailed on *Foncia*, was now working with us full-time, Oli was still there, of course, and Albert was now basing himself over there too. Charlie Darbyshire, Kate Steven and Rudi Steiness were over from the UK, and Hendo, from the Jules Verne crew, was with us to work on the rigging. We were aiming to launch Mobi before Christmas, so with four weeks to go the schedule was pretty action-packed. The team felt very much like family to me, and I was desperate to get stuck in with them properly. Mobi now looked like a real trimaran: her beams were attached to her huge hulls, and she was getting a little nearer completion every day.

I was collected from the airport by Oli, and I was in suspense. As we drove into the huge dockyard building where she was housed I saw her, and my heart started racing. I had flashbacks to the feelings I had had when I first saw *Kingfisher* sprayed and looking like a real boat for the first time. This time with Mobi things were no different. It was the biggest change I had seen in her, as the previous time she'd been black and grey, and in five separate pieces. Here she quite literally shone. I had a huge smile on my face; I was excited and I felt proud, really proud. I walked up to her starboard float and stroked my fingers along the perfectly smooth paintwork of her bow; she felt cool, being shaded from the bright Australian sunshine. 'Hello,' I whispered, as I felt just how perfect and precise the leading edge was. I didn't want to take my hand off her. She was real, beautiful and the culmination of so much work. I'd made it to Sydney, I could breathe now; our bond was forming and I had a comforting feeling that everything was going to be OK.

Those weeks in Sydney were accompanied by a mixture of emotions. I was hugely excited to be with the boat and the team, but at the same time I was trying to work hard on my fitness and spend time with Luis, who had come out to Australia to be with me. It had been a big decision for him to come out there, but we were incredibly fond of each other, and, after seeing each other only a handful of times over that summer, I knew that if our relationship was going to have the chance it deserved then we would need to be together.

We got on extremely well and had similar dreams and ambitions. Luis had even visited Derbyshire briefly and was fascinated by the countryside and the lush green scenery surrounding my childhood home. Each time we were together we became closer; I had never really had a partner around me while working on a project and I found it quite a change. On arrival in Sydney we bought a couple of bikes for getting around, and our daily routine would consist of training in the gym or swimming and then jumping on bikes and heading down to the shed. Though I wanted to spend as much time with the guys and Mobi as I could I was also desperate to give our relationship time and get to learn more about the man with whom I was living. It was hard knowing that, once Mobi left for the US, I'd be at sea for the best part of two months, and, though I desperately wanted to be with the team, I also realized that, if I were going to take any time off that spring, I should take it while we were in Sydney.

Though our time was so limited, we did try and do our own thing when we could. On one day we visited Sydney Zoo to learn more about Australia's animals, and on another travelled over to Manly on the coast for a few hours' surfing lessons. I loved it and was over the moon to get on my feet several times on my first attempt! Over one weekend we even managed to take a couple of days off in the Blue Mountains. That was a magical break. The mountains were spectacular, the scenery was stunning, and the depth of the wilderness and bush was astounding. We drank from each other's enthusiasm for all that was around us and shared the discovery of something which was new and special. Climbing trees, walking across streams and scaling rocky outcrops filled every day to the brim, and we saw species of plants and animals that we had never even seen in books before.

After weeks of blood, sweat and tears, Mobi was nearing completion, and we finally launched her just a week before Christmas. For the guys from BoatSpeed it had been a hard eight months' graft: 30,000 man hours in total. They had worked their socks off. To get her out of the shed required everyone to push her, literally, and on castors similar to roller-skates we edged her closer to the water. It was a stinker of a day – clear blue sky and boiling hot – which meant that the tarmac between the shed and the water was much softer than that indoors. It was a good incentive to keep pushing, knowing that if we stopped she'd sink into the ground! Once we had got her attached to the crane which was to lift her into her natural element for the first time we stuck two final stickers on her bows. They were two whale's eyes. They suited our Mobi, and from the moment she touched the water she would be able to see where she was going. It was exciting but nerve-racking to see her gently lowered, and my heart leapt the first time she hit the water and floated! Everyone was smiling, and there was a real feeling of achievement in the air. Though it wasn't her official launch, as that was to be on 8 January, I did ask Sari from the yard to spray her with a bottle of champagne. She was a wonderful person and, like Peter, her husband, she had put so much in. She was a small person but full of energy!

'Hey, look out for a lady,' she cried as she ran the length of the boat.

Crikey, I thought, *it's almost down to me now.*

From the moment we left our mooring in Neutral Bay I felt calm and in control on her. Our route took us out past Sydney heads, and with the blue sky and stiff wind we were all smiling. You have that horrible feeling before you sail a new boat that she may not handle well, may be unbalanced or just simply slow. But she was none of those. Nigel and the team had done the most incredible job, and my faith in him was reinforced the moment she accelerated. With the most effortless power she took off as she harnessed the wind for the first time in her life. She handled amazingly well in the waves, powering through them, and no matter how hard we seemed to push her they would rise up as if for more. I crawled all over her to feel every angle of her personality and wondered if it could be possible to sail on two perfect boats in one lifetime.

Having the whole team on board to pull the mainsail up made me realize just how challenging it would be to do it alone. Mobi was a big boat, and, though to me she had the personality of a gentle giant, I would have to put every ounce of energy I had into mastering her. Inside, though, I felt a quiet confidence, I was training hard and I knew that I could do it.

The days passed quickly once she was in the water and, aside from a brief break on Christmas Day and New Year's Eve, there was little respite for us: we were a very long way from the boat being ready for a 13,000-mile training sail back to Europe. Our trip was to be in four stages. The first to Auckland, for which we hoped to leave mid-January, and the second, third and fourth were from Auckland via the Falklands, and ideally New York, to home. We hoped to be away from there at the beginning of March at the latest. Mid-January meant we had less than two frantic weeks of preparations for her official launch.

I would have dearly loved for my Mum to be at the launch for Mobi to wish her safely on her way, but after a few phone calls to her back in Derbyshire I realized that she really wasn't well. Mum will always tell you how everyone else is and leave herself off the list, and that winter she was doing just that. I knew that she had been to the hospital for tests, and that she was beginning treatment for an overactive thyroid but that was about all she'd let on. The good news was that Fergus, my brother, had agreed to take her place; though he was working and would only be able to afford a brief forty-eight hours in Sydney.

I was so excited to see Ferg when he arrived, and the team were brilliant in taking over the preparations, allowing us to have lunch together. Ferg then went for a nap before the events of the evening were to unfold. That night was going to be very special for a lot of people. Nigel, Benoit Cabaret, his design partner, and John Levell were there, John being the structural engineer who had worked so carefully and methodically on her design. Peter and Sari were there with their family, and I remembered Peter's words as Mobi left the yard bound for Sydney: 'I hate boats leaving the factory, tears a part of you out every time they go.' Then, after a pause: 'That's OK; it's

Me with my Great-Granddad. In case you're wondering, those aren't his real ears!

With my brothers, Lewis and Fergus (carrying the fishing net).

Left to right: My Mum, older brother Lewis, Grandpa and Gran, younger brother Fergus and, at the front, me and Mac, my Border Collie cross.

The grid that I made to mark off every penny I saved towards buying my first boat.

The boat itself! *Threpn'y bit* may have been 'moored' in our back garden, but that didn't stop me from spending hours dreaming of the adventures we'd have one day.

On board *Iduna*, aged eighteen, during my first big adventure – a solo trip around Britain.

Taking part in the Vendée Globe in 2000 was nothing less than a
dream come true. Finishing in second place changed my life in ways that I
could never have expected. Having to leave *Kingfisher* at the end of the race
was heartrending – she had been my home and companion.

A shot taken just moments after leaving her.

Winning the Route du Rhum in 2002 was a 'coming of age' for me. Arriving in Guadeloupe was a euphoric moment, but the failure of fifteen out of eighteen boats to finish the race provided a sobering reality check.

The 'multihull massacre' of that year's Route du Rhum showed just how fragile these boats can be. Without the weight of a keel, they can be lifted from the sea by the wind and cartwheel through the air in seconds. Preparing to sail solo around the world in a multihull, I could not have been made more aware of the dangers I was facing.

Below and above: illustrations of what can happen even with a professional crew of ten people.

In 2003, Alain Gautier, Loik Gallon, Nicolas Bérenger, Philippe Peché and I took part in a crewed multihull race called the Challenge Mondial Assistance. On the second day of the race, we experienced the nightmare of a capsize, forcing us to pull out. It was the first time I had capsized a large multihull and having our world turned upside down made for an abrupt end to the race.

Shots from the 2003 Jules Verne: our crewed circumnavigation record attempt.

Top left and bottom: Our boat, *Kingfisher II*, was a 108 foot catamaran – built for taking on the rolling mountains of the southern oceans.

Top right: After experiencing a catastrophic dismasting deep in the Southern Ocean, we were forced to put together a makeshift mast, abandon the record and set sail for Australia.

Left: The fantastic crew of *Kingfisher II* that I had the privilege of leading.

Photos taken during the build process of *Mobi*, the boat that I would be sailing solo around the world. The team behind her was world class; together, they would contribute over 30,000 man hours preparing for the challenge.

better to see them in the water.' There were a whole host of journalists who had come over to Sydney from the UK, France and other countries. Mark was conspicuous by his absence, as he had made a decision to walk the final third of the distance to Antarctica that winter, like you do! Lou and Isabel Genis, also working on media relations, had come over from the UK to help out with the organization of things. The majority of the crowd at the launch, though, were the guys from BoatSpeed, and most came with their partners. I don't think they'd been invited to a boat launch before, and no one could have been more proud than me to have them there. The launch was done as a live link-up with a satellite truck to the UK, and Michael Pechard, the journalist, was there to be the compère. Even Ferg looked smart in his blue shirt and trousers, despite, like me, being nervous beforehand. Mobi shone and looked fantastic as she sat perfectly in the water moored just off the dock in Darling Harbour. Another milestone was achieved as the champagne bottle smashed, and Ferg and I hugged each other on the bow.

I do not remember that evening's events as I wish I could have, though, as tension between Luis and me had been escalating. Our relationship was intense, but rocky, and after the highest of the high it would suddenly plummet in a heart-stopping way to the bottom. New Year had been the best I could ever remember, but the night of the launch was the opposite. Luis was looking for something that I couldn't give him. He wanted me to be someone different. He wanted a girl who'd wear skirts and 'belong' to him, but I was a free spirit and felt trapped and frustrated by his feelings. That night brought things to a head for me. We were hopelessly in love but our relationship had culminated in a situation which had to stop. I realized that I could not become the person he wanted me so desperately to be. I was the kind of person who believed that if you really want something to happen then you should just go for it and never give up, but I finally realized it would only get worse. Throwing more belief and emotional energy at our relationship was like putting more and more charge through a broken connection, hoping that that and that alone would fix it, but it couldn't, and in fact nothing could. I was devastated, disorientated and perhaps even frightened by the notion that it wasn't fixable. I felt like my world had been pulled from under my feet. It should have been one of the most memorable evenings of my life, but instead it was a nightmare.

I was so glad that Fergus was there and that he answered his phone in the early hours of the morning. I joined him in his room, and we talked and talked. That time together in Sydney brought us closer than at any time I could remember, and it felt reassuring, familiar and safe to be with him.

I knew that I had to deal with the situation and that the inevitable would have to happen. If Luis and I were to stop ourselves from destroying each other we would have to be apart. Forty-eight hours after Fergus had landed we were back in the UK. I had bought two last-minute flights to London and then stayed with Luis until he caught his connecting flight to Portugal. Following that, I travelled back to Derbyshire; I have never been so glad to see my Mum and Dad.

Five days later, after a mad day at the London Boat Show, I was back on a flight bound for Sydney once more, this time to leave immediately with Mobi for New Zealand. I knew that what I needed was a total change of scenery, and that the memories of Australia would be better off behind me. I felt sick and empty and I realized that in my efforts to make the relationship work I had been losing the notion of who I really was. A close friend said afterwards that I was acting almost as though I was 'haunted'. It was unsettling and strange to recognize that I was trying to change my personality to make another person happy.

There had been one occasion when we'd had an afternoon off to visit the aquarium. I can't remember what happened, but I knew that things weren't good and that I had so much emotion bottled up inside that I thought I would burst. We visited Mobi on the dockside on our way back to the apartment, and, as a desperate exit for my frustration, I dived straight off the pontoon into the warm green-blue waters of the harbour. I stayed under as long as I could, finally surfacing by her bow, where I was away from Luis. Under water I could be my own person, and the blurred shape of Mobi made me feel safe as I opened my eyes.

It was the same feeling I had on the plane flying back. My confidence had been blown to pieces, and I was going to have to spend a long time on the water to find it again. I fell asleep. I was totally and utterly drained.

One thing which helped to take my mind off my relationship with Luis was the arrival of Francis Joyon in Brest. Just a few days after we had unpacked our container in Auckland he crossed the finish line, having made it round the world in 72 days, 22 hours, 54 minutes and 22 seconds. He'd not only broken the record but had taken a staggering twenty days off it. On that day the challenge before us got a whole lot bigger. It was no longer about being the first person to make it non-stop solo round the world in a multihull, and hoping to do it in less than the famous eighty days of Phileas Fogg, it was now to beat an outstanding record that most people believed would stand for a decade.

During our six weeks in Auckland I slowly began to be my old self again. I threw myself into the project like never before. All my spare time was spent with the guys there, working away on the boat and making decisions on how things should be on board. The bond that we had between us was strong, and the conversations we'd have while working on the most awkward of jobs were often funny or hilarious. Everyone would joke and mess around together, and when we stopped for lunch there would always be an entertaining story to be told. Week by week contact with Luis lessened, and bit by bit I could feel myself becoming stronger. I was almost surprised that I had let it happen to myself. I'd gone headlong into a situation which was perhaps destined to end in tears, but at least now I was beginning to be able to rationalize things. Considering that we had only known each other for a few months before our move to Sydney, things were never going to be easy, and though our relationship hadn't been a long one it had certainly been intense. I am sure that part of what happened was due to differences in our cultures, being in another country, speaking another language and the knowledge that I would be away for so much of the year.

We'd made what I felt were some smart decisions for Mobi's launch, and one of those was to put a decent-sized engine in her, so that we could park her and sail her without worrying too much. This meant that training sails and testing would be less stressful than they would otherwise have been, and with the strong winds that we had been looking to test her in in Auckland we would be able to get out with relative ease. The sailing and training went well, and the six weeks flew by. We were absolutely working our socks off, and the nearer we got to our leaving date the more hours we stuck in. In the whole of our six weeks in Auckland we can't have had more than a couple of days off, and when the day of our departure arrived it seemed too good to be true. We had worked on board for most of the previous night, and everyone was exhausted. We had to get off, though, and we'd set a date. It was time to sail in the Southern Ocean, and our Mobi was ready for it! Though for us this journey was simply the delivery of the boat to her new home, we were in fact about to sail half-way round the world.

Chapter Seven

I relished getting stuck in at sea again, and though there were problems on the way – a broken float rudder and a few technical hitches with the fuse system for the main rudder – we had a great sail. In the waves Mobi was miraculous, and I was relieved to find out that she was drier in the cockpit than the 60 foot tris. I practised changing a rudder with the equipment we'd made for it, and the whole operation was completed in forty minutes. Preparation was everything for these journeys, and despite having what felt like little time in Auckland to prepare, we had, in fact achieved a huge amount. For both Loik and Mark it was their first sail in the 'real' Southern Ocean. They were on part one of the delivery, the 5,000 mile leg to the Falkland Islands, which would take us around Cape Horn, and for both of them it would be their first rounding. We chatted and played music on Mobi's stereo, and for me it was a wonderful way to get to know her better. There were three of us there, which meant that, when things went wrong, they were easier to deal with, and the laughter on board was a welcome start.

Though I had become more of myself in Auckland, it was going back to sea which helped me more than anything else. I could not remember being so emotionally drained. Lou had been the closest to what had happened with Luis in Sydney, and, being a good friend, had helped me sort my feelings out bit by bit. Her e-mail summed things up really:

```
You have come alive again . . . Your emails are just
zinging and your energy comes pouring out. It is great
to hear you like this again - it has been a while but I
knew sailing Mobi would be your salvation.
```

Sailing in the south was fantastic: being back with the albatross, the huge waves and the isolated beauty of the Southern Ocean. We saw a few storms while we were out there and steadily pushed Mobi harder each day. I would sometimes do the manoeuvres alone to see if there were any hitches we'd find, or if there were any modifications we might need to do. After the Falkland Islands I'd be on my own on my route north, and with our last chance of modifying anything being during our stop-over there it was in my interest to go through every-thing with a fine-tooth comb. We tested her pilots, the charging systems, the lights and the navigation equipment. We tested her tracking and the data that we could send automatically from the boat. It was busy for those now back in the office in Cowes too, as this was our first real trial of how things would be for a large part of the year.

Though we knew the next port of call was the Falklands, we had still not decided where to end our journey in the northern hemi-sphere. If all went well alone with Mobi I would attempt the transatlantic record that spring before bringing her home to Europe. It would be a good test for Mobi and me, and a good warm-up at the pace we'd need for the round-the-world record at the end of the summer.

It was a lovely day with blue skies, and the sea had begun to flatten off as we sailed into the shelter of the Falklands. Loik and I were laboriously inflating our fenders on the trampolines, chatting about our delivery and marvelling at the cormorants which were fear-lessly flying just inches from our rigging. I'd never seen birds so close to the boat before, and their airborne formation skills were second to none. It was then that we nearly fell over backwards as the long-familiar sounds of the water passing our hull and wind in the rigging were replaced by the deafening sound of engines. Two Tornado jets screamed past us almost as close as the cormorants, and our hearts nearly stopped with the shock. We recovered, and in no time all three of us were standing in the cockpit grinning from ear to ear in disbelief looking round for the person that the air display was meant for! The show we received during that ten minutes was absolutely breathtaking. The jets went screaming past at lightning speeds; then they would bank off to the right or left or flip upside down alongside us. Each time they passed they would do something different, and we waited with bated breath for the next manoeuvre, trying at the same time to not run aground and keep an eye on the chart! I couldn't help but think that the cormorants must be modelling themselves on the Tornados – with such huge 'birds' flying past so precisely, every young cormorant must have wanted to be a pilot when it grew up! Each time they passed so low and close that we felt like we could touch them; and as they passed at what can't have been much more than Mobi's mast height we could even make out the figures in the cockpits. We smiled as they waggled their wings on passing, and then, as if that wasn't enough for us, they kicked in their red-hot afterburners, leaving us watching in amazement as they disappeared like rockets shooting into the sky. Perhaps if we'd been living in a city or driving down a motorway their presence might not have seemed so spectacular, but after 5,000 miles of nothing but the ocean a 600 knot flypast was pretty far out.

From a personal perspective the Falklands were a handful of treasured days which felt like a holiday and were the best medicine I could have possibly had. I was finally getting my confidence back, and after the emotional rollercoaster of Australia I was feeling that I'd found myself again. We spent happy hours working on Mobi in Mare Harbour, part of the Mount Pleasant military base, and were often visited by the nosy Commerson's dolphins, which were always keen to watch what we were doing on board. The welcome we had both at the military base where we stayed and from the people of the Falklands could not have been warmer. We had dinner at the house of the Commander of the British Forces, a tour of a Tornado at the air base, a drinks reception at Government House in Stanley and a visit to the Sea Cadets. It was action-packed, full of fun and even involved an element of relaxation, visiting some of the varied drinking establishments of the military base!

Sadly, and all too soon, just five days after arriving we were preparing for the off.

Just before we untied our ropes to leave, a lady whom I did not recognize, and with whom I had never spoken before, came rushing up to me. She introduced herself as Sally Poncet and handed me a book she had written, and a document about the declining numbers of albatross. We talked briefly, as our engines were already running and we were about to leave. Sally had been involved in counting the numbers of albatross in the Southern Ocean islands for thirty years. I loved the albatross, the most graceful bird I have ever seen, and a bird that had accompanied us through the Southern Ocean. Her final words were: 'I think that you might be able to help.' Little did I realize then the significance of the conversation I had just had.

The weather was perfect and the sail great. We sailed from Mare Harbour up to Port Stanley to check the systems on board, before dropping off the guys, and the four guests we'd taken for a spin from Mount Pleasant, to thank them for their hospitality. Having new people on board took my mind off the fact I'd be alone hours later, and the image of happily chatting while sitting on her forward beam, watching the sun set behind the islands as dolphins played on our bow, was one that I would not forget in a hurry. Once we were in the flatter water of Stanley Harbour our guests departed, and we sailed up and down in shelter while we did the final checks before Mark, Loik and Albert got off. I hugged them all as they climbed down into the boat that was collecting them and then waved goodbye as I watched them fade into the dusk to become just the tiny glows of distant navigation lights. It was the first time I had ever sailed Mobi alone.

As the final view of the island slipped away, I shed a single tear. It was one of those nights again: the stars blazing out and the sky black. The moon that we'd had in the sky had gone, and there was just an impressive glow to the west which I could only think was the Southern Lights. Not only that, but the sea was alive with phosphorescence. I was happy and excited and looking forward to the sail back, but I was not prepared for the shock of going so quickly from being surrounded by chirpy happy people to being totally and utterly alone.

The Falklands had been a huge boost, and I'd loved it, but I was also aware that it would be another month before I made landfall again. Though I was stronger inside after all that I had been through, it was not the best time to be alone. Those were on the whole a hard few weeks, and, though Mobi and I bonded well, I was tired. She sailed beautifully, but as we crept up the Brazilian coast with a disappointing amount of wind I had time on my hands and I ran through everything which had happened that year a million times in my head. I did more thinking than most would do in a lifetime, and I tried to learn from what had happened. The relationship with Luis had been a disaster, but it had in fact taught me a lot.

I was, however, slowly finding my sense of humour too, as my e-mail on 1 April showed:

```
I have just had one of the hardest nights at sea of
my life, battling with the thunderstorms along the
Brazilian coast. It's just getting light now – and
at last the night was long wet and at times quite
frightening . . . To be honest this morning I am tired
and wet – feeling very hungry and not even motivated by
the sound of the kettle boiling for morning porridge.
   I have made a decision – the winds are due to stay
like this for at least four days – so I am motoring at
about 6 knots and heading for Rio. This is ridiculous,
and I'm not achieving anything.
   I know this will come as a huge shock to all – but
after a month out here, and the months prior – I really
have to draw the line somewhere.
   sorry,
   ex
```

A reply from Charlie ended:

```
thanks for nearly putting me in hospital
  cx
```

And Mark, who had returned from Antarctica, replied to say:

```
nice job . . . had Lou on the phone immediately!!!
```

It was great to be able to communicate with the office, particularly in the light conditions when the sailing was easier. Charlie would send me a round-up of what was going on from time to time, what was in the news and happening around Cowes. Mark Turner, now back from his Antarctic expedition, would discuss everything with me, and Nick would send me long e-mails full of energy and enthusiasm. He was excited and busy preparing *Kingfisher* for the Vendée Globe later that year, having secured Skandia as a sponsor. Nick was one of life's wonderful people, and I could not think of anyone who I would rather have taken over *Kingfisher* than him.

Despite a setback of having to climb the mast to solve an issue at the head of the genoa, I was experiencing some wonderful sailing: the sea was pretty flat, there wasn't a drop of spray on board, and we were averaging 17 knots with a wind speed around the 13 knot mark. That was the beauty of multihulls, as they could achieve the impossible of sailing faster than the wind. The moon was so bright above us as we sailed north that you could have read a book in its light, but I was very aware that the record attempt was unlikely to hold much of this 'peaceful' sailing. I was learning that, though physically demanding, Mobi was a joy to sail, and I was so pleased to see how she performed under autopilot in different conditions. Even in the big waves of the south she was unbelievable – skimming over them, haring down them, then seemingly never sticking her leeward float in and stopping. It was a totally different experience to sailing the huge cat; her design meant she took less of a battering from the waves and handled more gracefully in the waves as opposed to driving through them using sheer power.

Despite a long list of work to undertake, during the voyage north I realized that I was growing happy enough with the boat's state to make a transatlantic record attempt on our way home to Europe. We'd sailed half-way round the world in training, but a high-speed transatlantic was going to be a measurable test of what Mobi and I could achieve together. The established record route is New York to the Lizard in the entrance of the English Channel.

Day by day we made our way north, tackling the doldrums and passing the island of Trindade and then the tiny archipelago of Fernando de Noronha, sitting just below the Equator. The final haul up to Newport Rhode Island was a long one, but one which showed so many changes in the sea. In the final 3,500 miles you would not believe things could alter so much. The water temperature had risen to 30 degrees, which made everything warm, including the sports drinks I was making to quench my thirst with water from the desalinator. The heat of the water gives the energy that the clouds need to grow so big and rise so high, and, looking at some, it seemed a miracle that they didn't fall to the water like lead balloons, they were so dense with water vapour. This area is unstable, in effect the boiling point of the earth. It's this energy that hurricanes use to form.

As we headed north, the sea temperature began to slowly cool and then stabilize before we reached the Gulf Stream, which we crossed a few days out from New York. The water temperature had sat at about 19 degrees for days; then, as we sailed into the Gulf Stream, it slowly rose to 21.5, and the wind suddenly swung through thirty-five degrees. Following that, the wind died, as the water temperature stabilized. Then, as we crossed its northern boundary, the water temperature plummeted down to 15, and the wind kicked back up to 25 knots. These aggressive changes were not good news for a multihull. A wind speed change of just 5 or 6 knots could mean three sail changes: get it wrong and you could be upside down.

We had decided to head for Newport Rhode Island as it would be an easier place to work on Mobi in the weeks before we would officially go on standby for the Atlantic record. Newport held many memories for me too, as I'd not only left there for my first trans-atlantic on my twentieth birthday, but I had also arrived there at the end of my first race with *Kingfisher* just three years later. It had been forty-four days since we had left Auckland, and to reflect on our journey I made a video recording before I was joined by Loik and Oli in a small rib.

It's been difficult. It's been a long time to spend at sea, when you know you're going to spend a lot of this year at sea and also the following winter, but above all I'm really happy with the boat. She's fantastic, and she's really looked after me. We've had problems, and we've solved them together, and she's really been great. I wasn't sure I'd be able to feel like that again but I can, and that's a great feeling.

Before going on standby for the Atlantic record, I flew home from the US and popped into the office in Cowes for the first time in five months. Then, after spending a horrible thirty-six hours in a cold and lonely flat filled with far too many memories, I headed north to Derbyshire for Mum's sixtieth birthday. I'm not sure that I realized how ready I was to go home.

I was shocked to the core when I saw Mum, still suffering with her thyroid problem. She just lay in bed looking grey and frail; there was no colour in her cheeks, and her smile was empty. I had never seen Mum like this before; she sometimes got migraines or felt a bit wobbly, but here she looked so poorly and helpless.

Dad was in a flat spin, almost to the point of struggling to function normally: he was so distracted that he'd stick coffee in the tea pot. I spent the week at home cleaning, trying to help all I could. I could hardly speak for the first few days. I was overwhelmed by my concern for Mum and exhausted by what I'd been through.

That week was the longest time I had been at home in a decade, and though it was a worrying time it was comforting too. It was wonderful to be back in the heart of the home in which I had grown up and spent almost every day of my childhood. The smells and noises were familiar; spring was in full flow, and the green shoots and cool air offered a stark contrast to the warm, dry summer air of Auckland and Sydney. I began to notice more around me, and as I walked through the garden memories flooded back into my mind like a river in spate. So many dreams had first taken root here. It was ten years since I had left home to work at the nautical school in Hull, but as I walked round the familiar garden I could have kidded myself that I had never left. It was the first time I 'connected' with home: before, I'd simply been a visitor. As I looked up at the spruce which had been planted as a seedling when I was just five years old I saw how time had moved on. Next to it were the apple trees I would harvest each summer morning before school, to supplement my lunch. Mac was at my heel, and I stroked her soft head. She had been one of my best friends as a child; from the age of twelve we headed off into the woods and the fields each night after school and in all my free time over the weekends we wandered for miles around the valley. Thanks to the open-mindedness of Mum and Dad I had grown up with a feeling of freedom, and that had, no doubt, led to me following my dreams rather than convention.

The ten years that had passed since I'd left held the most incredible wealth of experience and adventure. I had travelled, lived and set my eyes on places that I could scarcely have imagined when I was a child. Back then, my world was the forest, the footpaths, every corner of the garden and the tiny plants that grew in them. But, bit by bit, life had led me from one challenge to another, and though I knew nowhere as intimately as the area around home, the world was now a much larger place. I had seen incredible sights, but in doing so I had missed many of the precious events in the lives of my family. I had sailed around the world two and a half times, crossed the Equator seven times, raced across the Atlantic and been enchanted by the mystery of the Southern Ocean, but I had missed my Dad's sixtieth birthday and Ferg's twenty-first. Although I had been following my dream, it had perhaps been quite selfish.

Mum's birthday came along, and, though she was not well enough to celebrate, I could see the joy in her eyes at having her whole family around her. Lewis and Fergus were both there, Lewis with his wife, Lucie, and Ferg with Rosie, his girlfriend. My Auntie Thea came down from upstairs, where she had been bedridden since I sailed around Britain nine years earlier, and Gran came over for the day. There was a lovely atmosphere in the house, but it came with an overriding feeling of worry for Mum.

When I returned to the States the plan was to pass through London, meet up with my physio, Matt Todman, then head off to the airport for my flight to Boston. As usual I had got it wrong with the timings again, and unbeknown to me I had asked if I could see him on Bank Holiday Monday. Matt was not someone who would even point it out, he would just get on with it, and as I arrived at a very empty surgery he was waiting for me at the door. Matt was not only a really nice guy, but an excellent physio, and over the years we'd been working together he had become a friend. I had developed all sorts of creaks in my body, presumably as it had to work so hard to sail Mobi, and I wanted to grab the opportunity to see him to try and sort myself out.

What I like about Matt is he looks at the whole person and, on seeing how stressed I was as I walked in, he just said, 'Now sit down and tell me what's wrong. I'm not even going to look at you until you get it off your chest.'

Having bottled up my concerns in Derbyshire while keeping a brave face, it was a huge relief to download my feelings to Matt. Though there were a million worries on my mind, Mum's health was the only one that mattered. She was really ill, and with me about to shoot off to New York for a few weeks there was nothing I could do about it.

Matt listened to everything I had to say, and we continued chatting as he manipulated me, occasionally noisily, to put me back together again. He mentioned that he knew someone in London who was a heart specialist, and that if I felt it was right I could get in touch with him. I didn't sleep much on the flight worrying about Mum, and the day after we sailed down to New York I called Matt to ask if I could take him up on his offer.

It was Wednesday 5 May, and when I spoke to Matt's contact to explain the situation one of the first things he said was: 'Can your mum get down here tomorrow lunchtime? I could see her in my lunch break.'

'I'll see what I can do,' I replied; knowing how ill Mum really was, I wasn't sure she'd be up to it. I was totally taken aback by his offer and I never imagined that he might respond so quickly.

Though initially she said that she couldn't manage it, after making a few calls we managed to sort something out. My ex-partner and good friend Ian was driving from Scotland down to London, and, knowing Mum and Dad well, he agreed to drop them off. Helen King at OC, who was one of the most reliable people I have ever met, found a cab company who would be prepared to take them home. I knew that, if Mum was going to go, the journey was going to have to be as stress-free as possible.

I waited with bated breath for the result of the appointment, and it seemed afterwards that it had done the trick. The drugs Mum had been on were affecting her heart, and she needed another drug to stabilize it. I couldn't thank Matt, or Dr Violaris, enough. I had been desperate to know what to do, and they had found a solution.

It was not long after that Mum told me that she really thought she might not make it. Typical Mum, she never wanted to cause a fuss, and it made me remember never to forget that!

The relief was immense, but at the same time I was still exhausted. I had been non-stop for what seemed like for ever. Since the summer before the Route du Rhum things hadn't seemed to let up. I was struggling to cope with the pressures that I was under, and as a result I had a fear that the year would run away with me. When I finally saw the diary, which had nine days' hospitality in three locations in France, then ten days later fourteen days in the UK back to back, it was the final straw, and I began to write a long e-mail to Mark to highlight my worries.

Basically I am burning out, and in the current state I am in I am in no way in a fit state to take on the round the world record right now. It's a harsh, and from my point of view very frightening thing to have to feel,

but I have to face up to the fact its true. A
substantial part of this is my situation with home and
relationships - and on that front I have been through,
and am going through an absolute shocker.

It has to be assumed that I can sail the boat for
sure, but I really felt that I was more on my own this
time, and that there was a general feeling of 'of course
she can sail her' this time. I felt that the pressure of
sailing her was underestimated by others, particularly
in the state I was in - which did not help . . .

Do not think that you are losing the Ellen that you
know, I'm just going through the motions of self
preservation to try to get myself to a mental and
physical state where I can actually be proactive rather
than re-active, and spend time doing other things that
are important for me, which equally allow me to be able
to be realistic. Also I DON'T WANT TO LOSE THE
PASSION and I've been far too sodding close.

I STILL WANT TO BE THE FASTEST, FITTEST, MOST
PASSIONATE SAILOR IN THE WORLD!!

Talk soon

ex

I knew that at the heart of this lay my own sheer determination
to do the best job I possibly could. There are not many, if any,
sailors who sail half-way round the world in preparation for a round-
the-world attempt. I have always thrown everything I have at the
challenges I set myself, but on land I would give my all too, and it
was this that I struggled to pace.

The result was a list of conversations and the working out of some
time off before the record towards the end of the year. Mark suggested
I took a month off in October, but I knew that I needed to be with the
boat in her final stage of preparation. The one thing that I absolutely
wanted to do was see Nick off for the start of his Vendée, and the idea
was that when we returned from Les Sables d'Olonne at the beginning of November we would be on standby for the round-the-world.

Bit by bit that summer I realized that I needed to have fun, and try and chill out a bit. There had been a lot of intense stuff going on, and I had a strange feeling that my amount of relaxation that year was going to be the make or break of the record.

The following month brought a nice distraction from life as our company, OC, had taken over the running of a race called the Transat. In fact it was full of memories as it was the race that I had won into Newport Rhode Island in its previous edition four years before. I'd driven down to Plymouth with my kayak on the roof of the car, and I made the most of the early-morning light before most were awake by paddling around in the harbour. It was a nice feeling beginning to do things for my own pleasure again, and not be at the beck and call of a jam-packed schedule. It gave me time to mill around on the dockside, chatting to people I hadn't seen for six months. It was a nice way to get back amongst friends, solo sailors and team members alike, and I finally began to relax there. Though I too was on standby for my record attempt the weather window had not yet materialized, and it was wonderful to be there at the start and soaking it all in. Unlike them I had no specific start time that I was working towards. Mobi was ready, I was ready, and together we were waiting for the green light.

After a brief trip to Derbyshire I headed off once again to the USA. This time I made tracks towards Boston, rather than New York, as that was the finish line for the Transat. Having been there for the start, and it not being too far from Mobi, I decided to help with the arrival of the race. My job was parking the boats as they finished, and, as most didn't have engines, it was a stressful job. I loved being there to help people, though, rather than being at the centre of attention at the race finish. It was nice for a change, too, to see everyone else doing the interviews and see the whole game from the land-based side, though there was a concerning aspect to that. To be with the team as boats were dismasting, capsizing and breaking was a strange sensation for me, never so much as when Bernard Stamm called Mark to say that he had a major keel failure, followed an hour and a half later by his distress beacon going off. Before, it had been me on the other end of a phone; the one who was cold and wet and in danger. But here we were, sitting in a warm, safe, comfortable hotel in Boston, and I felt not only uneasy but totally and utterly helpless.

Following the end of the Transat, and having had no weather window at all for the two months, we waited in New York, resigned to the fact that we'd deliver Mobi back to Europe with a team. Loik and Oli had been taking turns to spend time boat-sitting in New York, and everyone gathered there for one final time to load her up for the off. Loik had been based there, and had even loaded up a Wendy house he'd bought out there for his daughter Maëna. Everyone was fairly relaxed, and we had arranged for our final crew member, Jean-Seb, to fly in from Montreal for the delivery. Seb had worked with us on the Jules Verne and once again was going to help us out during the summer as a break from his university course.

Seb arrived the day of our departure. The sun was shining, and we were due to leave that afternoon. In fact we'd planned to leave after a lunch together at the lightship restaurant on the pontoon by the boat. Just as we headed off to get lunch we received a text from Kate, who was luckily still in the office in the UK. She asked if I had seen the e-mail from Commanders Weather, who were routing the record attempt. I hadn't. I called her . . .

Summary:

Guidance today somewhat optimistic about a Tuesday departure. Think you should hold off on delivery another 24 hours to see how this looks tomorrow.

Crikey! I drew a long and unexpected breath before calling Commanders. It was like someone proposing you ran a marathon the next day when you were preparing for a nice long walk. They suggested I gave it a go, leaving twenty-four to thirty-six hours later, which would mean leaving the following day. We went to lunch to discuss the option. The guys said they were happy to work through the night to unload the gear, food and the fuel that we'd loaded on board. If we were going to stand a chance we were going to need to be as light as possible.

I was nervous as we headed out to the start line. It was 22 miles out from where Mobi was moored across the water from the huge skyscrapers of the city, and the distance gave a certain amount of thinking time. We had decided that the best time to cross the line was at the end of the afternoon, when the synoptic breeze would overpower the sea breeze. We made it out to the line just after 1700 local time, and, as the breeze was between 20 and 25 knots, we decided to give it a go then. It all happened so quickly. Up went the mainsail, the guys got off, and then I unrolled the headsail and was off.

Chapter Eight

The record I was trying to break had stood for ten years, and if anything was going to be a test, this was it. The North Atlantic crossing is less than a tenth of the distance around the world, but it's a sprint rather than a marathon, and I knew I would need to push Mobi very close to her limits to stand any chance of breaking the record. What made things harder was the fact that the record was set by a 60 foot trimaran like *Foncia*, which was smaller and therefore in theory lighter and faster than Mobi. It had been set by a Frenchman, Laurent Bourgnon, who had crossed in 7 days, 2 hours, 34 minutes and 42 seconds, which meant I'd need to maintain an average speed of 17.15 knots and cross the line before 00:34:42 GMT on Tuesday 29 June. It was going to be a hard one to break, and I needed to be realistic about my chances. The weather systems were far from perfect, but this was an amazing opportunity to learn, and I was going to give it my absolute best shot.

One of the risks of the early stages was fog; as Ken Campbell from Commanders had said, if we were lucky, we might outrun it until Tuesday. Fog at sea is pretty much the worst scenario possible, particularly in an area where there is shipping and relatively shallow water. You may ask: why shallow water? Well, just over one-third of the Atlantic crossing on the direct route is coastal; in fact the shortest distance from the Ambrose Light off New York Harbour entrance to the Lizard Point takes you through Martha's Vineyard, through Nova Scotia and right through the island of

Newfoundland. So although the distance is 2,857 nautical miles you will certainly be sailing further than that, unless you have wheels on your boat!

The first night gave us a real kicking. The wind was its usual changeable self. I can only have slept for fifteen minutes, as I spent most of my time changing sails. The mainsail on Mobi weighed just under 150 kg which was almost three times my weight, meaning each time it had to go up or down there was a huge physical effort involved. Mobi was a beast, and the loads she generated with her power were not insignificant. Plus the fact that everything on her was manual: pulling the sails up and down was done with winches; there were no hydraulic or electric aids. To give an idea of her power, her mainsheet was designed to go up to a maximum of 7 tons load, and her rigging up to 30. Her mast was in the shape of a foil, and sat on a titanium ball which was necessary to allow it to rotate. That was designed to a maximum dynamic load of 59 tons, which wasn't bad for a boat which weighed 9. Her mast was large enough that, if pulled up, I could ascend it inside, and it rose 100 feet from the sea. She had seventy-two watertight bulkheads spread between her floats and main hull so as to make her structure strong and light, and we had spent a lot of time working out what would happen if we crashed at high speed, building in a crumple zone at the front of her main hull float.

Though I knew that sailing her was hard work, this record was taking me to a whole different level. I was pushing her as hard as I dared, and that created a very narrow margin of error. With these record attempts you always hope that the first three or four days will be the ones where you have predictable and consistent winds, and then afterwards you take the cards that you've been dealt. This Transat was not like that, and while still in the cold water of the Labrador Current we battled with unstable wind and fog patches, struggling to keep up the average speed we needed. It was not only dangerous, but stressful, physically demanding and more importantly, slow.

The fog created that stress: sailing along in the freezing, moist wind, seeing nothing around you, just listening as hard as your ears will allow you for sounds that you begin to imagine. Every now and then the radar alarm bleeped, calling me to fumble on rubber buttons with my wet fingers to find a contrast that would indicate where the dangers lay. Sailing fast in fog isn't anyone's cup of tea, and I spent most of those first two days with my heart in my mouth. I was glad when I passed into the Gulf Stream, where the wind increased, the current was with me, and I felt like I could get stuck into the record.

DAY 1:
22:10:00 GMT 21.6.04 to 10:10:00 GMT 22.6.04
  Follows almost the exact course away from New York as Laurent Bourgnon (Primagaz) record course.
  Behind record: -42 miles / -2h 27m / DTF [distance to finish] 2674 miles
  10:10:00 GMT to 22:10:00 GMT 22.6.04
  First 24 hours completed at an average speed of 17.16 knots - right on the record pace. New weather model arrives forcing choice - risk poor forecast on the northern direct route (less miles) or head for the best weather (southern route) but having to sail an average 2 knots faster than the record pace.
  Behind record: -151 miles / -8h 48m / DTF 2490 miles
  Ellen quote: 'At most 14 minutes sleep and 8 sail changes since having left New York and now I have something on the rudder acting like a giant break on the boat, until daylight there is not much I can do. I also broke part of a winch during the night so its not been an easy start.'

We were stuck in the warm sector of a depression and we needed it to slip right by so that we could catch the north-westerly winds on the back side of it. The problem was that the front was not as clearly defined as we'd have liked: it was almost becoming occluded. The wind increased, but as it did so did the risk of squalls, and, knowing that in the unsettled weather we had fallen behind the record, I was pushing hard. Our boat speed went up regularly to 28 knots, and I pushed her harder and harder.

I spoke to the team: 'It's very, very stressful. You just spend your whole time hoping something doesn't break . . . Conditions change very quickly . . . You can't afford to break anything but equally you can't afford not to be pushing hard.'

I had never sailed her so fast, and the conditions were not letting up. The wind increased to 25 knots, 30 knots, 35 knots, but Mobi kept soldiering on, burying into the crests of the waves then cutting through them like a knife. It seemed like every wave she took on fed her with more energy and determination. She was being thrown violently from side to side, and many of the noises I was beginning to hear were new. Her foils were squealing with the speed and changing their pitch as we forged our way up the waves and then flew down them. The wind then began gusting to well over 40 knots, and still Mobi pushed on. I felt so proud of her and all who had built her; it was her first opportunity to really stretch her legs, and she was doing that in style.

However, on the second night I jumped out of my skin as the consequences of our speed finally hit home. We were flying through the water like a torpedo when there was a sudden bang, and Mobi was physically thrown sideways. Everything flew across the cabin in a fraction of a second, including me, and her angle was at least thirty-five or forty-five degrees. For a split second I thought we were going over, but as I was being pinned to the cabin side with the G force there was little I could do. The moment I could move I scrambled up to her cockpit, head-torch on, looking round. The pilot was still working, and remarkably we unfalteringly resumed course. The sea had picked us up and thrown us like a cork, demonstrating how small and insignificant a 75 foot boat could feel. I was a wreck by now, crouching in the cuddy, soaked to the skin with sweat and counting the heartbeats in my chest to calm myself down. It was exciting, though. I had never pushed a boat so hard, nor ever maintained such high speeds in my life. I can only have slept for one hour in those first forty-eight. The front was still behind us; we drove on.

```
By 0138 GMT B&Q covers 525.96 miles in 24 hours -
14 miles short of the world record distance set by
Laurent Bourgnon during his record in 1994.
  Behind record: -398 miles / -23h 12m / DTF 2000 miles
```

I also had an e-mail from Ian McKay, who probably knew me better than most. Typical Ian, with his great humour and wonderful way of encouraging me. He suggested that I tried to pace myself and to eat and sleep when I could. He ended his email:

```
And remember, you don't have to blow the bloody doors
off it; one minute early is fine!
```

We were still being pushed south, which meant that conditions were far from favourable, and until the front came over us we would not be able to gybe over and make a beeline for home. On the third day this took us twenty-four hours behind the record. It was devastating news, but I could feel that it was coming. During that night with the wind kicking in it took me an hour and fifteen to get the mainsail down. I was struggling to reduce its size, and with so much wind blowing it against the rigging my 57 kg was having little effect. It was all a learning experience, and I changed sails eight times in five hours as the front went through. I was a bit too close to fatigue for comfort and was desperately trying to find time to rest. I knew inside, though, that we still had a chance of breaking the record, which is why I was pushing so hard, but I also knew that the faster I would have to sail, the higher the risk was.

I managed to keep awake until the slightly more stable north-westerlies moved in. Mobi felt like a rocket ship, and, having had virtually no sleep for three days, I managed a miraculous ninety minutes, and ALL IN ONE GO! If ever there were a time to test skipper and boat this was it, and I resolved to push as hard as I could to cling on to any chance that was still out there for us.

Over the following days we were screaming along, during one period averaging 27 knots for two hours. The deficit went down to fourteen hours, then six, then three, then thirty minutes ... the weather for the moment was playing on our side, and, despite my exhaustion, I was managing to push her as hard as ever. It was brilliant.

But as the finish line drew closer I felt so nervous I struggled to eat – I had boiled the kettle only three times since leaving the States, which indicated how many proper meals I'd had. We were also approaching the shipping lanes now, and there would be a lot more traffic around: more boats, fishing boats and ships as we sailed over the continental shelf.

The night before the finish the wind direction was an absolute glam. Talking to Commanders and reading the forecast, I had been really worried it was going to go more into the west, but it didn't, and we sailed straight down the direct route for most of the night. Inside I still thought we had a chance of breaking the record, but I knew it was going to be very, very close, and it all depended on how long the breeze stayed with us.

I was incredibly tired, and, though I did manage to get some sleep that night, I was clearly running on empty. I had never pushed a boat so hard before in my life on my own, and living in what feels like a torpedo slamming through the waves was taking its toll. I was pretty close to my very first hallucination that night, though I didn't actually see anything. I had slept in the cuddy and then woke up with a start, didn't really know where I was, but stood up immediately and checked around the cockpit, from where I could see there were two ships in the distance. I could see their lights and I was convinced that it was another competitor in a race, together with a hospital ship sailing with them. My initial reaction while still standing there was that it was totally unfair that my competitor had assistance and that it wasn't allowed in the rules! It took me a few minutes to realize my competitor was a cargo ship!

DAY 7: Date: 28/06/2004
B&Q NOW 4 MILES BEHIND RECORD 'IT'S NOT OVER, TILL IT'S OVER ...!'

IN BRIEF

* LATEST DATA (1500 GMT) SHOWS THAT ELLEN
MACARTHUR HAS GAINED ANOTHER FEW CRUCIAL MILES to
climb within 4 miles of Laurent Bourgnon's record ...
only 13 minutes behind with 9 hours, 44 minutes and
42 seconds left on the clock and 152 miles to go to
the finish line.

* 'WE ARE IN THE HANDS OF THE WEATHER ...' that
up until now has provided a good south-westerly 20 knot
breeze but this afternoon that wind speed started
slowly to decrease to just under 20 knots.

* B&Q HAS AVERAGED OVER 17.8 KNOTS IN LAST
30 MINUTES and has to average 15.58 knots to beat
the record ...

It was so, so close: the record really was going to go down to the wire. But, though we pushed as hard as we could and timed our gybe perfectly, the reality for us was that the wind at the finish dropped and shifted. At 2200 on the final day it left us, meaning that we could no longer sail fast enough and we would have to gybe a second time. I was absolutely gutted and I stood in the cockpit almost in disbelief at the rollercoaster of emotion associated with pushing so hard. I had had less than fourteen hours' sleep in seven days, and it had all been for nothing. In that moment, with all the weight of the imminent round-the-world resting on my shoulders, and with the frustration at having come so close, I felt crushed. It felt as though everything I had touched in the previous twelve months had gone wrong, from the capsize and the dismast to my relationship with Luis. This record, albeit only in the final throes, was no exception.

We had missed it by just seventy-five minutes ...

By the time we arrived in Southampton, thanks to several solid hours of sleep, I had come to terms with our failure. Things in fact since we left Australia had not all gone wrong, and the record had certainly not been attempted with favourable conditions. Though we hadn't achieved the record, we had achieved something very important indeed. Mobi and I had a stronger bond, and I had a much better feel for where her limits lay. Hindsight is a great thing, but I was sure that without that attempt I would have not dared to push her hard enough round the world. I felt different about it then, and we were just six months from our standby time. Mobi was a tough cookie. Having pushed her so hard, I knew what she was capable of.

I just hoped that I, as her skipper, could live up to her.

My final six months on land were crammed with the usual summer madness, and, though there was some time for breaks, I was so exhausted when one came around that I struggled to get back up to speed. A few weeks after the transatlantic record we were over in France doing two weeks' back-to-back hospitality, entertaining our sponsors from the Kingfisher-owned Castorama. With Mobi having been in New York for two months, this meant that we had a huge amount of catching up to do when it came to sharing our project with those back in Europe, and this took a different toll on me. Each day we would sail with a group of guests and chat to them about the project. I always tried to make people laugh and bounded about the boat as my usual cheery self, full of energy and enthusiasm. When the guests were all in a line pulling the mainsail up, I would encourage them by saying, 'Come on, you lot! It can't be that hard. It's a girl's boat!'

The team were absolutely wonderful, and the atmosphere on board was unquestionably what carried me through that action-packed summer. Loik was the best person I could imagine as a boat captain, and we got to the stage at sea with manoeuvres where we could virtually just look at each other and know exactly what the other was thinking.

After France Mobi and the team returned to the UK for Cowes Week. This involved fourteen days' hospitality with just one free day, though beforehand there was the most wonderful respite as I joined two trips with the Ellen MacArthur Trust. There were several familiar faces that had sailed with us the year before: Katie, Dean, Alex and Maxine, to name a few. They were all a year older, and all had changed, physically as well as mentally, growing in confidence. But the biggest change was in Maxine, and it was not something that I was prepared for. She now had beautiful, shiny, dark curly hair to match her smile, and she looked so healthy. She seemed so, so happy too, and it was priceless to witness.

The Trust weekends were followed by Cowes Week, and in 2004 it was madness. Often we would have two groups of guests, one in the morning and one in the afternoon, and with Mobi, Nick's *Skandia*, and the 50 footer which he had successfully brought to victory in the 2002 Rhum, we entertained a staggering 396 guests. As in France, everyone had a wonderful time, and despite the bad weather, the fortnight was a great success. Though tiring, it did give me energy in a funny way, seeing face after face light up in amazement as they saw Mobi for the first time. I thought she was beautiful, but it sure was reassuring to think that others did too. Beneath all our smiles and enthusiasm, though, was an intense wish to get to Lorient and cross off the remaining jobs from our list. We were now only three months from 'standby' for the round-the-world, and there was much work to be done.

The following months remain a blur in my mind. Between the Southampton Boat Show and working on the boat with the team in Lorient, I had presentations to do in Sardinia, France and the UK. I had a distinct feeling that my calendar was running away with me. My problem was always that I'd give everyone and everything my energy; at presentations and events I would be my usual chirpy, chatty self, but inside there would be little energy left. I was not someone who was used to asking when I needed help, but I did. I sent a long e-mail to Lucy Horwood, my PA, who was looking after my diary.

Free time has been very, very difficult and finding time to organise my life very hard. What is going on is just about sustainable, but NOT interspersed with record attempts which take every last drop of energy that you have . . . I have a way of dealing with pressure which from the outside looks like I'm very happy. I can be cheery, and full of life, but inside there's sod all which is left as I give all my energy away to try to please more people, perform better and basically do a better job. I though, am the limiting factor . . .

I have tried to fight this battle on my own to try and deal with everything, but quite frankly as I'm sitting here in a service station in the car in France I realise that I seriously need your help!

In an attempt to download my feelings I'll describe how I feel right now . . .

I'm sitting in the car having spent 9 hours travelling. I've pulled over because I was so stressed that I was unable to drive at less than 100 miles per hour. I feel exhausted, and in terrible physical shape - i.e. I feel as far from a sportsperson as I possibly can . . .

My training recently has been a disaster, and everything else seems to exhaust me, leaving me with a head full of issues, and things that need solving.

Sardinia is an example of something quite destructive in this final run up to the record attempt. I had a reasonable start in Nantes, took two flights - got diverted to the wrong airport - then Mark and I drive for two hours to get to the presentation where I went straight in to perform. (I was travelling for 13 hours!) After ˄˄˄˄˄˄ all dinner and a 0130 bed time I got up to sail for the day. Mark decided not to sail, and went to the gym for an hour, ran for an hour, then swam for an hour. I was talking to guests onboard. Then we did the dinner thing - and I had time to get in to the pool for half an hour before hand. We got home about midnight, and five hours later I had to get up to leave. I got a taxi to the airport, and then took the first of three flights to get to Nantes . . . It's now 1630 - 11 hours later, and I'm still not in Lorient. On arrival my bags were lost, and I have a 2 hour drive back to Nantes.

I really need the time in my schedule to train without having to get up at 0600 every morning to do it, and have enough time around that to organise my life and other jobs onboard so that my head is rested enough to be able to train. I had to write this how it is so that you can understand how pissed off I am.

This is not in any way your fault - that's the last thing I want you to think. I just need you do understand a little of this anger and understand the reality that I'm not in the best shape ever, and that it's really my failing for not being strong enough to ask people to help when it's been necessary.

If I had not written this we would have spoken tomorrow, you would have asked how I was and I would have said Ok but a bit tired . . . then on we go again. SO this is hopefully going to break any barriers there are, and let you know that I really need your support, and that if we can get this right it will make more of a difference to my life than you can imagine.

Goals.

To be fit and physically ready to take on this attempt.

To do selective presentations which blow people away.

To be fun to work around.

To be very motivated, and communicate that motivation from the boat well . . .

To be rested enough to work reasonable hours with the guys . . .

To sleep as much as possible in the days leading up to trip.

and

To break this god damn record!

Perhaps it was stress, I don't know, but I was not in a great state. Time was running out, and I desperately needed to get myself in gear for the record. I needed to get back on track and feel that I was in control of my life again. As usual, though, being in Lorient with the boat and the guys was the best thing for me, and for the remainder of September I based myself there until I could head to Skye for a week for some rest and relaxation. I was kidding myself if I thought I could get the pressure out of my head, but in a funny way I didn't want to: I just wanted the time and the space to deal with it and prepare myself for it. On my return from Skye I headed back to Lorient and got into a rhythm where I was training every morning, running around the huge inland lakes close to where Mobi was. There I could relax, and as I ran for an hour each morning I was in a place which reminded me of Derbyshire, as the strong, damp smell of woodland teased my senses as my eyes darted round trying to spot wildlife as I ran. I got splashed with mud and tried to catch the early falling leaves. As a child there had rarely been a day when I wasn't in mud somewhere, and I found a strange sense of familiarity and safety in being there. In a way it was in those weeks in October I came to terms with what I was trying to achieve and became at one with myself. Slowly my confidence grew, and my persona perhaps changed. I was beginning to enter my 'other world', which was exciting, but daunting. A world that no one could follow me into.

Only too soon, the time came to sail from Lorient for Falmouth. It was strange really; you expect to be sailing into a storm in November, but we just had the most perfect conditions and the most glorious purple misty sunset. We had checked, checked and checked again, loaded all my gear and food on board for the record and removed Mobi's main engine – so now the only engines she had were the small 10 hp generators up forward. One, the main one, was in a box, and I had proudly called him George, scrawling his name across his protective box in black capitals. It was a perfect sail into Falmouth, little did I know that just two weeks later Mobi and I would be alone, powering south to the Southern Ocean.

Francis Joyon had circumnavigated the world in a staggering 73 days. The bar had been set so, so high, and in a boat which was 15 feet bigger than Mobi. I felt like David taking on Goliath. To break his record I was going to have to push Mobi harder than I would have liked.

This was the big one.

Chapter Nine

My time in Falmouth before the start had been a bit like being stuck in limbo. It's one thing to prepare for a race with a start day, knowing how your timescale will pan out, but when you might know only forty-eight hours before you go that you're leaving it's a very different story. It's a strange feeling, as if you have a huge exam to sit but you don't know when it is going to take place and you can never manage to relax. You know that what you're about to attempt will be harder than you can imagine, and, though in your heart you just want to get on with it, there is always a small part of you which would like to delay starting so that you can prepare more.

I kept sane by going running, weaving through the fields and along tracks and footpaths, guided by tiny pieces of photocopied map. The farmland and sounds of nature brought back warm memories of wandering the fields with Mac, my old dog, and the familiarity of it was once again comforting. I was also watching winter arrive and knew that, if all went well out there, I'd hopefully be home before spring.

I was fitter than I'd ever been, and my e-mails to people before the off were full of words like 'can't wait to get out there' and 'just want to get on with it'. My final e-mail to Commanders Weather in the US before boarding Mobi said:

Just to say a massive thanks . . . I know that this is
just the beginning - but I am really looking forward to

working with you guys . . . I know that this is going to
be the hardest thing I've ever had to deal with mentally
and physically, but I'm really up for it . . .

To know that you are all there, and going through this
with me makes a huge difference, and picking up the
phone to you all is a real pleasure . . . so let's get on
with this . . .

Thanks guys . . .

Ellenxx

Moments before I climbed on board Mobi to leave I was sitting
alone in a small room on the black leather sofa in the back office of
the Maritime Museum calling Mum and Dad on the phone to say
my final land-based goodbye. We had decided this time that it
would be easier if Mum, Dad, friends and family did not come down
to see me off. However brave you are, and however much you think
forward to the finish, it's a painful process for all. It's pretty hard to
know what to say when you're about to leave for a round-the-world
record, and 'bye for now' doesn't really do it. I thanked Mum for the
seventy-one pieces of her fantastic flapjack she had posted down
and which were safely stowed on board, and told them not to worry,
as we were as ready as we could ever be. But, as I said those final
words and told them both that I loved them, I felt my stomach
churning inside.

From the window of my safe but lonely little room I saw Mobi,
my home and friend for the next two and a half months. She looked
like a racehorse in the stalls, and I wished I could blink myself across
the start line and not have to deal with the final goodbyes. I was nervous, really nervous, and, ironically for someone who is happy alone,
I felt uncomfortable in that room. I left hastily, not wanting to spend
a second longer in my own company reflecting on what I was about
to do, I left to find Lou. It was time to get on with it.

The people who had gathered along the dockside cheered as I
walked down the gangway wearing my remarkably normal baggy
trousers and fluffy comfy boots. They were my favourite trousers,
totally impractical for sailing, being made of cotton, but they were

going with me and would remind me of home. I tried not to think about it but I knew all too well that an awful lot was going to happen, and months were going to pass, before I would climb back up that galvanized steel walkway once again. I recall clearly the sound that my feet made as I stepped on to it – now no longer on dry land.

I wondered what people were thinking. Did they think I'd make it, fail or perhaps never come back at all? But, whatever they were feeling, what I took from it was their support, and to me in that moment it made a huge difference.

I left the dockside in Falmouth at 1600 hours on 27 November 2004. It was a grey, windless afternoon, which gave no indication at all of the kicking we were going to get as we crossed the start line the following morning. Leaving is never easy at the best of times but you have to deal with it by treating it as a stage of the project that you have to go through to get out there. When I was busy it was fine, I was getting on with the process. It was when I had time to think that my nerves took over, and the pit of my stomach felt sick and uneasy.

Leaving the dock with the crew and knowing they would be on board with me for a final five or so hours put off that feeling of really going and made the dock departure a little easier. Mobi was towed out of the harbour gently, and we were all really touched when at least thirty boats came along to escort us out. I smiled inside as I saw a yellow Corribee, like my *Iduna*, the boat on which I first undertook a solo journey. Here I was, less than ten years later, about to take on the biggest challenge I'd ever faced.

When I was happy that we had everything ready for me to turn south for the start line, and I'd asked all the important questions that I couldn't remember the answers to, I went down below to try and steal a few moments to sleep. This was to be the last time for seventy-two days that there would be someone else to look out for us, and, more importantly, I would need to stay awake all night once they had gone, as we crossed the Channel to the start line.

It took me ages to fall asleep: I couldn't switch off, as I knew that the time with the team on board was finite, and minute by minute that time was drifting away. My brain was in mental and emotional overload, and I felt a huge urge to speak to each person who came into the cabin as I tried to close my eyes and rest.

For a split second when I woke all felt normal, then I suddenly remembered what was about to happen. For the first time ever before heading out to sea alone I felt sick with nerves and frightened, really frightened. It felt different this time. There were not another twenty friendly competitors in this race feeling the same emotions and going through the same experience this winter, just me, and me alone.

Seconds later Mark climbed down into the cabin. It was time for the team to get off, and I knew it. He could see how I felt from the look on my face, and words were not necessary as he wrapped his arms around me. In those moments my emotions came out, and we shared something that happens only rarely in life. The strongest moments for me have occurred without the need for words, and this was one of them. I remember sobbing to the point where I ceased to breathe normally, and Mark just holding me. I was so glad that he was there.

Watching the rib slip away was torture. It was like a piece of you that had been there to support you so closely was being severed. Physically they were still close, very close, but they might as well have been a million miles away. Though I wished them to stay, their waving arms grew smaller and smaller as their little craft faded away into the distance. This for me was without doubt the loneliest moment of the record.

It was just after 2200; night was falling. I reached down to the auto-pilot control and pressed the −10 button ten times. Her tillers swung over to starboard, and her bows bore away to the south, the direction of our start line, 100 miles away, and towards the Southern Ocean, some 6,000 miles beyond . . .

Though I felt at home on Mobi, at that moment, she felt quiet and empty. The chatter and voices were gone, and there was just the gentle glow of the instruments to keep me company as I sat at the chart table. I picked up a postcard that Mark had left on the desk there for me; the picture was a painting of a grey dolphin. I turned it over to read the words he had written on the back:

A donf!

Night and day; success or 'failure'; petole ou tempete; good day bad day; steady or variable wind; happy or sad; lonely or not; whether you need me or not; I will be here 24/7 on the end of the phone living it with you again.

xxM

The night passed slowly, emptily and nervously. The first night alone of many. It was an odd feeling as we wove through the traffic-separation scheme and crossed huge ships entering and leaving the English Channel. It's a very busy place, and in between sitting at the chart table and popping out on deck, I did a huge amount of thinking. It wasn't safe to sleep here, so my mind, for good or bad, was able to wander.

Perhaps for the first time in my life I was really contemplating my own mortality. I thought of things that I wished I had said to people, and goodbyes I'd been unable to make. I had odd thoughts about places I felt safe and things that I really wanted to do with my life. There were no tears now, nor was there panic. I was overwhelmed by an ominous feeling, the kind you get when you know you're about to have to deal with something really tough, and there is only one way to get through it – to go and get on with it.

I knew well that the best tactic was to concentrate on everything that needed to be done before I crossed the line in the morning, and that little by little over the first week things would get better. Once you gain some miles to the south, cross the Equator and feel the air cooling again on the other side you are on your way, well and truly – then it's the sleigh ride through the Southern Ocean and homeward bound. Sounds too easy, really, but you have to tell yourself these simple stories so that, when you're about to leave, the whole journey feels far more manageable.

Dawn approached slowly, and with it the sight of the lighthouse at Ushant. The wind was exactly what we'd been waiting for. The front had gone through, bringing a steady 28 knots. A quick call with Commanders Weather confirmed that we had the green light, and that they were happy with the latest forecast. I made the final adjustment to Mobi's sail plan, removing the staysail from its bag and hoisting it. I can't describe how nervous I felt as I moved around her deck. There was no turning back now.

We crossed the line at 0810 and 44 seconds on 28 November 2004. The wind was strong and from the north, and the sea conditions as we rounded Ushant were aggressive and unpredictable. Mobi's cockpit was being pounded with angry English Channel water, as, with such powerful currents flowing round the tip of France, the sea was kicking up a fuss. The motion on board Mobi was violent, and the water was shockingly cold. With my video camera I filmed back towards the cockpit, my thoughts drowned out by the smacking of waves hitting Mobi and the constant clatter of the helicopter engines near by.

I don't know why, but it surprised me when the helicopters flew in to film us. I'd got my head round leaving people behind during my crossing alone to the start line, but with the choppers about I could see faces again, and I wasn't entirely ready for it. There was even a figure I recognized in one helicopter: it was my good friend the photographer Thierry Martinez. Mark and I had spent several months living in his house seven years before. He knew me well, and it surprised me just how emotional I felt at seeing his figure waving goodbye. I hadn't seen Thierry since the summer, and it was a strange sensation saying goodbye through the air and not having the chance to give him a hug. Little did I know then, but he would be the first person to welcome me home as I approached the finish.

Once the helicopters turned and left, I felt quite uneasy. Mobi and I were finally alone, and the length of time I'd be away for sank in. Speed was good, and conditions eased once we sailed out of the rough current-fuelled tidal area off the shallow Atlantic coast.

It was a horrible time in those first few days, and, no matter how much you want to be out there tackling a record, it's only human nature to be nervous about what you are going to undertake. I'd glance round to see a face, finding nothing, no smile or reaction to something going on, and nor would there be, until the finish at least. I had flashbacks to Mobi's build as every single part of her reminded me of someone, a moment, and a job being done. It didn't help my feeling of nerves. So much energy, time, effort and so many sacrifices had been made by so many to get us to the start line. It was now up to me, and me alone, to get myself back to the finish line. It was I who had to run with the baton for the last part of our relay, and I was determined that, no matter how many times I slipped or fell, I was not going to drop it.

My first log from the boat sent later on that day read:

ELLEN LOG 1315 GMT:
Well, here we are out on the open ocean once more . . .
It's going to be a tough one this . . . I can feel it,
and really know that I am going to have to dig very,
very deep. The most important thing though - and I keep
hammering into the front of my mind is that I really
want to enjoy this. B&Q is the most unbelievable boat,
and she has such an incredible feeling about her - I
just really, really want to do the voyage justice for
her too. I am sitting here, obviously alone - and in
fact feeling very, very nervous. We are off - and the
Omega clock I can see just next to me is very definitely
ticking . . . How hard do we push, how gingerly do we
sail, how much will B&Q take, how much will I take?
These are all things which right now are in the front of
my mind. I just hope that I am able to relax into this,
and appreciate it for what it is . . . better go - I can
feel a genoa to solent change coming on . . .
    x
Back again - changed sails in a rather full cockpit
since I dragged the sails back there . . . I noticed a
few fantastic things as we left . . . There was an

unbelievable stillness as we left the dock . . . funny -
as if no-one really wanted to make too much noise -
all very odd . . . But it was fantastic to feel the
atmosphere there. Falmouth gave us all an outstanding
send off - I am overwhelmed . . . really overwhelmed. It
all seemed a bit like a dream really . . . as we were
towed out of the harbour there was a cormorant diving on
our bows and just a few hours later as we sailed out of
the harbour entrance we had dolphins swimming around
us . . . magnificent . . . time for a quick nap now . . . x

The clock was ticking, and no matter what I did I couldn't stop it. I was piling the most incredible pressure on myself to get the job done right. On day one I covered 400 miles, and I knew that I needed to average 369 per day to break Francis's record. Though Francis had been out on the ocean the previous year, it felt as if he was out there with me.

The record was a very different sensation to that of racing in the Vendée. In the Vendée there is a certain reassurance that the boat ahead of you could encounter serious problems, run into light airs or even not make it to the finish. Here in the record, things were different. Francis's time was set in stone: what I was now racing was a totally indestructible, infallible pace boat, which had finished its journey. Each error, slow period and problem would mean that the average speed Mobi and I had to maintain would increase, and with this speed would come more danger.

Our first hurdle was a nasty low-pressure system off the Portuguese coast, and with it came some extremely feisty conditions. We saw over 40 knots in the system and had a few difficult hours' sailing beforehand as we crossed a small high-pressure ridge to get to it: poor Mobi took a real battering. Changeable conditions are the killers on a multi, and having the wind change speed and direction relentlessly was unnerving.

The unpredictable weather was perhaps a good thing though in those first days of the trip. It made me focus on what was happening in that moment and distracted me from the worry about what we had set out to undertake. This helped me to adjust to my new world, and my new rhythm: I was kept busy by throwing my attention into keeping Mobi sailing at full speed. We also had a few minor technical issues on board, also good in helping you to focus the mind. Her central rudder flipped up just before midnight on the first day, and, as it was a rudder kicking up which led to *Foncia*'s capsize, it was something to be extremely wary of. Though I couldn't be certain of the reason, I guessed that it was due to being bashed around so much in the waves at the beginning of the record. We had designed a system whereby the rudder had two bronze fuses which held it down, and if the rudder hit something they would break, causing the rudder to kick up.

ELLEN LOG - 1300 GMT: 02/12/04
Well, I think that last night was my first real sleep since leaving a few days ago - and though I felt pretty groggy as the sun came up, I knew that it had been very, very necessary. Trying to sleep on poor B&Q who is relentlessly powering through the oceans is far from easy - this was never going to be an easy record to break. Now I think, and maybe just in the past few days, I realise what the scale of the task really is . . . I have felt under immense pressure since leaving - the pressure of that clock that never stops, and those minutes that never stop flowing. I've felt nervous, and tired, and generally pretty damn stressed since we left too. I've rarely felt any sign of hunger - though luckily have been doing this long enough now to realise that I need to just eat anyway - and luckily I have done that. That's at least one part of me that is working correctly and that's a start at least!

We have had our fair share of problems since leaving ranging from leaks in the water system, to a dangerous creaking noise from the rudders. Some frighten the life out of you and others just make you realise that the

list of things out here never ever stops. Each problem
is just a few more grams of your energy gently sapping
away . . .

The big storm we just went though was good for me I
think, as it made me go into 'survival mode' into the
'just get to the other side mode' which at least stopped
me thinking about all the stressful things. There's
nothing like a gust over 45 knots to focus the mind on
what is important in that moment!

But today whilst hanging off the back of the boat,
whilst lifting the main rudder out of the water I was
taken up sharp. I had my head in the rudder cassette
box, looking for damage in the case, but as I looked
down I saw a mesmerising flow of bright blue water
flying beneath her hull. Such a contrast it was to the
stressful hour of slowing the boat down for repairs -
that I smiled out loud (if you can do that!) and
lent down to touch this beautiful miracle of life. Just
water - but in that second it was priceless . . .

So, time for bed now. I need to sleep as much as I
possibly can as the weather is relatively stable. Having
said that though the winds been up to 25 knots and down
to 16 since I've been typing this mail . . .

later then

x

The relatively steady trade winds in the North Atlantic gave me
time to sort life on board, and get into some kind of routine, and,
despite the fact that there were often those big squall clouds lurk-
ing around ready to hose us with tropical rain and trying to blow us
over, things were relatively predictable, as you could at least see
them coming towards you. I was getting into the routine of life on
board, knowing what time I'd call in for our daily conference chat
and just how many pumps of water I needed in the kettle to make
a meal and a tea. I also knew how often I needed to make water to
ensure that I had enough to make up my powdered sports drinks

each day to keep enough fluid in me. I got into the routine of stowing my bags of rubbish in the back of the boat, checking the ball at the base of the mast for grease and charging the batteries, which were the life-blood of Mobi. Running her was becoming more and more like running me, and before long those two functions were going to become almost inseparable.

My food and 'consumables' were stored in one of ten bags which we had tied under the floor of the boat. Each bag was about the size of a sleeping-bag storage bag and was totally waterproof, and had in it everything from tiny gas bottles for the stove to vitamins, food, snacks and powder for my daily 500 calorie milkshake. The only other consumables bag had thirteen kitchen rolls in. These were to last me seventy-two days, and I used them for everything from loo roll to cleaning the galley and even wiping up spilt engine oil.

I had a range of meals, the majority of which were all freeze-dried, though I did have some which were crackers or oatcakes with cheese. I'd done this before, and though you wouldn't think that cheese could last in a boat with no fridge, I was constantly surprised by just how many temperature changes soft cheese spread can go through without it tasting or looking any different! The meals were scheduled so that in the hot weather I had cereals and milk powder and cold (ish!) lunches, but by the time I got down to the Southern Ocean I was on three hot meals a day, just like pot noodles. They are light as a feather, which is why we take them, and when you pick them up you would not think there could possibly be a meal in there. To make a freeze-dried meal involved boiling the kettle, adding an amount of boiling water to the packet and then waiting ten minutes for it to rehydrate. There are also sweet ones, like dried fruit, yoghurt or rice pudding. Breakfast ones are sweet too, generally like porridge, though there were cooked breakfast ones which had freeze-dried egg and bacon in them. They are not as bad as they were even seven years before when I started eating them, though you do get a bit tired of the fact that they are all, by definition, going to be mushy!

But the strange thing is that, despite the fact your body is working hard, you don't really feel hungry in the way that you do on land.

You never think to yourself, I really fancy a pack of freeze-dried yoghurt muesli, nor do you fancy something like steak and chips. You are nervous, very nervous, and, as we all know, in this state food is associated with necessity rather than luxury. It's that same feeling as waking in the morning knowing that you have an exam, or a difficult and important meeting at work: you don't feel like having anything for breakfast. If you ate then it would be because you needed to, not because you wanted to.

In fact, on Mobi all facilities were basic. There was no shower, no toilet – other than the small orange bucket I'd affectionately written B&Q BOG BKT in black text on the side of. For the whole round-the-world I had a tiny plastic container of the sort they give out in hotels containing special sea-water shower gel, and, bar the odd wipe down with a baby wipe, the only time you'd wash would be in a rain shower in the warmer part of the world at the Equator.

Mobi's cabin can only have been 2 metres long, high and wide, and the colours inside were blue, orange and yellow. To me her little shelter was perfect. Being a superstitious sailor, I could touch wood in two places: the tiny but beautiful fiddle rail around the galley and directly above the chart table.

Further forward, and behind the main cabin, were more compartments. The main ones were behind and in front of the main living area via watertight doors. The aft one housed engine parts, spare rudders, the satellite antennae and the steering system and autopilot computers. The forward one housed the main and back-up generator and all the electric cables, panels, control boxes and wires. The rest of Mobi was made up of ballast tanks, watertight doors and dark, small spaces, and with only the living area and engine room having any form of window or escape hatch, all other compartments were as black as mines.

One of the greatest challenges with taking such a high-tech craft around the world was learning about every aspect of it: from changing a rudder at sea, to scaling her mast, to understanding how to change the relays in the camera-system control box and even the circuit board in the anemometer at the top of the mast. You needed to be able to fix anything, be it splicing strops on to the sails, laminating the structure of the boat or fine tuning the satellite image receiver, and I loved it. I loved learning about it all.

On that southward leg in the Atlantic there was a need for it too. It wasn't long before I was in the tool kit cutting up a series of carbon wedges for the steering system, and monitoring our main generator, as it was using far too much oil.

```
ELLEN EMAIL - 0800 GMT: 05/12/04
Just a quick mail from the equatorial area . . . B&Q is
sailing along like a dream, and all ok onboard. It's now
very very hot onboard, and though I'm still in my
thermals at night, I'm not sure that they are really
necessary. The night time cabin temp is 29 degrees - and
the day time one higher. My hands are getting sores on
them again, as they always do in this heat and any tiny
scratch appears to become infected - better watch out.
But hopeful in a few more days things will start to calm
down, just better not forget that I'm leaving winter and
sailing into summer though! Better go, time to send
this, from a slightly nervous but happy ellen x
```

As we approached the Equator we had our first totally unexpected visit from the Royal Navy. Two ships, HMS *Iron Duke* and RFA *Gold Rover*, were on their journey back up from the Falklands, and they had decided to come and catch up with me. Though it was still the early stages of the trip, I was beginning to settle into the rhythm, and things were steady that day, as we'd had reasonable winds since sunrise.

The first arrival was the helicopter, which came out to see me when the ship was about 40 miles away. I was so excited to see them, and they flew up behind so close that I could just about make out the faces of the guys on board. The pilot called up on the radio, and the reply was the voice of a very excited Ellen. We chatted for a while as they hovered near by. They were on their way home for Christmas, and I pointed out to them that I would be away for Christmas and at least New Year, but was hoping to be back for 9 February.

The pilot, in a way only pilots can, replied, 'Well at least you'll be back for Valentine's Day!' I laughed out loud. It was wonderful to be around humour. I suggested that, if they did a fly past, I could send back the footage and possibly get them on ITN news the following night as I was doing regular interviews with them. And that they did, performing a manoeuvre as close to a loop the loop in a chopper as you can.

A couple of hours later the ships appeared over the horizon and stayed with me for over half an hour. I had a lovely chat with the captain of *Iron Duke* over the radio, and it was nice to talk to someone who had also been out here at sea for a while. The ships made a formation at the back of us as we spoke, and I couldn't help but feel happy at the morale boost they gave me. I was so excited to see them and couldn't stop grinning!

'*Iron Duke, Iron Duke – B&Q*,' I called up on the radio.

'*Duke*,' came back the reply.

'I didn't expect the full-on convoy here. This is unbelievable,' I replied, still grinning from ear to ear.

'The aim is to please.'

My spirits were soaring, and I called home, and Mum answered the phone.

'Mum, guess what's just happened to me. I've just been buzzed by a helicopter that's off a Royal Naval ship that's just 30 miles away with 175 guys on board! How cool is that! It's not like that happens every few days, is it?'

At the end of their visit the captain called up and said that they would be returning home now. Then, just like you'd imagine in a film, they both peeled away from Mobi's quarter, one to starboard and one to port. It made me feel very special; I had been really touched by their visit and, as I watched their silhouettes disappear off the horizon heading home for Christmas, I felt a surge of sheer delight.

Little was I to know that, bar a small strange-looking ship off the Brazilian coast I saw a few days later, that would be the last sighting of a ship until I rounded Cape Horn over a month later.

Chapter Ten

When you race or sail around the world non-stop there is only one route you can take, and, contrary to what most people assume, you'll be lucky if you see any land at all. The route essentially takes you down the Atlantic, across the Equator, then underneath the African continent, Australia, New Zealand and finally beneath the southern tip of South America before heading up the Atlantic all the way home again. Of the total distance, about half is the section sailing down and then up the Atlantic, and the other half is sailing under all the main continents, executing a lap of Antarctica and the South Pole. Though the equatorial part of your journey is hot and generally sunny, the vast majority is just freezing cold. If you think about it, you leave Europe in winter, then spend over a month in the Southern Ocean before returning to Europe having circled the world, and it's still – yes – winter!

Date: 07/12/2004

PRESS ALERT: NEW SOLO EQUATOR TIME FOR ELLEN MACARTHUR

Ellen MacArthur, on board her 75-foot trimaran B&Q, has set a new solo time to the Equator of 8 days, 18 hours, 20 minutes. MacArthur crossed the Equator into the southern hemisphere at 0230 GMT this morning (7.12.04) and subsequently took 14 hours and 3 minutes off the previous fastest solo time of 9 days, 8 hours, 23 minutes set by French sailor

Francis Joyon during his successful solo around-the-world record attempt.

Our crossing of the Equator went well, and we opened one of the tiny little bottles of champagne I had to mark one of the most important stages in the record. Passing into the southern hemisphere brings so many changes. The sun begins to pass through the north rather than the south, and the low-pressure systems and high-pressure systems turn in opposite directions. It really is a very different place. I called Mum and Dad to tell them we had crossed, and as Dad spoke, I scribbled his words in my log:

```
'at the end of the day the stars will either be with or
against you . . . and I think they might be with you'
```

Our descent of the South Atlantic was a challenging one. The weather cards we were being dealt in that section of ocean were far from perfect. The South Atlantic high I had used to my advantage to catch Michel Desjoyeaux in the Vendée Globe four years before was not playing ball for us, and had actually split into two halves. As you sail south into the Southern Ocean you are forced to cross the South Atlantic on its west side, but here I was forced further west than I had hoped, and there was a very real chance that the high would engulf us, stopping us dead in our tracks. I was hoping I wouldn't have a rerun of the Jules Verne. The upwind conditions after the Equator were, true to form, hot and wet. Far too hot to wear oilskins, but too wet not to! Gore-tex stuck to sticky legs and sun cream running off you with sweat is the name of the game there. In fact, everything you touch is covered in salt, as the constant spray is dried by the hot tropical wind.

A few days after the start I had checked the oil on the dipstick of the main generator and discovered that it was right at the minimum. With time I had been able to measure the speed of the consumption of oil in the main generator and had realized that it was drinking oil at an unsustainable rate. I had already pulled all the oil out of the back-up generator to see whether, by using that too, we could make it, but we couldn't. I would have run out of oil during the following two months at sea, and, literally, without a generator, there would be no life on board. A boat such as Mobi can't be sailed without an autopilot to steer her. It would be a challenge to even get her into the closest port, let alone finish a record attempt.

It was for situations such as these that we had installed the back-up generator; though it was much smaller, charging at only 55 amps, rather than the 200 amps of the water-cooled generator, it would hopefully do the job. I spoke to Albert back at base to discuss the issues I was having; we hadn't anticipated needing the back-up quite so early on in the trip. My notebook was strewn with calculations. The back-up was less efficient, and we were really concerned that it would get through the fuel I had more quickly, resulting in lack of diesel being the problem as well as potentially the lack of oil. After running it for a few days, I became aware that it had a whole host of issues of its own, and that these were just the beginning.

We were still in the tropics, and I was finding that the temperature in the cabin was rising to 50 degrees when the generator was running. The back-up generator was air-cooled, and though its exhaust went out into the centreboard case, I was forced because of the temperature in the cabin to have the fore-hatch open. This meant that the cabin, and then the cuddy, were being filled by acrid fumes, and as I needed to charge for so much longer with this generator I was getting headaches during the hours the generator needed to run. There seemed nowhere on the boat that I could escape from both the waves and the fumes, and I knew that there was no way I would be able to have the fore-hatch open in the south. On top of this I was having massive issues with the water-makers, which, bar the rainfall, were my only source of fresh water. Because the back-up generator was air-cooled, it was no longer sucking up water through the sea-water inlet, and so there was now no longer a powerful impeller helping the water-makers to pull in the water that they needed.

Heading down the Atlantic, I was really struggling, and by the time we were getting closer to the south I was down to just a few litres of drinking water. Things weren't looking good, and for the first time I felt a really sick feeling inside.

I was philosophical about the seriousness of the problem, but really angry inside that it was becoming a serious threat to the record. I remember calling Mark to give him an update as to how things were going. He could hear the frustration in my voice and, with a pause before saying it, suggested that perhaps I should pull into Cape Town while I still had the chance. I slammed the phone down. I was not going to give up and, full of will power, I immediately set to work.

Working under the floor of the boat would have been more straightforward if the waves had not begun to rise out of the ocean like endless running mountains. I was being hurled around the boat like a rag doll as I worked, and, as I'd had a brainwave that I could fill part of the emergency 7 ton ballast area beneath the floor, I had to give it a go. Soaked to the skin, being smashed against the floor above me and with water up to my knees, I attached a small filter to the end of the pipe, which I somehow managed to fix to the floor beneath the surging water. The noise was deafening as we flew through, and into, many of the waves. And as I'd had to squeeze through two of the tiny watertight doors sideways to get inside, once I was in there working I couldn't get to the autopilot controls, tillers or sheets quickly even if I tried. I felt massively vulnerable, more so as it was a very long process, but when I reprimed the water-maker and fired her up I was overjoyed: it worked!

At full chat it would produce water at the speed of a dripping tap, so I kept it going, making sure that there was enough water in the ballast, then, once I had enough, I bailed out the remaining ballast water with a pump, which was an awful job. As I worked into the night, the waves were growing inside my tank, and I felt like I was trying to actually catch the water rather than pump it by the end.

But I didn't stop there either, and once the system worked I was straight on to a solution to get cooler air into the generator. I tried everything from dismounting and fixing the fan I had by the chart table into one of the door hatches to taking the tiny heater apart and rewiring it beneath the floor to get it to blow into the air inlet using its fan. Nothing really worked that well until, virtually at the point of giving up, I came up with my final idea. That was to use the heater air ducting to get air from the main engine air outlet under my seat, through the watertight door into the engine room and into the air filter case I cut away to accept it. My final job was knocking out the carbon panel with which we had sealed the now redundant main engine exhaust. Fingers crossed, I finally started the generator, and when I realized that for the first time it ran at a reasonable temperature I sank to my knees with happiness . . . for a few seconds anyway, as I was immediately thrown clear of the floor by a wave, which virtually dislocated both my kneecaps on the doorway!

When I called Mark back with my news I was a very different Ellen. And when I spoke to my Dad, his knowing comment was: 'Sounds like a MacArthur!'

The storm strengthened, and we saw the worst conditions Mobi had ever experienced. I was literally bouncing off either the deck-head or the floor, and even in the little time I spent in my bunk trying to rest after my marathon session I actually got thrown clear of it six times. The wind was strong, nearly 40 knots, but the challenge was the waves; it was as if we were going the wrong way through them, smacking into the faces of mountains, rather than gliding down them.

This was our welcome to the Southern Ocean. As the front had arrived it had brought a sharp transition from hot air to cold winds, which marked a new phase in the trip. But as the weather eased off we saw the biggest symbol of change: our first albatross hovering before us, and the isolated islands of Tristan da Cunha on the horizon. I knew then that we'd fixed our charging problem just in time: we had stepped on the conveyor belt to Cape Horn.

14th December
the motto for today is SLEEP MORE - SUFFER LESS. I
tried to engrave this on my brain last night, and try
with all my energy to sleep - easier said than done
sometimes - but hey . . . we have to try . . . just as it
went dark I called into the weather routers and said
'I'll be sailing for the next few hours under solent and

full main, I don't care what the wind does, or where the
wind takes me . . . I'll call you in 3 hours. and I did.
I stripped off, jumped into a warm sleeping bag in my
bunk for the first time and, though just for two hours,
I slept . . . Conditions were thankfully quite calm last
night, and we spent a great deal of time sailing into a
high pressure system - after the horrors of the previous
36 hours upwind in over 30 knots and a mountainous
sea - everything now seems almost surreal . . .

   The sky is grey - but I like that . . . I almost prefer
it to the beating sun of the equator - but that will all
change soon i'm sure . . .

   THis morning ellen has found herself again. not only
that but she has rediscovered the magic of being out
here. the trials and tribulations of the last few days
seem miles away. Things are under control, and we're
heading SOUTH!!

   Xx

I had struggled to sleep after my two hours on the bunk, so I took
out the little plastic folder of photos I had and stuck those I'd been
given on to the foam lining we'd put on the inside of the cabin to
reduce condensation. Some were of my friends in Skye, a forest in
Derbyshire, a picture I'd taken out of the window of Fergus's car
once. Photos of Mum and Dad, Mac and the kids from EMT joined
them, including the wonderful smiling photograph of Maxine she
had taken when she sailed with the Trust. I was only just beginning
my journey, and I wanted Mobi to feel as much like home as she
possibly could. Lou had given me a white wooden Christmas decor-
ation in the form of a dove and on it she'd written: 'Have faith in
yourself, and have faith in Mobi, Lou x.' In addition to writing the
words 'SLEEP MORE SUFFER LESS' on the underside of the
coach-roof above my cuddy bean bag, I also was collecting phrases
such as 'ALWAYS TRY TO SEE THE POSITIVE SIDE . . . LEARN
FROM IT' and 'BELIEVE', I guess in a way to teach myself to be
stronger.

Not long before the start of the record I'd been to visit the local seal sanctuary during a day off, where I'd jokingly picked up this little purple pipe-cleaner worm I named Slinky, who had become one of my chosen companions for the journey. Slinky tended to hang out on my light fitting above the chart table, and he made me smile as I looked up at his goggly little eyes! I also had a tiny black and white bear I'd had since I was a kid, which had been with me for every single ocean journey I'd done. Around its neck was a little charm of a miner's lamp my Gran had given me. Things like this reminded me very much of home, as Great Granddad, Gran's Dad, had been a miner at home in Derbyshire.

ELLEN EMAIL - 16.12.04
A few thoughts for a very wet morning whilst we await the passing of a very wet and rainy front.

I look out of B&Q's windows and see big grey waves and monotonous drizzle. Our world has closed in around us, and we can see very, very little other than the 400m radius around us. We have more wind than I would have otherwise imagined - quite gusty around 25 to 28 knots. But we're sailing along ok - and with the changeable conditions I am sure that we are doing the right thing - not pushing too hard . . . We should be gybing in a few hours anyway - so pulling out the 3rd reef would not be the right thing now.

I was thinking in the early hours of this morning about life onboard, and what are the differences between what we have here, and what we experience on land. I think the first thing is that this little world of B&Q and I feels like a small island. We hope that we shall have all we need, and will have to improvise for what we have not. There is only so much of everything, so each square of kitchen roll, each few cm of tape used gets you closer to having none left. Everything is checked before it goes in the bin just to be sure it's not wanted. You need to be resourceful and tackle problems rationally and simply as they arise. There will always be problems, always . . . You just hope that they will be surmountable and deal-able with - the rest is a logical waiting game.

You check everything, because you don't have a million replacements. In reality, it's quite a simple life. I think that it's healthy to put other things before you sometimes, like putting the boat first. If I let her state slide, I know that she will be less able to look after me too.

I am very aware of the level of her batteries, and that keeps her functioning, and each drop of fuel for charging is measured. Lights are never left on unneeded, the kettle is always filled with 15 pumps of the tap - just enough for a freeze dried meal and a cup of tea.

Not more not less.

It's about managing this little space, keeping it dry, and as warm as I can. I don't have much here really, there are no luxuries - just a few CD's and the odd photo scattered around.

But I am lucky because the pleasure and luxuries are inside me. Those moments shared with friends and loved ones, the simple things that make people smile; they are with me all the time. They are priceless and, lucky for my endeavour, weightless too!

It's funny the way your mind works when you're sitting on a boat, in the middle of a huge grey huge expanse of beautiful ocean . . .

that's it for now

ellen

x

The temperature plummeted, and the wind increased, and now, firmly in the Southern Ocean, we had some blisteringly good days speed-wise as we saw 46 knots in our first big depression. It was colder than in the Vendée down there, thanks to the wind chill of sailing so much faster, but I was glad to be down in the south again.

Not only was it exciting, but we had something to celebrate, as, thirty-six hours after passing the Cape of Good Hope, Mobi had her first birthday! I was very happy and made the executive decision to steal the tiny bottle of champagne we had on board to celebrate Christmas. I drew a rosette on an empty envelope in my little folder of good-luck messages which I coloured in blue and red with the pencils I had for marking routes on the charts, and wrote in the centre '1 TODAY'. It sounds silly, but that act of celebrating that day with her brought a huge amount of pleasure to our little world out there. I opened the champagne and poured it on her deck, giving most of the rest to Neptune before taking a final sip myself. It seemed years since we'd first lowered her into the water on 18 December 2004 in Sydney, which was not surprising, as in our first twelve months together we had already sailed 30,000 miles, and we weren't even half-way round the world on this trip!

We had the most wonderful day of sailing. Though we'd been through some pretty hairy seas the day before, here things had steadied off a little. The sky was clear, with just a few white clouds, and progress was excellent. When Mobi's speed was out-standing so were my spirits and the two hand in hand led to an upbeat feeling.

The sea state was nothing short of mountainous and, though totally awe-inspiring, it also kept you on your toes. The wind was from the north, which made for a warmer, steadier breeze, and that evening, as the sun set vividly, wishing us goodnight in the western sky behind us, I was ecstatic.

Sitting at my Nav PC, I picked up the most recent satellite image on the dartcom receiver. I loved the dartcom, as it was able to receive a picture direct from the satellites as they passed overhead, and it was like seeing a real-time picture of where you were. The image was stunning, and though it covered an area as large as Antarctica to Mozambique, you could clearly see the yellow sunset to the west, shimmering on the water. I sent it home in an e-mail to Auntie Thea, with a message saying: 'I thought you might like to see the satellite sunset.'

But minute by minute the deep red sky ebbed away, almost, it felt, as if erased by the sweeping ocean washing over it on the horizon behind us. Each wave that rose and fell seemed to wipe it away bit by bit until it became the merest hint of a stain on the inky black sky.

It's about to go dark down here, and the waves are no smaller . . . In fact, now we've gybed they seem bigger and more powerful than before. I am completely in awe of this place. The beauty of those immense rolling waves is endless and there is a kind of eternal feeling about their majestic rolling that will live on forever. just watching them roll along - with nothing to stop then makes mobi and i feel completely insignifincant - they are hardly aware of our tiny prescence on their surface . . . The birds are numerous and varied, and they seem cheekier today - getting closer, and playing with thinwind on our forestay . . . I stand in the cockpit and stare - i think i must be the luckiest person in the world to be here seeing, feeling, smelling and touching all this with my own eyes and sesnses - I feel alive . . .

Though its quite frightening being here and feeling poor mobi being literally hurled down the saves as she was earlier - winds gosting not to 40 but over 50 too 55 in the squalls. Now the sun is setting there will be no visual idea of where we are on the waves, jsut that constant knot in my stomach wondering where we will end up at the foot of the wave before us . . . there is some kind of mesmerising feeling, some kind of completeness about being here . . . I feel this is not so far from the end of the Earth. we are isolated, isolated but on the other hand completely free . . . I am glad we have come down here and seen this storm . . . It's a reminder of how small and insignificant we are on this planet - but at the same time what a responsibility we have towards its protection.

I had this overwhelming feeling that I didn't want to let Mobi down. I felt like she was the strong one, and that I was the weak link. I felt that I would break before she did. I kept things in order on board to maintain the feeling of control, always putting everything in its place and keeping on top of the jobs list. The galley was always spotless, no matter how bad the conditions were; I always kept the chart-table seat dry, using absorbent cloths, and I made sure I always had batteries ready charged to go into the head-torches.

Occasionally, though, a message or note from home would bring me up with a start and remind me that there was another way of life. One of these came from my brother Ferg, which had me rolling round with laughter at the chart table.

```
Morning dude,
Looks like you've got it just about nob on so far.
Nicely done!
   Life's pretty similar to yours here at the moment . . .
conditions are pretty harsh . . . I've had to put a
t-shirt on under my work shirt to avoid catching a
chill . . . only had 7 and a bit hours sleep last night
as I've got the worry of the darts & dominoes 'Combine
Cup' looming on the horizon. Wednesday night's going to
be an emotional rollercoaster down at the Kingsfield,
we're going to have to pull out all the stops if we're
to top last years appearance in the final and our haul
of three delightful plastic trophies!
   Don't worry too much though . . . I'm sure the
MacArthur resolve will see me through (I'll keep you
posted)
   Oh . . . I get the keys to the house later. Little
brother's got himself some responsibilities.
   Glad to see there's been no ******* around!
   F
```

The highs out there contrasted so strongly with the lows. It almost seemed that the higher the highs, the lower the lows would be. Life existed as a rhythm. It was more a case of checking the vital signs than pleasure, but sometimes, when that pleasure came, be it from an e-mail or a sunset, it was the purest experience that you could imagine. I was well into the Southern Ocean when I laughed out loud, as I solved the mystery of the magic mug! I had a big insulated stainless steel mug which I loved, as it held a good big volume of tea. It was impossible to spill from as it had a huge, wide base with a non-skid bottom and it kept the tea hot for a long time even in the south. For weeks and weeks, though, I'd been wondering why it always held back a little tea from me each time I'd finished drinking. I'd even try shaking the mug while I was drinking, and tipping my head right back, but each time I removed the lid to check, there was *always* a load of tea at the bottom to tip out. It took me almost a month at sea to work out why: there was a tiny breather hole in the lid, and each time I tipped my head back to guzzle the last bit of tea my nose sealed perfectly on it!

As Christmas approached we had our first collision, and though I could find no damage on board Mobi, I certainly felt it as she slowed from 26 knots to 14 knots in the time it took to blink your eyes. I was on the phone talking to Loik about the water-makers, having spent eight hours during the night trying to fix one again, when suddenly I was thrown hard against the chart table. With that speed of impact I could not believe that there was no damage, but after a thorough check all seemed OK. I sat in the cuddy for a while after sighing with relief. I couldn't thank the design and build team enough for the incredible boat they had produced. Even the daggerboard, which I can only assume took the whole impact, was in a case which had rubber wedges both ahead and behind it. Without this I have no doubt that the impact would have shattered not only the daggerboard, but our whole attempt; 10,000 miles of racing would have been for nothing.

But I was not the only boat in the south suffering a collision. The very same day Sébastien Josse, one of the competitors in the Vendée Globe, ran headlong into an iceberg. He was in the process of passing beneath New Zealand, and luckily, as he was sailing slowly at 12 knots, despite bow damage and a crushed bowsprit, he was able to continue on with the race. I was regularly sailing at twice that speed.

I'm not sure that in the south my waterproofs actually dried out at all, as there was so much spray around. If I had been lucky enough to remove my waterproof jacket for a nap in the bunk, I was always reminded of what lay outside as I pulled the cold, wet rubber neck seal over my head shortly before I dashed out of the hatch.

The damp in the Southern Ocean seeps into your bones, and I was glad of the generator running to create some heat to help to bring my thermals back to life. They had by this stage been soaked so many times that each time I dried them they had white salt crystals all over them. My eyes were no different, and concentrated salt in your eyes is not a pleasant experience. With fatigue I would often rub my eyes and then wince as the crystals acted like sandpaper on my eyelids and stung my eyes like crazy. Occasionally in the deep south I would spread a layer of Fisherman's barrier cream over my cheeks and nose to stop them being chapped and burnt by the biting wind. The cream seemed to attract the salt even more, though!

Sleeping in the south was vital but not in the slightest way relaxing. Life on a boat flying through the waves is not peaceful, and the noise and movement penetrate deep into your soul. Mobi had a constant whining noise which came from her foils, and, depending on her speed, that noise was at a slightly different pitch. For two and a half months I would be tuned into its pitch and tone, and bar the rare days when we were sailing in light winds that noise was a permanent feature. It sounded almost like the noise you'd expect to hear from a monastery, like a constant ghostly chant, giving some form of message, twenty-four hours a day. Speed brings with it stress and to understand it a good analogy is driving a car. Drive at 20 miles an hour, and things are pretty relaxed, you could easily have a conversation. Take the speed to 40, and then you're beginning to concentrate a bit more, especially if you're steering round things. Increase it to 60, and you are concentrating pretty hard, and by 80 you are in a different zone. This trip for me pushed beyond that. Multis are different, and more like driving a rally car than anything else, plus this car has no windscreen wipers, in fact no windscreen, no headlights, no roads, and no brakes!

Because the ever-present risk of capsize was higher than ever while circling Antarctica, we had to be extremely careful. I would sleep with the ropes for her traveller and headsail sheet by me, and the control for the autopilot more often than not actually in my hand. I was so connected to the boat that I could almost change course whilst dozing, but my brain quite clearly just did not let up.

I had to sail Mobi as close to the edge as I dared, and that meant living on a knife edge. Sometimes I would sleep inside on my bunk, but the majority of the time, day or night, I was outside in the cuddy. There were two modes of falling asleep: one was when you were very cold and chilly, and the other was when you were soaked in sweat having completed a manoeuvre. Exhausted, I would slump down on the bean bag, which was in the shelter of the cuddy, under the side deck of the boat. From my resting position I could reach the sheet for the headsail, and I could see all three displays showing six lines of data which told me everything from wind speed and direction to water temperature. I would huddle up on my side in the foetus position so as to stay as warm as possible, my feet perpetually cold and damp in my boots thanks to the air temperature. I kept a woolly hat in the pouch just above the cuddy which I could put my hands inside as I slept and I would press my face into the damp blue pillow I left there and pull my grey fleece blanket over me. Having warm hands, I found, made a huge difference to getting to sleep, and I would often breathe out gently on to the pillow, almost in a pointless effort to warm it. Somehow feeling that warmth close to my face reminded me of how wonderful it feels to place your head on a pillow in a warm, still dry bed, with the knowledge that for eight hours the constant lullaby of silence will wrap its calming arms around you.

I felt more like an animal, sleeping with one ear open at all times, never letting go of the noises which surrounded me. I learnt that my instincts, rather than any alarm, would open my weary eyes for me, and that I could rely on the adrenalin which seemed to permanently run through my body, and would spring me into instant action. It was a strange sensation: when I woke I was always aware of why. Every single sound that I heard I knew. Every squeak, every creak and every rope I knew. Mobi was hollow, like a speaker, and each noise she uttered told me something. I was so connected to her that, if there was even the slightest of problems, I knew where to look if I felt something was wrong. It was an incredible feeling: Mobi had become a part of me which I could no longer function without.

Chapter Eleven

On 23 December we passed the incredible Kerguelen Islands to the north, and, though we were far too far away to see them, I did think back to our Jules Verne attempt two years before. In two days' time it was Christmas Day, and I could think of only one Christmas present I would like: to arrive home, before the countdown clock I had on my chart table read zero.

The next day I got an e-mail from Mark:

```
24th December . . .
Keep it up. Great speed.
  That cold front must be scared of you . . .
```

It was strange to hear news from what felt like another world. In his e-mail Mark spoke about how media interest in the record attempt was growing, and how he felt that people were beginning to understand that, if I even finished the circumnavigation, it would be an achievement. He was also in touch with Nick a great deal, who was having a really tough time over Christmas, and though Mark was at a friend's house for Christmas Eve dinner, because of not wanting to be away from his computer, he was going to leave early. As a result everyone moved over to Mark's and had their family Christmas Eve there, which he said was lovely. He finished by saying:

But half my brain is cold, wet and being thrown around
with you.
Call me anytime.
   Xx.

Christmas didn't happen at all for me. There was a huge storm to
our west, moving steadily towards us, and when the day came I spent
it literally hanging on to the boat, checking and checking again that
we weren't about to break anything, and hoping that we could maintain our ground to the north, which would stop us from being dragged
into the centre of the depression. I scribbled in my diary: 'Winds up
to 50 knots – not yet – just squalls – all OK – in one piece.'

I remember few things about the day, but eating a packet of
Wheat Crunchies was one, as was closing my eyes tight as the
waves slammed hard into Mobi's port side. I also had to restart the
generator time and time again as it stalled and, as we were thrown
around, I was reminded that doing so in far too many layers of
clothes for a room at that temperature was not pleasant. It was a 10
hp diesel engine, and not only was it a bugger to start, but each pull
of the start cord made that next sail change a little bit harder.

25th December
cannot get thro on phone
   have sent some clips
   have had well over 40 kn already
   shit night - generator takes 3 hours to charge as
stalled out 12 times during charge.
   hanging in here - literally
   x
   ps happy xmas m xxxxxxxxxxx

Oli sent me a Christmas message, which I saw when I logged on
for my weather information. It read:

Have a great Christmas on the big ocean. You are so in
touch with it that you will not be alone physically.

Oli understood – it was wonderful to read his words. He finished:

```
Be safe and give my love to Mobi.
  Take care
  Ol
```

The rest of the world felt so far away from us down here. We were not even near land now – thousands of miles away in fact. Strange to think that Christmas is such a 'calendared day', when life at sea has no calendar. I wrote a brief reply to Oli as I hung on to the chart table as we were aggressively punched through the ever-larger waves.

```
full on here - afraid no presents opened today . . . will
have xmas another day.
  hope all well in gaspe - mobi holding on about as
tight as i am to this planet's watery surface.
  lots of love
  miss and mobi
  xx
```

On Christmas Day I called home to Derbyshire twice. Once, speaking to my Dad at 0700, because I knew that conditions were going to get significantly worse, then again that evening – sixteen hours later at 2300. Mum answered the phone, and, though we spoke for a few minutes, I could not relax. I was really toughing it out in the storm. It was hard enough speaking to a warm, cosy house full of love and family, but I knew that I couldn't take my mind off what was around me; I needed to stay concentrated on sailing Mobi safe and fast. The further you headed round the world towards the half-way stage, the further away you felt both physically and mentally from those you loved at home. As you approach Australia and New Zealand your day is the UK's night, and this only strengthens the feeling of being out there in a different world.

I could hear the concern in Mum's voice and, though she put on a brave face and always asked how I was doing, I knew that, however difficult it was for me at sea, the whole family would be suffering too. Those at home are totally helpless. At least I can act in a situation; they have to simply wait for news, and will only get it when I am able to send it. In a way the communication makes it harder for them as well as you. They knew when I was in a storm and they knew when I had broken something and couldn't sleep. I felt about as far away from Derbyshire as I could have possibly felt on that day; I might as well have been on the moon.

I remember Mum saying that it was a white Christmas at home, which brought back all sorts of memories from my youth. I thought about the fire Dad would have lit, sending shimmers of warmth across the room to the Christmas tree, which would, no doubt, be proudly covered in the same decorations we had put on or made as kids. The warmth, love and happiness at Christmas were as far out of reach as they could be at sea; inside I felt quite churned up and incredibly nervous as I hung on to the edge of the chart table to concentrate on our conversation. Mum offered me the chance to speak to everyone else at home, but I declined. I daren't take my mind off the job. I said goodbye and put the phone down.

Earlier that day I had filmed a Christmas message.

Well it might not be a white Christmas, but there's enough breaking water out there to make it look like a snowfield. The front will pass, and the wind will increase . . . Speed OK, but we're getting thrown around and hammered. Happy Christmas!

ELLEN LOG: 26/12/04
Well I'm a bit stuck for words this morning . . . in fact it's about 3pm local time - that just about sums up my day really. I have no idea how much sleep I've had - though I know it's not by far enough . . . sleep is the rarest commodity out here, sleep and the time to eat. How many times have I said to myself - shall I eat or sleep. Basic but fundamental decisions.

Yesterday was a day from hell, with horrendous conditions, and a few 'full on' moments when your heart

Sailing *Mobi* for the first time was daunting but incredibly exciting. There was so much to learn . . .

Our training sail – which would take us half-way round the world – was with Loik and Mark. This photo was taken as we passed Cape Horn (note the celebratory Champagne!).

My final stage of preparation before the solo attempt would be a transatlantic record attempt. During it, I would put *Mobi* through her paces and test both her and myself, to see just what we were capable of.

Setting off from
New York on the
West–East crossing.

A life of lists . . . There seem to be endless jobs in every project.

Photos of the kit that I would take with me on the solo attempt. I had to think carefully about every item, from pairs of socks to rolls of toilet paper, as every extra ounce of weight would slow me down.

A shot taken on my mobile phone just before setting off around the world, looking out of the window in Falmouth towards the dock and *Mobi*.

We're off . . .

Hardship and happiness: having to fix a broken generator and climb
Mobi's gigantic mast were just a few of the challenges we faced during the
seventy-one days at sea. However, whatever challenges came, a positive
spirit normally saved the day! The little snowman I made after three of
the hardest days of my life may have been tiny, but he had a big effect on
my morale.

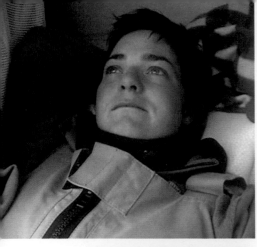

A picture of exhaustion. After Cape Horn we faced perhaps the most gruelling period of the entire record attempt, as we contended with a windless zone that demanded frantic, endless sail changes in a desperate attempt not to lose time. The total lack of sleep and constant physical pressure took me to a place that I have no wish to return to. Finding a few hours' sleep after we broke through the front of the weather system was a welcome relief.

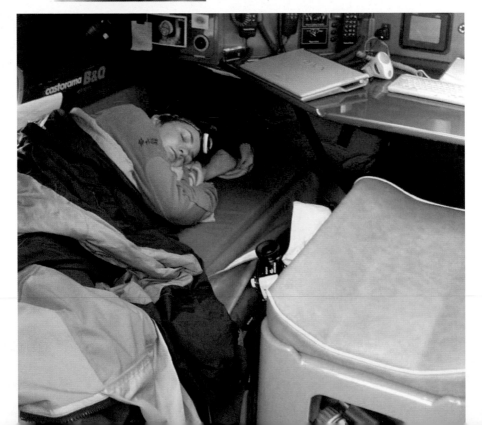

Right, a visit from HMS *Gloucester* and, *below*, a Tornado flies above *Mobi* as we pass the Falklands.

A satellite image which I sent to my Aunt Thea, showing both *Mobi* (the orange dot) and the remnants of the sun's light, shimmering on the sea as it set in the west.

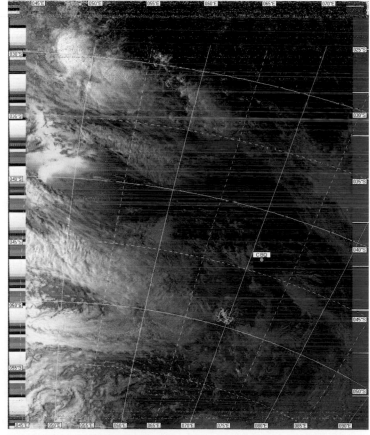

Reunited with my parents at the finish line. After 71 days, 14 hours, 18 minutes and 33 seconds, I'd made it . . .

The reception at Falmouth was incredible.

is literally in your mouth - well it's either than or
your stomach, it all feels the same . . . We got
physically picked up by a freak wave yesterday, which
made poor Mobi seem smaller than a duck in a swimming
pool, that was probably the most scared I've been in one
moment of the trip - just not knowing where or how we
would land. It's hardest when you have a few seconds to
think about it . . . normally when the waves hit you it's
bang - and the damage is done - when you're thrown, it's
a much more prolonged fear - like waiting for the
trigger to be pulled - or not as the case might be.

We had two 'hits' yesterday . . . the first was being
'thrown' and the second was a solid wave landing on the
boat as hard as if an elephant had been dropped on us
from heaven. I thank my lucky stars that I was down
below at the time, and that the damage was limited - but
just to see the elastic parted like butter and the rope
bags just ripped off was humbling, a statement of how
irrelevant we are out here, and how we have to 'earn'
our permit to pass out here. It's not a place for
bravado or complacency. This is real, very real, black
and white real. and when you close your eyes - that
reality does not slip away. The sounds are only
magnified in your head - reminding you that there's
no way out but to stay cool. There are no second
chances . . . After the storm yesterday I managed about
30 mins in my bunk as the wind began to moderate. Then
it was all hands on deck. Briefly we saw the beautiful
full moon - and the wind - which had been up at over 45
began to decrease. the start of my sail changes at a
time when I scarcely had the energy to feed myself. Over
the period of about 8 hours i did 12 sail changes - from
triple reefed main - and staysail - to full main genoa
. . . By the time the wind died to 10 knots at sunrise
this morn Up and down the decks that was swaying around
in a massively confused and violently undulating sea.

each time struggling not to fall over, or be hit by a
breaking wave through the nets. by the time I had to
pull out that final reef I was close to breaking. a cold
tired and emotionally drained wreck. Sitting, checking
for hours and hours with every muscle in your body
tense - just waiting for the next thing to go wrong
takes its toll - even the anticipation of a real arse-
kicker storm makes you feel quite weak at the knees ...
my mouth was dry felt quite out of sorts. fear and grim
anticipation work in funny ways ...

Now I'm here at the chart table, and for some reason
I felt like getting this down in an e-mail. I guess
somewhere in the back of my mind i know that this will
feel better tomorrow - those thoughts will drift anyway
and be faded by the next full moon and the sunset ...
Incidentally it seems a while wince we've seen the
sun ... another day of sailing through dense white
drizzly stormy clouds over a grey powerful sea ... the
generator's on so my feet are finally warming - and the
kettle's full ready for lunch. Got that third reef to
put in first though. we're surfing at 26 knots, and the
wind just reached 35. We've sailed back in to the front
that left us behind ... there really is no rest for us
out here ... no rest at all ...

I think we'll celebrate our Xmas at new year ... well
we can always hope. Christmas was sadly this year - just
another day, albeit a bad one in the office.

At least Mobi and I are in one piece ...

But when I spoke to Mark that day and heard of the Tsunami, my
problems seemed totally irrelevant. Though at the time no one
really knew the scale of what was happening, Mark had a good idea,
as his sister was in Sri Lanka. She had not only been an eye witness
to all that had happened, but like thousands of others had found
herself swimming in the water to escape. The more time that
passed, the more apparent was the scale of the devastation. I looked

on a few websites and was in shock at what I saw. Being at sea, surfing on the ocean which had caused so many deaths, felt peculiar. The Tsunami was in the Indian Ocean, and so was I. Where I was, in deep water, the wave was only about 50 cm high – negligible. But where it shelved on the beaches it reached 8 to 10 metres. Ironically Mobi was a safe place to be, but I felt distraught at what had happened and for weeks I couldn't get it out of my mind.

Date: 27/12/2004 03:34:01
Subject: Impossible is Nothing

Hi Ellen - we saw this quotation from Muhammad Ali and thought of you: 'Impossible is just a big word thrown around by small men, who find it easier to live in a world they've been given, than explore the power they have to change it. Impossible is not a fact, it's an opinion. Impossible is not a declaration it's a dare. Impossible is potential. Impossible is temporary. Impossible is Nothing.' Hang in there - you are an inspiration to us all!

  Love from Rebecca & Mark in NZ

We sailed on towards Cape Leeuwin, the third landmark in our trip. The important ones are the Equator, the Cape of Good Hope, Cape Leeuwin, Cape Horn, the Equator again and obviously home at the end! It was wonderful to celebrate the passing of another point. That was now three crossed off my little list. But after the exhaustion of the Christmas storm there were yet more challenging conditions ahead. We got spat out of the back of the weather front, which meant that the wind speed dropped back down to 10 knots after its previous 40. The number of sail changes was crippling, but we had to stay fast for a reason. We could see from the weather models that the front had stalled, and I had a slim chance, if I pushed it, to get back in and ride that weather system again. Out the back of the system the skies totally cleared, though I knew I couldn't let it last long, as we had to forge ahead back to the wind-filled clouds which would propel us along. It was unexpected and quite surreal spending a magic few hours surfing the sparkling mountains beneath the moon.

We made it back into the front after a few hours, and the clear skies once again filled with that heavy, penetrating pouring rain.

ELLEN EMAIL - 0330 GMT 29.12.04
Sitting here at the chart table soaked again . . .
Already changed clothes twice in the past 10 hours -
thank goodness for Arry the air cooled generator (as i
type this he's stopped for the third time in 20 mins -
back in a mo) . . . It's been another very hard slog . . .
yesterday winds much lighter than predicted - so more
sail changes, and the stress of hoping that when you
pull the reef out you won't be putting it in just an
hour later. Yesterday evening it became evident that
there was a storm brewing to the west that was going to
hit us hard again - and as the hours ticked by it
appeared to be worse than the Xmas storm.

I was right: it was, and we were now in it, landing gusts of over 45 knots. The sea was getting pretty damn nasty as it was taunted and goaded by the fierce weather heading our way. In the strengthening wind we set about our routine of changing sails. One of the nastiest was hanking the storm jib on to Mobi's forestay above the staysail. It involved dropping the staysail, then tying it down to the deck, then bringing out the storm jib through the small hatch by the stay and attaching it. The decks were constantly being hosed with spray and were getting quite dangerous. Working on the foredeck, I was holding on pretty tight; when your head-torch catches solid ocean water washing up through the trampoline like a knife through butter less than half a metre from you it's enough to make you swallow hard. If we'd had modes on board for safety I would have been on 'red alert'. Waves were breaking all over the place, and now even our tiny 15 m² storm jib began to feel gigantic.

I'd had a non-stop night, afternoon and morning. Just after dark I'd put up the storm jib, then spent half an hour adjusting the third reef. Both I did bearing away to avoid the risk of full-on hits with the waves, though there was always the odd one which caught me out. I got one wave as a full frontal while I was rearranging the gennaker in its bag, and it completely winded me.

It was not only the sails which needed dealing with, though, as there was time spent down below to tackle the now three-hour charge trying to keep other batteries up, which was a chore and a half, as in the rough weather the air-cooled generator kept stalling. It was like relentlessly waiting on a demanding person that you couldn't survive without. I guess if my stomach was in my mouth each time we fell off a wave, then I couldn't begin to think what was happening to the fuel and oil in there. I got the batteries up to about 70 per cent, which in the circumstances was not bad, I thought, then set about checking on deck again. Unfortunately the main had filled with a huge pocket of water, which was collected spray from the bows, so the next stage was another bear away and a forty-minute fight to pump the water out with the bilge pump. I could hardly stand up on deck let alone hold the pump down and work the handle. It took about twenty attempts, but on my last one it worked, and I managed to get the sail back on the boom – no longer loaded down with hundreds of kilos of water trying to rip it in two. As I pumped out I occasionally glanced up at the total turmoil of the ocean's surface and marvelled at the raw power of the wilderness for thousands of miles around me.

On climbing below I managed to get an hour or so's sleep on the floor after changing clothes again, then woke feeling hungry, but this time chose to ignore it and laid my head back on the damp fleece to snooze again. On awakening again there was another two-hour list of tasks. I bailed out the area beneath the pilot arms but couldn't work out where the water was coming from. Finally I discovered that it was from the old main engine bay, where there was about half a ton of water which, with the beating from the waves, had come in down the old exhaust, which I had to keep open as the air for the generator cooling now came from there. It was the area deep beneath my navigation seat in the cabin, and, as Mobi was such a huge boat, I could virtually stand up in there. For almost an hour I struggled with the same huge water pump and its hoses in the black hole under the floor which had originally housed her engine. There was no flat area down there and the water was slopping around and often out of the hole as Mobi was tossed by the waves around us. I pumped till it was gone, then replaced the floor again. I was exhausted and still hadn't eaten, but looking after Mobi gave me a comforting injection of energy and a feeling of calm amidst the raging storm.

Two days later we finally emerged from it into two days of fog, and when the water temperature dropped to just over 5 degrees I began to really worry. On top of everything we were averaging 20 knots, and had sailed the fastest twenty-four-hour run so far: 484.5 nautical miles. We were now sailing beneath New Zealand, and bizarrely for the wind strength the sea was quite flat, but the downside was that I could barely see the top of our mast 100 feet above us and I quickly realized that standing on deck staring into the freezing murk to watch out for bergs ahead would achieve little. Due to the flat sea it was possible to go outside with only fleece layers on, but with the freezing mist so dense, the damp drove through to your skin in seconds, covering the fleece in a delicate spider's web of minute, sparkly beads.

But there was another reason to be alarmed. A few weeks before us the Vendée fleet had passed through this same area. Though we were 300 miles north of the Antarctic convergence, which normally 'holds' the bergs there, there were bergs everywhere. I spent my time glued to both the radar and the graph I was recording of sea-water temperature. Though the radar had an alarm on it, I didn't trust it for a second, remembering back to the time in the Vendée when I had missed a berg by no more than 20 feet as I entered the Southern Ocean. Now we were travelling at almost twice the speed, and the effect of colliding at such pace was something we'd discussed at length in the design meetings. Even to the point of the orientation of the bunk, so I would be more likely to break my legs than my neck.

New Year's Day was a great day; the water was up in temperature to 9.3 degrees, and we were heading north-east with the gennaker up, smoking along. We were through the front we had been battling with and finally we were into clear air, and the fog which had been hounding us had been left behind. As we were not so far away from the islands to the south of New Zealand there was a great deal of wildlife around. Though we were not through the iceberg zone yet, I enjoyed seeing the horizon once more and looking out over the ocean at the stunning pintado petrels, with their delicate black and white painted wings that any designer would be jealous of. With the islands close by, the sea felt different.

Conditions were stable for a while, and things ahead, bar the iceberg field, were looking relatively all right for the south. I chose to welcome 2005 in by opening my delayed Christmas presents! What followed was a joyful hour of thinking about everyone close to me, which, unlike my Christmas in the Vendée, actually cheered me up a great deal. I think that because it wasn't actually Christmas Day it helped, and the presents that people had for me were incredibly thoughtful. Loik bought me a nodding 'Scooby Doo', which from the moment I opened it lived firmly fixed to the chart table. Ol got me fluffy dice, and there were socks from Gran, a DVD from my friends in Skye and a couple of T-shirts from Thea; Mum and Dad sent me a pudding and a tiny bottle of rum to go with it. Thea wrote me a poem too; it was so special to hear her words, as if she was saying them on board to me. It was a happy day, and one which had me crying out with delight, and giggling to myself for hours.

I knew that there were icebergs to the south-east, and, though I had hoped to be passing well to the north of them, I wanted to be on deck and rested when we entered the zone. And just before dozing off for a few minutes, with the horizon clear, I asked Scooby if it was rough, to which he shook his little head, and I then questioned the cheeky slinky worm as to what was going on. Despite the obvious dangers around us, it was wonderful to have a giggle and see the funny side of life!

A few hours later, when I was up on deck, I spotted two bergs, one after the other: not to the south, as I had imagined, but to the north of us. We were 60 miles north of the last reported position, and still they were to our north. That night I was very nervous.

We were approaching the international dateline, which meant we were going to relive the 2nd of January, which was all a bit strange, really. Our local time had shifted over the previous thirty-odd days, as we'd been gaining about an hour a day since passing beneath Africa, and from now on we'd be losing an hour each day. It was a confusing concept, but as all my weather data and our communications were going out daily in UK GMT, it helped me to keep track of things. I picked up the video camera.

Why do I enjoy this so much? Why do I feel so happy right now? I think it's the nature, it's the wildlife; you feel alive out here. You have to be careful; you have to look after the boat. I love looking after the boat, I absolutely love it. Servicing things when they need servicing . . . Hard work but simple, I guess. That's why I like it.

The main problem for us, however, was not the icebergs, but the weather which was forming on the front that we had just passed. A secondary low pressure began developing right above us, and for the next three days it was going to bring us living hell. Initially things were OK, I'd had some rest as we passed beneath New Zealand, but, as the storm persisted, I became more tired.

During the second morning of the storm I still hadn't lost my sense of humour though. I found myself standing by the galley making my morning milkshake. 'It's just like a milkshake,' I said, 'but it's made with powder because there aren't many cows down here!' But as the days slipped by, the cheeky Ellen who'd said 'nice hat' when she spoke to the camera about a monster black cloud full of rain and wind gave way to a completely different person, talking about how 'annihilating' the conditions were, and how it was no place for a multihull.

On 4 January we were just coming out of three of the hardest days' sailing I'd ever been through in my life. We had a secondary depression on a front develop right on top of us, and the weather system had a lot of energy in it, as we had discovered the hard way. That had never before happened to me, and as it was moving east at the same speed we were, there was nothing I could do to escape it.

154

The high-level clouds were totally new to me though the sky was mainly blue. But it was the wind which was totally mad, coming in towards us like angry demons to attack us with their icy gusts. In those three days the weather threw all it had at us. It was as unpredictable as a drunk wildly flailing his fists. I was always on edge, not knowing which way we would need to swing next. The wind had been shifting all over the place, and with its strength varying from 5 knots to 38 knots I was beginning to lose track of what stability felt like. Any one of the gusts could have had us over.

I was changing sails more frequently than at any other moment so far in the record, and was aching from head to toe. I'd done eleven sail changes in twenty-four hours. It was like having to run an assault course every time. Depending on the wind strength, each sail change would take anything from twenty to forty minutes. Soaked in sweat, I would slump down on my bean bag in the cuddy with the salt water stinging my eyes, and the freezing-cold Southern Ocean air burning away at the back of my throat.

I'm my own worst enemy in those situations. I couldn't rest if Mobi wasn't sailing at her potential. Two days in, I spoke to the camera:

> 27.6 boat speed, wind speed 38 knots. Let's hope that the worst energy has gone past . . . and it's all heading north-east to form a low that should carry us two-thirds of the way to Cape Horn . . . My cheeks are numb, and I can feel my mouth moves oddly My hands are dry, hard and splitting, it's so, so cold. In the north-west wind we should be able to sail more safely, as the warmer breeze will be more stable.

It was relentless. We had squalls of 44 knots, lightning and further problems. I had to resplice the solent furling line, which took me two and a half hours, without which I couldn't roll the sail in. I'd had what could not be more than two hours' sleep in the previous two days. Nothing allowed me to switch off, as I had to do everything to reduce our risk of capsizing. They were the worst conditions I'd ever sailed in and much worse than anything I'd experienced in the Vendée.

Over the three days we had some real 'shockers', where the wind reached over 38 knots, sustaining 35 for forty minutes. The sky went black and the sea a silky grey as the hailstones poured down from the heavens to batter the water's surface. Mobi was flying, surfing into the high twenties, then sailing deep, down the waves, on the limit – but thankfully not over it. The words Commanders Weather used to describe the situation were 'latently unstable'. I felt trapped and wrote in my own diary the words 'NO EXIT!!' I tried to make the most of the second such storm to collect some spare water – going forward to the mast to hold the bucket under the sail. The water fell, just above freezing temperature, as the hail which was falling melted off the sail. As I watched the storm pass over us my skin stung as the hefty hailstones belted us from thousands of feet above. They were hitting hard, and as they clattered off the deck into the sea below they echoed like popcorn exploding in a metal pan.

I managed a few hours of troubled sleep, waking each time to the ear-piercing alarm telling me once again the wind had risen. I would drag myself off the floor where I was huddled in my oilskins under my fleece blanket and look to the sky, facing into the icy wind to see yet another demon black cloud.

Though the nights were hard and exhausting, the sunsets were magnificent, with their orange glow lighting up the waves. The huge sea birds around us shimmered through this 'warmth' of light, which was so pure that, despite my state, I stood in total amazement. The dark clouds black in the sky ahead, but the boat before it glowing like a winter's fire. It was just stunning. On one rare night we saw the sky beyond the clouds above us and I realized that there was always a gentle golden glow on the horizon – dusk melting into dawn then bringing the new day. At least the nights were short, as it was allegedly summer here!

Between the squalls, and knowing that conditions were too dangerous to sleep, I made myself useful, putting safety lashings on the trampoline and bailing out the windward float, which had some water ingress. I tried to seal it better this time with silicone, as it seemed like only a matter of days since I'd last bailed it. It was a

bizarre feeling, sitting with my head poking out of the float –
it's narrow, but about as deep as I am tall – so when the hatches
are out you can stand on the hull. I felt like a character out of
Wacky Races, my little head poking out of such a huge, graceful
shape.

Finally, when conditions eased enough to write, I sent the following summary of those three tumultuous days by e-mail:

Jan 5th
Hi there world out there.
   Today I feel a bit like I have awoken into a new
world . . . I have an aching hunger inside me which has
been absent for a while, and the sea and sky that have
been so aggressive are now flat and grey - both.
   The last three days of sailing have been
undoubtedly the worst of my career. Never before have I
experienced winds more unstable, more aggressive, more
unpredictable. With a low pressure forming to our NW we
found ourselves getting literally 'run down' by the
energy and cold air rushing north to build it. My body
has been pushed beyond its limits, once again I found
myself screaming at the heavens. I am sure that I have
never been as tired as that in my life.
   Sleep - such an easy thing to say- but an impossible
thing to achieve in such unstable conditions. Winds have
been all over the place - changing in direction by 50 to
60 degrees at times, and changing at times in strength
by 30 knots in the space of a few seconds . . . in effect
the worst conditions for a multihull, as capsize is a
real possibility - and i have to say that flying along
with one reef and the solent in 44 knots of breeze made
me talk to myself constantly telling myself we were in
fact going to make it . . .
   Yesterday was the worst day, with massive squalls, the
same wind that was not predictable - the day began with
a constant 30 knots after a 47 knot gust, I was sailing

with 3 reefs and staysail. I'm now full main and genoa, reefs in, reefs out - body aching . . .

I apologise to the albatross that came closer in wonder what my cries were all about. I was past it, jsut past it - empty, exhausted . . . but at that stage with no escape, no button to push to make everything ok again . . . no way to hide from the alarms and wake ups from continuously interrupted doses . . . absolute exhaustion.

I tried checking the weather out, and characteristic of the day the grib I picked up came in 6 days out of date - I didn't realise so that threw me completely, and the end never seemed to be in sight - but one thing which does, did and will always help is reading the e-mails of support.

One from Oli, one of the team members who sent an unbelievable mail which could not help but pull you up on a bad day. and the thousands that are flooding in to the website . . . I sat there reading peoples encouragement, and quite honestly cried . . . cried just to see the support of so many people from so many places. It's humbling - I feel like they must be for someone else doing something incredible . . .

Yesterday evening the situation changed - i could feel things were improving after the final blast which was a hail storm. not just any storm - but an inch and a half of sleet in the cockpit. I don't know where the energy came from as my eyes had been burning red with tears just moments before - but I made a snowman . . . and after that - slowly but surely - everything began to get better. by daylight I was full main and genoa - and now I have a light breeze - but finally - thank god - a more predictable one.

This is Ellen out - about to eat something . . .

A few hours after my e-mail left Mobi via satellite to bounce back home to our website I caught this reply on our web page.

I had hoped that we were through the worst of the weather; however, we had two more huge storms to contend with before rounding Cape Horn. There seemed to be no let-up out there, and, unlike anything I remembered from the Vendée, the systems seemed to be rolling in and firing at us non-stop. On the night between the changeable conditions and the new storm when I should have been resting we had a wholly unwelcome incident.

I was lying in the cuddy, just closing my eyes and having a last look at the wind speed, when the alarm went off, and I saw the wind speed go up from 30 to 90 to 120 knots! Your brain gets used to marrying together noises and what it sees, and I instantly knew that it was a problem with the instruments. Despite the fact that I was already on my feet and running to the helm, the autopilot threw Mobi into a crash gybe, and, heart in my mouth, I ran out in the darkness to disengage it and grab the helm. Visions of crash-gybing *Kingfisher* in the Vendée flew through my mind. She had lain over at ninety degrees . . . Mobi would be upside down. I frantically fumbled for the off switch, dimly illuminated by the backlight in the driving rain, hit it and yanked the tiller across, only to feel it spin on its stock in my hand. Desperate, I ran across the cockpit, half expecting it to rear up as I felt her main crash over and slam into her running backstay and throw me, as *Foncia* had done to Alain, into the icy Southern Ocean. It was a race – just 3 metres, but a race – to grab the other tiller. I got it, and somehow managed to gybe her back. As if by some complete miracle it all happened while we were surfing down a huge wave. Ironically the waves which could have capsized us in seconds actually helped us to stay the right way up ... I stood there, gripping the tiller, my heart racing in my chest almost drowned out by the driving rain as relief flowed powerfully through every bone in my body. I settled into the rhythm of the waves, feeling where they were, and feeling the wind. The instruments were useless, but luck, at that moment, had definitely been on our side.

Mobi, unperturbed, almost as if nothing had happened, was back on track surfing over the mountainous waves once again, and, though it was now under my guidance rather than the autopilot's, she didn't seem to care. It was a while before I swapped the pilots over and re-engaged them in a 'stand alone' mode. I stood there steering her like a surfer on a board screaming down the waves. It was stunningly beautiful out there. Mobi felt alive, and I felt glad to be too!

In amongst all the turmoil I reset the instruments and studied the graphs to see what could have gone wrong, and from them it was clear that the compass had a fault and had lost its heading. When its heading changes, so do all the calculations and vectors in the processor, which makes the instruments tell lies. I swapped gyrocompasses over. I had only two: one down, one to go.

With the onslaught of yet another depression, and not being able to sleep thanks to just having been scared out of my wits, I realized that I needed some respite from the charging-system nightmare, so I made the decision that I would swap back from the air-cooled generator. It was not a complicated process, involving only swapping the thick alternator cables from one to the other, hopefully not electrocuting myself in the process. But in the seaway that we had, even brushing your teeth was a challenge, and, stupidly, I ended up burning myself on the exhaust, which was still pretty hot from the charge I had done earlier. With a yelp, I drew my arm away from it instantly, but I could feel that it wasn't so flash. I tore my shirt off to find a large blister on my arm – damn it! I grabbed the burns cream from the kit stowed next to the generator and smeared some on my arm. I looked at the stitches, needles, syringes and drugs . . . At least I was only reaching for a tube of cream.

The run of non-stop weather since Christmas had really taken its toll on my body. I was totally exhausted, and with this new storm on the horizon there was no respite. It was the worst forecast so far: very, very windy. The storm which lay behind us had 80 knots in it on its west side, and I was only too aware that there are places in the south that you can survive in a multihull and places that you probably can't. 80 knots was firmly in the can't bracket, and, as the storm rolled towards us, I knew in my heart that, if we slowed for any reason, or broke something on the boat, 80 knots would engulf us, and if it didn't capsize us it would likely smash us to pieces like matchsticks. The vision I had in my mind was one of Indiana Jones running before the huge stone ball chasing him down the canyon. I talked to the video camera.

> I lie here with freezing feet – can't sleep – brain won't switch off. To be honest, I'm feeling pretty scared right now. We've got a big storm coming and we're about a week from Cape Horn. Forecasts are saying that it's going to have 50 to 60 knots in it, may be up to 80, and I've just come out of three days of hell with very variable winds and no sleep, so I'm exhausted . . . My life is in Mobi's hands. Speed's going to be our saving, but equally speed is going to be what breaks the boat. We have some pretty difficult choices coming up. Eighty knots is a lot of wind. Far too much wind for a boat like this. Let's just hope . . . let's just hope it's better than we think

I spoke to the office:

> I just wish I had had more time to recover. Right now, I just don't know if I've got enough energy left to even get to Cape Horn. It's raining really hard and it's already rough – this storm is going to be big. We just launched down another wave and we are right on the edge of control here. To be honest, this is very, very frightening.

The low was chasing us, and staying alive was a pretty good incentive to stay ahead of it as long as possible . . .

The e-mails I was receiving were making such a difference to my days, which were, right then, filled with the concern and drama of storms. I got this one from Oli:

```
jan 5th.
In awe
   That is what my life is at the moment.
   In awe when I connect on the web site every morning
and every evening to see where you are and how you are
doing, in awe when I look through the window of my
living room and grab my skates for a little trip on the
river or a game of hockey with my mates, proud to be
part of such a great team of people living such a
fortunate life. I sometimes worry that all this immense
joy I feel at the moment is not for me but I take it
anyway. I consider myself, today, the luckiest man on
the planet and your determination and energy, your
skills and your bonne-humeur, all this is a serious
contribution to how I am right now.
```

Oli went on to talk about his friends, and the time they all spent at their computers making sure that I was OK.

```
They all, I mean all cross there 20 fingers and toes
for you and send there love. Trust me there's a lot
of it.
   I know I am not supposed to write that much because of
power consumption, but **** . . . sometimes you just have
to say these things . . .
   Take care of yourself, ride on, you are on your way
home.
   Proud Oli
```

There was one from Sari, Peter, all the boys and Bentley in Australia saying:

Please don't think we are ignorant for our lack of
communication, it's more that we are all watching in
stunned awe. Our days are a constant log-on vigil. Our
enormous thanks for letting us be part of this.

As usual, Fergus's e-mail cheered me up:

Oh and just in case your relentless motivation, drive
and determination to achieve in the face of
extraordinary adversity elude you for a moment . . .
please think of me and make sure you beat this French
dude so I've got a bloody good excuse for a couple of
days off and a great many beers!
   Doing well mate . . . keep going . . . you'll sh*t em!

The storm hit us, and I found myself sitting at the chart table
with my freezing-cold feet braced in the foot-straps. On one occasion Mobi was actually thrown clear of the water, something which
I would not be keen to repeat in a hurry. When you have heard
nothing but the ghostly yet familiar sound of the hum from Mobi's
foils for a month and it turns to silence, you worry. The window
just inches above my head was being constantly lashed with spray,
and the surface of the sea that I could see through it each time it
cleared was strewn with white water. The waves were huge. We
were sailing at an average of 20.04 knots with storm jib and three
reefs, and Mobi was just totally blowing me away. It was her
moment, and she was dealing with what was going on around us
with the biggest heart you could imagine. I was thinking aloud as
I wrote an e-mail home . . .

She is amazing - and right now - at this moment I owe,
and will owe my life to her. If only you could see and
feel the way she is riding these huge waves - faltering
rarely - and just picking herself up after each time she
is thrown.

I couldn't sleep and I was struggling to push food down I was so nervous. There was a very real risk of 60 knots where we were, which was not much more than the gusts of 47 we'd already seen. I could not bring myself to get out of my oilskins, and the motion was so bad that I was constantly holding on to something to stop myself getting injured.

but we are still here . . . for now we are soldiering
on. I am numb to the tiredness, as my veins are filled
with adrenalin and fear. my brain so active it cannot
switch off at all. with my oilskins round my ankles
I lie in the bunk and try to sleep - all I can do
is warm up a little and close my eyes waiting for
the next thud as we are thumped by on-coming waves.
Never knowing how big they are is horrible . . . I find
myself lying there wiggling my toes, clenching my
fists - and worst - clamping my teeth firmly together. I
wonder why - I guess it's either the stress, or the fact
that if I did sleep I would not bite my tongue with the
motion.
   Things have, to be quite honest been better . . . but
we're here and we will get through this - the horn is
getting closer by the hour . . . The support from you all
writing is just mind blowing. I mean mind blowing. I am
lost for words . . . I refresh the page each time I log
on for the weather and read as many as I can. YOU are
unbelievable . . .
   Exx

Mobi felt like a big dipper, like her hulls were on rails, but her movements were a constant surprise. She flew along as if her life depended on it. I was there for her, but I was effectively blindfolded and had to have the most incredible trust in her to handle the conditions. I never ever doubted her. Mark, through our e-mails and conversations, had a pretty good idea of the conditions. He had raced down in the south fifteen years before.

7th Jan.

Am thinking of you every moment. I was with Richard S
when you called earlier. We are both sick with worry,
and are seriously with you on every wave, every gust,
every missed heartbeat, every surf, every heel, every
bang and crash, and will be there with you until you
come out of the other side. Somehow try those 10 minute
naps if you can to keep your head together enough to do
the right things. You are the best sailor in the world
to deal with this, it brings a tear to my eye (now
included) when I say this to people all day.

    Love, m.xx

After throwing 50 knots at us, the storm stalled, and we ran out of the front of it. I can't have slept for more than an hour in the previous twenty-four: winds were still strong and the seas huge, and I just couldn't switch off. With conditions so rough, it was as hard to stand up as it was to wind down. Whilst we sailed as fast as we could, trying to keep as much ground as we could to the north for safety, the storm hovered behind us like a stalking assassin waiting for its moment to pounce. My instinct told me it was going to catch us, and that's exactly what it did, kicking the crap out of us at Cape Horn.

Feeling like the hunted prey, we had some fast days' sailing, and that speed was paying off too: as we approached the Horn we were only an hour short of a staggering five-day lead on Francis. But we still had just under 10,000 miles to the finish, and, though a lead was better than a deficit, I was brutally aware that we needed to actually get home to win. As if the risks weren't clear enough, the team had sent an e-mail to the boat warning of a 300 metre long iceberg drifting around to my north-east.

The e-mails of support continued to flood in:

Date: 10/01/2005 04:39:13
Subject: Hooah from Iraq!

Ellen, keep up the fight! You are doing great!!

Your biggest fan!

Sergeant First Class Gene Sizemore US Army Baghdad, Iraq

Date: 11/01/2005 16:04:37 Report
Subject: hi ellen

house work neglected, garage roof blown off, rain
leaking from roof into the bedroom, rang insurance
yesterday, but nothing seems more important than logging
on to see how you are coping i feel transfixed to the
screen like I am waiting for my exam results, my stomach
is turning over listening to you sounding so calm and
confident and looking so well, i cannot believe how
courageous you are. I am really hoping that you will be
safe, the night sailing must be worse, i hate it at
night you can get so disorientated. I suppose its a lot
easier just relying on the plotter and the radar, but i
do like to see where i am going its like driving with
your eyes closed. Do be careful i wish you all the very
very best with the wind and the sea looking after you
like its one of your thousands of fans. good luck for
tonight.bye for now,

the silver surfers irene and tom

Date: 10/01/2005 15:50:44
Subject: A Difficult Time For Ellen

Hi Ellen, As expected your extreme speed kept you clear
of the strongest winds and roughest seas. Well Done.
However, you are now in unstable conditions that will do
everything they can to catch you out, particular as you
are now clearly so overtired. Please take care; you CAN
afford to sail below 100% for at least 24 hours and cut
down on the number of sail changes as a result. You have
had some 'scary' warnings recently. Do heed them? By my
reckoning you may be a day further ahead of Francis Joyan

as your website lists his elapsed time to the Horn as 51
days 2 hours and 22 minutes? Your time is likely to be
around 45 days (0810 hrs. Wednesday 12th). Once again do
take care. I wish you a safe passage around the Horn.

   Ellen à donf.

   Alan in Dover, UK.

Date: 11/01/2005 04:09:11

Subject: KEEP FLYING YOU TWO. . .love Caz x

```
..........................................................
...................................ze$$e..................
.............ed$$$eee...........$$$$$$$P"""...............
..............z$$$$$$$$$$$$$$$$$$ee$$$$$"..................
..........d$$$$$$$$$$$$$$$$$$$$$$$$$$$"....................
.........$$$$$$$$$$$$$$$$$$$$$$$$$$$$$$$e..................
.......$$*****"""""***$$$$$$$$$$$$$$$$$$$$$$$$$$$$be.......
.....................""**$$$$$$$$$$$$$$$$$$$$$$$$L......
........................z$$$$$$$$$$$$$$$$$$$$$$$$$$......
.................$$$$$$$$$P**$$$$$$$$$$$$$$$$$$......
....................d$$$$$$$"..............4$$$$$......
...................z$$$$$$$$$$...............$$$P".......
.................d$$$$$$$$$$F.................$P".........
...................*$$$$$$$$$".............................
........................"***""............................
..........................................................
```


Date: 09/01/2005 17:22:40

Subject: We're all behind you

Dear Ellen, We are a survey crew working in the Bay of
Bengal. The whole crew are watching your progress via the
internet and would like to wish you the very best of luck
on your attempt. You are doing so well to date and we
will be cheering for you all the way. Keep smiling and
remember we are with you in spirit. With love and best
wishes, Graham Boniwell & the crew of the Geco Topaz XXX

Date: 10/01/2005 21:45:07

Just noticed that you are now into day 42. It took us 42 days just to reach Cape town from Southsea in the record breaking Whitbread of 1977 aboard Great Britain 11, and that was with a crew of 17 and you have almost reached Cape horn SOLO in the same time!!!! You are such an inspiration to all of us. Keep going - but above all keep safe.

John

(B&Q employee and fellow member of Int. Assoc. of Cape Horners)

It had been four weeks since we entered the Southern Ocean, and, though I was very nervous about all it was going to throw at us in its final hours, I was also feeling sad that, if all went well, I was about to leave it. I wrote a log:

ELLEN LOG: 12/01/05
We are sailing in 30 to 40 knots right now, and getting very close to our gybe just 45 miles off the coast off western Chile. The seas are monstrous, and as I stand in Mobi's cockpit I cannot [but] feel that I shall miss this wild and wonderful place. Somehow the south finds places inside you that you were unaware you had, it conjures up the most vivid memories, shows you the most unbelievable and breathtaking sights. Behind Mobi there is a rain filled squall - but from behind that peeps the setting sun. the light beams out a rich powerful dominant orange over the grey darkness of the clouds - it lights the spray flying from the crests of the waves, giving them a delicate, almost furry texture. how can such a powerful 40 foot wave be so delicate . . . ? As the light gets behind a breaking wave it seems to lift the crest higher. the striking turquoise colour seems as if it's artificially illuminated from another source - such brilliant colour in an otherwise grey blue sea . . . A lone albatross circles ahead. how many passing ships has he seen I ask . . . ?

A tear comes to my eye - because the albatross we see
on this voyage are now numbered, their graceful
effortless flight, and constant companionship will have
to remain etched in my mind till the next time.

For all being well . . . the next setting sun over Mobi
will be one as we leave the southern ocean behind . . .

for now . . . x

But the Southern Ocean had one last show of energy before it allowed us to leave it, and as the day progressed the wind got stronger and became more erratic. We began to see gusts of well over 50 knots; enough to flip Mobi like a cork, and the seas, due to the funnelling effect of the 'throat' between Cape Horn and Antarctica, became gigantic. In effect thousands of miles of ocean waves are squeezed through a gap which is just a shade over 400 miles wide. It's not helped either by the fact that, approaching the Horn, the sea can be anything up to 4,500 metres deep, but then it shelves to 200 or less as you round the corner. I had never rounded Cape Horn in a storm before, and it was not going to let me leave without showing me what it could do in all its glory.

At the Horn we had a lead on Francis of 4 days 2 hours and 45 minutes, but that seemed irrelevant at the time, as the goal was to actually get round. The seas were some of the biggest I've seen in my life. The waves were breaking, which is always a nightmare for boats, as the risk of being flooded from behind or breaking steering gear was high. The waves were steeper and larger than I'd seen else-where. It was like parts of them were painted, as huge areas of foam from the breaking water the size of tennis courts littered them.

Fearing for Mobi's safety, I took her mainsail all the way down to help to keep her the right way up, and I realized that it was the first time we'd done that since we hoisted it in Falmouth Harbour forty-seven days before. With just her staysail flying from her forestay, we surfed at 30 knots down the waves. My biggest fear was that, if we had to take the staysail down too and we still had too much, the area of her wing mast alone was an unreefable 45 square metres.

Having seen nothing bar two icebergs in the whole Southern Ocean,

I was startled by the beep of the active echo indicating that there was a ship around. I instantly shot outside, holding on tight to the pedestal, and it took me a while to work out just exactly where it was. It was the first time that I'd seen another boat in waves quite this big, and I was staggered that a huge factory fishing boat bigger than a cross-Channel ferry could be hidden by the waves so easily. It was literally only a quarter of a mile away, heading west round the Horn, but its huge red and white structure could have been easily missed. It was then that I realized just how big the waves really were down there.

Mark had said that there was going to be a plane flying out to film us as we rounded the Horn, but as the hours slipped by there was no sign. I knew both the cameraman and photographer who went up in the plane, and both said later that it was so windy, and they had to fly so low to stay under the clouds for visibility, that they feared they would not make it home. They never found us amongst the waves out there.

I stayed further south off the Horn so as to keep out of the worst of the weather. It was my fourth rounding of the Horn. The first had been under motor, as there was no wind on Kingfisher when we delivered her home, the second was blowing 25 knots in the Vendée, and the third was in 20 knots of wind and rain with Loïk and Mark Turner. Now here I was alone on Mobi with gusts of 55 knots.

As we passed the Horn itself I grabbed the little champagne bottle I had earmarked for it and climbed astride the cabin top so I could grip it with my legs to hold on. Celebrating wasn't for the event or the fun, but really just to mark officially the fact that we had passed it. It was more tradition than anything else.

That night was a night from hell. Just as I was getting ready to sleep for an hour after the most exhausting passage, the wind began to die. I couldn't believe it to begin with, but it did: it dropped from 40 knots to 8. I had expected a hairy night with a great deal of wind, and we were snugged down ready for that, but the wind shadow from the mountains on the west coast of Chile some 400 miles away had a different plan in store for us. That night alone I did ten sail changes, which left me shaking in a heap. Though I didn't know it at the time, it was going to set the tone for the whole South Atlantic.

Chapter Twelve

As HMS *Gloucester* came alongside to visit me I felt on top of the world. It was actually quite emotional to see people just the day after surviving the 55 knot seas of Cape Horn. I could not believe that twenty-four hours before we had been fighting to stay the right way up and had now actually made it into the Atlantic. The previous night's drama and fatigue were temporarily drowned out by something so incredibly uplifting, and it was a lovely way to be welcomed into the Atlantic Ocean.

Incredibly, as I was online getting weather that morning, I'd caught an e-mail on our website from Heather Somerset, whose husband was the flight commander on board. As the helicopter from the *Gloucester* flew over for the first time I chatted to the pilot and passed on the message. I was later told on the radio by the *Gloucester*'s captain that I had been speaking to Mr Somerset himself!

Not only did *Gloucester* turn up, but while they were alongside, a Hercules and two Tornados from Mount Pleasant Airport on the Falklands came over for a flypast. Each event moved me in a different way. The ship, as it carried personnel who knew what it was like to be out there on the ocean; the Hercules, as it was a huge and imposing aircraft which had been sent out just to see me; and finally the Tornados, as they brought memories flooding back from the previous year. The last time they had buzzed us was ten months before, when Mark and Loik were on board, and after we'd had a very different Cape Horn rounding. Those five fun days in the company of great people on the Falklands had made a great impression on me, and now here I was alone.

But that day I was shattered physically and mentally, and I knew it, so finally, with a half-reasonable breeze helping us along, I slept well.

The following day I was much better thanks to some respite, and for the first time in a month we had a reasonable sea state. The wind was quite a lot lighter, and despite slowing down I felt happy. I knew that that evening the wind would start to build from behind Mobi, and though it was going to be pretty feisty at 40 knots, at least, unlike the light head winds we had then, it would be pushing us along! The wind can't blow strong every day, and I rationalized this, spending most of the day tackling the jobs which I'd been adding to my list. In a strange way it was this attention to detail which made me feel settled and in control. Being on top of everything gave me peace of mind in the boat, and in myself.

I bailed the bottom of the boat out and fixed the leaky tap – again! I bound tape round anything worn to protect it and spread my favourite Lanocote (a grease from sheep's fleeces) on the ropes where they passed through fairleads, to stop them squeaking. The rising temperature made the Lanocote smell even more sheepy than normal and reminded me of Derbyshire. I repaired the tiller, which had been damaged in the crash gybe in the south, looked at the bottom bearing of the main rudder stock, then did a whole host of wiring work up the mast to fix the active echo so that it could run alongside the strobe without going off each time it flashed.

It was here that something extraordinary happened. I glanced up to look around from my fairly dodgy position hanging from the front of the mast and nearly fell off my perch as my eyes met with those of the biggest albatross I had ever seen. Its wingspan must have been over 3.0 metres. It made me smile from the bottom of my heart, and I had an overwhelming feeling that it had come to say 'goodbye' from the Southern Ocean.

I was more philosophical by this stage of the trip, and the sleep had done me the world of good. I felt much more in control of where we were, and, as it was day forty-seven and we had nearly five days' lead on Francis, things could have been a great deal worse. But what frustrated me was that I could feel the journalists at home saying that the record was in the bag and we just had to sail home, but I knew that this wasn't the case. I would need some time under my belt as the weather patterns for the South Atlantic were looking nothing short of horrendous; plus, both Mobi and I were a lot more tired than we had been.

The e-mails were still coming in thick and fast on the website, and I could feel the interest in what we were doing out there grow. It was like the Vendée: as I rounded Cape Horn the media attention increased, but the wonderful side to this was that the number of messages left on the teamellen.com site was growing, and I spotted one from Ben and Helen. Ben was one of my best friends at school.

Date: 13/01/2005 22:45:41
Subject: home run

Glad to see you back in your fav hunting ground we know what you did in this stretch of water in the vendee, get some sleep and come out fighting, spread those wings rare bird and fly, make this an unbreakable run. Well least for ten years! c u soon ben & helen Derby

When the wind came, it came with vengeance, and, though the weather was warmer, there was something really aggressive about the sea state in the South Atlantic. It was shallower for a start, and as we gybed our way up towards Buenos Aires things felt really awful on board. The worst thing was the waves, as they were short and steep in the shallower waters and felt like they were punching at Mobi and trying to make her crash into them. In the south she had ridden the waves beautifully, but here they felt like they were almost square, and Mobi was 'falling' off them. We needed to get into deeper water to the east, but the waves wouldn't let us gybe. It would have been suicide to gybe too early and take those waves on the beam. I spoke to the office:

We are falling off every third or fourth wave. It's hard, the whole boat is shaking, it's just terrible, it's terrible, it's ******* bad. Everything is creaking and groaning and smashing and grinding. You go over three waves and you close your eyes and hope it's okay, then the fourth one – 'WHACK'. I'm sure something is going to break.

The noises on board were ear-splitting, and I felt the most stressed and tired I had in the whole record. I think that it was the realization of my fears, that here we were going to have the worst conditions imaginable, and that we were going to have to fight with all our strength for every mile to the north. It was like trying to rest in a boxing ring: each time you closed your eyes, you were belted; but here there was no referee to stop the punches. They just kept coming again and again and again. I lay on my bunk for a while; I felt awful. My lead on Francis had already slipped by almost a day, but I knew what lay ahead, and it really wasn't good. Trying to drown out the crashes, I pushed my face hard into my pillow. I gritted my teeth. Come on, Ellen . . . hold it together. Get through this.

```
16th Jan
Where am I now . . .
   It's the morning here, and I'm feeling the most human
I've felt for days. Last night, after our gybe and third
reef episode yesterday I, for the first time had the
boat in a configuration where we were safe for a few
hours. The wind would decrease from its 40 knot gusts
- and the terrible sea conditions - should - in theory
improve . . .
The last few days have not been just testing, but have
taken me once again a long way inside myself to find the
strength to keep sailing safely . . .
Since cape horn which seems to me like weeks ago now
I have had nothing but changeable conditions. we've had
every sail up bar the gennaker, and the mainsail through
it's full range on several occasions . . . Yesterday I
was more tired than I have been in the whole trip - and
```

conditions worsening through the day. My body ached with
the strain of the trip so far, my joints throbbed -
together with yet another knock on my head, I just felt
like I was empty ... I have tried so hard to rest - but
when things are changing with the weather, and the boats
safety is in danger it's very very hard to switch off.
Disconnecting the brain does not come easily. in some
ways your body is exhausted, perhaps your brain ceases
to allow itself to switch off - and thought functions
like eating, drinking, charging the batteries, coiling
the ropes, can become tasks forced by habit - sleeping
is not necessarily something that comes on demand ...
We had a terrible time - the wind building, the seas
were horrendous, we needed to get east - but the waves
were pushing us west ...

Mobi was suffering, and so was I. i made lunch albeit
at about 1400 and after a frantic gybe in 35 knots,
and seas breaking all over Mobi (that ripped off the
starboard mesh protection!) I climbed straight on to my
bunk after putting on a new dry shirt - and thought 'at
least I've eaten' now sleep. then I realised that I
couldn't remember eating - and glanced over to the galley
to see my food still sitting there stone cold ... I ate
it straight away anyway - followed with some sports
drink - but that just shows how tired I really was ...

But last night - with a short break in the weathers
busy schedule we were able to get some sleep - how much
I do not know - but I forced it ... I lay till I had to,
and I do feel a bit better. I'm not back at 100 percent,
but I'm back ... looking forward to gybing out of the
horrible sea state, and pointing our bows once again to
the NORTH!!

exx

Within hours the wind began to die, and we ran once again through
the exhausting sail changes to get us from three reefs and staysail

to full main and gennaker. The order of events was, third reef to second reef, staysail to solent, second reef to first reef, solent to genoa, then genoa to gennaker, and then first reef to full main. The final two were brutal. Already moving the gennaker bag around on the deck meant I had to use my whole body weight to drag the bag, heavier than my own body, up forward. The process of getting it out and on to the deck was not a pleasant one, and I was glad Gran wasn't around, as there was an awful lot of swearing going on. Never more so than when the tack flicked up as I was attaching it to the bow and cut my forehead open. After a brief trip to unsuccessfully mop up the blood and stick a plaster on a sweaty, bleeding lump I was straight back to work. Once I had hoisted the gennaker, which wasn't easy on a totally unstable platform smacking up and down in the waves, I would unfurl it, and sheet it in. It was the biggest sail on board by a long way and went from the end of her bow to the top of her mast and almost to her back beam. Then the most brutal bit of all: hoisting the final section of her mainsail, to the top of the mast. It's the hardest reef, as you're literally lifting the whole sail, and with the boat still smashing into the waves it made the winch impossible to even budge at times.

When I'd completed this, I lay there in a jerking Mobi totally exhausted, but what made matters worse was that this weather was caused by the front of the low pressure we had sailed most of the Southern Ocean with. Now this was quickly passing off up to the north above us, with its associated rain and wind, there would be a calm zone of no pressure moving in from the west which would engulf us if we didn't sail fast enough. Though the centre of the low was now 4,000 miles away, its slow-moving grey front was just ahead of us, stalled, and we were sailing back towards it. It happens quite regularly here, that a huge, rainy, windless band just sits there just east of Punta del Este, but we *had* to get through it to the breeze on the other side, and we could only move if there was wind.

I don't know how to describe that twenty-four-hour period. When you don't think things can get worse, they often do, and living on board Mobi during that day was hell. We had all her sail up but were going nowhere, as the wind was so light. What made matters even worse was that the winds we were trying to reach were only a matter of a few miles ahead of us. Each wave came and lifted her bows high, then fell away so that they smacked hard on the water, stopping us dead. The sea was taunting her. I couldn't help but feel something was going to break. Her ropes were snatching hard each time her sails filled: SMACK, SMACK, SMACK . . . On and on it went, hour after hour, tormenting, goading, bruising and exhausting us. I couldn't sleep, I couldn't rest, I couldn't even think.

Once again I had tried a different course to make better progress towards and through this barrier, and once again it hadn't worked. I stood in the cockpit; there were ropes everywhere after the manoeuvre, and I slipped on them as I worked my way around her shaking cockpit. I simply slumped to the floor and cried . . . Nothing could make it better, nothing could stop it, nothing could control it. As the hours slowly, sleeplessly and helplessly slipped away, so did our lead on Francis . . .

I was right on the edge and I knew it. I didn't want to get off Mobi, I just wanted to sleep. Everyone in the office was worried, and that day I lost it on the phone to Mark. I called him, and then things went quiet while he switched it to record mode. There was a loud beep. I just wanted to speak to him, not his voice recorder. I screamed down the phone, then hung up and switched it off.

Sleep deprivation is not like torture, it *is* a form of torture. I was running on empty, and for the first time in my sailing career I was learning what that really meant. I was on the brink of despair, my actions went beyond the realms of logic, and I was reduced to functioning like a robot to stay alive. It was intense; more intense than anything I had been through before, and physical and mental exhaustion in this extreme form was new to me. I had found a place inside me which I have no wish to visit again, but a place that I am grateful to have seen and returned from.

Finally, we did make it through the front, but what met us the other side was not a steady flow of breeze with which we could make our way north, but another run of problems. When we finally touched our new wind the effect was instant: one minute we were going downwind in 5 knots of breeze, the next we were going upwind in 27! I had already changed the genoa to the solent and put the first reef in, but it was not enough. I eased the main out to slow us down and decrease the apparent wind speed, but the load on the solent was too much. The tack line shot through its jammer, and the bottom of the stay broke free, blowing straight off the deck and shooting high into the air and tearing the furling system off with it. My brain went into overdrive; the only way to sort this was to turn back south away from the wind. Adrenalin flowed and an exhausted body sprang into action. If we sailed back into the front we would be back to square one.

I bore Mobi away, working as fast as I could, attaching another rope to the end of the furling line and then, foot by foot, winching the flogging, angry sail down towards the deck. I then set about working out how to furl it. The furling line was damaged, as was the system to lead the line. Somehow I managed to get the sail rolled away, before heading upwind and hoisting the staysail and pulling her bows north once again. We were right on the edge of the clouds, but we'd got away with it.

Once we were through the worst of the squalls and showers in the front, the sky slowly cleared a bit, and, though the horrible swell was still there, I was grateful we had some good wind now to power through it. I spent hours getting sprayed on the foredeck repairing the furling system, even managing to get superglue in my eye. At least the water was a bit warmer than in the Southern Ocean, and the temperature meant that the glue went off a bit faster! I felt relieved to be back on track; though upwind sailing was far from fast, it did mean that we were at least moving. As it went dark I finished my final repairs and that night, for what felt like the first time in a week, I slept.

Rubbing my eyes, I looked up through the window in Mobi's cabin roof. It was daybreak, and the office had informed me that we might well get a visit from HMS *Endurance*, the ice-breaking Navy ship, which was on her way south, and I was thinking of the rendezvous as I looked up, as I had hundreds of times, to check her sails. This time, however, my heart skipped a beat. Something serious was wrong. Having somehow torn off, her headboard car was floating away from the mast track. I instantly knew if I couldn't fix it the record was over.

HMS *Endurance* came that day, but as I spoke to the captain on the radio and waved to her helicopter as it flew over us, my mind was elsewhere. I had managed earlier that morning to replace what we call the 'crayons' in the headboard car, which was undamaged as a result of the problem, but that meant that the track itself was going to be badly damaged. After replacing the parts I had rehoisted the sail, but could only do that to the position of the second reef. Above that, the track was torn, and the only way to find out if it was repairable was to climb the mast itself.

The rest of that day was just one huge concerted effort to get Mobi back in a state where she had any chance of sailing at record pace again. I went into automatic pilot to get the job done and climbed the mast twice: once to the second reef point, and once to the first, a few hours later. That climb was the hardest I'd done in my sailing years, as not only did I have to physically pull my way up the 100 foot mast, but the sea state from the front we'd crossed only the day before was bad: each wave Mobi sailed over smacked me hard into the mast, and I felt like I was in a fight with it. I wore thermals to try and preserve the skin on my legs, which worked, but my biggest concern was breaking a limb, or worse, my neck. I wore a helmet on to which I had stuck some bands of tape to help me spot the damaged areas of the mast from the deck, and I had with me files, a camera, glass-paper and tools in a bag tied to my harness. As I climbed it swung into my leg, actually puncturing my skin, which was testament to the violence of the motion up there; and it got worse with each metre I climbed. I felt like a bird that someone was trying to shake from a branch, except I had no wings and no way out. The mast was rock-hard too, being built of carbon, and it shook unpredictably and aggressively, taking all my energy just to hang on, let alone defend myself from it. All the time the sun beat down on me as I hauled myself up to that final point at the second reef where I could see just how damaged that part of the track was.

The aluminium was torn badly, and, as I tried to stabilize my body, which was pounding against it, I managed to cut my thumb.

At this point I laughed, as I knew that what Kev, our doctor, would suggest was elevating the limb and 20 metres up a mast was pretty elevated! I worked up there for what must have been an hour, filing away at the track to remove the burrs and smoothing it enough so that it wouldn't damage the crayons. A long way below me Mobi sailed on alone, surfing down the waves and firing through the ocean, with the shadow of my body up the mast flicking across her beam as she went. When I returned to deck I was massively dehydrated and, though I have no idea where I put it, I drank 4 litres of sports drink mix straight down.

Several hours later after descending the mast I climbed up once again. I thought initially I'd wait till the next day to file down the track at the first reef point, but, as the wind died enough to enable me to get up there, and all my gear was out, I decided to go for it then. The second time was higher and harder, and, as my legs were trashed, it hurt much more, but I got the job done, which meant that I could actually hoist the mainsail to the top of the mast again.

There was no question in my mind that what we had been through in the front had caused the damage. The load on her had been huge, and each time we'd slammed off those waves the crayons had been rubbing away on her track until they were so worn they fell out. There is always a price to pay somewhere down the line; the question is always: when?

I called the office the following morning:

I feel like I've been beaten up this morning: stiff as hell and moving round with the speed and elegance of an arthritic robot! I just want the pain to go away, I'm just so buggered. Everything hurts so much – if I move it hurts, if I move my legs, my arms, anything. Every muscle in my body feels like it's been torn. It's horrible. I'm glad I went up again yesterday – if I had had to go up again today, I wouldn't have done it, I couldn't have done it.

My legs were black with bruises, and, though our lead on Francis had fallen to 1 day and 20 hours, we were at least in fighting shape for the final dash home.

Mark sent me a photo to cheer me up. It was a stunning picture of a Tornado flying over Mobi, taken from another when they flew past, off the Falklands. Apart from the photo the e-mail was blank but the title read: 'Another fighter, just like you.'

Date: 22/01/2005 12:07:17
Subject: Help!

My name is Slinky and I stowed away on a boat to see the
world but the owner found me and is making me do lots
of work, changing these things called sails and then
2 days ago, she made me climb up the pole in the middle
of the boat to repair these rail type things. It was
very scary. When I am not working, she hangs me up by my
neck (very uncomfortable) near the computer station. I
managed to escape to type this message . . . please can
someone rescue me? Arr, help, she is coming back down
now . . . help!

As we headed north we were presented with our next challenge in the form of a high-pressure zone, with no quick route round it. The swell and waves from the front disappeared and were replaced by a flat, and eventually almost motionless, sea. Bit by bit the wind died down, and bit by bit Mobi slowed down. Though the South Atlantic had been Francis's slowest section of the trip, ours had been much worse, but I tried to sleep as much as the light, changeable winds allowed and tried to rationalize all that was going on.

The sun set each evening over the most unbelievable still sea and it seemed strange not to feel Mobi tossed around by the water, having her every move dictated by the waves around her. The huge, watery mountains of the south were now a lightly textured, slightly undulating carpet stretching further than the eye could see.

I seemed to have found some kind of inner peace, and, though the days were hot and restless, I felt surprisingly good. The weather could not have been worse for the record, and our speed was down to 4 knots. But we had what we had, and I could not alter the weather. I tried to forget the almost five-day lead we had had at the Horn and take each day as it came. I knew that until the descending clock ticked its final second I would not give up. All we could do was the best we could; and the rest would happen on its own. We had given our all, and would continue to do so, and only time would bring the outcome. I wrote in my log:

Easy to say, but tonight i feel in control . . . that's a better feeling than the past few weeks.

I knew mentally it always helped to get on with jobs on board and on that day I tinkered away in the scorching heat, as it was too hot to sleep anyway. I rewired both ends of the earth protector for the active echo, checked the steering bearings, replaced some protection on the mast, removed the damaged netting protection from the port side, checked all the seals on the float hatches and fixed the fixings in position, epoxied the bull's-eye back on the deck for the solent, and also re-bonded the carbon deck that had been torn up as it went flying. I was now back on the water-cooled generator and, as the team back at home had run one lubricated by just olive oil and rapeseed oil for several weeks, we had come to the conclusion that I could too. It smelt quite strange as the engine ran, but it worked a treat and meant that I had two charging systems functioning again, which was a huge relief.

I took the opportunity to rest and get Mobi in shape for her final sprint home. We would need to sprint too, as we were three days away from the Equator and we had fallen behind the record for the first time since day seven of our attempt. I was absolutely gutted. After everything we'd been through I felt the record was taken out of my control. Powerless to do anything about it, we were starting out again from zero, but at least it felt like a beginning rather than an end, and there was still a record to fight for!

Chapter Thirteen

24th Jan,

Here and now . . .

It's flat calm outside as we spend another 24 hour
period on this incredibly flat sea . . . It's a strange
sensation to be out here, still with the clock ticking
but at the same time feeling utterly helpless and unable
to make a difference. Here we have light winds, and
that's that . . . We can sail our optimum upwind - and
that's the best we can do for now . . . It's actually
quite beautiful, and having just a little time to rest,
and recover in stable conditions has probably done me
the world of good before what I am sure will be a
stressful, stormy and tense final two weeks. Mobi is as
ready as she will ever be, I have checked, rechecked and
hope that we can do no more.

I am OK - I think I've managed my time pretty well to
try to de-tune a little and find myself again after the
last few weeks of near exhaustion . . .

That's a good thing I guess that's come out of this . . .
Its incredible to think that we've been out here for
almost 60 days, and that Xmas and New year are all behind
us. it seems like only yesterday that we slipped our lines
from Falmouth, seen off by a fantastic flotilla of boats.
but on the other hand it feels like life onboard is almost

all I know now, and that re-adjusting to another life
'the' other life will be hard.

  But hey . . . we're still a couple of weeks away, so
life here goes on . . . In some ways I really am looking
forward to finishing, to see everyone again, those I've
been apart from for almost two months, I am tired and a
bit beat up - and this journey drawing to an end will
help that.

  But I think the main draw to the finish is to finally
end the worry, pressure and strain that my mind and body
is under right now . . . It's the not knowing - how we'll
finish, what will break . . . that's what takes it toll,
take the record away, and it simply becomes a voyage
around the world - add the record again, and it becomes
a very real and very arduous race. A race against time;
my invisible competitor - but perhaps above all - a race
against my own capabilities and myself . . .

  exx

Two days from the Equator, we had dropped to twelve hours behind
Francis, but some of the pain was taken away by the most beautiful
moon I had ever seen at sea. It was perfect in every way, full to the
brim, and an honour to sail beneath. It was one more reminder of
how lucky I was to be out there and it brought my nights to life.
That and the e-mails which were flooding into the website now at
a speed we'd not seen before:

Date: 26/01/2005 04:39:17
Subject: Fill the Stadium

Hi again Ellen I see you've had nearly 34,000 emails
sent to the website. WOW. Just think. That's a very
decent sized football crowd. Imagine a stadium full of
half-crazed fans yelling and cheering their favourite
team on. The score is one all (1-1) at the moment. Late
in the first half Ellen MacArthur of Castorama City

opened the scoring when she opened up what looked like an unassailable lead. Midway into the 2nd half, Francis Joyon hit back with a pile-driver of a strike and IDEC United draw level. The crowd is going mad. The atmosphere is absolutely electric. The dolphins are sprinting up and down the sidelines, but the albatross couldn't stand the heat anymore and disappeared long ago. But these are just the fans that came to the stadium Ellen. There are untold thousands more sitting at home following as best they can. Beyond them, all over the world there must be tens of thousands willing you on. Many of them will be deriving great strength from the sheer guts and grit you display in the face of all adversity. There are surely many children learning from your bloody-minded determination to succeed that their dreams can also come true if they take matters into their own hands. Then there are all those with their own demons to face - their own battles against the odds. Cancer, leukaemia, polio, autism or just plain crippled either physically or mentally. They will be realising that there might be a life for them as well too. All they need is hope. When they've got it then they mustn't give it up. You were never a giver upper and you've surely given them hope. Get the record for them Ma Petite Ellen . . . Now then Ellen, have a quick look around you. What needs to be done? What haven't you checked recently? Are there any jobs you could do that will help you return home quickly and safely? Hear that crowd roar Merde alors!!!

The following day we crossed the Equator. The doldrums further south had treated us quite well, but the biggest fear for me had been the massive white cloud which was visible on our satellite pictures. I had visions of it eating us up for a day at least, and a day was not something we had to spare. On top of that we also had a worrying system ahead of us, as once through the equatorial area we were going to have to navigate the Azores high-pressure system. This could play the game or not, and if it parked itself over the finish line as it looked like it would for a while we would have a rerun of our transatlantic record the previous June. I calmed myself: we still had 3,000 miles to sail.

But luck, for what felt like the first time in the Atlantic, seemed to be on our side, and we touched the new breeze without drawing to a halt once. In this unpredictable zone where Francis had slowed considerably, we had been allowed to sail straight through. The huge white cloud miraculously disappeared the morning we were due to run into it. As we crossed the Equator we were over one day ahead of Francis, and I called out to the heavens in delight. I had thought long and hard about what gift I would give Neptune as we crossed the line, and had settled on a tiny silver charm I'd had round my neck. I wanted to give him something that mattered to show our appreciation for allowing us to pass there again. Our equatorial crossing was done swiftly, and happily. When the new breeze came in I was shocked into silence, and it must have been hours before I could believe it was there to stay. I was quite emotional as I broke open my tiny bottle of champagne and flung the charm into the sea. Grateful emotion though.

29th jan 2005
'just so that it's on the list'
  there's some movement in the gooseneck – there's a mm or so of play in the horizontal pin just above deck level – the carbon appears to be worn . . . also bearings ****** in the trav. cars and mainsheet blocks at top.
  Skipper ****** – hopefully not beyond repair, but fairly easy to replace – easier to carry out alongside.
  That's all for now
  Ex

Wildlife was a theme for that part of our journey, which I took as a good sign. We had thousands of flying fish around us, and, as we'd passed Trindade on our way north, we even had a booby bird flying along with us. But the greatest of them all was the whale which swam beneath us. My heart was in my mouth. I was in the cockpit, and as I looked forward I saw the huge fin right in front of us. It was so close that there was nothing I could have done to steer round it, and I held my breath, hoping that we didn't hit it. Mobi's noise must have alerted it to our presence, as it appeared to wake, then spin round and swim right beneath our net! As it went beneath us it blew out through its blow hole. I stood there in awe of this huge creature which must have been half the length of Mobi . . . It totally took my breath away.

```
29th Jan 2005
hi m,
    please read this and pass onto the rest of OC . . .
thanks exx
    Well day by day, hour by hour and minute by minute
we're getting closer. Mobi and I are heading North, and
beginning to feel that the end may just be in sight. My
overwhelming emotions right now are those of worry, fear
and doubt. Am I choosing the right sails, have I checked
the right equipment, are we sailing fast enough . . .
many many questions. Though there have been a few
highlights over the past few days, (like mobi meeting
her first whale this morning!) these days are very hard.
I'm stressed - and the next week will feel like a
month . . . But I am thinking about the finish, and about
that moment when I can actually switch off my brain a
bit - knowing that Mobi is safely in the hands of those
who have and will care for her so well . . . Most of all
though, the thing I'm looking forward to the most - is
seeing all of you guys - the team. Seeing your smiles,
and hugging you all . . .
    This really is OUR project, what we are achieving is
down to every one of us - I think I'm just the unlucky
sod that pulled the short straw to be alone for a couple
of months!!
```

Seriously though, I can never begin to describe how
much I am looking forward to seeing you all again, and
being with you all . . .
    I feel frightened, nervous - but probably above all -
very PROUD . . . and that's what we've achieved until
this minute of this day . . .
    savour it . . .

    exx

Though part of me felt we were nearing home, another part was petrified that after all we'd been through we wouldn't make it. Once through the equatorial area the sea got rougher, and we were upwind once again in a boat-breaking, stressful motion. I worried that the headboard car would not hold out, and that I'd not only have to go up the mast again, but that we might damage the mast track irreparably. The further we got, the more we had to lose, and the pressure of that was immense for me on our final leg of the journey home. Though I was being carried by the incredible e-mails and support from those who were close to me, I was in a strange place. I was exhausted but aware that I was nearing home and, almost feeling like I was running out of time, I was more reflective than I had been before. I spoke to the video camera:

It's funny really – it's four o'clock in the morning, and it's black outside. There is no doubt about it there will be a fight to get across the finish line, and there is a huge question mark over the record. But I was sitting out there and looking at the stars and the clouds and I realized how much I love it out here. The hard part of this record is the pressure, it's the constant changing, and it's the fact that you're driving yourself so hard. But just being out here under the stars, being on board the boat, it's a different life; so different. Twenty-four hours a day you're thinking about the boat and the weather and what's around you. It's a huge change from life on land, where you're thinking about so many other things. Here there is a lot to deal with, but in so many ways it's simple; very, very simple. It's amazing really. I was just sitting outside thinking how happy I am. How fantastic it is just to be here in the middle of the Atlantic. I must be one of the luckiest people in the world.

I picked the camera up again the following day. The mixture of emotions was still flowing through my brain and my body like electricity. At this stage in the journey everything was more intense and, as I lay in my bunk about to take a nap, I realized that I couldn't sleep unless I had shared what was going on in my head.

You know, it's funny – I'm lying here, and we have about six days to go, and it feels like eternity really, and half of me, a big part of me, wants to get in just to kind of end the tiredness and the constancy of this which is a huge weight on your shoulders . . . and it has been now for over sixty days, this weight of performing and giving everything you've got. But as I lie here I look at the window, the sun's shining in. We're about a day and a half from the Azores, and I'm sailing a magnificent 75 foot trimaran. And I think all these things and think that I'm so lucky. Just how cool is it to be here coming up to some islands, how cool is it to be here on a sunny day sailing along.

I felt either drunk with happiness or nervous with fear. Not fear of the weather or dying, but the biggest fear that had been hovering over me for the whole trip. Fear of failure.

Back at home the team could feel my exhaustion. We were now just ten days from running out of time, and, though we were nearing home, we all knew too that it wasn't over yet. On the phone, during an interview on our daily conference call, I was asked: 'Will you have to give more than you have already given to get to the finish?' My answer showed them all that I was at low energy ebb:

I've put everything in – my heart, my soul, my flesh, my blood, just everything. I've never pushed this hard, I've never driven myself so hard, and I've never got so close to the edge for so long – never, ever. And it's not through choice, it's just through pushing so hard in the changeable conditions with the demands of a boat like this. It's been a real rollercoaster.

30th January - 2005

I think you do know I understand how deep you have dug
on this. I have never experienced what I have this time
with you, and never want to again either. A record isn't
worth it to be honest. But now we have come this far we
have to do whatever we can together to get to the finish
line, as otherwise it will have been wasted. We are far
enough still away to screw it up, and close enough for
you to feel mega-pressure - the worst place of all
probably! Too early for adrenalin to carry you through,
so far through that the reserves are nearly empty. They
are NOT empty though. I know it. I know it because I've
listened to you on empty, and you are not right there at
the moment. And that gives me hope. As you get closer I
think it can get better as there are some really hidden
reserves that will come in to play for sure, and
ultimately adrenalin as well for the closing stages.

We (especially, me, Lou ('cos she is close to it) and
Kate who was with me on the worst day of all a couple of
weeks ago) really do get it, we really know how fragile
you are at present. And we know how to help you when you
get back for sure, it will be another challenge, but at
least the physical aspect will improve rapidly . . . But
right now it feels very hard for us to help you, we can
just listen and be there. And we are there, believe me,
we are there day and night, more than ever.

You know you can finish, but to break this record you
need to somehow focus what energy you have on yourself.
Whilst you say you are empty now, it is still 100% the
reality that your mind and body are still every hour
fighting back, recovering, restacking, re-energizing,
whenever they can, even in small amounts. You have to
believe that and help it whenever the conditions allow
you. It WILL make a difference, its not a downward
slippery slope, it really isn't. People that have gone
further, in concentration camps, in wars, in the middle

of deserts after a month alone with no water, in much, much worse places have made it. And we can make it.

And you need to do whatever you can to help it. Because each little nugget in is going to help you get there.

Whilst the boat is undoubtedly going to throw something else at us, the constraint I would say is more likely you right now - so treat yourself as a job, a repair task, and although you don't have all the tools and time you need to mend yourself totally, a bodge job will do for now! So whatever DIY you can do, do it! It's obvious you can't disengage, but you can get perspective, you must. Think about the big picture, how much you have done already, and how relatively short the last part is. As Lou says, one day at a time, it was Peter Blake's best ever quote - one watch at a time.

Do your best and we will make it.

Massive hugs and love and as much energy as is possible to send down an email.

M.

Xx

It wasn't just Mark who was sending messages to the boat either. The tension in the office was clearly across the board. Charlie had been as close to Mobi as I had during the training sails and had covered for Mark many times on the phone.

From: 'Charles'
To: 'TRI'
Sent: Tuesday, February 01, 2005 2:31 AM
Subject: Re: email accounts change of settings

I can't really begin to think what it's like - although of course we try to put our selves there for you. the last week will be incredible for you I am sure a huge mixture of emotions, and experiences returning to the

cool, the more familiar areas of the maxsea charts,
stepping down the chart resolutions just like the end of
every trip just take every hr as it comes and goes, every
sunrise and set, each food bag ... just treat them like
any other - do your stuff ... let Mobi do hers, and
what ever will be will be ...

Date: 01/02/2005
Message from First Sea Lord attached:
  We in the Royal Navy are enthralled by your progress
in this ultimate challenge. In this special year for the
Royal Navy as we commemorate the 200th Anniversary of
the death of Admiral Nelson, and as a nation celebrate
our rich maritime heritage, I am especially proud that
we continue to have such outstandingly courageous and
determined seafarers such as you. The finishing gun
beckons and all of us in the Royal Navy will be cheering
you over the line. We wish you God speed for a safe and
truly historic homecoming.
  Admiral Sir Alan West, First Sea Lord.

We'd sailed well in the horrible conditions, and after our luck with
the weather at the Equator, by 2 February we'd managed to claw
back time to be over three days ahead. Though this was great news,
it was also very necessary, as between us and the finish lay not only
a humungous low-pressure system, which was going to test us once
again, but we still had to get through the centre of the Azores high-
pressure system, which, funnily enough, was sitting bang over the
Azores. In the meantime, conditions worsened, and though the
lumpy seas continued, the constant manner of the breeze did not.
At a time when we desperately needed to keep up a good pace to
make gains on the record, the wind was going from 14 knots to 27.
I dozed overnight in the cuddy with my oilskins on, trying to switch
my brain off, but was constantly woken by the horrible motion of
an uncomfortable and over-pressed Mobi, resulting in a night filled
with worry and sail changes. The following morning I managed an
hour in the bunk, but I couldn't sleep at all. I was getting thrown

hard against the side of the bunk as if someone was shaking me violently each time my eyes closed.

Date: 03/02/2005 19:51:27
Subject: Hope Reynolds aged 5 says

Dear Ellen. I know that you are close towards the end of the race. Hope you win. Love Hope ps. Daddy tells me its bed time now – I'll have some sleep for you because he tells me you are very tired now

Two days before we had passed the latitude of the Canary Islands, and we were now coming up to the Azores. The waves still felt square as we approached the islands, making it impossible to sleep: I'd had twenty minutes in twenty-four hours and when the wind slowly began to decrease it made Mobi even more uncomfortable to be aboard. As we neared the Azores and pushed upwind, it was clear that we were going to end up sailing between the islands, and, as wind between islands is often disturbed, we might be in for a difficult time.

It was dark when the islands approached, and it was strange to see the lights of the land for the first time in over two months. I felt they were a distraction that I wasn't looking for at that time, and, as we spent the night battling with a lack of wind, and with Mobi literally going round in circles, I wanted to wish them away. The wind was all over the place for forty-five minutes, then stabilized, and we began sailing upwind. Then it crapped out and swung through 360 degrees four times.

For two hours we stopped totally, I had to roll the genoa and sit there waiting for some wind from some direction. But it's not the still environment you'd imagine: you have 120 square metres of sail above you flapping aggressively from side to side, and each time you change tacks or gybes you have to mess about with the cunningham so that you can push the ten stiff battens which run the full width of the sail through so that their camber is the correct way. The top one is 100 feet above your head, and flicking them from one side to the other was a nightmare. The night was filled with noises of an angry, flogging mainsail, and the autopilot alarm screaming, which kept telling me that it couldn't steer the boat. Nor could I for that matter: if the boat's not moving, you can't make it point where you want. I handled that night badly. Though I did what I had to do for Mobi, I felt like my own emotions were in their first stages of shutting down. I could only just bear what was being thrown at us, and I knew that, if it carried on much longer, I wouldn't be able to.

Finally, by 3 a.m., the wind had steadied, and I managed to eat some dinner. I threw it down so fast that I burnt my mouth, as I was also desperate to sleep with the wind strength relatively stable. After our six-hour battle I was struggling. In the final two hours I'd done seven windless gybes. I dozed, once again totally exhausted. We were five days from our record time running out, and I calculated that we were four and a half days from the finish line. Twelve hours was not much slack after almost seventy days at sea.

The following day I wrote an email to the office:

Hi team.
I'm sitting here with tears in my eyes. Not really knowing what to do with myself. I cannot articulate how I feel, I doubt I shall ever be able to express what this trip has put me through, or continues to put me through . . . there have been some incredible moments, but there have also been those moments which are far too painful to bring back . . . The hardest part is that I know there is little resilience left . . . I'm running so close to empty.

I'm running so close to empty that I believe it's only the energy from others that's keeping me going.

Physically I'm exhausted - not just from the effort of sailing Mobi so hard, it also from the constant motion which makes even standing still impossible. On a scale of one to 10 this has been a 9 point something, and I'd stick the Vendee Globe on a 5 max.

To put it briefly, this trip has taken pretty much ALL

```
I have, every last drop and ounce. It has taken
everything to get this far - and we're still not there
yet. I have never attempted something as hard as this
before - all I want to tell you now is that this will
take a long time to recover from . . . mentally more than
anything else . . . though you know that I will be brave
and give my return to 'normal' life all I can . . .
please note that there are NO reserves, and that I'm
pretty fragile right now.
   I just want you to know how I am inside . . . I'm a
pretty tough person, but this has taken everything. I
chose to do this and I really don't need any sympathy
from anyone, quite the reverse, but I do need to know
you understand how totally exhausted I really am.
```

That afternoon I slept properly for a few hours – the first proper
sleep in a long time – and it paid dividends. The weather gave me the
chance to stay in my bunk for three and a half hours, and I felt amazing. Sleep changed everything. I was calm, collected and rational
despite losing fifteen hours to Francis. The following night we had
really fluky conditions once more which threw the wind all over the
place, but with the sleep I coped better. We were still not out of the
high-pressure centre, which was moving with us, but we were struggling, and I was haunted by visions of being stuck there for a week.

   The following morning the breeze steadied. The sky was clear
and bright, and the contrasting grey sea was now calm and soft.
Mobi could rest for a while, and we could breathe once more as we
slipped quietly along to the gentle sound of the bubbling water.
The sea was a deep but clear blue, and, as I leaned over and filmed
it, I spoke to the camera:

So beautiful. The water's so pure; so, so clear. What's down there?
Millions and millions of animals, and millions of miles of ocean we
don't know anything about. All there, just underneath us now, going
down for miles. Each fish has an incredible story and a life that we'll
never understand.

I spent a good hour on deck that morning, almost to soak in the relief of the steady wind and prove to myself that it really was reality. As the day broke, the golden clouds of the morning sun held their rounded shoulders high for all to see above the horizon. I popped below to check our position and I wrote an e-mail to the team.

```
4th Feb
888
  FALMOUTH IS 888 nautical miles away - and that's our
number!!
  Feel a tad better today, though we're in for a real
arse kicking now ... Not too long ... see you all in a
few days time ...
  love e and mobi!! Xx
```

And when the storm hit it did kick arse. We were forecast to have just 18 knots of breeze, but it was already 28 and gusting 33, and suddenly the finish seemed a very long way away. The storm moved in quickly, and with the huge beam seas forecast of over 25 feet we were getting bashed around again. The sea state wasn't helped by the fact we were approaching the continental shelf, and the active echo was going off much more regularly now. It would inform us of ships it could detect long before my eyeballs beneath my newly donned face mask could see them. Life on board was very rough, and that night I was colder than I had ever been in the Southern Ocean. The freezing northerly wind seemed to be trying to eat right into my soul, and I couldn't stop myself shivering as I stood in the cockpit, staring out. My feet were like ice, and nothing I did warmed them up; I tried jumping up and down, despite the violently moving deck, but it was hopeless. For half an hour at a time I'd try and go below to warm up a little, but it was so rough that I actually had to shut the door. One wave hit us side-on so hard that I was thrown from my bunk, and at the same time it filled our cockpit with water. I feared for Mobi. I was going to be glad to see the sunrise!

The following day amidst the rough sea our first visitors arrived.

We had HMS *Liverpool* for a while, with her helicopter up, a light aircraft which came out of Spain and a Nimrod. I remember feeling that we needed air traffic control out there! I felt quite numb as the vessels and aircraft all disappeared. We'd lost a further fourteen hours to Francis, and that night, as we tacked over towards the Bay of Biscay, we were kept on our toes. Getting through the Bay of Biscay was vital, and with a small low off the coast of Spain there was a risk that we could get stuck in it. Over the previous twenty-four hours we had only managed to make 100 miles towards the finish line, whereas at this point Francis had been storming towards the finish with over 400 miles covered in his day. Though in theory it should have been our last night at sea, I was beginning to doubt it. The wind had died, and we had a really shitty transition to get through. Not only that, but now we were approaching the coastline there were more and more ships to avoid. Time seemed to stand still, and we had everything from lightning to 40 knot gusts to not a lot of wind and a horrible sea. That night I only managed fifteen minutes' sleep, and with the erratic wind shifting through 100 degrees I ended up having to tack eleven times. I could not have been running on anything but adrenalin, as we fought our way north through the temperamental darkness to get to some decent wind. Despite our efforts our lead had dropped down to just over one day by daybreak, and the following morning we were still searching for clear air 200 miles from the finish.

But I knew we were getting ever nearer to home, and, despite the struggle, the record was still on. It was not over till it was over; what with rocks, ships and other obstacles more numerous now than at any stage since the start, but we were close. And as long as the wind did not do to us what it did at the end of the transatlantic record, we were in a strong position. Once the breeze filled in from the east as forecast our chances of making it would be significantly increased, and that day, for the first time in the record, I let myself feel that first glimmer of hope that we really were in with a chance.

I felt utter joy when the new wind filled in and we began to speed towards the north-west tip of France. Just before dark that night Thierry came out in the helicopter. I was 60 miles offshore, and

I was just close enough for the chopper to make it to spend fifteen minutes around me. There was something very special about that visit, and, though our record wasn't over, I began to realize that soon it would be. On seeing Thierry I felt like I could share what we had achieved in some way, and I waved as hard as I could possibly wave with a huge smile on my face and ran around to check that Mobi was as tidy as she could possibly be for her photographs!

As that evening drew in I made my final meal alone at sea, and for one of the rare times during the record I put on the stereo. I bopped along to the music, singing out loud as my head-torch bounced light around our dark homely cabin. Filled with a feeling of contentment, it wasn't just my voice alone which was singing: it was joined in a duet with my heart.

When I smelt land for the first time it was a feeling of total and utter sensual overload. It was the most powerful familiar yet unfamiliar smell I'd ever smelt and the first reminder to me of just how different my life would be less than twenty-four hours later. By that stage I could clearly make out the lighthouse which marked the south end of our finish line, and when I thought back to the morning seventy-one and a half days before when we had last set eyes on it I had a lump in my throat. So many adventures had happened since then, and now we'd come full circle, to stop in exactly the same place we started from. As we approached the line, the bright white light made Mobi's sails shine . . .

The finish gun fired. It was 22:29:17 GMT on 7 February 2005. We, Mobi and I, had sailed 27,354 miles in 71 days, 14 hours, 18 minutes and 33 seconds taking 1 day, 8 hours, 35 minutes 49 seconds from Francis's record.

We had done it.

Chapter Fourteen

I slumped down on the cockpit floor. It was over. The record was over, and now nothing – no breakages, squalls or problems – could take it away from us.

Strangely, at that moment, there was nothing inside but a numbness, almost as if my body was working out what it should be feeling. Everything seemed familiar, but inside I felt empty. The sole focus of every minute of every day had suddenly gone, and it had taken any direction we had with it. The constant was that we were still alone, though finally, second by second, the adrenalin could cease to flow.

I turned Mobi into the wind, and we waited; then the breeze died and we floated aimlessly in the water. I laid my head back on to her cockpit side, something I had done many times before. I looked up – the little strobe light was flashing away at the top of her mast. The night was pitch-black, apart from the odd searchlight from the helicopters above us, and the symbolic beam of the lighthouse rhythmically lighting up our mainsail, which marked the finish line and the end of our relentless journey.

I shut my eyes to momentarily close the world off around us and drew in a long breath of the cold evening air. My head was spinning, and slowly the emptiness began to be replaced by a feeling of pure relief. It was almost as if I needed a few moments to work out what relief felt like again, as adrenalin had been pumping hard into my veins for months. I no longer needed to be tuned into the instruments and alarms, live with that constant anxiety that an increase in wind speed or a sudden change in wind direction could lead to capsize, or listen for the tiniest noise which might indicate a problem. I just couldn't believe that it was all over; a huge part of my life was missing. I felt quiet, empty and alone.

Although I knew that the team were nearby on HMS *Severn*, the Navy ship from which the finish gun had fired, for now I could see no one. No faces, no figures, just a few distant lights, in one of the dark nights which blended into the days that we were now so very accustomed to. I silently thanked Mobi. There were no words, just an exchange in the language in which she'd talked to me out there, a language through which she'd wake me from my sleep to let me know she was in need of a little help. She'd withstood so much, faultlessly dealing with every problem which was thrown our way; averaging over 20 knots through a force 9 gale deep in the Southern Ocean, creeping along in the light airs, protecting me as I slept in her womb-like cuddy. Whatever the weather threw at us to try to trip us up, she dealt with it. She was always there watching out for me, as I was for her. If a boat could ever have a soul, then she did.

Looking back, I am glad that I had that time to slip over the finish line alone, to make sense of what we'd been through. In a way it was what I had craved four years earlier at the end of the Vendée. Back then, when I crossed the line, it was already too late. When that focus suddenly goes you travel to a strange place inside where you feel relieved, but at the same time there is a huge hole which suddenly appears. This time at least I was prepared for that, and, unlike the finish of the Vendée Globe, I did not feel so afraid.

Despite coming to terms with what we'd been through I could not have been more aware that there was a big piece missing, as so many other people had also put their heart and soul into this project, and without them around me the fact we'd broken the record meant nothing. For years we had lived and worked like a family, supporting each other and working on our beloved boat as if there was no tomorrow. We'd shared each other's worries, solved problems, found solutions – together. The team had followed every heartbeat of our journey from afar, but none of them were here. So that night, when the tiny boat appeared out of the darkness, my heart began to leap. And when the survival-suit-clad guys, my friends and team members, scrambled up and over Mobi's back beam to hold me safely in their arms, I knew we'd done it. *We finally had our record.* It was the most all-consuming emotion you could imagine: as if every e-mail, every thought and every bit of the preparation beforehand was encapsulated by each of their embraces. My mind was drunk with the feeling of gratitude and pleasure; seeing them all meant the absolute world to me. I nearly exploded with happiness, and if I could have leapt up high and reached the stars to show them all how much they meant to me then I would have. I held them all so tight, as they did me – it was the most unbelievable feeling to contrast with the long months without any human contact. It was at that moment the reality of what we had achieved came alive for me. I felt so safe and so happy that I was sure I was in heaven; I could have closed my eyes and lived in that moment for ever . . .

After swapping stories and sharing as much as I could with them all, I lay down in my bunk, utterly and totally burnt out. Mobi was sailing gently along under the cover of darkness, and I smiled to myself as I heard the totally unfamiliar sound of footsteps moving around in her cockpit. It all felt so safe and secure. I was finally able to remove my boots and waterproofs and snuggle up in my sleeping bag – knowing full well that on deck were the most incredible people, who were now watching over us.

Kevin, the team medic and my friend, had come on board and, as I lay in my sleeping bag, with my head on my salty pillow, he was taking my blood. As he worked we chatted to Nick, who'd had his hopes dashed of completing the Vendée Globe in my old *Kingfisher* when his keel had sheared off near the Brazilian coast. He had put his head through the hatch, and we compared our lives at sea. I remember lying there looking up at the chart table. 'It's so strange looking at that wind graph,' I said. 'I've been watching that every day since I left – and looking at it now it's hard to comprehend that it doesn't matter any more.' As my eyes finally closed I began to fall asleep to the sound of chatting and laughter in the cockpit above me. And in that moment – to me – it was the most precious sound in the world.

Waking in my bunk now the record was over was an unnatural experience. How my brain and body knew that I could sleep for a whole night I have no idea, but it did. Perhaps it was my self-preservation mechanism kicking in? You certainly pace yourself pretty accurately to arrive at the finish on the few energy reserves you have left. My first thought as I woke was one of nerves and stress, like waking from a nightmare. I knew I had been asleep for a long time and I was still at sea, and I knew that I had dropped my guard. It took a few seconds to realize that it was all over, and, as I opened my eyes with a new-found relief in my heart, the first part of our welcome to land was before me. On my chart table seat was a foil-wrapped package with a Post-it note saying 'Ellen – with love, Severn'. It was a still-warm bacon and sausage sandwich, and its wonderful smell had probably been what woke me from my sleep!

As the sun rose on that chilly February morning I appeared on deck to smiling faces. I felt so excited! Today was the day I was going to be able to see my Mum, Dad and family, the remaining team members who had not been able to come out to the finish line and those who were dear to me. I was taken aback too as I could see that we were no longer alone, and, bar the Navy ships that had briefly visited me on the round-the-world, it was something quite new compared to our previous months of solitude. There were a few ribs out with us, HMS *Severn* of course, and, minute by minute, hour by hour, there were more and more boats heading out to see us in. I felt as if I was in the middle of someone else's life. It was the beginning of February in Falmouth – surely this must be a dream. I waved to people and shouted hello back to so many, but the sheer numbers were really quite staggering. There were many familiar faces, which I saw one by one, people I'd worked with, people I'd sailed with, people who'd helped so much in my career. It really was like being in a dream: too good to be true. The early-morning eastern light warmed all it touched with its gentle pink haze, and its presence signalled blue skies for our first sighting of the UK coast.

Then I spotted a very familiar face: that of Mark. I had been keeping my eyes open for familiar faces in the boats all around us, and in that moment there was the most incredible transfer of emotion between us. Over the previous seventy-one days we had shared everything. He had been on the end of a phone for twenty-four hours a day since I had left Falmouth, and, though we could speak and discuss things, he, like the rest of the team, had been entirely helpless. The rib drew nearer, and I climbed down on to the platform at Mobi's stern; I could see excitement and relief on his face. He stepped on and threw his arms around me, holding me tight, with one hand on my head ruffling my hair. I could feel him sobbing with pleasure, and, as I pressed my face into his shoulder, I began sobbing too.

Soon after, Mum, Dad, Fergus and his girlfriend, Rosie, appeared in a boat, driven by my old friends Howard and Pete, who had towed *Kingfisher* out for the start of the Vendée Globe. It was so wonderful to see them all again, Mum had almost not come down for the finish – but I was so glad that she had made it. To be able to see them in the flesh was absolutely fantastic, but to be able to see the happiness in their faces was even better. One of the things which really told me I was at home was Mum throwing me a mango. In typical Mum fashion she called 'They were two for one' as she tossed it to me. I smiled from ear to ear, and even more inside. We hadn't even had time to hug at that stage. Luckily enough I had a knife on me all the time, so amongst the total madness of all that was going on around me I sat on good old Mobi's deck and devoured Mum's mango! That was the first fresh food I'd tasted for two and a half months.

The number of boats which came out to see us was staggering. Never in a million years could I have imagined something like this. There were canoes, dinghies, huge motorboats, tugs, fishing boats, yachts and ribs. It seemed like anyone who had access to anything which floated was out on the water. The sea was quite flat, which was a relief, as it made the 'sortie' a bit easier for some of the smaller boats. To be in the middle of that whole event was an incredible feeling for anyone out there on the water, but it seemed to me totally implausible that I was the reason everyone was there.

As we rounded the headland, the Maritime Museum came into view. Though perhaps I should have been thinking of other things, I smiled to myself inside. I was overjoyed by the fact that seventy-three days earlier we had left from the same place, and the hands about to tie those lines back to the dock were the same as those which had cast them off. There is something quite comforting about returning to somewhere which feels familiar after such an ordeal, and despite all you've been through there is a certain sentiment of coming home to a place which will not have changed too much during the months you are away. My mind flicked back to the countryside I had gone running through in November while preparing for the record. I had thought long and hard then about returning to this same place, and now we were here. I could see the hills behind the beautiful town of Falmouth, but as I glanced down at the docks in front of the Maritime Museum my mind flicked into action. It was time to get Mobi back on to the dock, where finally she would be able to rest. Her huge mast dwarfed all around her, and as I concentrated on proudly steering the most wonderful boat in the world back on to her berth, the mayhem around us momentarily disappeared. Yes, we had managed to break the record, but now, at the end of it, we really were home.

Moments later, amidst the most incredible air of excitement, I was in the arms of my Mum and Dad. In the Southern Ocean storm on Christmas Day they could not have felt further away, now they were so close I could touch them. Being able to look into their eyes with joy, relief and a million stories shared from afar seemed surreal. Everything shut off for me at that moment: the crowds huddled along the railings, and the hundreds of people crammed on to the pontoon. I was relieved it was over. I had not let them down and I had made it back in one piece.

Chapter Fifteen

Nothing could have prepared me for the feeling I had as I walked up and on to the stage outside the Maritime Museum. There were literally thousands of people, waving, cheering. It was too much to take in that everyone had come here, to Falmouth, to see Mobi and me come home, and I found myself smiling, with two words bouncing round my brain: 'thank you'. Individual moments stand out: I remember seeing that huge digital clock which had been placed on the stage behind me – STOPPED! That was it, it was over, done and dusted.

I was joined on stage by Sir Robin Knox-Johnston, a man whose exploits I had studied as a child. It was the second time he had stood on a stage beside me, as he was joint Yachtsman of the Year when I won the Young Sailor of the Year award aged eighteen, almost exactly ten years before. Robin was the first person in history to sail solo non-stop round the world, and I was over the moon to share my homecoming with him. Robin knew what this was all about. He not only understood what it was like to sail solo round the world, but later became one of the few people to have done it crewed in a multihull. There we stood, as my good friend the sailing presenter Richard Simmonds, our MC, stated, 'the first; and the fastest'. What a memorable moment in my life.

After I spoke on the stage and answered Richard's questions, I talked about the Southern Ocean and the storms we had weathered. But, as I spoke, I felt uncomfortable, and to some extent insincere; I really felt I had not achieved the record on my own. Even in my first hours since crossing the finish line I knew that what had brought me the most pleasure in the whole project was the spirit we had in the team: those incredible individuals who had brought so much to all that we did, who had kept me going when times had been difficult, not only through their e-mails at the time, but through the sheer amount they had given of themselves to the project. 'I'm very proud to have the round-the-world record, but I'm even more proud to be working with the best team of people as far as I'm concerned in the whole world.' They were inspirational people in their own right, and I was so proud to know them all. For me sharing this high point with them was priceless.

At this moment they came up on to the stage to join me, and for me the day could have ended there. It was perfect, we were together, we had done it, and it was over . . .

Looking back on the videos of the finish there was one question I was asked just as I was leaving the stage steps: 'Is this the best day of your life?'

I paused briefly before answering: 'I'm sure that's still to come – but it's not a bad one!'

In the middle of all that was going on, on reflection I thought that was an interesting answer.

It's funny, though, that amongst this mayhem I felt that though the world around me was advancing at a ridiculous pace, I wasn't. Inside I felt calm and measured; I felt in control and as if I was 'looking in' on all that was unfolding around me. I was not as shocked as I had been after the Vendée. This time I had a much better idea of what to expect, and knew that, though I was mentally and physically exhausted, it was no longer life-threatening. Life on land felt very trivial compared to life at sea on the boat in some ways. Not the big things, of course, but the stress people feel about things that really don't matter in life surprises you when you've been some-where quite different for a while. I don't think I could ever imagine being more stressed and ground down than I was on board Mobi. One measured and calm response to a question asked by Richard

Simmonds said it all: 'I honestly believe I cannot go further than I went in this trip, else I won't come home – that's the reality.'

There was something else which surprised me too. Mark had received an e-mail from Claude Breton, the Chairman of the World Sailing Speed Racing Council, who had been standing on the finish line in the lighthouse on the island of L'Ouessant in France.

It said:

```
Dear Mark,
I am back home and took the time to check something I
thought this night. I had not all my documentation with
me on Ouessant, but now I can confirm something which
could be interesting for your communication:
  In 1997, for his round the world crewed attempt on
'Sport Elec' (the current 'IDEC', Joyon's boat) in the
framework of the Jules Verne trophy did a new crewed
around the world, world record in . . . 71d 14h 22m 08s
and Ellen, single handed, yesterday night did . . . 71d
14h 18m 33s!
  It is so amazing, just 3m 35s less, so I wanted to
tell you that.
  Regards,
  Claude
```

When we'd announced my five-year plan back in January 2002, *Sport Elec* held the record for the fastest ever circumnavigation, crewed or not; three years later, solo, I'd just beaten them.

The press coverage was unbelievable, and, though at the time I was unaware just how much live TV had gone on as I'd crossed the finish line and arrived in Falmouth, the following day I did see that the *Telegraph* had produced a 'supplement' which covered just about everything about the record you could imagine. There were satellite trucks all over the place, media everywhere. The team did a fantastic job of keeping things as simple as possible for me, though, and I managed to grab some time with my folks and friends that day. We went back to the place we had stayed while on standby at the beginning of the record attempt, and I well remembered the terrible state of nervousness I'd been in as I had left there on the day of the start. Now I was returning to the same cottage and about to take my first shower in seventy-three days exactly where I had taken the last one. I remember vividly the feeling that night of how lovely it was to wear normal clothes, to feel clean and to do all these things with a warm feeling of relief.

But what I hadn't expected to be doing on my first night on dry land was spending an hour on the phone to Luis. The intensity of all that I'd been through had pushed those memories into the filing system of time, but that night he came back to the fore. He was calling because he didn't know what to do: he was being hounded by one of the tabloids with an offer of thousands of pounds to sell his story. It was hardly new news, as we had not spoken for a year, but that didn't seem to worry them. I could have done without it, but after all I had been through at sea I took it in my stride, which was lucky, I guess, as, despite my advice, he sold it anyway.

Trying to put that behind me, I climbed into bed between clean fresh sheets in a room with no background noise, movement, motion or surprises.

One other factor helped me deal with everything with pragmatism and composure on that first day back, and that was the six hours' sleep I'd had while we sailed to Falmouth across the Channel! Though six hours would be regarded as a short night for most, it was twice as much as I'd had in one long uninterrupted sleep since the start. During the record the most I had slept for was three hours, just once. So on arrival in Falmouth I was not only buoyed by the feeling of being home, but I was also more rested than I had been since I'd left there several months before. On land, for that moment at least, I felt settled.

My time in Falmouth had been a happy time, and now the record was over and we'd made it that happiness was lovely and pure. I was with the team I loved, in a place I loved, with a boat that I loved, and even Mum had been well enough to make it down to the finish. The interviews continued, and the e-mails flooded in, not just to the website, which was struggling to cope with the number of hits we were getting, but also personal e-mails from friends and colleagues.

There were a few comments at the finish from the media about how much easier it was to sail a 75 foot trimaran round the world with modern electronics and navigational aids than it was in the old days. It was almost implied that in the modern era of technology you just need to climb in the boat, press the 'send' button and you will miraculously arrive at the finish – ideally within the required time frame. I'd love to say, 'Just jump on board her and try it for twenty-four hours,' but I can understand why people may think this in a world where we have a piece of technology for virtually every task. I have never had a problem answering the question. I can assure anyone that, if they climbed on Mobi and felt her surge through the waves at 20 knots, they would realize that that couldn't be further from the truth. It's fast, it's stressful and it's brutal. There are rules with a solo record, and one of them is that you are not allowed any hydraulic or electric winches, which means for a start that, when you move the sails around, you do it by hand, and when you hoist the mainsail, you are literally hoisting three times your own body weight up the mast.

When Sir Robin Knox-Johnston became the first person ever to sail solo non-stop around the world he not only achieved something outstanding, he made history. It was unique and extraordinary, and I'm not sure that any record by anyone will ever top what he achieved in 1969. He sailed in the best boat which was available at the time, but it was by no means a racing boat. Robin had quite different challenges to face compared to me. Thirty-five years of technological evolution for a start have made huge differences to the boats themselves. Robin's boat, *Suhaili*, is a 35 foot monohull, compared with Mobi, a multihull at 75 feet. I suppose it's like comparing a modern WRC rally car and a touring car from the late 1960s – apart from having four wheels and an engine, they are totally different. His journey took him 312 days; mine took seventy-one. I have no idea if I would be capable of spending close to a year solo on a boat; it's the most unbelievable amount of time to be alone.

In trying to think of a comparison for the two voyages I came up with the following: it's the difference between driving from Lands End to John O'Groats at an average of 20 mph with only a map in fog, or driving there at an average of 80 mph with a GPS but no brakes.

The way that I see it is that there are positives and negatives to racing now as opposed to when Robin took to sea forty years ago. The positives are that you know where you are, and if you are in danger you are able to alert someone – albeit that they might be five days away in the Southern Ocean. The negatives are that, though your boat is very fast, the loads are much greater, and sailing her twenty-four hours a day, seven days a week, has to be one of the most stressful occupations I can imagine. It's intense – very intense, and for a very long time. I'm not sure forty years ago that the stress levels would have been the same because of the speed, but they may have been the same because you had no sun appearing from behind the clouds to navigate with, or you did not know where you were. I knew what weather was going to come my way, Robin didn't. At the end of the day they are different journeys, and are almost impossible to compare. But if there is someone to ask, it's Robin, as he's done both and inspirationally: at fifty-eight, he has just completed his third navigation under sail. He is a total legend.

There was one evening, just a few days after the finish of the record, when the whole team got together for a dinner, and a few friends joined us. It was the fiftieth birthday of Albert, our technical director, who had been an absolute stalwart in the project, and his birthday was a great excuse for our get-together. It was a great event at which we could finally all catch up and talk properly for the first time since I had returned, and it felt like a family outing for us. We had a great laugh about Oli's observation that all visitors who had come to Falmouth to visit Mobi from Derbyshire were described as being from 'landlocked Derbyshire', as if it could not be said in Falmouth without first pointing out that it was 'stranded' from the coast! I pointed out that I'd looked everywhere for the pair of gloves that I'd used in the Vendée to take round the world with me but, as

I couldn't find them, I had to buy some more – only to discover, on arrival in Falmouth before the start, that they were locked in an exhibit cabinet in the Maritime Museum together with other items from the Vendée Globe! We talked, laughed and celebrated a project which everyone round the table had played a role in somehow.

We continued our evening by going into the room next door and watching the ITV documentary for which I had filmed an interview just days before. I was quite excited to be sharing the record with the team in this way. No one, not even I, had seen any of the footage since I had shot it at sea, so it was with great anticipation that we all gathered round together in the little room at the hotel, some of us on chairs, some on the floor. The first thing which hit me was the level of emotion. I knew that of all the original twenty-four hours of footage perhaps only ten minutes of it was emotional. But the reality of TV is that, when the programme is made, all of the most moving emotional footage will be shown. Perhaps I would have seemed much more of a 'hero' if I'd come back without the footage of the bad bits. It would certainly have been a much easier task if I hadn't filmed those parts of the journey; but I chose to share the downs just as much as the ups, and though I didn't *need* to film myself in a totally exhausted state, in doing so I was being honest about what really happens out there. In the Vendée four years before I had also made a decision to film the hard bits. I know for a fact that the only part of the race where I 'cracked', if that's what you'd call it, was a few weeks before the finish. I had to climb the mast two days in a row, following which I went into the lead briefly; I then lost any chance I had of recovering the lead when I hit a submerged object and broke my daggerboard – and, to add insult to injury, the forestay snapped five days from the finish. That was a pretty nasty run of bad luck, and, exhausted after pushing so hard for two and a half months as I was, it's probably not surprising that I had a fairly large sense of humour failure. I know that the winner of the Vendée Globe I competed in, Michel Desjoyeaux, and Roland Jourdain, who finished a day behind me and third in that race, both screamed at their cameras and punched various parts of their boats. Putting yourself under that much pressure for that long is something you can cope with; you can pace yourself. But when something serious goes wrong it does feel like your world is falling apart; in many cases, the boat, your world, quite literally is.

Watching the programme also triggered off a reaction which I would experience more than once during the year. It showed me how our bodies adapt to a situation and often deal with crisis instinctively. This feeling was triggered by a piece of footage which I'd filmed on one of the rare occasions I tried to sleep in my bunk. You could see me climb into my bunk, then just moments after I had pulled the sleeping bag over myself the wind speed alarm went off, and the strange thing was that, sitting on the floor of that room, my body filled instantly with adrenalin. My fingers and arms were tense, and I was ready to leap into action. There is no question that my mind knew that the record was over, and that I was sitting in the safety of a building with a group of people I would trust with my life. But the 'instinct' in my body did not understand this: what I experienced was that same reaction which over the previous two and a half months had almost certainly saved my life. That's not something which you can easily just switch off once the journey is over. From my experience our memories tend to favour the good moments in life over the difficult moments; I would think that this is one of the reasons we are able to go out and do something again that we have already found extremely difficult, if not fairly traumatic, once before. Though the excitement of finishing had temporarily wiped some of the more painful memories of this record away, they were soon to return while I watched this programme.

But it wasn't just the adrenalin which flowed either; there were other changes in my body I noticed with time. The total lack of interest in food was one. As food had been purely a fuel and in no way a pleasure, I didn't care at all about what I ate as it no longer mattered to me, and it felt strange seeing food on land 'advertised' for how little energy it had in it rather than how much!

Most people assume that it is loneliness or physical hardship that is the most challenging part of a record; the being at sea for so long without company, the lack of facilities or fresh food of any sort. The reality is, though, that the hardest thing is the sleep and the stress – and the two are integrally linked. During the record five hours was the average sleep I would get per twenty-four hours, and the longest amount of sleep I had uninterrupted was three hours – just once. The stress comes from living constantly at a fast pace, and with a very real risk of capsizing the boat in almost any of the conditions you would experience at sea. It's not just the worry of sailing in storms in the Southern Ocean, but also the risks associated with squalls in the trade winds, or unstable conditions after the passage of a front. It really doesn't take many more knots of wind to be too much wind.

Even if I managed to survive inside the boat then there would be no chance of saving Mobi. For me that was unthinkable – to lose her would have been wrong. The thousands of hours of work which had gone into building the most unbelievable boat did not warrant such a disastrous end. I simply had to keep her in one piece. The team had written me a little note – 'THIS WAY UP' – just inside the doorway; it was put there with a smile, but underneath we all knew that there was a very real risk.

People often ask if I've ever fallen overboard on a race or record, and seem rather shocked with the answer that if I had I wouldn't be here. The boat is steered by autopilot the majority of the time – and the autopilot has no idea if you are on or off the boat unless you are able to tell it. We looked at trying to stop the boat if I fell overboard, but the reality was that, even if I could tack or gybe the boat, being so light and with so much sail area she'd drift along faster than I would ever be able to swim. So our idea for a system that would try to alter those odds was a one-man life-raft that would launch from the back of the boat if I went overboard. We even talked about what would be stored in the life-raft. It would be unlikely that you would survive for long in one in the Southern Ocean, but it would at least give you a small chance. We talked about putting a satellite phone in there, but I decided that as soon as you could speak to someone you'd probably give up. You'd be so comforted by words that you would drift off into hypothermia. I chose to put a pager in there so that messages could be sent to me, but I couldn't communicate back. I felt that would keep me fighting.

In the end, though, our survival system was never put on board Mobi, as the device I would have had to have with me all the time would have been too bulky. We consoled ourselves by deciding that I'd just be more careful and not fall off the boat anyway. Luckily I lived up to that expectation.

Chapter Sixteen

Following Falmouth the homecomings in London and Cowes were incredible, and to have so many people come out to see us in the middle of the winter really was astonishing. Both times I was intensely humbled by the size and enthusiasm of the crowd: it was all so overwhelming. Life was crazy, though there was some time off – and a few things happened that I would never have imagined. Returning home to be decorated by the Queen with a Damehood was not only unexpected, but a huge honour. I wished the whole team could have received honours too. What was also incredible was that President Chirac also chose to bestow France's highest award, the Légion d'Honneur, on me.

Once our beloved Mobi had been properly welcomed home we took her to our European base of Lorient in France to be refitted ready for our next attempt at the solo transatlantic record later that summer.

Though working with the team had always been such a great pleasure despite the pressures we were under, there was no question that, now the round-the-world record was secure, everyone's attitude was much more relaxed. We had more time to talk, more time to discuss each other's interests, hopes and dreams. And, perhaps, with the record over, we had more time to look outside the almost insular world we had all been living in for years which had enabled us to concentrate singularly on the task in hand.

We were based in one of the modern hangars of the old BSM, or 'base sous-marine', an old submarine base from the Second World

War. A sailing centre of excellence had been created there, and it had become home to several sailing teams. The old concrete submarine bases were imposing buildings: huge walls, many of which were 3 metres thick, and high roofs, again thick with concrete, covered in layer upon layer of boulders to protect them from any falling bombs. There were massive bays underneath where the submarines would have moored: long, dark watery corridors. Inside the place was eerie and damp, with the sounds of water slowly dripping from the roof into puddles and echoing along the unlit walkways. You expected to hear voices, commands, and huge, thunderous noises as the building was rocked by explosions . . . The doors were huge and made of steel, and some were wedged either closed or open as the bomb damage lowered the roof. It's the kind of place that sends your senses and imagination into overdrive as you wonder just who or what has been entombed in those rooms from that terrifying moment. You feel like you have entered another world in those buildings; in fact, in many ways you have. It is a world that no one of my generation will have experienced, but a world which is not far from any of us. My Mum and Dad were both born at the end of the Second World War, and my Gran at the end of the First. My immediate family were lucky in that neither my Grandpa nor Great Granddad were killed in the wars. My Great Granddad spent his life down the pits and, as a coal miner, essential to the functioning of our nation, did not go to war. My Grandpa did go: he went to Germany, and one of the most moving things I've read in a long time was his tiny little diary written while he was out there. Grandpa was not a strong man, and I cannot imagine how scared he and his fellow soldiers must have felt confronted with the brutality of war.

It had proved impossible to demolish these buildings as they were built so that they couldn't be destroyed. For years as I remember they had diggers on the roof removing boulders by the hundreds of tons so that they could seal the roof in some way. Some of the submarine bays were now being used by industry, though those by the water were not.

There is a specific day that I remember: 1 May 2005. There was a small pause in our schedule: we had delivered Mobi to Lorient, and, though nothing dramatic happened, it was one of the first times that my mind actually had space to think. That day was a Sunday, and with the afternoon free (an almost unknown occurrence for us), we decided to take a look around the *Viktor Pleven*. She was a retired factory fishing boat built in the early 1970s, was painted cream and light green, and had been there as long as I could remember. She was there as a museum piece and, at just under 300 feet long, she towered over the other boats tied up in the dock, including Mobi. She had been built for cod fishing, and up until 1992, when French fishermen lost their right to fish in the waters of Newfoundland, that's just what she did. As we walked around we were all quite shocked by her sheer size. She didn't feel like a fishing boat at all, but more like a ship, as she was just so big. Looking inside her cabins and accommodation made you feel quite uneasy, like walking around uninvited in a house you knew was someone's home. Feeling the chill of her steel hull, the dampness of her packing areas, the galley and cabins, was really odd for me. It was like looking into a dead space. Like something dramatic had happened there, and everyone had left. It felt quite unnatural to be there, and you could almost imagine that a fisherman would appear from behind a bulkhead and ask us to get off the ship as it was about to leave. In the wheelhouse was ancient equipment which was still being used up until 1994, and there were photos, one of a ship in the Arctic Ice – clearly a place she had sailed in her days. There was a photo of a net bulging over her decks absolutely crammed to the brim with fish. But the thing that shocked me most about that tour of the *Viktor Pleven* was looking at some of the paperwork on display. There was an accounts sheet placed under glass showing that in one trip 341 tonnes of fish were caught, with profits of £500,000. That's an awful lot of fish to land in one go. I felt sad for her, firstly because so many fishermen who crewed aboard her had obviously lost their jobs, but also because her era seemed to be over.

That afternoon, feeling in rather a thoughtful mood, we decided to do something different, and as Joni, a girl who had just begun to work with us on Mobi, and I were at a loose end we decided to jump in the little white rib we used to shunt Mobi about with and head up the Blavet River. There are two rivers which head inland from Lorient, the Scorff and the Blavet, but looking at the charts, we thought that the Blavet with its green banks and wiggly waterway seemed like a great place to go exploring. Our little cruise up the river was strange really, like an ultra-short break, and a pause in time. The river was absolutely stunning as we wound along it on the tide. We passed the huge concrete submarine base followed by the tiny Ile Saint Michel in the middle of the estuary. We passed beneath one of the main road bridges which crossed the river high above us before things quietened off, and our world became closer to nature again.

The Blavet was your classic beautiful coastal river, with trees reaching almost down to the water, seabirds calling as they fed on the exposed mud banks and the sound of what little wind there was blowing in the trees. It was idyllic, really, apart from the gentle throbbing of our little engine, which broke the peace. I had expected to creep up a green river and see nothing but the river itself, but as we turned the corner we saw fishing boats, not one, two or three, but over forty, all lying there in the mud. We had stumbled upon a boat graveyard ... Some were in reasonable condition, still with paint on, but others you could only just make out beneath the water. It was ghostly and strange to see these craft, people's life, joy and livelihood, left, abandoned and rotting away. Some were ancient and still had masts standing, with rigging hanging limp from them; some had broken masts with the remaining section looking like a broken bone sticking up out of their decks. All looked to be wooden, and the older ones even further up the river were absolutely beautiful when you looked at the graceful curves of their decks. I have heard that it is said that you must not destroy an old boat or else you release evil spirits, and that day I could well believe the old seamen's tales.

The experiences of the day made me think about the past, and about how we have 'forged ahead' with our fishing methods. Funnily enough, Oli had bought me a book by Mark Kurlansky called *Cod: A Biography of the Fish that Changed the World*. I'd read it with fascination and surprise, as it described the rise and dramatic fall of the cod industry. My visit to the *Viktor Pleven* encouraged me to go back into its fact-filled pages to try to understand more about the subject.

It spoke of the introduction of steam trawlers and the fact that they allowed fishing to become a huge industry; with the first steam ships reporting catches six times the size of sailing trawlers it was clear to see that we could take so much more from the oceans and so much more quickly. To show the speed at which the industry developed, the first steam trawler was built in Hull in 1881, and by the 1890s there was not one sailing trawler left there. I remember going into some pubs ten years before when I'd lived in Hull and seeing photos of how things used to be. There was one of Grimsby which had so many fishing smacks in there that you could walk from one side of the docks to the other across the boats. I had sailed to Grimsby many times during my time on the river and remembered the name of the dock, which, like so many other fishing harbours around Britain, had now become a leisure craft marina. Number 3 Fish Dock it was called.

The book described how the 'moratorium' on fishing in New-foundland led to the loss of 30,000 jobs in the fishing industry, those on the *Viktor Pleven* included. Though North Atlantic cod were not biologically extinct, they were commercially extinct in that they were so rare they could no longer be considered commer-cially viable.

As we had walked around the *Viktor Pleven* that morning, her future had been unknown, but on 29 September 2008 she was towed away to be cut up for scrap, having been sold at a token price of €1.

The submarine base, the *Viktor Pleven* and the fishing boats all ap-peared to be linked, as though they were trying to tell me something, carried through a message in an echo of the same forgotten song.

In May and June alone I did presentations or appearances in London, Barcelona, Lisbon, Austria, Oslo, Wales, Scotland, France, Lausanne and Geneva, received a Laurius Sports award in Portugal, and still found time to spend a few days in Skye, compete in the Bol D'or, go on a long offshore training session in France, attempt a Channel record on Mobi, spend time in Chamonix with Mark discussing the future and wear full military dress for the Royal Navy Fleet review in the Solent. It was a busy time!

The plan for the rest of the year once the refit was over was to undertake corporate hospitality in France, return to the Isle of Wight for Cowes Week and more guest sailing, then head for America to have another crack at the transatlantic record in Mobi. In tandem, I would be training in France with Bilou on his IMOCA 60; *Sill et Veolia*. He is one of the nicest people I have ever met, and I'd agreed to sail the Jacques Vabre with him that November. We had become friends ever since we'd raced against each other in 2000, some five years before, and when he asked me it was an opportunity I just couldn't resist. It was also an exciting prospect for me, as there was a more serious agenda behind it for me. I had begun to think once again about my next sailing challenges, and the boats I could see myself in were the IMOCA 60s. I loved them, it was an amazing fleet, and with Bilou's boat being a new-generation 60, it would bring me up to speed.

Knowing that there was a lot to achieve if I added the training and race-qualifying journey with Bilou into the mix, we decided that it was best if I sailed only the second part of the Atlantic delivery of Mobi to New York, where once again we were to sit on standby for the transatlantic record. I would sail from Newfoundland onwards with my faithful training companion Charlie, and Loik, Kate, Seb and a French friend of ours called Lalou would do the first leg to Newfoundland. Ever since watching the film *The Shipping News* during the delivery of Mobi I had been interested in the region, and to have the chance to sail out of there was going to be fantastic.

After a crazy schedule of sailing in the UK and France she left at the end of Cowes Week, allowing me a few days to head off up to Derbyshire to see Mum and Dad. It was the strangest sensation ever watching her sail off into the sunset without me. I didn't know what to feel.

But there was a different aspect to that year too, one which had not been in any plan, and nor was I expecting. Ian and I had known each other since the previous summer and we got on well, sharing many of the same interests. We had met as we worked together during Cowes Week, as he drove one of the boats. We had chatted often, waiting for guests to arrive, or while ferrying people here and there, and we were both aware that we were on the same wavelength.

The good thing about Ian was that he knew who I was. I'd borrowed his air tools the previous autumn at the workshop where he lived, as my old rusty truck was in such bad condition. He had seen me working away under the chassis in my filthy boiler suit and rigger boots, with as much of the delicious paste of Waxoyl and rust on me as you could imagine. He knew the real Ellen, and it was the real Ellen that he began to go out with during the year after the record attempt. Though he respected me for what I'd done, he didn't give a damn that I was someone who might be well known, and having met me in the 'media spotlight' of Cowes Week, he was under no illusion of what my life could be like.

Ian reminded me of home, and a trip out for the day for him wasn't going out to a nice restaurant or dressing up for the races. Like me, he was happier packing a few sandwiches and a flask and heading off on a boat or otherwise for a bit of exploring. I'd grown up like that, and I found our similarities reassuring. He also liked projects and making things, and we were as happy talking about adventures as we were philosophy or even the downside of carburettors! Thanks to playing sport and being active outdoors he was strong. He was also quite a bit taller than me, though admittedly that's not hard, and his tanned face sat nicely with his sun-bleached mousy brown hair.

Despite how busy I was Ian and I somehow managed to find time together, be it heading west along the coast road, sleeping in the back of his truck under the stars, or visiting Derbyshire and joining Dad at the farm-sales. I even called Gran for her incredible sausage, egg and tomato pie recipe, and we made it in my flat for Ian's birthday. He seemed to slot into my life in the most natural way possible, and it was wonderful and reassuring to have him around. He was a reliable person, and whether he was driving a car or boat I had total faith in him. When he smiled at me he made me feel immensely special, and as we began to fall in love I couldn't believe that I had found someone so perfect.

By the middle of October we could see that the record attempt was not going to be possible, so the team flew to New York to bring Mobi home whilst I headed to France to prepare for the TJV. Ian joined me at the start, and his presence was calming as we prepared for our race. The forecast wasn't too good, but Bilou was a great sailor, and we'd spent a fair bit of time sailing together over the summer, so we were as confident in the race as we could have been. Bilou knew his boat well, as he'd already raced her in the Vendée Globe.

My memories of that TJV are priceless, and probably some of the best I have ever had at sea. Bilou and I got on like a house on fire, and I am not sure I had ever giggled and laughed that much on a boat before. Though we were unquestionably out there to race, we were also out there to have fun, and in my book the two can sit nicely hand in hand. Bilou and I share such similar values and passions that, if we hadn't gelled, it would have been astounding. He, like me, has a huge love of the ocean, but also for the world and people that are around us.

It was a hard, fast and stressful race, and together we encountered all manner of hitches, from a flooded engine and drained battery to a crash gybe in a 38 knot squall. But throughout it Bilou and I managed to see the humour in just about everything that happened. The weather dealt us its worst hand at the Equator, where we lost our lead to our nearest competitor, *Virbac-Paprec*, prompting a close-run contest for the remainder of the race. In the final days nothing we seemed to do could get us ahead of them, and it was terribly frustrating, but we never, ever gave up. Thirty-six hours out we were 28 miles behind them, and in just twenty-four hours we reduced that lead to 14.8. Bilou and I were determined, and we had both seen races won or lost just metres from the finish lines. We made two tactical choices; the first to gybe inshore, which was a gamble that took us down to the 14.8; the second was to try something different at the finish, which took their lead down to 8 miles. When they finished they were just thirty-five minutes ahead of us, and we were pretty disappointed. Together we had made a special team, and even in the final stages we were joking and laughing, making funny gestures with our hands, pointing out to each other what was going on.

The race had been one of the best of my life, and even with a second place finish I wouldn't have been on any other boat out there.

Chapter Seventeen

That year brought with it another sailing event, one which had nothing to do with racing but which would nonetheless make an indelible impression on me. Ever since sailing past Marion Island in the Vendée Globe I had dreamt of sailing down to the islands of the Southern Ocean. I remember vividly seeing the lush green slopes of an island over 1,000 miles away from mainland South Africa, and I had expected that an isolated island only 100 miles from the Antarctic convergence would be black and icy, not green and lush. It took me totally by surprise and had a great impact on me, and it was an image that I would not be able to ignore. For days after we'd sailed past we had sea birds following the boat. It felt like the island created a haven for wildlife and provided a home, nesting and I guess a whole wealth of foodstuffs as the deep waters pushed around its shores bringing nutrients up from below. It wasn't until two years later, though, that my imagination would revisit those islands.

Almost exactly two years before my round-the-world record we had been dismasted on *Kingfisher II*. At the time we were only 60 miles to the east of the Kerguelen Islands, an archipelago of islands 1,200 miles to the east of Marion Island, and still, of course, deep in the Southern Ocean. It was during this period that I began carefully to study the possibilities of visiting the Southern Ocean islands to actually land on them and communicate what I found there. Since being a small child I have always had a fascination with islands. From my early years reading Arthur Ransome's children's books, I had often dreamt of sailing to and camping on uninhabited islands. I'd spend hours drawing maps of the tiny island on the pond up the road, then sticking it on to my bedroom wall with Blu-tack and falling asleep dreaming of the adventure it held. I'd plan where the settlements would be around it, and where the campfire and tent would be. My imagination has always been quite strong, but where islands were concerned it was unstoppable.

All things considered it was perhaps not so surprising that I sent an e-mail to Sally Poncet, the lady I had met briefly in the Falkland Islands, just ten days after our arrival in Falmouth. Sally had spent a good half of her life exploring these Southern Ocean islands and probably knew them as well as anyone else on the planet. She is a very special person, and one who has done some fairly extra-ordinary stuff herself.

Just before we had left the dockside Sally had passed me several documents. Among them was a wonderful book on her Antarctic experiences, and a report on the dramatic decline in numbers of the wandering albatross on an island called South Georgia. Isolated in the Southern Ocean as part of the South Georgia and South Sandwich Island chain, it's 1,000 miles east of Cape Horn and is below the Antarctic convergence, meaning that it sits in the colder iceberg-strewn currents which circulate around the Antarctic con-tinent. It's 100 miles long, crescent-shaped and has a rugged west coast and a protected east coast with some beautiful off-lying islands. The whole island is covered in the most spectacular scenery: magnificent glaciers and mountains, the highest of which stretches 3,000 metres into the sky. The wandering albatross are the largest birds down there, and birds which I believe sailors have a great respect for. On the darkest days in the most aggressive of storms, with huge waves and breaking seas, they will be there, appearing to fly effortlessly. I have always been amazed by these birds, their huge wingspans of up to 3.5 metres reaching out of their bodies like the most delicately built but powerful glider. You only see them in the Southern Ocean as you circle Antarctica, and they are your companions in the most desolate and hostile part of the world.

I remember Sally's words vividly: 'I think that you might be able to help.' Now, hopefully, I could.

My decision can't have been easy for my family or Ian, as I would be gone for just over two months again, and, worse, immediately after a transatlantic race which would take me away for another month prior to leaving. I am sure that they were reassured by the fact that this time I would not be alone, I'd once again be away for Christmas.

I had managed to meet with Sally several times during the summer, and we discussed our plans for the winter. I had always been fascinated by the south, and the plight of the albatross gave me a rare and valued opportunity to discover this icy wilderness. But what I didn't know then was that in South Georgia I'd be finding something that I wasn't looking for. Far greater than the sum of its parts, it was going to be one of the most important moments in my life. In South Georgia I would begin to see the whole world in a different way.

On my return from the finish of the Transat Jacques Vabre I had just two brief weeks at home before heading off on my journey to South Georgia.

But before I left I had a number of commitments, which included interviews in London, the Paris Boat Show, two days' team-building with the team at OC, my lap round the *Top Gear* race-track and finally the BBC Sports Personality of the Year award.

I surprised myself with just how nervous I was the morning of the *Top Gear* event. On arrival I got the prize for the biggest entourage ever, as half of the team decided to come and watch as well! It was an OC day out for many of us, and there had not been many of them over the years. I was surprised to find out that the filming was going on in the adjacent studio while I was out on the track. The legendary Stig was there of course, and he began by driving me round the track. First he drove slowly, then he drove quickly, and already my adrenalin began to flow. He seemed like a nice man, quite calm and collected, and was, luckily for me, patient with his students! We then swapped. I would drive twice round with him in the passenger seat before he stepped out to leave me to it. My first comment on seeing a full fuel gauge was: 'Does everyone start with a full tank of fuel?' It was natural for me: less fuel is lighter and faster.

'Yes, Ellen,' the track team said, 'everyone's the same.'

The Stig's advice was clear and encouraging as he told me where I should be in the road, and just when, and how hard I should be braking. I was totally focused, listening to every word he said. I'm one of those people who can choose to be competitive or not, and this time I was quite definitely choosing to be competitive.

This was all pretty new to me. I'd done a few days of karting before but was never very good, and had only ever had one go on a track. The funny thing was that I didn't pass my test till I was twenty-one and hardly drove, thanks to spending most of my time at sea. My aim was to make it at least to the top third, then I hoped that I wouldn't disgrace myself.

My laps began, and I wellied it, giving it all the concentration and acceleration I could. It was the most incredible buzz, even in a family car like the Suzuki Liana, and I enjoyed every single minute of it. The more laps I did the more I got the vibes that I was actually driving quite fast. I could tell from Stig's body language and enthusiastic instructions that he felt that I was close to the pace. He began encouraging me loads, saying, 'Remember, where I said brake, don't brake, count to three then stick your foot down so hard on the brake that you think it'll go through the bottom of the car.'

I did a couple more laps; on one I spun off, totally losing control, but I was straight back to the start line, with the bit between my teeth and raring to go. I had been asked to speak to the camera in the car as I drove, but there was no way I had enough brain space to even open my mouth. I was on a mission.

Stig then started saying: 'I know that you've got more in you than that; I know you can do better.'

I gave it all I had, but, as they didn't tell me the times, I had no idea how I was doing. On my final lap I could see that the cameramen had gone. I arrived at the finish line to be told that I had to get out of the car now. I felt that I could have done better, and I begged for another lap.

'No, Ellen, we have to edit the footage. You have to get out,' they replied.

'But the cameramen has already left on the last lap,' I replied. 'Please . . .'

The definitive reply came back: 'Ellen, please get out of the car.'

I was mortified, I really felt that with just one more go I could at least have done what I was capable of. The team and I were ushered to our Portakabin, where we had a brief drink before we were taken into the studio for the interview.

I sat down on the comfy seat, and Jeremy began chatting. He introduced me as a 'goddess', which was quite a shock really. I hadn't even thought about the interview, and, with adrenalin still running through my body, I was perhaps a bit quieter than I could have been. Jeremy asked about the southern oceans, life on board, how much sleep I got . . . and then finally he got on to the lap times.

'Where do you reckon, then?' he asked.

Not really knowing how to answer I said 'The question is – do I have to put it on there because I'm small, or do you have to put it on there because you're tall?'

There had been at least sixty other 'stars in reasonably priced cars' before, so the list was a high one. I doubted very much if I could have made the top set.

'I've no idea,' I said. 'All I know is that I would have liked another go.'

'Trust me, I have to put it on there with a lap like that . . . You're not tall enough to reach it.'

Jeremy pointed out that this was a much greater challenge than anything I'd undertaken before, and I pointed out how nervous I had been. Then his words began: 'You did it in one minute – pause – forty-six – pause – point seven!' Then he jumped to his feet, throwing his arms in the air shouting, 'You've done it!' I watched as he put my name right at the top of the list. I was astounded. When the clapping finally died, he said: 'The other thing I have to say is that's why we wouldn't let you do another lap . . . Not a lot of point, love. Faster than Jimmy Carr. Fastest person ever. Your life is now complete. Ladies and gentlemen, Ellen MacArthur.'

I swear that after that lap more people came up to me saying, 'Nice lap,' than had ever spoken to me before. And they were obviously referring to the *Top Gear* track rather than the planet!

The journey to get to the Falkland Islands, from which we were due to sail down to South Georgia, was a long and convoluted one, but I made it – despite being weighed down by over 30 kg of bags with cameras, solar panels and batteries in. I travelled via Santiago, then Punta Arenas, where I stayed for a day and a half before my connecting flight on to the Falklands. Punta was a world apart from the Sports Personality of the Year event I'd been to the day before my flight, and it was quite refreshing to wander round in a place where no one knew me. I spoke hardly a word of Spanish but found the people of Chile absolutely fantastic. They were so helpful and so happy, working out where I was trying to get to (the camping shop!) using sign language. It was great.

The Falklands were just as I remembered them, with everyone there really friendly and open. We were looked after incredibly well, including a dinner at the Governor's house in the few hours we had before leaving. We were even met by the Commander of British Forces at MPA (the military base and airport) and got to meet 'Deefor' (dog!), who was the current base mascot. We had got off the plane in the afternoon and had cast off our lines by midnight – a brief but very welcome stop.

We would sail from the Falklands on a boat called *Tara*, which was designed for this kind of journey. She was all aluminium, the plates in the hull on her bilges about an inch thick, her twin masts stocky and solid, and her hull form designed for ice – the idea being that she would pop out and rise above it. We were so lucky to be able to travel on her, as in effect we had thumbed a lift. She had been chartered by a man called Frederik Paulsen, who was heading down to South Georgia, not only to see a place which he clearly adored so much, but to take his two sons down there too. They were going to attempt to climb Paulsen Peak with two French alpine guides. There was also a mountain on South Georgia called 'Mount MacArthur', which was named at the finish of the Vendée Globe, when a bunch of marines climbed it for the first time. They'd called their support crew on the radio from the summit and were informed of my second place in the Vendée Globe. At that time I never in a million years thought that I might visit the place!

As I stepped on board *Tara* for the first time, though, something else other than our trip to South Georgia was on my mind. *Tara*'s previous name was *Seamaster*, and it was on board her that the legendary sailor Sir Peter Blake had lost his life. I have rarely admired anyone as much as Peter. He made a huge impression on me when he jointly won the Yachtsman of the Year with Sir Robin Knox-Johnston at the same time as I was presented with the Young Sailor of the Year award back in 1995. At that stage he had already won the Whitbread Round the World Race and the America's Cup for the first time. His lovely wife, Pippa, had launched *Kingfisher* for us in New Zealand shortly after Peter had successfully defended the America's Cup in New Zealand, and following his victory he had headed off into the southern oceans to document and raise awareness of environmental issues and find out with his own eyes just what was happening on our planet. It was during this venture that he died, shot by pirates who boarded his boat at the mouth of the Amazon, and eight years later it still sickens me. He was a truly inspirational man, and his absence has left, and always will leave, a totally unfillable hole.

The sail down to South Georgia made me realize just how remote the islands are. They lie 700 miles from the Falklands and there is no airport there. Some of the worst weather in the Southern Ocean can be found just to the east of Cape Horn – which is exactly where South Georgia is situated. On our journey down we sailed through an absolute stinker of a storm. The Beaufort scale on which wind speed is measured stops at 64 knots (Force 12), and we saw 71! I have to say that I felt pretty glad to be in a 120 foot boat, but all the same we still turned round for a few hours to avoid the worst of it. It was pretty full-on. Getting the final piece of mainsail on the foremast down in over 60 knots was quite interesting. You could hardly even stand up on deck!

The four days I spent on that passage were the first moments I really had to think in since I walked Mac in the hills as a youngster. Back then I would sit in the grass, Mac lying next to me, and I would think about everything. I'd dream of adventures, contemplate life, look at the world around me and find the best blackberry bushes in the area! Everything that I had done since then had been about goals, my own goals and achieving them. It was all quite selfish in a way. I had always been focused, always moving on to the next challenge. From leaving school at seventeen I'd been on a mission. Now, here in the Southern Ocean, I was beginning to find space in my head which I had forgotten was there.

There were lots of books in the on-board library, which I would read and reflect on as I was cuddled up wedged between the table and the comfy cushions – a stark contrast to my previous voyages in the south. I was beginning, for the first time, to wind down and see beyond my narrow focus: I was watching the birds and the wildlife without worry or stress; I was taking in all that was around me. My thoughts were in a place that I hadn't dared to let them go to for a long time, I felt in a way like I was letting my guard down, but I could feel the good that it was doing me. I was beginning to find my old self again.

It was 22 December 2005 when we first spotted the shores of South Georgia. It rose bit by bit out of the sea as dawn broke just after 0200, and presented us with a mystical sight. The silhouette was dramatic and quite unforgiving and made me think back through the centuries to when lands were first being discovered. We knew that the islands were there, and we had radar; I tried to imagine how it must have felt not knowing if you would stumble upon an island or rocks during the hours of darkness. Along the closest shore there was a blue-white iceberg, almost parked up alongside the island. A harsh but beautiful reminder that we were not in snowy Scotland, but somewhere much more remote.

As we first approached the north-west tip of the island the icy peaks were hidden in cloud, so only the black rocks and the snow-covered slopes were visible. As we neared, though, the cloud lifted, and the peaks came into view. It was stunning, and as I stood there, mouth open, a window in the grey cloud appeared, allowing in the most delicate shafts of light and showing the island in all its glory.

We followed the coast for what seemed like hours before our final destination was close. We were heading for an old whaling station called Grytviken, and the adjacent scientific base at King Edward Point (KEP). As the rusty steelwork of the whaling station could be made out in the distance, I realized then just how important whaling had been in South Georgia. It felt so exciting to be landing in this new place and to know that, for at least the next month, it would be home and shelter.

It was wonderful to see Sally again, and, once we'd exchanged stories about our hairy sail down, we got straight to business, discussing what our plans would be for the coming weeks. It was the first time I'd been on board *Golden Fleece*, and on approaching I could see that she was a sturdy steel boat, with a fantastic wheelhouse almost like a fishing boat. Her cabin was warm as I climbed down the companionway from the wheelhouse; she had a cosy, friendly feel, and I felt at home instantly. Sally and her team had already been down here for several weeks, undertaking research all around South Georgia, counting the albatross nests, plotting their locations and monitoring the numbers of birds. Previously the study had been based solely around the albatross, but now Sally was also monitoring the giant petrels.

Sally invited me for a cup of tea in the main cabin and I was pleasantly surprised to see the Captain of HMS *Endurance* – the Navy ship I'd last seen on the way back up the Atlantic the day I had ripped the headboard car from Mobi's mast track – which was also moored at Grytviken. We would stay in KEP for an extra day, as *Endurance* had offered us the opportunity to fly over South Georgia in one of the Lynx helicopters she had on board. I had not expected that for a minute. The flight was one of the most amazing experiences I have ever had: it's only when you see the inland part of South Georgia that you realize just what an incredible place it really is. The size of the glaciers just blows you away, as their crevasses appear dark against the icy channels slowly weaving their way to the sea. At the point where they break off into the sea there are high cliffs of ice, tinted with blues and greens. The water around them is fresh, and of a green milky consistency when compared to the clarity of the salt water. Higher still towered the black rocky peaks with their striking strata rising starkly out of the pure white but immense valleys of snow. The sky was blue, and the scattering clouds cast stunning shadows against the white wilderness. This was the island which Ernest Shackleton crossed on his historic journey back from the Antarctic. The lower slopes were green, with a mixture of high cliffs and streams running down through the mountains, some falling as spectacular waterfalls as they travelled their final metres to the sea.

We saw an iceberg offshore, and I asked the pilot if we could fly over to see it. Jerome, a French cameraman who had joined us in the Falklands to record my experiences, filmed the most incredible sequence as the berg grew closer to fill his lens as we circled it. There was a handful of penguins on the iceberg, tiny black dots, like people, watching in amazement as our huge red bird flew over them. Probably a first for them, like me, I thought, as they disappeared into the distance. It was from the air that the scale of the whaling industry really hit home to me. Grytviken had been cleaned up to a huge extent compared to the others, and it amazed me that as human beings we had created such a large industry so far away.

The evening after our flight we were due to head up the coast overnight to Bird Island, which was at the opposite end of the island, for Christmas. With the excitement of this journey and our arrival in South Georgia, Christmas celebrations had slipped to the backs of our minds.

Before we left, Sally briefed us on how to behave around the animals, and what the protocols were. We talked about the birds, but also the seals, which can be quite dangerous. We were there during the end of the mating season for the fur seals, and the males in particular can get very aggressive. Their teeth are like dogs', and their saliva carries about forty different types of bacteria, and if you let them get close to you they are very capable of biting you. Unfortunately one of the types of bacteria actually melts your bones, so if you do get bitten you need to get yourself on to an IV drip pretty quickly with a certain type of antibiotic which is capable of combating it. We learnt that one of the new scientists on Bird Island at the beginning of his two-and-a-half-year placement there had recently been bitten in the thigh. It was sobering stuff, but important to know – particularly for Jerome, I felt, as he was walking around with a camera to his eyes.

With the plan in place Jerome and I headed off to do some filming in the whaling station and to pop in and see the Carrs, an English couple who lived on South Georgia. They had renovated an old whaling house, now their home, and set up the museum in Grytviken to illustrate the history of the island for the ever-increasing numbers of visitors who arrive by ship. They had sailed down to South Georgia in their 28 foot 100-year-old wooden boat at the end of a twenty-five-year globetrotting adventure and had fallen in love with the place; they have lived there for the past fifteen years as the only two permanent inhabitants.

Tim and Pauline were inspirational characters. Now doing more skiing than sailing, they would head off up the mountains behind the whaling station in the depths of winter. They offered us hot tea and home-made cakes baked on the Aga; and in a funny way it reminded me of home in Derbyshire. We had a fascinating chat about the island, its history and their sailing exploits. I wished I could have spent all day with them there; I was eager to learn as much as I could.

After a good long chat we headed over to the museum to find out more and were welcomed by a stuffed wandering albatross hanging from the ceiling. This was the first time I'd ever seen an albatross quite so close, and its huge wingspan and general size really took my breath away. How a stuffed animal can look wise, I have no idea – but to me there was a majestic spirit about it.

South Georgia is thought to have been sighted in 1675, though it was not landed on until 100 years later by none other than Captain James Cook. Though it lies over 6,000 miles from the UK, it has been a hub for industry since the late 1700s, when sealing was prevalent. The Americans and Brits were down there in the search for seal skins, and the industry was so successful that it was estimated by 1825 we had taken 1,200,000 seal pelts. This sealing continued until 1908, by which time British legislation was put in place to protect the breeding grounds of the fur seals, as they had been slaughtered virtually to extinction. It was around this time that a new and bigger industry began to establish itself: whaling.

In the museum were fascinating pictures of the whaling stations; looking out of the windows at the tons and tons of steel and engines which filled the bay, it was impossible to forget that history. The photos of the whaling were graphic, and it was quite shocking to see hoards of people working on huge carcasses the size of buses. The regular method was shooting an exploding grenade into the whales then filling them with compressed air so they would float on the surface until the ship could reach them. It was all pretty grim, especially as they were often still alive as they floated there, waiting to be picked up.

Whale oil was used extensively from the 1700s onwards, and was the first of any animal or mineral oil to prove to be commercially viable. It was used as a primary source of candle wax and lamp fuel, and later for producing soap. Other uses included the manufacture of leather, varnish and linoleum. New uses were found in the early 1900s which included food, pharmaceuticals and in the production of nitroglycerine for explosives – an important product in both World Wars.

Grytviken was the first whaling station in South Georgia and was set up in 1904 by a Norwegian called Captain Carl Anton Larsen. I have heard it said many times that there were so many whales there that for three years the whalers never had to leave the bay. That seems hard to believe now: we hadn't seen a single whale on our journey through the Southern Ocean, let alone here in the bay at Grytviken. The largest whale that was landed on the shores of South Georgia was 33.5 metres in length and was caught in 1912; the second-largest was 29.5 metres long and weighed 177 tons. The first station was so successful that other whaling stations began to crop up all over the east side of the island, and just eight years later there were seven in operation, employing 4,500 people at their peak, two-thirds of whom were British.

Whale oil was precious, and the industry therefore was hugely lucrative – worth billions in today's money. Suddenly then you begin to realize how it made financial sense to build whole towns down there – and that's exactly what happened. We took enough materials, supplies and ships to build a 'new world'. In these new towns we built shops, churches, dentists' surgeries, cinemas, dormitories and offices. In some stations there were even light railways for moving things around, and that's not including the huge cylinders for heating the whale produce to remove the oil and vats for storing it afterwards. There were ships filling the harbours, some of which still line the shores today, and spare propellers and patterns for producing spare engine parts by making a mould in sand for molten iron. The scale of the whole enterprise is hard to get your head around, but in South Georgia it was all there laid out in front of us to see.

I looked at the dates and was staggered at how recent it all felt in relation to the life spans of my family members. My Great Granddad, Peter King, was born in 1894, ten years before whaling even existed on South Georgia, and I remembered sitting on his knee listening to his stories. He was of an age where he could well have worked in the whaling stations as they first began; he would have been ten years old when they began building them and he would have surely used whale-oil candles and lamp oil. Gran, my Dad's Mum, was born when whaling was at its peak. It staggered me just how little time it takes for so much to change in our world.

That day, as Jerome and I walked around Grytviken doing some filming, there was an eerie silence. It felt almost like a war zone: there were all these buildings but not a soul to be seen. It reminded me of the *Viktor Pleven* and the abandoned fishing boats in Lorient; all sitting there forgotten and lifeless. There were huge ramps of thick steel plate, several storeys high, presumably for dragging the carcasses up, and equipment everywhere. The size of the engines made you feel tiny. In awe, I spoke to the camera: 'It's like an isolated beauty but yet you see all this here and you can't believe it. This was a massive industry with thousands of tons of steel work employing thousands of people and now it's a dead, empty space.'

We sailed to Bird Island and had the most amazing walk there on Christmas Day. Sally introduced me to a whole range of birds which nested there. Following this, we sat down to a great Christmas dinner in the BAS station, and the atmosphere was lovely, almost as if we had all known each other for a long time.

It was on Bird Island that I saw the black browed and the wandering albatross for the first time. The wandering albatross are the birds which are the most striking at sea, as they have a wingspan of up to 11 feet, and they seem to soar effortlessly, just skimming the surface of the water with their wingtips. They are absolute perfectionists with their flying, never faltering, never making a wrong move, and living at sea. Incredibly, a young albatross, once it leaves the nest for the first time, will not touch land again for at least three and up to seven years. If I were an albatross I'd be pretty excited about leaving and discovering flying for the first time, but I think I'd be fairly apprehensive about my first landing! If it wasn't for finding a mate and breeding I guess the albatross would not need the land at all. The adults and full-grown chicks stand at the height of a large dog, but they are so very, very gentle.

The wanderers that are still nesting on Bird Island lived up in the meadows above the station, a stark contrast to the raucousness of the beach with the territorial and aggressive fur seals. Suddenly, as you walk over the hill through the wild tussock grass, the world changes: there is the call of the tiny pipit and the noise of the wind whistling up over the sea cliffs from a cold, inhospitable ocean. As we looked down over the slopes, we saw the windswept Willis Islands, which form the north-west tip of South Georgia; they looked bleak and dark, especially with a solitary iceberg creeping past. We stood near one magnificent bird, and Zac, a BAS research assistant, pointed out that he was about twenty-eight years old. That's only a year younger than I was then! When you consider that an albatross can live until it's sixty to seventy years old, you then realize that there are birds flying around now who'd have been here when there were 4,500 people down below manning the whaling stations of South Georgia. They would have encountered fishing boats that were much smaller than the massive factory ships of today and probably accompanied the sailors as they threw scraps to the birds. There is still food available from the fishing boats, but a large proportion of it these days comes with a 3 inch hook inside, as tasty for the albatross as it is for the deep-sea fish it's destined to catch.

Sally was with us on the hill, and her comments really shocked me. Twenty years ago, there were about 1,800 nests on Bird Island, and last year was the first year that there were under a thousand. With a young albatross having to wait for five to nine years before it's mature enough to breed, and only able to lay one egg every two years thereafter, they are not reproducing quickly at all; in fact humans reproduce more quickly than the albatross can. Even the chicks that are hatched only have a slim chance of making it: research shows that only one in five chicks survives to maturity. They have many things against them from the word go, and current trends are leading to extinction. I really felt that we humans need to give these birds the best chance we can.

We left Bird Island after Christmas and headed down the coast of South Georgia in a south-easterly direction, continuing with the survey Sally and her team had been working on before our arrival. We visited Prince Olaf whaling station, Possession Bay, Blue Whale Harbour. The weather was marvellous, and quite unlike the South Georgia I was expecting. From my experiences of the Southern Ocean the sun rarely shines, so I knew how lucky we were to have blazing sunshine. Our final stop was the Bay of Isles, in which were Salisbury Plain, Prion Island and finally our new home for the next few weeks, Albatross Island.

Each place was fascinating for its own reasons, whether it was the glaciers which towered above us, breaking up into the bays, or the huge whale jaw bones on the beach. On Salisbury Plain we were interrogated by baby penguins, all brown and fluffy like 1970s shag-pile rugs. Animals and birds weren't afraid of us down there and they didn't run away. They would come and peck at our gloves gently to see what they felt like or look us straight in the eyes sometimes to fathom us out. Jerome and I loved it; we soaked it up as precious moments in our lives.

The team helped us set up camp before we returned to *Golden Fleece* for dinner; then, once fed and watered for the last time on board, we said our goodbyes before we were left alone on a beach. It was quite emotional watching the tiny boat disappear over the horizon with new-found friends aboard, especially as she was headed direct for the Falkland Islands. But it was also quite exciting: we were literally in the middle of nowhere, and the middle of nowhere was about to become our home.

Our arrival on Albatross Island had been timely, as 2006 was upon us just hours after we disembarked from *Golden Fleece*. The sky was a deep ruddy-pink, and the air quite still, with just the odd puff of cool wind blowing over from the glaciers on South Georgia across the bay. We celebrated New Year by standing on the hilltop looking over the mountains and drinking a tiny glass of rum each!

The following day, once again, offered blue skies to us and showed the islands in all their glory. In my head I had thought that the most incredible thing that could happen down there was that I might be able to get close to the albatross, perhaps be able to see the expressions on its face, or look into its eyes as it sat on its nest. Never for a moment did I think that I would be able to sit on a hilltop with possibly the most stunning view in the world, almost able to touch the birds as they flew past. As their perfect feathers were lit by the powerful sun, they looked like polished sculptures, just their eyes and head moving occasionally. They were so clearly enjoying the afternoon warmth and having fun up there: not feeding or fishing, just playing in the updraught. They banked round so steeply that their wings were almost vertical, and sometimes, as they turned, almost stalling in the sky, they would pedal with their feet as if they were playing on the edge of their balance. Their eyes were always level with the horizon, which is amazing when you watch the speed at which they are able to manoeuvre, but they fly with the utmost precision: whether it's calculating a steep bank perfectly or wandering over the waves with their wingtips just millimetres from the water. I found myself laughing as they flew past. I felt a surge of such pleasure and excitement, and I began talking to them, asking them questions as they passed, sometimes like rockets, and sometimes so slowly and gracefully.

I immediately felt that I could never tire of the island. Though from the outside it appeared to be relatively barren, the reality could not be further from the truth. It was full of life and supported a diverse range of plants, animals and birds. I was stunned at the warm glows and different textures of the moss, which must have taken centuries to grow. In fact parts of the land were so delicate that each footstep taken was considered so as not to leave a mark on this priceless, pristine miracle of nature. It would have been there for thousands of years before I was born, therefore I felt it was only right that I should leave it as I found it.

Our campsite was a short walk up the hill from the beach, the same place Sally had camped in for years. We had pitched my small tent right next to the little freshwater pond, and Sally's on a clear flat piece of mossy ground 20 yards away. In the area where our tents were was a wanderer nest, though it was unoccupied when we arrived, like so many others. When we looked more closely we could see that it was a relatively new nest, and not long after our arrival a solitary male settled on it. There was huge excitement as he was finally joined by his mate. The welcome was joyous, their intimacy and the bond between them was so obvious that they appeared almost human. They also seemed totally unaffected by the presence of our tents, and they certainly made up for not seeing each other for a while. While the other birds from the colony were flying high in the skies, appearing to be having fun, our pair were happy in each other's company, gently preening each other's feathers, one at a time, with their huge beaks. It was wonderful to watch, just wonderful. It's hard to imagine how such a massive bird can be so gentle and be so loyal to its mate when, after raising a chick, it will often be a full year before they will see each other again. I found myself thinking for a moment just how a bird which spends so many months at sea can have this kind of relationship. There is a stark difference between spending time in a cosy protected nest and flying across the oceans for thousands of endless miles alone in horrendous storms. I was amazed that they really could be the same birds.

An excerpt from my log read:

```
The Pipits were singing flying high in the sky, their
song rarely heard so far and wide in the habitual
whistling wind. The morning sun is shining on the moss
above me lighting it like a majestic golden carpet. I
can hear our resident Albatross couple chattering away
to each other. This morning as we ate porridge in the
sun they were making the most of each others company
once more, completely oblivious to our presence. You can
get arrested for that kind of behaviour in public at
home, and they certainly put on a good show for the
camera!! It's so incredibly peaceful here, just peace
on a different level than I have ever felt before.
    I wish that everyone could feel the complete immersion
in happiness that I am feeling right now . . .
```

There was no sign of human presence on our island apart from two barbed fish hooks which we found next to the albatross's nest. They were from the long lines which are used for deep-ocean fishing, and those lines can have as many as 3,200 hooks on them and be up to 130 km long. Nothing could have highlighted the birds' vulnerability to us more graphically. You had such a strong feeling that on the island we were in their world, where only the weather is their enemy. It's out at sea, where they forage for thousands of miles, that they stray into areas where they can be in real danger – and those areas of danger are sadly where humans are fishing. But the tragic thing is that our unintentional catching of the albatross can easily be stopped. By towing a couple of streamers out from the back of the fishing boats or laying lines at night we can easily stop them from getting caught on the hooks. Just simple communication was all that was needed, surely. I felt in our world today that was possible: the fishermen wanted to catch fish, not alba-tross, anyway.

We spent our days wandering across the island, moving from nest to nest with our notepads and GPSs. We would collate our informa-tion in the evenings and spend many happy hours, particularly when the weather was terrible, chatting away in Sally's tent, which was the larger of the two, and we'd often look at the photos I'd taken during the day. I loved the time talking to Sally; I was learn-ing so much about a world that I had only ever sailed past. We talked about the months she had spent in the Antarctic, her time in South Georgia and the experiences she had been through there, such as the birth of her first child in Leith Harbour. That spurred conversations about the whaling stations and just how they were when Sally first arrived there. She spoke about how eerie they were and how they were like ghost towns; in fact, when she'd first gone in them, it was as if people had walked out just days before. There were films in the cinemas, bibles in the churches, imple-ments lined up on the shelves in the dentist's surgery, almost as if the next patient was about to walk in. Sally said that many of the stations are still like that today. I dreamt about those whaling stations that night and couldn't get the images out of my head. There was something that was jarring in my mind about what had gone on down there with the whaling. It wasn't the killing itself, but something else, and it was going to take me some time to work it out.

That afternoon, Sally and I were just over the hill and to the east of our camp, finishing our positions for the day. We were in an area where there were three chicks, and we were having a laugh, as one still had chick fluff all over its head – like a 1980s American hair-style. We nicknamed her Thelma, from *Thelma and Louise*. It was the time of the year that all the chicks should be upping and offing, as the next round of birds was already sitting on eggs. Sally was sur-prised that these three were still here. We wrote in our books all we could, noting down the length of the tussock grass around the nests, and whether there was much destruction of the nesting area from the onslaught of the fur seals. As we got to the final nest I sat down on a lump of tussock grass and was writing in my notebook when something extraordinary happened. The young albatross which had been sitting opposite me climbed down from its nest, walked over to me and stopped. As I was sitting down, his head was at the same height as mine. He looked me straight in the eyes, paused for a few seconds then sat down right in front of me.

Alfred, as we called him from then on, was quite a character. Sally had been working with the wanderers for over thirty years but she had never seen this kind of interactive behaviour before. We were both flabbergasted. From that moment on, whenever Alfred caught sight of me, he would get off his nest and try to join me. He would follow me, come to me and sit with me; he basically just appeared to want to be around me. Though he was fully grown he was not a very stocky albatross, and it did not take long for us to work out that the most likely reason for this behaviour was that he was starving to death. When a young albatross hatches from its egg it's fed on the nest for nine months until it's big enough to fly. The parents alternate – heading off to sea in search of food to regurgitate for the chick. Often the parents don't even see each other during this period, as it's pretty intensive feeding a young chick who will grow up to 15 kg in weight. By the looks of him Alfred was well under this, and our worry was that one, or both, of his parents had died. You could also tell from his movements that he was weak, as he would often stumble in the tussock grass, putting his wings out to try and stabilize himself. He often tried to stand next to me, but his legs were not very strong, and he would sit back on his heels with his bottom touching the ground.

I had heard people say that birds are not intelligent, but I have a story which will illustrate otherwise. One afternoon I went over to see Alfred. I sat a little way from his nest in case he decided that he wasn't interested in saying hello or that he wanted to be a normal albatross again. But he climbed off his nest, waddled over and sat down next to me. We seemed to be communicating just by being with each other, and, though it probably sounds stupid, I would talk to him as we sat there together, just contemplating life. I hadn't taken many pictures of Alfred at this stage, but as I was fearful that

Following our return to Falmouth, the team headed to Lorient in France for the boat to be refitted and set up camp at a vast submarine base, left over from the Second World War. It was the first time for years that I felt I could see outside our project. We visited a disused fishing vessel, the *Victor Pleven*, and a boat graveyard. Both experiences set off a new train of thought

In the year following the record, we took *Mobi* to Asia to establish a new record circuit. Here, she sits in front of the Shanghai skyline.

In 2005 I was given a life-changing opportunity to visit the remote islands of South Georgia and help communicate the plight of the albatross. Ever since passing near these isolated yet beautiful islands five years earlier, I had dreamt of visiting them. Seeing the cliffs of blue and green ice from aboard HMS *Endurance*'s helicopter was breathtaking.

One of our first stops on the island was Grytviken, a derelict whaling station. Established in 1904, it was abandoned in the 1960s as the limitations of whale oil became apparent. At its peak, the industry employed some 4,500 people in this far-flung corner of the world.

Sally Poncet, who had invited me to join her on her trip to South Georgia, and I were given a rare chance to camp out on Albatross Island to film the wildlife. As you can see, seals were a fairly regular sight!

Spending time amongst the albatross on South Georgia was unbelievable, and for the first time in so many years I had the opportunity to pause and reflect.

Our Alfred.

Building a home together on the Isle of Wight became an exciting challenge for Ian and me, but neither of us had anticipated quite how much of a challenge it would be! Without the help of a 7 ton digger, we would have had an even tougher time.

Right, the space that would eventually become our vegetable patch.

Ian and I chose to adopt Floss after a visit to the Isle of Skye. She was timid and badly injured, and looking after her tested us more than we'd thought possible, but it also taught me so much about life.

In late 2007, Ian and I decided to take a holiday and go off on a very different type of voyage: a tour through the canal and river systems of the UK. In our boat, *Gads*, we saw some incredible sights and were struck by the beauty of these forgotten motorways of the past.

he did not have much time left, I took off my rucksack and pulled out my video recorder and camera. I always kept them in plastic bags, so I removed these and popped them back in my rucksack.

No sooner had I picked up the camera to take a photo than Alfred was looking straight into the lens. I smiled to myself; he was a natural performer and clearly wasn't camera shy! Then the most incredible thing happened. Alfred moved over to my rucksack and proceeded to put his head inside it. I couldn't believe it. Seconds later he removed his head, and I was stunned. Alfred had picked out the plastic bag gently with the tip of his beak. I laughed out loud at his antics. I took a picture of him removing the bag. He then placed it neatly in the grass and put his head in my bag once more. Now I felt nothing would surprise me. As he removed his head for the second time he had the second bag in his beak. He then placed it next to the other one. I was totally blown away by him! How can a bird which had never seen a human being, or a rucksack, or anything that wasn't a seal, a mound of tussock grass, his parents or the sea, possibly know that there was even a place to put things in a rucksack. I had tears of emotion running down my cheeks by this stage. This little fellow was quite special. It was then that he did something which left me totally speechless. He placed his head in my rucksack a third time, picked up the tiny knotted string which I had attached to the inside zip, and, yes, he undid the zip to the innermost compartment of my bag. What more can I possibly say?

I thought about Alfred so much, and we talked about him often in the evenings and over dinner in Sally's tent. For me he was a symbol of what I was trying to communicate, and his plight was a result of human interaction in their world. I popped over the hill a few times to check on Alfred after our initial encounter. I wanted to know that he was OK but also to monitor his progress, hoping that a miracle would happen and one of his parents would return to feed him and give him strength, or that he would fly away himself to feed. But he couldn't leave, he wasn't strong enough, and when the chick in the nest next to him died a few nights later during a storm which swept over the island, I had to accept the painful fact that his days were probably numbered too. We would have loved to have whisked Alfred away and taken him to be fed at the base at King Edward Point, as I was absolutely sure that he would have allowed them to feed him. But the rules back in 2006 were that you were not allowed to interfere with nature, which frustrated me. I couldn't help but think that we were always interfering with nature, in fact we are part of nature, and the fishermen who had inadvertently killed Alfred's parents were quite possibly interfering with nature too.

We had a three-day spell of absolutely wonderful weather before we left. Bright blue skies, light winds, then blue skies *and* enough wind to kick off the mating calls of the wanderers, lifting them high into the sky. In the still moments we sat in the camp, and one morning I was in a T-shirt, just writing, and soaking in the real quietness. I never thought that such tranquillity could be found below the Antarctic convergence.

On one of these last days we went to survey the south-western corner of the island. It is one of the areas most hit by the fur seals, and the tussock that was light green and almost spring-like is now just muddy flats surrounded by thick dark-green tussock. Sally told me it was once a thriving area for wanderers, with many nests and frequent displaying, though now it felt more like a graveyard, with scattered old nests and the roar and growl of fur seals wherever we walked. There were five birds there when we passed, several on eggs on their nests, but a few without eggs. Often at the stage we were at then it's the males that are on the eggs and the females that have left the island to feed.

It was reassuring to see a few eggs there, though the most south-westerly bird was a different story. His nest was one from a few years earlier by the look of it. He was sitting there and had obviously been there for some time; his head was pointing over to the mountains, which gave the impression that that was where his mate last flew away. He obviously had no mate with him when we saw the state of his nest, and it appeared that he was waiting, just waiting and waiting, for her to return. His feathers were nearly all white, so he could have been fifty or sixty years old, and that waiting could have been going on for years. He looked so, so sad. I never thought that a bird could show emotion in its face, but, seeing that old albatross in the seal-damaged ground, I was overcome with sadness. The area is not a good one for mating as it's now all damaged, so no young bird will display there – just old, old nests and a guy who had given up. When we passed a week later, he had gone. Gone until he returns next year alone, who knows, maybe still with a glimmer of hope?

As our time on Albatross Island was drawing to a close, I would head off up the slopes in the afternoon with camera and tripod in a final effort to capture the beauty around us. I would sit in an old wanderer nest, which was lovely and warm, surrounded by tussock, with birds flying over the ridge, just a couple of metres above my head. I was in their home, their place, and I felt like the luckiest person on earth to be there. Each time the sun set I was blown away by the light and colour around me. It was magical; I could have watched the sunsets every day for a lifetime and never tired of them.

It was during this time at the end of the day that I would sometimes drift off into long periods of thought. My trip to South Georgia had been planned as an adventure, but in going there I had surprised myself by discovering something I had not come across for a decade: time to think. My glandular fever at the age of seventeen had unexpectedly interrupted my life. Though I wasn't looking for it, it had forced me to take a step back and think and to acknowledge what perhaps I always knew: my dream of being at sea was in fact possible. South Georgia gave me a second pivotal pause. Wherever I went thereafter, its echoes seemed to speak to me. The time I spent there had placed another corner piece in the jigsaw of my life.

Since sailing for the first time I had been fascinated by the water. I had fallen in love with something so powerful that it took over my life, and I had treasured every minute of it. I felt close to that passion in South Georgia, perhaps due to its proximity to the element I felt so at home in. I could look out across the ocean from pretty much anywhere we went; watching its ever-changing moods beneath the inhospitable and changeable weather of the south. The diversity and immensity of all that surrounded me was enchanting, constantly moving, changing and evolving: from the huge waves of the Southern Ocean lit up on magnificent moonlit nights to the bright turquoise-blue wave crests and the contrast of breaking waves, to the bitter, foggy nights of the ice fields. I loved the challenge, beauty and adventure that the sea had to offer, and, even better, it was always there.

But to achieve results in my sport I had needed to be focused. I had not grown up amidst the magic of boats and had thus treasured every moment I set foot on one. As a child I had longed, simply longed for the sea and when I was old enough to leave home I fled to it, never looking back. Everything had been about learning and improving, being fitter, stronger; driving myself for hours in the gym, then at sea pushing myself harder and harder to learn every minute detail about the boat, weather, my sleep patterns or the technology. I had sailed half-way round the world not once but twice in training, and as many miles in the Atlantic Ocean as I could possibly cram in. And as I lay my head back into the soft, thick moss and closed my eyes, I felt lucky; so lucky to live the life that I lead, so lucky to be following my dream. But as I lay there, my mind wandered to the incredible teamwork; the people over the previous decade who had helped me to achieve goals: the most amazing team at OC, who had become like a family, and, of course, my Mum and Dad and brothers, who really were. I thought a lot about my Mum and Dad and life back in Derbyshire. I thought of the days I spent with my dog, Mac, out up in the hills, scrambling around in the woods, and Dad teaching us what pignuts, cuckoo spit and oak apples were and how to sharpen a knife on a stone. I had such fond memories of the adventures we went on as kids, which were often just family walks, but they brought the countryside around us to life and gave us an appreciation for just how special it is.

But in recent years life had been the opposite. It seemed I had always been away; missing Christmases at home through building boats in New Zealand, Australia or sailing in the Southern Ocean. I had never been around for more than a few days at a time at home, always having something more pressing or urgent than family time. I guess I realized for the first time just how driven I was, almost to the exclusion of all else, and how self-centred I had been in following my dream. The pace had been relentless, and, frankly I had not stopped for long enough to give any of it a second thought.

For the first time I also realized just how young I had been when I competed in the Vendée, and how much harder that would have made it for Mum and Dad. To me I was just another sailor, but to them I was still their girl. I had moved away from home at seventeen to sail; at twenty-two I began building *Kingfisher*; at twenty-three I won my first race in her and at twenty-four I entered the Vendée Globe, which was to change my life for ever.

I thought back to the feelings I'd had watching the rough-edit of the programme the BBC made about the Vendée five years before. For the first time I was marrying my memory of the moment with images from the cameras from which no one could hide. Oddly, I felt no significant emotion watching the experiences I'd had at sea; but it knocked me flat watching my Mum and Dad say goodbye just before I set off. Thinking back to their expressions, I could feel my eyes welling up. My Mum had smiled when I looked at her, then kissed me, but after, as I watched myself nestle my head against her cheek, I could see her face slowly change to one showing worry. As we hugged, her voice over the pictures said: 'Your imagination goes to what can actually happen. But, on the other hand, I'm pleased she's doing it; it's what she's always wanted.' Then, as I turned to my Dad, Mum stood there and watched, one hand clasped tightly against the other. My Dad looked strong as he said, 'OK,' in almost a question rather than a statement. He then hugged me tight, slapping me hard on the back like he always did, and smiled at me before kissing me. As he hugged me, his voice over the images said, 'Ellen wants to compete; she's always wanted to compete; she will fight to finish the race.' I tried to smile back, then to put me at ease he kissed me on my forehead. I hugged him tighter, pushing my head hard into his neck, where it felt safe.

'I'll call you from the boat,' I said, as we ended our hug.

'I'm sure you will,' said Dad, hunting to say something appropriate, and then smiled . . .

It was time to go. I turned away, but something made me glance back, and it was then that I saw it. Though he winked at me, he was struggling to hold it together. His expression had totally changed, and there was a suffocating look of pain in his eyes. I wished I had not looked back.

Once I'd walked away in the film, I saw Mum and Dad glance at each other, and then, almost overwhelmingly, I could feel their strength. They knew how dangerous it was, but they also knew what it meant to me. It was then I realized that neither of them had ever tried to stop me. In never questioning my dream they had made a selfless decision: to give me not only love but freedom.

Perhaps the greatest gifts any parents can ever give . . .

I wiped my eyes. I was sobbing, and tears were now running down my face. I was so lucky . . . I looked out across the water to the stunning orange sky and realized the sun had set behind the mountains. It would go cold quickly now, and it was time to head down to the tents for dinner. Not wishing to leave behind the thoughts I'd had for ever, I lay back on to the soft moss one more time and, looking up into the sky, said: 'Thank you, Mum. Thank you, Dad.'

For some reason I felt I had to say that in the Southern Ocean . . .

Chapter Eighteen

I returned from South Georgia to my home on the Isle of Wight, where I'd been based since 1998. I'd never really cared about a home before, as I always seemed to be on the road, or more often on the sea! For the first three years I had lived either on the office floor, in Mark's sister's old room at his Mum's house at the west end of the island, or, for a few months, in a flat in Yarmouth. When I returned from the Vendée Globe I was staying on the sofa bed in Mark's flat in Cowes for the time I was there, but soon after I felt quite strongly that I needed my own space, as I'd been living out of a bag since I'd left home at seventeen some eight years before. It was at that point during the summer of 2001 that I found a small flat in Cowes, in the centre of the town, which I knew instantly was going to be my base. It was a cosy little flat with character, and despite being in the middle of town it was totally hidden away and very private. That had been the appeal, I think, finding a place to hide away from the publicity and pressure which a successful Vendée campaign left me dealing with. During the following winter I spent months working on it, making it homely, fixing sinks, plumbing, sorting the electrics, sourcing the wood-burning stove and generally making the little place feel like mine. Since then, though, I'd actually spent little time there, as I'd been away so much with the sailing projects. In fact, on one occasion I returned to the island to collect some clothes and realized that I'd spent six hours there in the previous six months!

It was in the spring of 2006 that Ian and I both stumbled upon the same advert in the local paper for a plot which was for sale on the outskirts of Cowes. Though we'd been living in my flat together for a while, we both knew that it wasn't really the place for us. It had no garden to speak of bar a 3 metre by 3 metre square out the back, and, though you could walk down the hill behind it and look at the sea, there was no outside space at all.

Our first visit to what was to become our new home was exciting for both of us, and once we stood in the garden behind the old bungalow it was like stepping into a little haven. At a quick glance the garden, though small, felt really secluded, and, though it had clearly been untouched for years, there was a superb feel to the place. We wandered round the bungalow, which felt quite sad in comparison. The old lady who had lived there had passed away in her nineties, and it seemed many of her possessions were still there. There were pictures on the walls of people, and a photo of a cat. In the little kitchen pantry there were vases, jugs and the old cat's bowl – thickly lined inside with lime scale. In the lounge was an old piano, which was out of tune but still working. The décor looked like it had not been changed since the house was built around the 1930s, and there didn't appear to have been much maintenance done at all. Though there was a little insulation in the loft, the rest of the house had been pretty much untouched, and there was woodworm in everything from the piano to the fire surround. The house was generally in pretty bad repair, and the reason it was being sold as a building plot was that the house basically had to be knocked down. One side of the house had fallen away by the height of three courses of bricks, 9 inches, and its concrete foundations were broken. Few of the windows would open, not unlike the door, which would jam all the time. There was a huge crack right through the house which in places you could push your hand through. It looked like the crooked house from a fairytale, and it didn't take long for us to realize that it was going to have to go.

The garden was overgrown and grassy in the middle, and, though there was a rather dominating corrugated light-green-painted galvanized shed on one side, the thing that caught my eye was the little bird table next to it. It was painted green too, was clearly home-made, and just had a friendly aura about it. At the end of the garden was a huge old oak tree, so overgrown that its boughs almost reached the ground, and beyond that was just overgrown darkness. We knew that the plot had some land with it out the back, so we pushed our way through the foliage, feeling like explorers. It felt like no one had been there in a very long time, and as we picked a path through the brambles and bushes we discovered how hard it was to make progress. The plants had totally taken over; it must have been really hard going for the wild animals too! On our first visit we didn't discover the full extent of the plot, for, although it was fairly narrow, it went back quite a long way. At the bottom of the plot was a copse, and the trees in it were quite mature, and I could see Ian's eyes light up with each step we took. It was a lovely place; we felt like we were entering a different world; and the noise of the road now seemed a million miles away. Though the top part of the copse was very scrubby and overgrown, this bottom part wasn't too bad at all. There were huge beech, sycamore and sweet chestnuts, and a plethora of holly trees. You could just about walk between them all too, and there were some clear areas on the steeper part of the bank which were still scattered with beautiful golden leaves from the autumn. I think we both knew that this was a place we could make our home.

After a bit of toing and froing, as always seems to happen when you buy a place, our offer was accepted, but as usual for me my time to be around and get involved was limited, as the next journey was a flight out to Yokohama, Japan, for the start of our next challenge with *B&Q* – the Asian record circuit. Several weeks before, and shortly after returning from South Georgia, we had loaded Mobi on to the deck of the cargo ship *CMA CGM Bizet*, ably commanded by Captain Jaspard, a lovely French 'commandant' who would safely transport her from Southampton Docks to the incredible city of Hong Kong. Luckily the shipping company had decided that they would sponsor us by charging us a token amount for the transport itself, not only to take Mobi out there, but also to ship her back from Singapore at the end of our tour. The only condition was that

I was able to launch their new container ship, *CMA CGM Fidelio*, at the time one of the largest in the world, later on that year.

We had been talking about the possibility of a record attempt from Shanghai to London for some time, and had always had it as a fall-back record in case I had not felt that taking Mobi round the world was a viable or safe option. But, after completing the round-the-world, I felt that there was no point in taking her out there and breaking a 'half-way-round-the-world' record. It simply didn't make sense. We decided, therefore, that we would try for something a bit different. We'd take her out to Asia, and we'd go for establishing a new 'record' circuit out there. Our plan was to start off in Yokohama and sail ten legs via certain checkpoints, but we'd actually stop in Dalian, Qingdao, Shanghai, Hong Kong, Terengganu in Malaysia and end up in Singapore for the finish. Another part of the appeal for this was that B&Q had a whole host of stores in Asia now, so there would also be a benefit to them when we went out there to share our story as we visited stores in China and Taiwan on our journey south.

The Asian Record Circuit for us was about establishing something new, but also sharing the experience and Mobi's adventures with the local people. We had translated our video and my book about my round-the-world record into Mandarin so that people in China could really understand. One large part of this was taking people on board her and showing them what an incredible boat she was, but this wasn't always easy. We managed to take some guests of B&Q Asia sailing, and for them to be allowed to even set foot on the boat, let alone actually sail her, they needed papers from the government as well as their identity cards. The tour was full of paradox and contradiction: the friendliness with which we'd be embraced by the local Chinese would give way to what seemed to be an European obstructive red tape from officials. Whilst the cities we visited showed violently contrasting sides, between the high-rise hotels and the shanty towns beneath them.

It was a difficult trip, for the constant store visits, events and promotional work placed a mental challenge alongside the physical one of sailing. Not only was I skippering Mobi at sea in conditions that were frequently difficult, but the relentless schedule on land was just too much. I was performing and smiling on land, but inside I was toast.

We had classes of children come to visit the boat, and I loved interacting with them. Getting a smile from one of them was absolutely priceless. Moments like this made the trip worthwhile, but it taught me a lesson that I was taking on too much all at once.

My memories of the whole trip, though, are as colourful as any I have, from the lush green mountains of the coast to the greys and browns of the floating cities of Hong Kong. Perhaps my strongest memory is of these water-borne shanty towns. Round the corner beneath the main road flyover in Hong Kong we discovered a whole community of boats living on the water, boats with washing hanging out, babies crying or dogs on deck. The boats varied, some large, some small, some more like barges, and some just square boxes built on anything that floated. Some were so small it was hard to believe anyone could fit inside them, let alone live there. There were faces of different ages peering out from behind the makeshift curtains and doors, made of café parasols, lorry tarpaulins, cardboard boxes and scrap timber. Some of the roofs were made of corrugated iron, and many had small trees in pots, next to barrels I could only imagine held fresh water. I was curious and would have welcomed the chance to have been invited aboard one. Though it was clear that these people had little, in a funny way their homes displayed a greater feeling of homeliness than the clinical hotel in which we were staying. My lasting impression was how incredibly resourceful these people were, building homes out of other people's waste.

The Asia tour was the last real adventure we were to have with our Mobi as at the end of that summer we were to bring to a close our incredible eight-year sponsorship with Kingfisher plc. We spent a good few hours tying her down to the ship which would bring her home, and when it came the time to say goodbye I popped my head inside her cabin, stowed my head-torch away in the pocket where it always lived and thanked her for looking after us. Her work was done. Mobi was about to begin her journey home, and so were we.

*

There was a huge amount of change and uncertainty when we all returned from Asia. With the Kingfisher sponsorship drawing to an end, new sponsors needed to be secured. Even before Asia I'd put a huge amount of thinking time into my future and I'm sure subconsciously part of the reason to head to South Georgia had been to continue exactly that. When sailing with Bilou just a few weeks before leaving for the south I had laughed until I cried. It had been fantastic to get back out there racing in the IMOCA 60 fleet again, made even more special by Bilou, and I was seriously considering two options. One was building a boat, a new version of the now outdated *Kingfisher*, with which to rejoin that fleet, and the second was a short-term plan to sail with Bilou on his boat for the two-handed Barcelona World Race. Thinking of racing round the world with Bilou appealed hugely to me, but if I built my own boat I could also sail the Vendée Globe. But, despite all the pleasure I was getting from the water, deep inside I was uneasy. Something I couldn't put my finger on was stopping me, and though I now had the corners there were going to have to be a few more pieces in the jigsaw for me to see what it was. I kept thinking back to things I had seen and felt in South Georgia, Lorient and now Asia. I had no idea where this process was taking me, and perhaps I wouldn't want to see what I found when I got there.

Ian and I managed to take a few days' break and head up to Skye, which was great fun. It was a brief trip, lasting only three days, but we caught the sleeper north and drove over from Inverness. The trip to Skye was for a purpose, as on 22 June I had the honour of being presented with the 'Freedom of Skye and Lochalsh' in Portree. I had asked if it would be possible at the same time to present to some of the youngsters from the local secondary school too, specifically about the trip to South Georgia. I wanted to try and give something back for the time and effort that everyone had put into the evening. It was very special to me to be accepted up there, and though I'd spent at least a month or two on Skye each year since 2003, I was far from being a local. I had really appreciated going up there and talking to people to discover more about my family, finding out that they were fishermen, and in which croft houses they had lived. It was fantastic too that two of my elder relatives from Skye, Anne and John Patience, were able to come up for the evening. Many of our friends were there too, and I really enjoyed the evening, nattering to people and catching up. I was presented with a framed text, hand-painted on to skin, which was absolutely beautiful. As I had sailed around the world I had taken photos and cards from friends on Skye with me, and the incredible soul of the island had certainly kept me going. What made it really special was that Anne was wheelchair-bound with MS, and it wasn't until afterwards that she told me that she hadn't left the house for five years. Despite her situation she never complained and was always full of humour and the most wonderful spirit.

With spring established and the weather warming it was time to get Mobi back in the water and sailing again, and the year picked up to its usual fast pace as we flung ourselves into our final summer of corporate hospitality. We were again to take guests sailing from both B&Q stores in the UK and Castorama stores in France. It was still always lovely to see people's faces smile as they helmed the boat, or peered into her tiny cabin, wondering how one person, let alone the four or five in Asia, could possibly have lived in her. French hospitality was going to be in Dinard and then Vannes for most of the month of July, followed by UK hospitality in Cowes at the beginning of August for Cowes Week. I travelled back to the UK a couple of times so that I could sail with the young people who were taking part in the summer trips of the Ellen MacArthur Trust; in fact I even made it back to spend my thirtieth birthday with them!

I also had another job to do while we were waiting for our hospitality in Vannes and that was to go and become the godmother of the *CMA CGM Fidelio*. I knew that the *Fidelio* was a big boat, but when we approached her from the dockside she looked more like a steel-clad skyscraper than a ship. The letters along her hull sides were almost too big to make out when you were standing close to them, and I worried just how big the bottle would have to be to be visible. She dwarfed anything and everything which was near her, and my first thought was how utterly unbelievable it was that human beings could build something so huge. On our arrival we were met by the Saadé family, who own the line CMA CGM, and that day I discovered they were the third-biggest shipping company in the world. We walked along to the entrance of the ship and, being someone who has always loved learning, I immediately started asking questions.

Fidelio was so long, at 349 metres, that you would almost need a bike to go from one end to the other, and I later calculated that if you walked around the perimeter of the ship you'd be walking for just a fraction under half a mile, and it would take you fifteen minutes! Her engine room was like a factory, and the cylinders were so big you could almost have had a party in them. The engine itself was, at the time, the biggest combustion engine, dimension wise, which existed in the world, measuring 24 metres long, by 12.5 metres high, by 4.5 metres wide. But the size was not surprising when you considered that it was the equivalent power of 92,000 horses pulling the ship along. I felt like someone had 'shrunk' me as I looked down at her huge propeller shaft, which was solid steel and probably a metre across. Her actual prop, which we couldn't see as it was under the water, was 9.6 metres in diameter; significantly higher than your average two-storey house. I was also intrigued that she had no gear box, which meant that, if you wanted to go astern, you had to stop the engine totally and then restart it in reverse! That taken into account, it took 13 miles to stop and over 5 miles to turn – unbelievable. She could also go round the world non-stop on one tank of fuel, which would have her sit at her cruising speed of no less than 25.4 knots. It was a strange sensation launching something so large – almost too large to comprehend I felt. I was honoured that I had been invited to do so, though; it's not every day you get to stroll across a 42.8 metre bridge!

Another opportunity came up in the UK before the onset of Cowes Week. I had been offered the chance to drive a rally car for a UK team. The offer was of a car, preparation team and training to compete in the UK. I could only imagine that it had come about after the performance on *Top Gear*, though I'm sure that Mark said he'd had some contact before that.

I can't say that I wasn't excited by the prospect. I got a huge kick from *Top Gear* and had absolutely loved the challenge. It was exciting driving a car on the edge, and I knew that I would relish the opportunity. I was first invited to meet the team and learn more about it, and when I had the chance to sit in the navigator's seat in a WRC car I was totally and utterly blown away. I really warmed to the team at M-Sport; they were great and passionate people, and I was intrigued by the technical side, which actually had a lot of similarities to sailing. Seeing the guys designing and making the parts, followed by the skills of the team welding the cars, was fascinating. I had always loved messing about in my Dad's garage, and this for me was like an extension of that. The facilities there were second to none, as not only did they have a track to test on down the road, they could run an engine on a test bed in a unit which could recreate the heat, cold and moisture that the engines would have to deal with on different legs of the global circuit.

The objective of the day was that I could have a go in the Fiesta car and see if I was any good or not, and being one who's generally up for the challenge, I saw it as exactly that. The unfortunate part was that as I started the car to drive it over to the test track I stalled, and then continued to stall three times. How embarrassing. Luckily I was subsequently told that you would normally change gears in a rally car at about 6,000 revs. I was used to changing at 2,000, so I learnt that just a little bit more accelerator was necessary!

When we arrived at the track we were lucky that both the 2005 and 2006 WRC cars were testing there, and before the spin in our car I was given the chance to do a couple of laps of the test track in the navigator's seat. It was a strange experience climbing into a bucket seat from which you can't even see out of the window. I did my seat belt up, quite proud that I knew how to connect the straps correctly on a five-point harness; luckily, however, someone came to check it, took one look at it and said, 'That's not tight enough.' He hauled them in and then said, *'That's* tight.' He was right, and, though I was unable to wriggle at all in my seat, I was glad, as, when the turbo start engaged and we were off, if there had been any slack in my belt I think I might have had to change my pants!

That car was one of the most startling experiences I have ever had. I didn't expect it to be so fast; nor did I expect to have absolutely no idea of what direction we were going in! The G force was extraordinary, and I swear we were actually going sideways, as opposed to forwards, for 95 per cent of the time; it felt like we were blasting into orbit. Talk about adrenalin, I was riddled with it, and I was in awe of the cool confidence that the driver had, whilst everything to me appeared out of control. After a couple of laps I was released from my seat and I climbed out. I tried to look unflustered about it but totally failed. It was an awe-inspiring experience.

It was my turn, and despite spinning off the track once, and having to change a brand new exploded tyre, I think I did OK. I was amazed how much faster I was on the track at the end of the session compared to the beginning, and, though it took a while for the adrenalin to wear off afterwards, I loved it.

After a long period of contemplation, though, I decided that rally driving was not the right thing for me to do. It was a difficult decision to make, as I would have absolutely loved to have done it, and I would have given it my best shot. But for some reason I did not feel entirely comfortable, and though I had already discussed the fact that I would only race the car if it could run on bio-ethanol, it was not enough to satisfy my conscience. I guess I did not want to become a celebrity who got all the opportunities because of what she'd done, and I was absolutely certain that there was some young up-and-coming rally driver who had dreamt about that since they were four years old and would have given anything to take that car on. I had worked damned hard for years to be successful in sailing and I didn't feel I deserved to be able to just hop across into another sport. Though I didn't know it at the time, I was in the process of finding my way; but something inside told me that this wasn't right. Strange as it may sound, it wasn't important enough to fit into the jigsaw.

Cowes Week came and went quickly, and, as we neared the end, we realized that the atmosphere we had with Mobi as the centre of our team simply couldn't last for ever. Oli had already departed for Canada, where he now lived, Loik was about to return to his family in France, and Mobi was about to be repainted white while awaiting her next journey. There was sadness in the air, but we did go for one final sail, and with pretty much the whole OC team on board it was a special one. The following day she was due to come out of the water and be repainted so it really was the last sail with her as Mobi. I had some time off, as we had now reached the end of Cowes Week. I was quite excited too as my Mum was down for a few days on a special visit straight afterwards, and I was so pleased for her to have the experience of sailing her. Ian even came along and tried water-skiing off the back. It was nice to have the time to try things we'd always wanted to do, and everybody loved it.

Since I had returned from the south something had been gnawing away in my mind, and despite the good moments we had experienced during the summer of 2006, it was a really confusing and difficult time for me. Since the visit to South Georgia I knew something inside me had changed, and that change had taken place in a way that would not allow me to simply 'reset the switch'. Bizarre as it may sound, I felt that I was living in a world which I was beginning to question; I was seeing everyday things that I had previously ignored differently. It was as if a page had been turned before I had finished the last, and I could no longer return to the place I was at. For the first time I had been uncertain what to do next. The freedom and challenge of the sea was my passion, and since I was four years old I had dreamt about it, lived it, breathed it and never wanted that to change. But something had happened I didn't think possible. For the first time ever something was interfering with that passion, and, frightened though I was, I was beginning to realize that there was another challenge out there far greater than sailing.

Though South Georgia had been one of the most incredible experiences of my life, it had brought on a dark summer for me. Little did I know back then just how much it would teach me, but as I reflected on my thoughts that year the scene of the whaling stations kept returning to my mind. Horrific as it may sound to have killed 175,000 whales on one island, I don't believe we went there to be barbarians. We went down there because we needed the resource. We were using what whales could give us to feed us, make medicines for us and keep our bombs exploding, and, as whale oil was precious, it was worth travelling to the other side of the world for. But what felt so strange in those whaling stations was that everything was left as if we'd walked out yesterday. That felt odd to me, and in the back of my mind I was trying to work out just why. But as I sat on the sofa in the flat that difficult summer it came to me: we left because the industry had died. We'd taken the whales out at a speed many times faster than they could reproduce and virtually ran out of them. Then, in the nick of time, we discovered mineral oil, a seemingly endless resource from beneath the ground.

To me it was a symbol of how spectacularly we can miss the point. How we as a species can not only watch a resource deplete before our eyes, but then quite simply walk away, and, as if nothing was amiss, move on to the next one. *This is what we do.* My gut instinct was telling me something was wrong. I had relied on this instinct so many times to keep me alive at sea, that now I struggled to ignore it.

Imagine if someone said to you, 'Go now, go and find every single item you will need for your survival for the next three months.' How many pairs of socks? How many tubes of toothpaste? How much diesel for the generator? You may find it challenging, but that's just one of the tasks you have to complete before leaving on a non-stop round-the-world journey. Get it wrong, and you are going to fail in your mission, or, if you get it really wrong, you may quite simply not come home. If anything will concentrate your mind, then that will. Run out of food, and you will starve; run out of diesel, and not only will you have no batteries for the autopilot, or GPS, but you'll have no electricity for the water-makers either, and you could even die of thirst. But the other side of the equation is that you cannot take too much with you either. If your boat is too heavy, it will never break a record, and, in the case of a multihull, if the boat is too heavy it will exceed its design tolerances and break.

The battery voltage is like a heartbeat, and the batteries like a heart. No matter how exhausted you may feel, you take care of this and, if you missed a charge because you forgot or fell asleep, then you would likely find yourself thrown violently across the boat and swimming in darkness as your home takes the one-way trip of a capsize.

I would never have entertained the idea of leaving on a light or a computer screen unnecessarily; I couldn't afford to: I would have run out of fuel. Everything on board was finite, and the reality of that was never more evident than on the descent to the south, when our record was nearly scuppered by the sheer lack of lubricating oil in the generating engine.

Basically, there is no room for error at sea, and you are aware of everything you have. For my last seventy-two-day trip I'd taken thirteen kitchen rolls, and I knew that was the right number as I'd experimented during the Falkland Islands delivery. That kitchen roll was the only paper I had and I used it for everything from loo roll, to oil spills, to cleaning. When I needed some, though, I didn't tear off a whole sheet, because someone somewhere in the world had decided that that's where the perforated line should be, but I tore off a corner, or just what I needed. No matter how tired you are you have to be careful. There is no one to help you do this, and there is nowhere within thousands of miles to stop and restock on something you have run out of. Your boat is your world; your resources are finite. That is until you return to land. You think.

But there was a much more important lesson that I had learnt which did not revolve around *how* I tried to use less but *why*. For me looking after my resources was a survival instinct. I knew that they were limited. And I knew that when they were gone, they were gone.

Though I was not sure what I should take on myself I *was* aware that, in order for our company, OC, to stay alive, we needed to find new funding for new projects, and a lot of our discussions during that period were about that. The best part about the last round-the-world record for me was the teamwork; I had absolutely loved it, and I was really keen to see the team not only kept together, but buzzing again and taking on new challenges. But my mind had moved on, and my heart told me I couldn't skipper another Vendée.

I knew that, if I were to make the decision to race, once again the project would take over every aspect of my life. It was pulling me apart, and I felt I was letting everyone down. But inside I knew I was embarking on a very different journey.

But in deep discussions with Mark, and to keep our fantastic team together, we decided at this point to propose the creation of a sailing team. This would bring together three sailors, including me, and continue on with the successful skill set we had, but this time share the pressure and responsibility amongst us. The idea was that I would effectively 'lead' the team. This way we could use all our expertise in communication, sailing and boat-building skills to compete in a range of events with different boats to give the maximum number of opportunities to the team members and our sponsors. With this plan I could follow my instincts too, which were telling me to learn more about this new subject I'd never heard of before: sustainability.

At OC we agreed that this would be a 'theme' in our communication too, though we were in the very early stages. Whether my role would mean reporting from far-off places about issues, travelling back down to South Georgia or the Antarctic, I didn't know, but I knew inside that for my own commitment to any project this needed to be highlighted as one of my main roles. It seemed the perfect solution; I could continue putting my skills and time into the build and sailing programme and be with the team, and I'd get to spend more time learning about the subjects I'd begun to touch on in South Georgia. It was a great solution for everyone. But there was a consequence to all of this. There was no way I could possibly sail with Bilou in the Barcelona World Race.

The first company we contacted was BT, as we'd been officially sponsored by them as our communications partner since 1998, when I'd competed in my first properly sponsored race. In fact, I'd met a lady called Kim Fitzsimmonds at BT back in 1995, when I won the BT/YJA Young Sailor of the Year award, and we were still in touch with her. We had begun to talk to them about supporting us for a much bigger campaign, and we presented for the first time to them to see what they thought.

We were aiming to find a single sponsor who would be able to fund the whole campaign, and therefore get the most benefit from our activities. We began talking to a well-known insurance company through a lead from a good friend called Hugh Morrison, who had been instrumental in my career by introducing us to Kingfisher. Then, out of the blue came a link to an energy company and a bank. Surely one of these would come off, we hoped. All saw pretty much the same presentation, but it was interesting that both the energy company and the insurance company were more interested in the sustainability part of the presentation than the sailing bit. BT was into the sailing project, though the sustainability work became key to them too.

They say 'put your money where your mouth is', and that's exactly what we decided to do with every single bit of cash we could pull together in OC. Perhaps we'd have acted differently if we'd have known that we wouldn't secure a sponsor for the sailing team for over six months, but we had an ambition of keeping our team together and faith in finding a sponsor. That's why we decided to begin the financing of a boat that we could not even remotely afford to finish. It was a huge gamble, but we were determined she should be on the start line of the Barcelona World Race, which started on 11 November the following year; after all, it was a race that OC was organizing too.

The conversations with the sponsors were very positive on all fronts, though as always quite convoluted, and we knew only too well that until the contract is signed there is no security. Towards the end of the year, the discussions with the insurance company had progressed, and there was a significant deal on the table to do a huge project in the area of sustainability. I felt massively motivated and sorely tempted by this, as I really liked the people there, but for some reason something blocked me. I suppose that in my heart I knew that I didn't have experience in this area, and my instincts told me that I was maybe biting off more than I could chew at this time. I was devastated when we finally turned it down, but I knew I needed to learn. I had one chance to get this right, and if I tried to run too fast too soon I could blow it. It was difficult trying to make clear decisions too when the financial situation at OC was a constant cloud over us.

The other option of a company to work with was E.ON, the second-biggest generator of electricity in the country. My first reaction when the contact was put through to us by a friend was to say absolutely no; but I was curious, and it interested me. If my mission was learning, then I had a good chance of that working with one of the industry leaders in power generation. I saw it as a way in to understanding their challenges, and I agreed to a first meeting.

I was really impressed by the attitude of the people there, and the fact that they realized that they were as much a part of the solution as the problem. I was under no illusions as to how unsustainable the industry was, and I was pretty blunt with my questioning; but I couldn't help but feel there was will power in that room to really make a difference. Surely an industry so large could really change things. This was going to be a common theme moving forwards: working with industry rather than against it.

E.ON talked about their challenge to try and get people to use less energy, which I questioned instantly; as, consequently, they'd sell less of what they made their profits with. It didn't make sense to me. But their answers to our questions were clear and concise; they wanted to offer the best advice possible for people to do exactly this, and through that be the market leader. They were keen that my involvement would be working with the business-to-business part of E.ON rather than the retail part, and therefore learning about their industry and small business clients' energy savings would also be a valuable experience. We discussed the fact that, if I didn't agree with what they were doing, I would absolutely stick with my own point of view. They were in agreement. My role was to help drive change in the business. That I felt was a good thing, and just after the first Christmas I'd had at home with the family for four years, we signed E.ON as a sustainability partner to the sailing team.

Chapter Nineteen

Through this whole crazy summer of discovery and research there had been something else going on: Ian and I had been dreaming, planning and designing the house we would build at the plot.

We had set about clearing the brambles away to see what we actually had there, and to try to get a sense of the space that we had. On my return, and all through the summer, we had worked away, clearing metre by metre: Ian with a spade and garden fork, and me with an old scythe I'd found in the overgrown wooden tool shed.

We got to know our fantastic neighbours too. Norman and Paddy on one side taught us about what the plot used to be like, how the garden was, and how the area had been forty years before. We learnt about the history of the copse, and about the personality of the place. We would often go round for a cup of tea and a sit in their cosy area before we had any facilities to make anything of our own. They were caring and welcoming people, never worrying about how dirty we got working on the plot. They had both retired and both had enjoyed interesting lives. Norman had begun his working life as a cobbler, a trade learnt from his father, before becoming a fireman. As a result of this he was on the island during the war, and the stories that both he and Paddy told were absolutely captivating. Norman was a smallish man, and fit as a fiddle. His bright eyes twinkled, and his sense of humour was astute. Paddy had been a schoolteacher and had lived next door for over forty years. Her aim was to always have a plant 'in flower' in her garden, and her knowledge of species was enviable. In the summer they would come and sit outside together, chatting and reading in the shade of their swinging garden chair. I loved everything about the house in which they lived and the space around it. I was beginning to feel a real sense of community; something that I had not felt since I'd left Whatstandwell, my childhood home in Derbyshire.

It was really therapeutic for me working on the plot clearing the land and doing something physical but constructive. The thoughts I was having when I reflected on South Georgia were quite negative and almost depressing, and seeing what I had actually achieved at the end of a day, be it moving a shed or making an area useable, helped me be more positive. The trees were absolutely wonderful to be working around too, standing timelessly and majesticly by us. I had always loved woodland as a kid, spending hours in it making dens, it felt familiar and good for my soul. One of the trees on our plot must have been 200 years old, and I marvelled at the fact that, though we can build huge massive high-rise buildings in a matter of months, trees take their own time, and you can't hurry them. If you wanted to put a beautiful magnificent tree next to a new house, you couldn't: you'd have to plant a small one and then literally wait a lifetime.

Our first task was to build a garage, which we designed ourselves. It was quite captivating working out how it would all fit together, how we'd cut the roof and what we would build it out of. As we slowly cleared out the back, it became evident that there was actually quite a lot of space there, and though there were two beautiful old oak trees, between them was enough space to put a house. The planners were happy in principle with our idea, which gave us the green light to get on and build our garage.

We had discovered quite a lot about the site by this stage. It used to be a market garden, and, as we had cleared away the brambles, we found everything from cold frames, to greenhouse bases, to brick floors and foundations for buildings. There was even a hydraulic ram pump in the copse, which had clearly been used to deliver the stream water to the greenhouses using a method which did not need electricity at all, just water pressure. When I had stumbled upon it I had no idea what it was, but on speaking to a good friend, John, and doing a bit of research, we worked it out. These discoveries even on our micro scale made me think a lot about how things used to be. A pump that did not use electricity sounded very exciting to me, and it made me think more about the management of our little plot. I liked the idea of having a simple device which not only ran for free, but had very few moving parts. I also warmed to the idea of being as self-sufficient as possible. Perhaps it stemmed from the upbringing I'd had, but it gave me an intriguing sense of freedom, and of being more in control of my own destiny.

On uncovering bricks in the ground we looked into their origins; some said 'Gunville' on them and appeared to be the same bricks the house was built from. I was intrigued that they had been made on the island, and that our pond in fact was likely to be an excavation hole connected to our local brickworks. During the eighteenth, nineteenth and twentieth centuries there had been 101 working brickworks on the Isle of Wight. It was a sign of the times, I suppose, that now there was not even one; the last one having shut two years before I was born.

After moving the corrugated garage, we set about pegging out the new building. As we had designed the garage ourselves on paper, the marking out seemed all the more exciting. When we saw the footprint for the first time the yard looked dry and lovely; it's a shame when the autumn rain came down it didn't stay that way! The first task was to dig out the foundations, so we hired a 3 ton digger, and, with Ian's instructions, I set about learning how to drive it. It was a new skill for me, and one that needed a good deal of coordination. I was absolutely amazed at the power of the machine. We had dug a few test holes by hand, and it had taken two hours to dig each one; the digger could make a hole that size in two seconds. If we had been trying to dig foundations that size by hand I really think that we would have been there for a good few months.

As the summer progressed, so did the garage. We sourced some old hardwood windows from a reclamation yard on the island and found doors and chairs from the local car boot sale at a snip of a price. One of the internal doors was solid oak which we got for a bargain £3. I loved the feeling of using something again, things that otherwise could have easily ended up in landfill. It felt fantastic just being there, and was a great antidote to my worries for the future. I found it calming to watch the seasons change around me and to be working outside, and when I really got screwed up worrying about the right or the wrong thing to do moving forwards Ian had an uncanny knack of getting me involved with a consuming job so that the difficult moments were replaced by the more rewarding feeling of creating something. Other than being at sea or preparing a boat on the dock my work had mainly been indoors, and it struck me then that young people aren't really encouraged in school to be roofers or bricklayers, which is surprising given how rewarding it was! Though it was hard work, it was great work. I absolutely loved it. It was the closest I'd felt to being myself in a long time.

On 26 March 2007 Gran died, aged eighty-eight. She had been ill for some time but had always fought hard to stay with us. In fact, Gran was one of those people who on paper should not have really been around. Her mother was told that she would not make it beyond a few hours when she was born, but not only did she survive, she went on to give birth to two sons. She'd had a replacement heart valve, two plastic knees and a terrible thyroid problem which took her down to 8 stone before it was properly diagnosed.

Gran loved running the home and absolutely adored making meals for her family. You couldn't leave the house without being fed something delicious, and her Christmas puddings were the perfect culmination of eighty years' experience. She was a natural carer and spent a great deal of her life looking after others, which she did with such strength. Gran was someone who was calm and capable, and though she never sought to achieve great things in her life, what she did take on, or was faced with, she did with pride. She was a fighter and had lived on her own in the house for over fifteen years since Grandpa had died; it was just where she wanted to be. The house was very special to her; it was her home and it held so many memories from her own childhood, and that of her children. My Great Granddad worked all his life to buy the place, and it was his labour-intensive efforts to hang on to the house which turned it into something very special.

After Christmas 2006, Gran began to go downhill. Her health had been poor for years, and she had been into hospital numerous times for various operations. In her final few years she had struggled to do things: her heart was weak, and the slightest activity made her out of breath.

Towards the end of March Gran made a decision to leave us. In true Gran fashion she had planned her own funeral, and once she'd seen each and every one of her family, it was only a matter of hours before she died. Her mind was at rest with her loved ones around her, and it was almost like she chose this peaceful moment to slip quietly away.

I found it hard to rationalize why she chose to give up. Even though in our hearts we all knew that her time was over, to sit with her and hear her say that she'd 'had enough now' was very painful. I tried to talk to her and encourage her by saying that we were all here for her, but deep down I knew that she was tired of fighting. Selfish as it may seem, it made it harder for me to hear her say those words. Knowing someone very close to you is dying is distressing enough, but when they tell you that they must leave you, as their warm hand squeezes yours, it hurts in a way that I had never experienced before.

Dad and I both spoke at her funeral just one week later, and, though Dad got through the eulogy he had written for Gran with great strength, I choked up totally reading my words. I repeated a line that Gran had said to me in that last conversation, just a few days before she had passed away. We were talking about how beautiful the spring birdsong was, and how the morning light lit up the bright-green buds beginning to emerge in the trees. 'Nature is so beautiful and it's free for everyone,' she said. How right Gran was. They are words I shall never forget . . .

After these words I had to pause to compose myself. And in those brief seconds before reading on I tried to concentrate on the happiness Gran would feel at being reunited with Grandpa, just an hour away from being buried alongside him. They loved each other dearly, and I had a sense that finally Gran really would be able to rest in peace. I read on to get to my final line: 'The end of a life should not be about what is lost and gone, but about what lives on in all of us. Thank you for those memories, Gran.'

Gran didn't want for much; she sought company, conversation and her family, and visitors around to fuss over and look after. She was happy with her lot and only wanted the simple things in life. She had only ever been abroad once – for my brother Lewis's wedding – and in all the years I can remember Gran outside that, the furthest she ever travelled was Southampton to see me arrive with *Kingfisher* after sailing her solo to the shores of the UK for the first time. As a child she picnicked in the fields and collected berries from the hedgerows. She made jam with Nana, her mother, and strolled in the field with her boys and our Grandpa. These are the simple things in life that I am so grateful have been passed down the generations.

Dad had been so very lucky to grow up there at the house where Gran lived for eighty-six of her eighty-eight years. It was a proper family home, and there was always something going on. When I was a child I can remember sitting on Grandpa's knee, milking the Jersey cow which provided the family's milk, butter and cheese. I can remember riding the cow in the two fields either side of the yard. I loved it there, running round with a feeling of freedom, hiding in the hay bales and throwing sticks into the brook after damming it to create little ponds. The vegetable garden had always been well stocked, and I remember sneaking in there in the summers and pinching pods of peas, which were better than any sweets to us. Then there was the yard in which Grandpa had built his stonemason's workshop, which had a pig, turkeys and chickens running free. I remember the old long wooden shed, in which the chickens and the hay lived, which was so old that the grain of the wood was raised on its blackened walls, seasoned with layers of creosote. Dad is full of stories of the area around where he grew up, about the old windmill on the hill which still grinds corn today, which generations ago my ancestors used to run. I love walking with Dad in his old stomping ground and learning just how much has changed since he was a boy.

Gran was the last of a generation in our family, and with her death I felt not only a huge sadness but also a massive loss. She was born six months before the end of the First World War and had grown up in a house with no fridge and as a child had ridden in a horse-drawn cart. She had never learnt to drive, relying on walking or lifts from her friends and family. She knew how to make butter and cheese, how to salt a ham and preserve any fruit or vegetable for the winter, and I wished that I had asked her so many questions, but then it was too late. It seemed to me that the world had probably changed more in Gran's lifetime than in any other period. When Gran was born things were built and made to last. So much so that in thirty years I can never remember any new furniture appearing in Gran's house, including the ancient sofa which Gran always used to sit on, which has now moved to the Isle of Wight.

The night of Gran's funeral Ian and I headed up on the overnight sleeper to Skye. I have loved travelling on the Caledonian sleeper ever since I took it on our first family holiday in Scotland in 1998. I will never forget the train pulling into Crianlarich station late at night; Mum, Dad, Ferg and Mac were on the platform with me, and the station was so small you doubted that the sleeper could possibly stop there. Bang on time the train pulled in, and the guard stepped out on to the platform. 'Miss MacArthur?' he questioned as the train pulled in. He beckoned me into the carriage, and then asked me whether I would like tea or coffee with my breakfast. It felt like I had gone back to a time when people knew your name.

I like the sleeper best when it's heading north, though I never sleep well, as I am always too excited. I love watching the sun rise as the train travels through the Cairngorms at dawn, and I never want to be asleep to miss it! I would find myself glued to the window, watching the mountains, streams and wildlife pass by. It is not uncommon to see deer close to the tracks, and in many of the valleys through which the train travels there are no roads or signs of human presence at all. The air always seems so much cleaner and purer in Scotland, and looking at the mountains, many still with snow on them, reminded me so much of South Georgia.

I was feeling quite drained after Gran's funeral, and travelling somewhere further afield helped me to get on with things and think ahead. It had been a busy six months, and the two-week break we had ahead of us was something we were looking forward to very much. Once in our little cabin on the train, we settled down on the bottom bunk with our flask, oatcakes and snacks. It already seemed as if we had started our holiday, and, as the train rolled out of the station and began its long journey north, we were happily chatting about the excitement of where we would be when we woke.

The freedom I felt up in Scotland was hard to explain; being there somehow redressed the balance in my life. As we approached the Skye bridge on the bus my heart began to sing; the clear waters surrounding the deep-green rocky islands felt so refreshing. Those two weeks were fantastic fun, and we walked all over Skye, climbing up to the jagged Cuillin Ridge, almost 1,000 metres above sea level, and staring out across the sparkling sunlit water to the islands to the west.

One day we went up the north end of the island to visit the memorial to the MacArthurs, hereditary pipers to the MacDonalds, which sat high on the cliffs in the grounds of Duntulm Castle, then went to find an ancient MacArthur gravestone in the nearby graveyard at Kilmuir. They call the Isle of Skye the misty isle, and there is a very good reason for that. It was a moist, moody day, and you couldn't see from one side of the graveyard to the other. We were startled when we were met at the gate by a black cat, as the graveyard is not exactly in the centre of a township, but when we searched the graves for the one we were looking for we were quite surprised!

Seeing the cat sitting on the gravestone, however, brought back memories from when I was about nine years old, as it's not every day you stumble across a gravestone erected in a public place to commemorate an animal. We were off on one of our usual family summer strolls, out somewhere different for a change in the heart of Derbyshire. On this occasion we'd gone to the Derwent Dams, and it was here that I discovered the gravestone. The inscription read:

IN COMMEMORATION
OF THE DEVOTION OF
TIP.
THE SHEEPDOG WHICH STAYED
BY THE BODY OF HER DEAD
MASTER Mr. JOSEPH TAGG
ON THE HOWDEN MOORS FOR
FIFTEEN WEEKS FROM 12TH
DECEMBER 1953 TO 27TH
MARCH 1954,

ERECTED BY PUBLIC
SUBSCRIPTION.

I was pretty young at the time, but I remember vividly the emotion I felt at reading that story and, travelling home in the car, I could think of nothing but the story of a dead man and his loyal companion. It had somehow entered my conscience, and from that moment on the Border Collie (sheepdog) was my favourite dog. After taking this in, I began to watch bits of *One Man and His Dog*, to see the dogs working. I loved the intelligence that they showed and their incredible abilities. I was fascinated by them so much that I'd paint pictures of them and by the time I went to secondary school I had two life-size paintings stuck to my bedroom wall: one of a black-and-white Collie, with the name 'Mac' already chosen for it, and one of a browny-black tricolour Collie with big brown eyes and a puppy-like stare.

When a friend from school said that there was a rescued Border Collie pup 'going to be put down', we ended up with our Mac, the most understanding Collie cross you could imagine. Mac became my childhood friend, and as soon as she was old enough she was my companion for all adventures in the surrounding countryside. Unbelievably now, Mac was still with us at almost twenty, but she lived with Mum and Dad, where her home was, and more importantly where she was happy. I don't know what made us decide to look for another dog, but Ian and I had been scanning the rescue sections of the newspapers for a while.

When Floss came along it was quite unexpected. On the last day of that holiday, literally just a few hours before we left the island, I realized I had a message on my answer phone. It was the lady from the SSPCA on Skye who we'd been in touch with over the past weeks. Her message said that, if we wanted to go and see the ten-month-old Collie with the broken leg at two o'clock, then we could. I don't know why; because it was a pretty crazy thing to do, but we decided to change our plans, stay around and, rather than getting the bus from Portree, take our old vehicle to Inverness to catch the sleeper that night.

I'm not sure if part of it was the reaction to Gran's death and replacing part of that loss, but my gut told me it was the right decision, and we met at 2 o'clock in the planned parking area right next to the main road. We said hello, then the SSPCA lady opened the back doors of her van. We were met by a pair of huge, wolf-like amber eyes, set in the face of one of the most delicately framed Collies I'd ever seen. My first reaction was that she was not at all what I was expecting: she had incredibly short hair, a lot of brown in her coat and extremely long legs, one of which was covered with the biggest plaster cast I'd ever seen on a dog along the whole length of her back leg. As she lay there she looked at us in a sideways fashion, as she was too shy to look us in the face.

She was basically an unwanted sheepdog; for one reason or another she had failed as a working dog, thus spending much of her time in the shepherd's croft garden, digging and tearing roots out of the ground. Breaking her leg was really the final straw, so the SSPCA had taken her on to try and find a home for her.

Taking on a dog was by no means a decision to be made lightly, but I think that we both knew in our hearts we would give her a go. After all, we were due to be back in Skye a month later, so if she really didn't get on we had the opportunity to bring her back home all fixed. We agreed, and ten minutes later we drove off with our new dog, Floss. It was perhaps a good thing that we didn't know then just how traumatic the following few months were going to be.

We prepared for our journey home by popping into the local hardware store in Portree and buying her a lead, a collar, some food and a dog bed. We didn't have too long to hang around, as we had a three-hour drive to get to Inverness, so we set out hastily on our way. On the journey I called the Caledonian sleeper to book Floss into our cabin. I knew that there was an extra cleaning charge for a dog, so I wanted to make sure we had everything sorted in advance. Unfortunately the phone call did not go quite as well as I'd hoped. I was told that you needed to book a dog over forty-eight hours in advance, therefore it simply wasn't possible. We were in a difficult position and could not even stay over for an extra night, as on Saturday night the sleeper didn't run. I tried to explain the situation to the person on the end of the phone, but she wasn't really interested. We decided to make a rash decision and take Floss on the train with us anyway. We were both booked in the same cabin, so it wasn't as if someone else would have to travel with her. She wasn't in a state to leave her bed anyway – so we thought that we'd risk it! In the end it all turned out fine. We took Floss into the cabin without any problem; she stayed in her bed, so we didn't feel bad that she'd left any dog hairs. We did speak to the guard about it and paid for the cabin to be cleaned anyway – so hopefully in the end we hadn't upset too many people.

Once settled in our cabin, we began to relax after five hours of worry, and to check out our arrival time in London I pulled out my computer. It was then that I saw Floss's ears for the first time. I'd earlier been playing a CD, and it burst into a tune; she looked up instantly, head on one side, showing off two huge furry radars. I had never seen such big ears before in my life!

In the middle of the night I got a bit of a surprise, though. As I lay there in the dim light of the cabin next to Floss in her bed I leaned over to check her. The reaction I got was quite a surprise to me, as what I saw was a lovely set of white teeth, which she was baring at me: I didn't understand her behaviour and I lay there in silence, worried about just how much we had taken on. It was therefore with great relief that we arrived in Euston Station, and I was able to deal with my thoughts in a more logical daytime thought process.

Our next Floss drama made my night of worry pale into insignificance, though, as that very afternoon, just hours after our arrival on the Isle of Wight, her plaster cast fell off.

The next six weeks were horrific and worrying. The Isle of Wight vets were not able to put a new cast on her, as her bones had passed each other in her leg, so she would need an operation. Without even going home for anything we drove straight to a specialist surgery that was based in Surrey, as she was going to need a plate in her leg to fix the break. We arrived there late on the Saturday night, to find the vet still in a consultation. The first question we were asked was: 'Is your dog insured?' which I have to say was not really something we'd had time to do. Needless to say, the receptionist seemed quite surprised when we explained that we'd only picked her up the previous lunchtime! When we saw the vet we explained as much as we could about what had happened, and I mentioned that her foot had swollen hugely over the past few hours. Since the cast had fallen off it had doubled in size; I felt a sick feeling inside which worried me deeply – I could not understand what could have happened.

We left Floss at the vet's for three days while they assessed her and carried out the operation, and when Katie, my new PA, and I went to pick her up on the Tuesday afternoon she looked quite washed out. She did, however, seem to show some pleasure in seeing us, which was nice. Her leg was shaved all over, and she had a neat stick-on bandage taped over the long incision on her leg. We were shown the x-ray of the repair – she had sixteen screws and a sizeable plate along the whole of her upper back leg bone. Her foot had also been x-rayed, but it showed nothing. I had a nagging feeling inside about her foot: I knew that what I was seeing was not normal. Whether that was just my gut feeling or bits of knowledge I'd picked up in the three years I'd worked at a vet's in Derbyshire, I don't know, but I felt that there was something bad going on there.

The following weeks it just seemed to get worse and worse, as her foot split open and went a grey-green colour. It then very quickly started to decompose, with her side toes and pad hardening and turning black. At the same time she had to have a second operation, as she was twisting the plate through using her leg. The answer was to fit an external carbon bar and two stainless steel pins, which were attached to her bones. Several days after that same operation it became clear what had happened, and the vet on the island explained what it was. Floss's foot had developed gangrene. Unfortunately the cast which she'd had on when we picked her up was also placed over her foot, and when her foot tried to swell up it couldn't, causing the blood to stop circulating. The worst part of it, though, was that gangrene is an infection which can spread, and we had no idea how much of her foot or leg would be affected. It was possible that after all we'd been through she might have to have her whole leg amputated. The best we could do was to take her to the vet's on a daily basis to have the dead tissue removed and to see how her foot was doing. She had to be sedated each time. After a few weeks of this we got the call from the vet that he was going to have to amputate her two toes and pad from beneath. The news was quite traumatic, but at the same time I was pleased that for now at least she'd still have two toes. The vet did say, though, that if she lost one more, he would advise removal of her whole leg.

I was surprised how emotional the whole journey was with Floss, taking her into the vet's and picking her up after another bout of sedation. I was really surprised by her attitude – almost as if she knew that we were trying to help her. She was still terribly timid, and each time we returned to pick her up she would roll over on her back and pee on the floor in submission. But despite this she never once resisted walking back into the vet's building. She must have been petrified but she always took her tablets without any hassle at all. On one evening she scared us as her foot bandage just fell off. It was after the amputations and it was really quite shocking, as we hadn't seen her foot since it had begun to turn black. She simply didn't seem to have one any more, just a couple of pads on the end of her leg and raw skin and stitches everywhere. We tried to keep calm and keep her from getting it dirty. I quickly sterilized some scissors, slit the bandage along its top and somehow, thanks to her incredible patience, we managed to get it back on again, hearts beating hard in our chests. She was amazing. It was such a relief when finally her ordeal was over, and her frame and bandages were removed.

She was a pretty brave dog, I thought, but we were soon to learn that, despite her timid nature, she had a will of steel! They say that dogs take after their owners, and I have to say that if there was ever a determined dog it would be Floss, so there could be a distant similarity there!

Floss was at the 'highly strung' and 'sensitive' end of the scale, and I began reading every book I could about Border Collies from cover to cover. I was desperate to try and understand exactly what was going on in Floss's mind. I wanted to provide what she needed to come out of herself, but most importantly at the same time feel safe. She had issues in a few areas such as meeting other dogs, being fussed over by people she did not know, and was very stubborn when it came to handing over the ball and such like. When she met other dogs she would walk up boldly and wag her tail; then after a few seconds in many cases she would bare her teeth at the other dog and then snap under its neck. She has never actually bitten anyone or anything, but she looked fierce, and it wasn't a very nice experience to go through as an owner!

As it transpired, these were all signs of fear-aggression, and it became clear that she was certainly not convinced that we were the leaders of her pack. I felt I'd done everything I could, trying to put into practice everything I had read in the books, but we weren't making too much progress. The frustrating thing was that you knew that she knew what you wanted her to do, but you also knew that she was choosing not to. One example of this was back up in Skye, where she was being an absolute nightmare. She had bared her teeth at a friend of ours, and tried to 'round up' another friend's child. Both were a surprise as they were the first signs of her acting like this, both with a friend, and with a child. She was on a lead too, but you could see it in her expression, she was behaving as *she* felt fit – not as we wanted.

To illustrate her thought process, I can describe an incident when we were trying to involve her in a game with a tennis ball. Each time we threw the ball to her she ran off with it. When we called her she didn't really seem so keen to come, and so we got a bit fed up with going up to her and prising her mouth open to return the ball. Ian and I therefore decided to play with each other and leave her out of the game. We had a few happy minutes playing with the ball;

278

that was, until I dropped it, and, before I could get to it, Floss had run to it, crouched over it and then actually peed on it right in front of us! That summed up her attitude; if you don't want to include me in your game then screw you – I'm claiming *my* ball! At that point in her life, if she had been capable of making snide remarks behind our back, she would have done. She was the delinquent teenager multiplied by ten!

Helping us through this time was a lady called Barbara Sykes. She was able to read dogs like no one I'd met before, and we got on well from the word go. She had just set up a new charity which rehomed Border Collies, after having worked with them for years, and her commitment to the dogs inspired me to gratefully accept her offer of becoming its patron, and a good friendship followed.

The subsequent months were deeply frustrating. Trying to get Floss to walk behind us, we might take thirty minutes to do a journey that would normally take three. She was stubborn, very stubborn, but luckily so was I, and, for her own wellbeing, I had to be the pack leader. Basically we learnt that, though she was head-strong in some ways, she was a frightened little dog, and what we'd been unwittingly doing was putting her into a situation where she felt that she had to take control. As Barbara said, you wouldn't thrust your child into a stranger's arms for anything, so why would you do that to a dog! No wonder she showed her fright somehow. I felt bad that we had got this so wrong and made her feel vulnerable, but that feeling made me all the more determined to put it right.

But bit by bit, little by little, we began to feel that her attitude to us was changing. She was becoming more responsive, she trusted us, she was no longer taking every situation upon her own shoul-ders, and she was letting us deal with things for her. I cannot now believe that the dog we took on in Skye is the same dog that we have with us today. Sure, she still has her issues, she will always be timid, and if you let her she'll try her hardest to cunningly manipu-late you, using her cheekiness and humour, but she gives so much back with her devotion, loyalty and character. Now, not only will she give you the ball, but she will put it in the exact place you ask her to. She will not only walk behind, but she will run for miles at your heel. Now, no matter what has surprised her enough that she wants to chase it, you can stop her, and then she comes running back to you with love in her eyes. You can command her with body language or a facial expression, and raising your eyebrows is enough for her to stop being naughty. You can teach her a new word by associating it with something and saying it only twice. You can talk to her, and she listens, cocking her head from side to side in the most inquisitive fashion, as if she's straining to understand every single word you say. She knows your moods, she gets excited with you if you are happy, and if you feel sad she will come to you and lick the tears away. Barbara summed it up well: Floss was feeling that she had found her 'for ever' home.

Perhaps in my early years I had lived in an idyllic and simple world; we had been so lucky with Mac, but Floss had shown me that life sometimes is not like that. And just because life is not like that it doesn't mean that success can't shine through in the end. I'm not sure I have ever been through such an emotional roller-coaster with an animal as I experienced with Floss. The torment of not knowing what would happen to her leg was the only thing I could think about for weeks, and that worry for her health was all mixed in with her behavioural issues. I suppose I also had the fear of failure with her, and that, even though I believed in her, perhaps I could not sort this. I had been through a traumatic experience with Luis during which I thought will power and effort could sort it out, but it didn't, and in the end I realized it never could have.

Floss renewed my confidence and taught me not to give up, to be patient and that rushing at things doesn't solve every situation. She taught me to be consistent, caring and to control my own stress to be strong for her. But above all, in the process of learning to understand her, I've learnt a lesson I didn't expect: how to understand people better too.

Chapter Twenty

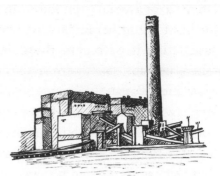

The following year, 2007, for me was the year I felt torn in two directions. I was trying to learn as much as possible about sustainability, but at the same time trying to keep the funding streams flowing and keep the boat build alive. As the year progressed, the pressure increased, and, though we'd managed to secure E.ON as a partner, we still had a title sponsor to find. It was a strange time for me; OC employed twenty-five people by now, and I felt, in part, responsible for them.

Luckily, there had been another development, as we'd been approached by a Spanish beer manufacturer, Estrella Damm, who wished to sponsor a boat for the two-handed round-the-world Barcelona World Race. With the cash flow as it was, we did not take long to decide to go for it and, using the capital from that partnership, we were able to plug the gap on the boat build.

At the same time BT were happy in principle with how we were planning the project, though we were still in negotiations about just how exactly the team and the project would work. The pressure was off from the boat point of view too, as it was clear now that our project would begin for them with the Transat in spring the following year, if, of course, they were still up for it. As a result of the positivity of our negotiations the team was coming together too. We'd been in discussions for some time with French sailor Sébastien Josse, who was excited to be skippering the 60, and we agreed he'd take over the boat straight after the Barcelona World

Race. The Vendée Globe was the big goal, and, as Seb had competed in that before and had just returned from skippering a Volvo 70 round the world, he was the perfect man for the job. Nick was going to take the helm of the Extreme 40, which was an innovative fleet of large high-performance inshore catamarans in a new circuit we at OC also happened to be organizing called the IShares Cup. Then there was me, the Ellen in Team Ellen, who would primarily race the third boat in the fleet. Not as big or as glamorous as the others, she was a Formula 18 two-man catamaran dinghy, and, as Nick and I had failed to complete the Archipelago Raid some years before, I felt there was some unfinished business there.

Everyone at OC was over the moon later that year when BT together with Cisco decided to go with the sponsorship of the sailing team. We celebrated with our project launch in September on the Seine in Paris, where we had the Extreme 40 in her new BT colours; Nick, Seb and I were all there to announce 'BT Team Ellen', our sailing team partnership. I was chosen to do a speech but found it difficult to stand on the podium talking about the guys skippering the boats, but as I began to speak about my role as sustainability ambassador I found a powerful, but subtly different energy in my voice. After well over a year of negotiations we finally had our title partner signed up, and with the good fortune of the Estrella Damm charter everything was beginning to fit together quite nicely.

I had embarked on a new journey, and the more I learnt the more I realized what there was to learn. I spent most of my time hungry for knowledge and trying to collect it anywhere and everywhere I could. I was seeing things differently, and it was fascinating me.

The end of 2006 had involved visits to the Buildings Research Establishment (BRE) in Watford, BedZed in London, and CAT, the Centre for Alternative Technology, based in Machynlleth, North Wales. I had visited CAT as a child. It had been set up back in the early 1970s, when a group of people took over an old slate mine and began trialling new ideas there. But things appeared to have moved on, and twenty years after I had first visited they were building a £3 million education centre there. I remembered the solar panels and the ingenious system of water-powered cars on tracks which took you up the almost vertical slope to the centre.

Ian and I had gone together to try and learn more for our house, and we were hugely excited to find a hydraulic ram pump there, working identical to the one we'd uncovered at the bottom of our garden. On the little plaque was written 'BLAKE'S 'HYDRAM'', just like on ours, and at the bottom it said 'JOHN BLAKE Ltd ENGINEERS' and underneath 'ACCRINGTON ENGLAND'. Seeing the name on there made me wonder who John Blake was. The serial number on the pump was 28616, so I guessed he must have got something right! It was great to see that it was made in this country too, and it reminded me of the many Saturdays I'd spent with my Dad at the farm-sales, collecting all sorts of old tools, implements and bits and pieces. A hydraulic ram pump is a brilliant system: it needs no electricity, and with only one real moving part it uses the power of a stream to create a vacuum and lift a proportion of that water up a significant height. It ran with a lovely put, put, put sound. We would have loved to get ours going again, but there would be little use for it now. The spring from which it was fed apparently used to provide the water for most of Cowes, but now the water table was so low it was merely a trickle.

They had displays of how solar water heaters worked, with little temperature sensors in the different circuits, so you could see how, by doing simple things, the water came out pretty hot. The first thing was pushing cold water through a normal radiator painted black; then they covered it with glass and insulated behind it; finally it came out at 69.8°C, not bad for a day with patchy cloud at the end of September.

They had a house there too which was massively insulated. The walls were really thick, and you could see a cross section of what was in it. It was simple when you thought about it: when it gets colder we just put on a jumper, and if it is windy we put on a water- and windproof coat as well. Why should a building be any different? It's got heat in it because of us being in it. We as humans are capable of living in -50 degrees by not letting the heat from our bodies escape, so with the heat of several people in a house, I wondered why it should be so different. Wall insulation was like wearing a jumper, and roof insulation like wearing a hat. It took me back to my childhood days when I used to watch a cartoon called *Gran*, which was about a very dynamic Gran who tried all sorts of activities when inspired by her Grandson Jim. One of the programmes had Gran knitting a very long scarf to wrap her house up in for the winter!

I spent a lot of my time trying to understand the basic principles of sustainable buildings, and from what I was learning it appeared to me that there were two schools of thought. You either went with what's called the 'thermal mass' building like BedZed, which is kept at a constant temperature through summer and winter by the mass of concrete or stone in it, or you went for the lighter, more sustainable wooden box, which would heat up quickly if you needed the heat, but which would also cool down quickly. In short, there was little heat stored in the fabric of the building other than the heat in the air. Older buildings fell into these two categories too, as the old stone cottages like my Nan's house in Derbyshire had big, thick walls, a huge fireplace and little windows to keep the heat in. Once the walls were warm the place always felt cosy, but it took a lot of energy to get to that point. A wooden hut, on the other hand, would heat up pretty quickly with a small fire.

We decided that it would be sensible to incorporate as much as possible of what we were learning into the flat, as we were still living there while we were building the garage. We changed the regularly used light bulbs from incandescent or halogen to low-energy. I had tried it a few times before, but had always been disappointed with the brightness of the light, so I had changed back. It was now that I realized that CFL low-energy light bulbs take a few minutes to get to full brightness, and I was frustrated that I hadn't known that at the time! I felt silly really that when I'd fitted the flat out six years earlier I hadn't given any thought to all this; in fact, two of the lights I'd had in the kitchen were 150 watt floodlights! The flat, though cosy in winter, was always quite dark inside, so we also decided we'd try out something called a sun pipe. It's essentially a roof window that's designed to let light in through any loft space, creating a skylight effect where you can't fit a skylight. It's a small, flat glass window on the outside, and a silver foil tube bringing light through the roof space or loft to the ceiling of the lower room. It transformed our relatively dark flat, as the back wall was for the first time flooded with natural light.

My inquiring mind was keen to know how energy generation worked on a broader scale in the UK, as I wanted to understand it before I jumped to any premature conclusions. It was here that the relationship with E.ON came to the fore as I was able to visit several power stations, among them Radcliffe in Nottinghamshire and Kingsnorth in Kent. Both of these were coal-fired power stations, and, though I knew that coal was about as far from renewable energy as you can get, it still accounts for more than a third of the electricity generated in the UK today, and I wanted to find out more. The most staggering thing about a coal-fired power station is the size of everything. In the distance the cooling towers always look huge, but when you stand next to them the word huge takes on a whole new meaning. I even had the chance to walk through one, which was like stepping into a concrete tropical forest, with warm rain constantly falling. Each team of workers, whether the guys who manned the control rooms or the engineers who maintained the burners, reminded me of the teams I'd been part of at sea, and everyone was welcoming. They were a close-knit group of people, and the feeling I got from both stations was that each team was clearly engaged in a mission to keep the nation's lights on.

At Kingsnorth we were allowed to look into the active burners, which was quite supernatural. In the sides at various heights were small doors, about the size of a small wood-burner, and to check that the burner was lit you manually opened them, keeping your distance, of course, to see. The first we saw was just like peering into a bright orange room. If you looked carefully through squinted eyes you could see the fly-ash like dust in the air. The second door was quite different, and was hotter, being higher up. It was slightly narrower, which was a sign, and, as our guide, Gary, opened it, we looked in with amazement. What we could essentially see was the combustion itself and we could clearly make out the raging inferno with its yellow, orange and white hot roar. It gave the impression that whatever was in that boiler was fighting to escape. The noise was quite surprising, and I found myself quite stunned by its power.

In an attempt to lighten my own mood at least, I turned to Gary: 'Don't tell me you've never tried to cook a sausage in there,' I said, slightly cheekily.

I liked Gary, he was a nice guy and I thought I could get away with it.

'Sausage?' he joked. 'We've done better than a sausage. We've cooked a whole chicken in there before.'

We also had the opportunity to stand in an unlit burner. Occasionally they pull them out of commission for a day so that the welders can scale the walls and make repairs to the miles of pipes that line them and which are filled with high-pressure steam to drive the turbines. We climbed through the tiny hole at the bottom, which I guessed was normally used to remove the ash, and then stood up, to be met by a group of guys all smiling with blackened faces and harnesses on. We said hello to everyone working in there, and then I was passed a powerful torch to look up to the roof with. I switched it on and looked up, and I'm glad it was dark in there, because my mouth must have fallen open. The burner disappeared into the roof, and even my torch could only just make out the ceiling, which must have been nearly 200 feet above us. The walls, though grey in colour from the fly-ash, reminded me of the pipes in an organ, and at different heights you could see the holes where the coal dust was blown in to combust. I stood in there gazing up, totally speechless.

The scale of the whole place astounded me. We had the chance to stand on the roof of the building, and, though we were 200 metres below the flue gas chimney, it felt like we were on top of the world. I talked with Gary about my feelings around sustainability, and we found we were on the same wavelength. He'd felt that energy prices could only go one way, and, as a result, over a decade before he'd put solar panels on his house to heat his water. When we looked out, we could almost see the North Sea, and below us were the estuaries I used to cruise in as a child with my Auntie Thea. To the south we could see the huge jetty where the coal for the plant was landed, with a 14,000 ton ship alongside. It looked much smaller now than it did when we were clambering over it a few hours earlier.

What didn't look smaller, however, was the huge pile of coal which lay to the east, and it took a while for me to realize that the tiny yellow Tonka toys were in fact huge earth-moving machines. There were 1.1 million tons of coal in that stockpile, and, though it looked like a mountain, it would only actually last for sixty days. That meant that the station at full capacity burned over 125,000 tons per week, 30 tons every *two and a half* minutes – the equivalent of one huge truckful. It would have taken my Great Granddad an awfully long time to have pulled that out of the mines with his pit ponies!

I'd learnt back at school in Derbyshire that coal was buried sunshine, old dead plants superheated underground and compressed for millions of years. That is until we came along with picks, shovels and then huge machines, having found a miracle rock that could keep us warm and light our homes. Seeing the speed at which we were now turning it from a dense black powder to an intense inferno, I began wondering how much of this precious stuff we had. I went to the World Coal Institute website for information, and on their home page, in big orange text, it said 122 years. Admittedly, it did say underneath that coal will last us for *at least* the next 122 years, but I was expecting it to say 500! I had sat on my Great Granddad's knee, listening to stories of his life, until I was eleven years old. I could remember his big hands and the vivid descriptions of his life down the pit as if it was yesterday. My Great Granddad was born 117 years ago.

Ultimately, I guess, coal is a renewable resource, but 290 million years is a long time to wait for the next batch.

Being someone who goes through life questioning things, I have to admit that a significant part of my time was spent wondering why I was thinking so much about this subject in the first place. When I looked around and saw the changes that were happening around me, I did sometimes worry that my thoughts were coming from another planet. I would see posters and billboards being replaced by

TV screens, at the same time as TVs just got bigger and bigger. Despite the fact that a 'green revolution' was underway in 2007, our country's energy usage was still increasing year on year. It was the year that Al Gore's film *An Inconvenient Truth* came out, and also Leonardo DiCaprio's *11th Hour*, which got a huge amount of coverage, and there was a growing feeling that green issues were stepping up to a higher level.

I was keen to try to learn what people could actually do if they felt passionate about this, so I went to a few conferences to learn what was going on. I went to a WWF conference about One Planet Living, based on the principle that, if everyone in the world used the same number of resources as we do in the UK, then we'd need three planets to support us. I liked their idea, and I thought that it was a clear way to put the point across. I was impressed too by the importance of the people who were there, and by what they were saying. David Miliband, then the Environment Secretary, was speaking, as was Sir Stuart Rose from Marks and Spencer. I was encouraged by the number of CEOs there, which I thought was a pretty good indicator of how seriously people were taking the issue.

As someone who is passionate about communicating, I was finding it hard learning all this stuff and not knowing how to share it. I knew I wasn't an expert at any of this, but I had real fire inside me. I had begun writing a blog to try to share what I was learning, but at the same time I wondered how many people even knew what the word 'sustainability' meant, and when compared to logs from a racing boat deep in the Southern Ocean it must have sounded pretty dull.

But I had come across something which was actually eclipsing sailing and taking priority in my mind. Day by day, I was realizing that it was far more important than any race or any record I could compete in, but also that communicating the message of sustainability was going to be an uphill struggle.

Chapter Twenty-One

Almost all of my sailing in 2007 before our BT Team Ellen launch was centred on the work of the Ellen MacArthur Trust, and I absolutely loved it. Since 2004 the Trust had had an inspirational leader in the form of Frank Fletcher, and we were going from strength to strength. He was not only a great visionary for what the Trust could achieve, but he was a great friend to the young people who sailed with us. Around everything that the Trust did there was a certain magic, and being with young people who were discovering things for the first time, with their huge, precious smiles and enthusiasm, was a joy for everyone involved. I couldn't think of a better reason to get out on the water, and, above all, every time we had an absolute ball.

My only actual race that summer was the legendary Round the Isle of Wight Race, and it left a lasting impression. I had competed almost every year since I had moved to the south coast, beginning with my mini-Transat boat ten years before. It's the biggest yacht race in the world and covers the water with sails, and there is always a real buzz in the air around it. Everyone is out there, from tiny cruisers to huge racing boats, kids, families and professionals, and the spirit amongst the sailors is quite special.

As we were still in the process of signing our sailing-team sponsor, I chose to take up an offer to helm an Extreme 40 catamaran. Extreme 40s are not exactly slow; in fact, at 40 feet long, with a mast over 60 feet tall and weighing in at just over 1.3 tons, they go at lightning speeds. They are built almost entirely out of carbon fibre, have no electronics whatsoever, and when they accelerate as the sails fill, if you are not holding on tightly, you will fall over. JP Morgan Asset Management were sponsoring the race and, as they had given a significant donation to the Trust, I had agreed to helm their boat. Of course we were out there to be competitive, but at the same time we were realistic about our goals. There were four other 40s out there, all, I believed, far more experienced than us, plus we were by no means the biggest boats in the fleet – the biggest monohull was a staggering 98 feet. Our start was very early, at 0510, though the biggest boats had started ten minutes before us. We met on the dock at 0415 before it was even light, which was a big ask for our guests. We had explained to them previously that it would be a good idea to use the loo before we sailed, as on board there was no cabin, let alone a toilet.

The wind was due to be pretty strong too, and there had been much talk of whether the 40s would sail at all if there was too much. I think our guests were quite surprised when I handed them a knife each, as, if the boat capsized, they could get trapped under the net. Though I had little doubt that between us we'd get them out, I wanted them to be as safe as possible. Extreme 40s are designed for inshore, round-the-buoys racing, where a long race would last twenty minutes. This race was 60 miles round an island, and for the majority of boats it takes all day. That day we were going to be racing out of the sheltered waters of the Solent into the English Channel and off St Catherine's Point, the most southern point of the island. We were all aware that conditions could be a little feisty! On board we had Nick Hutton, George Skuodos, Greg Homann, me and our two guests: Jo Kent, a BBC South journalist, and Campbell Fleming, whom I had met before, a wonderful, happy character, who just happened to be the head of JP Morgan Asset Management. No pressure, I thought to myself as we clambered on board.

As we were gently towed out of the marina at Cowes, the sun was just beginning to rise, and the Solent was slowly filling with masts and anticipation. We were nervous about the race. Extreme 40s are very easy to capsize, having so much sail, but we decided to give it a shot none the less; if the weather was too bad, we could always turn back. But we didn't turn back, and the following four hours and six minutes were going to be one of the best rides of our lives. The boat was fast, very fast, and, as the sails filled for the first time, my adrenalin soared. The water was filling up with thousands of boats, and at the speeds that 40s cruise around we all had to be on our tocs to avoid them.

Half an hour later, the start gun fired, and we were clear – off to the west with our sights set on turning the corner at the Needles lighthouse. Conditions were gusty, and, though we tried to stabilize our windward hull, where our guests were sitting, it frequently lifted 2 or 3 metres above the water. With the boat heeling over so much it can be quite disconcerting, but the calm faces of the crew created relative contentment on board.

After just over an hour we rounded the Needles, and the silence of our guests, well Campbell's anyway, was replaced by loud, whooping cries. Our boat, freeing off the wind, was getting up to speed and feeling as if it would fly off into orbit. Everyone was right at the back, guests included. The aim of the game was to use the weight to keep the bows from digging into the water, sending us into a cartwheel. At the same time, concentration on the helm went up to another level. Though we didn't know it at the time, one 40 had turned back at this stage, and on another my good friend Charlie had been catapulted off the back with the acceleration. The following hour and a half was extraordinary: concentration was at its peak, and the sailing was more like the surfing you'd see on a Hawaiian beach. Water fired up through the nets, soaking our guests, but through the spray could be seen the widest smiles on their faces. It was so wet that Campbell claimed he was getting a sea-water enema; he clearly loved the ride. Helming was so challenging that George, sitting next to me, with whom I'd never sailed before in my life, had to sit on my knee to stop me from being chucked out of the side of the boat by the power of the helm. A millisecond's lack of concentration and we'd be upside down, and with the bigger waves of the English Channel that was not a nice prospect.

As we surfed past the lighthouse at St Catherine's Point we all had smiles on our faces: we had taken the lead overall in the race and we aimed to hang on to it. The next corner to turn was the east side of the island, and it meant changing the angle of the wind on the sails. With a multihull, when you are up- or downwind you have a safe angle you can quickly turn to, but when you are reaching, with the wind across the side of the boat, safety is a long way away. Once the sails are eased there is little else you can do to stop the boat going over, and a few times on that reach we were right on the very edge.

Though *ABN Amro* got close to us off Bembridge, we managed to hang on to the lead until we crossed the line at 0916. Not only had we made it back in time for breakfast, but we were the first boat to cross, taking line honours. I have to say that, despite the fact that his BlackBerry was out of action due to water ingress, Campbell Fleming was one of the happiest people I have ever seen that day. He, the head of JP Morgan Asset Management, had won the JP Morgan Asset Management Round the Island Race, on a boat called *JP Morgan Asset Management*.

But for me it was a different feeling of happiness. It was absolutely wonderful to be back out on the water again.

In addition to our boat, we had two of our Trust Ambassadors, Dan Monk and Katie Miller, sailing for the Trust on Katie's *Corribee* and two other boats, each with five young people from the Trust on board, too. The land-based side of our activities involved ten walkers circumnavigating the island on foot, starting at 0430, and forty cyclists, who cycled the course and beat us! Some of the young people on the boats described the race as 'wet and fun'. I could certainly vouch for that as the atmosphere on board our boat too!

A few weeks later, at the Trust we began to run our four-day yacht trips, which as usual spanned the month of July. I always tried to meet every single young person who sailed with the Trust, and over the previous five years I'd not been too far off managing it. My normal routine was to meet them all in Yarmouth Harbour on the Wednesday morning, which was the third day of their trip. Crabbing is a common pastime amongst the kids, and it would not be unusual to see a few crabs in buckets, and bodies sitting on the pontoons with lines at hand! If I was there early enough there would be time for a bacon sandwich and a cup of tea before they were pleasantly surprised by two black ribs arriving to take them for a spin round the Needles. They absolutely loved it and would often scream as the boats did donuts and sprayed them with water. It gave them a chance to go just a little bit further, see a little bit more, experience a different aquatic activity from that they would have on the yachts, and I got so much pleasure from sharing that with them. The highlight would be seeing someone either come out of the door of the lighthouse on the westernmost rock of the Isle of Wight or leaning over the side of the rib in Scratchells Bay, looking down through the water at the seabed.

That evening would be their last one, and it was spent in the most beautiful setting of Newtown Creek. One of my favourite spots on the island, it's a tranquil estuary in a designated nature reserve. We usually hang out on the western spit, on the beach by the entrance, and with Frank manning the barbecue and the rest of the team playing games, the whole atmosphere is just pure magic. We would walk down the long shingle beach looking for driftwood, the young people in little groups, nattering away to their new-found friends as if they had known each other for ever. There might be campfires on the beach or a guitar might come out, and then, as the sun prepared for bed, passing through yellow to pink to red, so did we. Group by group, the dinghy would pick everyone up, and they would return tired to their boats. Their final night at sea would be spent falling asleep to the gentle sound of water lapping on the hull and the evening calls of waterfowl on the marshes.

After our marathon of four-day yacht trips it was Cowes Week, and 2007 was the second time we had been the official charity to the event. The previous summer we'd raised almost £90,000, so we were going to have our work cut out! One of the most successful events the previous year had been the Ellen MacArthur Trust Ball. For me, like many, it was not just any ball, and the response from the guests was astonishing. I can't quite describe just how special the atmosphere was during that evening, but it seemed to convey everything the Trust did in the most positive way possible. A long time friend of OC, Richard Simmonds, was the master of ceremonies and was extremely talented at getting people to engage and have fun. It was made a little easier for him at the beginning, though, when out of 480 people in there I ended up winning the heads and tails game! Richard at this stage tossed the coin over his shoulder and gave the prize to the other guest. But it was hilarious, spontaneous and a real surprise to everyone. Moments later he told a story which, in usual Richard style, had everyone rolling in the aisles. He described how he and our good friend Erik the cameraman were due to go out on the water to film the boats crossing the finish line of the Volvo Ocean Race. It was the early hours of the morning, and when the phone call came there was no time to waste. They were already a bit on the late side and didn't want to miss the finish, so they met in the corridor and ran for what seemed like miles to get out of their lodgings. Then, as the exit was in sight, Erik said, 'Richie . . .'

'What?' Richard replied in what was perhaps a slightly irritated, short-of-sleep fashion as he hurried towards the door.

'Richie!' he cried out again as he stopped dead in his tracks.

'What *is* it, Erik? Come on!' Richard exclaimed, now quite frustrated, as they really were late.

'Richie, I have to go back,' was the reply.

'Why?' Richard asked, exasperated.

'Richie . . . I've forgotten my camera.' And with that the whole audience fell about laughing. What a contrast that was, though, to the silence when Richard told the story of the phone call he received whilst he was driving down the motorway, hearing that same voice saying: 'Richie, I have something to tell you . . . I've got cancer.'

There are few people in our lives who've not had a friend or relative who has suffered from cancer, and when you translate that to the young people who sail with the Trust, it puts everything in our lives into perspective.

The extra funds we'd been able to raise in 2006 had allowed us to attempt something different that year, and it was with great excitement that we put together plans to go to Bradwell-on-Sea outdoor activities centre for a week at the end of the summer.

There is nothing special, but yet everything special, about Bradwell. The buildings are pretty standard 1960s architecture, like much of my old school, but the atmosphere inside the centre just felt right. Young people and staff mixed in a lovely way, and I felt totally at home there. On the estuary side of the centre was the huge grass-covered dyke, typical of the east coast, which ran all the way along the coast as a flood protection, and that first night I arrived there memories of my childhood came flooding back. I remembered walking along them with Auntie Thea, or Nan, and then running off along one late at night with tears streaming down my face, as everyone waited in the car, because I didn't want to leave the sea. Bradwell was on the river north of the Crouch, where I had first sailed as a kid, and the sights and sounds were all exciting and familiar. It was the first time I'd been back for years.

The activities at the centre were varied, and whether we were sailing the little catamarans, climbing the high ropes, canoeing or even just eating breakfast in the canteen, they were always accompanied by laughter. I loved the canoeing especially, and when we went to a nearby canal with the canoes and messed around laughing until we could laugh no more it was one of the happiest times in my life. We had lunch by a lock gate with the boats out of the water and then we carried them round to the weir, which was surrounded by overhanging willows and reminded me of a tropical jungle. I couldn't believe it when it was suggested we all shoot the weir. The guys from the centre had a challenge for me: 'extreme vacuuming'. Yes, you guessed it, it involved an old, bust-up vacuum cleaner, and my challenge was to go down the weir as I was casually vacuuming over the side! It was clearly pretty funny to watch, but the passers-by were not half confused when they saw a canoe paddling along the canal with a large red vacuum cleaner in it!

The other task I loved was the high ropes, and climbing to the top of such a huge structure got the adrenalin pumping for everyone. Staff and kids included all had a go. Though it sounds pretty dangerous, it was in fact very safe. We were all in helmets and climbing harnesses to catch us in case any of us slipped. The whoops and screams of excitement must have been heard on the other side of the estuary. The final task was called the 'leap of faith' and involved climbing to the top of a telegraph pole and then scrambling on to a square plate on the top. Once you got up there, which was easier said than done, as it didn't half wobble, you had to jump out to grab a trapeze bar which was just out of reach. The looks on the kids' faces when they achieved this were priceless, particularly as, when you're on the top, you don't believe you'll make it. As I was last, everyone thought that it would be funny to slide the trapeze bar out much further to see if I'd be able to get it, and Frank, knowing that I was a sucker for a challenge, began getting all excited. I totally missed it the first time. Then, determined, I climbed again. It was starting to get dark. I jumped a second time, and just managed to touch it. The third time, I was ready to give my all and crouched as low as I could and sprang into the air. I grabbed it, and was grinning from ear to ear. It was lovely to hear the cheers from below and to be sharing such special moments. Frank made a video, which had everyone in hysterics when we watched it at the end of the week. Beneath the images of me climbing for the first time, he put a caption: 'Having sailed around the world in seventy-one days, Ellen MacArthur takes on the Bradwell high ropes course'. Then a few seconds later, having shown two misses: '. . . and 71 days later she was still trying'!

Chapter Twenty-Two

The first two weeks in October Ian and I went away on a holiday, a holiday which had unquestionably been inspired by the fun I'd had while paddling a canoe at Bradwell. I had also read a book which was lent to me by a policeman on the Falkland Islands several years before called *The Unlikely Voyage of Jack de Crow* by A. J. Mackinnon, which was about a teacher who'd taken a tiny Mirror dinghy from north-west Wales to the Black Sea. I have to admit that that was certainly taking the word adventure to extremes: from passing out of the huge lock gates in Bristol to being boarded by pirates in Romania, the stories were quite gripping!

So, not surprisingly, this holiday involved boats and a bit of sailing – but more surprisingly it was on the inland waterways of Britain rather than the coast. The goal was to try to paddle a canvas canoe for roughly 300 miles to circumnavigate the industrial heartland of Britain.

No one could have been more excited about unpacking a canoe for the first time than me. After all the research I had done into the right kind of craft, I was really hoping that she would live up to our requirements. It was going to be quite an expedition, and the level of preparation if we were to be successful was going to have to be pretty high. As we opened up the package, out popped a long and floppy piece of red PVC: it was very hard to imagine that in a few weeks' time it would become our home for fourteen days. As we inserted her frames, held in place by long aluminium poles, any worries we had were quickly put to rest: our craft looked magnificent. It was at that moment I thought of a name for her: we would call her 'Gads' after the walks and the wanders that we used to call 'gadabouts' when we went off as children with our Nan.

We had realized quite early on that we would have to sleep in the canoe, not least as Floss would be joining us, as trying to stop at places where there was a B&B or a campsite was going to be impossible, and, not only that, but we couldn't really leave little Gads either, as all our gear and possessions would be stowed in her. There were three items that we needed to make before we could head off on our journey: the mast and sails, the sleeping tent, and a shelter for cooking under on land if it was racing, as we were not too keen on the idea of cooking in a canoe.

The most complicated by far was the sleeping tent, which I made by modifying an existing 'throw-up' tent and sewing some waterproof fabric on to the ends. Because we would need to sit up in the tent to get in and out we decided to raise it on thin glass-fibre rods, which were bent over and inserted into sockets in the frame of the boat. The result was quite strange in that Gads almost looked like she had another canoe lying upside down on top of her! I inserted a window and little vents so that the inside wouldn't get too wet with condensation and modified the original entrance zip of the tent so that we could get in and out with relative ease. I worked on the tent using the old manual Singer sewing machine which Mum had given to me. It was the machine with which she made her wedding dress and with which I made my first set of sailing trousers, and much else besides. It had been a while since I had used the machine, and it brought back happy memories as I worked away on our tent, as well as a last-minute thought, a small bean bag for Floss to sleep on, just like the one I'd slept on for the round-the-world. The fabric was a thin plastic mesh, which I knew was not only warm and comfortable, but more importantly wouldn't get waterlogged if it rained on us, and bearing in mind that the trip was in October, that was highly likely!

The next task was making the sail and rig, which ended up based around lengths of replacement tent poles. We chose the lateen-style rig, putting two poles together in an A-shape to form the short mast, welded some steel tube up to make the bracket for our mast head and used three others as the gaff and two as the boom. While visiting the Southampton Boat Show, I found some cheap offcuts of rope, some toggles and a few bits and pieces to finish off our kit. I popped down the road to the old Ratsey and Lapthorn sail loft in Cowes to get some sailcloth and clear plastic and material for the shelter. I had never made a sail before, so I had to work out how to do it. The mast, rigging, sails and sheets all fitted into a little bag I made which was about 40 cm long and 5 cm wide. Then all that was remaining were a few final touches like building a steering system using the paddles, finding a mattress, which ended up being a blue inflatable ready-bed from Woolies, and finding a way to pack all the gear we would take into a manageable amount!

Our first test trip was quite exciting, as we tried the sails for the first time. We launched Gads in Cowes and headed up the Medina past the chain ferry and up towards the river moorings. Floss, who had been a slight worry in the back of our minds, did not seem in the slightest concerned with her new home and, sporting her new yellow lifejacket, revelled in the challenge of making her way around the boat. The tide was running well at the time, but luckily the wind was relatively strong, so it was a good test to see if the sail was beefy enough to push us along and to see how our Gads would fare in a blustery wind. The tent poles worked a treat, as, being flexible, they 'bent off', spilling some of the wind and therefore not capsizing us. There was a great feature in the boat too, which was that you could inflate two full-length air pockets down her sides to increase her beam, making her much more stable. As we carried Gads back through the town we had a feeling of excitement and anticipation about our journey.

As we slipped the dock in Shardlow in the first week of October, there was a great feeling of adventure in the air, though as people were beginning to recognize me in the boatyard, we wanted to slip away quickly and disappear. One thing that I hadn't really appreciated about a canoe journey was that, if someone did want to follow you and talk to you all day, then they could, and we had come out here to get away from it all. We needn't have worried, though, as the season was tailing off now it was October; it wasn't too busy at all, and we had some lovely conversations with some super people. My biggest concern as we left was that we had such a huge amount of food and gear in the boat that there did not seem to be any space for people or dogs, but we left the dock and decided to find a decent stowing system later that day when we were somewhere quiet. Mum and Dad had dropped us off and said that they would meet us a little further down the canal before saying a final goodbye.

We were excited to be off but a little daunted by our target of 25 miles a day. We had guessed that we were going to need to paddle for about eight hours every day – and that was not including the time spent stopping for locks. We hadn't actually slept in the canoe before this point either, and though we'd tried out the sleeping arrangements on land to make sure that we would fit in, we had not done that with all our gear or while in the water! Everything was new to us at this stage, as Ian had never been on the canals before, and I had only tried it a couple of times before at Bradwell and on *Iduna* when I had passed through Scotland on my round-Britain trip in 1995. There was one new thing we discovered that was really useful about being on the canal network, though. British Waterways had a key that you could buy which allowed you to use all its toilets and showers, and we had seen that the locations were marked on the maps we had. When you are living on a canoe with extremely limited facilities it's quite useful to be able to use the loo or even take a shower!

We had no restrictions about where we would stop that first night, as we had enough food with us for the first few days, and nor were we too worried about miles on the first day: we just wanted to find a nice quiet place we could settle and try out our little home. After a couple of hours of paddling we found a lovely spot under the branches of a weeping willow on the inside of the bend of the river, where the water was flowing less quickly. As a child, I would have thought it a great place to hide from hostile natives! We pulled over, took out our ground-screws, found our mooring lines and got ourselves sorted for the night. It was wonderful to step out and on to the banks, for our little home to be there parked up in the reeds, and for Floss to be able to have a sniff about and explore a little while we put the kettle on. We didn't make a hot meal that night as we'd had a lovely pub lunch with Mum and Dad, so we ate a few cold snacks with a cup of tea in hand and took in all that was around us. We stowed Gads properly that night, and devised a packing system which saw us well through the trip – putting the food and kit bags in one end and our clothes bags at the other. Floss's bed sat on top of the biggest bags, where she could snooze in her own space; though on that first night she had us in stitches. Just moments after the final head-torch had been switched off she gingerly crept off her bed, climbed over our bodies and into my sleeping bag. It would have been funny enough in itself, but she then turned round so her head was on my pillow, rolled over on her back and promptly fell asleep snoring with both her front legs bolt upright like fence posts.

Sleeping in Gads for the first time felt very special with the sound of the water so close by, and once I had got over the initial giggles about Floss's antics I slept like a baby, despite the restriction in space.

Waking on board was as fantastic as falling asleep, and in those first few seconds as I woke, I felt totally at home and bursting with excitement! We were aboard the 'good ship' Gads and we were off on an adventure! That first morning we were keen to pack up to see how many miles we could really cover in a day and to see if our voyage plan was realistic. Ian opted to boil the kettle to make our flask for the day, and I chose to take our tent down. It was quite an intricate job with many tiny clips which attached along the little safety ropes around Gads's gunwale, and then the final part, once the tent was removed and rolled up, was to remove the hoops from their sockets. This, of course, went wrong, and I watched in horror as the end one flicked high into the air, before falling straight in the water and sinking. Not a great scenario on day one, and we didn't have any spares either. I looked over the side of the boat and was amazed to see the tiny red tape on one end of one of the poles. I'd taped them with a colour so we always put them in the right order, and luckily the river's water was so crystal clear I could see down to the bottom. There was only one thing for it – I was going to have to go in! So, on the first morning of our voyage, I stripped down to my underwear and waded into the freezing October water. I held on to Gads's bow and managed to catch the tiny pole with my toes by ducking down under water and feeling around with my feet in the mud!

The first part of our journey involved heading down the river Trent, partly on the river, and partly on the canal. We were aiming for a place called Keadby, where there is a sea lock from the river into the canal system called the 'Yorkshire Navigations'. We were trying to get there by day five, but to make that paddling progress was going to have to be good! The river was going to be pretty straightforward for the first half, as we'd be taken along by the current for most of it, and it was non-tidal. However, after Cromwell Lock the river becomes tidal, and, though it was going to flow with us more than against us, we would struggle to make decent progress, if any at all, with the tide out of favour. In those first few days we had some beautiful still conditions which could not have been better for paddling and we began to enjoy the variety of landscapes we travelled through: countryside, industrial areas, towns and even central Nottingham.

Our second day was spent in the most idyllic location. We always stopped for the night in the countryside, where there were fewer people and we could find a quiet place to tie up Gads. We pulled her up into the reeds near Hazelford, where there were huge, dark-coloured trees along the far bank opposite, and, as we approached, their reflection in the glassy water was quite breathtaking. There was not a breath of wind that night; sounds carried well, and you could hear the bird calls echoing eerily like in a jungle. As we snuggled down in our sleeping bags that night we could have been in the rainforest.

The following morning there was still no wind, and with a thin mist hanging over the water that 'jungle atmosphere' was still there. Being there at the crack of dawn before the world had woken was a very special experience. We crept along the river and decided to let Gads drift for a while in the river flow so we could drink in the silent atmosphere. As she was drifting at walking pace, I decided to go ashore with Floss for a morning stroll along the top of the dyke. On my left I could see farmland, villages and church spires going far into the distance and on my right our beautiful red boat being effortlessly carried along. There were thin patches of foam on the water's surface, a byproduct of the weir we'd just passed, and their delicate pattern slowly changed as the river wove its way between its banks. Watching Gads make her way down the river was so peaceful, and for the first time in a long while I could feel my mind really beginning to switch off. I returned to Gads with Floss to continue on our way, and it was just moments later when we saw a flash of blue over the water, then another immediately afterwards. We realized that we were watching a pair of kingfishers. I had rarely seen them in the wild, and they have always held significance in my life – not only because of their beauty, but as the first boat I sailed round the world carried their name. Both of us felt so privileged to have seen them.

Weaving our way closer to the sea we felt the river's energy more and more. We passed through Newark-on-Trent, and popped ashore for a quick stroll and a sausage roll while the lock-keeper kindly watched over Gads. It was one of the few places we went ashore together. We fed shire horses from the canoe with some carrots we had on board and marvelled at the age of the buildings. One had a black-and-white painted sign saying 'TRENT NAVIGATION Co.' and another had a Colman's mustard sign on the warehouse door. Seeing the scale of the warehouses along the river made us realize just what an important part they had played in our country's past. As we continued on our journey, the importance of our island's waterways became more and more evident, though signs of change were everywhere visible too. As we left Newark, we passed a huge old brick warehouse right on the bank of the river, which intrigued me with its interesting shapes. It was derelict but in one piece and had some broken and some boarded-up windows, though the most startling thing was that above it, and almost passing over it, was the A46 road bridge crossing the river. Gliding along, listening to the noise of the traffic above, we became aware of the two railways which crossed at that point too.

We tried sailing Gads for the first time, which worked a treat! It was such a break for us to be pushed along by the wind rather than having to paddle, and we felt cheerful as we powered along. With the chance to relax, I pulled out our guidebooks and read up on the waterways we were travelling on.

After Cromwell Lock things all began to change. The beautiful river banks turned to mud and sand, and we could see that it was going to be harder to pull Gads out of the water, as was necessary on the tidal water. We had known for a while that this section would be the most problematic, as from the map we could see there were no exits on to the shore. Once we passed Gainsborough and evening drew in, we looked for a place to stop. Bar a few rocks and plants, all we could see was a mud bank, which must have been at least 25 feet high. It was going to be a messy operation! The first thing we did was strip down to our pants and head into the shore. My plan then was to carry Floss up the bank first, which was steep and had the stickiest mud I had ever encountered. On my second step my shoe got stuck, and, as we'd taken only one pair each, it was not looking good! By this stage I was in fits of giggles, and poor Floss, suspended in my arms, was wondering what on earth was going on. My amusement wasn't shared by Ian, who was having a sense of humour failure at this point! I managed to find my shoe in the mud with my free hand and decided swiftly that with shoes it wasn't going to be possible. I managed somehow to get Floss to Ian, and then set about doing a recce up the bank.

It was then I realized that climbing the bank was nigh on impossible. The mud banks resembled hard, wet clay and were as slippery as anything I'd stood on. I tried to hold on to the plants, but to no avail, as they too were slippery and felt like they would pull out of the mud. I often find that in a sticky situation you somehow come up with a solution, and that I did – finding that if I pressed my toes really hard into the mud I could make a foothold! So, making our own climbing wall, we somehow managed to empty the boat, put everything on a groundsheet and then slowly but surely drag Gads up the bank, which must have been 45 degrees. When we arrived safely at the top we washed ourselves down with a bag of river water we had collected, washed Floss and the groundsheet on the little floodplain before the dyke, and, after about an hour of work, we put up our tent and prepared for the night. We didn't make a flask or a hot meal that evening, just ate some cheese, oatcakes and a bit of fruit, then bedded down for a few hours' sleep, wondering what lay in store for us in our final river section.

We were up at 0630, and outside it was twilight. The river was covered with its own layer of fog, and from our elevated bank we could hardly make out the water. We took down our frost-covered tent, which reminded me for a fleeting second of my time in South Georgia, and checked round to make sure there was no trace of us on the bank. We were both keen to be getting on our way and would be relieved to spend the next night out of the current and safely moored up alongside a still canal bank. It was easier dropping the bags down the slope into the boat, and we worked silently and swiftly to wash everything as we loaded it in. Dog, bags, paddles, me and then Ian, all present and correct; just time to stick the layers of clothes on, as there was a real nip in the air that morning.

I loved the feeling of paddling down our foggy river; it was mysterious, eerie and exciting as floating objects appeared ahead of us and then silently slipped past back into the gloom. As we began to hear signs of other craft on the water the fog had thinned, and by the time the thump, thump of the old diesel engines felt close enough to be a worry we could see exactly where they were. I have always loved old workboats: there is something quite solid, honest and dependable about them which appeals to me. Paddling along, I began to think of the old 'death and glory' boys in Arthur Ransome's 'Coot Club' books. They had an old, scruffy, tar-covered ship's boat they kitted out themselves, with a stove, cabin and a little mast. I loved those books, and I was swept, albeit only for an hour or so, into memories of my childhood once again.

We had no choice but to enter the sea lock in Keadby with our trusty little boat. We had called ahead to say that we were coming, and the lock-keeper was fantastic – having the lock ready and open for our arrival. That day was the first real sign of commercial traffic we'd seen, and around the lock were several docks with ships on them, loading up. Being commercial, the lock was also pretty big, and as we paddled in the sides towered above us. The lock-keeper threw us down some life rings just to be on the safe side, and we held firmly on to the ladder as the water rose.

To see the lock gates open on to the tranquil, still canal was fantastic. Now we no longer had to deal with the tidal Trent and could climb out of our boat wherever we chose. The sun had burnt through the mist by this stage, and it felt like we were entering a new phase of our journey.

Life was very different on the canals. We could 'see out' again, as the canals weren't lined with dykes, and there was a towpath for Floss to run along and stretch her legs. There were stopping places everywhere now; in fact you could nose anywhere into the side, as there were no reeds or brambles. We sailed once again on this stretch, and found that even with the slightest puff of breeze Gads would slide along quite nicely! The other thing we discovered was towing Gads with a rope and we were surprised at how easy it was. Either Ian or I would stay in the boat, and the other would take a long line positioned in the correct place to balance her. With this travelling method, one of us at least got to use their legs, which was a welcome break from sitting for hours paddling, and the other could nestle in the bags on the floor of Gads with the guidebook, reading out facts about the canals, villages and points of interest.

It amazed me how easy it was to pull the boat. Her weight was about 25 kg. Ian must have been near 80 kg, and the food and gear at least another 20 kg. That meant that I could fairly effortlessly pull twice my weight using a boat for transport, and we quickly realized that was exactly why the canals had caught on so well! In the days of horse-drawn barges a single horse could transport 30 tons of goods, ten times what it could transport by cart. That sounded like a lot, but it was a world apart from the 96,000 'horses' that powered the *Fidelio*, a figure which, I later found out, constituted

Left: In 2007 JP Morgan Asset Management sponsored the annual Round the Island Race and I helmed their Extreme 40 class entry to victory.

Above: IDEC, the boat on which Francis Joyon beat my record, and the moment on the stage afterwards.

With Greg Homann on board 'Foxy Lady' on the Archipelago Raid and, *above*, sailing through the Archipelago.

Sailing with the Ellen MacArthur Trust. Whatever the future holds, sharing time and fun with the kids involved with the Trust will always be a central part of my life.

Messing around
on the river!

With Jess.

Maxine.

The photo Maxine took of herself
on her camera during her first
Trust trip.

From an early age I can remember visiting farm sales in Derbyshire with my Dad. Here, he's cradling a very young Norman and inspecting a potential bargain!

With Eamonn. Working dogs had fascinated me since childhood, so to have the chance to learn with someone as skilled as Eamonn was fantastic.

Floss and 'Norm'.

My journey towards setting up the Ellen MacArthur Foundation has led to many unique and interesting experiences that I could never have imagined having, from tours of power stations and test-driving new generation electric cars to becoming involved with local councils and schools.

The CMA CGM *Fidelio*, a boat which I had the privilege of launching, was at the time one of the world's largest container ships. Just in the last four years, 72 ships of the same or greater size have been built.

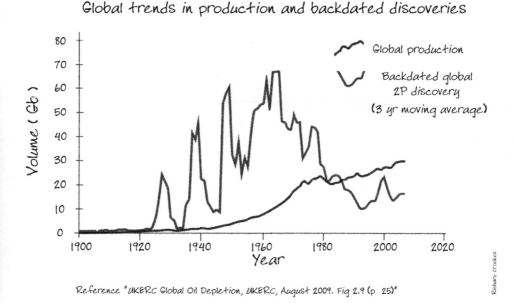

Global trends in production and backdated discoveries

Volume (Gb)

Global production

Backdated global
2P discovery
(3 yr moving average)

Year

Reference "UKERC Global Oil Depletion, UKERC, August 2009. Fig 2.9 (p 25)"

Richard Crookes

A graph showing the increasing gap between the amount of oil we use and the amount we have discovered. The stark reality of the situation is something we find all too easy to turn away from.

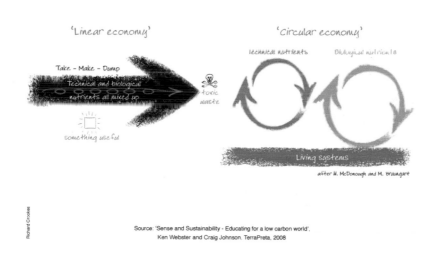

'Linear economy'

Take - Make - Dump
Technical and biological
nutrients all mixed up

toxic
waste

something useful

'Circular economy'

Technical nutrients   Biological nutrients

Living systems

after W. McDonough and M. Braungart

Richard Crookes

Source: 'Sense and Sustainability - Educating for a low carbon world',
Ken Webster and Craig Johnson. TerraPreta, 2008

A diagram illustrating the difference between a linear and circular economy.

A photo of the vegetable
garden taken earlier this year,
in all its glory, and the house
finally taking shape. Building it
together with Ian was a journey
in itself.

My Nan, on her graduation
day. At the age of eighty-two,
she fulfilled her lifetime
ambition of getting a degree.
She has always served as an
inspiration to me.

about 10 per cent of the total number of horses and ponies we have in Britain today! This opened up new thought processes, and we began to take more interest in the history of the canals.

As we travelled we realized that there were often railway tracks (some now disused and turned into cycle ways) following the routes of the canals. The canals were there first; they were the motorways of the past, the main mode of transport in the early industrial revolution. The first canal was built in 1759 and proved to be so successful that between 1791 and 1795 Parliament authorized fifty-one new canals (4,000 miles of waterways). Incredibly, just twenty years later, and after all that effort, the money had already moved on to the railways. It then became apparent to me that many of the canals must have carried the goods which led to their own demise. That was the reason that railways were built so close – because of the need for a form of transport to get the materials in.

Our journey unveiled a gallery of images of transport through the centuries: canals replacing tracks, railways taking over from canals, and then the tarmacked roads and motorways of the modern age.

The following days were happy days, as we had stunning, windless weather. We paddled beneath glorious bridges, with stalactites dangling from the high brick arches above our heads; we paddled over amazing aqueducts with intricate ironwork. Parts of the canal here were rivers once again, and we noticed how many plastic bags were clinging to the trees and bushes along the banks. We knew at some point we'd see the classic shopping trolley dumped in the canal, and we had to giggle to ourselves when our first sighting was not just one, but a whole row of them still chained together! The other thing that we could not believe was the number of footballs we saw in the water: we counted well over 100! It was startling to see the height that the water could reach too, and the amount of rubbish that had somehow made it into the water.

Our journey took us past Wakefield and into Huddersfield, where the quiet countryside quickly gave way to the town. You could feel the difference between the towns that were built around the canals and the towns they were built to serve. In the original canal towns the water's edge was lined with warehouses, quays, little wharfs and the odd public house. You could see how vibrant an industry it was when you studied the remaining warehouses, with their windows and doors which originally opened straight on to the water, now blocked up with bricks or stone. Where the newer developments have grown to meet the canal you had back gardens and parks adjacent.

There were hundreds of bridges built over the canals, some old, some new, some between fields for the farmers, some in villages for the carts; now you see whole motorways going over the canal – a scale of construction incomprehensible when the canals were built. As we had left Wakefield we had paddled under both the M62 and the M1 twice.

Huddersfield grew up around us slowly, and, as we closed in on the city centre, that vibrant canal feeling slowly turned to one of neglect. One section of the canal had been drained by vandals, and it was so shallow that Ian got out to lessen the weight, so that the boat wouldn't scrape the bottom. I crept along slowly, looking down into the water, weaving my way along between the motorbikes, shopping trolleys, scooters and beds that had been dumped there. It was spooky and dark, that section under the trees, and both of us felt quite vulnerable.

Closer to the town the buildings by the canal had graffiti on them. There were anti-theft metal spiked railings to separate their doors from the towpath, and the windows which weren't bricked had external shutters so that no one could break in. The next lock still had offcuts of blue and white 'POLICE CRIME SCENE' tape attached to the lock gates. It felt quite eerie, as if we were entering the town down a dark, unadvised and forgotten corridor. We had not seen, and nor did we see, one other boat making its way along this canal. Soon our dark corridor was shaded not by trees but by huge industrial buildings as we entered the centre of town – the canal really did seem to weave through Huddersfield's industrial heart.

The following morning we entered the Huddersfield Narrow Canal, which was to weave us through the Pennines before joining the Peak Forest Canal, brushing the eastern outskirts of Manchester, where we'd turn left at the Portland Basin. The canal began adjacent to Huddersfield University, and, despite the clue in the name, we were really surprised by its narrowness. Until then we had only travelled the 'broad' canals capable of taking larger vessels. This canal at its narrowest can only have been a little wider than twice the width of little Gads, and was clearly built for the smaller canal boats. We had our first morning of rain, but crossing the Pennines by boat was nothing short of spectacular: you could see everything far into the distance, as the huge hills rose up around you and fell away below the watercourse.

Passing a place called Linthwaite, we saw a gigantic old mill in the distance. It was amazing to think that someone would have built a six-storey mill here in what seemed like open countryside. I counted the windows: there were twenty-eight in its length, so the building must have been over 100 metres long. More and more mills appeared on this stretch, and it became quite clear that the majority were being converted into apartments.

When we arrived in the small town of Slathwaite, we learnt that the following section of canal was closed. We had been worried about this stretch for a while, as ahead of us lay the 3 mile long (yes 3 miles!) Standedge Tunnel, which we knew we were not allowed to paddle through. Our plan had always been to get there and then see if we could get a tow through, but with the canal closed we were going to have to find another option! Luckily, Slathwaite had a train station, and, not surprisingly, the line followed the canal. The decision was made that we would wait until daybreak the next day, pack up Gads and our bags on to our tiny trolleys and take her to the train station. Ian did a recce to find the station while I packed things away. Tent, clothes, food, paddles, tent poles – everything we had we had somehow to carry. It must have only been about 400 metres to lug our gear, but the road to the station was steep and rough, and the trolleys' wheels were tiny and kept overbalancing and falling over as we hauled them up the road to the station. Though it was quite a palaver, we managed to make it, hot, sweaty and a bit flustered, but with a good few minutes to spare before the train. When it eventually pulled into the station we were worried that we'd struggle to get everything on, but the conductor was lovely – and we all boarded, Floss included!

We had decided to go on to a place called Stalybridge on the outskirts of Manchester; though still on the Huddersfield Narrow, it was only a stone's throw from our next leg, the Peak Forest Canal. Getting to the water at the other end went really well – better than we'd expected, in fact – and we were so relieved to get Gads back in the water and ready to go that we celebrated with an ice cream from a petrol station across the road. We had travelled 16 miles on the train, but, if we were to have a chance to finish our circuit, we knew that we had to make up for the time spent packing and unpacking. Luckily, bypassing Greenfield and Mossley meant that we had missed the 'obstacle' of twenty-nine locks.

Skirting Manchester, we saw yet more derelict warehouses. This contrasted sharply with the parks, fields and gardens all butting up to the canal after we'd passed Portland Basin. There were old bridges once again, and tunnel after tunnel, some long, some short. The highlight of this stretch was the Marple aqueduct, 94 feet above the Goyt river, a fantastic piece of engineering that has stood for over 200 years.

The end of the Peak Forest brought a nasty night for Ian as we reached Marple Junction after a long haul up a hill which sported sixteen locks. We had arrived in a picturesque village, but unfortunately Ian had managed to get blue-green algae poisoning, so spent the evening vomiting. So, for the first section of the Macclesfield Canal, I towed Gads most of the way with the rope to give Ian a rest and some quiet, gentle recuperation time.

The huge Goyt cotton mill was the last big building we saw before heading off on the Macclesfield Canal, which had a wonderful peaceful feel to it, as there were no major roads along its length. It circled the edge of the beautiful Peak District too, which reminded me of the cross-country races I used to compete in as a kid. The Macclesfield Canal was stunning, and we monitored progress by counting the bridge numbers which were displayed on each one on a steel plate above the arch. We crossed Bollington aqueduct and headed on to Macclesfield itself, seeing the huge Hovis factory by the water, which is now converted into flats.

The next morning, though there was misty drizzle, we decided to push on. It was day twelve, and we were both quite tired. We were also quite worried that there was another tunnel coming up – the Harecastle Tunnel – and, as at Standedge, we knew that we would not be able to paddle through it. We were in luck, though, and managed to hitch a ride on a lovely old workboat. As it turned out, we could not have found a better solution, as we were able to lift Gads straight into her cargo hold, throw the bags in and then sit up front for the passage. *Cassiopeia* was a fantastic boat – long and very narrow, and suitable for any of the canals on the UK network. Though she was a workboat she was still beautifully painted in blue and yellow, and she had a really solid, trustworthy feel, with her riveted steel plates and gentle thudding engine.

We were so excited at the chance to travel in the hold of a workboat, and our excitement was not let down by the experience of travelling through the tunnel. The sound of the engine was reassuring as we slowly motored through the dark, damp, cold stillness. I was glad that our helm was experienced, as in certain parts of the tunnel I swear that we were only inches from the roof. It is staggering to think that it was built in just three years 180 years ago, before we had anything like the machines we have today. Though the Harecastle Tunnel is not as long as the Standedge Tunnel, it is still over 1.5 miles long, and it took us half an hour to get through. It was exciting to re-emerge into daylight at the other end. What was more impressive, though, was to look back at the exit in the wall which looked no more imposing than a large garage door!

We were now on the home stretch, and felt motivated to give the last two days a real push, which meant that our final few miles involved some pretty intense paddling. We passed Stoke-on-Trent and Burton-on-Trent, paddling alongside the A38, and towed Gads along towpaths within which were concreted huge road signs for the drivers on the dual carriageways above. It was noisy and smelly by the roads, and we were feeling the slight unease of being on the canal in a town once again. Past industries were still visible, with ceramic factories and breweries right by the water; we had learnt that pottery was more safely transported by boat in the past, as it didn't get shaken around as it would on a cart. I was surprised to see the Armitage Shanks factory still operating, with its palettes of conveniences which could be admired from the water!

As our voyage was drawing to a close I began to reflect on the journey. I found that by crawling along at paddling speed you take in so much more: you can hear the wind in the trees, the song of every bird, and you almost feel as if you are breathing your surroundings in as you go. It was magical moving so silently, with no engine noise, brakes or traffic. Even in a sailing boat, especially when you go fast, there is a huge amount of noise, but here it was different: the only sound was the paddles hitting the water and the lovely bubbly sound at the bow if there was any wind on the water. But the other thing I found was that we also had time to talk, laugh and joke and share with each other everything going on around us. It was such a different way of travelling from what I was used to. You are not travelling too fast to talk to people heading along the same waterway as you, and you are outside and not cocooned in a car with the windows shut so you can't speak to people. The whole experience felt quite liberating in a strange way, like being in touch with something basic you had forgotten you knew.

We could have driven that distance easily in six hours, but our holiday showed me that perhaps life is as much about the journey as the destination itself.

This particular journey had offered me a lot. It hadn't just been fun and a wonderful break for Ian and me, it had shown me a side of our country and our history that is very close to us – nestling behind the riverside flats in our cities – yet all but hidden. But, more than that, seeing canals lying alongside rail tracks, rail tracks abandoned and used for leisure as cycle tracks, and, looming above them all, vast motorways and roads, the new waterways of the modern world, it had struck me just how quickly things move on.

Chapter Twenty-Three

As OC was running the Barcelona World Race, I travelled out to the start, both to wish our new 60 off, and to be with the Mayor, who would start the race on 11 November. It was familiar to me being around the boats in a pre-race scenario, but there was a certain part of me which felt terribly lost. Being around all the sailors was great, but the uncomfortable anxiety of being stuck between two worlds was not. Over the previous two years my life had begun to move on, but I felt like an addict being taunted by all that was around me.

On the first morning I went running at dawn and, not knowing Barcelona at all, I decided to run round the port. As I stepped out of our apartment into the city I was surprised at the silence after the raucous welcome of the nightclubs of the previous evening. The only people around seemed to be a group of street cleaners who were hosing the previous night's vomit down the drains. As I entered the port area, I ran over the bridge adjacent to the boats, which all appeared to be snoozing in the safety of the dockside. With their mooring lines relaxed, they sat silently in the water and in the early-morning light it was a peaceful scene. In a couple of days' time it would be a different story: sailing day and night, non-stop, for three whole months. My mind was full of excitement for those sailors about to embark on this adventure.

I circled the dock, feeling how different this November was to the November three years before in Falmouth, as I waited to leave on my round-the-world. Falmouth was cold, and winter was setting in, and I thought how nice it was for the teams to be spending their last days on land in clement, relaxing conditions. If the weather followed its normal pattern for November, there was a good chance that the first bad weather the boats would see would be in the Southern Ocean. I passed the yacht club, looking up at the boats out of the water for winter, and thought back to the days when I was working on *Iduna* before my round-Britain. Keen as mustard, I even slept beneath her in the yard. Each boat in that yard told a different story, but the same spirit of adventure was there.

I ran around the rest of the harbour basin, then back towards the race village and the tents. It was 0730, and the sun was just rising. The dockside was empty, neither the teams nor the crowds were around. Barcelona appeared not to have woken up.

I slowed to a steady jog. The final part of my run was past the nine boats which were to compete in the race. They looked inspiring, all lined up there, pointing the same way, clean and ready. Some were aggressive-looking and angular, and others more friendly; some had shallow cockpits, and others deep and small. Some had tillers, and others had wheels. And, as I passed each boat one by one, I couldn't help but think of the personalities of their skippers.

But with three of the boats there I had a special relationship. Bilou's boat, *Veolia Environnement*, was there. He was racing with an old friend, Jean-Luc Nelias. I thought back to those moments being thrown around in the forepeak during a howling gale and laughing until we could laugh no more. It was hard to believe it was now two years since we had sailed together, and my memories of that trip were still some of the strongest ever. His boat looked great, and with a smile on my face I wished him well.

Also on the dock was *Kingfisher*, and, as my eyes fell upon her for the first time in months, I stopped jogging. Despite her different livery, I was struck by the familiarity of her deck. As I looked up at her huge black mast, the memories washed over me like a tidal wave. I remembered sitting on her bow during the final night of the Vendée Globe, my tears dripping into the sea with pleasure. I thought back to the first time I had sailed her in Auckland Harbour, and the trust that had built between us over the thousands of miles since. She was the boat on which I had crossed the Equator for the first time in my life, and then twice more within a year, all solo. We had begun to design her eight years before, and, looking at her, it was as if time had stood still. She looked as perfectly proportioned and beautiful as the day she was launched. *Kingfisher* had been the boat of my dreams, and I was so lucky to have been her skipper. I was in a daze of memories. I'd forged so many opportunities to be on the water over the previous twelve years – why was I stopping now?

I walked on, then stopped again. The next boat was *Estrella Damm*. She was the boat which had had the most of us all in her. Seb, Nick and I had sat in design meetings, all putting our experience into one boat. All three of us had taken part in the Vendée, and all three of us had sailed around the world three times. Albert had put his heart and soul into her build, making her the lightest, strongest craft possible, and the boys in Cowes, slaving over a whole winter, had turned her from a set of drawings into a beautiful weapon. She was the most awesome boat, and as I looked at her I felt so proud of the team. I firmly believed she was one of the fastest IMOCA 60s in the world, and I felt that because I had seen the blood, sweat, tears and time that had gone into perfecting her. Here she was, race ready, two days before the off, and I wasn't going out there.

That afternoon was the skippers' press conference. I felt confused and sad. I sneaked in at the back, not wanting to be noticed by anyone. The eighteen skippers were all sitting there, visibly excited about the race they would be starting just forty-eight hours later. They were in pairs, chatting, exchanging jokes and smiling. I stood there feeling like I was looking in as an outsider; there might as well have been a huge piece of glass between us.

The video about the race began playing, the music loud, almost spiritual, the clips of the boats sailing powerful, and my heartbeat increased. It showed different boats in different seas, and in the mix of images I saw Mobi, followed later by me, in my element, on the bow of *Kingfisher* under a Southern Ocean wave. As the music grew to a climax, I could feel pure emotion overflowing inside me. It was a feeling of emptiness and loss, of loving something so much but knowing that it was being taken from you. I felt uprooted and vulnerable.

Teeth gritted together, I felt my eyes mist over, but I couldn't turn away from the screen. Why the hell wasn't I going out there? All I saw in those images was home.

At the end of the press conference Bilou came up to me. I had stayed out of the way as the meeting broke up. We hugged each other, and, as he looked in my eyes, I knew he understood.

'You could have been out there with me,' he said.

'I know,' I replied.

That afternoon I drifted in and out of the media centre as if I was drifting in and out of consciousness. In the end it was so bad I had to go and sit out the back behind the tents on the tow ball of one of the trailers.

It was the day before the start. The crowds would be growing and the atmosphere building, and from the moment I got up I knew that I couldn't bear the thought of being down there on the docks. I hadn't slept much at all and felt awful and knew I just had to get out, so I headed off to find somewhere to think. On the map in the apartment I'd seen there was a park to the west, so I headed off through the grid-like streets, keeping the rising sun on my back. After a while the buildings parted to reveal the park on a hill, and it looked refreshingly lush, despite the fact that some trees were changing their colour for autumn. I found one of the winding paths which would take me up to the plateau and, as I steadily climbed, I could see more and more of the city. Beside me were tiny waterfalls leading to reed-lined ponds with beautiful clear water, and high above I began to see huge stone walls which belonged to a castle. I have always found that there is something both grounding and liberating about looking out to the horizon, and from the hillside by the park I began to see not only the city, but also the sea.

I drew a long breath; the scene was beautiful, all but for the pungent brown layer which covered the city. Once up at the castle, I strolled through the gardens, exploring the park. I sat in grassy glades beneath trees, watching children roll down the slopes, and then almost dozed off lying on walls forming lily ponds which one after the other ran gently down a slope. I had soaked in the peace of the morning and I was ready. I was in a quiet place, and there now was time to think.

Deep down, I knew that sailing round the world again would not achieve anything. There was a real simplicity in the sailing, and if my next challenge had been to break my own round-the-world record, it would have been straightforward. I would know the designer to work with, the guys to work with, the boat to build, and the way to train. I even knew which brand of stove and sports drinks to use. I may not have managed it, but I knew exactly how to do it. In essence it would be the continuation of a dream, and be wonderful for me, but it wouldn't be helping to find solutions to the problem I was only just beginning to get to grips with.

I sat down on a bench in the shade and went online with my phone. I did a search for the word 'sustainability', perhaps in an effort to remind myself of its definition.

It came up with 'sustain': '1. To keep in existence; maintain. 2. To supply with necessities or nourishment; provide for. 3. To support from below; keep from falling or sinking.'

They all sounded very positive. But then that was the word 'sustain'. With almost all the energy we use in the world coming from fossil fuels, then we must be living *un*sustainably, and that would mean the opposite. If that really was the case, then why had I, together with every other child of my generation, not been taught this at school? I had never questioned in my teens or even twenties that the framework within which my life operated could be something which was ultimately flawed. I never thought that there might come a day when fuel is so expensive that our family wouldn't be able to afford it and I never thought that my Great Granddad's work may one day be a trade of the past. At first I felt a bit angry but then reassured myself with the thought that perhaps back then we simply didn't know.

I walked under a beautiful bridge, then up some stone steps, which were quite different from any I'd seen before. They were light grey in colour and had gaps at the back of each tread which were filled with grass. Above me in the trees I could hear birds. The day was still sunny, and the clear blue sky above us was enough to make anyone feel like singing. I found a comfortable place on the grass by a tree and sat down to watch the bright red-and-yellow flash of a goldfinch above me. I remembered learning as a kid that some migrate from the UK, and I smiled to myself, wondering whether I'd seen this tiny character somewhere at home before. I lay back, watching it flit from one branch to another, presumably looking for food.

I returned from my pleasant distraction to my thoughts. To me sustainability was a crap word. It sounded boring and uninteresting. And anyway, why did we need a word for what we should be doing anyway? Surely sustainability was just common sense? If we as humans live in a way which can't be sustained, then what about other species on the planet? Could that little bird above my head survive for generation after generation? Is it dependent on something which will not be around for ever? Not being an expert on goldfinches, I was unaware of their needs, but I guessed that, so long as there were plants with seeds around and places to nest, they would probably be just fine.

But could we? Could we continue to live in that same way?

I glanced out across the city, just being able to make out under the canopies some of the most beautiful buildings in the world. We humans seem capable of doing anything we set our minds on.

And, with that thought, I dealt with the difficult decision I'd made. It was the unequivocal tipping point in my thinking. Having learnt what I had, I simply could not carry on as before. The sailing had given me a voice, and my new challenge was to work out the best way to use it.

A door to a whole new world lay before me. In that moment I walked through it, and, though I felt like I was walking into the unknown, I knew I couldn't turn back. Looking only forwards, I let the door click shut behind me.

That day, 10 November 2007, was to be the first day of the rest of my life.

Chapter Twenty-Four

It was wonderful to get home to Floss and Ian, and really exciting to see the blank canvas of our plot. I felt like I had turned a page in my life, and it was time to start down a new path. Autumn was now well upon us, and it was a sign that we needed to get our planning permission in if we were to build our house the following summer.

The following months were exciting and demanding as we worked, often long into the night, drawing partitions, windows and shapes. We filled books with sketches, made models with matchsticks and read everything we could get our hands on. We wanted to create a home that would fit naturally into a woodland setting, which looked as if it belonged there, and, as we were keen for the house to be there for a long time, we wanted to try and make it 'timeless' in its appearance. We didn't want it to date, and we didn't want it to break either. If we were going to put that much time and effort in, it would be nice to think that it could still be there in a few hundred years, like the handsome oak trees standing near by. We wanted to build a house that was sensible too, a house that would waste little energy and would be cheap to run. It was our moment to invest in our future, and we were keen to get it as right as we could.

We ended up with a design which had a slate roof, and 2 feet thick half-brick, half-wooden-clad walls packed with insulation. We tried to use basic principles to keep it cool in the summer and warm in the winter: we put bigger windows on the south side than on the north, and put an area of glass on the south which would act like a heater from which we could blow hot air into the house. The pantry was located on the cooler north side. Because we had to build on concrete piles due to the clay ground we could take the house right up to the canopy of the oaks, which we hoped would mean that the upstairs would feel like a tree-house. We planned for all the bedrooms to catch the eastern morning light, and for the kitchen to have the midday and afternoon sun, and placed the glass so it would be shaded from the hot summer sun by the huge oak tree once it had its leaves. We drew a vegetable garden and a small lawn out the front. I had always loved sketching and drawing, and the process of filling a blank piece of paper with a house reminded me of the design meetings for *Kingfisher* and Mobi. Ian drew up the final drawings, and before the first buds came out for the spring we had submitted our very own planning application!

Since we'd had Floss I'd been spending a lot more time out in the fields just wandering, like I used to as a kid. I'd stumble upon a pheasant tail feather, and it just made me think how lucky I was to have grown up in the country, and how grateful I was to Dad for teaching me all sorts of interesting things. It's that funny feeling of just knowing that you know something, but you're not really sure where it's come from. Then you reconnect the neurons in your brain and realize that you've not thought about that for over a decade.

One was the little brown balls that you get forming on oak tree twigs – oak apples. I knew somehow that every oak apple had a hole in it, left after an insect has bored its way out. I did a bit of research and found out that it's the larva of the gall wasp, which works its way out in June or July. The larva actually creates the gall itself using the tree's woody cellulose. Nature is pretty fascinating; if only we could do something to a tree that would make it grow a home for us rather than the rather more labour-intensive method of cutting it down to build something!

But it wasn't just through the wanderings with Floss that I was reconnecting with my past; I was to find another connection – quite by accident too. When we were having problems with Floss early on, Katie had suggested contacting a farmer she'd seen working with geese at a local show on the island. The reason she mentioned him was that he seemed to have a wonderful relationship with his dogs.

I loved the feeling as we headed down the track to his farm. The road was not tarmacked, and it reminded me of visiting farms in Derbyshire with Simon Reeve the vet when I was doing my work experience. As we pulled to the side of the yard we saw no one, but a short while later we heard a voice from the barns. Eamonn was busy feeding the animals, but after a few moments he walked over, and we spoke about Floss. The question I remember the most was 'Do you really want to work her?' and the answer for me was clear. I would absolutely love to learn how to work her, and from that moment on my apprenticeship began! Eamonn had a way with the dogs, and he had an incredible confidence and ability to understand what they were about to do just before they did it. Though we were unaware at the time, he was a bit of an expert at trialling too, and his dedication to his dogs had led him to some impressive results.

Eamonn was a kind man, and not unlike my Dad in many ways. His background was in riding, training and then teaching people on horses and, though he'd worked with Collies during his first farm job in Wales, he had done little with them until he replaced his riding-school horses with sheep, when he began working with dogs once again. We went to see Eamonn with Floss as often as possible, always taking some of his dogs down the fields too, so that we could watch them work and see what we were aiming for.

I loved everything about the farm, from the little vegetable garden outside the kitchen to the little dairy next door. I loved the fields and nature which were all around us; the ducks would waddle down to the little pond every day, the geese wandered around the yard, the cheeky Muscovy duck would always be by the back door, and the cats would be watching everything from their chosen vantage point. It was a place where we could turn up in our muddy work clothes without offending anyone, where we could always pop in for a sit-down and a cup of tea and where we were always made welcome. As we walked down the fields with the dogs there would be buzzards flying high overhead, the rabbits would scarper into the ancient hedgerows, and the air would be alive with birds whose families must have lived there for generations. The sheep would be sheltering from the sun under the statuesque single trees, almost in a role of 'watchfulness' over the field. At that moment, I would forget all my worries and, albeit for a few hours, I would enter a different world. Working with the dogs required total concentration, and it was that that I loved.

Meeting Eamonn led us to our next arrival, and when he bred a litter of pups we ended up with one. It was Ian who chose the dog in the end. He rather liked the little tricolour lad with the lopsided white patch on his forehead and one brown leg. We didn't have to travel far from the plot to get the inspiration for his name. We called him Norman, and, though it's not the most common name for a dog, it somehow really suited him. It was wonderful watching him entertain himself for hours with a stick or a ball. He would watch the dragonflies patiently or study what the ducks were up to on the pond. It was lovely to see him run full pelt down through the woods, with leaves flying everywhere, marvel at the interactions between the pigs, or get worried when the ducks began fighting. There was the most beautiful innocence and impressionability of youth.

I loved working Floss, and this feeling sent all sorts of thoughts and memories shooting through my head. But one of the hardest facts was that dogs don't live for ever, and, no matter how ready I thought I was to hear the news, I was devastated at the inevitable death of Mac as she closed on twenty years.

The next time I returned home I went for a walk with Floss and Mum, and we spoke a huge amount about our wanderings about the countryside with Mac. On our return we climbed over the wall into the bottom of the field as we had done for years and walked over to where Mum and Dad had buried her. We both instantly broke down in tears, seeing what lay before us. Dad had somehow carried the most enormous stone down the field and placed it over her grave. In it he had carved the words 'Mac 87–07'.

I don't know if Mum and Dad had more faith in me or Mac, letting me wander off into the hills for hours on end. But I couldn't help but feel that we all knew that Mac would look after me. She had been so special in my life. I thought back to the times as a child trying to get her to herd the ducks around the field. As she was cross-bred, her instincts weren't there, but it didn't stop me trying to teach her. And then I thought about how things could have been. I thought back to lying in the car with her as Mum and Dad drove around Skye on my first visit. I remember the bright-green slopes and sheep up on the hills, and the feeling of contentment that I had there. Things could have turned out very differently in life, and I honestly believe, looking back, that if Mac had had the herding instinct in her, the girl who spent her weekends at farm-sales with her Dad would have probably become a shepherd.

On 20 January 2008 Francis Joyon broke our record. In fact he not only broke it, he smashed it to pieces. I was there, peering into the darkness off the French coast as his tiny strobe light came out of the cold Atlantic night. My emotions were all over the place that evening: I felt overjoyed for Francis, so privileged to be there to see him arrive, but I was reminded, fairly unexpectedly and brutally, of what I had been through to get to the same place three years before when it had been my strobe light coming over the horizon. Now, it was Francis's turn, and I felt nervous for him. I knew his arrival would be crazy, and I was mindful of the abrupt switch he would soon experience.

When Francis had established his seventy-two-day record, the record which I had broken three years before, he had dealt with the finish in his usual Francis way. He had descended from the boat, waved to the public, sat in front of the journalists for twenty minutes answering questions, then got up and gone home. Not only that, but he had a flat tyre on his car, and before driving home he calmly changed it.

I have known Francis since I first set foot on his boat in 1996 at the start of the Europe 1 STAR solo transatlantic race. My friend Alan Wynne Thomas, with whom I crossed the Atlantic for the first time in my life, introduced me to Francis, who showed me round the 60 foot trimaran in which he was competing in the race. I had never been on a big multihull before, and I was totally awe-struck by the sheer size and power of his boat, but at the same time its apparent fragility.

Francis and I next spent time together almost exactly four years later, as in spring 2000 we were competing in that same race. I was racing *Kingfisher* in the 60 foot monohull class, and he was on the same boat once again in the 60 foot multihull class. Before the start I was nervous, very nervous. It was my first solo race on *Kingfisher*, and I had no idea how I'd perform against the rest of the monohull fleet, all of whom would be racing against me later that year in the Vendée Globe. Despite my own nerves I remember Francis clearly. His sponsor had chosen to end their partnership with him shortly before the race, and, what was worse, someone else in the race was now sponsored by them. He had a boat, but no money, and he had had to sell his good mast to raise the finance to compete in the race.

He arrived in Plymouth, alone, picked up a mooring alone and was preparing his boat alone – which is no mean feat in a 60 foot tri. We were stretched to get *Kingfisher* ready for the race, and I had four people working on my boat. Francis did not have this luxury. Not only that, but the mast he had put on his boat was an old, heavier one and needed tweaking. He spent days up his mast, soldiering away.

He fought hard in that race, really hard, and when he came out on top of every boat in the fleet as the first tri to finish in America I was so happy for him. His story really had been one of triumph in the face of adversity, and the brief time we spent together at the finish was superb. Francis must be close to a foot taller than me, but he's a gentle giant, strong but kind. I respect him hugely as a person.

Shortly after tying *IDEC* up at the dockside, he addressed the public on a stage. It evoked memories for me when I saw the fatigue on his face. Looking into his weathered eyes, I understood totally what he had been through, and instantly identified with all that moment stood for. I was asked to stand on the stage beside him, at which point we greeted each other and exchanged so much in just one glance. I was in total awe of what he had achieved, and, despite being the only human being on the planet at the time to understand what he'd been through, I frustrated myself by struggling to find words which could even begin to describe the enormity of his journey.

He had taken two weeks off my time.

A short while after the public address he spoke to the journalists in an auditorium which was right by the harbour. I sneaked in the back to hear the questions and answers, fascinated not just by what he would answer, but also by the questions he would be asked.

'Did you cry at the heavens?' Francis was asked.

'Only last night, when you lot tried to scramble on to my boat,' he replied. Just hours from finishing his record Francis was one step ahead.

Later that day I was invited to climb aboard *IDEC*, which I accepted with excitement and anticipation. My first reaction was a surprise to me in that I felt that I was stepping on to Mobi. Despite being 25 per cent bigger, her extra size was mainly in the huge bow she had protruding beyond her forestay. Her designer was the same as Mobi's – my good friend Nigel – and I could sense his talent and style as my eyes flitted from fixture to fitting. The biggest difference with Mobi, apart from her size, was the lack of a generating engine, or any high-speed communications. Francis sent back only a handful of images from the sea, as he had less power than I did. He took a wind generator, hydrogen fuel cell and solar panels, and they were enough to power him round the world. With no satellite antennae he needed less power, and without the half a ton of diesel I took, he was lighter. I was offered the chance to go below but I couldn't bring myself to do that. It was Francis's world, which had been his home for so long. If he had invited me in it would have been different, but without him there it felt wrong to enter a space that was so personal to him.

Despite the fact that there were other people on board, for a good fifteen minutes I disappeared into my thoughts. As I walked her decks I felt a mixture of emotions: a real sense of belonging, and that huge yearning for the sea and the adventure it brings. But I had made a decision, and, as I stood there full of emotion, I knew it was right. I smiled – I was still glad that I was feeling such a strong pull towards the sea. I would have been worried if I hadn't.

Though the record, the culmination of a five-year dream for me, was now gone, I was happy for Francis. No one could deserve that record more than him. I left Brest hoping that he would be able to slot back into life on land without too many challenges, and feeling how lovely it had been to share that brief moment with him.

I had followed his journey closely, and, though he communicated little, his e-mail sent two days before Christmas was an interesting one, echoing my thoughts entirely:

```
To all the children, who want to share my dream.
   I realize now that the planet isn't as big as all
that. Previous generations thought it was infinite and
drew on its resources, but we have now reached a key
moment . . .
   I believe children understand that better than adults,
who are often too deeply involved in their daily lives
to see what is going on.
```

There was a whole new wave of questioning once Francis broke my record, and everyone and their dog seemed to think that the best thing for me to do would be to try and take it back. Would the right thing be to sail around the world again, doing what I do best and to try in the process to raise awareness of the issues we all face? What would I do – sail a boat which had 'live sustainably' emblazoned on its side? It would surely raise a huge number of questions, but I had to ask myself, was it just a stunt and what would it actually achieve? In a way, it would have been the easy option. Not breaking the record itself, of course, but the knowledge that I knew how to do it. But I didn't feel that this would actually solve anything. If I tried to break the record it would take four years of my life, four years in which I could be learning more, rather than just putting my name to something. In my heart of hearts I knew that this new journey on which I was embarking was not about using sailing as a vehicle, it was about heading into an unknown territory which would have its own storms, challenges, nightmares and victories, but, unlike the others, I didn't know where I was going to find the start line, let alone the finish line.

Through our sailing-team partnerships I was doing talks for E.ON, BT and other organizations, and my message was becoming clearer. I tried my absolute best to convey to everyone what I was learning, talking about the need to conserve the resources we have. I talked about managing my energy, diesel, food and water on board Mobi, and the fact that I was doing that when I was more tired than I would ever be at any other stage in my life. I spoke about how I took just thirteen kitchen rolls with me to get me round the world. It was all real for me, but as my speeches focused more and more on sustainability, and the final part covered more and more of what I'd learnt, I found that people began to fidget in their seats. Without realizing it, I was conveying the fear which I felt for our futures, and it was leaving the audience at the end of the presentation with a negative vibe. I knew that it was coming from my frustration. I wasn't being the positive Ellen people were accustomed to. Standing before me like an overpowering menacing figure was the greatest challenge I had ever come across, and I felt scared. I felt scared because, despite two years of research, I could not see a way out, and everyone, I felt, could see right through me.

Chapter Twenty-Five

Perhaps it was meeting Eamonn that had triggered something off in my mind, but I felt the need to learn more about farming. It was a subject which I was sensitive to, having grown up around the farm-sales, and, though I didn't have much practical experience, I'd spent enough time around farmers with my Dad to realize that things were not perhaps as they should be. The number of farms was dropping, small farms anyway: either they were being sold as country estates, or the land was being sold off to the larger neighbouring farms. I found it really sad to see everything those farmers had worked for being sold. Walking down the rows of items at the sales you'd see everything from furniture to well-handled chain saws to old milk churns. Often the thing that struck you was that much of the equipment was generations old, and with my Dad's fascination with old tools he was the perfect person to be there with. He taught me a lot in those years, and in fact still now, if we're up in Derbyshire and there's a sale on, I'll be the first to jump in the car with the dogs and head off with him. I remember leaving a farm-sale recently with him with a couple of bits and pieces in the back. There was an old boy on the gate, and, as we queued to leave, he leant over to us in the back with the dogs and said, 'I sat a good few broodies in those.' He was referring to the galvanized 'broody coops' we'd bought, which you can use for transporting chickens or housing hens sitting on eggs. I realized that he was the farmer who was selling everything off.

'They'll be going to a good home,' I promised him. I was quiet for a while as we headed off down the bumpy track, thinking of the figure leaning on the gate, paying his respects to his memories passing before him.

Many, it seemed to me, were older farmers, who had kept the farm going as long as possible but had got to the point where they physically couldn't cope, or were financially left with no options. Their children were rarely going into farming, as there was not enough money in it to support a family, and they felt compelled to leave the way of life behind for a career which would give them a future.

When my Dad first started work, there were 200,000 more farmers in the UK than there are today. Farming now is on such a large scale that it rarely exists without huge and expensive machinery. An average-size modern tractor is 75 to 100 horse power, and a little bit easier to feed than 75 to 100 horses! If the farmer replaced his tractor with 75 to 100 horses, he'd need to cover half his farm with horse paddocks. Again I came back to how dependent we are on oil, not only for fuel, but also in fertilizer. But it's not just in the farming process that we use so much energy, it's the transportation of the animal, the energy in the feed, the energy in the abattoir and even the cooling of the steak.

We've come a long way over the past 100 years, but I wanted to get under the skin of how sustainable that progress was. I thought it would be a good idea to see both a large and small farm which were both trying to be as sustainable as possible. A lady who worked for E.ON suggested going to Sheepdrove, a huge organic farm in Berkshire. I had not realized at the time, but it is owned by the Kindersleys, previously of the publishing house Dorling-Kindersley, and thanks to their unwavering dedication it had grown to its present size of 2,250 acres. I really liked Peter Kindersley and his wife, Juliet, and as we sat in the eating area of the incredible conference centre they had built there we chatted. The place was fascinating, with its stunning rammed-earth walls made from the chalk dug out for the foundations, and the huge wooden structure of the roof above us. They mentioned that when they had first built the centre it wasn't so popular, but when they started calling it an eco-conference centre, it suddenly got quite busy.

We talked about the subject of sustainability, looking after the land, and looking after animals as well as organic farming on a large scale and how things were doing generally at the farm. Their meat and many local organic vegetables were provided in the eating area there so that people could really taste the difference. They really knew all about the farm, and I liked that. Knowing their stuff was important to them, and they had clearly spent a great deal of their lives learning. We spoke about some of the compromises that still have to be made, like the fuel for the tractors, and we discussed some of the discoveries they had made about genetically modified crops through studies that they'd been doing with another farm. We talked about planning permission for a wind turbine to create enough energy for the farm's power needs, but that there was a great deal of push-back on that from the local community.

It was great that they were doing something on a large scale which really was working. We went for a tour of the farm, saw the moveable free-range hen houses and learnt how their chickens are able to scratch around in the hedgerows and get the vitamins and natural medicines that they need. The pigs had a huge shelter to hide them from the summer heat, the sheep had simple scratching posts so that they could scratch away and relieve an itch or remove a parasite. We discussed the use of pesticides, and the fact that even forty years after their land had ceased to use them they were still there deep down in the chalk and could still be monitored in the water beneath. There were electric gates which were solar- or wind-powered, which meant that they never got left open. It was all a fascinating experience, and we could not have been made to feel more welcome.

I found the whole wind-turbine debate a very interesting one. In the UK especially it is a hugely emotive subject. Most people seem quite open to the idea of windmills, but they just don't want them on a hill near their home. I think that one of the big problems is that power is generated centrally, so people have begun to take it for granted. I am not sure that anyone living near Radcliffe was particularly over the moon to have a huge set of cooling towers in view of their house either, and nor are the people who are in the vicinity of electricity pylons. But as I learnt more I began to see a different way of looking at things.

Generations ago my family ran the windmill at Heage in Derbyshire, and I do wonder whether, when the windmill was proposed, all the locals were up in arms because they didn't want to see it on the hill above their house. I doubt that very much. They probably built it with their own hands, because they needed to grind the wheat to eat. It was part of the community, it was their windmill. And it still is: so much so that they renovated it, ran it, and it still grinds corn today. Would I rather see a hill with or without a wind turbine? Without. But if I lived in a house with no electricity, then perhaps I would think very hard about having one there.

Next, I visited the much smaller, 70 acre, Blacklake organic farm in Devon with Katie and her family, who lived near by. It was run by Catherine and Nick Broomfield, and it had the best hedges and pastures I had seen in a long while. It was in an idyllic setting, with rolling hills, tiny brooks and happy animals. As we wandered through the fields with Catherine and her son, she spoke of what they were doing there and how they were making it all work. The grass was varied and really established in the ground, and they use age-old methods to care for it. The feed for the animals was all produced on the farm, and they used crop and animal rotation together with common sense and knowledge to get the best out of the land and keep it in a healthy, balanced state. We spoke about the whole farming system too. Catherine, having worked on farms in her youth, had experience behind her and strong views. One of her points concerned the subsidies introduced after the Second World War. 'Subsidies were given to the farmers,' she said, 'to keep the price of food low after the war, but the result is now that people don't know what the real price of food is. The subsidy should have gone on to the food, and then people would have been aware of the true cost.'

This was not just a UK phenomenon. In the late 1950s the Common Agricultural Policy was introduced across Europe, and by 2009 nearly £50 billion, over 40 per cent of the EU's annual budget, was spent on funding it.

Blacklake Farm felt homely, warm, the kind of place you could call in for a cup of tea and stay for ever. It seemed perfect in every way, from the beautiful green pastures running down to the tree-lined goyle to the orchard above the road, from which they produced apple juice. The cob-walled farmhouse was ancient, with its irregular shapes, whitewashed walls and the kitchen floor worn away at the doorway with a huge curve carved by footsteps over centuries. It was sad to think that, when the Broomfields bought the farm, it had been advertised as a 'country estate', though reassuring that they had pushed against that and kept it working as a farm. They use local breeds of cattle and sheep and sell their produce to nearby towns and villages. The fantastic thing is that, even though the farm is very small by modern standards, as a business model it works. Although the weather and luck can move the line of profit, they survive well and happily. The farm is small enough to cope with and handle, and small enough to understand and manage. I liked that: they knew their farm intimately. And as Bertie, their son, pointed out, not only are the animals on the farm healthy and happy, but they are also 'very tasty'!

What these two experiences made me realize was how different these farms are from the norm. The availability of cheap oil has allowed us to get more from our land than ever before. Mechanization, artificial fertilizers and large-scale farming make more money, and, as long as oil remains cheap, these will continue to be used to vastly increase our yields. What I had seen at these two farms was a step in the right direction, but both farms still had tractors in their yards . . .

I had started off on a mission to learn about growing food and ended up with my head stuck in a book about economics. Everything I was learning about led to an expansive thought process where I had to understand the much bigger picture. I had no concept of economics when I left school, but now I was actively learning about it. My hunger for knowledge was also taking me further afield, and thanks to the relationship between OC and Renault developing through my interest in sustainability, I was learning fast. We had worked with Renault for years as our sailing-team car partner, but they now had a new agenda, and, having worked on their sustainability policy for years, they were ready to communicate it. I was reassured to see that the car industry was taking the subject so seriously, and with Renault I really felt that they meant it. I was actually taken aback in our second meeting, when I entered really fired up with my questions on their policies, only to find that I was being questioned about my own credibility! When they stepped up to become the final sponsor to our sailing team I had a new opportunity to step inside the world of industry, and this time learn more about the reality of how cars are designed and made.

I visited Renault's techno-centre, which employs a staggering 12,000 people, as well as being an actual working factory. It was an eye-opening experience. The techno-centre is on a site of 370 acres and is like nothing I have ever experienced in my life. Everything happens there, from design to engineering to making prototypes and even the first trial runs of the production lines. I walked round with my mouth open and learnt everything from how to increase fuel efficiency by changing the bolts in the vehicles to which parts of a Laguna door can be recycled into what. I was equally amazed by the scale of the factory, and watching the 40 ton weight of the huge steel presses lift up and down, literally printing out car doors on their hydraulics, was mesmerizing.

Aside from seeing how things really worked, I had some incredible opportunities. I was allowed to drive the prototype of the new Twizy in the workshop, get a sneak preview of the future of their cars and have a go in their new hydrogen car before it was even released to the public. I was surprised at the hydrogen car; it was not sluggish at all as I had imagined, but was actually a great driving experience. It was powered by a fuel cell that converted hydrogen into electricity to run an electric motor. The impressive thing was that the only thing to come out of the exhaust was water. It made no big roaring sound at all when you started it. It was really truly amazing, and, with an autonomy which could theoretically reach 700 km, as I drove it I felt convinced that it was the car of the future.

If it was a fast car, with great autonomy, then surely it would be the solution, but the stumbling block is perhaps the hydrogen. If I was thinking that it could replace oil, then I guess eventually we'd need to have access to it in the same quantities we have of oil today. But there is one big difference between hydrogen and oil. The oil industry is extracting a product we *already have*. It is possible to make hydrogen by passing electricity through sea-water, but the electricity to do that has to be generated in the first place. Bio-fuels are a renewable fuel, but also, like hydrogen, involve creating something we don't already have: the fields devoted to bio-fuels could otherwise be used for food.

But it wasn't just the hydrogen car that I was lucky enough to drive thanks to Renault. They also, as a total surprise, lent me an electric car. I must have bombarded them with so many questions that they thought that, if I had the chance to actually drive one, I might shut up! Renault didn't currently produce electric cars, though planned to do so again in the future. Mine had been built in 2003, six years before. Charging it was simple, as you literally plugged it into any 13A plug socket, anywhere, and it was a strange sensation opening the bonnet to see nothing there but an oversize Scalextric engine. No moving parts, no glow plugs or spark plugs, no gearbox, no oil. Never having ever driven an electric car before, I did not really know what to expect, and it might sound silly, but I was quite surprised when I turned the key to start it and there was no sound at all. Before I moved off I thought I'd stalled, but of course you can't stall an electric car, as it doesn't have an engine. It's quite nice too to trundle down a country road and listen to the sounds around you. I loved it, and the dogs loved it so much too that they would actually jump into the boot if it was left open in the yard. I'm sure that the quietness had something to do with it. The other thing I noticed was that, even when you've started it, you can have that lovely sensation of being able to continue to have a conversation with someone you were talking to out of the window, and, as electric cars have no exhaust, nothing unpleasant comes out of the back, so you don't worry about starting it next to your strawberries!

I couldn't talk about the car without mentioning the inconveniences, though. Once fully charged, which takes eight hours of being plugged into a standard plug socket, the autonomy is only 60 miles. For me, 60 miles wasn't a problem, as it's the total circumference of the Isle of Wight, but for someone needing to drive further it would be a bit of a problem. But the good thing is that, at current energy prices, those 60 miles will only cost you about £1.50, ten times cheaper to run than my efficient diesel car.

Major car manufacturers are devoting a greater part of their research and development to electric cars. Future models will travel further, have changeable batteries and will be less expensive. In the case of Renault, this has moved on so far that in 2011–12 the general public will be able to buy one of their *four* new all-electric production cars at a very similar price to their combustion-engine equivalents. In fact, the Renault–Nissan alliance deems it important enough to be investing 4 billion Euros and employing 2,000 people in their electric-car team. That's amazing, considering that their electric Kangoo failed less than five years before due to a lack of orders: surely an indication that the world is changing.

As I studied everything from cars to tractors I couldn't help but do the maths in my head about the energy involved in their use and production. And not just that: if all the cars were going to be electric and we were going to revolutionize our farming system, then we'd have to produce even more energy. I thought back to Radcliffe power station and challenged myself to work out whether we could actually make that much energy sustainably.

I looked into the figures for how many onshore wind turbines you'd need to replace Radcliffe, and I was really surprised to see that it was as many as 676. But that's working at 100 per cent capacity, and we know that we don't have wind blowing all the time. I looked into the numbers and found that wind turbines seem to work on an average of about 25 per cent capacity in the UK, which would mean that, in order to be able to produce as much power as Radcliffe could running at full chat in one average year, you'd need to install over 2,500 of the biggest wind turbines available in the world today. That's not only a lot, but it's twice the current wind-generation capacity in Great Britain – to replace what just one power station could generate!

I was realizing that in the long term there was a need not only to revolutionize farming, but also to work out how we might adapt to our new set of circumstances as we leave behind us what we know as the industrial revolution. So if car manufacturers and farming are beginning to future-proof themselves, how could you and I do the same? How could we future-proof ourselves?

When Ian and I bought our plot on the island, we'd never read a book about sustainability in our lives. But when we set out to build something, we wanted to build the right house, a house that was cheap to run in the future. But were we living in a bubble? Was what we were learning applicable to everyone?

As we were finalizing plans for our house, the Isle of Wight Council approached me to ask me if I would be interested in becoming the figurehead of their new vision for the island, called 'Eco-Island'. Despite feeling really motivated, I made it quite clear that I didn't want to become the figurehead of the idea straight away, but would be very happy to become one when we'd actually achieved something, so after a couple of meetings I said that I would be more than happy to get involved and spend time with the council and other island bodies to actually try to help in any way I could to make things happen on the island.

My first engagement would be an Eco-Island conference in February, which would encourage local businesses to come along and hear of the plans for the island. It was all about sustainability, and I agreed to be a speaker. The hall was filled with over 300 people; it was great to see that there was clearly so much support for what the council were proposing.

There is something special about the Isle of Wight. It is a beautiful island, with huge chalk cliffs, sandy beaches, ancient forests and well-managed farmland. It is separate from the mainland – obviously – but there is no bridge, and anything that comes on to or goes off the island still does so by boat. So, if you want to measure change, there cannot be a better place in the country than the Isle of Wight. If you managed to insulate everyone's houses on the island, then, as the electricity and water comes to the island through several metered pipes and cables, you should be able to assess the improvement pretty easily. In a normal county it's much harder, as wires and generation don't usually correspond that well to the boundaries.

It was an interesting learning curve for me. I spent several days there to begin with on a crash course, to learn about how the system works. I was not aware of the structure of a council, and over the nine months of working very closely with them I have to say I had to learn a lot! The chief executive was a visionary and had a real passion for putting ideas together and making things really happen. It was he who had first contacted the office to ask if I would be interested in getting involved, and when he came to see us he arrived with the leader of the council and his colleague. It seemed that everyone there saw the incredible potential the island had. Eco-Island was an initiative that aimed not only to make the island a net exporter of renewable energy by 2020, but also to improve people's lives on the island. It was about health and wellbeing, pride and happiness. It was about what a community should be working towards anyway, I guess.

Energy was something which was discussed a great deal in the meetings, in terms of both waste reduction and generation. Wave and wind turbines were discussed as well as solar and biomass boilers. The only current power station on the island was an automatic gas-powered back-up one, and all other power came from the mainland. It wasn't always going to be the case, though, as I learned that in 1965 a nuclear power station had been planned for the Isle of Wight. Understandably, local people didn't want it, so local yachtsmen and naturalists raised the funds for the purchase of Newtown Creek, its planned location, so that they could gift it to the National Trust.

Meetings on the island led to more meetings further afield, as I discovered very quickly that finding solutions, whether in energy, transport or home insulation, was going to involve more than just the island. I subsequently ended up in all sorts of meetings with Defra, Ofgem, SEEDA, E.ON and the Crown Estate. I found out about the CERT scheme, a £600 million pot created by a surcharge on our electricity bills which is available for us all to insulate our houses. Roughly 50 per cent of that is for vulnerable people, or people on benefits, or anyone over seventy, who can get their walls, lofts and light bulbs done totally for free, and the remaining £300 million is for a 50 per cent grant towards the same things for everyone else. I was staggered when I found out and wondered if people actually knew of its existence. I knew that my Gran certainly hadn't. There seemed so much to do, and so many different paths to go down.

The reality was that the council didn't have vast amounts of money spare to put a team on to the project, so the resources there were limited. I could understand that they were funded by taxpayers' money, so it was a difficult situation, but in trying to find workable solutions alone I was beginning to feel I was banging my head against a wall. I felt totally ineffective on my own, and, even if I'd wanted to spend all my time on it, I couldn't due to my sailing-team commitments. I was also working free of charge, because I was passionate about finding a solution, but I knew that I couldn't ask other people to do that too. Now on a bit of a funding trail, I began trying to find out how the project could gain more momentum.

I spoke to one government department about the island's vision. They were really positive about the whole idea and agreed that it was an ideal place for measuring just what a difference could be made. We discussed everything from mass insulation schemes to testing lower-energy street lighting to renewable energy offshore. Finally, I asked about the possibilities for seed money to employ a small team of people to help the council, but the response was: 'Have you tried the National Lottery?'

At that point I decided to look elsewhere.

Chapter Twenty-Six

Ian and I spent the first week of July 2008 trying to complete the foundations of our house, and I remember well spending the larger part of my birthday in the trenches, shoring up the clay ground until we were ready to pour the concrete in. There was something hugely satisfying about levelling off those foundations on which we were to build our home. The shade kindly provided by the huge oak tree was welcome as we worked away, both excited about the prospect of seeing the house take shape but slightly worried about whether we had the windows in the right place to let the sun in! The entrance of the site was now clear, and finally mud free, as, when we'd sadly demolished the old bungalow, we'd used the bricks and concrete from its foundations to form the drive. The pond, which we'd cleared out ourselves the previous year, was now beauti ful, clear and green, with dragonflies by the dozen and several clutches of wild ducks already hatched on it. The site was once again coming alive, and we couldn't wait for the time a year later when we'd be living there, watching the seasons change around us from the warmth of our home.

Alongside the house and more research it was also a busier year for sailing. It kicked off with the sad return of *Estrella Damm* from Cape Town after pulling out of the Barcelona World Race with rudder damage. But at least on land we'd had more positive news, when we'd secured the funding for the sailing team from Renault. Once *Estrella Damm* was rebranded *BT*, we christened her in London, and, through BT's connection with the Isle of Wight Festival, the Sugababes sang live on her deck as she sailed beneath Tower Bridge. She looked spectacular in her new colours, and just weeks later it was the start of the Transat in Plymouth, and her first race in her new livery awaited. I felt different about the boats now; having dealt with my decision in Barcelona, I was itching to be there.

Just weeks later, though, it was my turn, and with Australian Greg Homann I was lining up on the start line for the Archipelago Raid. It was time for my main event in our BT Team Ellen project, and, though it was very different from an offshore race, I was really looking forward to it.

It wasn't the first time we'd sailed together, as Greg had been one of the crew when we won Round the Island the previous year, and we'd also been out to do three days' training in Sweden a fortnight before. Our session went really well; it was an opportunity to get to know each other better, and the chance to work out how we'd function best as a team.

Neither of us were pros in any way when it came to sailing small cats, though Greg had significantly more experience than me, having tried to sail one solo non-stop across the Atlantic! It was quite refreshing to be sailing with someone who may even have been classed as crazier than me, and from those first three days of training it was clear that we were going to get on well. Even before arriving in Sweden we had nicknamed our craft 'Foxy Lady', and it was clear that the more we sailed together the more jokes, banter and sarcastic comments we were going to be throwing at each other.

One moment I remember well was fumbling about with the charts, trying to find out where we were when we'd gone off the edge and over the fold on the chart. I'd had two pushed safely in a plastic wallet around my neck, and, as our GPS hadn't got the charts loaded at that stage, we had to rely on finding our position on paper. The charts were already pretty wet, as that's what happens when you refold them several times with wet hands; but in this instant they were about to get a whole lot wetter. We were both hanging out over the water as we were fully extended on our trapezes, and, as I normally steered, Greg had taken over by holding on to the tiller extension behind my back. With the strengthening wind firing spray all over us, to say that I was struggling with the task would be a massive understatement. Trying to get the one from in my mouth and the one shoved down my nappy (which is what you wear to clip on to the trapeze with) back in the plastic case the right way round with the scales readable was like trying to balance on a ball whilst juggling. Although it was a serious situation, as we were not exactly sure where we were any more, we were both giggling so much that we nearly capsized!

The Raid was visual paradise, though; to have the luxury of spending six days sailing amongst the 100,000 islands of the archipelago and through their most spectacular waters was a joy. Seeing the wooden houses nestling in trees on tiny islands was magical, and it seemed totally impossible that there could be so many of them. We went everywhere, from tiny creeks we had to paddle through to really huge expanses of the Baltic Sea heading over to Åland. Our nights were spent camping in little tents near the boats, sometimes on the beach. Waking with the most beautiful pink skies, still mornings and scenery to die for was the most incredible experience, and, even if we were absolutely exhausted, we couldn't help but appreciate the most magical places we were sailing in.

Greg's hands were not in great shape by the end. He had been working the mainsheet, and, though he always wore gloves, they were covered in blisters, and he had three fingernails about to fall off. On the third day I'd had to stick a red-hot needle through his nail to relieve the pressure; I took the Mickey out of him, because I didn't think he was very brave about it! I reminded him that I'd had to do it twice to myself, and one of those alone at sea! Everyone suffers physically – but in the Raid it always seems they have a smile on their face. The atmosphere on our boat was fantastic, and, bar a few exhausted hours or the odd stressful landing, we managed a pretty constant level of healthy banter. Greg and I made a strong team, we worked together well, always tried to do better every day and were honest about each other's strengths and weaknesses.

We did not win the Raid; in fact, we finished ninth out of

twenty-two. But then again the guys that did win were back for their fifth attempt! The best thing for us was that we progressed well throughout the week, and we ended up in fifth place on the final leg of the final day, which would have stood us in good stead if our rudder hadn't fallen off! It was the strangest thing to happen just a couple of hours from the finish. We were sailing along when there was a sudden 'bang', and the boat slowed. We continued racing after that with just one rudder, surprisingly only losing one place to other competitors, but when a 30 knot squall came in as we were closing on Stockholm in the final thirty minutes of our race we suddenly looked in pretty bad shape, as with only one rudder we could not actually tack the boat! Greg had to jump in the water to turn the boat through the wind, and, as we struggled, we snapped our bowsprit on a buoy. Knowing full well that turning was difficult, we ended up having to hide in a bay for shelter to escape the waves. Once the squall had passed we headed out once again, and we did manage to finish, but, as in so many other races, we had been taught once again that it's not over till it's over!

It was a tough race, and concentrating so hard for so long really does take its toll on you, but flying along at sunrise between the rocks makes you feel alive. I had loved it, absolutely loved it, and it had been a wonderful challenge. I had been excited by the competition element, fallen in love with the Archipelago and absolutely revelled in the challenge of learning to sail a new boat well. But for me there was something quite special about being out on the water again. It reconnected me with the adventures of my childhood and reminded me that I didn't have to give up sailing just because I was not haring off round the world in a race.

With Sébastien competing in the 2008 Vendée, pretty much the whole team headed out to Les Sables d'Olonne in November for the start. Everyone was really excited, as the most incredible period of hard work had gone in to get *BT* to the state where she was completely ready for the race. For me this time was going to be quite interesting. This was to be my fourth Vendée Globe start, and at each one I'd had a very different perspective on the race.

It was in Les Sables that I thought back to the moment in South Georgia when I realized just how young I was when I had first competed in the Vendée. At the time I felt like every other sailor in the race, focused on what I had to achieve and just wanting to get on with it. I remember feeling that, no matter what happened out there, I was going to give it my best shot. The staggering thing was that, eight years later, I was still only eighteen months older than the youngest competitor. It made me realize how much pressure I put on myself at such a young age, and how some of the experiences that a 'normal' young person would surely have had must have passed me by.

The first time I was there in 1996 was with my friend Alan Wynne Thomas, who sadly is no longer with us. He was a total inspiration to me, and for whom I had been working to prepare a boat for this very race. Unfortunately, he had not found the funding, but we travelled over to the start together to watch the fleet leave all the same, and for me as a twenty-year-old it was a pivotal moment in my career. As I walked down the pontoons with Alan I was totally fascinated by the boats, the people and the atmosphere – everything was new, and I was totally in awe of it. It was then, in Les Sables with Alan, that I made the decision to do everything I could to compete in the next race.

Somehow, with a hell of a lot of luck and a huge amount of work, I was one of those twenty-four competitors on the start line four years later. So in 2000 it was a very different story. I was filled with nerves, excited about the race, but petrified of something going wrong and not making it. I was concentrating on how I would need to perform for the following three months, trying not to take in the atmosphere too much as I did not want to lose my focus on the race. Then, for the first time, I knew how it really felt to be one of those solitary figures disappearing over the horizon for a very, very long time.

In 2004 I was still on edge. Though I wasn't competing in the Vendée Globe, I was on standby for the round-the-world record attempt. The start of the Vendée was on 7 November, and I ended up leaving exactly three weeks later on the 28th. So in 2004 my head had not really been in the Vendée, nor had I been able to stand back, watch and take it all in. With my own journey just around the corner, I was tense and preoccupied, but none the less glad to be there to see many of my friends leave.

So it was really strange to be there this time, my fourth start, but, though we had Seb in the race, and I was nervous for him, I wasn't about to sail. I was able to take in all that was going on around me and spend time with friends I'd not seen for some time. I went along to Seb's leaving party shortly before the start, which was fantastic. He was on fine form and didn't seem in the slightest bit stressed. Anyone would have thought that it was his birthday party, watching him act the fool and mess around with the team, who were ultimately his mates. I knew that Seb felt ready, and I knew that his boat was ready, as, with the amount of time, care, effort and attention to detail that had gone into building her, there could be no other outcome!

As *BT* motored out into the channel to follow the previous 60, I stood on the end of the pontoon with Albert. It was he who had been responsible for building the boat, not just *BT*, but Mobi too. There was not a need for many words; we had already been through a lot together, and we knew the score.

What felt like moments later I was whisked through Les Sables on the back of a scooter to get to the castle, where I'd be doing a live TV commentary for the start. It was incredible to see the thousands of people – children and adults of all ages – all walking from the spot that they had found on the harbour wall to watch the boats leave, or on the beach to see what they could of the start. It was a fine spectacle; and there, hidden under the cover of my visor, anonymous on a scooter, I was able to take it all in.

I felt quite alone that day in a strange kind of way, having such a strong insight into what would be going on in the heads of those sailors, some leaving for their first Vendée Globe. I had more in common with those who were leaving than those on the dock. I wasn't going this time, and it was impossible to describe the emotions I was feeling to those around me who had never gone.

It had been a successful year for OC. We had run the Transat, competed in it and organized a new Extreme 40 circuit, in which Nick finished on the podium. But what we were struggling to do was to find a way to communicate sustainability within it.

Towards the end of 2008 at an OC management team meeting we made a fundamental decision: that OC was not the vehicle through which I could communicate the sustainability message. We'd had people in to speak about the subject and had employed someone one day a week to work on it within OC. Mark had tasked Jamie Butterworth, who managed the BT project, to spend time with me trying to communicate sustainability. In the meeting Jamie asked whether, in view of the impending recession, we should refocus OC towards working with companies together on sustainability rather than sailing sponsorship. But it was clear from the outcome that my 'sustainability' project in whatever form it took would have to exist outside OC and be something totally separate. It was common sense, really, as OC's core business was managing sailing campaigns and events. I felt a real wave of sadness that the passion which was growing inside me was not something that I would, or could, be sharing with the team at OC, but life has a funny way of working itself out, and, just when I was struggling to find a solution, I met someone who could help.

After watching Seb leave for the Vendée Globe, Katie, Joss, Jamie and I had travelled to the ferry port of St Malo before heading to the Isle of Wight. It had been a big day for all of us – it's not like the Vendée Globe comes round each year. Joss had been to many starts and, as a sailing journalist, he had put a lot of time into following the race and knew many of the skippers. It was Joss who had written about their lives. Jamie was the account manager for BT and had lived as close to the team as anyone possibly could. It was Katie's first Vendée Globe, though she had heard me talk so much about it in the three years we had worked together, it must have felt like her tenth. We all had a passion for sustainability, and Nicolas Hulot, the person we were about to meet, did too.

We met for the first time as we rang the bell at his garden gate. Nicolas looked to be in his mid-fifties; he was tanned, with mousy brown hair that was longer than most and, though small and slightly built, was clearly very fit. He was an unassuming character, very natural; dressed in an orange jumper and a pair of blue jeans, he warmly welcomed four strangers he had never met in his life before. As we stepped into his garden he smiled and beckoned us in. On the front step of the house were two dogs which I couldn't resist going to say hello to.

'He's called Picchu,' he said. 'I found him on Machu Picchu while on the Inca trail. He followed me for days, so I brought him home.' I liked Nicolas instantly.

Nicolas was a TV presenter, a kind of cross between Bruce Parry and David Attenborough, though in France he is the one and only Nicolas Hulot. I knew he had been travelling the world for many years, visiting different cultures and places; and to me his eyes conveyed a real need to communicate what he had learnt. He talked about what he felt about the state that we, human beings, were getting ourselves into as a result of our unsustainable consumption of the earth's resources, and then, over lunch in a tiny makeshift beach restaurant, we spoke about why he felt the way he did. By his own admission, when he had begun travelling the world over thirty years before, he was not an ecologist, but the more he travelled the more he began to realize that the world we live in was not infinite, but instead finite and vulnerable. In 1990 Nicolas set up a foundation, which had the objective of communicating what he was seeing with his own eyes.

The following hours with him passed quickly as we discussed the work of his foundation. He spoke of the years he had spent struggling to get traction; he felt he was trying to communicate a subject, but that it wasn't getting the interest it deserved. It was during the French presidential election in 2007 when everything changed. Having been deeply concerned about the candidates' views on environmental policies, he considered standing himself, and the moment that went public the polls showed that he could in fact score big. The other candidates were suitably concerned. He used this pressure to ask them to come to him to define how they would tackle ten specific points relating to sustainability. Then, once the main candidates had done this and signed up to it, he stood down. One of these points was to choose a number two to the President who would look at the sustainability implications of each decision that the government made. It really was a bold and brave move, and the effects of it are still very much present today.

Meeting Nicolas had been quite inspirational for all of us. We not only shared many of his views, but we had spent time with someone who had really done something concrete, real and measurable. After three years of trying to work out how I should go about tackling this topic I had finally met a man who understood it.

The most fascinating thing for us was the structure of how his foundation worked, and a few weeks later we travelled over to Paris to see just that. It was an organization which was totally independent of any other body. My experience with both the sailing team's sustainability work and Eco-Island had shown me that, with the best will in the world, when trying to fit into a bigger organization there were real challenges involved. Pursuing both relationships had taught me so much, but the freedom and flexibility to achieve what I believed was possible was simply not there. After meeting Nicolas I was convinced that the right thing to do was to set up a charitable foundation through which to communicate, and the reason for this to exist outside OC was now quite clear. Like Nicolas, I didn't want there to be anything in this for me, I didn't want to draw a wage and I wanted to be independent. A foundation could also become the structure through which I could pull together a team. Not unlike a sailing project, it was clear that I couldn't do this on my own, and having the right team who could focus solely on our goal was essential.

Like Nicolas's foundation we could attract funding from corporates. My experience during previous years had taught me that the capability of a huge organization to change itself, but also to influence government, was great. Since beginning sailing solo at eighteen I had begun to work with companies through sponsorship, and I was now feeling much more relaxed in board rooms. At the foundation we would work with industry, not only to learn, but also to really make things happen on a tangible scale.

Things were beginning to fall into place, and the map for the future was becoming clear. I had a good feeling inside, that everything had happened in my life for a reason, and perhaps the sailing had been there to give me a voice. But, despite clarifying the structure, there was one element I wasn't yet at all convinced about: what our message was.

There was something which happened in 2008 which would be a wake-up call to everyone. The vast majority did not foresee the timing or severity of the financial crisis. Everything was going so well, we were booming, the City was making a fortune, and many big companies were expanding like there was no tomorrow. Who could have anticipated the front pages of the newspapers talking of billions of pounds of fresh new money being invested into the economy? It was not long before we began to talk about trillions, and perhaps in a funny way money meant very little any more. I don't think I'd heard of a trillion before, and it certainly wouldn't fit on my calculator.

It's interesting in this day and age that we describe ourselves in the developed world as a *consumer* society, and until recently I'd never thought about that phrase very much. But when you actually look it up, the definition of the word to 'consume' is: '1. To destroy or expend by use; use up. 2. To eat or drink up; devour. 3. To destroy, as by decomposition or burning. 4. To spend (money, time, etc.) wastefully. 5. To absorb, engross.'

We are always told that we need more and more, we need to travel faster and faster, and that it should cost less and less, but is this a model which can continue indefinitely? We went from hunter gatherer, to farmer, to industrialist, and now to consumer: all three bar consumer imply that we are actually working and doing something constructive, rather than destructive. We need things for sure – clothes, furniture, toys and goods – but can more stuff at a cheaper price really mean we're paying the true cost of what we are consuming? Crucially, societies in the developed world are founded on the consumption of irreplaceable natural resources.

It really scares me to think that we could be in a similarly disastrous situation as the financial crisis but through a shortage of resources. I'm sure that the belief as the crisis unfolded was that something or someone would sort it out, and that there was little time for questioning whether the whole system itself may have been wrong. I'm sure that everyone thought that it would just readjust itself. But it didn't. It went catastrophically wrong. Though it's hard to say, that phrase 'it's only money' does spring to mind . . . the problem with sustainability, however, is that it's not just money, a value printed on paper that rises or falls, it's real stuff that actually exists. To plug the gap of the financial crisis we printed more money.

And the problem is that we can't just print more coal, gas or oil.

The biggest oil tanker in the world is a quarter of a mile long, 30 feet longer than the Empire State Building is tall, and when fully loaded is so deep (at 80 feet) that it can't even get up the English Channel. It can carry 4.1 million barrels of crude oil, which, at 2008 consumption levels, will last the UK less than three days. In the UK we use 4.4 litres of oil per man, woman and child each day. If we had to produce 4.4 litres of it in our garden we would struggle in a year, let alone in a day.

The use of oil has crept into our world at an alarming rate. Since my Dad was born the world's consumption has gone up tenfold. Since I was born the number of motor vehicles on our roads has quadrupled to over 800 million, whereas when my Great Granddad was born only twenty-five had been sold in the entire world.

Oil is now an essential part of industrial farming, used in fertilizers to increase our yields on the land and in transporting the food to processing plants and then shops. There are six barrels of oil in just one cow by the time its meat reaches the shelves of US supermarkets. But it's not just meat. It is so crucial now to our industrial farming methods that there are 10 calories of oil in every calorie we eat. If oil disappeared tomorrow, millions more people around the world would quite literally starve.

We use oil for making half our clothes, seeing our family, popping to the shops, TVs, mattresses, deliveries and even pharmaceuticals. It is in everything we do, but this level of use is quite understandable.

As I write this book, crude oil costs about £50 a barrel, and in that single barrel is the same amount of energy as ten labourers working every single day for a year. So of course you'd go for the oil – why wouldn't you?

Our oil discovery peaked in 1965, when we found 55 giga-barrels. In 1975 we found 35, in 1985 we found 15, in 1995 we found 8, and in 2005 we found 5.

The International Energy Agency (IEA) is responsible for advising twenty-eight governments in the world, including the UK and the USA, on their energy policies. They were set up as an independent body by the Organization for Economic Co-operation and Development, so they are about as far from an environmental group as you could get. To find out more about oil, I thought that they'd be a good bet.

> Estimates of remaining proven reserves of oil and NGLs range from about 1.2 to 1.3 trillion barrels (including about 0.2 trillion barrels of non-conventional oil) . . . This is enough to supply the world with oil for over 40 years at current rates of consumption.

That brought everything home to me: forty years was in my lifetime. The hard fact is that oil won't be around in the quantity we have today for ever. In a handful of generations we have ripped through a staggering amount of what is effectively a one-off gift. As the IEA put in the first paragraph of their executive summary:

> The world's energy system is at a crossroads. Current global trends in energy supply are patently unsustainable – environmentally, economically, socially . . . What is needed is nothing short of an energy revolution.

Central to the problem is the issue of peak oil. Peak oil production is the point at which the depletion of existing reserves can no longer be replaced by additions of new flow capacity: that is, you can no longer get out of the reserves what you want or need, a bit like trying to squeeze more out of the bottom of a toothpaste tube.

Once they are 'past the maximum', the amount coming out decreases, and the risk is that demand will outstrip supply – hence in the UK we are now a net importer of oil. This notion of peak oil was originally put forward in the 1950s by a man called M. King Hubbert, a geoscientist working for the Shell Oil Company. It is only with time that the importance of his discovery has shown itself, as illustrated in the words of the former chairman of Shell, Lord Ron Oxburgh, in 2008: 'At the time Hubbert was regarded by many as a crank, and the industry line was that new discoveries would continue to replace what had been used. We now know differently.'

The theory became reality as the USA hit peak oil production in 1970, and our North Sea oil platforms in 1999. Perhaps it's stating the obvious, but if we continue to use more and more of something that is not replenishing itself, then at some stage, we are going to get to the bottom bit. It's not that we will run out of oil, but when it gets harder and more expensive to get out, the consequences will ricochet across the globe.

On my boat fuel was finite, but I could refuel once I'd crossed the finish line. In our world we can't. And that is exactly the issue. When the price begins to skyrocket many industries which are dependent on the stuff for their very survival will be held to ransom by the limits of the planet. As the chief economist of the International Energy Agency said, 'We should leave oil before oil leaves us.'

Something out at sea had changed my outlook and had made me realize that many of our currently essential resources are limited, but as I had never even questioned this until two years before, why on earth should anyone else? Not everyone has the opportunity and space of South Georgia to think, and nor would they all choose to either. What had happened to me was that I had slowly embarked on a journey driven by my curiosity which was taking me through the process of changing my mind. No one likes to change their mind. It's almost as if a part of your soul is questioned, or your previous life is put on trial. My brother Lewis and I sometimes argued as kids, always about something to do with sailing, but neither of us could bring ourselves to change our mind. A quote by the American economist John Kenneth Galbraith sums it up: 'Faced with the choice between changing one's mind and proving that there is no need to do so, almost everyone gets busy on the proof.'

How would I in what I was doing convince people that there was a need for things to really change? I was beginning to do more talks on the subject, introducing what I'd learnt from my journey, my story from South Georgia and managing my resources on board. But I found that I began to touch on so many subjects – farming, transport, industry, energy, economics and even allotments; they were all relevant, but I was struggling to tie them all in together, other than using the word 'sustainability' that is, which many people still did not really understand.

Though I thought hard about attaching myself to just one part of the argument – which initially people encouraged me to do – I couldn't. It wasn't about saving the oceans or pollution on our beaches, or even just about oil. The whole point about 'sustainability' is that it encompasses *everything* we do in our lives and is relevant to the whole framework within which we live. So what exactly *was* it that I was trying to communicate?

For me this wasn't about saving the planet, it was actually about mankind's future, and our ability to sustain ourselves, man being the single species on this planet that is dependent on non-renewable resources for its survival. When I spoke about South Georgia and my adventures there, people would link what I was doing to the environment, but for me it went way beyond that. I felt frustrated that I wasn't communicating what I really meant. What I needed was a unifying concept to bring this all together, and the word 'sustainability' didn't do it.

Chapter Twenty-Seven

The following year, 2009, was the year of real commitment, when a passion and an interest became the thing that was going to take over my working life. I was excited, really excited. It felt like the passion which had been rattling round my head for three years had burst out with real direction. Not only that, but, as the path became clear, so did so much else.

On reflection it would also be a pivotal year, where I either went for it and made the Foundation come alive or gave up. The previous time this happened to me was in 1998, before the Route du Rhum. Back then, I simply didn't have the funds to pay the entry fee. I had no sponsor, no way to make it to the start line, yet I had total belief that I would get there. And when Mum let me know the day before the deadline that Nan had left me £5,000 in her will, I didn't hesitate for a second to commit the whole amount to the non-refundable entrance fee.

I had thrown my inheritance into the Rhum as I knew that it was the only way to make the race possible, and I knew that the right thing to do was something similar for the Foundation. I decided to fund it for its first eighteen months so that it could actually get on and make things happen. I did not want to be running around trying to find funding to the extent that we took our eye off the ball. Moreover, I had total faith in the Foundation, and I was absolutely certain that it would succeed.

Our trustees included myself, Philip Sellwood, the CEO of the

Energy Saving Trust, and Peter Morgan, who at the time was Head of Communications for BT. The Foundation's day-to-day operations would be based in Cowes, and at the beginning of 2009 Ian and I found an office in which to put it. It was a wonderful feeling, to be setting up our own base, and, as the year progressed, the people who would work for it fell into place. The greatest surprise of all for me was that Jamie decided that he wished to leave OC and work with the Foundation; having spent several months working with him, I couldn't imagine a better person for the job. Katie, as my PA, also moved across to work partly for the Foundation too, and Joss was also very keen to be involved. Over the year the team and the office became established; the pure setting-up of something new was creating a wave, and we were all overjoyed to be riding it.

At the same time our very own house had become a place that we could actually live in. Its personality had grown with time, as we'd found bits and bobs in the paper, like the ancient old butcher's block we had collected from a dusty garage. It was an interesting concept, giving a new house character, but we did all we could putting as many quirky items in as we could muster. The downstairs floor we covered with leftover slate roof tiles, and the furniture was made mainly of old stripped doors and whatever we could uncover in Dad's barn. That was, apart from the bed, which Ian made in an evening in an attempt to get the mattress off the floor! The chimney mantelpieces and stairs were made of big chunks of chestnut we had dragged from the woods with the help of Terry the farmer and his tractor. We made the doors for the kitchen out of leftover wood from the cladding on the outside of the house and at the same time expanded our animal menagerie. Three and a half years after we had first walked on to the site, home felt like home. Though we lived in the house for three months before we actually fitted the front door, we were in, and it felt fantastic.

But, despite the house nearing completion, I hadn't been able to be there for much of that summer. The Ellen MacArthur Trust was setting sail round Britain. It was its biggest challenge yet, and I was eager to be a part of it. The intention was to sail almost 2,000 miles on a boat called *Scarlet Oyster* and in the process take eighty-five young people as crew on seventeen different legs round the country.

What made it more special was that the young people would go into hospitals at the end of each of their legs and talk to other young people going through treatment. It was so clear from our experiences just what a difference some positive role models can make at a time when those young people are really toughing it out. We financed the tour with donations from Skandia, BT and the Energy Saving Trust, which covered every aspect of the trips, enabling Bradwell and the usual summer trips to continue on as before, which we all felt very passionate about.

Though I would have loved to sail the whole tour, I knew timewise I simply couldn't, so I settled for next best, which was to visit the boat at nearly all of her seventeen stopovers. My contribution to the tour would be a series of lectures. I would speak about my life for an hour, and people would pay to come and hear about it. All the money would go to the Trust. I thought long and hard about that presentation and decided on breaking my life down into three defining moments. The first would be the love of the sea and sailing for the first time as a child; the second would be discovering the most incredible enthusiasm of these young people with cancer; and the third section was going to be about South Georgia, the Southern Ocean and my discovery of sustainability.

The idea for our round-Britain trip came from my voyage on board *Iduna*, and the adventure of a lifetime I'd had when I was just eighteen years old. As we discussed the planning of our journey, my memories came flooding back. From my stopover in the tiny Scottish harbours of Stonehaven and St Abbs to the huge industrial estuaries I sailed in, like the Humber and the Bristol Channel. My experiences from that voyage changed my life. I grew in confidence, and I met new people; I learnt new skills and I discovered so much beauty. Seeing my first wild dolphins in crystal-blue water as I sailed out of Stonehaven was one of the most exciting moments of my young life, and I dearly hoped we could give some of those same experiences I'd been lucky enough to have to the young people from the Trust. My trip around Britain had taken four and a half months, which was a month longer than it took me to get round the world for the first time!

As I'd experienced fourteen years before, we were welcomed wherever we went with open arms. The generosity of people on the stopovers was outstanding: they organized everything from free taxi rides and meals to tours of just about every place of interest on the way. There was always something to do, and the fantastic team worked like clockwork. Our boat crew of Cath and Karen could not have been topped. They worked extremely well together and brought out more smiles from the young people than you'd have thought could have possibly been in them! But it wouldn't have worked without Simon, who did the shore support, and Joey and Katie, who helped with the lectures. Simon was one of the most capable and competent people I'd worked with, and at each stopover his white Trust-shirt-clad figure would be there waiting. He was a big guy, always smiling and brilliant with people of any age. He, like Cath and Karen, got so much from the journey, and they were so wonderful to be around.

The talks went well and were held in all sorts of locations, nearly all of which we secured free of charge. I ended up speaking everywhere from Falmouth Maritime Museum to Holy Trinity Church in Hull, a wonderful community centre in Dover, corporate auditoriums in London, the council chambers in Newcastle, yacht clubs all over and university lecture halls in Liverpool, Edinburgh, London and Glasgow. Frank would pop to different locations, often with me, and we spent hours chatting on trains about our lives and all that was going on with the Trust. Joey would sometimes be with us, and we'd have an adventure on the sleeper train, followed by Simon meeting us in the car at the station.

It was special to see the young people speak in public, often having come out of their shells over the previous week. One face who was present at the beginning of the tour was Dan Monk, one of our Trust ambassadors, and to see him speak in the hospitals was really touching. His story was so moving, and the way he put across what he had been through was really inspirational. The highlight of the talks, though, was always the video that the young people had made on each of the legs. They were rarely anything other than hilarious, and their passion for life shone through like a beaming light.

But in contrast the end of my talks felt different. The young people were talking about all that they *could* do, whereas I was talking about what we *couldn't*. In the past they'd been about picking a goal on the horizon and just going for it, whereas here I felt like I was telling people that they shouldn't even set off. So much that I had heard about sustainability was 'do less' and 'use less'. In fact when asked by the audience at the end of my talks what they could do, that was often my answer: 'Use less.'

Was I really trying to tell people that they had to use less and less stuff until they returned to the Stone Age? Was the whole purpose of sustainability to reduce our consumption and just 'harm the planet' a bit less? I felt like I was the doom and gloom monger, and, though everything I was saying was fact, I was just turning people off. Because I didn't have the solution, I'd been communicating my fear, and though fear would perhaps galvanize a small percentage of the population into some kind of action, it certainly wasn't motivating for everyone. Surely there is some mileage in finding some other kind of solution. Something troubled me about the conventional 'use less' approach. 'Use less' will only go so far before it becomes *useless*.

Surely there was something more simple to grab hold of, a goal that I could chase after then run with. A goal that, through its appeal, like sailing, would motivate me to give every ounce of energy that I could muster. Instead of running away from the problem, I wanted to turn round, face it and take it on, just like those kids had.

At the end of the trip, we had an emotional reunion with as many young people as could come to Cowes, which had been our start and finish port. It had been a great success, and both the young people and their families alike were extremely happy. I had loved being a part of it, but that summer had been different for me. I realized just how much I'd missed actually sailing with the young people. Despite the Foundation taking over my life, there was a piece in the jigsaw that, for my heart and soul, I could never remove. That wasn't only sailing, but the best sailing I could ever imagine: sailing with the young people from the Ellen MacArthur Trust.

*

Towards the end of the year I was invited to go on to Radio 4's *Desert Island Discs*, and it was one of the better interviews I did. I liked Kirsty Young, I relaxed in the interview, and she asked questions about my past which took me deep into my thoughts. I talked about sailing and the Trust, I spoke of my Mum and Dad, I talked about the freedom they let me have as a child, and the fact that they never pushed me to do anything, but let me follow my dreams. As I spoke I often had tears in my eyes as I explained that I didn't know how they let me go when they knew that sailors had not returned from that race before. It had not been at the forefront of my thoughts since South Georgia, and suddenly here, in a radio studio, it all came flooding back. I was glad of the music interspersed in our conversation, as it gave me a chance to breathe deeply and recover for the next questions!

The final part was talking about the round-the-world record and the fact that the previous year Francis had taken it away. I explained, as I had in many interviews before, that something had happened in my life to make me think differently. Something 'that has really scared me to the point that I can't go back to sea and go around the world again, because this really matters'.

It was October, and my marathon of seventeen talks all over the country was finished, as was the Trust round-Britain trip. Ian and I went to Derbyshire to Mum and Dad's before heading north again for a holiday on the Isle of Skye.

Then, on day one of the holiday, I was on the front page of *The Times*:

Ellen MacArthur gives up the ocean to save the planet.
Four years ago she broke the record for the fastest solo circumnavigation of the globe. Now Dame Ellen MacArthur is giving up ocean racing to become an eco-warrior.

My heart sank. I was not an eco-warrior. I travelled straight down to London to meet Jamie, who by this time was running the Foundation. We had not wanted the Foundation's existence to be public until we had actually achieved something. The article went on:

The sailor, who is 33 and 5ft 2in in wet socks, says she is so alarmed about the threat to Earth that she wants to concentrate on stopping mankind destroying the environment rather than embarking on new marine adventures.

Never once in that interview had I mentioned eco, or the environment, or in fact man's destruction of it either. I had purely and simply spoken about resources and hoped the reality was that I was a realist who wanted to help do something about a problem spoken about by governments, in boardrooms and in living rooms. It was hugely disappointing to see the conclusions, but none the less a true reflection of people's perceptions. If I was a journalist, I wonder what I would have said. I knew we were on the right path, but we had to get our message right.

I spent what was left of those two weeks off worrying about the Foundation but slowly, with the time to think, I began to realize I was perhaps blinded by the enormity of the problem and was still looking for something.

The small team at the Foundation had been spending a lot of time working out exactly what it was we were going to set out to achieve. We all felt that there was no map from which to plan, and we all knew that even Nicolas's foundation in France wasn't doing exactly what we wanted to do. We'd spent many an evening together throwing ideas around, sampling each other's cooking and trying to put our finger on our identity. As a result of this we'd decided to work in four sectors. We wanted to do a local 'action' project, a general communication project, work with industry in the form of our partners, and finally work with young people, as we really felt that was a great way to get the message out.

The avenue of education led us to meet the Nuffield Foundation, which creates teaching material for schools. The meeting came about as a result of the *Desert Island Discs* interview, and my interest in sustainability, and during it the name Ken Webster came up. Ken was, as far as we could see, one of the UK's few experts in sustainability education.

I have rarely met anyone with the same clarity of thought on any subject as Ken, let alone the tricky subject of sustainability. Jamie, Ken and I hit it off immediately, and just seventy-two hours after we met him he was with us on the Isle of Wight, and one of the first people to stay in our new house (though at this time we didn't even have a front door!). Meeting Ken made me realize that I was in fact the stumbling block in my own thinking. He made me realize that I knew the solution to the problem – we all did. Ken had spent much longer than me absorbing information and ironically as a result saw things in an incredibly simple way. He showed me that I had made two fundamental errors and that I needed to deal with this challenge as I had done when faced with challenges at sea.

Firstly, I had always dealt with challenges and obstacles at sea by imagining that what lay the other side of them would be better. I would visualize life after the event with a sea less dangerous or aggressive, and time to sleep and eat once again. In a way you need to make your imagination run wild, finding hope and faith in a moment of acute anguish which has momentarily washed the positivity out of you. Sometimes at sea I was wrong in my assumptions, and things got worse before they got better; but it was that mindset that carried me through. Always looking forwards and always striving for that next moment, be it simply seeing the dawn of the following morning or holding your family again. Spending time on the edge taught me to always have hope and to always look forwards, and here I was on a new mission, not even listening to my own advice.

Secondly, at sea, I was guided by a single, simple goal: to sail around the world, to travel full circle, to return to where I had left. My trip was about the journey, not the destination. And the journey fascinated me, as its boundaries were endless: it was full of decisions, challenges and unknowns. Ironically, I would finish exactly where I started, but I would be ready to sail again, with new knowledge, a greater depth of experience and the possibility of doing it even better next time.

Now I couldn't see through to the other side, because I didn't have a goal. I couldn't see where I was going. I couldn't see the future with clarity and I failed to realize that the lessons which we needed to use to get there were all around us. Like a sailor who thought the world was flat and who was trying to slow down their boat to stop it falling off the edge of the earth, I was failing to see that there was another way, and a horizon beyond which was the true freedom I'd sought as a child.

I wanted to be an advocate for ambition, not restriction. And if everything was about harming less and doing less, then what the hell would we be able to do in the future? Back to that old adage again of less and less until we ground to a halt? Or do we continue as we are and smack headlong into our limits and fall off the edge of the planet? I felt that our system wasn't working. But why not? If life itself had existed on our planet for millennia, then why was *our* present system unsustainable? And the answer began to come clear. Now we were beginning to bump up against limits and we needed to begin to see things in a different way. Through our rampant pursuit to grab as much energy as we could from the world, we thought that we could be excluded from the basic rules of life. Unknowingly, perhaps, we had begun to live in a linear system, and the laws of nature exclude that from working long term.

And all of a sudden, the big picture came into focus; in fact, it hit me like a ton of bricks. The very framework in which we live is *broken* – the structure of our boat is fundamentally flawed. Rather than plugging holes in a sinking ship, should we not be aiming to build a new one that can sail for ever?

I began to think differently, and the issues I had come across before looked different. The goal was simple: it was about rethinking and redesigning the system itself. I now saw a different framework which promoted opportunities rather than took them away. It wasn't about the world being a mechanical system that we can control, but rather an intricate web of systems from which we can harness power and resources.

One of the rules is that we put back what we take. In nature there is no waste, but there is a profusion of nutrients. One acorn is needed every 500 years to replace an oak tree, but each year, none the less, thousands fall to the ground. The leaves fall too, and though in time they form a dark, moist blanket, they don't stop the bluebells pushing their shoots through them in March. Year after year, the leaves keep falling, and the bluebells keep growing, and another golden carpet nourishes the next year's growth. Nature has nowhere to throw things away; it doesn't need to as the waste of one species is food for another.

If you had ten sacks of grain and you ate them all in one year you would have created a linear system. If you ate some, then fertilized the land with your waste, then planted the remainder to grow next year's crop, you would be living in a cyclical system. And obviously that's the one that works. We're currently kidding ourselves if we think that we can continue to take, make and dispose of the stuff for eternity; it's a primitive view, about as outdated as the view of the earth as flat. But I'm not naive either. This isn't an argument to go back to a pre-industrial time, with its back-breaking labour. These lessons for life are as applicable to a modern industrial world as they are to understanding how a forest works.

If we put back what we take, then we need to be able to take stuff that we can put back. But with metals and plastics that's impossible; once we've gone to the trouble of having them in circulation, then we don't want them to degrade and sink into the ground. So perhaps there are two kinds of 'stuff', or let us say 'nutrients'. The ones which we send back to the ground, and then the ones which we keep in circulation for ever. And this concept of for ever I found a fascinating one. We need to keep the precious materials we have in constant circulation. Even recycling these days is in fact down-cycling. A glass bottle does not stay a glass bottle for ever. It often gets turned into aggregate for putting on roads. But should a jam jar get crushed down then turned into another jam jar anyway? Surely it would be much more energy efficient to sort it to a certain size, then sterilize it and use it again?

I thought about electric cars: that's already thinking differently. How on earth could you charge the batteries? Images of Radcliffe sprang back to mind, and the seeming impossibility of replacing like for like with renewable power. But I wasn't thinking differently enough.

Combustion is very inefficient, as there are many losses through the process of burning a fuel. The most efficient diesel engine in existence works at about 45 per cent efficiency and petrol 30 per cent. The rest of the energy is lost in the engine as friction and heat. An electric car, however, works at 98 per cent efficiency. Suddenly you are only looking for half the energy. But then look at the weight of the electric car. Does it need to be built of heavy steel? Just like Mobi, lighter is faster. Suddenly the energy required is a fraction of what I originally thought. I had been trying to tackle the wrong problem. But we'd also need the parts of the car. What if half of the car could be composted down, like the seat covers, tyres and parts of the interior, then the copper and steel could be collected from the motor and drive shaft, and the body could perhaps be made from a plastic which became the next car body? But what about building a car plant which runs on renewable energy? Again, it sounds impossible, but when you totally redesign a vehicle there is the opportunity to make it without the need for stamping huge sheets of steel out with 40 ton presses. You build a composite or a plastic body with a polymer that allows you to melt it and turn it into a different-shaped car part when the time comes, not one that becomes rubber matting for a playground in the next cycle, and landfill the next. This part can stay the same car part for a very long time. You also don't need so many moving parts – there are no engines, and parts and oil – so the factory becomes less complex. You perhaps negate the use of most of the paint due to the polymer doors and wings. You are now looking at a whole new set of variables, and through simple redesign, the bar is significantly lower. Perhaps now you connect the car to your house via a smart grid system and it can act as 'storage' for your energy needs, ironing out peak demand for national energy generation.

Then, perhaps, we rent things rather than buy. Maybe we rent a mobile phone, or a floor covering, or our chairs, or even our clothes, so that when they need replacing they are collected to become new products. And if you take the thinking to its furthest point, there is no place now for landfill.

I was no longer looking at a 'no more' solution, but a 'do more' solution, and it wasn't a case of saying that the developing world can't develop because of the issues with declining resources. If we keep resources in the system at the right quality they can develop. In addition, many developing countries are very rich in solar energy potential.

If waste equals food, then everything changes, we don't have a sewage treatment plant, we have a power and fertilizer plant.

At school we need to teach these rules; the most important rules of life.

Teaching future generations how to think differently will mean that, when the world decides it's time to push the button and change 'systems', then our young people will know exactly what to do.

And now I was excited. Now, I realized, this was the biggest challenge that we have ever faced. Here we have the opportunity to adopt the rules which have been proven to work for millennia. This is not just about redressing the balance, but to do so by redesigning our future. It's about using our boundless ingenuity to get this one right, and we have no excuses. The blueprint is already there.

The message was simple. As simple as the difference between a straight line reaching an edge and a circle which could go round and round for ever.

Chapter Twenty-Eight

With 2010 came a new dawn, and a realization that the track we were on with the Foundation was the right one. My gamble to sink everything into it had paid off, and with our message now clear, pretty much everyone we spoke to agreed with us. Not jumping in with both feet had paid dividends, and the years of research were slotting together wonderfully. I was so glad that I'd not gone out and performed some kind of PR stunt, and that I'd kept my head down till I knew exactly what I was trying to achieve. The Foundation was in the starting blocks with the best chance possible, and its mission statement said it all: RE-THINK THE FUTURE.

And our message made sense to people. They understood that it wasn't just about going backwards, but striving forwards towards something more positive than where we were at the moment. They understood when we talked about the 'framework' being flawed, and that it wasn't about using less and less and being gloomy, but about redesigning the future as a challenge. From this moment I never doubted what we were saying, and people suddenly believed in what we were setting out there to achieve. Rethinking and redesigning the future was something really aspirational, and the more we took our message out there, the more people were keen to get on board.

Through this whole process we had been looking at our funding strategy and had decided to choose the same route as the Nicolas Hulot Foundation in France. This involved working with businesses to become 'founding partners' and we were motivated by how well our plans were received as we got verbal agreements from two companies in our very first meeting! Renault were the first to sign up, and their commitment to 'thinking differently' was highlighted when they presented to us a graph of oil demand versus supply as a reason for their investment in their new range of cars. Negotiations with BT went well, and they too stepped in as a partner, seeing the benefit of education for the future. Then there was a call out of the blue from Kingfisher, the company I'd first met twelve years before. They felt our goals fitted well with their plans for B&Q, as they were already working on products centred around this new 'redesign' model. All in all things were going well, and we felt energized by our progress.

Ken, the man who had walked into our lives with the key to unlocking our message, was so excited with what we were trying to do that he began to work for us, becoming Head of Learning at the Foundation.

Ken lead education, Jamie and I worked more on linking education with business. Katie took over the management of communications for our Isle of Wight case study, the 'Chale Community Project', for which we secured £500,000 through a government initiative, and Joss began working on the content for the new website to go live when we launched the Foundation at the end of the summer. By spring 2010 there were eighteen people working on our new vision. I felt that, since our inception in June of 2009, we had come on a long way. Our message was clear, and our growing team pulled together more strongly than ever.

Our trustees worked together beautifully, each having strengths we could draw on through our common goal. We enrolled a fourth trustee, Jim Moffatt, a man who understood digital communication, and helped gather a team of experts to shape what the Foundation would look like to the rest of the world. Meetings were exhausting but full of adrenalin-filled hope, and the level of excitement we began to generate around our plans grew by the day.

There was also a natural end to working with OC, and as my sailing team obligations drew to a close, we went our separate ways. Things had moved on a long way since I first met Mark at the

London Boat Show when I was nineteen years old. I'd just finished sailing round Britain, and he'd been like a big brother to me, helping to lead the way. We'd faced seemingly enormous challenges together, but despite them had managed, not once, but over and over again, to achieve the impossible.

But fourteen years after Mark and I had met, our priorities were very different. What I never believed possible had happened: something in my life had eclipsed my childhood dream of sailing. I shall not know to this day why this happened; perhaps I felt so content that I'd made my dreams come true that it was time to give back. I don't know, but I'd reached a turn-off in my journey, and, though I'd be leaving something behind, I knew I had to follow it. Now I realized how different Mark and I were, and though, when we had shared the same goal we had pulled strongly together, those times were now behind us.

As 2010 powered along, so did the Foundation. We hadn't even launched, but I knew that something big was going to happen. One indication was when I joined Ken at an Educating for Sustainable Development conference run by a colleague of his in Sheffield. Ken had earlier spent a day with a group of young people from an arts college in Wakefield, and they were going to give the final presentation of the day. He had taken them through a familiar briefing around the resource limitations with which we are ultimately faced. He'd outlined the linear, 'take, make and dispose' economy and drew out the notion that the framework is fundamentally flawed, but then introduced them to natural cycles, about how the rules dictated by life itself, based on feedback, have been generated by trial and error over millions of years and proved resilient. Ken turned the argument on its head and changed their minds. He showed them that we didn't have to accept the inevitability of doing less and less, but that there is another way. He taught them that it wasn't about doing less harm, but getting things right. Once and for all.

So when those young people, who would have been sixteen or seventeen years old, stood up on the stage to present their take on sustainability, they blew everyone away. They talked about a handful of basic principles which would turn the way we make things and take decisions on their head. After just one day of learning they'd nailed it. It was the best presentation of the day.

Sitting there, I made my mind up. What the Foundation needed to do as its main priority was to get that message out to all young people in the country and to ensure that the next generation has the necessary skills to rethink, redesign and ultimately rebuild our sustainable future. We were on the brink of something, and I felt it. It was so overpowering that night that I couldn't sleep. I felt the same feeling as I had when I crossed the Atlantic for the first time, and made my first landfall on the skyline of Les Sables d'Olonne.

From this moment on my talks began to change too. Those young people had shown me the way forward, as they wanted to feel the freedom I had felt as a child. For me freedom had been about hoisting a triangle of cloth and sailing for ever, but shouldn't every generation have their freedom?

And it was this with which I began to finish my talk: highlighting what we could achieve rather than what we couldn't. I went back in my talk to the photo of my Great Granddad and covered what human beings had achieved in his lifetime. I showed a picture of lightning and said that, after seeing this, someone somewhere realized that we could actually make this stuff. Just three years before Great Granddad was born we built the first power station in the UK, and at the time it was the biggest in the world. I showed a photo of the first car and said that there were only twenty-five in the world when Great Granddad was born; now there are over 800 million. I showed a photo of the first human being flying, which we somehow managed to translate in 100 years to 4.9 billion passengers per year in 2008. I showed that we discovered penicillin just eighty-two years ago, which has saved millions of lives, and in the last half century we've invented the personal computer, the microchip and built the first nuclear power station. I put a picture up on the screen of the moon taken from Mobi. For thousands of years man has looked at the moon; then, just forty-one years ago, only eight years before I was born, man actually got up there and stood on it. I put up a picture of the first mobile phone, which became available thirty-one years ago; now we've produced enough for two-thirds of the world's population to have one. Finally, I put up an image of 'Google' to represent the internet. It was only invented twenty years ago, and now 1.8 billion people have access to it, and as a result information can be shared across the world like never before.

So, yes, sustainability is a big problem, and yes, it's probably the biggest challenge we've ever faced. But we humans are good at taking on challenges. We do it well, and, if you look at history, we can pretty much achieve anything we set our minds on.

As spring kicked in, our home was complete, and the images we'd had came to life more vibrantly than in our wildest dreams. We had created not a house, but a home, and we felt like we totally belonged there. For the first time we could watch life unfold around us from the security of our own four walls: nest boxes for the birds, bright green leaves in the oak trees tinting the rooms, and animals every-where. Norm was now a fully grown dog, but had kept every bit of his boyish charm. The little vegetable garden which had been bur-ied beneath rubble outside the kitchen window came to life, at the end of which sat our makeshift greenhouse, sitting on our rain-water storage tanks. On the other side of the path beneath the huge oak emerged delicate shoots of newly planted grass seed, and a clutch of wild ducklings hatched on our pond. Over the previous four years we had slowly worked on the land, planting everything from dreams to apple trees, and they were all flourishing. The land around the house had matured before it had, and when we moved in it looked like it totally belonged there.

For the first time in almost a year Mum and Dad came down to see us, and it meant the world to me to see their smiles as they wandered around. Everything was full of character, and it had a story, from the rug upstairs which had been given to my Nan some seventy years before as a wedding gift, to the pictures from my

Gran's loft which decorated the walls. Mum and Dad fitted in like they'd always been here, Dad out in the garden tinkering with the greenhouse, and Mum finishing off the curtains she'd made for us in the snug. Floss and Norm ran through the house, and outside, the ducks, geese and chickens strolled around just as they had in Derbyshire.

It felt like I'd returned home.

It is here I have come to write, in my Nan's old cottage, nestled on the hillside in the village of Whatstandwell, sitting by the window where she always used to sit herself. The kitchen is warm from the heat of the Aga, and what is around me is familiar. Though it has altered a little in the years since Nan lived here, the aura is the same. On the mantelpiece are her old pens – fibre-tip pens with white ends, which you probably can't even buy these days.

I have so many memories of this cottage, as a child, playing on the rug in front of the fire and sitting on Nan's knee on her big brown reclining chair. I remember her numerous piles of books, and her blue folding side table with silver and coloured paper under the glass, one of her few prize possessions, given to her by a neighbour, who had made it out of shiny coloured sweet wrappers. I remember the little trinkets she used to have in her little glass-fronted cabinet opposite the door, which, if we were lucky, we'd be allowed to play with. I remember the day she got her word processor, which she learnt to use in her seventies; it used to sit on the table which I am typing on now. The kitchen reminds me of the dinners she used to make in the pressure cooker, and the quince bushes outside remind me of her jelly. The houses on the lane remind me of her friends, and the little gate, with the worn steep stone steps, reminds me of each and every time we would visit Nan as kids – excited to see her and rushing to be the first for a hug!

Nan died almost exactly eleven years ago, but my memory of her is as vivid as if she popped out half an hour ago to see her friends in the village. Being here is special to me. It's a place where I am able to write but, more importantly, it's a place my soul feels at home. I loved my Nan dearly, and I still miss her terribly. She was an honest grafter and above all she led by example. She had a hard life, and had little, but she would *always* give so much. I sometimes wake in the mornings having dreamt that I have seen her again, with that warm feeling inside that she looks healthy and well, and I feel happy that we have been able to catch up for a natter.

I have a little lamp shining over my shoulder, as the sky outside has just turned dark grey again, but we have just had the most fantastic half-hour walk that feels to me like we've been gone a week! Norm and I headed down to the quarry again, grabbing a half hour before lunchtime. It had been raining incessantly since we returned from our run, so when I looked out to see a clearing in the sky (well a lighter patch anyway!) we set off for a quick spin.

We climbed over the wall next to the old wooden gate and on to the track which bends round past the allotments. On the right is the old stone drinking trough we used to play in, where the water flowing through a hole in the dry stone wall above. I think back to the times we threw sticks in the source to see whose would make it out of the trough first. I remember playing there in the sun, with the birds singing in the trees, sitting on the grass leading to the primrose-lined path. We followed a pair of pheasants, scouting out, no doubt, for the site of their annual nest. It's lovely to watch them move along before us, not running away at speed or flying off in a panic. To the left of us was woodland, and to the right were the allotments, each with their own character, where Nan used to grow her veg.

As you cross the stile the land falls away each side, leaving the trees to cling to the slopes, growing between huge boulders in a statuesque sign of the past. On the vertical cliff faces which surround parts of the quarry there are hanging ferns and mosses, with water slowly pouring out from the seams between the rocks. On one, the highest face, is a horizontal shelf running its whole width – I was fascinated by this as a kid, dreaming of shuffling along it, high above the forest floor – either rescuing an injured or trapped animal or using it as a magical doorway to enter into another far-off land . . .

Everything there reminded me of Nan, and our walks back then, 'going for gads'. Nan would put on her thickly woven marmalade-coloured woolly hat, and we'd wander about the village for short walks, the most common of which was this one from her cottage. Nan always had an inquiring and imaginative mind, and I have a sneaky feeling that she helped to stimulate mine.

Nan was the middle of three girls from a poor family who lived in the city of Bradford. Her Dad worked in the Salts, and Black Dyke textile mills, and her mother made and sold socks from home. Nan had a real passion for learning and she loved languages and writing. It was clear at school that she had talent, too, as she won a scholarship to go on to further education. But, as she came from such a poor family, her future was pre-determined, as her father forbade her from pursuing her studies, saying she had to go out and earn money for the family. Being the hard worker she was, Nan got a job at a building society. Though her husband died young, she made sure that all three of her daughters went through university to have the chances in life she didn't have. And once her work was done she retired and moved to Derbyshire, where she helped bring us up, her grandchildren. Those years we spent together, in her own words, were the happiest years of her life.

But Nan's drive to learn had not decreased, and, despite being in her seventies, she decided to join us in secondary school. She came on our school bus, having walked down the hill from the village of Whatstandwell, and I would often eat with her in the school canteen. Nan was a pupil in my brother Lewis's class for GCSE German, and then, with the bit between her teeth, she carried on to do A-Level French and A-Level German in one single year. She just kept going, always with books in her bags, always on a mission, and always losing her reading glasses!

After her A-Levels Nan decided to fulfil her lifelong dream of getting a degree, and as part of her course went to Ludwigsburg in Germany on a six-month student exchange. Nan was eighty by this time. We heard tales of her going to pizza parties, feeding squirrels in the park and socializing with the students. She was amazing, and if given an opportunity she would grasp it with both hands and carry it as far as her aging legs would carry it. She nearly didn't achieve her dream; she returned from Ludwigsburg very ill and had to be admitted to hospital. She had fibrosis in her lungs, which gave her pneumonia; then she developed cancer. The prognosis was not good at all, but the hospital's advice to Mum was to send Nan back to university, as they genuinely felt that finishing her degree would keep her alive. Despite struggling through her exams, Nan gave it her best shot, and she graduated at the age of eighty-two with a degree in European Studies.

As Nan had made such an impression on the university, she was asked to give an acceptance speech on behalf of all the students on their graduation day. Nan was clearly nervous but overjoyed to have been asked. I don't think that Nan had ever given a speech before, but her tiny figure, all bent over and frail, determinedly made its way to the lectern. It was a funny set of circumstances. Her hat wouldn't stay on, which was a bit of a shame, so Mum had taken that, and unbelievably one of the lenses fell out of her spectacles the moment she stood up. Luckily it was her bad eye, which she had little sight in anyway, though I'm sure she must have known her speech off by heart by that stage anyway. Her speech was written in her favourite purple fibre-tip pen, and as she stood by the microphone she rustled her papers while she calmed her nerves.

But when Nan began to speak, the whole hall fell silent. Parents and offspring alike were attentive. For fifteen minutes she entertained the audience, and with her every word she had them in the palm of her hand. She talked of her life, her past, the lessons she had learnt; then finally she came to the subject of her lifelong ambition – her degree. With a totally straight face she then said: 'At the age of eighty I went to Germany as an exchange student and scored . . .' The room erupted with laughter. '. . . but not in the way you think,' she added. There was silence. 'I scored because in Germany old people are respected.' And I bet not one person in that room has ever forgotten that.

Dearest Nan died three months later. She had patiently waited seventy years for the chance to hold her degree, and, after putting two generations of her family before her, in the nick of time she had done it. But through the realization of her lifelong dream she was given a chance she wasn't searching for: the one chance in her life to be listened to. And she took that chance, not for the notoriety, but because for the first time in her life she had the opportunity to make a difference. And despite being daunted by the experience, she put everything she had left into it.

Nan was not going to let that chance go. And nor am I.

I sit here in the cottage. In a folder on my Nan's old table by my chair is the rosette I made for Mobi on her first birthday in the Southern Ocean and the photo Maxine sent me of her smiling into her camera. Everything feels like it was yesterday.

Norm is lying on the floor on the grey fleece that I'd pulled around me as I slept beneath the stars aboard Mobi. So much has happened, yet the view from this little window is the same view that I saw as a child sitting on my Nan's knee some thirty years ago.

The best things go full circle . . .

A donf A French expression meaning 'full on!'

Astern Behind a boat or going backwards.

Backing A backing sail has the wind on the wrong side.

Backstay The cable from the masthead to the stern, holding the mast up.

Ballast The weight in a boat.

Bearing away Turning away from the wind.

Bilge The part of the hull that's below the waterline. It collects any water that's entered the boat.

Block A pulley.

Boom The spar that extends backwards from the mast to which the foot of the mainsail is attached.

Bow The front of the boat.

Bowsprit A spar that extends forwards from the bow.

Bulkhead The structural wall, either full or partial, across a boat's hull.

Buoy A float that acts as a navigational aid.

Cabin The living area below deck level.

Cassette box The box the rudder sat in which slotted into Mobi's hull.

Catamaran A twin-hulled boat.

Cockpit Where the boat is steered from. Most of the control of the boat happens here.

Code E A cross between a spinnaker and gennaker.

Crash gybe An unplanned gybe where the boom swings in an uncontrolled manner across the boat.

Crayons Long cylindrical smooth sliders.

Cuddy The small roof-like shelter over the cockpit.

Cunningham Tightens the luff of the sail from the deck.

Daggerboard A retractable fin that extends vertically from the hull to prevent leeward drift when upwind.

EPIRB Emergency position indicating radio beacon.

Fairleads Guides for ropes.

Fenders Used to protect a boat from the dock.

Float Hull of a multihull.

Float rudder Rudders on a trimaran which are not on the main hull.

Foredeck The area of the deck in front of the mast.

Forepeak The area of space in front of the mast below decks.

Forestay A metal rod supporting the mast from the bow. *Kingfisher* had three.

Furl To roll up a sail around its stay, a bit like a vertical blind.

Fuse system A system to stop the rudders breaking if they hit something.

Gennaker A large sail that is a cross between a spinnaker and a genoa.

Genoa A large jib sail that sets in front of the mast, but extends aft of the mast.

Gunwales The upper edge of the boat's sides at deck level.

Gybe To change direction so that the stern passes through the direction of the wind.

Halyard A rope used for raising and lowering sails.

Hank Metal clips used for attaching a sail to a stay.

Headbound car A metal slider which runs up the mast on a track to hold the top of the sail to it.

Headsail Generally any sail which can be used to go upwind before the mast.

Heel When the boat leans away from horizontal because of the action of the wind.

IMOCA International Monohull Open Class Association.

Impeller A wheel used to pump water.

Jammer A fitting on a boat to hold a rope under tension.

Jib A triangular sail which sets in front of the mast.

Jumar An ascending device that grips a rope so that it can be climbed.

Jury rig A temporary, improvised repair to a broken rig.

Keel A vertical fin that extends downwards from the bottom of the boat. Ballast in the keel helps keep the boat upright.

Kite See Spinnaker.

Knot One nautical mile per hour.

Lazy jacks Ropes or canvas used to 'catch' the sail and help control it as it's lowered.

Leech The trailing edge of a sail.

Leeward Downwind.

Mainsail A large triangular sail that hangs between the mast and the boom.

Mainsheet The rope that's used to control the mainsail.

Martingale Cables strengthening the bowsprit.

Mast ball The titanium ball on which the base of the mast could rotate.

Maxi catamaran A very large catamaran.

Occluded The warm and cold front of a low pressure system merging together.

ORMA Ocean Racing Multihull Association.

Pad eye A U-shaped bolt attached through the deck as a strong fixing point.

Port The left side of the boat.

Reach Sailing with the wind perpendicular to the side of the boat.

Reef Reducing the area of the sail in high winds by partially lowering it.

Rib A Rigid Inflatable Boat. A powerboat with a rigid hull and inflatable tubes around the top edges.

Rig The arrangement of the mast, shrouds and sails.

Rudder A vertical fin at the stern of the boat that steers it.

Running backstay A removable backstay.

Seaway A word used to describe a rough sea state.

Sheet A line used to control the sails.

Sock Fabric used to slide over a spinnaker to control it for hoisting or dropping.

Solent The intermediate jib sail, between the staysail and the genoa.

Spinnaker A very large light balloon-like sail used when sailing downwind. Sometimes referred to as a kite.

Starboard The right side of the boat.

Staysail A triangular sail similar to, but smaller than, the jib.

Steering deep Steering as far away from the wind as you dare.

Stern The rear of the boat.

Storm jib A very small, strong sail used in rough conditions.

Tack The direction the boat is sailing in relation to the wind, or to change the direction of the boat so that the bow passes through the direction of the wind.

Tack line Rope holding the front corner of a sail to the deck or bowsprit.

Tiller Attached to the rudder and used for steering the boat.

Trampoline Netting hung between the hulls of catamarans or trimarans.

Trim To adjust the sails in relation to the wind.

Trimaran A three-hulled boat.

Trinquete A staysail.

Water-ballast Sea-water compartment filled to trim the boat.

Windward Upwind.

Wing mast A mast shaped like an aeroplane wing to give a sailing boat more power.

1995
BT/YJA Young Sailor of Year award
Sailed *Iduna* single-handed around Great Britain

1996
First transatlantic passage, leaving Newport, Rhode Island (USA)
  on Ellen's twentieth birthday
First transatlantic race in the Quebec–St Malo on board *Anicaflash*,
  skipper Vittorio Malingri. Result: third in class

1997
Mini Transat single-handed transatlantic race in 21 foot boats on
  board *Le Poisson*, number 116. Result: seventeenth overall

1998
November: Route du Rhum solo transatlantic race from St Malo to
  Guadeloupe on board Open 50 foot monohull *Kingfisher*. Result:
  first in Open 50 class (20 days, 11 hours, 44 mins, 49 secs)

1999
January: Won BT/YJA Yachtsman of the Year award
June: Round-Europe race on board Open 60 foot *Aquitaine Innova-
  tions*. Co-skipper with Yves Parlier. Result: first in Open 60 class

August: Fastnet Race on board 60 foot trimaran *Kingfisher* (ex-*Primagaz*). Co-skipper with Yvan Bourgnon. Result: fourth in multihull class

November: Transat Jacques Vabre two-handed transatlantic race, Le Havre to Salvador de Bahia, Brazil, on board 60 foot monohull *Aquitaine Innovations-Kingfisher*. Co-skipper with Yves Parlier. Result: sixth in Open 60 class

2000

June: Europe 1 New Man STAR solo transatlantic race on board Open 60 monohull *Kingfisher*. Result: first in Open 60 class (14 days, 23 hours, 11 mins) – youngest person to ever win race

November–February 2001: Vendée Globe solo, non-stop round-the-world race on board Open 60 monohull *Kingfisher*. Result: second (94 days, 4 hours, 25 mins, 40 secs) – fastest female and youngest sailor to race around the world solo, non-stop

2001

May: Challenge Mondial Assistance on board 60 foot trimaran *Foncia-Kingfisher* with co-skipper Alain Gautier. Result: first

3 July–25 August: EDS Atlantic Challenge crewed five-leg race from St Malo with stops at Hamburg, Portsmouth, Baltimore, Boston on board Open 60 monohull *Kingfisher* with co-skipper Nick Moloney. Result: first place overall. Also on 60 foot trimaran *Kingfisher-Foncia* during 2001 season:

30 April–5 May: Trophée Coralia at Fécamp. Result: second.

19–24 June: Sardinia Grand Prix

30 August–2 September: Fécamp Grand Prix. Result: first

11–16 September: Zeebrugge Grand Prix. Result: second

4 November: Transat Jacques Vabre two-handed transatlantic race from Le Havre to Salvador de Bahia, Brazil, with co-skipper Alain Gautier. Result: second in the ORMA 60 class

2002

January: Ellen MacArthur and Kingfisher plc announce five-year plan to include Jules Verne record attempt and culminating in the solo Route du Rhum race in November 2006

9–23 November: Route du Rhum solo transatlantic race from St Malo to Guadeloupe on board *Kingfisher*. Result: first in Open 60 class (13 days, 13 hours, 31 mins, 47 secs), setting a new mono-hull record

2003

30 January: Jules Verne record attempt on board 108 foot catamaran *Kingfisher II*, departing with fourteen crew to try to break the existing record of 64 days, 8 hours, 37 minutes and 24 seconds. *Kingfisher II*'s record attempt ended on 23 February when the boat dismasted in the Southern Ocean, 2,000 miles from the coast of Australia

April: announces build of new 75 foot trimaran to race under the colours of B&Q and Castorama. The sole objective of the new trimaran is to attempt to break solo speed sailing records

November: Transat Jacques Vabre two-handed transatlantic race from Le Havre to Salvador de Bahia, Brazil, on board 60-foot multihull *Foncia* with co-skipper Alain Gautier. Result ninth overall (suffers sail/halyard damage on day two of race)

2004

8 January: launch of new 75 foot *B&Q* trimaran in Sydney, Australia

March–April: delivery trip of new trimaran from New Zealand via Australia and the Falklands Islands. Leaving the delivery crew at the Falklands, Ellen sails *B&Q* solo to New York

June: solo transatlantic record attempt on board *B&Q*, missing the record by just 75 minutes in a time of 7 days, 3 hrs, 49 mins, 57 secs

November: departs on solo round-the-world record attempt. Finishes in February 2005, a new record of 71 days, 14 hrs, 18 mins, 33 secs

2005

New SNSM (St Nazaire to St Malo) crewed maxi record set on board *B&Q*. New record stands at 1 day, 3 hrs, 23 mins, 29 secs

November 2005: Transat Jacques Vabre race on board Open 60 monohull *Sill et Veolia* with Roland Jourdain. Result: second

2006

March–June: Asian Record Circuit

2007

JP Morgan Asset Management Round the Island Race. First to finish (Extreme 40 catamaran). Completed the course in 4 hrs, 6 mins, 3 secs

2008

June: Archipelago Raid with Greg Homann on board F18 *BT*. Result: ninth overall

2009

Artemis Challenge at Cowes Week on board IMOCA 60 *BT* skippered by Seb Josse. Result: first

Accolades

Raymarine YJA Yachtsman of the Year Award, 1998, 2001

ISAF World Champion election of Woman Sailor of the Year by 113 sailing federations throughout the world, awarded 14 November 2001

The Cup of the Chief of Staff of the French Navy, awarded 30 November 2001

FICO World Champion ranked by number of points obtained in the year's ocean races, awarded 7 December 2001

BBC Sports Personality of the Year Awards overall runner-up (behind David Beckham) plus Helen Rollason Award, awarded 9 December 2001

Sunday Times Sportswoman of the Year, awarded 11 December 2001

MBE awarded 12 December 2001 at Buckingham Palace by the Queen

Nomination for the title of Femme en Or ('Golden Woman') sport-adventure in France, election on 15 December 2001

Listed in *Time* magazine '100 Heroes and Icons', 2005

DBE awarded 24 April 2005 at Buckingham Palace by the Queen

Alternative Sportsperson of the Year 2005, Laureus Sports Awards, May 2005

Nominated *Sunday Times* Sportswoman of the Year 2005 (third overall)

ISAF World Champion election of Woman Sailor of the Year by 113 sailing federations throughout the world, awarded 8 November 2005

BBC South Yachtsperson of the Year, 2005

BBC East Midlands Sportswoman and Personality of the Year, 2005

Third BBC Sports Personality of the Year, 2005

Raymarine YJA Yachtsman of the Year Award, 2005

Morgan Stanley Great Briton in Sport, 2005

Guest on BBC's *Top Gear*, winning 'Star in a Reasonably Priced Car', 4 December 2005

ISAF Hall of Fame – one of only six inaugural members – November 2007

Légion d'Honneur presented by Président Nicolas Sarkozy, March 2008

The CITY under
SIEGE

Also by Michael Russell

The CITY *under*
SIEGE

MICHAEL RUSSELL

CONSTABLE

CONSTABLE

First published in Great Britain in 2020 by Constable

1 3 5 7 9 10 8 6 4 2

The moral right of the author has been asserted.

A CIP catalogue record for this book
is available from the British Library.

ISBN: 978-1-4721-3037-2 (hardback)
ISBN: 978-1-4721-3038-9 (trade paperback)

Typeset in Dante by SX Composing DTP, Rayleigh, Essex
Printed and bound in Great Britain by Clays Ltd, Elcograf S.p.A.

Papers used by Constable are from well-managed forests and
other responsible sources.

Constable
An imprint of
Little, Brown Book Group
Carmelite House
50 Victoria Embankment
London EC4Y 0DZ

An Hachette UK Company
www.hachette.co.uk

www.littlebrown.co.uk

For my mother and father

Dark Angel, with thine aching lust
To rid the world of penitence,
Malicious Angel, who still dost
My soul such subtle violence!

'The Dark Angel'
Lionel Johnson

PART ONE

A MAN OF NO IMPORTANCE

We are sorry for the Irish people if the storm breaks on their shores and over their land. We know what others in a similar situation have suffered, but Mr de Valera and his friends have sheltered behind neutrality, and they may have cause to wish that they had drawn the sword with the remainder of the great representatives of freedom and democracy. We in Malta have no regrets. In Malta we have suffered, and we are prepared to suffer more until final victory . . . We must not forget that there are many Irishmen fighting in this war against Nazism – with units of the Imperial forces in Britain and over-seas. It is the fact that the Free State is still neutral that is regretted by all who love Eire. The poet sings that a nation born where the shells fall fast has its lease of life renewed.

Times of Malta, 1941

1

The County Hospital

Naas, Co Kildare, 1939

In the white, tiled room the two porters carried the body from the mortuary drawer and laid it down on the porcelain slab in the middle of the room. Detective Inspector Stefan Gillespie turned the pages of a manila file of statements, reports and photographs. The photographs showed the body as it had been when it was discovered, in a grove of trees by a river, surrounded by the debris of a picnic: a tartan blanket, a wicker basket, a piece of cheese, a half-eaten loaf of bread, apples and apple cores, two empty beer bottles, a bloody kitchen knife, a bicycle on its side. Then the body up close, partly clothed; the stomach and the tops of the legs drenched in blood. In black and white, the pictures of the picnic site and the river, in wide shot, looked almost elegant. The sun had been shining. In some photographs its light reflected off the water. The detective looked from the photographs of the body to the body itself.

Beside him Sergeant Dessie MacMahon smoked a cigarette, looking at the young, dead man with disinterested curiosity. He had read the State Pathologist's report. There would be no more to learn. They were in the mortuary at Naas Hospital for reasons he didn't much like, checking up on the work of other police officers, looking for mistakes, failings, shoddy work. It was the kind of thing that went with the job he now, suddenly, found himself doing. He didn't much like that either. It was a job he hadn't asked for.

Stefan Gillespie continued turning the pages of the file. The only other sound was the slow tick of a bank clock that hung above the mortuary door.

The body of James Corcoran was a fortnight old. Cold storage in the hospital at Naas was cold enough to slow decay, but not to stop it. The smell of rotten flesh had risen up as the porters pulled open the drawer. It wasn't strong, but as the Sweet Afton Dessie MacMahon was smoking went out, he lit another. Stefan Gillespie closed the file and moved closer to the slab.

It was a boyish face. He looked younger than his twenty-four years. A mop of dark hair covered his forehead, the only part of him that was unchanged by death. The opening that reached from the throat to the chest and stomach, where the flesh had been pulled back for the examination of the internal organs, had been closed up and loosely stitched. As always, with the State Pathologist, it was neat, tidy work. He was a man who gave the dead care and attention; it was something the dead were always owed, whoever they were, whatever reason had brought them to the slab. For Stefan, his work was unmistakable. The body was immaculately clean, washed and tidied, ready for the undertaker when that time came, as it would do soon. The flesh was pale, almost luminous. The colour was deceptive. In reality it spoke not of the cleanliness outside, but of the rot spreading beneath the skin, which would eventually break through and consume it.

There was nothing to surprise Inspector Gillespie, having seen the photographs taken at the scene of death and after-wards, as the body had been stripped and opened up and explored. The wounds around the groin were obvious. They

4

were what made this so striking. There were seven: in the lower stomach, in the thighs, in the penis and the testicles. Now they were only uneven tears in the white flesh, thin, broken lips lined with black, long-dried blood. What was visible did not record how deep the kitchen knife had gone, how hard and how furious the strokes had been. The gushing blood that had covered James Corcoran's body and his clothes, his trousers and his clean, white shirt, had long been washed and sponged away. The bruising around the throat was still clear, though, grey and yellow, red in places. The fingers that had throttled him had pressed so hard that the hyoid bone had broken. But the savagery of his death had been left behind now. His face was oddly calm.

The doors into the mortuary opened with some force and the tall, bearded figure of the State Pathologist, Edward Wayland-Smith, entered, with the air of impatience that was familiar to Stefan and every other detective.

'What's all this to do with you, Sergeant Gillespie?'

'Your office told me you were here today. A good time to catch you.'

'That's not an answer, is it? I'm in the middle of an important meeting. Administration, that's the thing. Never mind the dead.' Wayland-Smith grinned. 'Still, you gave me an excuse to leave the buggers to it. This one's done, isn't he?' Wayland-Smith glanced at the body. 'Inspector Charles's, Maynooth?'

'You might call it an administrative matter, sir. The case seems to have ground to a halt. I've been asked to look it over . . . see if there's more to do.'

'To see if Inspector Charles has made a bollocks of it, you mean? It wouldn't surprise me. I don't think it's an investigation that fills anyone with . . . I don't know if enthusiasm is the right word, but if it is, there's probably a considerable lack of it. There's an element of the proverbial bargepole with which some things are not to be touched, however. I'm sure you know all that.'

'Do I?' Stefan smiled.

'You'll have read he was training to be a priest.'

Stefan nodded.

Wayland-Smith shrugged, as if that explained everything.

'But I'd forgotten, they've moved you into Special Branch. And it's Inspector Gillespie now. Good for promotion, but not for making yourself popular.' He looked at Dessie. 'He's dragged you along too, MacMahon.'

'That would be the word. Dragged. Special Branch wasn't my choice.'

A look passed between Stefan and Dessie. There was a smile in it, or at least the hint of a smile, but something else from Dessie that wasn't a smile.

The State Pathologist registered the exchange.

'You've lost weight, MacMahon. That's no bad thing.'

'That'll be something to thank Special Branch for, sir.'

Wayland-Smith laughed.

'Well, I'm sure we can't have too many policemen keeping an eye on what we're all saying, now that there's a war on that we intend to play no part in. I'm sure Ireland will have a lot to thank you for. I don't think the state has a great deal to fear from Mr Corcoran, however. You've seen him. Is that all?'

Stefan Gillespie said nothing.

All three men were silent, looking down at the body.

'It was a very vicious attack,' said Stefan quietly.

'Very. Unusually so, I'd have to say.'

'An attack by someone he knew?'

'I can't say that, but it seems a reasonable conclusion.'

Stefan opened the file and turned several pages.

'In the investigation, there seems to be some resistance to talking about the details you've given. They beg certain questions that I don't see asked.'

'I can imagine that's so, Inspector. Are you surprised?'

'Can you tell me what happened – what you think happened?' Stefan asked.

'You've read my report.'

'I'm a great believer in the horse's mouth.'

'He was strangled. Asphyxiation was the actual cause of death.' Wayland-Smith moved closer to the slab, looking at the young body with a kind of tenderness, unlike his brusque, impatient manner with the living. He walked around the body slowly as he spoke. 'The wounds around his groin were inflicted immediately after death. I mean immediately, almost simultaneously. The quantity of blood left that in no doubt. He could barely have been dead.' He stopped and looked up at Stefan and Dessie. 'Perhaps he wasn't, not quite.'

'He was partially dressed. Did that happen before or after death?'

'He was as you will have seen him in the photographs, Inspector. His shirt was open, as were his trousers. That's how he was when he was attacked.'

'The trousers pulled down.'

'Some way down.'

'And he was lying on the ground, before the attack.'

'Yes. That would be my interpretation.'

'Was he killed where he was found?'

'Not for me to say. Given the circumstances I can't see it could have been otherwise. And I gather that was the conclusion Inspector Charles came to.'

Stefan Gillespie turned over another page in the file.

'There was semen present.'

'There was.'

'Not only from the victim.'

'No. I would have made that observation, simply on the basis of common sense, from the two areas semen was found on the body, but I was able to establish the two specimens of semen do represent two different blood groups.'

'We know the killer's blood group?'

'In all probability.'

'So, we assume some sort of sexual act took place, possibly – even probably – consensual, followed immediately by a brutal, murderous attack.'

'I can only give you simple facts. That's what it feels like. And you can see, already, why there are a lot of questions no one would be eager to ask.'

'There's no evidence there was anyone else involved?'

'Nothing that I've seen. My evidence stops with the body.'

'There's nothing that gives us any more information about the other man?'

'Nothing I could find, Gillespie. I understand there are some fragments of a fingerprint that don't belong to the dead man. On a beer bottle, I think it is.'

'Would the killer have had a lot of blood on his clothes?'

'Some, certainly. Whether it was a lot would depend on how he was positioned when he delivered the blows. There was no resistance, obviously. The wounds were inflicted with . . . I suppose frenzy was what came to mind when I first saw the body. That still doesn't mean the murderer was covered in blood. I gather the investigation has produced nothing on who he was, where he came from, where he went. An isolated spot . . . did anyone see anything at all?'

'No. There's barely a thing,' said Stefan. 'He's almost invisible.'

'Is that so surprising, Inspector?'

'I'd have hoped for something, sir, more than we have, working out from the scene of the crime. It is isolated, but there's not even a sighting of two men cycling together. And there's nothing in terms of the victim's associations, his friends, things he might have said. He set out on a picnic, after all. This wasn't something that happened by chance. Time, place . . . must have been arranged.'

For a moment, again, they looked at the body. It offered no answers.

'However this encounter came about, Inspector Gillespie, it was, by its nature, secret, utterly secret. Whether the second man was someone James Corcoran had just met or knew well, what they were doing had to be hidden. That's the point, isn't it? It's what we're fighting. Every effort, presumably on the part of both men, went into trying to make sure they were invisible.'

The black Ford pulled away from Naas Hospital. Dessie MacMahon drove.

'Maynooth?' he said in a flat, unengaged tone.

'Yes. St Patrick's College.'

'Not Donadea?'

Stefan Gillespie reopened the file on the death of James Corcoran.

'I wouldn't mind, if there's time. But the scene of the crime can't mean much after a fortnight. If we were actually investigating this, maybe. We're here to tick Inspector Charles's boxes and see if he needs to go back and do it again.'

Stefan didn't notice the sour look from his sergeant.

'But I think we should speak to this man Dunne. He seems like the only one in the seminary who was close to Corcoran at all. He wasn't exactly blessed with friends. Or if he was, Maynooth CID didn't get very far unearthing them.'

'There's a good reason for that,' said Dessie. 'They'll all know enough about what happened, however tight Andy Charles tried to keep it. If any of them are queer they'll be more worried about that coming out than a dead body, friend or not, and for the rest, they'll all want to keep well away from it.'

'We'll take what we've got, Dessie. And I'd like a look at his room. I'm assuming that's still locked up as part of the

9

investigation. There's a list of things that were taken to the barracks in Maynooth. Nothing that matters; at least, nothing that produced any evidence. But that doesn't mean they didn't miss something.'

'This is a fucking waste of time, Stevie, you know that?'

'You could be right.'

'Andy Charles is a good detective. What are we chasing him for?'

'We're not chasing him.'

'We're looking for what he's done wrong, what he missed, what he didn't do. What else is this for? Does he even know we're on it? Have they told him?'

'I'm sure he'll find out.' Stefan smiled.

'Yes, he fucking will, Stevie.'

'A friend of yours?'

'If he is, he won't be for long.'

Stefan took out a cigarette. He lit it, glancing sideways at Dessie.

'You're not that pissed off about Inspector Charles, Dessie, or a couple of fellers in Maynooth CID. You're just pissed off. Well, I am too. I didn't ask to go into Special Branch. And I didn't ask for you to be pulled along to work with me either. I don't want to spy on anyone, let alone other Guards. It's shite and we both know it. But it's Superintendent Gregory's shite. It's his decision.'

'His shite is our shite now,' muttered Sergeant MacMahon.

'All right, Dessie. I don't know what the hell it's about, and I'm no happier than you are being in Dublin Castle with the Commissioner's collection of old IRA men and narks and all-round arseholes. But if you don't like it, get used to it, because Terry Gregory will cheerfully tell you it'll only get worse. I don't trust any of those gobshites in the Castle, Gregory least of all. And I'm not even welcome there. Anyone they don't know is an informer . . . and since they're all fucking informers themselves, why not? But the last thing you and I need to do is stop trusting each other. We're here, Dessie. We may get on with it, so.'

Dessie MacMahon did not reply. Eventually he produced a shrug.

2

St Patrick's College

Inspector Stefan Gillespie walked across the grass of St Joseph's Square, the great quadrangle of St Patrick's College, Maynooth. With him was a young man in the black priestly uniform of a seminarian. The small square of white at his throat was the only break in the black. He wore wire spectacles and a look of seriousness that reflected the conversation he was about to have, as well as his nature. He looked to Stefan unsettlingly like the young man he had seen earlier in the mortuary. He was about the same age. He had the same pale features, even the earnestness that was still, somehow, in James Corcoran's dead face. There was no real sense that the trainee priest was nervous being asked to talk about his dead friend, but because Stefan could see he was wary, he had said nothing yet. He had asked no questions. He had left Dessie MacMahon to search out a cup of tea and talk to the porter, who had extracted Aidan Dunne from the library. He wanted the conversation to be as informal as he could make it.

St Joseph's Square was empty save for a few young men hurrying along the straight central drive, late for a lecture. The square was laid out as a garden and Stefan and the young seminarian were walking among trees. The buildings of the college made up the quadrangle, surrounding them on four sides, but the buildings felt a long way off. The space was huge. Long, high, grey walls full of windows, hundreds of them, with the spire of the chapel at one corner. It was a place that had been built to declare its seriousness and its immutability. The rows of windows carried the barest echo of the grace and light of the Georgian terraces being built in Dublin at the same time. In the dark stone and the insistent formality, in the relentless repetition of mullioned windows, there was something fortress-like. The college had been established at the end of the eighteenth century, when the Penal Laws, which tried to make Catholicism invisible in Ireland, were being abandoned. The Penal Laws failed. St Patrick's was a grand statement of Catholic visibility. This was the biggest seminary in the world. Training priests was one of the few things that Ireland did on a bigger scale than anyone else, anywhere. If there was one place that proclaimed the permanence and the power of Catholic Ireland, it was calmly, peacefully here.

'I don't know what I can tell you that I haven't said already, Inspector.' Aidan Dunne spoke quietly, breaking the silence Stefan Gillespie had let sit uneasily between them as they walked slowly through the college gardens.

'You can tell me about your friend being happy.'

'What do you mean?'

'That's what you said, when you were talking to Inspector Charles. He had been happy, noticeably so, in the days . . . the week before all this happened.'

The young man nodded. He looked slightly puzzled.

'I don't know how much you know about what happened . . . the details.'

'I only know he was attacked and killed.'

'Maybe that's all you want to know,' said Stefan.

'Maybe it is. I know it was . . . it was all very unpleasant.'

'Unpleasant is certainly one word for it, Mr Dunne.' The words were spoken quietly, but there was an edge that was

13

almost an accusation. 'I think you know enough to know . . . you don't want to know more. You're not alone.'

The seminarian looked away; it was true enough.

'But back to what you told Inspector Charles, Mr Dunne.'

'If I knew anything, do you think I wouldn't have said?'

'You say he was noticeably happy, does that mean he wasn't usually?'

Aidan Dunne frowned. He wasn't sure how to answer. Questions he had been asked before were about times, dates, facts, when he last saw his friend.

'It's a simple question.'

'He had his ups and downs; we all do. A vocation isn't an easy thing. We all face questions, all the time. You can be very sure about your faith and still be unsure whether the priesthood is the right way, if you're doing the right thing.'

Stefan Gillespie said nothing for some seconds. Then he continued. 'That's not what you meant, is it? Is that what you think about when you're asked about a friend who's dead, who's been murdered? His vocation? You were talking about something else you were conscious of. It was in your head. So, there was something unusual about it. It stood out. When I read it, in your statement, it stands out for me. It was . . . exceptional in some way, is that fair?'

'Yes, I suppose that's right, Inspector.'

'What made him so happy, then?'

Aidan Dunne shook his head and walked on in silence.

'Let's look at it from the other end. If being happy was so obvious, his unhappiness was more than the ordinary ups and downs of life at St Patrick's. If he did have doubts about his vocation, they must have gone deep, is that true?'

'I don't know what you want me to tell you, Inspector.'

'Were those doubts there only because he was homosexual?'

Aidan Dunne stopped, staring at the detective. There was a startled look on his face, but not only shock; there was a sense of fear, as if something that should not be said had been spoken, casually, idly; others might be listening.

'It's just the two of us, Mr Dunne,' said Stefan. 'I won't be writing down your answers. I simply want to understand your friend, and to see if there is anything at all, anywhere, that can help us find the man who killed him.'

Aidan Dunne walked on, looking at the ground.

'You knew he was homosexual?'

The young man nodded.

Stefan took out a packet of cigarettes and offered him one. Dunne took the cigarette. Stefan took one himself and lit both. They walked on again, smoking.

'You did know?'

'Yes.'

'Did he talk to you about it?'

'Never.' There was a hint of uncertainty in the word, but only a hint.

'Until those last few days?'

'He still didn't say anything, as such. But I knew. I guess he knew that.'

'There are other men in the seminary who have the same problem.'

Dunne frowned and said nothing. He looked straight ahead.

'I'm not asking about you.'

'I'm not! Jesus! I'm not that way at all.'

'I'm only interested in your friend. Did he associate with other men, other men here who were that way? I'm sure you have a sense of it. It may be that no one says anything, or looks too hard, but sometimes it's not so easy to hide, is it? James was your friend. He didn't say a word about it. You knew anyway.'

'I can't talk about this,' said Dunne.

'It's another simple question. I'm assuming he was happy because he'd met someone. Isn't that what it was? Isn't that what he said . . . in some way?'

'James was very shut in on himself, that's the only way I can put it. He didn't make friends easily. I'm not sure he wanted to. I knew because he had the room next door. We got on. I sensed things about him, yes, but I know he had little to do with anyone here. He worked all the time, that's almost all he did. I think he wanted to work himself into believing he really did have a vocation.'

'But he didn't?'

'I thought . . . he was using the priesthood to run away from something.'

'Suddenly he was happy. Someone had made him happy, is that it?'

'Not someone here. I know that, Inspector.'

'So, what did he tell you?'

'He'd been in Dublin for a few days, working at the National Library. He'd met someone. I suppose . . . he was in love. He didn't use those words, but it's what he was saying. And it had made everything clear. He knew what he had to do. He couldn't stay at St Patrick's. He knew he didn't have a vocation.'

'And that didn't trouble him?'

'No, quite the opposite. He said he was going to go home the following week and tell his mother and father. He was going to leave the college. He said he might even leave Ireland. He talked about going to England . . . I don't know what that meant, and he didn't either. Most of what he said didn't make sense. When I asked what he thought he was going to do . . . in the middle of a war, he laughed and said it would all be fine, it would all be grand. All he had to do was find a way to live his life the way he wanted. And he believed he could.'

'And what about the day out, the picnic? You've said he talked about it.'

'He said he was going to meet his friend. That's all he called him . . . I think somehow he managed to avoid even the word "he". It was a day out, they were going to cycle down to the country . . . there was a place he knew, a place he loved . . . They were going to make plans about a holiday in England, that's what he told me. These weren't long conversations, Mr Gillespie. He was in and out of my room . . . talking, then going away. He came back to borrow a picnic rug I had . . . and then he needed a knife for the bread or something . . . and I had one . . . that was the last evening he was here. And the next day he was gone . . .'

'James told you nothing about how he met this man, where he met him, what the man did? There was no name, no description? There was nothing?'

Aidan Dunne shook his head.

Stefan nodded. He had more than Inspector Charles had got. He had a clearer picture of James Corcoran's last days, but that's all. The killer had an existence in his head that he hadn't had before, but it was only a shadow. Stefan knew Corcoran better, but he knew nothing that helped. He did not tell the dead man's friend what had happened to the borrowed bread-knife. Stefan looked round to see Dessie MacMahon walking towards him, a mischievous smile on his face.

'The Dean wants a word with you, Stevie. Canon Mulcahy.'

'Does he now?'

'He's profoundly unimpressed by your lack of courtesy.'

'Is that what he said?'

'His exact words: "profoundly unimpressed".'

'Thank you, Mr Dunne. And I'm sorry for your loss.'

Stefan Gillespie and Dessie MacMahon walked back towards the college. The young seminarian stayed where he was, as if unaware they had gone. He wasn't looking at them. He was looking at nothing. He was crying, noiselessly.

Detective Inspector Stefan Gillespie stood in the Dean's study. Behind him stood Sergeant MacMahon, and behind him the college's head porter. The room was lined with books on every wall, except where the large windows looked out to the drive and the gardens where Stefan had just been walking with Aidan Dunne. Canon Mulcahy sat at his desk, a slight, tight-faced man, wearing a look of almost puzzled benevolence on his face, as if he had been done some small but inexplicable wrong. Stefan imagined he had been standing at the window, not long before, watching the conversation with Dunne, and not liking it. Mulcahy's face softened into something like a smile. He was comfortable giving instructions.

'I think your sergeant can wait outside, Inspector.'

'As you wish, sir,' replied Stefan. He looked at Dessie MacMahon. The sergeant grinned and walked out of the room. The porter left too, pulling the door shut. Mulcahy did not offer Stefan one of the chairs in front of the desk; instead, he stood up himself and walked round to stand very close to him.

'I am surprised, Mr Gillespie, that you should come into the college to speak to one of our seminarians without asking to do so, without approaching a senior faculty member. In matters of discipline, I am the first port of call here.'

'There is no issue of discipline that concerns the college, Canon Mulcahy, just a conversation I needed to have with Mr Dunne that continued conversations he had had with Inspector Charles and detectives from Maynooth.'

Canon Mulcahy drew himself up, regarding Stefan with less benevolence.

'There is an issue of courtesy, Inspector. It may not be your strong point, but no one walks into this college to question its students without permission.'

'It's about the investigation into the death of one of your seminarians.'

'I'm glad for that information. But you might want to enlighten me about what precisely you have to do with the investigation into that tragedy. I have only just put the telephone down from speaking to Superintendent Mangan at the barracks in Maynooth. His men have been conducting the inquiry ever since poor Corcoran was found, in particular Detective Inspector Charles. Superintendent Mangan has no idea who you are, Inspector, even less idea why you're here. He was flummoxed altogether, though he put it more colourfully.'

If the last words were some sort of joke, the Dean did not smile.

Stefan did. 'Ah, I'm sure he'd know me if he saw me.'

'Then perhaps you'd like to do something about that. He's in his office in the town, and he asked me to tell you to call in there, as soon as you leave here.'

'I see,' said Stefan.

'Thank you. Before you do leave, perhaps you'll tell me exactly what you wanted to know from Mr Dunne, given that he has already made a statement.'

Stefan was surprised at the ease and assurance with which Mulcahy asked that question. He obviously had every expectation that he would get his answer.

'I don't know how Superintendent Mangan and Inspector Charles do things in Maynooth, but that's not how police inquiries work, Canon. Not quite the confessional, but still, as these things go, it's near enough, at least until it comes to court.' He shrugged. 'Judgement . . . well, not so different even there.'

'Do you think you help your case by insulting the Church?'

'The case is not mine. The case is about finding who killed your student.'

'And it is a very sensitive matter. I shouldn't have to say that, Inspector.'

'Perhaps a little too sensitive.'

'What do you mean by that?'

'I mean that so many questions have not been asked from the start, particularly about homosexual associations or relationships in the dead man's life, that more work has gone into what isn't being said than trying to find the killer.'

'Do you think being blunt and offensive is clever, Mr Gillespie?'

'I think being honest might have brought us closer to a brutal murderer.'

'If you want me to be honest, there are things we now know about Mr Corcoran that mean he should never have been here at all. He was not a suitable candidate for a vocation. He must have known himself that he was . . . in sin, perhaps very deeply in sin. He needed to be closer to God, certainly, but not as a priest. We can only hope that he is now closer to God. The problems he had, which are still only conjecture, are not the business of St Patrick's, except in so far as he was a seminarian. He was, however wrongly, one of us. We pray for him. The whole community prays for him. As for the questions you seem so interested in, I'm not frightened by the word homosexuality. I'm not frightened by any sin. But we all owe something to James's memory and to his family, his mother and father especially. They have been hurt enough by his death, without having to suffer the exposure of things in his life that, if true, should be decently forgotten. Any judgement on that belongs . . . in a more compassionate place.'

'Surely his parents know what happened?' Stefan pushed aside most of the Dean's words, except for what told him again that questions had not been asked.

'I don't doubt the Guards left many details alone, out of charity.'

'You mean they probably said nothing and asked nothing.'

'You seem to have an unpleasant appetite for all this, Mr Gillespie.'

'You should look at what the killer did to your seminarian,

Canon. Charity's grand. Maybe begin with making sure he doesn't do it to anyone else.'

The Dean looked at Stefan with cold contempt, as if he was something very grubby. He didn't expect anyone to speak to him like this. He didn't expect anyone to disagree with him. It certainly wasn't the place of a policeman. He turned away towards the big window, his back to Stefan. He looked out over the quiet lawns and the elegant drive to the college. He would not show anger.

'There is nothing more to say, Inspector. I think you're finished here.'

Canon Mulcahy walked back to his desk and sat down, smiling.

'I'm sorry, Canon. I suppose I wish the investigation had been more urgent when it started. Time was lost. I still . . . I wanted to look at his room.'

The Dean opened a cigarette box and took out a small, dark cheroot.

'Did you? I'll repeat myself. Whatever it is you're doing you're finished with it now. Anything else, you can discuss with the superintendent. He can discuss it with me. If there is a reason for you to come back here, we can discuss that as well. It may be that if you're with him, I will agree to it. My impression, however, is that the investigation is in good hands, and that won't be necessary. In fact, when I did speak to Superintendent Mangan, he suggested that the best approach to you would be to tell you to fuck off. I think he has you summed up well, Mr Gillespie, but I'll let him elaborate himself, as I'm sure he will.'

The Special Branch offices took up one side of the Police Yard at Dublin Castle, away from the buildings of state that had, not long ago, been the heart of British rule in Ireland, away from the chapel and the gardens and grand spaces. The entrance to the yard, through the stone archway of the Carriage Office, owed something to the look of the rest of the Castle, but the yard beyond, circling the Special Branch building, consisted of scruffy rows of garages and old stables and stores. Inside the building, Stefan Gillespie sat in a chair facing Detective Superintendent Terry Gregory. Gregory stood behind his desk, turning the pages of the file on the murder of James Corcoran, smoking a cigarette. The superintendent sniffed and shut the file. Stefan was aware his boss had looked at nothing at all in the file. He had certainly taken nothing in.

'You spoke to Superintendent Mangan?'

'I phoned him from St Patrick's. It was a one-sided conversation. He wasn't happy the case file had ended up in Special Branch. There didn't seem any point going into the station to see him. I did . . . well, what he told me to do. Fuck off.'

'I had a similar conversation with Andy Charles.' The superintendent grinned. 'Let's just say I was shocked by his lack of due deference to my rank.'

Stefan smiled. It wasn't much of a smile, but he had worked out, in his short time in Special Branch, that when the boss made a joke, you smiled. He wasn't yet sure what he made of Terry Gregory, except that he didn't like him.

'And the Commissioner has had a phone call from the President of St Patrick's. Obviously, the Dean thought your attitude required some comment from the top man. Insolent, rude, offensive, all those things that I wouldn't particularly have you down for, but then I'm not a fucking priest, am I? It would have all been very polite, but it hardly puts you in Ned Broy's good books.'

'You told me it was the Commissioner who wanted the case looked at.'

Gregory sat down and leant back in his chair.

'I wasn't expecting quite as much of the Protestant work ethic, Stevie . . . I can cope with a bit, but you're going to have

22

to learn to keep it under control. Ned Broy gets a letter that expresses concern about the fact that the investigation into this murder has ground to a halt. The daddy of the dead feller is an up-and-coming member of parliament. So, since the letter's from a TD, on Dáil Éireann notepaper, Ned asks for the file from Maynooth and then he asks me to make sure it's all been done by the book. I ask you to have a look and tell me what you think. What you think, Inspector, that's all. I didn't tell you to go out and start the fucking investigation up again, all on your fucking ownsome.'

'You might say it was done by the book, sir. It's a shite book.'

'And so you thought you'd show Maynooth CID how to do it?'

'Why ask me the question if you don't want an answer, sir?'

'The answer the Commissioner wants is along the lines of: there may be a few minor criticisms, a few things to chase up, but apart from that it's a thorough, workmanlike job. Is that so hard? You didn't have to leave the office, let alone start a row with CID in Kildare and the bloody Catholic Church. Three years ago, Ned Broy put you back in uniform for punching a priest. You're in CID a couple of weeks and you've got the hierarchy foaming at the mouth about you.'

'I didn't ask to come into Special Branch, Superintendent.'

'Don't try to be clever with me, Inspector. If I want you, you're here.'

Stefan didn't reply. Now there was an edge to Gregory's voice.

'So, what should Inspector Charles have done, Stevie? You tell me.'

'It starts with a lack of urgency, sir. You can't list the consequences of that. You can't buy back the time. But the main thing is the relationship between Corcoran and the man who killed him. They must have met shortly before the murder. A week, not much more. I'd say they didn't know each other

23

before. They probably met in Dublin. They arranged to meet again at Donadea. This was a big thing for Corcoran. Not some quick pick-up. So, where they met, how they met, these are questions that should have been asked. There's not so many places in Dublin two queer men can hook up, or many places to go if they did. I'm not saying that's the way it was, and I'm not saying it was that obvious, but it should have been tried. Were there places Corcoran regularly went to in Dublin – pubs, bars, pick-up spots? Was he known? Had he ever been noticed by the Guards? We should have been in Dublin with photos of him. Who saw him? Was he with anyone? It's a shocking murder. The investigation was too small.'

'And what do you think the Church would have made of all that? Not to mention his family. Photographs of a seminarian in every queer pub and public convenience in Dublin? And for what? You think every faery in town would queue up to tell us who was at it on a dark night in the Phoenix Park bushes?'

'It's not just any killing, Superintendent. It was fucking grim.'

'You know the complaint came from the lad's father?'

'He's a TD. Yes, you said.'

'A Fianna Fáil man – with a career ahead of him right now. Word is he's about to become a junior minister. A Cabinet seat soon . . . if he doesn't mess up.'

Stefan looked harder at the superintendent's smile. It seemed as if those words were meant to offer an obvious conclusion; they were self-explanatory.

'Your man has a feeling the investigation wasn't what it should have been. He passes that on to the Commissioner, because he's an important feller, and he can. But he doesn't know very much, except that his son was killed, brutally killed, in an attack that must seem almost random. He knows about the brutality. But it all came out of nowhere. Maybe a madman, what else? And does he know his son had sex with the man who killed him? I don't think so. And I doubt anyone's stuck a piece of paper in front of him and his wife with a description of what was happening by the lake minutes before their son was killed, with details of two different specimens of semen. Discretion, Inspector, doesn't make for good investigation. But do they want pictures of their boy up in every Dublin toilet now? I doubt it very much. And one thing's for sure, if that was happening, Rory Corcoran TD could say goodbye to his ministerial career.'

Stefan Gillespie nodded. That was the simple truth.

'He'd be finished. Unfair, unreasonable bollocks, but who can doubt it? So, I'll send this file back, with a few critical observations. Ned Broy will write a letter expressing his full confidence in his officers in Maynooth. And life goes on.' Terry Gregory got up abruptly. 'That's it, Inspector. If you want to fit in, don't show too much initiative. If you can't be arsed to fit in . . . same advice.'

Gregory looked at Stefan, as if waiting for a response. There wasn't one.

'Why did you join the Guards?'

'I'm not sure I had a reason.' Stefan shrugged. 'If I had, I've forgotten it. I left Trinity because . . . I didn't like it. There was no point staying. I needed something to do. Maybe it was because my father was a policeman. Or maybe because they were looking for recruits and I couldn't think of anything better.'

'That'll do. As long as you didn't bring any principles with you.'

'Perhaps that's what I've forgotten, sir.'

Superintendent Gregory laughed. He walked across the room and stood looking out through the glass at the detectives in the room beyond. He had his hands in his pockets. He watched his men as if he didn't much like what he was looking at. It was clear, without more words, that the conversation was over.

Stefan walked to the door. As he opened it, Terry Gregory turned.

'You're right. The investigation was shite. If there was a chance of identifying the killer, it's long gone. Too much time spent keeping too much quiet. And if you read between the lines, a bit of . . . well, your man was fucking queer, and he got what happens to queers. So, you're right about all that too.'

The man who killed James Corcoran left Ireland long before Stefan Gillespie saw the body in the mortuary at Naas Hospital. He left even before Inspector Charles arrived at the picnic site by the lake at Donadea, the morning after the murder. He took the mail boat from Dún Laoghaire on the night of the killing. By the time a poacher found the seminarian's body, walking out of the Donadea woods towards the lake early the next day, the murderer was getting off a train at Euston Station in London. A great calmness had come over him after the frenzy of the assault. He knew the danger he was in and he knew he had to get away unobserved. He had gone to Donadea almost unseen from Dublin, taking two days to cycle by a roundabout route, sleeping the first night in an empty lock-keeper's cottage by the Royal Canal and the second in the ruins of the castle at Donadea, among the all-enveloping trees. That morning he swam at the lake where they had arranged to meet. The water was cold and clean. The September sun was still warm on his body as he lay on the grass to let himself dry. They met at midday. James had cycled from Maynooth, taking backroads and boreens as well. All the secretiveness of getting there, unknown, unnoticed, was part of the excitement. This would be their place, this deserted estate, overgrown and unworked, thick with trees, with a sparkling, hidden lake at its centre. It was James's place first, at least somewhere he had discovered, a secret space. But the man he came to meet was good at finding his way. And afterwards the man had to find his way back to Dublin, even more unnoticed, more unremarked than when he'd come. That was the sole thought in his head. He had an Ordnance Survey map and a compass. He had a change of clothes. There was blood, of course. That was easy to dispose of. He stripped naked and swam in the lake again. He put on new clothes and wrapped the old ones in a tight bundle. He wheeled his bicycle out of the trees to the road and set off, heading north towards the Royal Canal. He saw no one for several miles and when he did hear a car, then later a tractor, he had time to slip through a gate into a field. When he rode through a village, his head was down and whatever attention he attracted was the work of seconds. And it wouldn't matter. Someone would have to stumble on the body, in a place few people went. He would be gone. He made good, fast progress. He disposed of his clothes, weighted down with stones, and then of his bicycle, in a deserted stretch of the Royal Canal. He followed the towpath into Maynooth, where he got the train into Dublin, making sure he arrived at the station with only seconds to spare, so he wasn't standing on the platform, waiting, noticeable. By then he was very confident. And Dublin asked no questions. He ate a meal in a restaurant on Stephen's Green, with more to drink than he was used to, then travelled out to Dún Laoghaire for the night boat to Holyhead. He had never killed before. The thought had been there sometimes, the anger had been there, perhaps a need, building in him. It had still happened without him wanting it, or knowing he wanted it. He was sorry for what he had done. He wished it hadn't been James. He shed tears for what had happened, looking back from the boat as it steamed away from Dún Laoghaire's lights; tears for himself rather than the dead man. Yet there was a sense of relief, too. And for a time, a very short time, it made him feel that he had torn something out of himself, that he had rid himself of the darkness, of all the passions filling him with disgust about who he was. It was done, and done in such a terrible way that surely none of those feelings could ever come back again, those feelings he could not control. Hadn't he put a stop to it? Hadn't he done that at least? It was a kind of sacrifice. He didn't often pray, but he did as Ireland disappeared into black night; not for James Corcoran, the man he had butchered, but in the bright hope that what he had done had truly cleansed him.

3

Kensal Green

London, 1941

Row upon row, across London's great suburban cemetery at Kensal Green, the avenues of the Victorian dead stretched in every direction. A derelict community of black slate and mildewed stone, modest headstones and crumbling mausoleums, miniature Greek temples and skewed Egyptian obelisks, and the red Gothic arches of a dozen tiny Albert Memorials. Watched over by angels with broken wings and chipped and blackened faces, the straight paths echoed the streets that spread out around the cemetery for mile after mile, with a kind of cacophonous decay that brought a hint of chaos to the solid certainty of the houses the dead had inhabited when they were alive.

A middle-aged man was walking along one of the tomb-lined avenues on a clear, chill January afternoon. He knew the place well. It had been a part of his childhood. He had lived in one of those solid streets. Walking through the cemetery had been the ritual of so many endless, empty Sunday afternoons. Now the cemetery had an easy, casual familiarity that he felt more comfortable with than the roads he had just taken from the Underground station at Kensal Green. Perhaps it was that hint of chaos in the tumbled stones. They reflected a truth of sorts. You had to wait for death to discover all had not really been well, in the best of all possible worlds; nothing had been certain or solid. It was part of an unwanted past as far as the man was concerned. But it was there even if he had made himself a stranger to it.

He was just over forty. A fastidious, almost obsessive concern with his appearance meant that he did worry about being forty. It felt older than it should. There were plenty of people to reassure him it was really no age. He was, after all, Ireland's greatest actor and theatre director. He liked to say he wasn't, but he was not unhappy to be contradicted. If growing older concerned him, mostly he pushed it aside, amused that it mattered to him at all. But here, in this forgotten place from a largely forgotten past, the awareness of age was less easily shrugged off. He already felt coming had been a mistake. The streets beyond the cemetery walls were dead to him. That hadn't changed. They always were. They were before he knew they were. He had grown up here, but he'd left it behind in a strangely absolute and final way. He had invented a past for himself in which Kensal Green played almost no part. The child who had lived there was a ghost. It was fitting that on this rare visit his companions were ghosts too.

Along the avenue, between bare trees, in front of a crop of tombstones that leant in every direction, several dozen people stood by a heap of newly dug earth, watching as the undertakers lowered a coffin into the ground. The smell of fresh soil was in the air. The drum of a rusty gasometer rose up behind them.

Micheál Mac Liammóir was late, though there were others still behind him. No one was in a hurry. The actor's presence was a gesture, one he was unsure he should have made. There wasn't even an audience to appreciate it. It was unnecessary; it was inconvenient. It had involved the mail boat from Ireland, and a train through an England full of delays and wartime darkness. But as the Irishman he had become since leaving

Kensal Green, funerals mattered. He had decided this one did. He owed the man a lot, though he hadn't seen him in many years. It was the kind of sentimentality he was usually too scrupulous to allow himself. But there was a debt. There had been kindness, generosity, friendship, when he'd been unsure how to find that. The man had helped him become who he was.

Most of the mourners were men, older rather than younger. Mac Liammóir recognised some: actors, directors, artists; people he would have expected to see. He nodded and smiled the quiet, uncommunicative smiles that go with a funeral where the deceased doesn't matter so much to the mourners' lives. But for a moment he mattered enough. The words of the burial service surrounded these people briefly – friends, acquaintances, strangers – and bound them together. They were words that somehow you were born knowing.

'Thou knowest, Lord, the secrets of our hearts; shut not thy merciful ears to our prayers; but spare us, Lord most holy, O God most mighty, O holy and merciful Saviour, thou most worthy Judge eternal, suffer us not, at our last hour, for any pains of death, to fall from thee.' The minister looked round at the faces for some seconds, blankly, then continued. 'We commend unto thy hands of mercy, most merciful Father, the soul of this our brother departed, and we commit his body to the ground, earth to earth, ashes to ashes, dust to dust.'

The look was an invitation to come and cast earth on the coffin. No one moved. Then one man stepped forward. An undertaker handed him a brass trowel of soil. He tipped it on to the coffin. Micheál Mac Liammóir moved to the grave more dramatically. He bowed his head and scattered the earth, with purpose and flamboyance. As he turned there was a queue. He smiled. This was a performance at least. The dead man had every right to expect it to be properly done.

As the actor turned away from the graveside, he passed a young man, dark – Indian, he thought – looking at him with a fixed, frowning gaze. Their eyes met for only seconds, but Mac Liammóir felt a surprising intensity in the other man's stare. There was a sort of smile, too, boyish, awkward, but it was the intensity that unsettled him. The young man wore a grey overcoat, well cut, elegant. He clutched a brown, square canvas box to his side. It hung from his shoulder. The gas mask case that not long ago everyone carried, but now seemed less essential than a tin hat. The actor nodded uncertainly and carried on. The man was still watching him. He could feel it. It was someone who knew him, perhaps someone he should have known. He didn't recognise him. The man saw that and didn't like it. He expected a response. There had been anger in those eyes. Mac Liammóir shrugged it away. The Indian was attractive, unquestionably. A forgotten encounter? It must have been a long time ago. Those days had gone. Well, gone for the most part.

The last scatterings of earth fell on the coffin.

'O Father of all, we pray to thee for those whom we love, but see no longer. Grant them thy peace; let light perpetual shine upon them; and in thy loving wisdom and almighty power work in them the good purpose of thy perfect will; through Jesus Christ our Lord. The grace of our Lord Jesus Christ, and the love of God, and the fellowship of the Holy Ghost, be with us evermore. Amen.'

Micheál Mac Liammóir crossed himself.

Then everyone was leaving, turning back into the avenues of the dead, exchanging quiet words about plays and friends and the war and last week's bombing in London, unfinished sentences. The great actor was conscious of the dark young man again, gazing from some way off. He walked on, following the other mourners. He was puzzled, but more than that, he was annoyed. It was as if the man wanted something. There was an etiquette. Not remembering was a part of that. You never imposed. You never reminded. Except by invitation. It wasn't about politeness. For some men it was about survival.

A brief encounter, if that's what it had been, should be exactly that. He had almost decided to speak to the young man, but something stopped him. It was that intensity again. Mac Liammóir's instincts were to go. There was something troubled in the young face, a mix of desperation and anger.

A familiar voice pushed all that away.

'Alfred!'

There was no mistaking the voice, lazy but razor-sharp, or that the name he had once been called was from the past. No one used it now. In Ireland hardly anybody knew he once carried this most English name.

'It's a while, Noël.'

'Well, I suppose we've nodded across a crowded room from time to time. Not so long as all that. Let's not make ourselves any older than we are, Alfred.'

Noël Coward took out a cigarette case. He offered one to Mac Liammóir. They stood for a moment, saying nothing, as one actor lit the other's cigarette and then lit his own. The two men had known one another in childhood. They had acted together as children. For both of them it was a world that had been left behind, though only one of them had entirely erased it from his present.

'I'm sure you're rather a stranger to London now,' said Coward.

'I thought I should come. Eric did a lot for me.'

'I saw him last year. Very ill. I can't say I kept in touch with him, but at least I did something. He spoke a lot about old times. I have to be honest and say I couldn't remember most of what he was talking about. I think he invented some of it, and even that wasn't particularly entertaining. Well, nothing wrong with that. If I am ever so ancient that I find myself spending most of my time talking about the past, I shall make everything up. Anyway, there he lies. He mentioned you. I think he'd rather you'd come to see him . . . when he was still alive.'

'I should have done.' Mac Liammóir smiled. 'Thank you, Noël.'

'Not often I can be self-righteous, Alfred. Don't begrudge it me. And I still can't call you Michael, let alone say it the way one is supposed to in Irish. I don't do it to irritate you. It's how I see you. I still resent the fact that you're a serious actor.' Coward laughed. 'And rather too serious, I sometimes think.'

'If my father had given me a more interesting name, I might have kept it.'

'There's something in that. As a child I took some pleasure in you having an uninspiring name. I might have come to nothing without my diaeresis.'

The two men joined the drift away from the graveside, heading along the avenue towards other avenues and the entrance to the cemetery, walking slowly.

'I have a car waiting, if you want a lift into Town?'

'I think I'll get a breath more air and take the Tube.' Mac Liammóir wasn't sure why he suddenly said that, except that he wanted some time on his own. 'I gather a few people are going for a drink, at Billie's. I might do that. I don't know. I have a night in Town before I go back to Dublin. Are you going?'

'I have work to do. Well, dinner with tedious people is always work.'

'I'm sure you'll amuse them.'

'You see what I mean, Alfred. You're the serious one, I'm the clown.'

'Ah, but what a clown!'

Noël Coward laughed. 'There is that.'

They walked on for a moment, silently. Mac Liammóir smiled.

'I remember you at ten, Noël, auditioning for a goldfish in one of Miss Lila Field's thankfully forgotten productions. We met at the audition. You asked me if I'd done much work. I'd no idea you meant acting. You also asked me if I knew what I wanted to be when I grew up. I didn't. You were unimpressed. You said people should always be clear about what they want. You were. I don't think you ever doubted or lost your way. I opted for uncertainty.'

'You finally discovered what you wanted to be, Alfred. An Irishman.'

Micheál Mac Liammóir laughed.

'I hope I make a better Irishman than I did a goldfish.'

'I'm sure you do, but I have never forgotten that Miss Field cast you as King Goldfish. I was stuck with Prince Mussel, not on until the third act.' Coward grinned and shook his head. 'The *Morning Post* review singled you out as the pretty little boy with the curls. It left a scar on my heart that never went.'

'I don't remember that at all,' said Mac Liammóir.

'Terrifying that I do,' replied Noël Coward. 'Ten or not, a low point in my career. You were earning two pounds a week and I was only on thirty bob!'

'You've made up for that since, Noël.'

'Money is a small compensation.'

'But you're busy enough, from what I read.'

'I suppose so. I've tried to find an obviously heroic role in the business of war, swanning around the world on some vague Intelligence mission, all grand hotels and secret assignations. They did give me a diplomatic passport, but it seems Winston didn't think I was achieving much by travelling the empire. They decided I'd be better singing while the guns fire, or words to that effect. Jolly songs for the troops. Positive propaganda. Which sounds like an exercise in boring the Germans into submission. I hope it doesn't do the same to Britain.'

'I doubt it will, Noël.' Mac Liammóir said what he knew his old friend expected him to say, but perhaps without the conviction that was required.

'It is a work in progress, dear boy. Some argument about whether a dressing gown and cigarette holder is good for morale or not. However, Herr Hitler has been helpful in making me a normal Londoner. The Luftwaffe dropped a bomb on my flat. I'm at the Savoy now. Beggars can't be choosers.'

The last joke, as if scripted for it, coincided with Noël Coward's arrival at his Rover. It was perfectly timed. The chauffeur was holding open the door.

'You're sure about the lift, Alfred?'

'I'm sure. Take care.'

The Englishman took out another cigarette, fixing it into a black cigarette holder with a shrug that was a rare moment of self-deprecation. He was on stage, even in the back of a car driving through suburban London. But the conversation with Mac Liammóir had been a performance too. It was something the Irishman understood. They were very different men, with very different ideas about what they did, but they shared something in that need to keep performing, whether on stage or not, in public or in private. Performance was a way to survive. It always had been. They knew it as children, even before knowing why survival was necessary.

Leaving the cemetery for Kensal Green Underground Station, Micheál Mac Liammóir slowed down. There were several people ahead of him from the funeral. He chose not to catch up with them. He might talk to them later, over a drink. For now, he turned away from the station, towards College Road. Burrows Road, Ashburnham Road; the turnings were still familiar. They were in his head, though he had forgotten they were. And the houses were as drab and as heavy as they had been in his teenage years. On Purves Road he stood outside number 150. He looked at it for only seconds before retracing his steps. He had a dread of this place that bore no real relation to what it was, or what it had been. If he felt any guilt about the battered scenery stored in the back of his mind, perhaps it was because his mother and father had never been as interesting as his story needed them to be. They were as solid and as ordinary and as English as these houses. They belonged in a place where he had been unable to breathe. But it was the reason he couldn't breathe that separated him from this place. That was the truth. The real desires that were his real identity.

The platform at Kensal Green Underground Station was empty now. The funeral contingent was gone. Only a few people stepped forward on to the red Bakerloo Line train as the doors opened. Micheál Mac Liammóir got in and sat down, conscious that a drink would be no bad thing now. He had not noticed the young Indian man who had been waiting by the platform entrance and ran to get into the next carriage at the last moment. He had already forgotten the uncomfortable encounter at the graveside. He had not registered that the man had been following him, keeping far off in the quiet streets of Kensal Green. He would not notice, as the journey into London continued, that the man had him in sight through the windows at the end of the adjacent carriages and was ready at every station for him to disembark. He was less likely to notice anything as the train went into the tunnels and filled up with passengers, and as it passed through stations closer to the West End, where the platforms were filling with people settling down to spend the night underground, in anticipation of the bombing. He was absorbed in what he was looking at, interrupted by the stretches of darkness in the tunnel. It was a rhythm he still knew, the rhythm of the stations that had been like a heartbeat when he was young. Queen's Park, Kilburn Park, Maida Vale, Warwick Avenue, Paddington, Edgware Road, Marylebone, Baker Street, Regents Park, Oxford Circus.

He counted them, as he used to count them once. He did not notice, at Piccadilly Circus, getting off the train, threading his way through the crowds to the escalators and emerging into late-afternoon London, that the young Indian man was still following him.

4

Billie's

In the bar at Billie's, in cellars beneath Little Denmark Street, a quartet of black musicians played 'Somebody Loves Me' with lazy familiarity. A woman with a peroxide-blonde perm, who might have sounded better without the American accent she was failing to imitate, sang in a breathy, slightly off-key whisper.

> Somebody loves me, I wish I knew
> Who can he be worries me,
> For every boy who passes me
> I shout, 'Hey maybe
> You were meant to be my loving baby.'
> Somebody loves me, I wonder who,
> Maybe it's you.

There was a buzz of conversation and laughter from the bar and the tables that were barely visible along the dark walls. There was little light anywhere except around the bar. No one was listening to the music, not even the dancers who shuffled round the small dance floor in front of the band. The couples dancing, most of them draped around each other, would have been unusual elsewhere. There were men and women dancing together, but among them white women danced with black men and black women with white men. Men danced with men and pressed their bodies close, slowly and sinuously, keeping time to what their bodies were saying more than to the music. Women dancing with women, in the face of men too busy at the bar, was familiar in any dance hall, but here two women's lips touched in the darkness. The club was full, though it was still early. It had been barely dark when Micheál Mac Liammóir had walked down the steps from the street. But things happened earlier in London now. What the night had in store in terms of bombing, no one knew. At any moment the silence and the darkness outside could be pierced by the moan of engines overhead and the sounds of the first explosions. There were nights when nothing happened. There were nights when the bombing was elsewhere. Some ran to shelters or hurried home to the suburbs at the first sign of German planes. Others made fine judgements, forcing another half-hour of pleasure from an evening before seeking safety. Some diehards stayed in Billie's basement, drinking their way through a raid.

Mac Liammóir had walked from Piccadilly Circus in the dusk. He had spent only two nights in London since the Blitz began. On neither occasion had bombs fallen close to where he was. He registered bombsites and shattered buildings, the broken windows of shops he knew, the sandbags at every entrance, the criss-crossed tape over every window. He had not seen the dead; he was conscious of that. But tonight, he was conscious of more. The walk from Piccadilly, along Coventry Street, to Leicester Square and Charing Cross Road, was another return. Coming out of the Underground he saw the Café Royal, still the safest place in London for a man like him; if you were welcome there you were important enough to be safe. Passing the Criterion, he smiled. The site where Eros stood was boarded over, but some things didn't change. Two young men, barely boys, were eyeing passers-by, wearing too much rouge and too much lipstick. The Dilly boys, bombs or no bombs. Outside the Lyons Corner House in Coventry Street a noisy gaggle waited for tables. The queue was full of men in uniform, like everywhere, but this was a Corner House where the codes and signals of queer London were learnt and practised. He had learnt them as a young man, with a kind of bewilderment and then with joy, finally knowing he was not alone. No one said anything; all was discretion. No one suggested the first-floor restaurant was different from any other floor. But the waitresses never sat women there. It was a public space but a private club.

Mac Liammóir didn't like the centre of London any more than its suburbs. It had always felt as if it was crumbling behind its imperial façades. The theatres mattered, but nothing else. Yet he felt an unfamiliar warmth for the city that night, with darkness closing in; such complete darkness, like a curtain coming down in the blackness of an auditorium, but with no lights to come up. Now the London he had turned his back on was being destroyed, he had time for it.

In Billie's, a handful of men who were at the funeral occupied one end of the bar. Micheál Mac Liammóir joined them. The conversation was bright enough. They were theatre men, in one guise or another, acquaintances rather than friends. The talk was of before the war, of old friends, and as ever on such occasions, who had died. But the war was quickly there, even in the cheerful relief that the theatres had reopened. Someone had decided entertainment mattered; that meant there were still jobs. The bombing was always present, too, though mostly in black jokes and unlikely stories. Mac Liammóir listened and laughed, but he offered no jokes of his own. He had some, but it felt as if the right to joke came with being under the bombs. And if these old acquaintances were amiable enough, he knew that not every comment about him being safely tucked away in Dublin was well intentioned.

41

There was no sign of an air raid, though the maître d' appeared at intervals to say that there were bombs along the Thames, beyond Greenwich. No one took much notice, but people were beginning to drift away. Whether the West End was to be spared for another night or not, evenings finished early now, just as they started early. Micheál Mac Liammóir ordered one more drink before setting off to his hotel. Suddenly the drummer at the side of the dance floor delivered a crashing drum roll that had nothing to do with the slow version of 'Caravan' being played. The trumpeter blew a discordant wail before, abruptly, resuming a muted solo. The actor noticed several customers moving across the dance floor at speed to disappear through a back door, among them a couple of men in uniform. Everyone else continued as before, talking, drinking, dancing. Two men in raincoats, hats still on, approached the bar. The maître d' stood in front of them, smiling his broadest, apparently most welcoming smile. He knew who they were, as did most. The warning had already been sounded.

'Are you friends of Dorothy, gentlemen?' asked the maître d'.

There was chuckling from the onlookers.

One of the newcomers produced an identity card.

'Military Police.'

'Lovely, dear,' continued the maître d'. 'I wish you'd come in uniform.'

'We're looking for service personnel. This club is off-limits.'

'Really? That makes us sound very exciting. Would you like a drink?'

'Don't come the faery with me.'

The second MP walked away from the bar, through the club. He was watched with distaste by some and laughed at by others. He looked ill at ease, uncertain what exactly he was supposed to do, unless he actually saw someone in uniform. The music continued. The first MP glared at the maître d'.

'I have information that men in uniform were seen entering this club.'

'Well, I don't see any. Are you going to ask us all for our identity cards?'

The military policeman looked more doubtful.

'I'm only interested in service personnel.'

'I don't blame you. Aren't we all, dear?' There was more laughter. Then the maître d's tone changed. 'I'll give you a bit of advice, soldier boy. A lot of people who come in here are VIPs. That means Very Important Poofs. The police know that. And we're surprisingly friendly with the police. They leave us alone. That's how it works. You need to do the same. Or you could find your cushy job patrolling the West End cut short. If you bump into a senior officer, who knows where they'll post you? Could be somewhere you might get shot at.'

The second MP returned from a fruitless circuit of the club.

'Now piss off,' said the maître d', grinning cheerfully again.

As Micheál Mac Liammóir watched the two military policemen head for the exit, he saw a figure at the bar, watching him. The man was familiar, the young Indian from Kensal Green. The actor was unaware that the man had been sitting in Billie's for some time, at a dark corner table, waiting until Mac Liammóir was finally on his own. He was smiling. He walked forward with his hand outstretched. The actor responded as he had to and shook, but he knew now that he had been followed.

'Mr Mac Liammóir, you don't remember me, do you?'

'I'm sorry. You'll have to remind me. I did see you at the funeral, and I had a feeling I really should know you. You'll just have to put it down to age!'

'Vikram Narayan. It was Cairo, the Royal Opera House, 'thirty-six. I was a stage manager. You gave me a part in *Romeo and Juliet*. One of your chaps was off with the usual Delhi belly, or whatever the Egyptian equivalent is.'

The young man grinned. Mac Liammóir nodded.

'Yes, of course. I remember now.'

He did remember. The Indian had played Sampson in the opening scene of *Romeo and Juliet*. He remembered that it had been a mistake, all the more glaring because it was the beginning of the play. It was a mistake born of another mistake and a row he'd had with his partner, Hilton Edwards. There had been a night, a very drunken night, when he had fallen into bed with the, admittedly very beautiful, young stage manager. He had barely recalled anything the next day. He wasn't convinced anything had happened except that he had passed out, though Hilton was never going to believe that. But he felt some kind of awkward obligation to Vikram Narayan; the result was the second mistake. That was the one Hilton Edwards had not let him forget. Narayan was appalling.

'I can handle you fucking the boy, Micheál, but not fucking the Bard!'

Hilton's words came back to him and he smiled.

Vikram Narayan was smiling too, an oddly fixed smile.

'You're living in London now, Vikram?'

'I spent some time back in India, after Cairo, but I've been here a while.'

'Are you still . . . working?'

Mac Liammóir was not finding it easy to say anything. It was not a problem he had normally, but the man unsettled him. As the words left his lips, he regretted them. For someone in the profession, the word working meant one thing. He knew, before he finished, that it was unlikely Narayan was acting.

'I'm not in theatre at the moment, no.'

The great director thought that was probably an understatement. The season in Cairo was in focus now. The man hadn't been much better as a stage manager.

'I want to get back to it, though. That's where my heart is.'

The young man stepped closer, smiling more broadly. Mac Liammóir wanted to step back, but he was wedged against the bar. He thought Narayan was going to make a pass, there and then. He couldn't get away. He glanced at his watch. He was usually better with words, much better, but he felt he was going to be reduced to something like, *Good God, is that the time already?*

Narayan said nothing. The Irishman began to waffle.

'You knew Eric Lake, anyway? He was a very old friend. I hadn't seen him in years. He was a very kind man, kind to me . . . but you knew him too.'

'Not well. He helped once . . . with a job. Front of house. It meant a lot.'

The words were pointed, as if they connected to Mac Liammóir.

'I think we were meant to meet again, Mr Mac Liammóir. I had no idea I would see you today. But I have thought about you. The idea of coming to Ireland, you see, that's the thing. The idea of working with you again. So, when I saw you, I was more than surprised. I was delighted. If I hadn't gone, it wouldn't have happened . . . Things are destined sometimes, don't you think?'

Mac Liammóir didn't think so at all. He was more uncomfortable than ever. And something in Vikram Narayan's voice reminded him of what he had seen in his face before. A kind of desperation. His eyes were fixed, unwavering.

'I think I can be honest with you. I need help. To get out of London. That's what's in my head.' He reached forward and touched the actor's arm. 'I'm sure all sorts of things are in my head, seeing you again . . . all sorts.'

Jesus Christ! Mac Liammóir barely stopped himself saying the words.

'I have some money,' continued the young man, changing his tone suddenly. 'Enough to get to Ireland, maybe enough to keep me a while. But I need the papers to travel. I need a job to go to if I'm to stay. And we're old friends, aren't we? We've worked together. You see why I was thinking of you. And of course, the opportunity of working at the Gate with you . . . wonderful.'

The Irishman could hear an emptiness in those last words. Narayan's face was blank. The words meant nothing. All that was there, behind the smile, was the desperation. He didn't appear to be drunk. For a moment Mac Liammóir wondered if he'd been taking drugs. He was sweating profusely.

'You will help me, won't you?' he spoke quietly, but it was a plea, deep and troubling. He whispered, 'I have a room we can go to . . . if you want to go.'

'I don't, Mr Narayan,' said Mac Liammóir. He tried to sound kind.

The young Indian reached into his pocket. He took out a business card.

'Take this, please.'

The actor took the card.

'My address. I'm sorry if I said the wrong thing. We should approach this professionally, of course we should. Please . . . if I am too eager . . . forgive me.'

'Vikram, I can't take you into the company just like that. I hardly know you. We met for a few days, five years ago. We're a small company . . .' The actor trailed off. He could hardly tell the man there were no circumstances on earth in which he could offer him a job, even if there was a job. 'Impossible.'

The young man shook his head. He spoke more softly.

'It's not safe for me here. Something happened . . . Ireland would be safe.'

Mac Liammóir said nothing, because the words meant nothing.

'It's the same for all of us who are working for Indian independence. I have, I always have. I told you, in Egypt. We

46

talked about Irish freedom, Indian freedom. Do you remember? Ireland showed the way. We all look to Ireland.'

'I see.' The actor said something because he felt he must. He remembered no such conversation, but it could have happened. It was the kind of conversation he might have had. It was a conversation he had had with others.

Vikram Narayan moved closer, almost whispering now.

'If you could offer me a job, then I could get into Ireland. I need the papers, that's all. You shouldn't believe what you hear about India. There are those of us who don't want Britain to win this war. We feel like you. We know the words. We hold the thought.' He smiled, as if he knew he was saying what Mac Liammóir would want him to say. 'England's difficulty is our opportunity too. Aren't we all fighting in the same cause, in Ireland and India?'

Micheál Mac Liammóir had no ready answer to this unexpected appeal to his Republican instincts. It wasn't long ago that he might have echoed the Indian's words with enthusiasm. There was a cause that India and Ireland shared. There was a fight for freedom in the face of the British Empire that Ireland had not fully won, and India had still to win at all. But the war that was happening now made for less easy conclusions. His antipathy towards Britain had to be put beside his hatred of the darkness that was sweeping Europe. He could have that conversation, as people across Ireland did, and find himself in conflict with himself, but he didn't want it now, here. And he didn't believe Vikram Narayan wanted it either. These were words meant to impress him or put pressure on him. He could feel it. They were spoken with the intensity that was driving the young man's voice. But they carried no conviction. Mac Liammóir wanted to get away. Narayan could see it.

'You should help me. You have to help me.'

'Mr Narayan, please . . .'

The young Indian's tone changed.

'I don't care what I do. I need to get away. Do you understand?' There was a quiet aggression in the voice. 'I think you owe me that.'

'Owe you?' The actor frowned. 'Dear boy, what do you mean?'

'You know what I mean.'

'I don't think I do. But I do think I've had enough. A brief encounter in Cairo that memory tells me probably didn't even happen . . . is hardly a debt.'

Narayan's face came closer.

'How does being queer go down in Ireland, Mr Mac Liammóir? It doesn't go down well here, but with all that Irish holiness, what would they make of you, if they knew what you got up to? How about a story like that? I could say a lot that would make the newspapers sit up. I wouldn't stop at Cairo. Papers don't care if it's true. What would Ireland think of the squalid old man you are?'

Micheál Mac Liammóir stared in disbelief. This had come from nowhere.

And then he laughed.

'You think I'm a candidate for blackmail?'

'Every queer's a candidate for blackmail. I could do it.'

'My dear boy, you're right to say this isn't a topic much talked about after Mass of a Sunday in Ireland. And you might think that Ireland, of all the places on God's Holy Earth, would be the last to give a man like me protection. But you'd be wrong. Ireland is a land of glorious hypocrisy, and if I made a paragraph in the *News of the World*, the whole island would pretend it was never there. There may be a couple of deaf old ladies in Cahirciveen and Malin Head who are unaware of my sexual predilections, but that's about the extent of it. Perhaps you missed the conversation with the military policeman just now, but on Eireann's sacred shores, I really am a Very Important Poof.'

It seemed that abruptly all the energy had drained out of Vikram Narayan. But Mac Liammóir could see there were, surprisingly, tears in his eyes. At that moment the maître d', who had watched for the last few minutes, approached.

'Is there a problem, Mr Mac Liammóir?'

'No, not at all. I think Mr Narayan is leaving.'

The young Indian looked deflated, beaten. He glanced nervously at the maître d', as if he was a new kind of threat. He turned quickly and went, pushing past people as he did.

'Do you know him?' The actor looked at the maître d'.

'He doesn't come in often. I don't think he has the money. Rather down on his luck. I'm sorry if he upset you, sir, but I'm sure he meant no harm.'

The maître d' walked away. Mac Liammóir was less sure Vikram Narayan meant no harm. He finished his drink, collected his coat, and left.

Walking back towards his hotel in the blackout, Micheál Mac Liammóir was still troubled by the face of the young Indian. It pushed aside his awareness of the dull thud of explosions. They were a long way off. Along the river, the maître d' had said. Only a few days in London had made that seem ordinary. The sense of desperation he had seen in Vikram Narayan's face, even at a first glance, across the coffin at Kensal Green, would not go away. Whatever was wrong went deep. It was not idle, and whatever anger the actor felt himself about the attempt to blackmail him into helping the young man, he felt something else too. There was no reason why he should feel sorry for Narayan after what had happened, yet he did. Something made him think he should have tried to help. It was an uneasy feeling. It was the kind of thing you might feel for a stray dog that snapped at you in the street. What could he do? Why should he bother? But the tense, hopeless face remained in his head when those last angry, mad words were already fading.

He put his hand in his pocket and found the business card. It was bent and dog-eared. It read: *Vikram Narayan, Actor, Flat 6, 24A Greek Street*. Mac Liammóir shook his head. There was something almost pitiful about the printed declaration. The man was afraid of something. And there was a connection, however slight. It meant almost nothing, but perhaps it was wrong to turn aside on the road. He had five pounds in his wallet. If he could help in no other way, he could give him that. He was very near Greek Street. It would take only minutes.

Micheál Mac Liammóir reached the door at 24A Greek Street, sandwiched between an Italian restaurant and a delicatessen. There was a list of names and some bell pushes. Narayan's name was there, but when he pressed the bell, he knew nothing was happening at the other end. Probably none of them worked. A man cycled past, an air raid warden in a tin hat.

'The front door'll be open. You won't get nowhere pressing those!'

The man disappeared into the darkness.

Mac Liammóir opened the door. It swung back to reveal a corridor and some stairs. There was a faint light from the landing above. It didn't seem the best idea to be here, but he had made his decision. For whatever motive, a conscience he had no reason to salve needed salving. He walked up the stairs, looking at the door numbers. A second flight of stairs took him to the top of the house. There was only one door: Flat 6. It was ajar, and the room exuded a warm, orange glow. Narayan was home. Mac Liammóir wished he wasn't. He could have stuffed the money under the door. But he would do what he had come to do. He knocked on the open door. There was no answer. He pushed the door and looked into a small, cluttered room, lit by a bedside lamp. There was an armchair, a table, a chest of drawers, a bed in one corner. The blackout blinds were closed. There was another door across the room.

If Narayan was in the other room, maybe that would do as well as being out. He would leave the money on the table and scoot. He took the five-pound note from his wallet. He laid it down. It was as he looked up that he saw the bed in the corner. And the body of Vikram Narayan stretched across it. He saw the blood everywhere on Vikram's clothes and on the sheets. The young Indian was dead. There was so much blood Mac Liammóir could taste the iron in the air.

5

West End Central

Inspector Stefan Gillespie sat at a table in the window of the Lyons Corner House at Piccadilly Circus, looking down at London going to work. The night had been quiet in the West End and he had slept well enough in the small attic room at the top of the offices of the Irish High Commission, across the road in Regent Street. No one lived at the High Commission, but for two months now, either side of Christmas, Stefan had shuttled back and forth between there and the Department of External Affairs in Dublin, carrying the briefcases that were the diplomatic bag. A train of Irish and British diplomats, politicians, businessmen and Army Intelligence officers followed the same route. He knew many of them now, British as well as Irish. Sometimes they spoke on the mail boat or the train, sometimes there was merely a nod, often there was nothing. He knew those whose journeys were public property and those whose travel arrangements led them into the offices of the British Army and British Intelligence – the men who weren't meant to be noticed at all. Irish neutrality was a business that showed itself, clear and transparent, above the waterline, in all its necessary dealings with the British, but what mattered was the invisible iceberg beneath the surface.

In many ways Stefan's work as a courier was about what could be seen and defended, even if some of what he carried might not have been viewed positively in Berlin. There the conviction that Ireland was a constant thorn in the side of the British war effort was an article of faith.

Stefan found the job tedious and repetitive. It meant a lot of time doing nothing except sit on boats and trains, but if it was undemanding, it kept him out of Special Branch. He didn't mind that his time wasn't spent spying on other Irishmen and cataloguing dissent. He was used to London now. He knew the routines of the shelters and the Underground. He knew its atmosphere, intense and resigned, slow, yet full of a strange energy. He didn't dislike being there. He found the anonymity of the city an easy thing.

It was still early, just after eight o'clock. There was a newspaper in front of him, but he wasn't reading it. There was a break ahead, when he got back to Ireland: two days at home in Wicklow, with his young son, Tom, and his parents. He would take the mail boat that night. He looked at his watch. Shortly he would walk up to Charing Cross Road to find a book to take back for Tom.

He smiled. He knew he had to do better with the book than his effort at Christmas. It was the price of being at home so little. The *Beano Book* had not been unwelcome. It lasted for Christmas Day and it provided a series of bad jokes to repeat for several days more. But he had lost his sense of what Tom read, even what he thought. He had seen the book next to Tom's bed was a translation of *The Iliad*, from the library in Baltinglass. It was something he had never read. Tom would be twelve before long, and in the last year, without Stefan seeing it, he had changed. He had grown quickly into someone Stefan didn't know as well as he had. Being away so much it felt as if it had happened abruptly, when it really hadn't at all.

'Gillespie!'

Stefan looked up to see the High Commissioner, John Dulanty.

'Miss Foye said you were here.'

Dulanty pulled back a chair and sat down. He had just arrived from his commute into London from a quiet house in the suburbs. He travelled into Waterloo every weekday, like any Londoner, and he was as unnoticeable as anyone else on the Southern Railway trains through Wimbledon and Clapham Junction. Stefan was barely ten years younger than the High Commissioner, but Dulanty's balding head made him look older. His voice gave little indication of his Irishness. He had been born in Liverpool; he grew up in Manchester. He was one of a cohort of British civil servants and diplomats with Irish parents, who had left the service of Britain to work for the Irish state when it came into existence. His loyalty to his country now did not disguise the fact that the skin he inhabited seemed, at times, as English as Irish. In the midst of London's war especially, he was as much a participant as an observer. He took out a cigarette. The Nippy, the waitress, in crisp black and white, hovered.

'Just a cup of tea.'

The waitress disappeared.

'I had a message from Scotland Yard when I got in. One of the assistant commissioners. I don't know quite what to make of it. He didn't know much himself. It was something he picked up, that he heard, that could become . . . I don't know if embarrassing is the word . . . but awkward. As I say, I don't know exactly what's happened. I imagine you know who Micheál Mac Liammóir is?'

'Yes, of course. I know him . . . well, I've met him.'

'That might be helpful. I suppose, if you know him . . . you'll know that he is a man with . . . with some less than normal social . . . when I say—'

Stefan smiled. 'He's queer. I'd say we can take that for

granted, sir.'

Dulanty frowned. It was what he meant but he didn't like it said. The waitress brought the tea. The High Commissioner waited as she walked away.

'So, Mac Liammóir has been arrested. I don't know if arrested is the right word, but he's in custody or he's being questioned. He was in some club in Soho.' The High Commissioner said 'club' with an expression of distaste. He glanced round and lowered his voice. 'That's the gist of it. That's all the Assistant Commissioner knew. Something happened between Mac Liammóir and . . . some chap . . . and the long and the short is that someone – I assume this man – is dead.'

Stefan Gillespie found it hard not to smile, listening to Dulanty's delivery of a narrative he did not relish talking about, but those last words were serious.

'Dead?'

'Yes. It seems Mac Liammóir is . . . a witness . . . perhaps a suspect.'

'Well, I find suspect very hard to believe, sir.'

The High Commissioner shrugged. He stubbed out his cigarette.

'It appears Mr Mac Liammóir was over here for a funeral. I have had no request for consular help, but he may need it. I hope this is a mistake of some kind, but I'd like to know what's happening. He is . . . a prominent figure at home – and to some extent here. It is a private visit, but he does . . . Well, with the Gate Theatre, as a director, an actor, he has represented Ireland all over the world. He is much admired. If he is involved in something . . . squalid . . . it's not what we want splashed all over the newspapers. And if it's more serious than that, it is something that Dev won't . . .' Dulanty shook his head. 'He will go berserk.'

Stefan said nothing. He was a policeman. If there was a dead man somewhere, whatever the circumstances, his first thought was not what the Prime Minister of Ireland might object to in the newspapers.

'We need to find out what is happening, Inspector. Do you see?'

'Do you know where he is, Mr Dulanty?'

'A police station . . . West End Central.'

'I can't just walk in there and ask what's going on, sir.'

'The Assistant Commissioner recognises . . . a diplomatic element to this. That's why he called. No one wants waves, wherever they come from. You can't tell where anything leads just now. Mac Liammóir has influential friends here. And if we want to avoid embarrassment this end, the British don't want to see him turned into a cause célèbre in Ireland. Mac Liammóir is strident about his nationalism. If it looks like he's being persecuted, nobody needs him dressed in the Green and turning himself into a martyr. The man is not beyond that.'

Stefan laughed. 'No, he probably isn't.'

The High Commissioner ignored the laughter. He wasn't amused.

'I don't want to involve a solicitor. That's not our business. Mac Liammóir may have done that himself. That's up to him. I'd rather the High Commission isn't directly involved at this point. The Assistant Commissioner is happy for you to go into West End Central. He will provide any bona fides.'

'Go in to do what exactly?'

'Help with inquiries, with anything they may want to know.'

'Why would they want to know anything from me, sir?'

'All they have to do is tell you what's happened, why the man is there, whether he is actually being charged with anything. They will be instructed to let you talk to him. I want to know what I tell Dublin. I want to know if this will stop where it is, or whether there is worse to come. As far as Scotland Yard is concerned, it's a request from me, and the request is being accommodated as a courtesy to the Irish government. You won't need to explain yourself at all.'

'I should think there's every chance they'll tell me to fuck off.'

The High Commissioner drained his tea and stood up.

'I think they'll do what Scotland Yard tells them. And if there's nothing to this, except keeping insalubrious company, I'd say the police will do us a favour and forget about it. If so, I want Mr Mac Liammóir out of London and on a boat to Dublin as soon as possible.' He smiled for the first time. 'You might offer up a couple of prayers to St Anthony for that happy outcome. I certainly will. He was my mother's favourite saint. I'm sure she's still got some credit with him.'

The sergeant on the front desk at West End Central gave Stefan Gillespie a smile that was almost a sneer. It was clear he was expected, but not welcome.

'Garda Síochána, eh, Inspector? We don't get many of those.'

'I think someone should have phoned, Sergeant.'

'From Scotland Yard, that's right. To the superintendent. If we'd known Mr Mac Liammóir was putting on a show, we would have sold tickets.'

The sarcasm was wasted on Stefan. He didn't reply.

'You'd better come through then, Inspector.'

The sergeant lifted the desk flap.

'Who do I need to talk to? Is it CID?'

'The super can't be arsed to see you. He said get on with whatever you're here for. As for CID, I think they'll leave you with the feller from the Yard. They've already sent a chief inspector. He beat you to it. In with them now, for what it's worth. My bet is they'll let you two at it . . . and go for a fucking drink.'

Stefan followed the sergeant along the bright corridors.

57

West End Central was a new police station. One day it would have the stale smell of sweat and smoke that all police stations had. Now it smelt of polish and new paint. The sergeant knocked on a door and went in. Inside were three detectives, standing at a desk, looking at photographs, statements and diagrams.

'It's the Irishman,' said the sergeant. He turned and walked away.

Stefan Gillespie stepped into the room. The three men looked at him. Only one of them smiled and walked forward, hand outstretched. He was tall, slightly gaunt, with pale hair and skin that was darker than it should have been, as if he had been a long time in the sun. He was older than Stefan; not by much.

'Frank Nugent.' He shook Stefan's hand and turned towards the other two, a man in his fifties, heavy and sour-faced, and a man in his twenties. 'Inspector Hardy and DS Dillon. They've been working on the scene of crime. And they've tied the murder into several other similar killings. The body was only discovered last night, but that's what's come out already. It's good work.'

Stefan registered the word murder. The English detective was talking to him as if he knew something. He had known about a death, but not a murder.

The older man walked across the room and shook Stefan's hand now. He did not do it with any good grace. The atmosphere in the room was uncomfortable.

'It's Inspector Gillespie, is that right?'

'It is. It's Stefan.'

'I don't know exactly what you're here for.'

'I'm not sure I do myself,' said Stefan, trying to keep the conversation as light as he could. He sensed that whatever the atmosphere was, it had been there before he walked into the room. 'You have an Irish citizen . . . I don't know if he's in custody or whether he's a witness to something . . . I think it's just that I was here, and the High Commission wanted to offer . . . some assistance.'

Inspector Hardy laughed. 'To us or to him?'

'Maybe both,' said Stefan more quietly.

'The man you want to talk to is Chief Inspector Nugent here,' continued the DI. 'He seems to be taking over. Who knows why he's here either?' He looked at the man who had introduced himself to Stefan a moment before. 'Murder. Why would they hand that to Special Branch, but what the fuck, eh?'

'No one's handing anything to anyone, Dick,' said Nugent.

'You're not here for your health, sir.' Inspector Hardy made a point of the formality of Nugent's higher rank. 'I don't suppose you are either, Mr Gillespie.' He made the same point, in a different way, ignoring Stefan's rank. 'When you sort out what you're doing, give us a shout. The office is yours.'

Detective Inspector Hardy nodded at his DS. He walked out and the younger man followed him. For a time Stefan stood looking at Nugent, who had a faint smile on his lips. The Irish detective had no idea what was going on. But he knew that if the chief inspector was from Special Branch, the West End Central CID man was probably right. He was there to take over, whatever the reasons for that.

'Not much of a welcome, Inspector.'

'I wasn't expecting much of a welcome. It's Stefan.'

'I think you're slightly more welcome than I am.'

'I'm here to find out what's happened to Mr Mac Liammóir.'

'I know.'

'Has he been arrested?'

'No. Helping with inquiries. I think Inspector Hardy had him down as a killer in the early hours of this morning, but it's clear enough that his own description of events is probably true. He discovered the body. And that's all. I say that's all, but if you look at what he found . . . he won't forget it in a hurry.'

Nugent turned to the table. He pointed at a row of photographs.

The wide shots showed a room, cluttered and small, lit by the harsh light from a flash. The close shots showed a bed and the body of a young, dark man; the full body, stretched out on the bed, then closer views of the head, the swollen neck, the legs, the stomach, the groin. The photographs were black and white, but the blood-stained clothing showed sharply all round the stomach and thighs. There was a great deal of blood. The man had been stabbed repeatedly.

'This is the crime. This is what Mr Mac Liammóir saw when he walked into the flat where it happened. The dead man is a young Indian, Vikram Narayan. Mr Mac Liammóir found a policeman and reported it. However, inquiries by CID established that he and Mr Narayan had met earlier that evening, at a club in Little Denmark Street – Billie's – where they had some kind of argument. The long and the short, as Mr Mac Liammóir happily told Inspector Hardy, was that the dead man tried to blackmail him in some way, threatening to reveal his homosexuality, which Mr Mac Liammóir has no problem revealing himself. The idea was that he followed Narayan back to his flat . . . and killed him.'

As the English detective spoke, Stefan stared at the photographs.

'That's extremely unlikely, however, Stefan. Even a cursory forensic examination shows that Mr Mac Liammóir did exactly what he said. He walked into the room, saw the body and walked straight out again. Still, you can't altogether blame Dick Hardy. This is a very distinctive murder. The knife wounds round the groin and the genitals, I mean, all administered, with great violence, immediately after death. There have been three similar murders over the last year. Two in London and one in Berkshire, in Reading. All the men were young, and they were almost certainly queer. Dick Hardy had seen reports of the other deaths. He thought he'd not only stumbled on a fourth murder, he'd caught the killer red-handed. He was right about the murder.'

Chief Inspector Nugent picked up a large manila envelope. He took out several photographs. He was too busy with his story to register the intensity with which Stefan Gillespie was gazing down at the pictures on the table.

'These are a couple of photographs from two of the other murders. I think one on Hampstead Heath, another along the Thames, near Richmond. I've only seen these today. The basics are the same. A man is killed, a blow to the head, strangled or suffocated. Then he's attacked with a knife, same way each time.'

Stefan looked up, frowning. He took the photographs Frank Nugent was holding out. He was not at all surprised by what he saw.

'This needn't concern you, Stefan. Mr Mac Liammóir has given a detailed statement. It seems to clear him of any involvement. The forensics tend the same way. So does the fact that there is a pattern of murders. Assuming he was not in England when the others took place. He says he wasn't, but you can verify that in Dublin. Hopefully, these are just loose ends. I think even Inspector Hardy recognises Mr Mac Liammóir's a lost cause. He's no use as a witness – he saw no one. So, I guess that's you finished.'

Stefan laid the new photographs on the table, next to the others.

'I don't know that I am, Frank.'

'What do you mean?'

For the first time Frank Nugent realised something else was going on.

'I've seen this before,' said Stefan.

'Seen what?'

Stefan glanced back at the photographs. He was familiar with what he was looking at. He had known straight away. He had not forgotten that image.

'The same thing. In Ireland, nineteen thirty-nine. A young man, strangled, then stabbed, over and over again, in exactly the same way . . . in exactly the same places.'

Stefan Gillespie stood in a small, square room. There was no natural light, simply a bright bulb overhead. Even in a new police station this room had been made as bare and uncomfortable as possible. The only furniture was a table with a chair on either side. Micheál Mac Liammóir sat at the table. He wore a grey overall. He looked tired. There was a cup of tea in front of him, but it was untouched. There were cigarette ends in an ashtray. The actor stared at Stefan without recognition. It was a while since the two men had seen each other, but hardly more than a year. They were only acquaintances, yet Mac Liammóir knew him well enough to recognise him. Now there was only bewilderment in his eyes; behind that something more fragile, a dull and uncertain fear.

'Mr Mac Liammóir.'

The actor kept staring, looking through him.

'You'll remember me, so.' Stefan smiled.

'I'm sorry, whoever you are. I can't think of anything else I can say.'

Stefan pulled out the free chair and sat down.

'I'm not here to ask you anything. My name's Stefan Gillespie, you've seen me in Dublin. At the Gate. And in New York, when you were on tour. I'm an Irish policeman. I'm a Guard. The High Commissioner sent me here. Mr Dulanty.'

'Dulanty?' Mac Liammóir still looked confused.

'You can leave soon. They're pretty well finished with you.'

Micheál Mac Liammóir shook his head.

'They think I killed a man . . . a man I knew . . . Jesus, the way he . . .'

A wave of shock seemed to roll over Mac Liammóir. He was shaking, but slowly. There were tears in his eyes. Then he was still again.

'How long have I been here?'

'Since last night.'

'I found him, that's all. I wanted to help him. Then he was there . . . just there. I can't believe how . . . like a piece of meat . . . blood . . . I ran . . . I ran and there was a policeman . . . Then I was here . . . they kept saying I did it . . . and they were talking about other men . . . other dead . . . I told them what happened. They wouldn't let me sleep. They—' Mac Liammóir stopped, staring harder at Stefan. He was looking at him now, not through him. And there was a smile, almost a smile. 'Stefan. Jesus Christ! What in God's name are you doing here?'

'Among other things, getting you out of this place. And hopefully home. The High Commissioner wants you on the mail boat, sir, out of harm's way.'

The life that had drained out of the actor was returning.

'I only came for a fucking funeral. A fucking funeral!'

Mac Liammóir stood up. He stumbled and leant against the table.

Stefan moved round to help him.

'I'm grand. I'm just exhausted. They did put me in a cell, but I couldn't get any sleep. The beds are terrible here. I shall say something before I go. There certainly won't be a tip.' He breathed deeply; the joke faded. 'There was someone crying. The next cell. It seemed like hours. Just crying. It didn't stop.'

'They have your possessions at the front desk. I think they want you to reread your statement and sign it. But that's all of it. Where are you staying?'

'A hotel, in the Strand, the Regent Palace.'

'I can arrange for a taxi.'

Mac Liammóir looked at the overall he was wearing.

'What about my clothes?'

'They were being examined by forensics . . . I don't know . . . it's just . . .'

The actor shook his head. He understood what the examination was about; the blood that the police were looking for on his clothes. He stepped forward and stumbled again slightly, his limbs stiff from sitting for so long. Stefan put his arm round him. The tears that had been there briefly before returned. Mac Liammóir's head was buried in Stefan's shoulder. He was sobbing. But it was only for a moment. He moved back, smiling, for the first time, the wry, almost insolent smile that Stefan recognised so well.

'I think I'd rather not have them back. But I can't walk through a hotel lobby like this, can I? I have a suit in my room, a shirt, a tie, and whatever else. I don't suppose you could be a real saviour and go and fetch them for me? And bring them back? I'm sure your consular services could stretch to it, Stefan. If they can provide me with some washing facilities here, that would be helpful. I'd like to exit this den of the whoreson English with rather more dignity than I entered!'

They walked to the door. As Stefan opened it, Mac Liammóir stopped.

'He was frightened. It feels like that, looking back. Desperate, anyway. But I couldn't do anything. When he threatened me . . . I've no idea what it was about. Afterwards, I felt guilty. I thought some money might help . . . but I don't think it was about money. How . . . why did someone do that to him?'

6

Charing Cross Hospital

Little more than an hour later, Stefan Gillespie left Micheál Mac Liammóir at the entrance to the Regent Palace Hotel in Piccadilly, now in a grey suit that had been brought from his hotel room. There had been not much conversation. Stefan had been surprised to find Chief Inspector Nugent waiting for him outside West End Central Police Station in a car, first to take him to the Regent Palace to collect Mac Liammóir's clothes, then to make a second journey to the hotel to drop the actor off. The first leg had been surprisingly silent. Nugent made only a few remarks about traffic and the blackout and fuel shortages. At the Regent Palace he went upstairs with Stefan to Mac Liammóir's room. He walked around the room as Stefan took clothes from a suitcase. He looked at a book by the bed and glanced into the suitcase. He bent down and picked up a pair of tan brogues that were on the floor, inside the door to the corridor, with a printed note on them to say they had been cleaned. Stefan recognised that despite everything, the English detective had the Irishman at the edge of his mind. He was getting a better sense of who the man was.

'He'll need shoes. The ones he had on are evidence. The soles are the only place they found blood. I don't know if he'll get them back. He'll miss them. From Lobb's, handmade. I don't suppose even great actors have many of those.'

'I don't suppose they do.' Stefan noted attention to detail.

They walked to the lift and down to the street. As the car pulled away, Stefan took out a cigarette. He was surprised the English detective had said hardly anything about the similarity between Vikram Narayan's death and the death of the young man by a lake in Ireland. It had been less than two years ago.

'Any observations about Mr Mac Liammóir? You were looking.'

'I didn't expect to see much in a hotel room, Stefan.'

'No.'

'Though it's not every Irish nationalist who gets his shoes in St James's.'

Stefan Gillespie laughed. 'Is that useful?'

'You never know, do you, in our line?'

Stefan heard the edge in Nugent's voice.

'Our line?'

'I checked on you with the Yard.'

'They have a list of Gardaí, do they? That doesn't sound very likely.'

'They have a list of Garda Special Branch.'

Stefan Gillespie lit the cigarette. It wasn't his business how they did things at Scotland Yard, but if Nugent had observations to make, so did he.

'I don't think it's odd the Irish High Commissioner asked the only Guard in London to see what the Metropolitan Police were doing to Ireland's favourite actor. I'd say CID at West End Central were more puzzled why the Yard sent a senior Special Branch officer to take over an investigation into a dead queer. Even if there's been a few of them. You get to be jack of all trades in Dublin Castle, but that's not how it works here. Not that it's any of my business.'

'Not that it is.' Frank Nugent laughed. 'Give me a fag, will you?'

Stefan passed him a cigarette and held up his lighter.

The Scotland Yard man went on. 'There's a list of dates. The killings I told you about. While there's no evidence I can see that says your actor killed Mr Narayan – in fact, I'd say the opposite – there is all the circumstantial stuff. An argument, threats, he was at the scene of crime and, of course, the whole queer business, which makes for suspicion in itself. You know what I mean by that. If a man's a pervert, then why not a murderer?'

'That's not much of a case, Frank.'

'Men hang on less,' said the chief inspector. 'Anyway, dates.'

'Dates,' said Stefan.

'Where was your actor on the dates of the murders, all of them? I'm assuming he's not going to turn up in the environs of London and Reading on the dates specified, but it's belt-and-braces from his point of view. And there's no point wasting time on a dead end from our point of view. With a murder in Ireland, those loose ends do need some tying up. But he's an actor. I'd expect to find fairly clear evidence of where he was on a particular day or night. Of course, that includes the date of the murder in Ireland now. If that really looks like the same killer. It doesn't help Mr Mac Liammóir. Quite the opposite.'

Stefan Gillespie nodded. He had already had the same thought.

On the second journey to the Regent Palace, Micheál Mac Liammóir had sat in the back of Nugent's unmarked car saying nothing until they reached the hotel.

'I'm booked on the mail boat tonight. If I'm able to get the train …?'

Mac Liammóir didn't finish the sentence. Despite the reassurances, he could not feel free of what had happened. Stefan looked round. The words were a question, addressed to him. But he couldn't answer it. He looked at Nugent.

'I'm sorry, sir,' said the chief inspector. 'There may be more questions. I know there's probably nothing you can add. But we would appreciate you staying in London a few more days. It's nothing to be concerned about. Something may come up. It's early days. You may even remember something.'

'I'm more inclined to forget than remember,' said the actor quietly.

'And you know you're quite at liberty, sir.' Nugent smiled.

Micheál Mac Liammóir smiled too. 'Except that I just can't leave.'

'I wouldn't put it like that at all, Mr Mac Liammóir. And if you need any reassurance, you have Inspector Gillespie here. Helping us out. Right, Stefan?'

Stefan nodded as he seemed required to do.

Mac Liammóir looked at him for a moment. He didn't look reassured. Stefan got out of the front passenger seat and opened the door for the actor.

'I'll keep in touch, Mr Mac Liammóir.'

'It's early, but I'll probably be in the bar. Until they carry me upstairs.'

He walked towards the entrance. The porter tipped his hat and opened the door for him. Stefan heard a bright, jokey voice he knew was a performance.

'Thank you, Stanley. Quiet night again last night!'

Stefan got back into the car. Nugent pulled out into Piccadilly.

'I'm helping you out then, Chief Inspector, am I? I didn't know that.'

'You know now. You're here, aren't you? I don't suppose you've got much else to do. I haven't seen the body yet. And it could be you've seen one of these before. You're one up on me. I need to know if you're right. You do too.'

In little more than six months, the mortuary that made up only a small part of the basement of Charing Cross Hospital had spread: from an office and two theatres and the refrigerated chamber where a handful of bodies could be kept in storage, to now filling the corridors all round. As other storerooms, off the same corridors, had been turned into emergency theatres and overflow wards, the living and the dead were in closer proximity than had been the case in peacetime, and for many the shift from one state to the other involved a short journey in every sense. For the living, only the seriously injured came to the hospital from where the bombs dropped night after night, so the numbers that died were high. But the dead came too, when they were pulled from the buildings and the wreckage, disfigured, crushed, torn, often burned beyond recognition. And if they were unidentified, they stayed until they could stay no longer. The refrigeration plant could only cope with so many corpses. Many waited in the corridors, in cardboard coffins and bags, men, women, children, for a vacancy that might keep their flesh from rotting long enough for someone to claim them.

It was along one of these corridors, stacked with the dead who had been brought in over the last two nights, from bombing in the East End and the Docks, where other hospitals and mortuaries were overflowing, that Inspector Stefan Gillespie and Chief Inspector Nugent pushed their way into a theatre. Mortuary assistants and pathologists gathered what information they could from the unidentified dead, most of them laid out on trestle tables and the floor.

No one could grasp what Inspector Nugent was looking for. The idea of a murder victim puzzled the men and women who were examining the dead. It seemed out of place as the waiting bodies came in and out, with the details that could be noted – noted as quickly as possible. The night shift had gone. There must be a note somewhere. There had been a pathologist on through the night. There would be one somewhere now, at some point.

'Would he be here? Was it a fire? There was a lot from the fire at—'

'The Police Surgeon sent him. It was the only ambulance he could get.'

'He'll be here somewhere then, won't he, Chief Inspector?'

'Narayan, Vikram Narayan.'

'If they know who he is he won't be in here. All these are unidentified.'

A nurse called out:

'Was there a man brought in who was killed?'

There was some laughter.

'They've all been fucking killed, haven't they?'

'I mean someone killed him.'

No one responded.

Trolleys with dead bodies wheeled in and out round Stefan and Frank.

An elderly man walked into the room.

'Police?'

'Yes, Chief Inspector Nugent. This is Inspector Gillespie.'

'Next door.' The man walked out into the corridor. The two policemen followed. 'Hawkins, I was on last night. I've looked at your man. I'm sorry, I haven't had time to write a report. I can tell you what happened, but I've only made a cursory examination. Cursory is what we do at the moment.' He pushed open two swing doors. They entered a low, dark room, with a bank of drawers at one end. The room was cold. There were bodies on trolleys and on the floor.

'The Indian chap. Narayan, is it?' Hawkins addressed a round, short man, sitting on a stool, reading the *Daily Mail* and smoking a hand-rolled cigarette.

'The poof?' said the man, with a sniff of disdain.

'The police want a look at him.'

The man on the stool got up and walked to the bank of drawers. He took hold of a handle. The coffin-sized drawer slid out of the wall. Hawkins walked forward. Stefan and Nugent stood beside him. The man went back to his paper.

The naked body of Vikram Narayan lay in the drawer. Stefan glanced at the dark face. It looked peaceful, like Corcoran's. Then he looked at the stomach and the groin and the knife wounds that formed a kind of wreath round his genitals.

'There's a blow to the head. Severe, but probably didn't kill him. He was then suffocated. That's an assumption at the moment, but the signs are right. Your inspector from West End Central mentioned a pillow. That would be about it. The wounds have nothing to do with his death. Inflicted around the same time, probably afterwards. The knife thrusts were through clothes. A sort of circle. Quite neatly applied, but not much of a knife. A kitchen knife of some sort. In fact, the end of the blade broke off in the wound, in what must have been the last thrust. I don't know if you have the knife, but you will want this.'

The pathologist picked up an envelope that lay in the drawer by the body. He handed it to Nugent, who opened it and looked at a blackened sliver of steel.

'Less to do with the violence of the blows than a poor quality weapon.'

Frank Nugent nodded.

'Is that it, gentlemen?' Hawkins asked.

'Will you be doing a full autopsy?' said the chief inspector.

'I can't think there'll be much else to say. Knocked on the head, suffocated, then, for whatever reason, decorated. If you need more, you'll have your own people. I've too much to do. I'll send a report. But we can't keep him for ever. If you want the body preserved, you should make other arrangements.'

'He was fully dressed?' asked Stefan.

'Yes.'

'Was there any indication of sexual activity?'

'I'm not sure what you mean.'

'Semen, for instance?'

'That's a very specific for instance, Inspector Gillespie, but no, nothing of that kind. I wouldn't think he had much time for dalliance between the crack on the head and the asphyxiation. All there was in that area was blood. A lot of it.'

Stefan Gillespie sat in a small office, high in the red-and-white brick building that was Scotland Yard. It was a building he had seen many times, standing at the end of London's great street of government, across the road from the Houses of Parliament. It was an oddly unassuming block set beside the classical stone façades of the government buildings that surrounded it. It could have been a block of flats in a Kensington side street, or a department store that hadn't lived up to the grandeur of Harrods or Selfridges. It was hard, even with the instinctive distrust of the British police that Stefan's Protestant heritage couldn't ignore, not to feel something about this place. Good, bad or indifferent, and inevitably a mix of all three, this was still where policing began. It may have been a monument as much to what policing should have been as to what it was, but it was still a monument. And it was reassuring to see that it was as dirty, as cramped and as full of people who looked like they didn't want to be there, as any police station he'd ever been in, big or small. And in the corridors the smell of dust and old sweat and tobacco was the same too, with the slight scent of ancient urine that always found its way, somehow, up from the cells.

Chief Inspector Nugent's office was close to the attics, to the side of one of the brick turrets that marked each of Scotland Yard's corners. It seemed a kind of outlier. They passed through no big office to get to it. Other doors along the corridor from the stairs were firmly shut. Stefan saw no one, though the floors below had been busy. He wondered who, as a chief inspector, Nugent was in charge of. It didn't feel like he was surrounded by men from a Special Branch department that must have been many times bigger than Terry Gregory's. The office itself was tiny, with a sloped ceiling and a small window that just about gave a view of a patch of the Thames. Nugent had disappeared for several minutes to make some tea. Stefan found himself looking past the box files that were piled up around the desk, a dozen deep, at a large-scale map of India. It looked out of place, taking up most of the wall next to the window.

Now the two detectives were looking at a row of photographs, all of them of the bodies of dead men, marked with some variation of the savage circle of knife wounds round the stomach, thighs and genitals. There were photographs of the bodies as they had been found, naked, partially clothed. The pattern was clear. Photographs of Vikram Narayan, on the bed in his flat and on the slab at the mortuary, were in position beside the others, the last.

'I spoke to my boss in Dublin,' said Stefan. 'He's sending photos from the Donadea murder. There are some statements. They don't amount to much.'

'But you have fingerprints . . . a fragment?'

'Yes, from a beer bottle. What have you got in the way of prints?'

'From the flat in Greek Street, quite a lot. That doesn't mean the killer left anything. Until we find something to compare them with . . . we can't know.'

Stefan Gillespie nodded; nothing led anywhere without a suspect.

'You think your man in Ireland, Corcoran . . . you really believe it's the same?'

'I can't see how it isn't. It has to be. But once you've said that, it just turns four into five. We had fragments of a print, but there was nowhere to look and no one to look for. It was a dead end. But what about the investigations here? What about these other murders? It doesn't seem you're much further.'

'Except in quantity. There's nothing, Stefan. I say nothing . . .' The Englishman turned the pages of a file, opened another and turned more pages. 'I've only just got these from the Murder Squad. Still getting on top of it. No prints at all. That's remarkable in itself. The man may be a maniac, but a meticulous maniac. If we can compare the prints at Narayan's flat with what's coming from Dublin, maybe we will get a break. A break . . . but no suspect . . .'

'So, this is your case now?' asked Stefan.

'It's too big for West End Central.'

'And too big for the Murder Squad?'

'There's the Irish angle now.' Nugent grinned. 'A delicate relationship.'

It was an answer of sorts, but Stefan Gillespie felt it was an answer after the fact. Frank Nugent had arrived at West End Central when the only Irish angle was the Irish actor who found the body and was, perhaps, a suspect. It might have been awkward. It wasn't about a relationship with the Irish police. That relationship was only there now because of new information from Stefan.

'Except for Vikram, all these murders have taken place outdoors somewhere,' continued the chief inspector, 'like yours in Ireland, James Corcoran. So, every time, no real surfaces to get prints from. A few footprints, but nothing substantial. Never the same shoe, but always a size ten or eleven. That's it. The killer leaves almost nothing behind. There are some hairs, a few pieces of wool or fibre. But looking at the file, so far, the fibres don't match each other. One detective wondered if the killer was even destroying his clothes after every attack. With the blood, maybe he'd need to. But he never appears to have worn the same thing twice.'

'You can't destroy your hair.'

'It's brown. That's about it. No hair so far at Vikram Narayan's. Well, two on the pillow, bleached, maybe permed,

74

a woman's. Presumably another visitor, another time. So, we have short brown hair and he may have used Brylcreem once. Hardly enough to identify anyone. No one to identify anybody anyway. Four bodies and we're no better off than you were in nineteen thirty-nine. No witnesses, no sightings of the dead men with anyone near the time of their deaths. Not necessarily surprising. You take the one on Hampstead Heath. It's a place men meet for sex. Men who don't know each other. Men who have never seen each other before and won't see each other again. I'm not saying it's all like that, we can't know, but we're dealing with a level of secretiveness . . . a hidden world. That's what these dead men have in common. They're all some part of that world.'

Stefan stood up, looking out at the patch of light that was the river.

'That's true of James Corcoran, too,' he said. 'But it's not the same. I'm sure he met the man who killed him, in Dublin, sometime before. A few days, maybe a week. Maybe more, but certainly that. They arranged to meet again. Nothing random in it. It was secret, yes, but it was no chance meeting.'

'That's what interests me, Stefan. You've got more there than a dozen detectives have put together over our four murders. We're still hoping for more from Vikram. There's at least a chance he knew the killer or that the killer followed him from Billie's. I know the man could have picked him up in the street, but everything that went before – the argument with Mac Liammóir, the mood Mac Liammóir says Vikram was in – makes that feel unlikely. And this wasn't long afterwards. It wasn't the middle of nowhere, either. It was the blackout, but not a dark night. It was the West End. There were people about. No bombing even close. Inside a building. All that makes for a much higher chance the killer left a trace somewhere, that someone saw him in the area.'

'They've never found a witness before?'

'Maybe one, maybe two. Not close enough to the scene of any murder to be sure, but the only descriptions we have. Two descriptions, both of a soldier.'

'Is that it . . . a soldier?'

'A tall soldier.' Nugent laughed. 'No, that was never going to be red-hot evidence, was it? A bloody soldier! Some place to start in the middle of a war. It could have been anything, anyone. It could have been a fucking Home Guard uniform.'

'So, where do you start?'

'I'm a fresh pair of eyes, Stefan. That's why they've put me on it.'

'Just you?'

'The Murder Squad will do the leg work where necessary.'

'They'll enjoy taking orders from Special Branch, Frank.'

'Maybe we're not as unpopular here as you are in Ireland. It might help that we're not a retirement home for ex-IRA men who still cherish our old comrades, the ones beavering away to overthrow the government, the ones who aren't beyond shooting the occasional policeman, for old times' sake. But I'm sure they're grand fellers, eh? Or don't I understand Ireland at all, Stefan?'

Stefan Gillespie heard the easy mockery in Nugent's last few words, but he wondered if he heard more. He had struggled to place the chief inspector's accent. It was English enough, southern, middle class, but there was something else in it he couldn't place. He wondered if there was something Irish in there. He looked at Frank Nugent and smiled. He didn't know what to make of the man. There was something about him that didn't sit right. He didn't belong in this murder inquiry. However dark, there was no political dimension.

'You don't have to be English not to understand Ireland, Frank.'

Chief Inspector Nugent laughed.

Stefan said no more. What went on in Scotland Yard wasn't

his business. Only James Corcoran was his concern. He had forgotten the dead seminarian, but now he remembered; he also remembered how little anyone had wanted to know about that murder. Something of that atmosphere was still there. Superintendent Gregory didn't relish the prospect of working with the Metropolitan Police on a killing that had been filed away and forgotten. From a phone call only an hour earlier, Stefan got the impression that his boss didn't want the failings of An Garda Síochána under the microscope at Scotland Yard. The Garda Commissioner wouldn't like that either. However, Terry Gregory was no slouch when it came to examining the clouds that came his way for brighter linings. With four bodies piled up, the failings of the police in Britain were on an even bigger scale. The pros and cons could wait till Stefan got home. They would have to look again at what had happened by the lake at Donadea. There had to be a chance of finding who James Corcoran's murderer was. And one thing that did raise Superintendent Gregory's spirits was the sudden realisation that the killer would probably turn out to be an English poof now, rather than an Irish one. There was the silver lining, however small. English homosexuality was safer ground.

7

Veeraswamy

Stefan Gillespie left Scotland Yard, heading back to Regent Street and the High Commission. Assuming the information from Ireland raised no more questions about Micheál Mac Liammóir, Stefan would return to Ireland the following night, carrying the diplomatic bag and bringing an unexpected operation with the British police that no one would be very enthusiastic about on either side of the Irish Sea. In Britain, with the dead all round, and the flow of telegrams arriving in homes to express regrets for the dead men overseas, it felt like there were bigger priorities. He had seen that in the faces of the Murder Squad detectives that Chief Inspector Nugent had sent out to talk to men in the queer pubs and bars and cottages of the West End. Those men wouldn't want to speak to the police and the police wouldn't want to speak to them. The only hope was that someone had seen something; if anyone knew anything, fear might break through the wall of secrecy, but the fear of exposure was still there to prop it up. In Ireland there were a lot of reasons why working with the police in England was viewed with suspicion, and the baggage from the past was complicated by present neutrality. It made every area of contact between the two countries something to be explained away or denied. Five dead men didn't alter the fact that every misstep the Irish government made brought criticism and diplomatic fury from London and Berlin down on Dublin.

It was odd that carrying a briefcase to and fro from Dublin to London had kept Stefan outside that for several months. He was simply part of the show. What he carried was the most official and least significant material passing between the High Commission in Regent Street and the Department of External Affairs on Stephen's Green. What was contentious found other routes. Men from Irish Military Intelligence, G2, who sat in meetings with MI5 along the road from the High Commission in St James's, but were never officially in England at all. Politicians and army officers who marketed a far more cooperative Irish neutrality than the fierce impartiality Éamon de Valera advertised in the Dáil and declaimed on radio for the Irish public. Most of what those men carried, they carried in their heads. It was never to be written down.

The messages Stefan brought related to the most innocuous tasks of John Dulanty, the Irish ambassador, who went by the title of High Commissioner because Ireland was still part of the British Commonwealth of Nations. The difference between Dulanty and the other High Commissioners, however – Canadian, Australian, New Zealander, South African – was that Ireland stood outside the war. It supported neither Britain nor Germany. And it was the only part of the Commonwealth that the British War Cabinet had plans to invade.

In London, as in Dublin, Stefan Gillespie's spare time was something he filled up rather than used. If he could not be at home in Wicklow with his young son, filling up time with not much was how he lived. In some ways it was easier to do that in London, where he knew hardly anyone, than in Dublin. The business of war, still a neutral's business too, was what occupied him in one way or another. And it was an occupation. The weary sea crossing from Ireland to North Wales; the slow, constantly delayed, constantly re-routed trains between Holyhead and London; broken nights shuttling from a hotel room or a camp bed in the High Commission to the Underground or a basement shelter.

There were days in London with nothing to do, waiting for instructions, for the bag; moving around the West End from pub to pub, on a now familiar route, staying long enough to drink but never long enough to do more than exchange a few formulaic bomb-and-war-and-weather observations. A drink in one pub, a drink in another. It passed the time. And anonymity suited him, not because of the job he did, but because he had no inclination for anything else. He drank too much, he knew that. Never enough to be drunk, but enough to know it was too much. He drank because it was something to do, the same way others smoked. He smoked too, but without the same conviction.

London was all motion and anonymity. Because he didn't belong, it didn't mark him out the way Dublin did. There was no need to be anything other than alone. He had worked on one mission in London already that year. He knew it. He was used to the bombs. And, of course, he could take a rest from it. But the darkness of the city at night was undemanding. Most of the time, that would do. It had been this way since the death of his wife, Maeve, eight years before. There had been times, there had been women who made him step away from it, but something always pulled him back. Sometimes that seemed more about laziness than anything else, but it was still where he was. It suited him, to be in transit. Even when he was at home in Wicklow, with his son Tom and his parents, on the farm that was the real fixed point in his life, it sometimes felt as if it was only a pause. It was a pause he needed, but if it lasted too long, he was restless. Movement was a purpose, however empty that was. The war that was not meant to be Ireland's war kept Stefan in motion.

He returned to the High Commissioner, having killed what remained of the afternoon in three pubs on his route from Whitehall to Regent Street. It was dark, and he expected the High Commission to be closed, but as he came out of the lift, heading for the stairs up to the room he was sleeping in, the stairs towards Dulanty's office, he could hear the sound of Miss Foye's Remington. Miss Foye was now somewhere around fifty years old. She was a spinster, as she had to be to work in the Irish civil service, and she used that word as a kind of claim to authority over the men who worked there, whatever their age. She had worked at the High Commission since it was established, with the foundation of the state in 1922. If the High Commissioner was head of mission, it was Miss Foye who ran it, whatever anyone else might think. She was from Cork but there was nothing soft about her voice. It was sharp and crisp, and it did not suffer fools. Stefan liked her, most of the time, but he had not worked out whether she disliked him or simply thought he wasn't serious enough for the job he did. But everyone had felt that at some time, even the High Commissioner. Stefan walked on towards Miss Foye. There was no other route. Three drinks were scarcely a misdemeanour, but he knew she was watching him, though she appeared to be gazing down at the typewriter. Her look would be one of familiar disapproval. She always knew when he'd been drinking. It was the fact rather than the quantity she disapproved of. She looked up, finally, as Stefan Gillespie reached the desk, and pulled a sheet of paper from the roller.

'This is for you, Mr Gillespie, from Superintendent Gregory. The details of Mr Mac Liammóir's engagements on the dates in question. I will send a copy to Mr Nugent at Scotland Yard, but I have telephoned him already with the information. I thought you would want him to have it . . . as soon as possible.'

'Thank you, Miss Foye.'

He smiled. There it was. The tone of voice to go with the look. He should have been there to do it himself and not, as she knew he had been, in some pub.

'The chief inspector says there is no problem with Mr Mac Liammóir returning to Ireland. If there are other questions, he assumes that you will ask them and provide the answers. I told him I was certain that was your intention.'

Stefan nodded. She would be pleased she got two bites of that cherry.

'And Mr Mac Liammóir has been on the telephone too.'

'Is he at his hotel?'

'No, but he wants to talk to you.'

'I'm sure. Anyway, it's good news. Where is he?'

'He's in a restaurant, over the road. The Indian one, Veeraswamy.' She spoke the name as if she didn't entirely trust the idea of an Indian restaurant. 'He said he'd appreciate you joining him. And he did say it was important.'

Stefan walked across the road, following Miss Foye's directions, and found his way up a flight of stairs to the first floor, where a large dining room looked out over Regent Street, though the thick blinds and curtains necessarily blocked the view. It was an unexpected sight. The furniture was full of ornate, intricate carving. The walls were hung with bright tapestries. It was something he knew, but only from pictures. Above the darkness of London's blackout, it was a small world on its own, full of subtle and unknown scents as well as the colours of India. There were only a few customers: several men in uniform, very senior uniforms; others in the dark jackets and pinstriped trousers that were another uniform of seniority, this time the civil service's. He was shown to a table in a corner, tucked behind a carved screen, away from the main part of the dining room. And he saw Micheál Mac Liammóir waiting for him there.

'Dear boy, sit down. Have a drink.'

A waiter in a turban and a kaftan smiled.

'A beer, that'll be fine.'

'I've ordered food,' said Mac Liammóir. 'Just soup and a pilau. Is that all right? I haven't eaten all day. I haven't wanted to. But I need something now.'

'I'm happy to leave it to you, sir. I wouldn't know what to order.'

'It's very good, the real thing – don't be tempted to play safe and have something English or French. This won't be too hot. I'm sure you'll enjoy it.'

Stefan smiled and nodded. The conversation wasn't really about food; it was about Mac Liammóir trying to recover a kind of normality out of the chaos.

'So, Stefan, what news?' asked the actor.

'You can leave tomorrow. The mail boat awaits.'

'Thank God. I gathered from the Gate that you wanted a résumé of where I've been and what I've done since nineteen thirty-nine. I had no idea Scotland Yard took such an interest in the theatre. If they want reviews, I'm happy to oblige. Well, in most cases.' He laughed and raised a glass of wine, as Stefan's beer arrived at the table. He was trying hard to lighten the past twenty-four hours of his life. 'I don't understand what all those dates were. Mr Nugent is satisfied. But why?'

Stefan had decided he would tell Mac Liammóir the truth. The actor had been pulled into this, however inadvertently, but there should be no secret about what was happening now, or about what had happened before. It was hard not to feel that too much secrecy, too much sweeping away what nobody wanted to look at, was one reason why the killer of five men was still killing. Mac Liammóir was surely owed the truth after being a suspect himself.

If it was a truth that Micheál Mac Liammóir was owed, it was not one he was easy hearing. The darkness he had started to push away came back, and it was darker. If he wanted somehow to leave it in London, it touched Ireland, too.

'I don't know what to say, Stefan. It's terrible . . . and it's terrifying. I suppose I wanted . . . I wanted to feel with poor Vikram it was some sort of awful accident. That sounds stupid; even as things stood it was stupid. We're all stupid when we want to hide, I suppose. Five men . . . dead. No one can hide from that.'

'No.'

'It's very strange.' Mac Liammóir drank slowly. He was puzzled now.

'I hope it won't stay that way,' said Stefan. 'We will find him.'

'You have to say that, of course you do. What I mean by strange . . . is that Vikram's sister came to see me this afternoon. She doesn't know any of that, what you've just told me. She went to Scotland Yard. She saw Mr Nugent. She wasn't expecting to see him . . . or that he was in charge of the investigation into her brother's death. She knows him, you see, from India, that's what she said.'

Stefan took this in. It was very odd information.

'He told her nothing, really,' said Mac Liammóir.

'To be honest, there isn't a lot to tell,' said Stefan.

'This will all seem very . . . I don't know what it's about, Stefan, but she doesn't like Chief Inspector Nugent at all. She is disturbed by his involvement. I don't know whether this new development . . . this poor Irishman . . . will help her in any way or if it's even relevant to that . . . ah, but here she is now.'

Mac Liammóir stood up and Stefan did the same as a slim, dark woman, with long black hair, stopped at the table. She was very striking. She wore a dark suit, with an orange and yellow scarf that said something of India. As the waiter moved a chair for her to sit on, it was obvious she worked at the restaurant.

84

'Mr Gillespie.' The woman reached out her hand.

'This is Miss Narayan, Hindu. Vikram's sister. She is the manageress here, so it seemed a good idea. Nearby for us both. And sort of out of the way.'

'Thank you for coming, Mr Gillespie.'

'I'm very sorry, Miss Narayan.'

'Thank you.' She shook her head. 'I tried to find out what had happened to Vikram. I got very little at Scotland Yard. I was taken in to see Chief Inspector Nugent, but he told me almost nothing. I was surprised to see him . . . There is a connection, an Indian connection . . . It is not a welcome one at all.'

Hindu Narayan was thoughtful. But she did not elaborate.

'I asked at Billie's, the club. Mr Nugent mentioned it. He said Vikram had been there. I got more there. They told me about Mr Mac Liammóir. I found him. I did know he had been a friend of Vikram's. I knew they worked together in Egypt. Mr Mac Liammóir told me what he knew. He said you'd know more.'

Stefan glanced at Mac Liammóir, who looked down into his wine glass. He wasn't as easy with this as he was trying to look. Stefan did not imagine he had told Vikram Narayan's sister everything in his statement. He doubted anything had been said about the young Indian threatening him with blackmail.

'I can tell you what I've just told Mr Mac Liammóir. It's not an easy thing to say. It doesn't find the man who killed your brother. But I hope it will.'

'You can't tell me anything worse than what's happened. But before anything else, I want to know what Mr Nugent has told you. When I asked to see the detective in charge, I didn't expect him. What did he say about Vikram?'

There was a look of anger on Hindu's face.

'I don't know what you mean,' said Stefan.

'He must have said something. It's not as if he doesn't know

85

him.'

Stefan frowned. This was now a conversation about Frank Nugent.

'You've got no idea what I'm talking about, have you, Mr Gillespie?'

'No, I'm not sure I have.'

'Nobody asked me to identify my brother's body. I still haven't seen it.'

Stefan wasn't sure she would really want to see it.

'But he was identified, wasn't he?'

'There was never any doubt. Mr Mac Liammóir found him.' The actor nodded. 'I knew him, Hindu. You know I did.'

'The sergeant at Scotland Yard said there was no requirement for further identification. I told him I wanted to see Vikram. "No need, miss," he said. "Don't upset yourself, miss," he said. "Chief Inspector Nugent has identified the body."'

Stefan registered the words. It was clear Nugent knew the dead man.

'You don't know Chief Inspector Nugent is IPI, do you, Mr Gillespie?'

'IPI? I'm sorry, I have no idea what IPI is.'

'Indian Political Intelligence.'

'He's Metropolitan Police Special Branch,' said Stefan.

'Yes, but he's come here from India. He's in London to spy on Indian nationalists, people working for Indian independence. He's a spy, that's all. India is not full of people who want to fight a war for Britain. We have our own struggle and it goes on whatever happens here. You're Irish, like Mr Mac Liammóir. You know what it means. Frank Nugent is a spy and a thug. In India, when people are arrested by IPI, they don't come out the way they go in. Sometimes they don't come out at all. In Delhi they took Vikram when he was only a teenager. He did come out, yes, but he was in hospital for weeks afterwards. That was Mr Nugent and his officers. My family

86

has been in the Congress Party since the beginning. They beat my brother because they dare not attack my father. I don't suppose Mr Nugent did it himself. They use Indian officers to do that. Vikram took it all. He never answered their questions.'

She said the words proudly, with a look of defiance, fighting tears. Micheál Mac Liammóir reached across the table and touched her hand. Stefan turned away. He knew what such a beating looked like, sounded like. They didn't happen often in the cells in Dublin Castle, but they happened.

'Mr Nugent has known Vikram for years, in India and in London. The details I won't . . . it is not relevant. They have been watching Vikram here, as he was watched at home, because he is fighting for India. The Congress is in his heart, his head. He has been followed. He told me. His flat has been searched. He has been threatened, questioned. The chief inspector's people report who he sees, who he knows, meetings he goes to. He has—' She stopped, dropping her head. There was anger, but there were still the tears she was not going to show. 'I must say "had", he had . . . it's all *had* now, isn't it?' She looked up again, calmer. 'Why is this man investigating a murder? Why do I go to ask about my brother's death and find *him*? He hasn't told you he knew Vikram, has he?'

'No,' said Stefan quietly, 'I can't say he got round to telling me that.'

It was an hour later that Stefan Gillespie and Micheál Mac Liammóir emerged from Veeraswamy on to Regent Street. The conversation had not moved much further. Who Frank Nugent was and what he was doing was no clearer. Stefan had explained something of the background to the murders that culminated in the death of Vikram Narayan, but he had not said everything. He wondered how the killings came across to Miss Narayan. He had skirted round the issue of homosexuality. And when he did, he felt it was what she wanted. Although she must know the truth about her brother, it was shut away somewhere out of sight, even now. She believed there was something political behind Vikram Narayan's death. She almost insisted on it. Yet none of that related to the violence dealt out to the five men who now included her brother.

However, if there was nothing political, why had Special Branch's top India hand pushed his way into the investigation? And why was he behaving as though Vikram Narayan was a stranger when he had known him for years and had officers following him around London, recording every contact he made.

A good place to start looking for evidence about who the young Indian had been associating with, and where he had been in the days before his death, was the information Chief Inspector Nugent and his officers must already have. And it hadn't even been mentioned. There was no doubt Nugent was hiding a great deal. But Stefan didn't have to look hard to find that less surprising than it ought to have been. In Dublin, Terry Gregory had made a career out of telling nobody anything. It didn't have to mean anything. It didn't necessarily mean what Hindu Narayan was convinced it meant. She had decided Frank Nugent was responsible for her brother's death in some way, whether personally or not didn't matter. Despite the evidence tying her brother's death to a killer who had murdered other men in the same way, she was unwilling to let go of the conviction that seemed driven by her personal dislike, even hatred, of Nugent.

There was something else, too. Stefan could hear it in her voice and see it in the fierce determination in her eyes. She didn't want to believe Vikram's death meant nothing, that he was simply in the wrong place at the wrong time. To find a way to accept his death, she needed him to die for India. She seemed to expect that Stefan, because he was Irish, would think the same way. She was frustrated that he didn't, that he felt, whatever Frank Nugent was, that the evidence that made her brother's murder part of a chain was real. Hindu didn't want it to be real. She had finally turned her distress on Stefan, almost accusing him of being in the pay of the English.

'I'm sorry,' said Mac Liammóir. 'I wasn't quite ready for that.'

'Me neither,' said Stefan.

'The deaths of the other men make it more complicated, Stefan. But I still thought what she said was odd. An English policeman, who turns out to be an Indian policeman, investigating the murder of a man he pretends he doesn't know, after following him round London, a man he beat up years ago in India. I thought you should know. It's still . . . I don't know what it is.'

'I'm glad I know. I am being lied to. That's always worth knowing.'

'Well, we're in England, Stefan. Would you expect anything less?'

Stefan Gillespie smiled. As they walked on, he was more thoughtful.

'I understand Miss Narayan feels . . . that she wants . . .'

'Yes,' said Mac Liammóir, 'if he had to die, she wanted a hero.'

The two men separated. Stefan Gillespie crossed Regent Street, Micheál Mac Liammóir walked on through Piccadilly Circus to the Regent Palace Hotel. Stefan stood, taking out a cigarette and lighting it. He thought he would walk up Regent Street and back before returning to the High Commission. He would probably stop at a pub. He needed another drink. Most of all he needed to clear his head and think how he would handle Chief Inspector Nugent the next day, whether to play the game and see where it led or call him out. What Nugent was doing was only Stefan's business in so far as it concerned James Corcoran and a man who had now murdered five times. It was easy to forget that with Hindu Narayan's face still in his head. And

Frank Nugent's callousness was in his head too. It seemed he had hardly spoken to Vikram's sister. He had been uncommunicative. He owed her more of an explanation, certainly more of his time, surely. He owed her the assurance that her brother's death did matter and that everything was being done to find the man who had killed him. Yet Stefan also wondered, did Hindu Narayan want to listen?

Drawing on the cigarette, Stefan moved back up Regent Street. He noticed a car pull out ahead of him. It moved to the left and drove away towards Oxford Circus. He recognised it even in the darkness. It might have been simply another black car, but it was the car he had been in and out of several times that day. Chief Inspector Nugent would not need telling where Stefan had been that night or who he had been talking to. Wherever Nugent got his information, he was good at his job. He had been watching the restaurant. Stefan smiled, then he groaned. The sound of sirens filled the street as they cranked up and wailed. He could hear bombs – one, two, a third – not close, south of the river. But coming his way. He turned round, heading for the Underground, joining the growing stream of Londoners.

8

Greek Street

The next morning Stefan Gillespie walked through Soho to Greek Street. He had called Scotland Yard and he knew Chief Inspector Nugent was at Vikram Narayan's flat. The morning was cold. In the air there was the smell of smoke; behind it the sour scent of the incendiaries. There had been bombs in Marylebone and the Euston Road, but nothing closer. The city went about its business and the streets were busy with people going to work. The street market Stefan passed was stacked with vegetables. A uniformed constable stood outside 24A Greek Street. Parked in front was the black Austin Stefan had last seen heading north along Regent Street the previous evening, carrying Frank Nugent away from his surveillance.

'Chief Inspector Nugent here?'

'He's upstairs, sir.'

'Inspector Gillespie.'

The constable nodded. His expression said, *Oh, you're the Irish one, are you?* A mixture of suspicion and wry amusement. But he spoke officiously.

'The room at the top, sir, right up. You'll find a couple of footprints marked on the stairs; if you could manage to avoid stepping on those, please.'

'I'm sure I can manage that, Constable,' said Stefan, smiling.

The door to Vikram Narayan's flat was open. It was no more than a room with a tiny bathroom, almost in the attic of the building. The small window let in little light; the bedside lamp and the overhead bulb were on, even though it was a bright day outside. Stefan stood in the doorway, unobserved, taking in the cluttered room. He could see the bed. He recognised the corner of the room from the photographs he had already seen. Elsewhere, books were stacked in piles against the walls. Several suits hung on the kind of rail you'd find in a shop. The room would have been drab and cold – that was its normal condition – but the walls and the chairs were draped with variegated Indian cloths and hangings. It was a kind of brightness that faintly echoed the Veeraswamy, and it made him think again of Vikram's sister. Frank Nugent was looking through a chest of drawers. There was a flash of light; a photographer in the bathroom, taking pictures. After a moment another flash. Across the room, a man in plain clothes placed items in a series of cardboard boxes on top of a small table. Another detective. The chief inspector stood up, catching sight of Stefan.

'Come in, Stefan. The place has been dusted to death, no worry.'

Stefan crossed the room towards Frank Nugent.

The photographer emerged from the bathroom.

'Is there anything else, sir?' he asked.

'I don't think so. You're happy?'

The photographer nodded, putting his camera into a bag.

'Give him a lift back to the Yard, Sergeant.'

The other detective nodded.

Stefan was standing by Nugent, as the two men left.

'Anything new?'

The chief inspector pushed the bottom drawer of the chest back in. It was full of books; it slid shut with difficulty. He struggled to push in two top drawers, overflowing with the unremarkable stuff of a seemingly cluttered life.

The wall behind the chest was covered with pictures of actors and film stars, cut from magazines. They were pinned and pasted over one another. Stefan scanned them, picking up some faces he knew. Humphrey Bogart, Marlene Dietrich, Katharine Hepburn, Cary Grant, Laurence Olivier, Spencer Tracy, Noël Coward. There were some he didn't recognise. He thought they must be theatre actors. He recognised a young Micheál Mac Liammóir.

On top of the chest of drawers were several photographs. Three were in frames, one glass crystal, the other two silver. One picture was of Vikram Narayan. He was in a suit, smoking a cigarette, wearing a monocle. It was a posed photograph, taken on a stage. He was dressed for a part. Stefan recognised Narayan's sister, Hindu, in the second photograph. The third was of an older man and woman, posing stiffly in a studio. Stefan could see they were the parents, from the images of the two faces he had in his head, the dead brother and the sister he had spoken to last night. There were other, smaller photos. They included pictures that must have been taken in India; groups of young men and women; a family gathering where he recognised, again, both Vikram and Hindu; a picture of what looked like a class of schoolboys. Then Vikram on a camel, with a pyramid behind him; a picture of him on the steps of the British Museum. Frank Nugent shoved the last drawer in with a grunt. He took the photographs of family and friends and put them in one of the boxes.

'There's a footprint by the bed, with traces of blood, paper over it now. The same inside the door. Replicated on the stairs. Someone going out and going down. Not Mr Mac Liammóir's print. In fact, his shoe is partly covering the one by the door.

Which confirms he was here afterwards. The killer had already gone.'

As Nugent packed several more items in the boxes, Stefan walked to the bed. It had been stripped of sheets and blankets. The pillows had gone too. It was only a bare, grubby mattress on a brass and iron frame, rusty in places. There was a book on a table by the bed. Stefan recognised the brown cover and the gold lettering of a book he knew, an anthology of poetry: Palgrave's *Golden Treasury*. He sat on the mattress and opened it. Inside the cover was a bookplate: *Vikram Narayan, For Excellence in English, La Martinière College, Lucknow*. He had the same book at home. His mother and father had given it to him as a present. There was a bookmark. Stefan turned to the page; a poem he knew well. He hadn't looked at it in many years, but he knew it. The poem began on one page, but it was book-marked where it ended.

> Ah, love, let us be true
> To one another! For the world, which seems
> To lie before us like a land of dreams,
> So various, so beautiful, so new,
> Hath really neither joy, nor love, nor light,
> Nor certitude, nor peace, nor help for pain;
> And we are here as on a darkling plain
> Swept with confused alarms of struggle and flight,
> Where ignorant armies clash by night.

Stefan closed the book and got up. He was here because of a dead man in Ireland, but he already knew more about the dead man in England. But not as much as the man now writing a list of contents of the cardboard boxes knew, though he pretended he didn't. Stefan watched Nugent. The chief inspector, wearing white cotton gloves, put a black camera and a long steel lens into one of the boxes. It was a striking item of equipment in this room full of books and clothes and bright oriental colours and ordinary clutter. It didn't belong.

'What's that?'

'The photographer tells me it's a Leica camera with a 50 millimetre lens and an Elmar 135 millimetre telephoto lens. He wouldn't mind the telephoto lens himself.'

'And it's Narayan's camera?'

'It's here, so yes.'

'What would all that cost?'

'Enough.'

'A lot.'

'Yes.'

'The conversation in the club . . . the idea that he was on his uppers. Bollocks. But that's why Mac Liammóir was here. Couldn't help him any other way, but he could give him a bit of cash. That camera equipment is real money.'

'He wasn't short of money,' said Nugent. He picked up an envelope from another box. 'Under the mattress. There's over a hundred pounds there.'

'So, what does that tell us?'

'I don't know.'

Stefan Gillespie looked at Nugent for a long moment, then smiled.

'I'd have thought Indian Political Intelligence could do better than that.'

Nugent grinned.

'I did assume Miss Narayan would have filled you in on that.'

'I suppose now you've stopped watching her brother, you've got time to watch her. Or were you just watching me, for the crack, one Special Branch man to another? You need to do better than the car you drove me around in.'

'I can do better when I need to. Come on, I'll buy you a tea, Stefan.'

*

Inspector Stefan Gillespie and Chief Inspector Nugent walked away from the wooden cabman's shelter in Soho Square with mugs of tea. Two taxis were parked outside the green, shed-like building that served hot food and drink to cabmen. There were similar buildings all across London. They kept strange hours and they were open in the early mornings when nothing else was. The steam from their metal chimneys was a welcome sight on a cold night, and all the more so in the blackout. They were meant to be the preserve of taxi drivers, but the men who ran them recognised a detective when they saw one. When there were no detectives around, they said it was simple: simply by the smell.

'I wasn't expecting you to meet Miss Narayan, I have to say.'

'She got fuck all from you. She wanted more.'

'She's a very determined woman.'

'She wasn't very happy to find you in charge of the investigation into her brother's death. And why should she be, given the background?'

'What background is that, Stefan?'

'They didn't send you from India because they're short-staffed on the Murder Squad. You're here to watch Indians, nationalists, politicians, whatever they are, and you've had people on her brother . . . I assume since he got here. It's only a pity someone wasn't watching him the night he died. You knew who he was, that's the thing. What sort of fucking conversation were you having with me about a dead queer in a mortuary, knowing who your man was?'

'I had to decide what was your business and what wasn't.'

'And have you, Frank?'

'I don't know yet. It depends what I'm investigating.'

'I would have thought that was the one thing that was straightforward.'

'Is it? What would you do with an IRA man in Dublin who'd been hacked about like that? Would your first thought be: *He must have been chopped up by a maniac*? Or would you want to know where the feller'd been, who he'd been talking to, what he'd been up to, before you settled on your madman?'

'It's hardly the same thing.'

'Isn't it? There are some very nice chaps who want an independent India, I can assure you, and I've lived in India long enough to think they've got some fucking right to want it. But it's like all these things, Stefan, some of these chaps are nicer than others. Some of them want to march through the streets and join Mr Gandhi in fasting for freedom, and some of them wouldn't mind a holiday in the Emerald Isle to take an IRA course in making bombs. And there are those, given the time that's in it, as you might say yourself, Stefan, who'd like to see if Mr Hitler couldn't help them do things faster than Mr Gandhi. You've got IRA men in Berlin. Well, we've got Indian nationalists there. A Mr Subhas Bose, in particular, there right now. You may remember him coming to Dublin a few years ago. Despite the meetings with Dev, and the reception at the Shelbourne, Terry Gregory was keeping an eye on all the IRA men Bose was talking to as well. Mr Bose has friends in Ireland that are not friends of Dev's.'

'You know more than I do, Frank. It's before my time.'

'I think I do, Stefan. It wouldn't have mattered whether your friend Mac Liammóir wanted to give Narayan a job or not. He's on a list of Indians who won't be allowed into Ireland whatever happens. I know, because I drew up the list. And I don't doubt your Superintendent Gregory has a copy of it, along with G2, Customs and Excise, the Department of External Affairs and Uncle Tom Cobley and all. But then I don't imagine Mr Gregory tells everyone everything.'

Stefan laughed. 'That would be putting it mildly.'

The two men turned back to the cab shelter and put the mugs down at the hatch. They walked towards Soho Square and into the gardens. For a time they said no more. Stefan was aware that he was out of his depth.

'Miss Narayan,' said Nugent quietly.

'Yes,' replied Stefan.

'A remarkable woman.'

'She wouldn't have a great deal of time for you, Frank.'

'No, she wouldn't, I am aware of that.'

'And you wouldn't blame her.'

'I could tell you that I didn't break her brother's ribs myself in Delhi, but I'd be lying if I said I told the men who did to stop. I left them to it. But that's how it works sometimes. You won't like the kind of man who'd go in for that sort of thing yourself, but I doubt you haven't stood by and watched it, or at least heard it. I doubt you haven't shaken your head and ignored it. We're in the same job. I don't do it because I like it. I've long forgotten why I do it at all.'

Stefan had nothing to say. It was a simple truth.

'I should have been prepared for Hindu Narayan. She arrived at the Yard. I didn't know what to say. She's not a woman with any predisposition to believe me anyway. Starting with what happened, the simple facts. Did she want to hear me say her brother was possibly killed by a man he'd picked up in the street? Probably a stranger. A man he'd gone back to his room to have sex with. And the details of the death . . . It's still something I can't put out publicly, for reasons that have to do with the investigation. You understand that. I have men out asking questions, trying to look for sightings, people who knew Vikram. I don't want too much knowledge on the street. I want to ask questions without creating panic. There aren't many homosexual men who will talk to the police. It's softly, softly. It has to be.'

'You'd think Hindu would understand that,' said Stefan.

'Up to a point. She knows . . . and then she doesn't. She's protected him for years, even from his family. I think she's kidded herself into the bargain.'

'But you've had men watching him, Frank. You know all about him.'

'I haven't had anyone watching him.'

'That's not what Miss Narayan thinks. Why wouldn't she be right? You tell me Narayan was a nationalist. He was too dangerous to let into Ireland because he had what . . . contacts with the IRA? If you weren't watching him, what were you doing? She knows it backwards. She knows who you are. She knows why you're here. That's why she thinks you've got something to do with his death. Why not, when she finds you in charge of the fucking investigation? I don't know you and it looks like a cover-up to me!'

'I didn't say there aren't things to cover up.'

'I see. Well, I suppose that's honest enough.'

'It doesn't mean there's not a real investigation. It doesn't mean I don't want to find the man who killed Vikram, as well as the others. I owe him that.'

Stefan heard something different in Nugent's tone, something more real.

'You owe him?'

'Yes. It's not something I can explain to his sister.'

'Because she wouldn't believe you.'

'I don't suppose she would. I'm not sure I'd want her to.'

'I think you've lost me, Frank,' said Stefan.

'The reason I wasn't watching Vikram Narayan was because I didn't need to. He was doing the watching, from inside the nationalist movement. I know what his sister thought. That's the lie. She didn't know. But Vikram had worked for me since he was in India. He was my agent. The first thing I had to do was decide if he'd been murdered because someone found out the truth.'

Stefan nodded. It wasn't pleasant, but it made sense.

'I can't see how that's likely,' continued the chief inspector, 'given what we know about the other murders. But what I have to ensure is that this investigation reveals nothing about Vikram being an informant. He has to remain the man his sister thinks he was. There's a whole chain of connections, other informants – going all the way back to India and the Congress Party – that could just disappear. You know how these things tie together. He wasn't that important, but he knew people. He was trusted. Because of his family. You know that, too. Isn't it the same with Republican families in Ireland? The Narayans are people who matter in the independence movement, in the Congress. It's in their blood. The daughter's not called Hindu for nothing.'

'I'm not here to cover up your shite, Frank. It's about murder.'

'I know. I am here to pursue that. As for what I've just told you . . .'

'I don't care. Just cut the lies. It's not my business to tell anyone else.'

'Not even Superintendent Gregory?'

'If you cared about that, you wouldn't have said it.'

'You'll be heading to Ireland now, but you might want to steer clear of Hindu Narayan. If she thinks you're useful, she's persistent. I don't mind her telling her friends her brother's death has something to do with Indian Political Intelligence. It even suits the story. But I don't want to make my lies your lies.'

Stefan had decided not to talk to Hindu Narayan again. He didn't want to lie to her and now he knew too much to avoid lying, even if what he knew was only part of the truth. He had just one thing to carry back to Ireland and it was nothing to do with India, Indian Political Intelligence or Chief Inspector Nugent's Special Branch operation in England. He would pass what he had been told on to Terry Gregory, though. There were issues between the Irish and British governments, even about what was going on halfway round the world, in India, that mattered to them both. It didn't have to matter to him. It was only another stone he had looked under by chance. But there was a murder no one appeared to care much about in Ireland that would now not be forgotten. In the middle of the mess that was Special Branch and Intelligence and the misinformation of war, there was a real crime and there was real police work to do. He wanted to hold on to that. Not for any principle, but because it was, out of nowhere, something solid. It seemed, despite his doubts, that it was solid for Chief Inspector Nugent too. There was little about Nugent to trust, but what there was related to the murder of Vikram Narayan. Stefan did not think that Nugent had told him the whole truth, but that didn't matter. He believed that when the shite was shunted aside, the IPI man wanted to find Vikram's killer. That would do.

He took the afternoon train from Euston to Holyhead. There had been a message at the High Commission from Hindu Narayan, asking to see him. She left a note with Miss Foye, saying there was something she needed to tell him. He ignored the message. As the train pulled out of London, he regretted it. He did not want to face her, with what he now knew about the brother she so loved and so believed in, but he felt shabby about sneaking away. She was, as even Frank Nugent acknowledged, a remarkable woman. If he did not want to confront her, with a head full of evasions, he was sorry he hadn't seen her again.

9

Thomastown

Thomastown, Co Kilkenny

It was three days later that Stefan Gillespie got off the train from Carlow at Thomastown, the next stop after Kilkenny. It was a small country town on the banks of the River Nore. Once it had been bigger; the street of scruffy buildings still clung to a kind of elegance. It was a Norman town, like so many in Leinster. It lay claim to a ruined castle and a ruined abbey that reflected a long-forgotten importance. Thomastown sat in a softer countryside than the town Stefan had left that morning before dawn, Baltinglass. Apart from the bright colours of the houses in the main street, the Kilkenny town could almost have been English. With the high, bare hill that rose up behind it, and the Wicklow Mountains beyond that, Baltinglass could never have been anything other than Irish.

Stefan had spent the night at home in Wicklow, with his eleven-year-old son, Tom, and his parents, David and Helena. He had been there only a few hours and was surprised to find an atmosphere that was colder than usual. Tom had little to say and spent most of the evening out in the fields or in his room. The book Stefan had bought in London, *The Hobbit*, was, at least, a success, and if Tom was in his room it was partly because he was absorbed in it already. But the atmosphere was not right. David Gillespie had a lot to say about nothing in particular, which was always a sign that he had something else to say that was being avoided. Helena produced more food than anyone wanted and worked at pretending nothing was wrong. There were things wrong that Stefan knew about. There were problems at the farm; there had been for some time now. The year before, the fact that David Gillespie was getting older came as a surprise to no one but Stefan. He could do less work and some of the land was let to a neighbour. There wasn't as much income. Stefan's Garda salary mattered more than it had done. His father didn't want to accept that it did, but he had little choice. There were tensions where there had been none before, but this time Stefan felt it was something else besides. If there was ill-temper, it was between Tom and David. He had not seen temper in his son before, not in a way that somehow felt quiet and resentful. It was more adult than Stefan was used to. Tom was changing. Things that had been simple, childlike, were more complicated. It had been there at Christmas, but barely. Now it filled the farmhouse. Stefan had no idea whether the atmosphere was a spat or something more serious. With only a few hours at home, he took the easiest way and ignored it. He left his questions unasked, hoping that next time he came home they would have evaporated.

James Corcoran's mother and father lived in a house on the outskirts of Thomastown, in the constituency Rory Corcoran represented in the Dáil. The TD was at home for the weekend; Stefan wanted to speak to him. It was there that the contents of James Corcoran's room at St Patrick's College were stored, in the trunk they had arrived in. It was well over a year now, fifteen months, because the months were still counted. There was still a room that belonged to the dead man. Stefan had established that it was virtually untouched. It wasn't unusual. When a death was so far-reaching in its impact, it could be a long time before the dead were allowed to leave. Things that mattered could not just be thrown away. Stefan was grateful for that. There might yet be something to find.

He left the railway station with directions to the house. He walked through the town and out the other side, along the River Nore. He did not call at the Garda barracks, as protocol required, though he walked past them. He knew Superintendent Carberry from his time in uniform at Baltinglass, but he had nothing to ask. He would give the Corcorans what privacy he could. One minute's conversation at the Garda station and all Kilkenny would know.

Stefan had arrived back from England to find that Dessie MacMahon had already established a murder room in a small storeroom, away from the main Special Branch offices. He had brought all the information that related to the death of James Corcoran from Maynooth. The files and statements, the photographs of the scene and of the body, the boxes of evidence from Donadea. The boxes contained the blood-stained picnic rug, the beer bottles, the bread knife that had inflicted the savage wounds, and even a bag that held the remains of the bread the knife had been used to cut beforehand. A note explained that a piece of cheese and some sliced ham had been disposed of. It was an example of attention to detail that Stefan Gillespie wished could be seen elsewhere in the investigation. Another box held the clothes that James Corcoran had been wearing, along with an envelope containing woollen fibres that had probably come from the killer's clothing. Against a wall leant the bicycle James Corcoran had ridden from Maynooth to Donadea. Both tyres were flat. Stefan would look at all this material. He would look again at the reports, the statements, the photographs, the maps. He already knew that he would be lucky to find anything. If there had been more to find at the time, something would have come of it. One thing mattered. One thing that, put together with the investigation in England, might lead somewhere, eventually: the fingerprint.

Superintendent Terry Gregory was less interested in the murder Stefan Gillespie was now investigating than he was in the Metropolitan Police Special Branch, Indian Political Intelligence and Chief Inspector Frank Nugent. That was what he wanted to talk about when Stefan finally sat in his office again. The presence of a small Indian community in Ireland, mainly in Dublin, was not something Stefan was unaware of, but he didn't know it had any significance, let alone that it was under surveillance by G2, Military Intelligence, and had been before the war. Terry Gregory's magpie-like passion for collecting information, including the least shiny and obviously useful information, was in full view. Stefan had information about the Indian community in London; there were links to Ireland. It didn't matter how slight. This was information G2 might want. That made it a precious commodity. Special Branch and Military Intelligence were as much competitors as colleagues. They watched each other as closely as they watched the various players who were in their sights. They had different roles and different targets, but they never let that stop them straying into each other's territory. Terry Gregory, in particular, had a loose sense of where his own remit began and ended. If there were things G2 kept to themselves, they were, by definition, things he wanted to know about.

'You remember your man Bose, Subhas Chandra Bose?'

'Nugent mentioned him. Isn't he in Germany now?'

'Yes. He was here in 'thirty-six.'

'I read something about it. I wasn't in Dublin then.'

'Bose was a big man in the Congress Party. In India he's not as big as Gandhi, but he's there with Nehru, at least he was. Now he broadcasts on Berlin Radio. He was the hard man, so. The others want constitutional change. He wanted a boatload of guns and explosives. The only thing different from Ireland is that the gunmen don't run the show there. I guess he got fed up. If they won't fight, maybe the Germans can instead. Does that sound familiar?'

Stefan nodded. He didn't reply. Gregory mostly was talking to himself.

'So, your man Nugent was in England when Bose was here. At the Special Branch office in Holyhead. One man and a dog to keep an eye on who's on the mail boat.' Gregory took out a cigarette, though he didn't light it. 'Busier now, I'd say. He didn't come here at the time, but they had people watching Bose. He wrote to me, though, Nugent. He said he was only being helpful. He suggested Mr Bose was trying to establish links between the IRA and the Indian Congress Party. He said Bose had met and conversed with people of all political classes of opinion.' The superintendent laughed and then lit his cigarette. 'It's a phrase I've always remembered. But he was right. Bose met de Valera and then proceeded to meet most of the people in Ireland who'd decided, by that time, that the Republican cause would be best served by a bullet in Dev's head. There was a distinct cooling towards Mr Bose on Dev's part. Your man was welcomed with open arms, because we support Indian independence, but the people he ended up with were either gunmen or communists. And his best friends in Europe were Herr Hitler and Signor Mussolini. Mr Nugent said we might want to know the Italians had been caught trying to get money and arms to anti-British elements in India. Elements being Mr Bose's part of the Congress Party. Anyway, Nugent wanted our cooperation. We declined at the time, though I suspect Dev made his feelings about Mr Subhas Bose known to Messrs Nehru and Gandhi. He wasn't asked back.'

'If the IRA can't get Germany to invade Ireland, it's a long march from Berlin to Bombay,' said Stefan. 'Haven't the English got bigger problems?'

'They had bigger problems than Ireland in nineteen sixteen. Look at us now! If the Congress Party isn't exactly supporting Britain in the war, it's standing back. If that changed, if India blew up like Ireland did . . . that would be some problem.'

'I'm sure it keeps Mr Nugent busy, sir.'

'But he's got time for a dead homosexual. Why's that?'

'Well, we have too. What's the alternative? There are people dying by the thousands, tens of thousands, everywhere. So, do we just forget about murder?'

'Is that a bit of principle I see surfacing? Be careful, Stevie.'

Stefan laughed.

Superintendent Gregory pushed a typed list of names across the desk.

'This is from the Department of External Affairs. A list of Indians not allowed into the country from Britain. You'll see your man's name: Vikram Narayan. It's a list the English supplied. We haven't even bothered to have it retyped. They don't give much detail but contact with Bose is one reason Narayan is on the list. In nineteen thirty-six, when Mr Bose was on his way back to India, his ship docked in Alexandria. He wasn't allowed off, in case he stirred up trouble in Egypt. Mr Narayan was one of the people who went on board to meet him. That's the year the Gate Theatre toured Egypt and Narayan had his brief encounter with our great actor. Narayan was one of Bose's people in Egypt.'

'Except he wasn't. He was working for Nugent and the IPI.'

'Who knows?' said Gregory. 'But he was up to his neck in it, one way or another. So? Well, Dev's got a lot to say in support of Indian independence, as ever, but when the political posturing's done, our interests coincide with our friends' across the Irish Sea, for now. Or at least as far as we can throw them.'

'And Chief Superintendent Nugent?'

'The short version is that G2 is now doing the IPI's job for them in Ireland. I doubt there's much that goes on in the Friends of India Society here that won't end up on Nugent's desk. Most of what the less respectable Indian nationalists are doing with the IRA in London lands on mine. Apart from what we chose to keep to ourselves and vice versa, as ever, ad infinitum, Amen! And it's always cosier than you think. Chief Inspector Nugent's boss in India is a Superintendent Philip Vickery, a Fermanagh man, and educated at Trinity, like you. Who knows? If he'd stayed in Ireland . . . he'd probably have my job now.'

'Is that some kind of warning, sir?'

'You can never know too much. These deaths are another contact with English Special Branch. If you get anything interesting from Nugent, tell me.'

'What about the murders, sir? Are they of any interest?'

'Is that a sour note of indignation, Stevie? Tut! The murders are yours. If I've got other priorities, that's what I'm paid for. It might look like my in-tray is populated by clowns playing at spies, and IRA men on the piss, but the line between the clowns and the tanks rolling down O'Connell Street, whether they're German or British, could be no more than a fucking clown with a stick of gelignite. You just do what you're told and leave the moral debate till there's no war to get in the way. There'll be time then and I'll be happy to listen. Assuming we come out the other end as we went in, with God's grace . . . and the fellers who follow the tanks don't arrive with a bullet . . . for every man here.'

Terry Gregory stubbed out his cigarette and grinned.

He crossed himself.

'This is the word of the Lord. Thanks be to God.'

He stood up. Stefan did the same.

'I'll want to talk to Mr Corcoran, sir, James's father. Since I am reopening the investigation, someone should tell him, before I pitch up on his doorstep. I will have to explain what's happened in England. That's what's brought us back to the case. It's hard to tiptoe round. I think we're beyond not mentioning his son's homosexuality out of politeness. Did he ever get his Cabinet post?'

'Not yet. He's still a junior minister. Agriculture.'

'You'll tell him?'

'He complained we weren't doing enough at the time,' said the superintendent. 'I don't know if he'll like it any better now we're back. But that's not a sin, is it? It's not easy looking into the darkness, Stevie. We forget that sometimes. Or we get too used to it.' There was something close to compassion in Gregory's voice. 'You'd hope the wound was healing now.'

He shook his head. He was brusque and businesslike again.

'He's an important man. The Commissioner can tell him.'

'Yes, sir.'

The superintendent frowned; the other story was still in his head.

'Your man Nugent will have a reason for this. Vikram Narayan.'

Stefan wanted to get on with the job; the rest didn't concern him.

'Does it matter?'

Terry Gregory gave him a wry, equivocal smile. It always mattered.

The Corcorans' house was some way out of Thomastown. It was a solid, square, Georgian farmhouse, but it had been built out from an older structure. Once it had belonged to planters; the equally solid English middlemen who bit by bit had become more Irish than English, though they barely knew it. They did the work that kept the Ascendancy, the rootless upper class that England had planted in Ireland, in the avaricious idleness that was its only reason for being there. Now the house was home to the family of a Deputy in the Irish parliament. It was kept with the neatness it always knew. The lawns were tidy. There were dark rhododendrons the size of trees, which an earlier occupant had brought from the Himalayas. The windows were big and bright; the frames had recently been repainted. Old, warped glass and new white paint shone in the winter light.

A young woman answered the door. Sorcha was a maid or a housekeeper; she worked there at least. Stefan recognised the accent of Kerry. He walked into a hall full of dark, heavy furniture. It looked as if it had come with the house. A man in his fifties came out from a room off the hall, thin, grey-haired, balding.

'Cé hé, a Shorcha?' He asked who it was.

'An tUasal Gillespie, an póilín.'

He was introduced, in Irish, as the policeman Rory Corcoran was expecting. The question was only asked so that the Irish-speaking habits of the household were established. Stefan recognised a particular kind of house, where Irish was spoken in a sea of surrounding English. It was a statement of what should be rather than what was. It was likely Corcoran and his family were not native speakers. Sorcha, the woman who let him in, would be. It was one reason she was there. Rory Corcoran stepped forward and stretched out his hand.

'You found us then, Inspector.'

'I did, sir.'

'Come through, will you? Have you come down from Dublin?'

'From Baltinglass, my family are there.'

'Another ruined Cistercian abbey by a river!' Corcoran smiled, but Stefan could feel the tension, as he followed the TD into a big room that was the politician's study. It was lined with books, meticulously tidy. Two sofas stretched out in front of a walnut desk. A turf fire smouldered, as turf fires do.

'Please, sit down.'

Stefan sat on one of the sofas.

'Will you have some tea?' The deputy stood by the fire.

'I won't, sir, but thank you.'

'Ned Broy spoke to me yesterday. I understand the investigation into my son's death is being reopened. There's new information. He didn't go into many details . . . I gather it's because of a murder in England that is in some way . . .' He left the sentence unfinished.

'There have been several deaths in England, in fact: four now. All in London except one.' Stefan spoke carefully. 'All very similar to your son's.'

The door from the hall had opened. A woman had come in. She was pale, slightly fragile. Her face was lined in a way that made her look older than she was, maybe in her late forties. Her hair was black, somehow younger than her face. Her lined features were accentuated by a frown of dark seriousness.

'Cén fáth nach raibh tú a glaoch orm?'

She asked why Corcoran hadn't called her. She was slightly irritated. The Irish didn't hide that. But her face softened. She understood why he hadn't wanted to. Her voice was gentler as she looked from her husband to Stefan and back.

'Ná déan iaracht mé a chosaint.'

She didn't need to be protected, she said. Stefan understood. He imagined that Mrs Corcoran must have been beyond the kind of protection that meant not talking about her dead son for a long time. She was looking at him again now.

'I'm sorry, Inspector . . . I'm Mary Corcoran,' she said.

'Inspector Gillespie.'

'You must think we're very rude.'

'Not at all, Mrs Corcoran. Más mian libh Gaeilge a labhairt . . .'

He had asked them if they wanted to continue in Irish. Corcoran looked surprised. He may have already made enquiries about the policeman who was coming from Dublin

Castle. He may have picked up, even in a few words, on the almost invisible signs that told any Irishman who was a Catholic and who was a Protestant. Mrs Corcoran smiled and shook her head. It was a gesture of politeness on Stefan's part, but he also knew the fact that here a knowledge of Irish made him a little more trustworthy than he had been a moment earlier.

'We'll stick to English, Mr Gillespie,' said Corcoran.

He sat down. His wife remained standing.

'You were talking about other men being killed,' said Mrs Corcoran. 'And you think the same . . . the same person was responsible. It's hard to take in. This was in England . . . how can you be sure? You are very sure, I take it?'

'We are very sure. I don't think it would help you for me to say . . .'

'No,' said the deputy. 'I don't think it would.'

'It's terrible,' continued his wife. 'How many . . .?'

'With your son, there are five murders. So, this investigation is now being led by the police in England.' He paused. The point needed making, even if it felt unwelcome. 'I don't know what more we can find out here, but I want to look at a number of things, in particular what came back from St Patrick's. Do you still have your son's possessions – the things that were in his room there?'

'Yes, Inspector,' said Mary Corcoran softly. 'It all sits where it's sat . . .'

'I don't know that there is anything we can really tell you, Mr Gillespie,' interrupted Corcoran. 'Every question that we could answer, we answered. But this awful thing . . . came from nowhere. We knew nothing. It simply happened.'

Stefan Gillespie was silent for several seconds.

'I am interested in how James was, in the days before.'

'He was in Maynooth,' said the deputy.

'Did you hear from him?'

Mrs Corcoran went to the mantelpiece. She took a cigarette from a silver box. She picked up a heavy, onyx lighter and lit the cigarette. She turned back.

'He did telephone to say he would be coming home, the next weekend.'

'And how did he sound? What sort of mood was he in?'

'He was quite cheerful. He didn't say a lot.'

'Did he say anything more?'

'That he'd sent a letter. And we would talk about what was in it . . .'

Stefan watched Rory Corcoran shift uncomfortably.

'And what was in it?'

'In what way, Inspector?' asked Corcoran. 'I don't know what anything my son could have written in Maynooth has to do with dead men in London.'

'I'm trying to understand your son. It may help, it may not. But the days that led up to his death are important. I think they are. I don't want to intrude . . .'

'But you have to.' Mrs Corcoran smiled.

'I do.'

'We have the letter. It arrived . . . after he died.'

'I'm very sorry. Did it tell you what he wanted to talk about?'

'He wanted to leave the seminary.'

Rory Corcoran stood up.

'I don't understand the point of this, Gillespie. Every priest will have doubts about what he's taking on. It's a vocation, not a job. A lifetime's commitment to God. He was dealing with it like any young man. He wanted to talk. He needed reassurance. How on earth does that relate to being killed?'

Mary Corcoran stepped closer to her husband and touched his hand.

'I'll take Mr Gillespie to James's room, Rory. I'm sure I can answer any questions. I know you have a lot to do before you go back to Dublin, darling.'

Deputy Corcoran nodded. He seemed to diminish in stature; the fragile figure beside him seemed to grow. She was the stronger. Coming into the room she'd looked timid, nervous. Stefan could see it was the other way round. The man who was a public figure, a TD, a government minister, a strong pair of hands for his party in Kilkenny, was the one who wanted to run from what Stefan was there to talk about. There was, after all, the Emergency, the word the Irish government used to describe the war that wasn't quite a war, yet. It was all-consuming. The business of running the country was no bad place to hide.

'I'll be here if you need me, Inspector.'

Corcoran walked to his desk and sat down. He opened a briefcase.

'If you'll follow me, Mr Gillespie,' said Mrs Corcoran.

Stefan Gillespie left the study with her. The junior minister looked down into the briefcase on his desk for a long time before he finally took anything out.

Mary Corcoran led Stefan Gillespie through the house and out into the back garden. They walked along a shaded path, where the rhododendrons were bigger and older. They came to a wooden shed-like building, painted in grey with two curtained windows on either side of a door. It was a peaceful, welcoming place.

Stefan followed Mrs Corcoran inside. She walked from one window to the other and opened the curtains. It was a single, large room. A bed, a table; a small kitchen at one end, with a basin and cooker. There were bookshelves against one wall. In front of one window was a desk; in front of the other was a chest with candles, a crucifix and a statue of the Virgin Mary.

'We call it the annexe, and Rory used to work here when we first came to Thomastown. But James always wanted some-where of his own – really his own – from when he was a teenager. And when he said he was going to be a priest, it seemed even more important that he had his own . . . a special kind of space.'

Stefan looked round, taking in the room. It was simple and calm.

'I do understand, Mr Gillespie, that these terrible murders . . . I don't want details. I know enough . . . I know too much . . . too much that will never go away . . . I understand that they have to do with what James was . . . in some inexplicable way these other men died because of that. I don't know what to say about James's homosexuality, except that Rory and I pretended it didn't exist . . . or that being a priest would end it. But if you have something to say, please say it. If there are things my husband can't talk about . . . I am far beyond that.'

'I'd like to look at the things that came from Maynooth. I'm not sure anyone looked at his room in the college. If they did it's not mentioned.'

'There's a trunk, over there, at the end of the bed. I've never opened it.' Mary Corcoran pointed across the room. 'I can leave you, if that's all right.'

She turned back towards the door.

'Thank you. I would like . . .'

'Yes?'

'The letter he wrote. It must have been one of the last—'

She cut him off, almost with anger in her voice. This was very hard.

'I'll get it, Mr Gillespie. You don't need to explain.'

Stefan walked slowly round the room. There was little to see. The bookshelves carried a mixture of books. It was what you would expect in the room of a young man who had not long stopped being a boy. Among the missals and the catechisms and the books on theology and philosophy, there were still books James Corcoran had read as a child. Stefan went to the trunk at the foot of the bed. He pulled up a chair and sat down, opening the lid. One by one he took out the items that were inside. There were clothes, neatly folded and pressed. A black overcoat, sweaters and corduroys and the black uniform of the seminarian. There were more books: bibles in Latin and Greek, a Hebrew Old Testament, prayer books, dictionaries, the works of the great theologians of the Church: St Augustine, St Anselm, Thomas Aquinas. There was a heavy missal, full of underlinings and abbreviated notes. Half a dozen novels, some maps, a guide to Rome. There were folders and notebooks full of essays and notes, in a small, tightly written hand, neat but hard to read. Then a bundle of letters. Most were from his mother; some from people Stefan worked out were brothers and sisters. There were letters written on Dáil notepaper, from his father, short, uninformative, but often funny. There were postcards with pictures of cities: London, Paris, Vienna, Jerusalem, Rome; some had been pinned on to a wall.

That was it. A torch, batteries, some glasses and cups. They were things that should be looked at for prints. There was no reason to believe that the man who killed James Corcoran had ever been at St Patrick's College, let alone in James's room, but it should have been done in any thorough investigation.

At the bottom of the trunk there was a small tortoiseshell box with an elastic band to keep the lid on it. Inside were several pieces of paper and a champagne cork. The pieces of paper included a bill from a restaurant in Dublin, a receipt for the purchase of a book from Hodges Figgis in Dawson Street, and two tickets for the Metropole cinema in O'Connell Street. The restaurant bill and the receipt were dated: five days before James's murder.

There was a knock at the door. Stefan got up and went to open it.

Mrs Corcoran held out an envelope. She looked less strong than she had.

'This is the letter.'

She turned and hurried away.

Stefan walked back to the trunk and the pile of the contents he had laid out around him. He sat down and opened the letter. It was the same neat, slightly cramped hand he had already seen, just made bigger and more legible. The letter was written in Irish. Not a long letter. There was only one paragraph.

I will try to get home next weekend, to talk to you both. I will plant the thought now, without explanation, so the thing isn't a complete shock! I have come to realise that much as I love it, the priesthood is not for me. I think I have to face that and do what's right, what's right for me. Surely God would want that? I think I have to look at my life in new ways. Don't worry about this. I am actually very happy, in a way I have never been, in a way I have never let myself be. I don't know what that means, and I'm not sure where it will take me. It may take me out of Ireland. My life has been all 'odi et amo' till now, even if I haven't let myself face it, hating what I love, hating myself most. There is another way. I have seen that in the last few days. So, don't worry. Trust me. I will make sense of it all. I can now. I know myself better. I'm happy, remember that. That's what I have to tell you above all else. I love you both. See you next weekend.

Stefan Gillespie looked at the date on the letter: four days after the restaurant bill and bookshop receipt; the day before his death. Stefan would not immediately have made sense of 'odi et amo' in the letter, except that the Hodges Figgis receipt told him where to look. The book Corcoran had bought was a Loeb edition of Catullus's poems, Latin with an English translation. Stefan had just seen another copy of those poems on James's bookshelves as he had run his finger along a line of titles. The phrase 'odi et amo' was in there, Stefan remembered. He found the book and flicked through it. 'Odi et amo. Quare id faciam requiris. Nescio, sed fieri sentio et excrucior.' *I hate and I love. Why, perhaps you ask. I don't know, but I feel it and I am tortured.* Stefan reread the letter. There had been torture, self-hatred, now joy. He recalled the conversation with James's friend at St Patrick's, over a year ago. Happiness, a different kind of happiness. Why keep a receipt and a restaurant bill in a box with two cinema tickets and a cork? The champagne was on the bill. A wild extravagance for a seminarian at St Patrick's. Love tokens; only love turned bills and cinema tickets into treasures. The date was right. James had met someone in Dublin. Someone who changed his life. The man who killed him the next time they met.

10

Scoil Naomh Iósaf

In the windowless storeroom that contained the flotsam and jetsam of James Corcoran's murder, Superintendent Gregory read Stefan Gillespie's handwritten report, a series of scribbled notes on two days' work. Dessie MacMahon sat on a chair, leaning against the wall, smoking a Sweet Afton, content, for once, that he was doing something that felt like police work. Gregory was in no hurry to finish. Stefan waited for a response. He had one more thing; some real evidence.

'It's nothing new,' said Gregory. 'You thought he'd met someone.'

'We know now. I can't see there's any doubt it's the man he arranged to meet for a picnic in Donadea. We know the date. We don't know how they met . . . if they'd met before, but we know what they did, where they went . . .'

'None of that identifies the man, or does it?'

'Not yet. Not a year on. CID should have been out in Dublin—'

'They weren't,' snapped the superintendent. 'Next?'

Stefan looked at Dessie. Dessie sat forward on his chair.

'Two assistants in Hodges Figgis recognised a photo of Corcoran, even though he hadn't been in there since then. He was a regular customer, over three or four years. He had an account. Mostly books on theology, the classics, some poetry. They don't remember that day, or him being in there with anyone.'

'The restaurant?'

'No,' said Stefan. 'I showed them a photo. They didn't know him.'

'I doubt they did at those prices,' said Gregory. 'Cinema? Not a chance.'

'I have a theory about the Catullus.'

'Does it identify the fucking killer?'

'No, sir.'

'That's helpful then.'

'There was no Loeb Catullus in his room at St Patrick's. He already had a Latin edition at home. It seems likely he bought it as a present for this man. We know there was one poem that meant a lot to him. It's even in his letter home.'

'I don't need a lesson, Stevie. I was no slouch at Latin.' Terry Gregory grinned. 'I was thinking of going into the Church at one time. You see, no one ever believes that. If they still had the Inquisition, I might have gone for it.'

Stefan and Dessie offered the laugh the head of Special Branch expected.

'When you find a maniac with a knife in one hand and the poems of Gaius Valerius Catullus in the other, I'll get straight on to Chief Inspector Nugent.'

'This has gone cold for over a year, sir. I'm putting together what I can.'

'I know, Stevie.'

'Someone is going to be picked up, sooner or later, probably in England. That's what it looks like. When he is, there's a lot to prove . . . it will all count.'

'All right, I know that too. What about this champagne cork?'

Stefan picked up a cellophane envelope. This was something real.

'You see the metal bit on the top, where the wire's attached?'

Gregory nodded.

'There's a thumbprint. Very clear. The print we have on the beer bottle, from the picnic, is also a thumb, the same thumb. It's a fragment. It might not even be enough to identify. But it matches this. And this is more than enough.'

Gregory sniffed. It was better. It moved things forward, a little.

'Good. That's something, Stevie . . . something solid.'

He walked to the door. He looked back; a decision made.

'It's time G2 put up some fellers for the courier run. You're back on Castle duties. You can keep an eye on this.' He shook his head amiably. 'When you pick up the feller with his knife and his Latin poetry, we'll be laughing. But keep your fingers crossed our friend Nugent is doing better in London.'

The weekend brought Stefan Gillespie home to the farm below Kilranelagh, and more days there than he had spent since a Christmas that had been brief. The conversation he had to have with his father, about the coolness between Tom and David, was unavoidable. When Stefan learned what had happened, though he recognised a problem, he also recognised his father's instinctive urge, shared with most of his Protestant neighbours in Catholic Ireland, to keep his head down. He felt that what had happened didn't mean much; it could be resolved without a lot of trouble. Ultimately it was about those things Stefan had seen himself recently. It was about Tom growing up, thinking new things, finding new ways to look at the world. But if he was rebelling, David Gillespie was right to be cautious about where that led. Tom's new ideas, combined with a stubbornness that made him not unlike his father, were touching on things that affected the family from outside, in particular ways. In the past they had caused deeper problems for Stefan, David and Helena, and for Tom himself, when he was too young to know it.

Stefan went to the fields above the house, the first morning he was home. He saw Tom coming out of the trees, where a steep wooded valley that marked one of the boundaries of the farm led down to a stream. The boy was absorbed in his own thoughts. The sheep dog, Jumble, walked patiently at his heels. Tom and the dog were still inseparable. But a year ago, there would have been a game; boy and dog running, chasing. It was a small thing, but it marked real change.

Stefan waited as Tom saw him and approached.

'You were out early,' said Stefan.

'I wanted a walk.'

Father and son moved together across the field of grubby, winter sheep.

'How's *The Hobbit*?'

'It's good. I finished it.'

'That was quick.'

'I read fast enough if I like something.'

'What's it about?'

'I don't know. *The Iliad* with dwarves and dragons . . . and a lot funnier.'

'I never read it. I wouldn't imagine *The Iliad* being big on fun.'

They laughed and moved on. Tom was anticipating what was coming.

'You're still doing Latin with Mr Cashman after school?'

'Yes, I like it.'

'You know he doesn't have to do the work to get you ready for a scholarship exam. Opa's tried to pay him something, but he won't take it.'

'I know. John Byrne's doing it too.' Tom grinned. 'He doesn't like it.'

They were both postponing the reason Stefan was there.

'I wish you and Oma talked German to me when I was young. I only know a few words. That's what I want to do, German and Latin, and Greek too.'

'That's very ambitious.' Stefan smiled. 'I don't know about Greek, but I did Latin because I had to. And I didn't much enjoy it. I did German because I spoke it, so it was an easy subject. But it depends where you go to school.'

Stefan had delayed long enough.

'You know the parish priest's been to see Opa and Oma?'

There was little left of the German heritage that Stefan's mother had brought to the Gillespie family as a young woman. Helena had spoken German with him, as a child; he still spoke it well. He had visited his cousins in Germany when he was a teenager. All that had faded with time and distance, but Tom still used the German words for grandfather and grandmother, Opa, Oma.

'I know.'

'You haven't been going to Mass.'

Tom shrugged.

'And you've been lying about it to Oma and Opa. You started off making excuses for not going and when you ran out of those, you pretended you were going and never got there. What have you been doing on Sunday mornings?'

'Nothing.'

'Nothing?'

Tom shrugged again.

'There's other lads than me who don't want to go to Mass.'

'Tom, you know enough about how difficult things are . . .'

'What's that got to do with me? Nobody asked me what I thought about all that. I don't want to go. I don't see why I have to.' His face hardened. 'I don't believe in it. What's the point? It isn't school. I'm not learning anything.'

Stefan and his son said nothing for a moment.

'You know some of this, Tom, but not everything. Let me say it.'

Tom sniffed, irritated, impatient.

'When I married your mother, because I was a Protestant, I had to promise that any children we had would be brought up as Catholics. That didn't change because she died. It was a promise. You might say a sacred promise.'

'And would you have kept it, Daddy, if they hadn't made you?'

It was a sharper question than Stefan expected.

'All right, maybe the answer to that isn't so easy. Maybe you're right. You know a bit . . . there was a time . . . before you started school . . . I don't know if you remember it now, but you went to stay with your uncle and aunt for a while.'

'I sort of remember. I've stayed with them other times. That didn't seem any different, but I know what happened. I know people tried to take me away.'

'Maybe taking you away is putting it more strongly . . .'

Stefan stopped. There was no point trying to retell the truth.

'There was a particular priest who didn't think you should be brought up in a Protestant home, even if we did take you to Mass and send you to a Catholic school . . . and do everything we had to. It got a bit out of hand, and yes, the Church did . . . but it was sorted out. I think they knew they were wrong.'

Tom was silent. He sensed there was pain, and anger too, which his father still felt. It opened up a memory that time had not softened.

'We've kept the promise, Tom. You went to school at Talbotstown, the way they wanted. We took you to Mass or you went with your friends. You took your first communion with your friends at school. We're still keeping the promise. You've got your confirmation coming up. Then suddenly we have the parish priest complaining you're never at Mass, and

Oma and Opa don't even know. They go off on a Sunday to church in Baltinglass. And you just piss off!'

'I wouldn't have to piss off if they let me do what I want.'

'And you've told Mr Cashman you're not doing your confirmation.'

'I don't believe in it. That's what it's about. Saying you believe it.'

'At least Father Brennan doesn't know that.'

Tom stopped. He bent down, scratching Jumble under his muzzle. He was holding back anger of his own. Stefan turned, waiting for him.

Tom stood up, then smiled slightly. 'Do you believe it, Daddy?'

Stefan saw that although they had never had this conversation, his son knew the answer. It was not something he could sidestep, let alone lie about.

'I believe in what I know about the teachings of Jesus . . .'

It was weak; even Tom, at eleven, knew how weak it was.

'I have read bits of the Bible,' said Tom. 'I quite like some.'

Stefan laughed. 'That's a start.'

'You don't believe it, Daddy. You don't believe what the Church says. And it's not just about Mass, is it? Do you go to the Church of Ireland in Dublin?' Tom walked by Stefan, more confident. 'Oma doesn't think you do.'

'Well, Oma doesn't miss much.'

Stefan took out a cigarette. It felt like Tom had the upper hand.

'But you're not old enough to make that decision. You will be. But you need to make it for yourself. To make it when you know what it is you believe and what you don't. I think that takes more time than eleven years, Tom.'

'Nearly twelve.'

'More time than nearly twelve.'

'Don't you mean, shut up and do as you're told? No one

needs trouble. That's what I get from Opa. He won't say it to me, but I hear him tell Oma.'

Stefan drew on the cigarette. He tried to bring conviction to what he said next, but he knew his son would hear its absence. If he believed what had to be done, what had to be said, it was for reasons that wouldn't bear much scrutiny. He wasn't far from telling Tom to shut up and do as he was told.

'Avoiding trouble isn't such a bad thing, Tom. You need to go to Mass. You need to make your confirmation with everyone else. Maybe, as time goes on, we can say . . . you made your confirmation, that's the promise fulfilled. You'll be leaving Talbotstown next year. You'll be somewhere else, if things work out. You'll be boarding. When you're home, it will be different. For now, it is like school. I'm sorry. That's how I have to put it . . . and you have to do it.'

Later that day Stefan Gillespie took the tractor from Kilranelagh towards the long, high hill of Keadeen and the school at Talbotstown that sat in its shadow, at the furthest edge of the mountains. The tractor's link box carried a heap of cut black turf for the fires in the school rooms at Scoil Naomh Iósaf, St Joseph's School. The turf was a contribution parents made to the school through the winter and it was the Gillespies' turn. There was little else at Talbotstown, except for the crossroads and a farmyard and a shop that was only really another farmhouse, with a bar in the front parlour. It was the school and the church that brought people there. Otherwise it was a peaceful, unremarkable place; a junction of quiet roads, a scattering of fields and then Keadeen beyond.

Stefan and the school principal, Michael Cashman, said little as they unloaded the turf in the store behind the low stone building next to the church. The teacher was in his fifties; a quiet, solitary man, now teaching his second generation of children. He had a lot to say to the pupils he taught but kept his own counsel with his neighbours. He was highly thought of, commanding a respect most priests in the area assumed they had, but rarely did. He was as unremarkable as his school and the battered pipe that was never out of his mouth and was mostly unlit. He kept himself to himself. He worked unassumingly, tirelessly for his school. People knew what they owed him.

'You'll want a cup of tea, Stefan.'

'I will, Michael.'

'And the chat you came for.' The teacher smiled.

'And that, too.'

The two men sat in front of the fire in the big classroom. The fire was too small for the room, and however much turf was piled on it the children sometimes sat in their coats in the worst of the winter. Michael Cashman filled his pipe and lit it till it blazed up, but it was soon out, and he would not bother to light it again.

'I appreciate what you're doing with the Latin.'

'Ah, I enjoy it. If I'd been a secondary teacher, that's what I'd have done. So, it's a bit of recreation. I'm hammering it into Tom because I want to.'

It wasn't true, but Cashman was uncomfortable with gratitude.

'I think Tom enjoys it too,' said Stefan.

'I hope so. It's not something he has to do for a scholarship, but he can, and it will help. They like some Latin. And it will help him when he starts.'

'Is he up for a scholarship?'

'Oh, I'd say he's well up for it. It might not cover everything.'

'I reckon if we had to pay, we'd find the money,' said Stefan. This was something he had only been thinking about recently – where Tom went when he left the school at Talbotstown – but his mother and father had thought about it longer. If they needed to pay, the way the farm was now, with Stefan's Garda salary subsidising it, it would be harder than it might once have been. But a way would be found.

Michael Cashman looked into the fire, chewing his pipe.

'There's the question of where he goes.'

'Well, Knockbeg would be first. It's closest, even when he's boarding. Maybe Clongowes with a good scholarship. I doubt we'd run to that otherwise.'

Stefan listed the two Catholic boarding schools that were nearest.

'That's the conversation the parish priest had with me, so I imagine he's had it with David and Helena too.' The principal laughed. 'He'll be having it with you soon enough, if you're not fast on your heels and keep out of his way.'

'I don't mind if he does. I've nothing to argue about with him.'

'No?' said Cashman, with a look that was almost conspiratorial.

Stefan frowned. 'Should I have?'

'We should talk about the other thing, Stefan. God and confirmation!'

Stefan laughed. 'A conversation I'd like to avoid having with Father Brennan.'

'He doesn't know anything about the fact that I now have a declared atheist in sixth class, nor does he know Tom's told me he doesn't want to make his confirmation. Obviously, he does know Tom's been missing Mass. He's on the warpath. I don't need to say he takes it seriously, more seriously than if Tom was living in a Catholic family. There's a point he has to make, do you see?'

'Oh, I see very clearly, Michael.'

The principal got up and bent down by the fire, knocking the contents of his pipe, largely unburned tobacco, into it. He stood up again and put the pipe in his mouth, not caring to refill it. He was serious, thoughtful.

'The trouble is all this goes quite deep with Tom. That's what I think.'

'How do you mean?'

'I only have the gist of what happened, before he started school here, between you and the Church. I'd be bound to know something when it involved you punching the curate in the face in Baltinglass.' He smiled briefly. 'And I'm sure Tom has only a bit of it himself, but he has enough, so. Too much, I'd say.'

Stefan nodded, not sure what this meant, but recognising a truth.

'I think he'd be better off out of it, Stefan.'

'Out of what?'

Michael Cashman sat down again.

'This isn't a conversation anyone else can know about. Tom is strong willed. I don't mean he's difficult, but he's hard to shift from what he thinks. That's true on everything. Sometimes it's good and sometimes not. At his age, not everything he thinks is reasonable. Not that I'm saying it's unreasonable for him to reach a point when he doubts the existence of God. He's got there earlier than most. What he now sees . . . is that in Ireland, you keep your mouth shut.'

'Yes. I don't think he takes to that idea.'

'He doesn't. He's too young to see why he can't say what he thinks.'

'It's a strange time,' said Stefan. 'I don't know him as well as I did.'

The principal smiled. 'You'll know him again . . . in a few years.'

'You still haven't told me what "getting out of it" means.'

'What Tom feels about the Church goes deeper than whether he believes in God, or whether he's asking questions and not getting honest answers. Whatever happened when he was younger, along with all the years he's had to lead a separate life from his family on a Sunday morning . . . they have left a mark. Some children would deal with that more easily. Tom's not easy. He doesn't take things easy. Partly, it's that thing about not knowing where you belong. Being outside. Even if you rebel, you need to fit first, I think.'

'And where does that take us, as far as school goes?'

'I don't mean you give up. He could go to the Tech in the town, and it wouldn't be hard. He'd fit in well and he'd come out in a few years looking for a job. And the only effort it would have cost him would be to sit tight and shut up. You're right to want more than that. My worry is that if you put him in a Catholic boarding school, it's doubling down on everything he doesn't want. He might be getting a great education, but he'll be in and out of the chapel, on his knees, on a daily basis. If he fights, they'll give him a hard time. I don't want to say they'll knock it out of him, but he has it in him to be bloody-minded. There's no room for that. Not believing is . . . he's turning it into a way of saying who he is. I wouldn't want to put money on him staying the course.'

'That all sounds good, Michael! Thanks.' Stefan shook his head.

'I'd say you need to take another course,' said Cashman gently.

'And do what?'

'Take on the Church again. Leave it behind. It's time to change.'

Stefan said nothing, waiting for the teacher to explain.

'Take him out of it all . . . and send him to a Protestant school. Not because it's Protestant, but because it's simply something else. Put him in for a scholarship at Kilkenny or Wesley College . . . Wesley's where you were. He knows that. He won't tell you, but he's talked to me. He wants to know why he can't go there. He won't even say it to David and Helena, because you'll all tell him he can't. You'll tell him he has to do what Father Brennan says. That's it.'

'If Father Brennan's on the warpath about him missing Mass . . .'

'Time has passed, Stefan. You've done enough. You've done what you promised. Tom's had eight years of being taught how to be a Catholic, most of it from me. Until the last few months, he was the best Mass-goer in the school. He made his first communion. He's about to be confirmed by the bishop. You can stand your ground now. He's a Catholic, in every way the Church means. You only have to say that's not going to change. Tom can say it too, whether he wants to or not. Send him to the school you want to send him to. Just do it. We'll keep it quiet as long as we can, so the fuss doesn't last when it comes. There'll be a row with the priests. But he'll be twelve, going on thirteen, when he moves. I'll pretend I'm disappointed . . . while I'm working my arse off to get him a scholarship. That's my advice, Stefan. But I never said a fucking word.'

Stefan laughed.

'You do one thing, though,' said the principal. 'You tell Tom what's happening, and you tell him to keep it to himself. He will do that. I know it. Then you tell him he goes to Mass every bloody Sunday and never misses it. You also tell him he will be confirmed . . . along with everyone else in the class.'

'I see,' said Stefan, taking it in. It was another way to think, after many years of thinking only one way. It seemed to bring clarity, though he was still unsure. 'It's one hell of a lesson in deceit, Michael!'

The principal took out his tobacco and started to refill his pipe.

'Maybe it's a lesson in survival. Sometimes we have to learn those.'

Almost a month and a half had gone by at Dublin Castle. The door of the room which held the evidence from the murder of James Corcoran was locked most of the time. There was nothing more to gather in Ireland, no more information to pass on to Chief Inspector Nugent at Scotland Yard, and no information from him to come to Ireland. The Metropolitan Police had pursued their inquiries, spreading out from the scene of Vikram Narayan's killing, looking for witnesses, for anyone who had seen anything, looking for the Indian's friends and contacts. The results produced nothing that tied anybody to the events of the night of the murder. There was nothing that led anywhere as far as witnesses were concerned. Shadowy figures in the streets of Soho in the blackout; a man on a bicycle, or maybe a woman; a car parked nearby, black or grey or dark green, quite big, not that big. All the other murders, with the exception of James Corcoran's, looked like chance meetings: two men who met for sex, in places where men did meet for sex; two men who almost certainly didn't know each other. But even putting together the last days of Narayan's life wasn't easy. The two areas of his life that the police were looking at were both environments where the police were unwelcome. In London's homosexual world the police were always to be feared. The ability to live any kind of ordinary life depended on secrecy. For some of the people who were working for Indian independence, the war had brought a new need for secrecy. They were being watched as they had never been watched before. For both of these groups, giving information to the police was to be avoided.

Stefan Gillespie had returned to the business of watching and reporting on his countrymen. On those who were at the fringes of the IRA. On the hard-line Republicans waiting for the defeat of Britain and, if it could happily coincide, the replacement of de Valera's government. On those with too many connections to Germany or Italy or, in anticipation of events elsewhere, to Japan. On those who were too loud in their enthusiasm for Britain as well, and on those who kept quiet about their connections with Britain but were working for the British government. As always, too, there were the reports and records kept on the men who left Ireland to fight with the British forces. The lists of these did not tell the whole story, as so many found their way to England to work and then joined up. For the first time, Stefan was sent to report on meetings of the Friends of India Society, who gathered at the Country Shop in Stephen's Green. Superintendent Gregory seemed to have decided that his relationship with Frank Nugent in London qualified him to do this.

He attended several lectures on Indian crafts and one on the life of the Buddha. The society was mostly a way for Indians in Dublin to meet socially, but there were a few IRA men who showed an unusual interest in the crafts of the subcontinent and occasionally disappeared into the back room of the Country Shop for tea and biscuits. The prime movers of the Friends of India Society were an enthusiastic English couple, Mr and Mrs Hurley-Davis, who had moved to Ireland at the beginning of the war. They were more vehement in their support of Indian nationalism than most of Dublin's small Indian community. Terry Gregory, who had little interest in what happened at the Country Shop, thought they were British agents. Stefan's reports on the society were passed to Military Intelligence, from where, once anything useful or revealing had been removed, he assumed they went to British Intelligence, probably to end up on Chief Superintendent Nugent's desk.

Stefan had not heard from Nugent on the murder cases for over a month, when he was called into Gregory's office one evening. Frank Nugent was phoning from London. There was a development, although it had not come through the investigation, and it had arrived from a very long way away.

'Nugent's got something,' said Terry Gregory. 'Another murder.'

Stefan took the telephone.

'What's happened, Frank?'

'Another one.'

'Jesus! In London?'

'No, not in London. In the Mediterranean, in Malta.'

'Malta?'

'That's right. It's come straight to the Yard because a Military Police sergeant in Valletta remembered something similar, when he was a copper. He wasn't on the case, but he couldn't miss it. The same way you didn't . . .'

'No doubt?'

'None, for my money. I've seen the photos.'

'Everything the same?'

'Yes. Happened in a park, near a queer pick-up place. The dead man was a young Maltese. No doubt he was queer. No evidence again, not so far. Don't know what the forensic work's like there. No witnesses to speak of, but maybe a sighting of the dead man with a solider, not long before. No real description of the soldier, but it fits in with what we already know. And there is some hope . . .'

'Which is?'

'Well, Malta's under siege at the moment. It's being bombed round the clock by the Germans and the Italians. No shortage of soldiers. But getting people in and out isn't easy. Everything comes by convoy, and they're being attacked. So, what we know is that since Vikram Narayan was killed in Greek Street, seven weeks have gone by. In that time only a couple of hundred soldiers have arrived in Malta. Some were already in Gibraltar when Narayan died. In terms of soldiers who were here seven weeks ago and are in Malta now . . . we're talking about less than a hundred. That's suddenly a small pool to fish in.'

'Very small.'

'He has to be there, doesn't he?'

'Well, I'd say so.'

'So, I've booked your flight,' said Nugent, laughing.

'Booked my what?'

'This is a Metropolitan Police and Garda inquiry. You're the one who's produced the fingerprints that are going to hang this feller. I don't know whether there'll be an argument about where he's hanged. I suppose we have the numbers. But I assume you want to be in Malta, to find him and arrest him.'

'And how do I get there, Frank?'

'Get to London and the RAF will do the rest. Plane to Gibraltar, on to Malta. Always a chance of getting shot down over the Med. Apart from that . . .'

Stefan looked up at Superintendent Gregory.

'Do you know about this, sir? Am I going to Malta?'

'I'll talk to the Commissioner, but we want this off the books.' He grinned. 'And done right. Plenty of room for Scotland Yard to cock it up.'

The words were for Nugent to hear. Stefan returned to the phone.

'Well, seems that's what's happening . . .'

'I'll fill you in when you get to London. You'll need to leave tomorrow.'

'All right.'

'One thing . . . Hindu Narayan, Vikram's sister . . .'

'Yes.'

'She was knocked down by a car. A month or so ago. She was lucky. The car was going some. She was injured but she came away with not much more than a broken ankle. It was her head more than her leg they were worried about.' Stefan almost heard a smile. 'But she was fed up carrying her tin hat, so she'd put it on. These things happen in the blackout, of course. You wouldn't think so with everyone crawling along. The car drove off . . . driver didn't stop.'

The last words were slower, almost hesitant.

'Anyway, she came out the other side,' said Frank Nugent after a pause.

'You make it sound as if you don't think it was an accident.'

'She doesn't think it was.' The chief inspector laughed. 'She reckons Special Branch did it, because she was asking too many questions about her brother. You've met her. You won't be surprised she doesn't trust anybody.'

'Let alone you.'

'Let alone me. I have tried.'

'So, who do you think would want to harm her, Frank?'

'I don't know what I think. It was very odd . . . that's all I can say. She was just coming out of the restaurant. I don't know why I'm telling you this. It's nothing to do with the investigation.' Nugent stopped, as if not convinced of that. 'Anyway, if we find the murderer, she won't need to ask any more questions. She might not want to know what really happened, but I think she ought to understand that I've done everything I can to find Vikram's killer.'

The change of subject had contained a change of tone. Stefan heard concern and uncertainty, different from the breezy assurance of what went before. And there was something personal in it. It seemed to matter that Narayan's sister knew what Nugent had done. But the breeziness returned. A few more words set up another phone call to finalise the arrangements. And then the Englishman was gone. Stefan handed the phone back to Superintendent Gregory, who was scribbling notes in his familiar, virtually illegible scrawl.

'What do they want me for, sir?'

Gregory looked up and shrugged. He considered for a few seconds.

'I can think of a number of reasons. Given where all this started, they still have it in mind this feller might be some mad Irish queer. Once the English get hold of an idea, you have the bollocks of a job getting them to let go. And if he is Irish, whether he's a British soldier or not, a Guard's name in the papers will hammer that home. And to be fair, Chief Inspector

Nugent needs to be sure. They've got a lot of murders, but they don't have much on this man. They're not going to catch him red-handed. Mad or not, he leaves no trace. It's only a bit of circumstantial evidence that will identify him. Now there's a chance. And we have the only solid evidence. You're the officer who found the complete print. So, if you're there when the arrest is made, that looks good in court.'

Stefan nodded.

'Then there's the politics,' continued Gregory. 'If it all goes wrong, and you don't find anyone, it spreads the blame. Scotland Yard won't mind shrugging it off as if we're the ones who pushed the thing when there wasn't enough to go on. Sure, wasn't it all about keeping on the right side of the fucking ungrateful, neutral, bastard Irish? Because you can bet your life there's already a row about this in London. The British Army won't take kindly to a civvy policeman poking his nose into their business in the middle of a war. They won't care about the other crimes. You know how these things go, Stevie. This is Military Police territory. If there's a butchering maniac in the ranks, he's their butchering maniac. Nugent will get a cold reception in Malta, I'd say.'

Superintendent Gregory paused for a moment, then grinned. 'It may do him no harm if an Irish detective gets an even colder one.'

PART TWO

DE PROFUNDIS

*T*he much looked-forward-to Charlie Chaplin film, The Great
Dictator, has arrived at long last in Malta, and will be
shown at the Manoel Theatre. The Great Dictator was
produced, written and directed by Charlie Chaplin, and in it he
plays the dual role of Hynkel, Dictator of Tomania, and a Jewish
barber . . . This is the first film in which Charlie Chaplin talks.
The Great Dictator has been shown all over America and in the
non-dictatorship countries of Europe and has been everywhere
acclaimed as one of his greatest comedies.

*The following qualified in a Colloquial Maltese Test and have
been awarded £10 each by the General Officer Commanding: -
L/Cpl. Gaunt, J., C.M.P.; L/Sgt. Andrews, W., 24ᵗʰ (F) Coy, R.E.;
Capt. Bolton, J.R., R.A.M.C.*

Times of Malta, 1941

11

Mare Nostrum

Malta, 1941

The Sunderland flying boat flew east from Gibraltar through the night. It would reach Malta just before dawn. The plane was safe enough leaving the Rock. It would not be at risk from the fighters of the Luftwaffe and the Regia Aeronautica until it came close to the tiny island that sat between Italy and the coast of North Africa. It was at its most vulnerable there, where German and Italian planes from Sicily dominated the skies, but as a solitary plane, emerging from the western darkness, close to dawn and a lull in the bombing of the island, it had every chance of slipping unseen into the RAF's seaplane base at Kalafrana. The Sunderland carried precious spare parts for the handful of decrepit RAF fighters that barely defended Malta against almost daily bombing. It also carried medical supplies, a generator, a dozen searchlights. It was little enough. The RAF kept its fighters flying by cannibalising the ones shot down in ever-increasing numbers. Food and fuel and ammunition, which were all running out on the island, and the desperately needed replacement aircraft could only be brought in by ship, and it was a long time since a convoy had got through from Gibraltar. Too many ships were being sunk to risk more losses. Malta was under siege and the siege was becoming costly in every way. In Berlin and Rome, it was believed that the island that stood in the way of the campaign to sweep the British out of North Africa and take control of Egypt and the route to India could not last much longer. If Britain was slow to put its ships in harm's way to save Malta, it was because some in London believed the same thing.

Stefan Gillespie sat in the front cabin with Frank Nugent. He had taken the usual route across the Irish Sea to London, then travelled with the English policeman to Poole on the south coast to board the Sunderland. The plane flew across the Bay of Biscay and followed the Spanish and Portuguese coast to Gibraltar, where it stopped to refuel and pick up cargo. The other passengers were senior army and navy officers, along with three young pilots, barely out of training, eager for action. The military men would travel on from Malta to Alexandria and Egypt, the Sunderland's final destination. The pilots were for Malta itself. The older men chatted cheerfully with the young to begin with, but after a while they ran out of things to say. They knew what the pilots hadn't yet begun to think about: outnumbered and with equipment the Luftwaffe could outpace and outgun, the young men would probably not be in Malta for very long. Like spare parts in the seaplane's hold, the pilots were there to replace what had already been shot out of the island's skies. The odds against them not being shot down in their turn were not high.

Between England and the Rock, Stefan Gillespie and Frank Nugent said little about the case. For a time, they asked each other more personal questions than they had before. Stefan spoke about his home in Wicklow, his son; he spoke briefly, in the matter-of-fact tone that went with the passing years, about the death of his wife Maeve, Tom's mother, simply as something that had happened that was no longer very different to many things that happen. At least that was how it could be talked about. Nugent spoke a lot about India. There was, as Stefan suspected, something Irish buried in him. His father had been from Waterford, his mother was English; he had been born in Cork. The family moved to India when Frank was a young child. He grew up in India; that was his place in the world, though he didn't say it. He went to school there; he spoke Hindustani and other Indian languages as easily as he spoke English. His father had worked for India's vast railway system and loved the country. His mother hated it. She did what she had to do, but when Frank's father died, she left for England within a week of his funeral. She lived in a bungalow in Worthing that contained not a single memory of over thirty years of her life on the subcontinent. Nugent had tried living in England himself. He lasted two years. He told the story easily, in little more than a few wry sentences. But Stefan was surprised how abruptly it stopped. The English policeman, who saw himself as an Indian policeman, was comfortable with the past and with some well-rehearsed anecdotes. However, he had very little to say about the present that wasn't work. He didn't say he was single, but no family was mentioned. Stefan recognised that silence as a barrier.

It was obvious to both Stefan and Frank that there was at least one Intelligence officer on the plane. He was the only one who showed interest in the two policemen. When they were waiting at Gibraltar for the Sunderland to refuel, he insisted on buying them a drink in the mess at the seaplane base. He introduced himself as Major Courtney, also en route to Malta. He expected some kind of explanation of what they were doing and was irritated by Nugent's cheerful refusal to give him one. He was more irritated to discover that Stefan was not even a British policeman. Frank Nugent offered no explanation for his journey to Malta, or for the fact that an Irish detective was travelling with him. Stefan offered no more than a polite interest in the Rock and went out to look at it. Nugent followed him, still amused. And then they boarded the plane again.

As the seaplane continued east in the darkness, the cabin was much emptier. The young pilots had drunk what they could during two hours in Gibraltar and had brought a bottle of whiskey on board. They started into that shortly after taking off, with the result that they were quickly asleep. Several officers sat further forward in the cabin, including the now sour Major Courtney, who sat as far from them as he could. Stefan Gillespie and Frank Nugent had the seats at the back of the cabin to themselves. Chief Inspector Nugent took a folder from his briefcase. He passed several sheets of paper over to Stefan: they were a closely typed list of names and army ranks.

'These are all – almost all – the soldiers who travelled to Malta between the date of Narayan's murder and the death in Malta. It may not be complete, but they should be able to fill in anything that's missing when we get there. Most of these men arrived on one ship, within a couple of weeks of Vikram's death. A few came in by plane over a longer period. There are only seventy-three. They include regular troops, Royal Engineers, medical corps and some Intelligence officers. I've also got a list of RAF bods. Naval personnel are more difficult to track. They come and go from Gib, North Africa, Egypt. But we start with the idea the man we're looking for is a soldier. If witnesses said they saw anyone in the vicinity of any of the murders, it was a soldier. That's consistent.'

'So, we just pitch up and fingerprint the lot of them?'

'That's the deal.'

'The deal?'

'This hasn't gone down well with the army.'

'Terry Gregory didn't think it would.'

'He was right. There's been a bit of political argy-bargy. In fact, we're only here because the Colonial Office managed to overrule the Ministry of War. I think they pointed out that the empire on which the sun never sets is asking the people of Malta to sit there while the Jerries and the Eyeties drop bombs

144

on them. From what I hear, apart from some Hurricanes, there's only a few clapped-out fighters, including fucking biplanes, for God's sake, to stop them. The last thing they need is a British soldier roaming the island with a carving knife. And that's what they've got. It's a small place. They want him caught and they want him out of there with a noose round his neck. Someone had the sense to realise the Military Police are too busy directing traffic and picking up drunken squaddies. Don't quote me. They do have an investigation branch. Officially, we're to assist the Provost Marshall and his merry men.'

'What about the Maltese police?'

'I don't know. Nobody mentioned them.'

'Isn't the dead man a Maltese civilian?'

'You're not in Eire now, old son,' laughed Nugent. 'In the colonies the military outrank the colonial police. I should know. I'm an Indian policeman. We're only a step up from the damned natives. Hardly to be trusted, let alone in the middle of war.' He looked more serious. 'And I'm not joking, Stefan.'

As the Sunderland droned through the night, more of the passengers drifted into some kind of sleep. Frank Nugent was one of them. Stefan Gillespie stayed awake for a time. He looked through the files the Englishman had laid out on the seat beside them. These were extracts from the investigations into all the murders that stretched from Donadea in Kildare to a park beside the Grand Harbour in Valletta. Stefan had seen the full files only briefly, in Nugent's office at Scotland Yard, fat yet empty of any useful content. He had not read them through in any detail but then there wasn't any detail, at least not detail that did anything other than describe the dead bodies. He was struck again by the barbarity and viciousness of the attacks. He was also struck, for the first time, by how little evidence had been left behind. It seemed unreasonable. So many killings, so little to hold on to. It was no different with the latest. No witnesses, no forensic evidence, no connections that led anywhere as far as the victim was concerned. They had only what came from Dublin, the fingerprints, and the assumption that the man was a soldier, now in the Malta garrison. Stefan Gillespie gathered the files together and pushed them into Nugent's briefcase. He took a cigarette and lit it and stared through a window at the dark.

Stefan had spent one night in London, sleeping in the room above the High Commission's offices in Regent Street. He knew from Frank Nugent that Hindu Narayan was back at the restaurant after the accident in Regent Street. She was only across the road. He felt he ought to see her. He phoned her at the Veeraswamy. She was cautious when she spoke to him. She assumed he was still in contact with Chief Inspector Nugent. He told her he was, but it wasn't the reason he wanted to see her. That wasn't entirely true. Frank Nugent had suggested he make contact with her, since she wouldn't talk to him. It wasn't a suggestion Stefan followed only because of Nugent, however. He was curious about Hindu Narayan.

He met her outside the restaurant in Regent Street, not long after arriving in London. They went to the Lyons Corner House at Piccadilly. She talked about her ankle and the time it took to heal and how inconvenient it all was.

'I did take to sleeping in a shelter or in the Underground. Otherwise it took me so long to get out of bed and get somewhere safe, if the sirens went off . . . normally, I used to wait for a raid and then make a dash.' She laughed. 'But dashing was out of the question for a while . . . So, I tried staying in shelters, but I gave up in the end. I hobble a bit, still . . . but I dash as quickly as I can, when dashing is required. I can't live down there like that . . . not every night.'

Stefan nodded. He had been in London enough to take more risks than he had at first. It wasn't entirely rational, but it went with the way of life in the city. There was a belief, almost in London's air at night, that if your number was up, it was up. Otherwise, you had as much chance as anybody else, inside or outside a shelter. It wasn't that people didn't care about their safety, but the bombing had been going on long enough to be familiar. People took chances.

Hindu Narayan pushed him on his contact with Frank Nugent.

'That's why I'm in London.'

'That's cosy. I'm surprised Indian politics is so interesting in Dublin.'

The remark was a kind of sneer, but Stefan was aware it interested Garda Special Branch and Irish Military Intelligence more than he had known himself until recently. He thought it was unlikely she wouldn't know that too. But if her words were meant to show contempt, they were also probing.

'I'm here because a man was murdered in Ireland. I did tell you about it before. It was over a year ago. He died the way your brother died. He was strangled, then mutilated with a knife, very violently, when he was dead. The reason I'm involved is because we're looking for the killer. That's all it is.'

Hindu said nothing. She stared past Stefan at Piccadilly Circus.

'There has been another murder now,' said Stefan. 'The same, exactly the same. In Malta. I think Chief Inspector Nugent tried to tell you that, didn't he?'

'He's tried to tell me a lot. Even when I was in the hospital.'

'Hindu, whatever's going on in terms of India and the English Special Branch and who Mr Nugent's watching and who he isn't . . . I don't know. You do know. You have friends who know. Your brother knew, I suppose.' Stefan spoke carefully; he knew more than he was saying. But he was used to half-truths. 'This is something else. Nothing to do with any of that. It's about a vicious killer.'

'Perhaps,' she said quietly. 'I wanted to believe something else. It makes it much harder . . . much harder, when a man like him . . . like Chief Inspector . . .'

'There is a good chance we can find Vikram's murderer now. That's why I'm going to Malta with Chief Inspector Nugent.'

'But why him? Why is he the one doing this?'

'It just turned out that way,' said Stefan.

It had turned out that way. He was unsure the word 'just' explained it.

The Indian woman nodded.

'I still can't be sure Mr Nugent had nothing to do with my "accident".'

'Why? What could he gain from that?'

'I kept asking questions about Vikram.'

'And did you find out anything?'

'I don't know. I tell myself it's all paranoia sometimes, I suppose. Or am I trying to make myself believe what I want to believe? Frank wants me to know he's trying to help. I don't want his help. I despise him. That's the truth.'

Stefan was conscious that Hindu had used Nugent's first name.

'The man still has to be caught,' he said.

'I tried to find out what I could,' continued Hindu Narayan. 'Whether I was right about what I thought or not, I didn't trust the police. Even if Vikram wasn't killed by them or IPI or some thug who worked for Chief Inspector Nugent, there were things nobody was asking. That's how it felt. My brother had been . . . frightened is the word, in the last few weeks of his life. He was suddenly desperate to get out of England. I still think . . . I thought that had something to do with why he died. I couldn't believe something so . . . arbitrary, so futile. I tried to talk to his friends, people he knew . . .' She waited for a moment. 'I am not talking about Indian friends, or political friends, I mean men he was close to. They avoided me. They got angry. There's a man he was . . . someone Vikram cared about a lot. He has a photography shop in Brixton. I went to see him. When I started asking questions he told me to go. He was shouting at me . . . upset, yes, but angry with me . . . then he cried. He begged me to leave him alone. It was the same . . . the same as Vikram, as if he was afraid of something. Yet the only people Vikram needed to be afraid of were the police.'

'You have to understand that the world your brother—'

'I know all that, Mr Gillespie. This was more. It was more.'

She looked at him for a moment and then shook her head. 'Am I looking for things that aren't there? I don't know any more.'

The conversation was over. Stefan knew Hindu Narayan believed what he had told her. It mattered that she did. He was aware that it mattered too, by proxy, that Frank Nugent wanted her to believe him. And it was the truth. What was happening in Malta, the search for the murderer, was all true. Stefan wanted to believe that the other things he knew, that Hindu's brother had been a double agent, working for Indian Political Intelligence, had nothing to do with it. He believed it, but he carried the deceit like a weight, nevertheless. By Lyons Corner House, at the entrance to the Underground, Hindu reached out and shook his hand.

'I hope you find this man in Malta, Mr Gillespie.'

'I think we will, Miss Narayan.' He smiled. 'You know it's Stefan.'

Hindu Narayan smiled too, for the first time with amusement.

'I do.'

She walked down the Underground steps, hobbling a little. He watched her disappear and turned away. He was glad most of what he said had been true.

★

The conversation with Hindu Narayan came back to Stefan Gillespie as he looked out of the window at streaks of pale, orange light spreading in the sky. The flying boat was descending. He could feel the change in pitch and hear a heavier drone from the engines. One of the crew moved through the cabin, telling passengers to fasten their safety belts. Frank Nugent had been asleep. He stretched, yawning. Dawn was barely visible, but as Stefan looked out again, he saw the waters of the Mediterranean, now darker than the sky.

'Almost there,' said Nugent. 'And still in one piece. Not bad.'

'You thought we'd be shot down?'

'Apparently it doesn't happen a lot.'

'I'm a neutral.' Stefan grinned. 'The word is probably out.'

Chief Inspector Nugent gathered up papers and clipped his briefcase shut. Stefan's head was still full of Hindu Narayan and the Lyons Corner House.

'When I saw Hindu Narayan, she was talking about a friend of her brother's. He has a photography shop in Brixton. Did you ever speak to him?'

'I think she was trying to run her own investigation at one point.'

'Because she thought you weren't.'

'Something like that.' Nugent's voice was brisker. 'But yes, I talked to him. Eddie Hopkins. I don't know if he was a boyfriend or they were just acquaintances. Hopkins is certainly one of the fraternity, put it that way. But he doesn't seem to know anything. He wasn't around at the time. He's not part of the Soho crowd. He hadn't seen Narayan for a week or more. What about him?'

'Well, I was wondering about that photographic equipment.'

'Yes, he bought it all there. Still can't see why. It was professional stuff. Expensive. And sod all use to anybody for taking snaps. Hopkins didn't know what he wanted it for. But I'd say he was happy enough to take the money.'

Stefan nodded. Nugent's investigation had been thorough, whatever Hindu thought. But it had been no more than a series of loose ends till Malta.

'You found a used film in his pocket, didn't you?'

'Yes. Didn't get anything out of it. Couple of shots of a man and a woman in a café, probably a railway buffet . . . could have been one of the big stations. Then there were some shots of the funeral at Kensal Green . . . where Mac Liammóir saw Vikram. Mostly out of focus. He could hardly use these lenses. Noël Coward was at the funeral.' Nugent grinned. 'The only surprise. There were some decent shots of Mac Liammóir with him. Who knows why?'

Stefan laughed. 'Perhaps he was a fan.'

Nugent shrugged. 'Whatever he was, he wasn't a photographer.'

The morning was suddenly there, as the heavy Sunderland glided down to the sea, closer and closer. There was enough light to catch the waves. Stefan could see the coast. Low, white cliffs, and beyond that what seemed like white, flat land and white stone in the pale light of dawn. What he glimpsed through the window was the corner of an island of tiny, stone-walled fields and bare, rocky land, scattered with small buildings that were simply another shade of white. The hull of the plane hit the water with a judder that could be heard as well as felt. The shock pushed Stefan into his seat. Engines raced; then they were quieter. The hull rocked as the Sunderland sailed into the RAF's seaplane base.

12

Kalafrana

The tender carried the passengers from the Sunderland flying boat to the quayside at Kalafrana. Even in the early morning, Stefan Gillespie could feel the heat the day would bring. At home winter was barely over, but the scent in the air, here where the sea met the shore, had warmth in it already. There was a brightness about the sky that gave clarity to the broad strokes that painted the dark sea, the grey-white land, the blue sky with its last tinge of orange on the horizon. At the quayside, a row of corrugated-iron sheds and breeze-block huts were draped in pale camouflage nets and painted in shades of brown and white. The soldiers and airmen, waiting by a row of Bedford trucks for the Sunderland to unload, wore the British Army's sand-toned tropical gear in various combinations of shorts and trousers, shirts and jackets. At either end of the quay two camouflage-covered anti-aircraft guns pointed up at the clear morning. Vans and staff cars waited by the steps up from a pontoon, and as Stefan Gillespie and Frank Nugent reached the top of the steps, a tall, lanky soldier walked towards them. He wore the red peaked cap of a Military Policeman. His shirt and his shorts were neatly pressed, in sharp contrast to most of the men in crumpled, sweat-stained outfits that were barely uniforms.

'Chief Inspector Nugent and Inspector Gillespie?'

He held out his hand. In the other he held two tin hats. He was older than either Stefan or Frank Nugent, but not much. His face was lined; dark and tanned from many months of Malta's sun. He exuded a kind of orderly calm, but a broad smile broke up the clipped officiousness of a very military voice.

'Jack Yates, Lieutenant, Provost Marshall's office.'

'Good to be here, Lieutenant, finally,' said Nugent.

'Bit of a trek. You'll need these.'

He handed them each a tin hat. They put down their cases.

'You'll want them soon enough. You've hit a bit of a lull this morning. It's not good at the moment. We get Jerry and Eyetie bombs. Hard to tell which is worse. The Jerries know what they're aiming at, so we can work out what they're doing mostly. The Eyeties drop them anywhere. No idea what they're after. If you're here long . . . you'll be glad to get back to London for a break.'

Yates turned to a younger man behind him, in a less well-presented combination of khaki shorts and tunic that bore an MP's armband on one sleeve and a corporal's stripes on the other. He wore thick-lensed glasses. In contrast to the officer's tanned face, his skin was pale. If Yates fitted, he looked out of place.

'I'll take that, sir.' The corporal took Nugent's case as the chief inspector reached for it. He took Stefan's too. 'And yours, sir . . .' He grinned. 'That's the way. Officers don't carry their bags. Can't have them straining themselves.'

'Jimmy Gaunt,' said Yates. 'If you want anything, ask him. Never mind if he looks a bit of a twit, he knows his way round this island, don't you, Corporal?'

'On a good day, sir.'

The lieutenant got into an open-topped, camouflaged Humber Snipe. Stefan Gillespie and Frank Nugent sat in the back. Corporal Gaunt was at the wheel. They left the Sunderland, Kalafrana and the Mediterranean behind.

The Humber pulled out of the base on to a dirt road. As it joined a metalled road, cracked and pitted, Gaunt stopped, waiting for a low-loader to pass. On it was the fuselage of a Hurricane fighter, along with sections of wing and cockpit. The fuselage was black, buckled. It had been burning not long ago.

'Bastards,' said Lieutenant Yates. 'Most of our fighters belong in a bloody museum. u/s the lot. They only keep them flying by cannibalising what's shot down. Let's hope the poor fucker got out OK. We're running out of pilots too.'

The moment of harsher reflection fell away almost immediately, and as they drove to Valletta and reached the perimeter road that ran between the city's great walls and the Grand Harbour, the lieutenant chatted idly about the city and the island, the bombing and the food shortages, and the weather, in more or less the same easy voice. The walls of rock and stone that rose up around the peninsular on which the tiny city of Valletta was built were enough to drown out Lieutenant Yates' commentary, for Stefan at least. The sand-coloured bastions soared high above them; massive stone blocks built from the hewn rock on which they had their foundations. It was monumental building on a scale Stefan Gillespie had never seen. He heard the Military Police officer describe the building of the city, almost four hundred years ago, by the Grand Master of the Knights of St John, Jean de Valette, after his tiny force of knights had defeated a vastly superior Turkish army of invasion. The city was to be both an impregnable fortress for the future and a celebration of victory. A recognition of sacrifice; a place of beauty that gave thanks to God. As far as the knights were concerned, they, and God, had saved European civilisation. Jack Yates delivered his words on the saving of civilisation with a wry smile.

'So, nothing new under the sun.'

He turned back, offering Stefan and Frank a cigarette.

'But times change. I'm not sure God allowed for German bombers.'

Stefan Gillespie had heard only snatches of what Lieutenant Yates had to say about the ancient siege and the siege that was happening now. Corporal Gaunt broke into the commentary intermittently, to correct his lieutenant. It was clear, when Stefan did catch a few words, that the corporal knew the city's history in detail, while his superior didn't think details mattered. Eventually the two Military Policemen were talking to each other. Neither Stefan nor Frank Nugent was listening anyway. Nugent was absorbed in his own thoughts. He had been here before, on a ship that had stopped over, en route from India. Stefan continued to take in the great walls of Valletta; they needed no explanation. He also took in the rubble and the broken buildings that lined the harbour; that needed no explanation either. Looking across the Grand Harbour to the buildings on the peninsulas opposite Valletta, which Stefan now knew were called the Three Cities, thick smoke rose from recent bombing. In the moorings along the road into Valletta, there were British ships, large and small, in battered disrepair, smashed and holed, many half-sunk in their berths.

The Humber Snipe reached the end of the harbour, with its breakwater on one side of the road and the seaward end of the city walls on the other. Here stood the fortress of St Elmo, guarding the approaches from the Mediterranean. Once the headquarters of the Knights of St John, now of the British Army, St Elmo was built of the same sandstone as everything else; and like everything else it was the target of the Luftwaffe and Regia Aeronautica. The Humber crossed the bridge over the great ditch surrounding the fort, into the outer bastion. Corporal Gaunt slowed to a crawl to negotiate a building and part of a wall that had been bombed the previous night. Dozens of soldiers were clearing rubble from the roadway. There was a heavy cast-iron skeleton in the debris.

'Lost an ack-ack last night,' said Yates. 'Junkers.'

Jimmy Gaunt halted the vehicle as two men walked across the road with a stretcher. The man on the stretcher was dead, only now pulled from the rubble. He was the drab colour of the dust and stone that had crushed the life out of him.

The Military Police vehicle turned up a ramp and drove through a dark archway, into an inner courtyard, bright and elegant, cloister-like. The corporal stopped in front of a pair of high open doors, leading to a cool, stone interior.

'Provost Marshall wants to have a chat first, gentlemen.' Yates smiled. 'That's how he is. Urgent, whether it is or not. Accommodation front . . . afterwards.'

The two policemen followed the lieutenant into the building.

Inside it was almost cold. The roof was high, leading up through two storeys with a wide stone staircase to one side. Ahead were more double doors, heavily carved, and a large, shadowy room. Stefan could see an altar on the far wall, but between the doors and the altar were packing cases and wooden crates. The Military Police officer turned to the left and knocked on a door. He opened it immediately and then followed as Stefan Gillespie and Frank Nugent entered.

It was another big room, with a huge mahogany desk at the centre. There were bookshelves and filing cabinets. The walls were lined with maps of the Mediterranean and the island of Malta. A small, nervy-looking man sat at the desk. He didn't get up, but simply watched Stefan and Frank curiously.

'Chief Inspector Nugent, Inspector Gillespie, Colonel.'

'Thank you, Yates.'

The lieutenant left, closing the door.

'Colonel Macgregor, Provost Marshall. IC Military Police, Malta.'

Only now did the man stand up and walk round to shake hands.

'So, welcome to Malta.' The accent was Scottish, though barely.

'Thank you, sir,' said Nugent.

'Yes, sir.' Stefan echoed the words.

'I'd appreciate your ID.' The colonel smiled amiably. 'Form's sake.'

The chief inspector opened his briefcase and took out his British identity card and his police warrant card. Stefan Gillespie took his passport and his Garda warrant card from his jacket. Macgregor took them and returned to his desk. He sat and peered at the documents. He wrote a long note in a ledger.

'I'll hang on to these for a bit. Jack Yates will get them back to you.'

He picked up Stefan's passport and looked at it more closely.

'A diplomatic passport, Mr Gillespie.' He used the word 'mister' purposefully, as if he was deliberately avoiding the use of the police rank. He laughed. 'Don't see many of those. It won't confer any special privileges here.'

'I wouldn't expect it to, Colonel.'

'Good.'

The Provost Marshall looked at them for a few more seconds. He was being scrupulously polite, but both men knew that they were not welcome.

'I won't say the announcement of your arrival wasn't a surprise, Nugent.'

The colonel made a point of addressing only the English policeman.

Frank Nugent made no reply.

'You do know what's happening here, I presume?'

'I know what I've read in the papers, sir. And I was briefed in London.'

'I take it you've read something in the papers too, Gillespie?'

'I have.'

'Really?' Macgregor sniffed. 'I'd be interested to know what the Irish papers have to say about the situation here. Since you get your news from Berlin as well as London, you may have a different perspective on it all, eh?'

The words were said pleasantly, but there was a sneer behind them.

'I don't know, sir. We're mostly kept in a state of terrible ignorance in Ireland. It's the censors. They do a grand job, altogether. We're so busy making sure what comes from Berlin doesn't offend London, and what comes from London doesn't offend Berlin, that we get hardly any news. A lot of blank spaces but plenty on what's happening round the country's cattle markets.'

Stefan spoke with an expression of almost puzzled seriousness. Frank Nugent's smile struggled to avoid broadening into a grin. The colonel pursed his lips. His words were intended to insult the Irishman, not give amusement.

The Provost Marshall got up and walked to where a map of Malta hung.

'Slap bang between North Africa and Italy, which means we're a pain in the backside for German and Italian convoys trying to get troops and supplies to North Africa. We sink a lot of their ships. It started with the Duce invading Egypt and wanting to make Malta an Italian province, but he made such a cock-up that Herr Hitler had to go into Africa and sort out the mess, and that means they have to see this little island rather differently. They're reluctant to invade for some reason, though God knows why. If they hammered us hard enough and put in enough troops . . . But in lieu of that the aim is to blast Malta into as many pieces as possible and starve us of supplies, especially fuel. They're doing a pretty good job. They assume a tipping point, at which the Malta Garrison surrenders.'

Colonel Macgregor returned to his desk.

'You might as well sit down.' He sniffed again, as if bored now.

The two policemen moved to chairs in front of the desk.

'Most of what we have in the way of aircraft consists of knocked-up Gladiators and obsolete Swordfish. The Messerschmitts fly them out of the sky. The RAF has some Hurricanes now, but too few to even things up. We've yet to see a Spitfire. There's a limit to how many ships the Navy can send to the bottom of the Med to get supplies in. And when you look at the map . . .' Macgregor gestured to the map on the wall. 'You see where Sicily is. Full of bloody airfields. They come when they like. And mostly they do what they like. Sorry if that's a statement of the bleeding obvious, but when we're being visited by one of our neutral friends from the Emerald Isle, it is worth stating.'

The Provost Marshall took out a cigarette.

'You won't find many people with a lot of time for Irish neutrality, Mr Gillespie. When people are dying, one does know where one's friends are.'

Stefan said nothing.

'So, the dead man, this Maltese chap. A very unpleasant murder.'

The colonel had said what he wanted to say. It was time for business.

'Of course, I'm very unhappy that this man was killed in Valletta – even more unhappy that it seems, as things stand, that the perpetrator may have been a British serviceman.' Macgregor opened a file on his desk. 'This is the information I have been sent from Scotland Yard, Nugent. These other murders, which I've only just found out about, do appear to be related. Hard to see it any other way. The thing is appalling . . . bloody appalling.'

'Yes, sir,' said Nugent. 'That is why we're here and why—'

The Provost Marshall cut the chief inspector off.

'Looking at this frankly disgusting evidence . . . we're dealing with a pervert. We know that. Let's be honest, with a world of perverts. In a world like that, we can't be surprised at some of the things that . . . shocked, but not surprised.' The Provost Marshall stubbed out his cigarette firmly. 'I have kept details about the death, the manner of the death, as quiet as possible. As far as these other murders are concerned . . . I have not let that go beyond these four walls . . . My Special Investigation Branch officers are handling it.'

Frank Nugent and Stefan Gillespie exchanged a glance. Macgregor had stopped, abruptly, as if he had said all that was necessary.

'Presumably the Maltese Police are involved, sir?' said Nugent.

'In so far as they need to be, I think, Chief Inspector. They were called to the scene when the body was found. They have attempted to find civilian witnesses . . . to no avail it has to be said. A couple of people saw a man in uniform somewhere nearby, around the time . . . in the blackout. There are thousands of soldiers in Valletta some nights. In reality, there's nothing. Looking through the details from these other investigations, it's much the same story here: no evidence, no forensic material, no fingerprints, and no weapon.'

Chief inspector Nugent nodded.

'It's very consistent, sir. Very brutal . . . almost frenzied. Yet the man has enough about him to make sure that nothing gets left behind . . . hardly anything. Isn't that a good reason to cast the net quite wide, in terms of the public?'

'I want this pervert caught as much as anybody,' replied Macgregor. 'But I will be frank with you: there are other considerations, as far as the public goes. This is no time to put an announcement on the front page of the *Times of Malta*, about something that could be a major embarrassment to the

British Army. We rely on the loyalty of the Maltese people; they have to have faith in us.'

Nugent looked at Stefan Gillespie again. Stefan shrugged. He already knew his opinion was not something the Provost Marshall would want to hear.

'And what if there's another murder?' asked the English policeman.

Colonel Macgregor didn't answer. He was not used to being contradicted.

'If it did happen again, sir, if it looks as if things have been covered up.'

'It's not a question of covering up, Nugent. It's a question of discretion.'

'As you have no suspect, sir . . .'

'I've told you that, Nugent. You know anyway.'

'But we do have the fingerprints, courtesy of the Garda Síochána.'

Colonel Macgregor looked at Stefan Gillespie, almost reluctantly.

'I can't say I'm happy with the way I'm being asked to approach that.'

'It seems like it's all there is,' said Stefan quietly.

'If it works,' continued Frank Nugent, 'if the man is identified, he can be arrested and returned to Britain. Minimum of fuss. You have your . . . discretion.'

'I am acting on it, Chief Superintendent. I have instructions to do so, after all.' The Provost Marshall did not like being told what to do either. 'Soldiers who arrived in Malta after the date you've given us will be fingerprinted. I have a good man in my Special Investigation Branch. Again, it is not necessary to involve the local police. It is an army matter. But it's wishful thinking to say some connection with the murder won't be made in the garrison. That kind of rumour isn't easy to control. Once loose, Extemplo Libyae magnas it Fama per urbes, etc.'

'Rumour than which no other evil is swifter,' said Stefan wryly. 'But in this case, six murders on, there seems to be a greater evil than a few rumours.'

'Thank you, Mr Gillespie.' Macgregor looked surprised that the words of Virgil he had thrown out as if they proved something had been understood. 'I take your point, obvious as it is. I think the interests of the British Army, in a theatre of war, are probably not best served by the opinions of an Irishman.'

Colonel Macgregor stood up.

'I know what I have to do. I'm doing it. If it produces the result we want, the man will be arrested and handed over to you, Nugent. You can take him back to England to be tried and hanged.' The Provost Marshall glared at Stefan. 'Or to bloody Ireland. I can't say I care. Dead bodies are the business of every day here, soldiers, sailors, airmen, civilians. Frankly I don't have the luxury of concentrating all my resources on what the queers are doing to each other. My men will take the finger-prints. You two will simply wait until the job is done.'

'Colonel Macgregor, I think as far as police work—'

'Don't give me a lecture on police work, Mr Nugent. You'll wait, whatever the outcome. My instructions are to cooperate with you. That's what I'm doing. The men on the list are not going to take too kindly to this. I won't be asking them to take orders from a bloody civilian. The top brass doesn't like this. They don't want you poking around on military establish-ments, let alone our friend here. I don't know what clown in the Colonial Office decided this was a good idea, but Malta is a battlefield. There's a fucking war on!'

'Whatever you say, sir.' Chief Inspector Nugent smiled amiably.

The Provost Marshall snapped at him.

'You think you could do this in Civvy Street, Nugent? Gather up a collection of Londoners at random and demand their fingerprints. How many would tell you to fuck off? You might find a lot of soldiers doing the same.'

'This is the army, isn't it, sir? I assume they'll do what they're told.'

'They will. But you have no authority here. My men will take the prints. As for the sodding Garda Síochána!' Macgregor was angry now, and his anger was directed at Stefan. 'I suggest you stick very close to Mr Nugent and keep your head down, Gillespie. For all sorts of reasons. Axis bombs and bullets won't be able to spot your neutrality, even if you wave at them as they fly past.'

A sharp look from Frank Nugent stopped Stefan replying.

'You're responsible for Gillespie, Nugent.'

'I'll do my best to keep him under control, Colonel.'

'Don't waste my time trying to be clever either. I have to tolerate this business, no more. My lieutenant will take you to your hotel. Your reason for being in Malta is simple. If this fingerprint process gets a result, you have a prisoner. That's the point at which you have a job to do: to remove him from Malta. Meanwhile, keep out of the way. There are military facilities you can use in Valletta. If you do have any reason to be on military premises, your ranks entitle you to use the officers' mess. You will be issued with temporary passes.'

There was silence. Macgregor had finished.

'I think that's all.'

'Thank you very much, sir,' said Frank Nugent, with pointed politeness.

He nodded at Stefan. They both stood up.

'Thank you, Colonel Macgregor,' said Stefan, with stiff obligation.

'We rely on your thoroughness, Provost Marshall,' continued Nugent.

'What the fuck is that supposed to mean?'

'I note there are a number of officers on the list for

fingerprinting, including two pretty senior ones. I assume the job will involve everyone, regardless of rank. That's my understanding from London. And it's only fair.'

The Provost Marshall eyed the chief inspector warily.

'We're looking for an ordinary soldier, Chief Inspector. That's what all this evidence about the other murders says . . . all this material you've provided. Whatever sightings there have been, here too . . . it's been an ordinary soldier.'

'It's a supposition, sir. Probably correct, but we can't be sure. And as you say, a lot of men will resent being asked to do this. Not without justification. But it won't be any use unless it includes every name. And if ordinary soldiers feel they have been singled out . . . officers need to set an example to the men.'

The chief inspector ended with a shrug, as if he said this reluctantly. The Provost Marshall didn't like the idea. He knew many officers wouldn't like it. But it was not easy to argue. He also didn't like Nugent having the last word.

The two policemen emerged into the bright sunshine of the courtyard at Fort St Elmo. Corporal Gaunt was sitting in the Humber Snipe, reading a book, too absorbed to see them. Lieutenant Yates was following them from the building.

'Come on, Jimmy. Start her up!'

The corporal put away the book and started the engine.

'All in order, gentlemen?' asked the lieutenant.

'Well, we've got temporary passes for the officers' club in Valletta.'

'Never mind.'

'You wouldn't recommend it?' said Stefan.

'No.' Yates grinned. 'But I'll show you a couple of bars in Strait Street. That's more like it, as they say. We can set you up there. You won't look back.'

Stefan and Frank Nugent got into the open-topped Humber.

'Isn't that right, Jimmy?'

'If you say so, sir.'

'Jimmy's a bit of a prude,' laughed Yates.

The two detectives smiled as if they understood the conversation, but as the Humber turned in the courtyard, Frank Nugent spoke quietly to Stefan.

'You in a hurry, Stefan?'

'Why?'

'Sightseeing,' answered Nugent.

Stefan looked puzzled.

'Hotel then, gentlemen!' announced Lieutenant Yates.

'Where's the body, Jack?' asked the chief inspector.

Stefan understood.

'What body's that, Frank?'

'The murder victim. We've come a bloody long way to see him.'

The lieutenant shook his head. He had no instructions on this.

'Where is he?' asked Nugent again.

'Mtarfa Hospital,' said Yates.

'How about a detour to Mtarfa Hospital, then?'

'Did the colonel say that was all right?'

'He didn't say it wasn't,' said Nugent.

'We forgot to ask him,' added Stefan.

Lieutenant Yates shrugged, then laughed.

'It's not a state secret. You heard the man, Jimmy. Mtarfa.'

13

The British Hotel

The open-topped Humber bumped out of the fort and turned north, away from the Grand Harbour, to follow the city walls in the other direction. Stefan glimpsed the streets of Valletta for a moment, rising up in straight lines inside the walls, and then they were gone. More walls; bastions and sea again; the city shut away, somewhere above. Stefan was aware of the sound of explosions. They had been there some time, he realised, barely heard inside Fort St Elmo. They were not close, but deep, heavy. There were also sharper sounds, harder to hear, faster, almost rhythmic. They were not close either, but they came from every direction. He was familiar enough with bombs and anti-aircraft guns to know how they sounded in tandem. There was a lower hum too, much closer. Looking up he saw a wing of aircraft in formation move across the sky, south of the city, coming from the sea. Lieutenant Yates glanced up. It was the daily routine.

'Heinkels, with some Messerschmitts to hold their hands. South and west. Looks like the airfields today: Hal Far, Luqa. Handy we're going the other way.'

They went west from Valletta. The landscape didn't change. There were few hills. The domes of churches stood out above everything, bigger than the small villages seemed to justify. They drove for half an hour, seeing few vehicles except army trucks. The sound of bombing, ack-ack fire and tracer bullets still rumbled and clattered in the bright, clear air, for now somewhere else. It was hot. At regular intervals the long nose of an anti-aircraft gun pierced the sky. By each one, half a dozen soldiers sat smoking and staring upwards, waiting to see whether the Luftwaffe and the Regia Aeronautica would come their way.

The Humber Snipe passed the hill where the walled city of Mdina rose above the island, on a high point that would be hardly a hill anywhere else. Close to it they came to a grand square building that occupied another hill, behind Mdina. The Naval Hospital had been built where there was light and air, and where breezes blew even on the hottest, stillest days. It had not been designed for war from the air. Around it was the familiar sandstone rubble that showed that the great red crosses painted over it offered little immunity.

The hospital was full of the island's wounded, both military and civilian. The business of war here, as in London, pushed the death of one young man into a place not so much of indifference as irrelevance. The dead, however they died, were the dead. The business of this place was with the living. This was a brighter place than Charing Cross Hospital, though it dealt with the dead and the dying in the same way. As Stefan walked along Mtarfa's chaotic, bustling corridors, to see a third dead body in a third hospital mortuary, there was a noisy, almost cheerful banter. There was a strangely intense sense of life.

The body of Anthony Zammit offered nothing new. He was as clean and well presented as James Corcoran and Vikram Narayan had been by the time Stefan Gillespie saw them. The wounds that ringed the abdomen and thighs were harshly delineated, but the fury of the blows was clear. They were gaping, ragged, as if the knife had twisted as it plunged. Stefan had forgotten that violence. The anger the wounds expressed had not been washed away. It had been there in the same way on Corcoran's corpse. On Narayan's body the stab marks were more tentative, shallower; the knife had to penetrate clothing. Zammit, like Corcoran, had been partly naked.

The inspector and chief inspector took in the details and mentally ticked them off against what they already knew. The sight left no doubt about the reason they were in Malta. The killer had killed again. He was close by.

Returning to Valletta, Corporal Gaunt dropped Lieutenant Yates at Fort St Elmo and drove back round the perimeter road to the great stone gate that was the main entrance to the city from the harbour. Two dark arches gave access to the city above, but the gate was a statement as well as a point of entry. It was named after the Queen and Empress in whose reign it was built. The arms of Malta and Valletta were carved in relief over each of the arches, but above them, at the top of the gate, standing alone, grander than both, dominating, were the arms of Great Britain, supported on each side by a lion and unicorn rampant.

The British Hotel was only yards from the Victoria Gate, a flat, sandstone building, sandwiched between others, that looked down to the gate and the Grand Harbour beyond. It fronted Battery Street and emerged at the back, that was really the front, on St Ursula Street; narrow, steeply cobbled, stepped, like many of the city's streets. Only in Battery Street could a vehicle get close.

Jimmy Gaunt carried the policemen's bags into the small lobby. There was little more than a desk, a brightly tiled floor and a ceiling fan that circled lazily overhead. A staircase wound up through several storeys behind the desk and formed a narrow, open stairwell. A round, dark man in his fifties, emerged from a door that led to a small bar. He smoked a thin, black cheroot.

'They're here then, Jimmy.'

'Il-pulizija Ingliż . . . u l-pulizija . . .'

The corporal faltered in Maltese; the English policeman . . . and the . . .

'Irlandiż, Irish,' laughed the man. 'That's easy enough, isn't it?'

Gaunt flushed and adjusted his glasses. He turned to Stefan and Frank.

'This is Mr Sacco. He runs the hotel.'

'The British Hotel,' said the hotel owner pointedly. He reached into a box for two keys. 'You're welcome. Rooms on the third floor, 301 and 302. Balconies and a view of the Grand Harbour.' He shrugged. 'Bombs allowing.'

Gaunt reached across and took the keys.

'I'll do it . . .' He stopped to say it again in Maltese. 'Se nag ħmel dan.'

'All right.' The hotelier shrugged, turning to the two policemen. 'You'll excuse us. Jimmy's doing his Maltese lesson. He has me confused sometimes.'

'This way, gents,' said the corporal.

He started up the stairs. Stefan and Frank Nugent followed.

'That's impressive, Corporal,' said Stefan.

'I wish it was. I've got a bloody army exam in Colloquial Maltese.'

'Do you have to do that?'

'No, it's just,' Gaunt looked down and mumbled, 'just an interest.'

Stefan stood in the high, square room, looking out through the blue shutters of the boxed-in balcony that pushed out above the street. There was an explosion, much louder than anything he had heard so far. He saw smoke rising, black and grey, a great pillar of it across the harbour. There, he now knew, on three fingers of rock, stretching out into the harbour between sheltered creeks, were the Three Cities: Vittoriosa, Senglea, Cospicua. There too were the dockyards of the British Navy. He saw cranes rising beside the sandstone buildings that mirrored Valletta in miniature. Another explosion sent up a plume of smoke.

'Jerries are dropping what they've got left after the airfields. Most days they drop something over there. Some days that's where they drop everything.'

Jimmy Gaunt stood in the doorway.

'I'm off, sir.'

'Thanks, Corporal. Not much to stop them,' said Stefan.

'Not a lot. They'll be back for Valletta soon enough. Maybe tonight, tomorrow. There are plenty of shelters, well signed. Caves and tunnels under the city are best. Mr Sacco can show you where. You've been in London?'

Stefan nodded.

'Same sort of thing,' the corporal grinned, 'but nowhere to run.'

The bombers had gone. There were no more explosions. No more anti-aircraft fire. Stefan sat in a chair in the balcony, smoking a cigarette, still looking out at the smoke over the Three Cities and a view that, in another time, would have been calm as well as beautiful. He heard laughter on the stairs, the sound of women's voices. The door to his room was open. He looked round suddenly.

'Are you the English policeman or the Irish policeman?'

A woman in her twenties, blonde, looked in from the landing.

Stefan stood up. 'The Irish policeman.'

'It sounds like the beginning of a joke. An English police-man . . . an Irish policeman . . . but there should be a Scottish policeman. There are always three.'

Stefan walked to the door.

'I'm sorry. We should have brought another one.'

'You'll do.'

Another woman appeared, a little older, dark.

'What's he like?'

'Not bad. For a policeman.'

'Has Jimmy gone?'

Stefan realised the second woman was asking him.

'Corporal Gaunt?'

'Of course, Corporal Gaunt.' She turned away, as a third woman appeared, the youngest, very much darker in complexion. 'You just missed Jimmy, Maria!'

'I'll see him later.' The woman called Maria carried on upstairs.

'I'm Jane,' said the woman who first spoke to Stefan. 'That was Maria.'

'I'm Alice.' The second woman looked back into the room.

'Stefan Gillespie. And the English policeman is Frank Nugent.'

'Is he any better looking?'

'You'll have to judge for yourselves.'

'Is he any funnier?'

'Not a lot,' laughed Stefan.

'Oh, well, beggars can't be choosers,' said Jane. 'Catch you later.'

And they were gone, still laughing, now running up the stairs to the next floor. They all wore the light khaki that was the colour of almost everything.

Stefan sat in the bar at the British Hotel, gazing out to the street. Frank Nugent walked in and sat at the table. There was already a glass of beer waiting for him.

'Sorry, I was waylaid.'

'You met the girls.'

'I did. They've just occupied the bathroom.'

'I hope you said something funny.'

'What?'

'It's a test. I think I failed.'

'Well, I did all right on the Intelligence front,' said the chief inspector. 'They work in the War Rooms. Up the road, underground. That's where they plot the bombers, fighters, what's coming in and what's there to stop them. Well, we know that's a bit of a one-way street. Jane and Alice come, respectively, from Bournemouth and Norwich. Maria is the daughter of Mr and Mrs Sacco. And she is the particular interest of Corporal Gaunt, who is, after a fashion, walking out with her, at least trying to. I think Jane and Alice take a more enlightened approach to these things, but this, of course, is a very Catholic country. In fact, I'd say if you were looking for a country more Catholic than your own dear native sod, Stefan, this is it. Jimmy has asked permission to walk out with Maria, which I imagine amounts to exactly that . . . if approval is given.'

'Doesn't sound too promising,' laughed Stefan.

'The problem is not the old man,' continued Nugent, 'but the old woman. We haven't had the pleasure, but it seems she is a woman of Gorgon-like instincts, with a dislike of soldiers, sailors and airmen; in fact, probably of any male under the age of sixty-five who crosses the threshold of the British Hotel.'

'What about policemen?'

'Even policemen, Stefan, I'm sorry to say. But love will find a way, as you know. Mrs Sacco has Corporal Gaunt on probation. He has to demonstrate his bona fides by learning Maltese. Fair play to him, he's calling her bluff.'

'Ah, that makes sense of . . . well, just an interest, he said.'

The two detectives were aware of a man standing by the table. He carried a tray with three glasses of beer. He wore another version of an all-purpose, sandy-cum-khaki uniform.

He had a sergeant's stripes, but the cap and the tunic didn't look like the British Army. He was younger than both detectives; dark-haired, olive-skinned. He put the tray on the table and pulled up a chair.

'Chief Inspector Nugent, Inspector Gillespie. A pleasure to meet you.' The man put out his hand to shake theirs. 'George Spiteri, Malta Police.'

'It's good to see you,' said Nugent. 'Colonel Macgregor didn't appear too keen on us meeting you. That's the impression I got. What about you, Stefan?'

'Well, it might be a Maltese corpse, but it's a British Army murderer.'

'Exactly.' Sergeant Spiteri laughed. 'We should know our place.'

'I take it you don't, though,' said Frank Nugent, 'know your place.'

'My inspector does. He's ex-British Army. I'm not here officially.'

'Good.' The chief inspector grinned. 'Do you know what's happening?'

'Most of it. I know about the fingerprint from Ireland. I know about some similar murders in England. I know there's a list of soldiers to fingerprint.'

'The colonel's right to distrust rumour,' said Stefan.

'Malta's a small place,' said Spiteri. 'We can do better than rumour.'

'What about the colonel's Special Investigation Branch?' asked Nugent. 'We've been told to leave it all to them. Has he got any real detectives there?'

'There are a couple. Ex-UK police. One from the Met, one from Liverpool. Shaw's the Liverpool man – Irish originally, I think. He did work in fingerprints. I don't know if anyone's even been near a murder investigation. They're mainly involved with pilfering stores, theft from the dockyards. But I can't knock them too much. We're not exactly the murder capital of the Med.'

'Well, you're still working on this,' said Stefan. 'And ignoring the fact that the Military Police have decided it's not the business of the Malta Police.'

'That seems to sum it up,' said Spiteri.

'And you're ignoring your own Inspector . . .'

'Inspector Simmons,' said the sergeant. 'Ignoring is over-stating it.'

'So, why?' asked Stefan.

'First, because I want to find who killed Anthony Zammit. He has a family. We all know each other here. That's how it is. I don't think the Military Police have any business shutting out the Maltese. And practically, I don't think that's going to help find the killer. Colonel Macgregor is more concerned about how it looks than getting results. I don't mean he doesn't want to find the murderer, but he has priorities. So do I. I don't want this man to do it again.'

'Yes,' said Nugent, 'none of us do. If this fingerprinting is thorough—'

'Secondly,' said Spiteri, interrupting, 'because you have it wrong.'

Stefan and Frank Nugent looked hard at the Maltese sergeant.

'What does that mean?' asked Stefan.

'The fingerprints. I don't mean you haven't got the man's fingerprint. I don't know, but I assume you're fairly sure of what you've got. But if you're only looking at men who came to Malta since the last murder in London, then there's a problem . . . and that problem isn't the seventy or eighty soldiers who are being fingerprinted from your list, it's the twenty-five thousand who aren't.'

'You've had a lot more than hearsay to go on,' said Stefan. 'You've obviously seen some of the material Scotland Yard sent Colonel Macgregor.'

'I couldn't possibly access that, Inspector.' George Spiteri smiled.

'Since you have,' said Nugent, 'you know the man was in England at the beginning of the year. A murder in London, the next here. The dates are clear.'

'They're not,' replied the Maltese policeman.

'Why not?'

'I can't explain away the evidence. What you have is convincing. I'm not arguing with that. I can't argue with it. But in spite of the evidence, the dates do not make sense, not here. This isn't the first murder in Malta . . . it's the second.'

'And when did the other murder happen?' asked Stefan.

'I'm not exactly sure about a date. But at the back end of last year.'

'That's impossible,' said Frank Nugent, 'unless we've got a soldier who was in Malta then, back in Britain after that, then back in Malta again. All right, well, that isn't impossible . . . but there hasn't been that kind of troop movement. Anyone moving around like that . . . you'd be talking about very senior officers.'

'I'm not offering an explanation, Mr Nugent. I'm just telling you.'

'All right, tell us, George.' Nugent glanced at Stefan and shrugged, puzzled. 'And make it Frank and Stefan. We're not the fucking army, are we?'

'A body was found in December. In bombed buildings on the other side of Valletta, Old Theatre Lane. It's an area that was badly hit. It took a while to start clearing. So, the body. Badly decomposed. Under rubble, but not much. Covered up by old doors and beams. But in an area that was very thoroughly checked after the bombing. The man could have been missed, of course. I don't think he was, though. I think he got there later. Either he died there or he was put there. Either way, I think he was killed. Nothing to do with the bombing.'

Mr Sacco hovered behind the bar. Stefan signalled for a round of drinks.

'The body was in quite a state. Hard to get much from it. Death probably from a blow to the head. Nothing to stop that happening when a building collapsed. But we still have the question . . . how was he missed? Then there's damage to the lower body. Abdomen, stomach, top of the legs. The flesh was falling away, but you could see the marks. What caused them? There was talk . . . had rats been at him? Did something fall on him . . . with nails or spikes? Where was it? It should have been on top of him. And he was partly undressed. That only makes sense now. Our suspicion was that the body had been put there after the building collapsed. The pathology and the forensics didn't tell us anything then . . . or anything that made sense. Not at the time. But it's become clearer . . .'

Mr Sacco put down three more glasses of beer.

'And when did it make sense?' asked Stefan.

'When I looked at Anthony Zammit's body. It explained what I'd seen on the first body, a man called Kenneth Borg. Wounds we couldn't understand . . . they weren't clear, half rotten . . . but the same circle of stab marks. It's not like anything else, is it? I've looked for parallels between Borg and Zammit. Borg's body was near a place that men meet. A pick-up spot. He was homosexual. I found out later, when I started to look into it. A lot of things do match.'

'Have you got any photographs of the body?'

'No. Once he was identified his family wanted him buried. There wasn't enough to justify us investigating. Some days there are just a lot of bodies. But there's a sketch of the wounds the doctor drew. And it's very striking. It's a lot more striking now I've seen other things that look the same. Once you've seen what we have all seen, when you know what it is, it's like stigmata.'

14

The Upper Barrakka Gardens

The day that followed Stefan Gillespie's arrival in Malta was a day of heavy bombing. It started in the late morning and continued with short breaks until dark. Most of it was directed at the Three Cities and the dockyards, across the Grand Harbour, but later it spread to docks and storehouses in Floriana, on the Valletta side of the harbour, beyond the Victoria Gate. It spread into the streets of the city and down to the end of the peninsula and Fort St Elmo.

Stefan and Frank Nugent spent most of the day in the tunnels under the Upper Barrakka Gardens that looked out over the Grand Harbour, close to the British Hotel. There were tunnels everywhere under Valletta, carved out of the soft stone that built the city. Now they were full of people. Families had claimed their own corners of these cavernous spaces; they had even dug deeper into the tunnel walls to create spaces of their own that could be curtained off and filled with deckchairs and mattresses. It was not unfamiliar to Stefan. It was like the Underground, rough-hewn and without trains. But beneath the Barrakka Gardens, it was as if the street above had been brought into the depths. Spaces were the property of a family or a shop or a business. In one large alcove there was an altar.

A young priest said Mass. There was the smell of incense, the tinkling of the communion bell. In the light of guttering candles, people cooked and read and slept and argued about who several yards of tunnel wall really belonged to. Children had lessons and played hopscotch and fell over their sleeping parents. The British Hotel had its own small recess, where two tunnels branched. There were several chairs, a table and three camp beds. Mrs Sacco provided soup to the hotel patrons and, it seemed, to most of her neighbours as well. Mr Sacco brought down a crate of beer in the afternoon. Corporal Gaunt arrived towards evening, looking for Maria, and quickly found himself pulled into a Maltese lesson that he had not bargained for by her mother. Everyone was bored. Everyone was tired of what was happening. Yet everyone seemed to accept it with an equanimity and good humour that Stefan had never seen in the Underground tunnels under Piccadilly Circus.

There were lulls in the bombing or times where it was further away. Stefan and Frank walked up and down to the Barrakka Gardens above them, all day, to smoke cigarettes and look out over the Grand Harbour at the smoke that was everywhere, and to watch the waves of bombers. Stefan watched his first air battle. He saw two Messerschmitts peel away from the bombers they were guarding, as two British planes suddenly appeared out of the smoke. The British planes were the old, slow Gladiators. The biplanes looked as if they belonged to another age. But they had the benefit of surprise. Black smoke burst from one of the Junker bombers. It flew on for some minutes and then its nose dropped. There were flames from the cockpit and it was falling. Almost straight down into the harbour. The biplane turned away, heading back into the smoke it had emerged from. The two Messerschmitts split away from each other, one to chase the retreating Gladiator, the other to tackle the second plane. The first British plane reached the smoke and dived into it.

The Messerschmitt followed. The second Messerschmitt flew straight towards the other Gladiator. The two fighters were firing as they tore towards each other, head-on. But the Gladiator was heavily outgunned. As the Luftwaffe pilot pulled up above the RAF plane at the last moment, there was smoke from the biplane. The engine coughed and stalled. Within seconds the Gladiator had followed the Junker into the Grand Harbour. The first Messerschmitt reappeared out of the smoke over the Three Cities. He had lost his quarry. The whole thing had taken a few minutes. Not even long enough for Stefan to finish his cigarette.

The next day was quiet. When the bombers came from Sicily that afternoon, they would leave the city and the Grand Harbour for another attack on the RAF airfields at Luqa and Hal Far. That morning Chief Inspector Nugent had gone to St Elmo for an update on what Colonel Macgregor's Investigation Branch was doing with the fingerprint list. Pointedly, Stefan had not been invited. The colonel told Frank Nugent that Military Intelligence had some reservations about an Irish policeman having free access to military bases. He was apologetic, but only slightly. He added that it was nothing personal, more a matter of policy. They were, after all, in a war zone. Frank Nugent thought it was probably a policy the colonel had dreamed up in the officers' club in Valletta over a couple of whiskeys with the Intelligence major they had met at Gibraltar.

Stefan spent part of the morning with Sergeant Spiteri of the Malta Police. Since neither he nor Chief Inspector Nugent could get into the Military Police investigation, it was useful that someone wanted to talk to them.

The day was warm and bright. It would be hot later. Although thin smoke drifted over Valletta and the Three Cities across the harbour, it was peaceful. Stefan Gillespie and George Spiteri stood by the Customs House, on the waterfront below the Victoria Gate. This was where the ferry from the other side of the harbour landed, and where dozens of dgħajjes moored, the small water taxies that shuttled around the harbour. This was where Anthony Zammit's last visit to Valletta had started, shortly before he was killed.

'He lived in Senglea. He worked in the docks there. He came over in a dgħajjsa, early evening, just getting dark. Quiet night here. No bombing. The man who brought him over knew him. He was on his own. Someone else saw him, minutes later. He took the Barrakka Lift. A girl he knew was getting off.'

The two policemen crossed the perimeter road. They walked through a dark archway into a kind of gully, cut out of the rock beside a turn in the city's bastions. A thin, almost fragile tower of criss-crossed scaffolding rose up against the rock to one side, reaching high above, bolted into the cliff face and the city wall. George and Stefan stepped into the lift and the iron-grille doors shut behind them. The cables creaked and groaned. The cabin shook. The lift rose noisily and unevenly upwards, over two hundred feet. Suddenly there was a narrow view of the Grand Harbour that slid upwards as Stefan looked out at it.

The lift opened into the arched colonnade that made up one side of the Upper Barrakka Gardens. Stefan already knew the gardens. This was one of the entrances to the tunnels he had sheltered in the day before. It was where he had stood, smoking a cigarette and watching German and British pilots die. This was the finest view of the Grand Harbour. Behind the colonnades was the dappled light of a shady garden where the people of Valletta came when they had nothing much to do and wanted to do it in a place that felt a long way from the heat of the sandstone streets. There were few green spaces; the walls that had been built to defend the city had become places where trees and flowers grew. Now the view of the Grand

Harbour from the gardens was framed by the guns of the anti-aircraft battery that took up the platform below the colonnades.

'During the day, it's like any park. People walk and talk and sit around. That's what it's for. Visitors come here to look at the harbour, but we go for the trees and the shade.' Spiteri grinned. 'We've seen the harbour now and again.'

They walked through the gardens. They were stacked with sandbags. A group of British soldiers was unloading crates of ack-ack shells from a truck.

'After dark, the atmosphere changes. At least, it does over here.'

The sergeant gestured to a clump of trees and some benches.

'It's away from the harbour. An out-of-the-way corner. And it's always been one of the places men come looking for other men. There are no lights, even without the blackout. No one takes much notice. We might move them on now and again. But there's never that many. If they don't cause trouble . . . if they keep out of other people's way . . . we leave them alone.'

'Did anyone see Zammit here?'

'No. No one I've managed to talk to. It's not easy. You know that.'

Stefan nodded.

'But someone saw him walking out of the gardens. There's a restaurant, by the gate, where you come out into Castille Place. Come on. I'll show you.'

The policemen walked on through the gardens and out into a wide square.

They passed a small café. A few customers were sitting at tables outside.

'I have a statement from the waiter. He saw Anthony Zammit with a soldier, walking towards the bus station. It was night by then. But not such a dark night. The man knew Anthony well. He only saw the back of the soldier. Probably a private. Tall, thin . . . maybe fair-haired.'

They moved on across the square. They turned towards the main street, which the British now called Kingsway, but the Maltese still called the Strada Reale, as the knights who built it had. They passed the great building that was the Royal Opera House, built by an English architect to bring something of Covent Garden to the city of the Knights of St John. Surrounded by classical pillars on every side, it looked like no other building in Valletta, but it had become a much-loved symbol of the city.

They crossed the bridge over the deep moat that cut across the peninsula from side to side. They were outside the city now, in a wide street full of small, colourful buses. George Spiteri turned to the left, following the city walls, past the bus station, to an area of stunted trees, scrub and parched, yellow grass. It was scattered thinly with rubbish. Stefan followed him. The sergeant stopped.

'We found him here. You've seen the photos. When men meet in the Upper Barrakka, they go somewhere else for sex. It's a kind of understanding. People leave them alone. They can find someone there. But they go to some quiet corner to finish the job. And this would be quiet enough, especially with the blackout. Hardly any buses run at night now. It would be empty all around here after dark. And it's out of the way . . . wasteland. It goes nowhere.'

Stefan looked around. There was nothing to see. It was just another place where a young man had died. It joined the list of dark, unimportant corners.

'So, when did Colonel Macgregor get involved?'

'It was our investigation for a couple of days. Then we had the evidence that Anthony was last seen walking in this direction with a soldier. And then the colonel's Special Investigation Branch came in. The investigation was theirs.'

'All theirs.'

'That's how they like it. Interrogating soldiers is not our business.'

'You're still pissed off,' said Stefan Gillespie.

'Pissed off enough to keep at it. I'm still looking. You'll hear a lot of people tell you this is a very small place. It is. It is for everyone. That includes the men who meet each other in the Upper Barrakka. Someone must have seen something. Someone must have noticed something. Someone knows something. I don't even mean about Zammit. Remember, I think I have two murders here.'

Stefan Gillespie walked on along the Strada Reale, Malta's widest street. He already knew his way round the streets that led here from the British Hotel, and continued on, the length of the peninsula, to Fort St Elmo and the sea. Valletta was built on a grid, like a miniature version of New York. Long, narrow streets ran the length of the city and shorter ones crossed it from shore to shore. In a different time, Stefan could have enjoyed the elegant city and the buildings that lined the Strada Reale: townhouses and palaces, churches and public buildings. But his mind was on the dead bodies that had brought him here, and when it wasn't, it was full of the sound of aircraft and bombs and the day he had spent underground. Suddenly a heap of stone stretched almost all the way across the street. It sloped up like a hill. Yesterday it had been a house. Men and women and children were working in the rubble, clearing the road. There were soldiers and sailors with them, filling trucks and trailers with the debris.

A few hundred yards on, Stefan passed the cathedral of St John. He could see ahead that the Strada Reale opened up into a square of palaces and grand buildings. This was where he had arranged to meet Nugent. He saw a sign for the Caffe Cordina. Opposite the café, beneath a stone arch, he saw the English policeman at a table with another man. The man wore the usual khaki fatigues; on the table was a Military Policeman's red cap.

Stefan sat down. He was introduced to Robert Shaw, sergeant in the CMP Special Investigation Branch. He was short, balding, with the accent of Dublin.

'Dead end,' said Chief Inspector Nugent curtly.

'No go,' added Sergeant Shaw with a shrug.

'All the fingerprints have been taken. No matches.'

'Did you get everyone on the list?' asked Stefan.

Frank Nugent sat back, lighting a cigarette. 'Near as dammit.'

The waiter hovered. Stefan asked for tea.

'We got through your list of soldiers,' said the Military Policeman. 'Two officers moved on to Alexandria. One Royal Engineer dead in a raid on St Elmo last week. That's it. No one's going to give you a guarantee someone didn't slip through Malta between your dates. People get transferred, die, go sick, get put in the glasshouse for robbing or fighting or getting pissed. But I think we had all of them. And the idea that the feller you're looking for just happened to be lucky enough to get missed off . . . that would be some fucking luck. Your knifeman isn't on the list. I'd say you're barking up the wrong tree, gentlemen.'

Sergeant Shaw delivered his verdict with a look of satisfaction. He'd done his job. It was the civvies who had fucked up. They had it wrong.

'Those were Colonel Macgregor's words,' said Frank Nugent, 'more or less. He didn't exactly say the fuck-up was entirely ours, but it cost him not to.'

The Military Policeman laughed. He got up.

'Good hunting, lads.' He looked at Stefan. 'How's Dublin?'

'Quieter than here.'

'Ah, you'll miss it when you get back. You get used to it.'

'I'm not sure I would,' replied Stefan. 'Where are you from?'

'The North Strand.'

'Is your family there?'

184

'They were the last time I was home.'

There was a note of reticence in Shaw's voice. The Irish State didn't take kindly to its citizens fighting in the British Army, even though it only made noises about stopping them. But the sergeant did not want more conversation about Ireland with an Irish policeman. There would be no Ould Irish bonhomie.

'Take care, lads.'

Stefan and Frank Nugent watched him walk away.

'Is he any good?' asked Stefan.

'He knows what he's doing. He was in fingerprints in Liverpool before he joined up. He's a proper copper; I'd say one of Macgregor's better specimens.'

'So, what's the colonel proposing now?'

'He's talking about inspecting a selection of poofs and pansies the army has defending Malta for the empire . . . Well, that's about as much sense as I got.'

'And what does that mean?'

'I think he's going to send his boys in their red caps to knock some heads together in a few queer bars on Strait Street and ask them if they've got any pals who are in the habit of murdering the men they've just buggered. They are, after all, perverts and . . . one thing leads to another in that line of work.'

Frank Nugent laughed. 'I'm paraphrasing his thinking, but unfortunately not a lot.'

'Jesus, that's not going to get him far.'

'No. But I'd bet on it giving him more trouble than he's bargained for.'

The two men sat looking out at the Strada Reale.

'So, that's that,' said Stefan eventually.

Nugent nodded.

'And is that it as far as the dates are concerned?' said Stefan. 'If we're not looking for a soldier who left England after Vikram Narayan was killed?'

'I don't know. That ought to be impossible.'

'It isn't if George Spiteri's right and there was another murder.'

'If . . .' said the IPI man.

'I've been thinking about Narayan,' said Stefan.

'Have you got an explanation then?'

'No,' continued the Irishman, 'but there are questions if you tot up the similarities, in all the killings. That's six, Jesus, seven if there's two here. One can't fit. Either the first one here or Vikram Narayan in London. So, look at them. All outside, in isolated or out-of-the-way places, except one. Most chance meetings in known pick-up spots for homosexual men. Not true in Ireland. Maybe not true for Narayan, but let's come back to that. In every case, except one, there was sexual contact. That's Narayan. The others had sex, whatever that involved. We can't know that for the first man in Malta, Kenneth Borg, but he was undressed, partly or completely, as in every case . . . except one. In every case, wounds to the lower body were so violent that it's still shocking to look at the photographs, let alone the bodies. The amount of violence hits every time. And that's true of all of them, wouldn't you say, all except for one? Vikram Narayan.'

Chief Inspector Nugent nodded, taking in the train of thought.

'He was fully clothed,' said Stefan. 'There was no sex. The knife wounds were shallower . . . almost neat. That's a subjective judgement, but it's one I'd make. It feels different. And where did he meet his killer? Did he know him? We don't know, but I've walked from that club, Billie's, to the flat in Greek Street. We know when he left. We know when Micheál Mac Liammóir found the body. It wasn't that long. Vikram had to meet a man in the street. They had to walk to his flat. Then the killer had to knock him out, smother him, then add the knife wounds . . . instantly. You'd almost say as they walked through the door.'

'You're right,' said Nugent, 'if there is one that doesn't fit, that's it. List it like that, and it misses a lot of the characteristics of the other murders. There could even be fingerprints, just not the fingerprints of the man who killed James Corcoran. We've never found a suspect. Well, we've only looked in one place.'

'Maybe that was a mistake,' said Stefan.

'But how about the stab wounds? They're still so similar. No one could come up with that, Stefan. The chances are . . . you'd have to know something already.'

'And if you did know something,' said Stefan, smiling, 'you'd be hard put to find a better way of making the police look in the wrong direction.'

Frank Nugent said nothing for several minutes. He called the waiter.

'I think we need a couple of beers.'

'What now?' asked Stefan.

'We're still here,' laughed Frank Nugent. 'As people will tell you.'

'What does that mean?'

'Well, since we won't be taking fingerprints from twenty-five thousand soldiers, I reckon we should forget Colonel Macgregor and his Special Investigation Branch. I'd say the feller we need to listen to is Sergeant Spiteri.'

15

The Lascaris War Rooms

The next morning, Inspector Gillespie and Chief Inspector Nugent found themselves with nothing to do. There was no communication from the Provost Marshall's office. Frank Nugent phoned Colonel Macgregor and found that he was either busy or elsewhere. There was nothing from Sergeant Spiteri either; since he was acting without the authority of his superiors in the Malta Police, who had no intention of treading on the toes of the Corp of Military Police, they had to wait for him to contact them. They were in Malta to find a murderer, but the fingerprint trawl had failed, and it seemed the Provost Marshall intended to take their mission literally. Fingerprints had produced no results; that was the end of it for them.

That morning no Axis bombers and fighters had appeared. Stefan and Frank walked the length of the city, down the Strada Reale, to Fort St Elmo. Bombs had fallen on the sea walls the previous day. More men had died; two anti-aircraft batteries had been damaged. The fort was full of soldiers clearing access to the walls and engineers trying to get the guns working before the next raid. The colonel was busy.

As they walked back into Valletta, they heard the drone of planes. German bombers; an escort of fighters; heading inland.

No one took much notice, apart from glancing up with weary resignation. People had good instincts now. There were no sirens, but they knew anyway. Sound, direction, height; you could tell when they were going somewhere else, as you could tell when the rain was coming.

A horn blasted loudly when the two detectives reached the cathedral, heading back towards the hotel. A Military Police Humber Snipe was parked at the corner. Lieutenant Yates was sitting in it, smoking lazily in the sunshine.

'Enjoying the weather, mes enfants?'

'Not a lot,' said Nugent. 'We did try to see your colonel again.'

'Did he have other priorities?'

'That word cropped up, believe it or not,' laughed Stefan.

Yates grinned.

'You're sticklers, I'll give you that. You didn't get the message?'

'I think we did, actually,' said the chief inspector.

'Well, yes, there is that message, Frank. The other one is that there should be a Sunderland in from Alexandria – two, maybe three days' time. Going on to Gib. The colonel thought it would be handy for you, as you've nothing left to do . . .'

'I'm not sure I see it that way,' said Nugent.

'That's between you and the colonel.' Yates shrugged. 'Why bother?'

'Why not? We're here.'

'This is the army. Don't volunteer. Don't do anything you don't have to.'

The lieutenant offered them both a cigarette.

'You've got a couple of days. With a bit of luck, the bastards won't be bombing round the clock. Take it easy. Go down to Strait Street. Next road along. You can drink all day and all night, and the women are so sick of fucking soldiers and sailors they'll eat you alive. And that can be free, gratis and for nothing. It's our job to keep all ship-shape down there, make sure the boys behave. I can sort you out something very nice, very clean. Just say the word.'

'You're too generous, Jack!' said Nugent.

'Up to you.' The lieutenant chuckled amiably. 'Offer's there.'

Stefan laughed. 'I'll pass. But don't let me stop you, Frank.'

'I'll pass too.'

'And there's me trying to do you two a favour! Oh, here's Jimmy.'

They saw Corporal Gaunt, on the steps of the cathedral with Maria Sacco. The two stood as people passed them, coming out of Mass.

'Come on, sunshine!' shouted Lieutenant Yates.

Jimmy Gaunt pecked Maria awkwardly on the cheek. She flushed, seeing the three policemen watching them, and hurried away. Gaunt ran towards them.

'That's the only place she's allowed to be on her own with him, at bloody Mass in the cathedral,' Yates explained. 'He's not even a Catholic! But you got to lend a hand when it's true love. And they say we don't care about our soldiers!'

Laughing again, Yates stubbed out his cigarette and climbed into the Humber. Corporal Gaunt got in and started up the engine. They pulled away.

'Lunchtime, lads!' the lieutenant shouted back at Stefan and Frank Nugent. 'Intelligence reckons bombs over the harbour around then. Stay safe!'

The reports from Intelligence were right. By midday bombs were falling on the docks in Floriana, on the Valletta side of the Grand Harbour, closer to the Victoria Gate and the British Hotel. Stefan Gillespie and Frank Nugent were underground again, in the tunnels beneath the Upper Barrakka Gardens. The routine they were already part of was in operation. The tunnels were filling up. It was cold after the heat of the afternoon, but it would get hotter as the number of bodies increased. They sat against a rock wall. Stefan was writing a postcard that pictured the Grand Harbour without smoke or fire or collapsed buildings or the battered hulls of broken ships. Nugent was trying to read the *Times of Malta*, with some difficulty, in the light from nearby lamps and candles. The sound of the bombs and the guns was there, in the distance. The sound of Mass was closer. In the cavern-like alcove across the tunnel, a young priest was saying the Credo. The people around him, jammed together in semi-darkness, were saying it with him, in Latin and in Maltese and in English.

'Deum de Deo, lumen de lumine, Deum verum de Deo vero . . .'

'Alla minn Alla, dawl mid-dal, Alla veru minn Alla veru . . .'

'God from God, Light from Light, true God from true God . . .'

It was as the Mass was ending, that George Spiteri appeared, standing by them.

'I thought you'd be here. That's perfect.'

'What's perfect?' said Nugent.

'You're where you need to be.'

'For what?' asked Stefan.

'The secrets of the confessional,' said Spiteri, grinning. 'Don't tell!'

The Mass finished and the congregation drifted away into the tunnels and alcoves. The priest saw Sergeant Spiteri and nodded. He moved to the back of the alcove, behind the table that served as the altar. He pulled off the chasuble he wore over his black robes, folded it and put it beside his tin hat.

'Father Zachary, these are the two policemen I told you about.'

They introduced themselves and shook hands.

'That's twice I've seen you in the shelter, Inspector Gillespie.' The priest smiled broadly. 'And never at Mass when it's going on in front of your eyes. And you from Holy Ireland! They say there's nowhere holier than Ireland, but if there is, you have found it. We're in serious competition with you in Malta.'

'I take it you've been in Ireland, Father.'

'I have. But don't worry, I won't report you.'

Stefan laughed and left it at that. It seemed no place to elaborate.

'Father Zachary has been talking to a few people . . .'

'I have. I know what's happened. I know about the deaths. But some of the men you want to speak to have no great trust in anyone, especially the police, and since we're blessed with more than one sort, in any kind of police. I try to give them something to trust . . . it doesn't make me popular with the Church, but that's another story. The story that matters to you is that I've asked a few men I know to talk to Sergeant Spiteri. I trust the sergeant and he says you can be trusted. There are people with things to say. I did hear one confession . . .'

The priest took out some tobacco and started to roll a cigarette.

'I can't tell you what the man said in the confessional, naturally, but I think he would talk to you. And I think what he has to say . . . might help you.'

'He's knows something about the murders?' said Stefan.

'He knows something . . . he saw something . . . please don't think it's very much. I'm hardly a detective, but it is only what he saw . . . and what he felt . . .'

Father Zachary lit the cigarette.

'But that was before . . .' he said with a shrug.

'Before what?' asked George Spiteri.

'It's common knowledge, among the men we're talking about, that the Military Police have carried out a series of, well, raids, I suppose . . . on bars in Strait Street. Bars that cater for a particular interest, let's say that. They can't touch civilians, but soldiers, sailors, airmen, have all been questioned about their associations, their friendships. I put it politely. You know what I mean.'

'We know that's going on,' said Stefan. 'Not a clever idea.'

'Not at all,' said the priest. 'Not if you want people to talk to you. And the result, I'm afraid, is fear. These men fear exposure. We're not only like Ireland in the amount of time we spend on our knees. So, I'm sorry to say that the men who were prepared to meet you and talk to you and tell you . . . perhaps something that might help you find this . . . monster . . .'

'They now think, fuck that for a game of soldiers,' said Nugent flatly.

Father Zachary inhaled, then blew out a cloud of smoke.

'That's about it. You put it very succinctly, Chief Inspector Nugent.'

It was quiet. The bombers had gone. The fighters had gone. Stefan Gillespie and Frank Nugent had spent an hour walking by the harbour. Fires still burned, in the darkness of Valletta and across the water in the Three Cities. The two men climbed the dogleg steps that led from the Victoria Gate to Battery Street and the British Hotel. The steps were closed in, with the street high above and the road from the Victoria Gate below. They were full of cats, as they were every night when people had gone; mangy, moth-eaten, half-starved cats, prowling, roaming, stretching, sleeping. There were dozens. Suddenly, the sound of a shrill screech: in a corner two cats hissing and fighting. A matter of seconds. Then one tore down the steps, past the policemen. The cats barely registered the two men, moving aside only at the last moment. This was their place at night. They held it for themselves and ignored humans unless there was no choice. Some of them glanced up and mewed. People often put food out for them, though there was little to get in a city short of everything, when even scraps were too precious to be thrown out. But the cats knew when someone looked like a provider and when not. These two humans only needed ignoring.

The silence was broken by the weary note of sirens revving up. It stopped almost as soon as it had started. It was a false alarm, quickly turned off. The sound came from across the harbour, from Senglea and Vittoriosa. But it was enough for the cats. They had long known what the sirens meant. They were gone in seconds, scattering up and down the steps, racing into their own shelter holes.

Turning where the steps bent up towards Battery Street, the two detectives saw several men walking down towards them, soldiers in different shades of khaki. The soldiers stopped, forming a line across the steps. For a few seconds Stefan and Frank continued, but then they halted, recognising that there was, suddenly, a threat.

'What's the problem, lads?' said Stefan cheerfully.

One of the men stepped forward; he wore a sergeant's stripes. 'You are.'

Stefan and Frank exchanged glances. For a moment they had no idea why this was happening. These men were looking for trouble and looking for them. This was not happening by chance. Stefan knew it had something to do with why they were in Malta. Things were being stirred up. Here it was. The Englishman shrugged. The same thought was in his head. The Military Police had done the stirring. This was the result.

'I think you've the wrong end of the stick,' said Chief Inspector Nugent. 'I don't know you . . . you don't know me. Whatever you think you're doing . . . whatever it's about . . . this is a mistake. We're just going back to our hotel.'

Stefan looked to one side. As he did so Frank Nugent caught the movement of his head and did the same. Below them, coming up from the Victoria Gate, were another half-dozen soldiers. There would be no escape.

'You don't even know who we are,' said Nugent. 'This is mad.'

Stefan took a deep breath. 'I'd say they know exactly who we are.'

'The Irish fucker's right.'

'OK, you know who we are. What do you want?'

The sergeant who was doing the talking nodded. Soldiers swarmed down the steps from above and up from below. Stefan and Frank were grabbed by the arms. There was no point struggling. They were not going anywhere.

'We want to give you a lesson in manners. You need to keep your nose out of other people's business. I don't know why you're so fucking interested.'

'I'm not interested in your business,' said Nugent. 'I don't give a fuck.'

'I'd hazard a guess,' said Stefan quietly, straining to look across at the chief inspector, 'that it'll be more like Colonel Macgregor's business, Frank.'

'Shut up!'

The speaker moved forward and punched Stefan hard in the stomach. He crumpled up, but the men who were holding him fast didn't let him collapse.

'The sodding Red Caps are pulling us in left, right and centre. You've only got to go for a drink in the wrong bar. They're there. Who do you know? Who do you knock about with? Where do you drink? Have you got pansy pals? Who do you fuck and how often? And do you like to give it or fucking take it, soldier?'

There was laughter from the men.

The sergeant grinned.

'I like to give it. Let's see if you can take it! Because it started with you. That's what we hear. Fucking civvy coppers! We'll give you information!'

'You've got it wrong,' began Nugent. 'It started with—'

The sergeant lashed out and punched him in the stomach.

'Shut it! You're not in Blighty now, Mr Inspector Nugent.'

Frank Nugent couldn't speak now.

'Listen! It started with a dead man, Sergeant,' shouted Stefan. 'A lot of dead men. A lot of dead men like all of you. That's why we're here. We didn't tell the MPs to question you. Why would we? We don't have any jurisdiction.'

'Too right, you Paddy bastard. We're here to show you that you don't.'

At that point there was the sound of laughter above them.

Stefan looked up; he knew the voices.

Several of the soldiers turned round, looking up too.

'Ignore your bloody mother, Maria,' Alice was saying.

'I can't. She never takes her eyes off me.'

Stefan saw Alice, Jane and Maria, starting down the steps. They were dressed in their uniforms, on their way to their night shift in the Lascaris War Rooms, he guessed.

'And lie, lie, lie again,' said Jane loudly. 'No decent mother would expect her daughter to do anything else when it comes to men. She lied once!'

Jane and Alice were laughing. Maria, more subdued, smiled.

They saw the crowd of men ahead of them. They saw Frank Nugent and Stefan Gillespie being held. They registered that Frank looked in some pain.

'Hello, Frank; hello, Stefan,' said Alice brightly.

Jane and Maria were frowning, still taking in the tense mood.

'We were looking for you. We said we'd show you the War Rooms?'

This was news to Stefan. He had a vague idea what the War Rooms were. He only knew the women worked there. But now he could think of nothing he would rather do than see them.

Alice looked at the sergeant who had been doing all the

talking. She could see the other men watching him. Whatever was going on, she could tell that he was the focus. She smiled broadly at him. The soldiers would know who they were, from their uniforms, but it had done no harm to remind them. The War Rooms were not far away. They were packed with senior officers. They were guarded by Military Police.

'Still quiet this side, Sergeant,' said Alice. 'Let's hope it stays that way.'

Jane took her lead from Alice's tone now.

'So, are you two coming, then, or have you changed your mind?'

The soldiers holding Stefan and Frank looked at each other, uncertain what to do, and now feeling doubtful. The mood was punctured. They let go.

If it was unclear what was happening, the sense of menace had been palpable in the darkness. There was silence on the steps. In the distance the sirens sounded from the Three Cities. Abruptly the distant thud of ack-acks.

'I hope we're not breaking up a party?' said Alice, yet more brightly.

She stepped forward, down the steps. Jane and Maria followed.

The soldiers moved aside, silent, slightly sheepish now.

'It's probably not the best time,' continued Alice pleasantly. 'Quiet enough here but bombs the other side of the harbour. Who needs that trouble?'

'War Rooms, then,' said Jane. 'You both look like you need a cup of tea.'

She took Stefan's arm, turning him round on the steps. Alice did the same with Frank Nugent. Maria was staring at the sergeant who had been doing all the talking, as Alice and Jane walked down the steps with the two policemen.

'You should go back to base, Sergeant, before a bomb drops on you.'

Jane and Alice walked on with Stefan and Frank; Maria caught them up. Behind them the sour group of soldiers was drifting back up the steps.

Alice grinned at Frank Nugent.

'Well, we've lumbered ourselves with you two now. Talk about "always ask a policeman"! Oh, dear! We'll look after you . . . till your chums have gone.'

Jane clutched Stefan's arm harder, laughing.

'I just think it's smashing you've made friends here so quickly!'

The three women, talking cheerfully about nothing much, took the two policemen along several dark alleys and arches and through two Military Police checkpoints to a dimly lit tunnel that was only minutes from where they had started. It seemed to drive directly under the bastions that rose up above in the darkness. Sirens were sounding in Valletta, but the sound of bombs and flashes of light in the sky came from the other side of the harbour. From the tunnel they turned into a brightly lit chamber where several soldiers and Military Policemen sat smoking and drinking tea. The Military Police sergeant who sat at the entrance grumbled about whether Stefan and Frank Nugent could go in, but he knew who the women were and was happily badgered into it by Jane and Alice. The tunnels that ran into the walls and the rock under Valletta here were the heart of the British defence of Malta, but there was a casualness about this place that mirrored what Stefan had already seen. What happened here, as elsewhere, had become a familiar and ordinary routine.

The corridors and the rooms were full of men and women in uniform, sitting at telephones and standing at great tables painted with the outline of Malta and the Mediterranean coast surrounding it. Stefan and Frank passed these rooms, glancing in at the maps and blackboards that filled the walls, looking like the boards at a railway terminus. They contained all the details of the airfields and the squadrons and the aircraft that could be put up to defend the island from the Luftwaffe and the Regia Aeronautica. The maps on the tables showed attacking and defending aircraft in the form of wooden markers, slotted with cardboard letters and numbers, which were pushed around by women who wore the same uniforms as the three ladies of Lascaris from the British Hotel. There was a constant buzz of instructions, from all directions, and mixed in with that were the crackling voices of men, pilots and observers, coming over Tannoy loudspeakers. In the background, behind the voices, there were explosions and the rattle of bullets. Jane and Maria disappeared into one of the big operations rooms. Alice offered a garbled explanation of what was going on as she hurried Stefan and Frank past the rooms to a canteen at the end of the corridor. It was empty except for four soldiers playing cards.

Alice produced two mugs of stewed, lukewarm tea from an urn.

She lit a cigarette.

'We'd all love to know what you two are doing here.'

'Ah, walls have ears, Alice,' said Nugent.

'He means we're here because we're here,' continued Stefan. 'If we did know when we started . . . who knows now? That's what makes us so popular.'

'We did try to get it out of Jimmy. He wouldn't even tell Maria!'

They were aware of the Military Police sergeant who had let them into the War Rooms, suddenly there. He looked awkward and uneasy and just a little red-faced. Not unreasonably: someone had just given him a bollocking.

'Bit of a cock-up, Alice.'

'You don't say, Sergeant. When wasn't there?'

'My officer said I shouldn't have let the two gentlemen . . .'

'Don't be silly,' replied Alice. 'They're only having a cup of tea.'

'They're not authorised . . .'

'Piffle. They're policemen, for goodness' sake!'

Frank Nugent grinned at Stefan. Stefan nodded. They both stood up.

'It's OK, Alice,' said Nugent, 'you saved our bacon. We're safe enough.'

'No bombing this side, sir,' said the sergeant apologetically. 'Orders from the Provost Marshall's office. That's the thing. Seems your clearance wasn't . . .'

'I'll take them up, Sergeant,' said Alice, irritated.

'Well, finish your tea, anyway . . .' The sergeant grunted and went out.

'Red tape,' sniffed Alice. 'They love it. It's not like what we do here's a secret. And don't you work with the Military Police? That's what Jimmy said.'

'Jimmy maybe says too much.' Nugent smiled. 'We do and we don't.'

'It's all nonsense, most of it.' Alice shrugged. 'Playing at soldiers.'

'It is,' said Stefan, laughing. 'You'd think there was a bloody war on!'

Alice led the two policemen back along the main corridor. They sidestepped the trail of men and women rushing up and down, in and out of every room. But then Alice stopped by the door into the main operations room. Stefan and Frank stood with her, waiting. They had not noticed anything, but she had. It was silence. There were voices along the corridor, but in the biggest room there was nothing, except the crackle of the Tannoy on the wall. No one was speaking. Everyone was very still. The women who stood round the map of the island, the men who sat above them, looking down at the table, the soldiers and airmen carrying messages back and forward from the telephones and the Intelligence and observation desks. They were all gazing at the speaker on the wall. It crackled, hissed again. Somewhere a dim explosion sounded, behind all the interference.

Then a man's voice.

It was the controller, sitting high above, who spoke.

'Striker to Echo 2, come in . . .'

The Tannoy hissed.

'We've lost you, Echo 2 . . . you need to break away . . .'

There was more silence.

Then a voice on the Tannoy, breaking through the interference.

'Striker, am not hearing you . . . not hearing . . . thing's fucked.'

There was a buzz of relief around the room.

The controller's voice again.

'Echo 2, bandits 20,000 feet . . . break away and return . . .'

The Tannoy hissed again. A long, empty moment.

'Hit over Senglea . . . I'll get her home . . .'

'Fast, Echo 2 . . . you need to break away fast . . . bandits above . . .'

'Not hearing . . . not . . . shit . . .'

Over the Tannoy's crackle, something like the rattle of bullets.

Everyone was still staring up at the black box on the wall.

'Shit . . . three of the fuckers . . . they're on . . .'

Another sound. Far away, dim. It could have been an explosion.

'Echo 2 . . . Echo 2 . . . Striker calling Echo 2 . . .'

No one moved. The Tannoy hissed intermittently, but that was all. Stefan saw a woman, standing next to Jane, reach out and put her arm round her. Then the voice of another officer, looking down on the room, broke into the silence.

'Three Hurricanes, Hal Far, now airborne . . .'
The room unfroze. Work continued.
'I'm on now, too,' said Alice softly. 'I'll take you out.'

16

Strait Street

The day was still after the night before. Malta came out of hiding to pick up the pieces, to shovel, clear away, mourn and bury the dead. They went about the life of the island with a quiet determination. Stefan Gillespie and Frank Nugent could only watch. Their part in it all would soon be over. In the morning after a heavy night of bombing, it was hard to believe that what they were doing mattered, especially when they had achieved nothing. If they had a job to do, the Luftwaffe and the Regia Aeronautica were doing everything possible to thwart it. Everywhere the dead piled up. Why should a few more count?

'Are you two busy this afternoon?'

Alice stood in the doorway to the bar of the British Hotel, where the Irish detective and the English detective were drinking coffee. It was a precious commodity in Malta and Mrs Sacco had a supply she kept quiet about. She knew the two policemen would be leaving soon.

'I don't know,' said Frank Nugent, as if he really didn't.

'When he says he doesn't know,' laughed Stefan, 'he means we're not.'

'Ah, but we could be.'

'What, busy packing?'

'I don't like walking away from it. The bastard's here, Stefan.'

'Talk among yourselves,' said Alice. 'Never mind me.'

'The short answer is we're not, Alice. Busy.'

The chief inspector shrugged.

'For an Irishman, you're not very big on optimism,' he added.

'You keep forgetting, I'm the wrong sort of Irishman, Frank.'

Alice was getting impatient.

'You two never say anything to each other we can understand.'

'It takes years of training,' said Stefan. 'Frank specialises in it.'

'Do shut up! Look, Jane's very low. You heard . . . in the War Rooms. He was a pilot she knew. She went out with him a few times. I mean, it's not . . . little things matter quickly here . . . sometimes there's not so long for them to matter.'

'You don't have to explain, Alice,' said Stefan.

'No. Anyway, Charlie Chaplin! That's what we all need.'

'Is it?'

'Yes, you too. Both of you. All you do is sit around doing nothing.'

Frank Nugent tapped his head. 'It all happens up here.'

'Well, the Charlie Chaplin film's on at the Manoel Theatre, *The Great Dictator*,' continued Alice. 'We all want to see it, but I can't get anyone to go with us. So, I've decided you two can come.'

'You have a way with invitations, Alice. How can we refuse?'

'You won't refuse, Frank.'

'It's the opportunity of a lifetime for me,' said Stefan.

'It's Charlie Chaplin. Don't overdo it, old son,' laughed Nugent.

'Forbidden fruit. They've banned it in Ireland.'

'You're joking!' said Alice.

'No, no Charlie. We can't be trusted with that sort of thing!'

'That's just silly!'

'That's neutrality. Hitler and Mussolini are no laughing matter.'

'You're coming, then?'

'Why not?' Stefan said.

Frank Nugent nodded.

As Alice turned to go, George Spiteri walked in.

'Can I smell coffee?'

'Guests only,' said Alice. 'That's what Mrs Sacco says.' She left.

Sergeant Spiteri walked to the table and picked up the coffee pot.

'What she doesn't know won't hurt her.' Stefan pushed a cup towards him.

'This was worth the journey. I haven't had real coffee in a month.'

'Is that all you're here for?' asked Nugent.

'No,' said the sergeant, smiling, 'but it's a good start.'

Stefan and Frank waited. George Spiteri drank the coffee.

'You know what I can't understand,' said the chief inspector, 'if we were in India, and there was a rumour of a British soldier killing Indians, we'd have riots and blood in the streets.' He grinned at the Maltese sergeant. 'Surely any self-respecting colony should have a few nationalists to stir up trouble and throw bricks through the governor's windows. It's not the way it's done!'

'Unfortunately, they're all in Uganda.' Spiteri laughed.

'Uganda?' exclaimed Frank Nugent.

'The British sent them off at the beginning of the war.'

'Well, that's one way of doing it,' said Stefan.

'But as nationalists go, some of them left a lot to be desired.' Sergeant Spiteri topped up his coffee. 'Their vision of independence was Malta becoming part of Italy. There was never a huge amount of enthusiasm for that. And since Mussolini started dropping bombs on us . . . Well, Uganda's probably the best place for them. In the meantime, most of us have made our choice. And it is our choice. We know what side we're on. The future . . . well, that's something else.'

He shrugged and drained the coffee, then he smiled.

'So, first things first. No rumours, no riots, just Strait Street!'

Half an hour later, Stefan Gillespie entered the narrow, canyon-like defile that was Strait Street. The street ran parallel to Kingsway, Valletta's widest thoroughfare. In the city's simple grid, Strada Stretta, too, stretched the length of the peninsula, down towards Fort St Elmo. It was so narrow that two people leaning out of balconies on the upper floors of opposite houses could touch.

Its buildings were high enough that they gave the gullied street a dark and secret atmosphere and kept it cool, even on the hottest days. Once the tall houses had been the homes of the Knights of St John and the wealthier citizens of Valletta. Now it was a row of bars and nightclubs, cheap hotels and brothels, over a hundred and still counting, though the line between any of those establishments was a narrow one. Alcohol, sex and jazz were the blood and the pulse in Strait Street's veins. The British presence in Malta had its pluses and minuses. People differed on where Strait Street stood in that reckoning. It had served the needs of the navy and merchant ships for a long time, and with ever-more soldiers, sailors and airmen arriving in the build-up to war, it had only grown in size.

Strait Street kept strange hours, but they had become more erratic as Malta came under siege from the air. Time had to be grabbed and business had to be done. Whereas the night and the early hours of the morning were when Strait Street had usually seen trade at its busiest, now, whenever there was a respite from the bombing, the bars and their ancillary activities opened up, and any servicemen who could find a free hour, whenever that hour was, made their way into the welcoming darkness of Strada Stretta.

George Spiteri led Stefan and Frank Nugent through the street. It wasn't busy, but there were bars open and soldiers and sailors moved from one to another. The sounds of several jazz bands emerged through open doors from dark interiors, blending and clashing cheerfully as the three men threaded their way along the street that was also known as the Gut. The sergeant stopped at a shabby door bearing none of the garish signs that advertised the delights of the neighbouring bars. There was a name in chipped, gold lettering: The Dorotheum.

The two detectives followed the sergeant inside. There was a bar and three or four tables. Music thumped away through a Tannoy-like speaker. Behind the bar a bearded man nodded at George Spiteri. Clearly, he knew the sergeant.

'Cisk?' was all he said by way of greeting.

'Yes, beer's fine, Karl.'

Only now, their eyes adjusting to the half-light, did Stefan and Frank see two men sitting at one of the tables: a young man, barely out of his teens; an older man, fidgety, suspicious. Spiteri went across to them. There were nods of hesitant uncertainty from the men at the table. The sergeant gestured at the two detectives to join them. More nods; recognition rather than greeting. They sat.

'We'll forget names, for now.'

The older man spoke in Maltese; telling him it was not just 'for now'.

'Mhux "biss għalissa", Surġent.'

The sergeant laughed. 'All right, we'll forget names, full stop.'

Karl put down three glasses of beer. He grinned.

207

'Friend of Dorothy One and Friend of Dorothy Two.'

'Fuck off,' said the older man.

'This is Mr Nugent and Mr Gillespie,' continued Spiteri. 'They don't know you. Or anybody. But they did come here to find the man who killed Tony Zammit and Kenneth Borg. And other men, too. I want to do the same.'

'You haven't got very far,' said the older man.

The younger man finally spoke. 'And maybe there's a reason for that.'

'And what is that reason?' said the sergeant.

The two men looked at each other, reluctant to say more.

'Father Zachary asked you to speak,' continued Spiteri.

The young man nodded.

'We don't know you from Adam,' said Stefan quietly. 'You can say anything. But we need something. Mr Nugent and I probably won't be in Malta much longer. What we came to do . . . we fucked up on. We came to collect a murderer . . . and we'll go home empty-handed. I know Sergeant Spiteri is doing what he can, but he's at a dead end too. And when the chief inspector and I get on a plane in a couple of days, the man who killed your friends will still be here. This feller's killed six or seven men that we know of. He won't stop. He's here. It's only a question of when he does it again.'

No one said anything for almost a minute.

Finally the younger man spoke.

'There is a soldier we've seen, some of us. I've seen him a couple of times. He watches. That's all you can say. And other men – other friends – have seen him. He watches, where we meet each other. Dark places, at night. He doesn't come close. I could only say he's tall, thin . . . a soldier in a uniform—'

The older man broke in. 'It's not so odd. Some men are very nervous. They want something, but they're frightened. It takes time to have the courage. There's a lot to be afraid of if you're seen, if anyone finds out. And there are other things that stop you. The shame of what you're doing. Some men watch a long time before they . . .'

For a moment again no one spoke.

'But with this man, something is different?' asked Stefan.

'Yes, I suppose,' said the younger man. 'Something doesn't feel right.'

Spiteri looked at the older man again. 'There is more, isn't there?'

The older man nodded.

'Yes. This soldier did come up to me one night. In the Barrakka Gardens. He didn't say much, barely anything, but that's not so unusual. He was English, I know that. I told him we could go somewhere. We could go down in the lift, to somewhere quiet. We walked towards the lift, and when it came up, someone stepped out. And the soldier ran. Fast. Back into the night. I saw his face for a second, just before he ran. He looked . . . I wouldn't say frightened, but angry, very angry.'

'Would you recognise him again?'

'I don't think so. I only saw this soldier briefly. He had a kind of scarf. Just round his neck, but it covered a bit of his face, his mouth. It was months ago.'

'And what about Kenneth Borg?'

The older man was silent again, before he continued.

'Kenneth had met this soldier too, at least once. He told me about it. You notice men. And we'd noticed him. It sounded like the same man to me. Ken tried to talk to him, but the man didn't answer. He just left, as soon as Ken went over to him. Ken had seen the soldier watching, like I had, the way I told you he watched. Ken was intrigued. He liked mystery and strangers. He said he'd have him next time. He'd give that soldier what he wanted. He said it like a joke.'

The man shook his head, looking down.

'And you think this could be the one we're looking for?'

The man looked up again.

'I can't know that. But I know there's something not right. That's all I'm saying. You're looking for a soldier. He's a soldier. You're looking for a man no one knows. That's him. You should look at him. You have to look at him.'

The man stopped, quite abruptly. He looked hesitant, as if there was something more he wanted to say, but he wasn't sure he could safely say it.

'But that isn't the end, is it?' said Spiteri.

'No,' replied the older man. 'There is one more thing. Ken saw more of this soldier's face than anyone else. He'd tried to talk to him. He had a feeling he recognised him. He wasn't a hundred per cent sure, but he said his gut told him he was right. He reckoned he'd seen the soldier somewhere else. He didn't think he was an ordinary soldier at all, even if he was dressed up as one, when he hung about at night in the Gardens. Ken thought he'd seen him in Strait Street, on patrol. He reckoned this soldier was really . . . a Military Policeman.'

That afternoon Inspector Gillespie and Chief Inspector Nugent abandoned the case for a few hours. They had something now, something new, something important, but the next move was going to be very difficult. They had to take what they had, along with George Spiteri, to the Provost Marshall at Fort St Elmo and to the sergeant's superiors in the Malta Police. One thing that wasn't difficult was anticipating Colonel Macgregor's reaction. It would not be pretty.

For now, it would be no bad thing to let it settle for a while. They both needed to marshal their thoughts before they stepped into the furore to come.

They walked to the Manoel Theatre with the three ladies of Lascaris. They sat in its old, golden interior, with its tiers of boxes, more opera house than cinema, and watched Charlie Chaplin mocking Hitler and Mussolini and their strutting dictatorships. Stefan had wondered how easily the laughter would come, with those same dictatorships raining bombs on the island outside the theatre. There had been dead to bury that morning, as there were every day. But it came easily, from an audience of British troops and Maltese men, women and children, laughing with a mixture of relief and some defiance; there was still a world in which simple laughter could triumph. For the British, it was Charlie Chaplin's absurd Hitler-Hynkel who provoked most laughter, but for the Maltese it was often Jack Oakie's Napaloni-Mussolini who produced belly laughs and boos. If Adenoid Hynkel captured some of the real darkness behind Chaplin's comedy, for the Maltese, Benzino Napaloni was their very own pantomime villain.

They came out of the theatre cheerful and refreshed. It was almost dark, but the night was clear and warm and quiet. The bombers might come, but such moments were to be grasped with open arms. Alice, Jane and Maria wanted to go to the Caffe Cordina for some tea and the only cakes in Valletta that still seemed to be made from flour that wasn't adulterated with something unspeakable and inedible. Stefan was happy to go, but Frank Nugent was preoccupied. Sitting in the cinema had not transported him as far from the business in hand as it had Stefan. As they came into the Strada Reale, he hung back a few yards with Stefan. The women walked on, laughing about the film.

'You go with them, Stefan. One of us should.'

'What's the matter?'

'We can't sit on what George has come up with. A Military Policeman. How many are there? Not that many. We have to go back to the Provost Marshall now. You, me, George Spiteri.'

'I know. He is going to love us,' said Stefan, smiling.

'I want to get it all down. Old stuff, new stuff. Point by point. We need to box Macgregor in. He has to realise there's no way round working with the Malta Police . . . and with us. We know more than he does. If he doesn't do it, and there's another murder, he's the one who'll be in the shit, army or no army.'

'I'll leave you to tell him that, Frank.'

Alice called back.

'Come on, you two, no dawdling. Cakes!'

'You go with the girls. When you get back to the hotel, we'll go through it together.'

Jane shouted back now too.

'Don't you two eat?'

Frank Nugent laughed. 'Tell them I've got a bit of Delhi belly!'

It was half an hour later that Stefan was walking down the steep cobbled steps of St John's Street to the junction with St Ursula Street and the British Hotel. He had left Alice, Jane and Maria with tea and cakes at the Cordina. The break that the afternoon had offered was over. Like Frank Nugent, he wanted to get back to work. There was a possibility that the journey to Malta would not be a waste of time. There was a chance that the man who had killed so many could be caught. The answer lay in the British Army. But the Provost Marshall and his men had to be battered into looking for the killer among their own.

The streets were silent, away from Kingsway, but there was a small crowd as Stefan turned into St Ursula Street. The road was blocked. Two Maltese police constables stood talking to an agitated group of men and women. Further up the stepped cobbles more policemen were walking slowly, shining torches in front of them. The conversation Stefan heard was in Maltese and English. He couldn't make out what anyone was saying, but as he moved through the crowd, people stopped talking. They were looking at him, concerned, awkward, nervous. He felt tension. Something was wrong.

A woman spoke to one of the constables in Maltese.

'Dan huwa il-pulizija l-ieħor, il pulizija Irlandiż.'

Stefan could guess the meaning; the other policeman, the Irish policeman.

'Inspector Gillespie . . .' said the Maltese constable.

'What's happened?'

'Mr Nugent, Chief Inspector Nugent. He was attacked.'

'Attacked?'

'The ambulance has come. It's through the hotel.'

The Maltese constable turned towards the St Ursula Street entrance to the British Hotel. Stefan followed. The policeman was almost running, so was Stefan.

'What do you mean attacked?'

'We think he was robbed, at the corner.'

The policeman pushed open the door to the hotel.

'There was a knife.'

'For fuck's sake! Is he all right?'

The two men ran along the corridor to the bar and the lobby and the doors out on to Battery Street, where there was road access.

'They carried him through . . . so the ambulance could . . .'

Stefan came out on to the street on the other side of the hotel. A stretcher was being carried into the back of a British Army ambulance. There was another crowd of people, among them Mr and Mrs Sacco, white faced, staring. Jimmy Gaunt was by the ambulance door. Stefan stood, frozen, unable to grasp what had happened in only seconds it seemed. Corporal Gaunt turned towards him. Stefan could see blood on Gaunt's shirt and shorts and, as he walked towards him, blood on his hands.

'I found him, Mr Gillespie. I found him . . . just lying . . .'

'Is he . . .?' Stefan couldn't get the words out.

The ambulance's engine started up.

Jimmy Gaunt turned to one of the army medics.

'This is Inspector Gillespie . . . he's the policeman with . . .'

'All right then. Better hop in, mate.'

213

Stefan, hardly knowing what he was doing, climbed into the back of the ambulance. The medic got in beside him. He pulled the door shut and sat down opposite the stretcher. Stefan sat next to him. The soldier took out a packet of Woodbines. He offered one to Stefan. Stefan shook his head. He gazed across at the stretcher and the face of Frank Nugent, now unconscious. The army medic lit his cigarette. Stefan sank back on the bench.

'What do you think?' said Stefan Gillespie quietly.

The soldier drew heavily on his cigarette. He did not reply.

17

Fort St Elmo

The next morning, Stefan Gillespie waited in the Provost Marshall's office at Fort St Elmo. An ATS corporal brought him a cup of tea. Stefan walked across the room and looked out at the sunlit courtyard. Apart from a truck and a staff car, it was empty. It was a strangely peaceful place. Created by knights who numbered priests in their ranks and had started out building hospitals, the heart of Fort St Elmo, behind its heavy bastions, still contained the faint memory of a monastery. The silence would not last long. Stefan took in the map of the island next to the window. Sicily loomed over it, far bigger; dotted across the Italian island were the locations of dozens of German and Italian airfields. Bombers would leave them again soon enough.

A bookcase reached up to the ceiling next to the map. Stefan let his eyes wander over the rows of books. He saw a shelf of small red and green books; red for Latin and green for Greek. They were sandwiched between bigger volumes; a thick Liddell and Scott *Greek–English Lexicon*, a Lewis and Short *Latin Dictionary*, books of grammar and classical history. This was what the British brought to war. Then he remembered the last time he had looked at one of the small red books, in the garden annexe in Thomastown that was James Corcoran's refuge. There was a Loeb edition of the poems of Catullus and there was a receipt Corcoran had kept for another copy of the same book, probably bought as a present for the man who killed him a few days later.

Colonel Macgregor's books were kept in neat, alphabetical order. Between Gaius Julius Caesar and Marcus Tullius Cicero were the poems of Gaius Valerius Catullus. An old copy, no dust jacket, battered and well read; sandwiched between volumes that looked almost untouched. Stefan took it and opened it. On the fly leaf: *Haydon Macgregor, Edinburgh University, 1919.*

The door opened. The Provost Marshall entered, flustered, irritated.

'Sorry to keep you, Inspector.'

Stefan noted that for some reason his rank was acknowledged today.

'I've been with my SIB chaps . . . and the Malta Police.'

The words were simple, but they contained the suggestion that this was Stefan's fault. Macgregor didn't sit down. He paced as he spoke.

'It's a relief about Nugent. A great relief. You've seen him?'

'Yes, sir. I was at the hospital till this morning. He's grand.'

Grand was stretching it, but Nugent would come through.

'I really don't . . .' Macgregor was shaking his head. 'It's not Malta. Not the Malta I know. People get robbed, yes, but even that is rare enough . . . you know? It's a quiet, peaceful place.' The Provost Marshall smiled. 'Well, you might not think so when you're in a shelter under the Barrakka Gardens, but people are not bombs. They put up with the bombs, though. I've got men who can't stick it the way the Maltese do.'

Macgregor looked at Stefan as if he needed his words justified.

Stefan gave a nod. He had seen the truth of that.

'This business . . .' The Provost Marshall stiffened. 'I have no doubt you and the chief inspector will see something else in what's just happened. I am sure Sergeant Spiteri does too. I don't know. I will admit that. But it still seems . . . if you take one appalling event and shove it next to another one . . . is that evidence or just piling up a series of coincidences?'

'I'm not a great one for coincidences, Colonel, especially when it comes to people getting murdered and then, hey presto, someone trying to murder a policeman who has found out . . . who's stirred things up.'

'You've certainly done that, both of you. You and Spiteri.'

'You can't stir something up if there's nothing to stir.'

The Provost Marshall walked to the window and gazed out.

'I have seen Sergeant Spiteri this morning. It's clear there are issues we need to work on more closely with the local bods. Spiteri's boss will be working with Sergeant Shaw and the SIB, and Lieutenant Yates. I accept that I may have been slow on this. But, who knows, perhaps I might have been more active if you and Chief Inspector Nugent hadn't arrived to lead us up the garden path. It was Scotland Yard, as I recall, that insisted we only had to fingerprint a few dozen soldiers, and it would be done and dusted. Not bloody so, Mr Gillespie.'

'No, sir.' Stefan smiled. The Provost Marshall had enjoyed saying that.

'So, we are on to this. The Corps of Military Police and the Malta Police. I have to say that these allegations about a Military Policeman . . . supposedly from one queer with the habit of picking up men in the Upper Barrakka . . . I simply don't believe it. I won't ignore it, but it's no basis for an investigation.'

Stefan was sure that meant Colonel Macgregor would ignore it.

'It's one place to look, Colonel, if there's a reason to look.'

'Well, "if" is the word, Inspector. I don't go by "if"s. Meanwhile, you and Chief Inspector Nugent are surplus to requirements. You failed to do what you came here to do. You find it impossible not to stir up trouble where there is none. And now, regrettably, Mr Nugent has been seriously hurt. I've spoken to the Officer Commanding and I know he's passed it by the Governor's office. As soon as the chief inspector can travel, there'll be seats on a plane to Gibraltar.'

Stefan nodded. He was in no position to argue. His presence was never really tolerated anyway. Nugent probably would argue, but to no purpose.

'Thank you, sir.'

Stefan realised he was still holding the Loeb Catullus.

'I'm sorry, Colonel. I was just looking at this.'

Macgregor took the book. His face softened, in some surprise.

'You're a classicist, Inspector Gillespie?'

'Not at all. Small Latin . . . and no Greek whatsoever.'

The Provost Marshall leafed idly through the book.

'Looks like you read a lot of Catullus, sir.'

Macgregor's sharp voice was quieter. Somewhere there was regret.

'It's funny, isn't it? I spent a lot of time reading this stuff, two thousand years old – getting on for three, some of the Greek. I carry it around with me, I don't know why. I never look at it. But I remember reading it. That was something . . . worthwhile. It's not a word that comes into my head much now.'

As Stefan Gillespie left the colonel's office, Lieutenant Yates and Sergeant Shaw were walking towards it. Yates smiled and slapped Stefan on the back.

'They make them tough at Scotland Yard!'

'Tough enough,' said Stefan.

'Thanks for leaving us all your work!'

'It'll give you something to do, Jack.'

'Yes, Lieutenant.'

Shaw grinned. 'Bugger all going on in Malta!'

The SIB man knocked on the colonel's door and went in. Yates followed. He looked back at Stefan for a moment.

'You seen Jimmy Gaunt, my corporal, Stefan?'

'No, not since last night.'

'He's disappeared.'

'If he's at the British Hotel, I'll say you're looking for him.'

Yates laughed. 'Whatever's going on with Maria Sacco, if he's not back ASAP, he's on a charge!'

The first thing Stefan saw when he came out of Fort St Elmo was George Spiteri, leaning against the bonnet of a black Austin 10, smoking a cigarette.

'Do you want a lift?'

Stefan nodded. He took a cigarette from the packet held out by Spiteri.

They got into the car. Stefan lit the cigarette.

'I was up at Mtarfa,' said the Maltese sergeant. 'Frank looks good.'

'He's not so bad.'

The car pulled away.

'He knows we've got our marching orders? Back to Blighty.'

'I told him that's what I'd heard at HQ. I've got mine, too.'

How do you mean?'

'I can drive the car and carry the bags, my boss is running the case. He'll do it Colonel Macgregor's way, whatever that is. And that won't impress the people who might be able to give us more information. There's not so many places homosexuals go. The man we're looking for was hanging around them. We know that. Other people must have seen him too. And they all know each other. I think there's more to get. I think we could even start to build up a description. That's the only way to go. But now? It's the kiss of death. You think our friends from the Dorotheum will sit in an interrogation room with a Military Policeman and repeat what they said? It'll be a know-nothing, saw-nothing, heard-nothing job from now on. Not only that. They'll be thinking about what happened to Frank Nugent. They might not want to risk being . . . robbed.'

Stefan Gillespie stepped out of the bathroom at the British Hotel. He had shut himself in there, in the middle of the afternoon. The ladies from Lascaris had come back from their night shift that morning. They were still sleeping. There would be no hot water for them when they finally came to. He knew the consequences. It was the first time he had won the battle of the bathroom. They were sleeping late; he had taken his chance. A bath was not at the top of his list of priorities but being alone was. The skies were still over Valletta; half an hour of silence was worth the wrath of the three women upstairs. Frank Nugent was all right. Stefan had left him recovering in hospital at Mtarfa. That was what mattered most. It had been close, closer than the English policeman chose to say. But he had been lucky, not only in the organs the knife had missed, but in the hospital they had taken him to, where the trauma of bloody wounds was a daily routine.

For the rest, there wasn't much left that Stefan could do. He could only wait to leave the island. If Frank Nugent had little authority, he had none. Colonel Macgregor wanted them both out of Malta. The colonel's predictions had been fulfilled. Sending civilians into a theatre of war, as if ordinary life – even the ordinary investigation of a murder – could somehow continue showed the ignorance of the civilian authorities. There was too much trouble that was beyond the Provost Marshall's control, or anybody else's on an island under siege. The only way to deal with anything troublesome that Colonel Macgregor could realistically control was to remove it. But what Macgregor saw as trouble, Stefan and Frank Nugent and George Spiteri knew was a breakthrough. A Military Policeman. Somewhere behind it all, in Ireland, in

England, in Malta, was a man who was now a Military Policeman. It was something so fragile that it could easily be punctured. And it was likely it would be.

The claims came from people Macgregor would give no credence to; they were only homos, poofs, queers, perverts. And they were making allegations against the Corps of Military Police. Where would Macgregor even start? He'd start by refusing to believe it, thought Stefan. And then another thought, a mad thought. Macgregor was a Military Policeman. It was a wild, unexpected idea, but it was there. Stefan could feel he was grasping at straws, reaching for anything when everything was falling apart again. That's how it was. Anyone could read a Latin poet. A coincidence. And if he was always suspicious of coincidences, wasn't that what they were made of; something here, something there, slammed together only because they were in your head? But how many soldiers in Malta carried a copy of James Corcoran's favourite Latin poet? Stefan Gillespie knew he was leaping at nothing because he had control of nothing. There was only vagary and hearsay.

He was on the landing above his own room, about to go downstairs. He had closed the bathroom door quietly. He had stepped gingerly along the landing. He did not want to wake Alice, Jane and Maria, particularly Alice and Jane. Bath water was a precious commodity. At the British Hotel, the ladies of Lascaris insisted it was their property. He needed a drink before he faced them.

It was the silence of the hotel, in the silent street – where a rare afternoon of peace meant a siesta for most of the residents – that let Stefan hear the noise of a door opening on the floor below. He looked down over the banister. He saw Jimmy Gaunt come out of Frank Nugent's room. The corporal turned to the door and locked it. He waited, listening, looking down the stairs. But he did not look up. He moved quickly, quietly downstairs. Stefan could see the lobby and the desk. No one was there.

Corporal Gaunt disappeared. He was putting the key behind the desk. He stepped across the lobby, visible momentarily, and hurried out through the door to Battery Street.

Stefan waited a few seconds then went down. He passed his own room and Frank Nugent's and continued to the lobby. He walked behind the reception desk and picked up the key Gaunt had put down. He went upstairs and into the English detective's room. He walked to the open shutters of the balcony. He could see Jimmy Gaunt, making his way towards the Victoria Gate. He looked back into the room. It was neat and tidy, as Nugent had left it. On the table next to the bed was a briefcase, files, papers, pages of scribbled notes. There was a map of Valletta marked with hieroglyphs, intelligible only to Frank Nugent. Stefan knew they showed where two bodies had been found, where a witness had seen a victim or an unidentified soldier, where two men may have been picked up by another man at different times. And there were accounts of conversations with George Spiteri and the men at the Dorotheum in Strait Street. Gaunt could have no reason to come into the room secretly, except to look at all this. There was nothing else there. And people had been looking for the Military Policeman too, earlier. Jack Yates had made a joke about it. Gaunt had disappeared. He was AWOL. Why? He must have been at the hotel all along. He had been there to search Frank Nugent's room.

Chief Inspector Nugent was a meticulously tidy man. Stefan, who wasn't, had found himself almost irritated by the way the Englishman squared up piles of documents and numbered and renumbered notes to keep them in chronological order. It was close to obsessive. The state of the papers on the table in Nugent's room was normal for most people, but Stefan had a clear image of what the desk looked like before. The material had been searched. Much of the information it contained was already with the Military Police at Fort St Elmo. Stefan didn't know how difficult it would have been for Jimmy

Gaunt to get access to it. Not that difficult, if he was determined to see it. He wanted more, to risk doing this. But why? What did he want to know so badly?

It was unlikely, even if the corporal had been at Fort St Elmo that morning, that he would have been party to any conversation about a Military Policeman, in the uniform of an ordinary soldier, cruising Valletta. It was something the Provost Marshall was sitting on; something he didn't want talked about publicly. It was also something he didn't believe. It would not be common knowledge. But Jimmy Gaunt must have known something and he had been desperate to find out more. And he must have done in Nugent's room. He must know things now that George Spiteri had told neither his own boss, Inspector Simmons, nor the Provost Marshall. He would know the names of people who were talking. He would know who had pointed to a Military Policeman in disguise, picking men up for sex in the Upper Barrakka Gardens.

The rest of the afternoon was as unsatisfactory as it could have been. Stefan Gillespie thought Jimmy Gaunt might come back to the hotel. He was always hanging around there. But so far, the corporal had not returned. Stefan didn't know what to do next. He wanted to get some perspective on what he had just seen but there was no one to talk to about it. He thought of taking a taxi to Mtarfa, to see Frank, but decided he should stay in Valletta. He needed to know more about Gaunt. Sitting in the bar at the British Hotel, he was interrupted by two Military Policemen who were looking for Gaunt themselves. They were good-humoured enough, but it was clear that Lieutenant Yates was no longer making jokes about the corporal's disappearance. Jimmy was in trouble.

Stefan walked along the Grand Harbour to Malta Police Headquarters. George Spiteri wasn't there. He left a message and was caught, and briefly interrogated, by the sergeant's

superior. Inspector Simmons was an English colonial policeman, who was simultaneously curious about what Stefan
wanted and half afraid he might tell him. Stefan knew from
Sergeant Spiteri that Simmons lived in a state of permanent
genuflection to the British Army in general and the Provost
Marshall in particular. The inspector was now working with
Colonel Macgregor on the investigation of what were two of
the most brutal murders the island of Malta had seen, not to
mention the ones in England and Ireland that came with it. He
would do what the Provost Marshall told him. Stefan knew
that anything he said would go straight to Macgregor. The
inspector showed all the signs of being a man who worked
hard at avoiding trouble. If he ever found it, his first instinct
would be to pass the ball on. There was no point telling him
anything.

Fort St Elmo was close to Police Headquarters. Stefan had
left the fort earlier, with nothing more to say, but something
had happened. Corporal Gaunt's behaviour meant something.
But what? He couldn't be sure the corporal hadn't been sent
there by Lieutenant Yates, or by the colonel himself. Gaunt
was handy for a bit of spying. He was never out of the British
Hotel, waiting for Maria, being dragged off for lessons in
Maltese by Mrs Sacco, to keep him away from Maria. That was
a standing joke. But searching Frank Nugent's room wasn't.
And something was growing in Stefan's mind: the night before,
in Battery Street, the ambulance taking Frank away. Blood on
Jimmy Gaunt's shirt and shorts. A lot of blood. The corporal
helped carry the chief inspector to the ambulance from St
Ursula Street. But hadn't he been the one who found him? The
first one on the scene? Wasn't it Gaunt who saw a figure
running away in the dark, at the top of the steps? The robber.
Wasn't it only Gaunt who had glimpsed this supposed robber?

Frank Nugent had seen nothing himself. He'd sensed someone behind him in the night, on an empty street. Then the

knife, like a sledgehammer in his side. Pain, blackness. He remembered nothing more until the hospital. It was still being called a robbery. And, yes, Frank Nugent's wallet had gone. But he was no more inclined than Stefan or George Spiteri to believe in a chance theft. They had stirred the black pool. Something had come up from the depths.

Stefan returned to the hotel to find Gaunt back again. He was outside, talking to Maria. She was in uniform, on her way to the War Rooms. She was laughing, teasing him about something. It looked like he was hard work. By the time Stefan reached them, Maria's voice showed irritation. She turned as Stefan approached, smiling warmly. Jimmy Gaunt nodded. He looked uncomfortable.

'Mr Nugent's all right,' Jimmy said. 'That's some relief.'

'He'll be fine,' said Stefan. 'I think he was lucky.'

'I can't remember anything like it,' said Maria, with genuine disbelief. 'People do rob. Bags and purses. But no one would do that. I've never heard of it.'

Gaunt shrugged at neither of them in particular.

'Long as he's OK, Maria.'

Alice and Jane came out of the hotel.

'You bastard,' said Jane.

'You Irish bastard,' added Alice.

Stefan was puzzled. He had long forgotten.

'Water, bath,' continued Alice, 'ladies of Lascaris for the use thereof.'

Stefan smiled. 'You'll survive.'

'Don't do it again!' said Jane. 'We'll send in the MPs if you do.'

'Won't we, Jimmy?' laughed Alice.

Jimmy attempted a grin, without much conviction.

'Don't mind him,' said Maria. 'He's been drinking.'

'I have not!'

'I can smell it, Jimmy.'

The three women walked away.

Jane called back. 'If you see Frank, give him a kiss – from us, that is!'

They hurried on.

Stefan headed into the British Hotel.

'Good thing Mr Nugent's OK.' Jimmy Gaunt said it again.

Stefan wondered if he should say something about the MPs who were there earlier, looking for Gaunt, about a now angry Lieutenant Yates. He didn't.

'Yes, it is,' Stefan said, and carried on into the hotel lobby.

An hour later Stefan Gillespie came downstairs. He walked into the bar and stood with a beer. He nodded at Jimmy Gaunt, who sat at a table in the corner, on his own. The corporal nodded in return, but he made no attempt to join Stefan. And Stefan stood at the bar, drinking, because he had no inclination to talk to Gaunt. Not now. When he did, it would be a different conversation from anything that had gone before. But he would do nothing at present. He had to wait for George Spiteri. He had promised the sergeant and he needed his authority.

Mrs Sacco bustled into the bar, looking busy as she always did, but a little put out. Her eyes fixed on Jimmy Gaunt. Clearly, he was what had ruffled her.

'Jimmy, have you got nothing better to do?'

Corporal Gaunt looked up.

'Lieutenant Yates was here earlier. He was looking for you.'

'He can look, can't he?'

'Are you off duty, then?'

'I suppose so.'

She tutted. This wasn't a Jimmy Gaunt she knew. She smiled.

'Come on. If you have nothing to do . . . why don't we do some Maltese?'

She spoke almost tenderly. Stefan saw she was concerned.

'Aħna nitgħallmu l-Malti . . . we'll learn some Maltese, yes?'

Jimmy Gaunt stood up, irritated, almost angry.

'For fuck's sake, give it a break, woman.'

He rushed out of the bar, leaving Maria's mother close to tears.

Stefan put the glass of beer down. He walked out quietly. He went to the door and stepped out into the street. He could see Corporal Gaunt heading towards the junction with St John's Street. If Mrs Sacco was surprised by Jimmy Gaunt's behaviour, so was he. The corporal was obviously anxious, disturbed. He was a worried man. Stefan wanted to know where he was going.

18

Triq Marsamxett

Stefan followed Corporal Gaunt up the steep steps of St John's Street, keeping back as far as he could, always to one side of the street, in the shadow of the shops and houses. There were not many people about, a few Maltese men and women going home, or searching the thinly stocked shops for something that might not be there tomorrow, soldiers and sailors moving from bar to bar, probably working their way from the harbour to Strait Street. Jimmy Gaunt was as preoccupied as he had been in the bar at the British Hotel. He was easy to follow, but full of indecision. He slowed down, stopped, lit a cigarette, walked quickly, threw the cigarette aside half-smoked, slowed and stopped again. As Stefan came up behind him into St John's Square, Valletta grew busier. There were people in the cafés, standing in groups talking in the laziness of an evening that was still calm. There was a line of men and women moving towards the cathedral. The bell was tolling for Mass. Jimmy Gaunt almost passed the Cathedral of St John, but he turned to the cathedral steps and the open doors.

Stefan Gillespie waited, then he walked into the cathedral. It was filling up with people, but he could see the Military

Policeman sitting on one of the chairs that covered the blaze of colour that was the marbled floor. He was close to the doors. He would only have to turn to see Stefan. Stefan went back outside. He walked to a café under a colonnaded archway that partly hid him and ordered a beer. The doors of the cathedral were in front of him, across the square.

It took ten minutes before Corporal Gaunt emerged. He walked on along St John's Street and crossed the central street of the city, the Strada Reale, Kingsway. Stefan followed.

Jimmy Gaunt swung abruptly into Strait Street. The bars were busy here, some behind closed doors, some with doors open on to cave-like interiors that showed no lights. The tight space of Strait Street was crowded with servicemen. Stefan struggled to keep Jimmy in sight, as he brushed off the calls for business from the open doorways and the balconies above. He lost Gaunt for a moment, then almost ran into him when the Military Policeman had to stop to speak to two MPs on patrol. Clearly they didn't know he was AWOL, but Stefan could see Gaunt didn't want to talk.

As Strait Street began to slope steeply down towards the end of the peninsula that was Valletta, the corporal turned into St Christopher Street. There was a red telephone box – a piece of London coming out of nowhere. Jimmy went into it and picked up the phone. He was there several minutes. He came out of the telephone box with irritation, almost anger, adding to the confusion and indecision he already exuded. It was darker now. St Christopher Street was empty, and Stefan needed to stay much further back. He thought he had lost Jimmy Gaunt, but then he saw him, walking across a low hill of brick and stone, to a terrace of houses beyond. Stefan crouched, watching. The corporal passed the row of buildings, looking up at the windows, many of which were broken and unrepaired. Black, empty interiors lay behind them. The houses' fronts were cracked and scarred from shrapnel. Stefan registered a sign in chipped stone at the corner of one of the buildings: *Triq Marsamxett, Marsamxett Street.*

There was a shout from another street and a peal of laughter; it was somewhere behind Stefan. Two voices were arguing. There came the sound of something smashing. The young Englishman stopped at a door now. He pushed and went in.

Stefan walked slowly towards the building. He saw a light in a window at the top of the house. Then it was gone. A lamp had been lit and a shutter had been closed. Stefan reached the door of the house. It was open. Inside was a dark hallway and a set of narrow stairs. There was silence. As he started to climb the stairs, he saw that some doors had pieces of planking nailed across them. There was a smell of warmth that was somehow dry and damp at the same time. There was the smell of rats and mice. Jimmy Gaunt had to be at the top, in the room behind the shutter. Stefan moved carefully, quietly, upwards, listening all the time.

When he reached the top of the staircase, there was a narrow landing. There were three doors. The third was open. The other two had padlocks screwed to them. He could see clearly in the dim light that came from the doorway to the third room. He moved towards it. There was a black alcove and a steep, ladder-like stairway that had to lead to the roof. He could see a padlock on the floor. The door had been broken open. At his feet there was a heavy iron bar. It must have been used to force the lock. Suddenly, he felt his vulnerability. He was unarmed. He had no idea where he was. There was a chance that Jimmy Gaunt had put a knife in Frank Nugent. Could there even be a chance that he had killed six men? It seemed mad, but was it? Gaunt was a soldier, a Military Policeman. The man that had to be found was a soldier, a Military Policeman. That fitted. And Jimmy Gaunt's recent behaviour didn't fit an innocent man.

Stefan picked up the bar. He looked through the open door. He could see a wall and part of a bed in the room. The corporal was bending down at the side of the bed. He pulled out a heavy leather suitcase from underneath it. He undid two straps and lifted the lid. He stood up, looking into the case. He pulled something out, a piece of clothing. He dropped it on the bed and stepped back. Stefan moved out of sight, into the alcove. As he did, he kicked an empty bottle into the stairwell. A few seconds, then the sound of the bottle smashing below. He heard Corporal Gaunt's footsteps on the bare floor. The light from the lamp in the room was casting his shadow along the landing now. He was walking towards Stefan.

'Who is it?'

There was a rustling, a clip unclipped.

Corporal Gaunt had taken out his revolver.

'I said who is it?'

The corporal's voice was trembling.

'Is that …? Who is …?' Jimmy seemed to gulp. 'I am armed, right?'

The outstretched hand and the revolver it clutched moved slowly into the opening to the alcove. Stefan Gillespie lifted the iron bar above his head, and brought it down with all his force. The gun spun away along the landing towards the open door. Jimmy Gaunt collapsed on his knees with a scream of pain. Stefan came out of the alcove and used the bar once more, against the side of the Military Policeman's head, even as he looked up at Stefan in fear and bewilderment. Now Jimmy lay on the floor; out cold.

Stefan Gillespie breathed deeply, leaning against the wall. There came a familiar sound, winding itself up and wailing across the night, over the square streets of Valletta and into the house. The sirens were going, all around. An ordinary night. The bombers were on their way.

*

Stefan dragged Jimmy Gaunt into the room. He was unconscious. He groaned but didn't come round. Stefan pulled him to the iron bed frame that was against a wall, under a shuttered window. He took one of the leather straps from the open suitcase and wrapped it round the corporal's hands, buckling it tight. There was blood on Stefan's hands as well as on Gaunt's. The bar that had smashed into the wrist had a sharp, jagged edge. Stefan could feel the inertia of a broken wrist bone too, drooping as he tied it to the other one. He wound the second strap round the Englishman's ankles and buckled them together. He saw the MP's service revolver in the doorway. He picked it up and put it beside him on the bed.

The room was small and dark. The walls were cracked; there was crumbling plaster. The paraffin lamp lit only the area around the bed. It sat on a box across from the bed, where Gaunt had put it. The bed was quite new; carved, heavy mahogany. There was an armchair next to it, new too, in smart red morocco, with brass studs that gleamed. It was as if someone had started to furnish the room and abandoned the effort. Why? Against one wall there were a dozen boxes and packing cases.

Stefan lifted one of the lids of the boxes. There were bottles of Johnnie Walker whisky stacked inside. The room looked like it was a place where goods pilfered from the army were stored. On a line, stretched across a corner of the room, a suit hung on a hanger; there were trousers, shirts. A pile of unwashed clothes, military and civilian, lay against the wall underneath; shorts, underwear. Yet the room did not feel as if it was lived in.

There was only a dirty sheet over the mattress of the bed. On a packing case, there was a half-empty bottle of Johnnie Walker and several maps of Malta and of Valletta. On the bed was the open suitcase Stefan had seen Jimmy pulling clothes from. Next to it was a khaki army tunic and a pair of khaki trousers. Stefan looked into the case and saw more khaki. He pulled out the clothing. There were two more uniforms in khaki serge. They were the uniforms of an ordinary soldier, with no markings of rank. There were shorts and shirts in the sandy-yellow of tropical kit and two forage caps. Stefan laid the items on the bed. There were no regimental badges, no signs of identity. This was the unidentifiable, barely registered soldier who might have been glimpsed somewhere near so many killings. In blackout, in cities full of plain khaki, these uniforms brought a kind of invisibility. There were two heavy commando knives in oil paper. And there were papers he recognised, copies of reports and statements from the Scotland Yard files Nugent had sent to the Military Police at Fort St Elmo. In the bottom of the case, Stefan found a bag that contained thin, pale kid gloves, almost the colour of flesh. Four pairs. There were never any fingerprints. It was obvious now. All these things were disposable. Uniforms of the night. And whatever bloody state they got into, they could be thrown away. Afterwards.

There was a moan from the floor. Then a cry of pain. Jimmy Gaunt had discovered the pain that was a broken wrist. Stefan sat on the edge of the bed, staring at the young Military Policeman's wide, blinking eyes. Gaunt pushed himself up, his back against the wall.

'Ow, shit!' He held up his bound hands. 'You bastard!'

Stefan said nothing. He couldn't relate this to the pale, boyish face.

'I can't see a thing. Where are my bloody glasses?'

Stefan stood up. Jesus, what was the man talking about?

'You want your fucking glasses? That's it, is it? That's what you say?'

'That would be a start, sir. Why the hell did you do this?'

The note of injured indignation was not what Stefan expected.

The corporal grimaced in pain again, but his mind was somewhere else.

'I knew he had this place, I found where it was. I couldn't fathom what was going on, but I saw him, that's the thing, after Mr Nugent was stabbed, later, near . . . I couldn't make sense of it. He said he wasn't there! I never imagined this, I never . . .'

Stefan stared at Gaunt. What was he talking about? There were tears in his eyes, but it was something that pushed past the pain.

'I didn't know who . . . I was afraid, I tried to phone Sergeant Spiteri . . .'

'What?'

The corporal was staring away from Stefan now.

'Fuck,' he said quietly.

He was looking at the door.

Stefan Gillespie turned the same way.

The uniform was as neat and sharp as ever; the red cap was tightly fixed on his head, at exactly the correct military angle. It was Lieutenant Yates.

'Bit of a party, lads?' He walked forward, smiling. As he did, he unclipped the holster at his side and took out his revolver. He glanced down at Jimmy Gaunt, battered and in pain, his hands tied. 'So, is that an arrest, Inspector?'

Stefan gestured towards the bed and the pile of uniforms.

'You'd better look at what's here, Jack.'

It did not occur to Stefan to wonder how Lieutenant Yates got there, at precisely this moment. He did not register that the revolver was pointing at him.

'Follow my leader,' said Yates. 'There's Jimmy Gaunt, pride of the Corps of Military Police, heading along Strait Street . . . and down here to Marsamxett, with Gillespie of the Garda Síochána in hot pursuit. Not easy to miss. I didn't.'

Stefan saw where the gun was pointing.

He looked at Gaunt. The corporal shook his head.

'Might have been better asking what was going on, sir, instead of . . .' The corporal held up his bound hands.

'Yes.' Stefan nodded. 'It might have been a lot better.'

Yates moved closer, with an expression of weary irritation.

'Don't poke your nose in. That's a lesson in life, Stefan. You and Frank, now Jimmy. What's the point? Nobody cares, not really. It's a fucking slaughterhouse out there. Why fucking bother? But I knew Jimmy was going to pitch up sooner or later. He'd been asking about my little hide-away. I'm sorry to say some idle fucker said something. My fault, maybe. I probably mentioned I had a little place, didn't I, Jimmy, after a drink? Somewhere to bring a woman, eh?'

'You can't walk out of this now, Lieutenant,' said Stefan. 'You have a gun, but where's that going to get you? We're not some fucker in the darkness.'

'You're not clever, are you?' said Yates. 'But then you're a Paddy.'

'Sir,' said Corporal Gaunt, rank still dominant, 'I think it's over, sir.'

Lieutenant Yates turned the revolver from Stefan and pulled the trigger.

Corporal Gaunt slumped back on to the floor.

The revolver was pointing at Stefan again, even as Yates spoke.

'I'm pissed off about Jimmy. I mean that. Your fault, Inspector.'

'How the fuck does shooting him help?' Stefan was almost shouting.

'You're an Irishman, of dubious antecedents. I had Intelligence take a look at you. Irish Special Branch, not your average detective, eh? Trip to Berlin not long ago, right? Family in the heart of the dear old Thousand-Year Reich. You'll be found in the docks. Areas verboten to non-military sorts. When I say you'll be found, I'll find you, taking photos. I'll just do my job! It won't surprise Colonel Macgregor. Neutral, my arse, is his line. He didn't like you poking around. You shot poor Jimmy when he saw you. He'll get a medal. Posthumous. I shot you as you ran. I might get one too. But I won't begrudge Jimmy his if I don't. That'll be that. So, you see, I can walk out of this.'

'Why? To do it again . . . How many men do you need to kill, Jack?'

'You mistake your role here, Inspector. No questions, thanks.'

'Was James Corcoran the first? Or were there others?'

'Shifting you both, that's the bugger,' said the lieutenant to himself.

'He had a name, though. The others didn't have that, did they?'

'Keep me talking? Oh, dear.' Yates shook his head. 'None of us have real names, you see. Queer, that's the name. None of us asked for it. God-given. Can't get shot of it. Whatever you do. You try. Never clean. Never clean again.'

'You can stop this, Jack. Wouldn't that be better?'

'Ah, the old trick-cyclist routine. Don't bother. I'm not going to break down in tears, Stefan. There's a job to do. Marsamxett's empty now. Bombed out, not a lot of people about. That's good. But moving two of you will take some doing . . .'

Yates was talking to himself again, more tense, working things out.

'Even with hardly anyone about . . . getting the two fucking bodies . . .'

Stefan had not moved since he first realised the lieutenant's gun was aimed at him. Now he stepped forward slowly. The slightest shift. Then again.

Still covering Stefan with his revolver, Lieutenant Yates knelt down by Jimmy Gaunt. At that moment there was an explosion. It wasn't close, but it was loud. It shook the building.

Another explosion followed. Yates smiled.

'That's what I want . . . Yes, everyone in the fucking shelters!'

There was the sound of ack-ack guns. More bombs. Yates stood up.

'That's my boys,' said the Military Policeman. 'We need a bit of noise!'

Stefan could see, as Yates stared at him, what he had not seen before. It wasn't something that spoke of madness, but it was a cold detachment. It wasn't confusion, it was more like emptiness. He could also see the MP's attention was no longer on him. Yates was thinking hard, still working out what to do. Stefan used that moment. He inched closer to the bed. That was where he had put the gun down earlier. A khaki tunic covered it. He could see the edge of the grip. He would have to take it and shoot almost instantly. He had one chance. If he missed, Yates would have several. He could not fumble it.

There was a groan from Jimmy Gaunt, half-conscious. Yates spun round.

'You're not dead, you fucker! I need you dead. Damn you, Jimmy!'

Lieutenant Yates levelled the revolver back at Gaunt.

'I didn't want to kill you, you arsehole. But that's how it's got to be.'

Jack Yates' attention was off Stefan for only a second. There was another explosion outside, closer than before. The room shook. Stefan chose that instant to kick out at the box and the lamp. The lamp spun across the room, smashing against the wall. As it did so the light went out. The room plunged into darkness. Simultaneously Stefan had thrown himself hard at the bed.

Yates had turned round and now he fired, but into thin air.

Stefan's hand found the grip of the revolver. He fired two rapid shots towards where Yates had been standing, then pushed himself off the bed. Now he was behind the big armchair. But the MP had moved too. As he did, he fired in Stefan's direction again. But as he pulled the trigger he stumbled over Gaunt.

'Fuck!'

Stefan fired in the direction of the voice.

He heard Yates stumble again.

Something hard, metallic, clattered across the room.

Stefan shot again. He thought Yates had been hit. The noise could have been the gun falling. He fired one more time. There was the sound of feet on stairs. Yates was running. Stefan waited in the darkness, listening. He could hear the steps for a moment more. Another blast outside. The ack-ack guns.

He walked to the door and moved slowly down the stairs.

It seemed lighter outside. He didn't know why. The sound of the anti-aircraft guns was a more distant rhythm, dull, insistent. The raid had passed.

At the bottom of the stairs, the front door was open.

Stefan edged towards it, revolver ready. Yates would be running. Or would he hide? Maybe he'd been hit. Stefan couldn't know. What about the gun? Did Yates still have it? Would he be waiting somewhere, in all the rubble? Stefan knew if he saw the lieutenant, he would have to kill him. If Jack Yates had the gun, he would not hesitate to shoot. Stefan could not wait to find out.

Suddenly, the hall of the house was filled with a bright, almost blinding light. Stefan Gillespie shaded his eyes. He walked through the doorway, out to the rubble-strewn street. Ahead of him was Jack Yates, his hands in the air, yet standing as if to attention in the unexpected brightness. A truck and a car had their headlights on the street and the front of the house, and from the back of the truck a searchlight shone out. Two Maltese policemen had pistols trained on the CMP lieutenant. Walking towards him, over the rubble, was Sergeant George Spiteri. The phone call Jimmy Gaunt had made, in a moment of panic, on his way to Triq Marsamxett, hadn't got through. But his garbled message had. Spiteri stopped. For a moment he looked at the Military Policeman. Lieutenant Yates stared straight ahead, unmoving, with a slight smile on his lips. He lowered his arms slowly. He nodded at Spiteri. He raised his hand and saluted.

The priest had known first, almost before the boy had. All that time ago. It was in confession, after his first communion, that the priest asked him about his thoughts, the bad thoughts, the dirty thoughts. Those were the words. The thoughts were there, of course, thoughts the boy knew he shouldn't have. That they were about sex was bad enough, but it was the wrong sex. The thoughts were still shapeless. Even the guilt was closer to confusion. The boy hadn't grasped how guilty he was meant to feel. The priest told him. He wasn't so old, maybe forty, but he seemed very old to the boy. He was always probing, giving the thoughts in the boy's head a shape they didn't have. They would have found a shape, but in a way that was the boy's own. The priest took hold of those thoughts and gave them a darkness and a bleak, bitter reality the boy could not have imagined. And when the priest pushed the boy's face on to his stiff penis and filled his mouth, calling him names under his breath – filthy, black, hateful, damning names – the boy, barely knowing what was happening, already felt that something inside him had broken beyond mending. The priest knew that too. Breaking was part of it. He knew the shame the boy felt when he found, sometimes, that he was hard too, though he hated the man's every touch and every breath. And the priest made him know how deep that shame had to be, how complete, how everlasting. Only prayer could save him. And silence. But the priest knew, too, that the boy would fight the silence, one time at least. And before the boy could ask for help, the man in the grubby, black, tobacco-flecked cassock whispered a warning, prayerful and kind, heartfelt and compassionate, to his mother and father. He had stopped their son interfering with other, younger boys. He had to tell them that. And when the boy began to protest that it wasn't true, that it was the priest who had— The words were never finished. His father was already beating him, so hard and so long that blood poured from one of his ears. His mother simply walked away. She always knew the truth. But she said nothing. They moved, eventually; that was it. That was all his mother offered. Still she never spoke. And till they moved the priest continued from where he'd left off. Only now, instead of prayers afterwards, there were more threats, darker threats: exposure and shame in this world; damnation in the next. The priest would hit him too. And the priest would weep, calling the boy, between tears and incoherent, pleading prayers, every filthy name he knew.

It was a long time since any of that had been in Jack Yates' head. It was there fleetingly when he stared down at the sea, through the window of the Sunderland flying boat that was carrying him back to England. He had learnt to keep his mind in tight, separate compartments. He was good at it. But the compartments were suddenly not as watertight as they had been. There was seepage now. And there were things to be left behind. Lieutenant Jack Yates, CMP, affable and easy-going, popular and pleasant to talk to, yet a man you never quite got to know. He was gone. There was no room for him. That Jack Yates, along with the Military Police and the war, had been a refuge. He had joined up when he came back from Ireland, after the holiday that had ended in such an unintended but somehow inevitable way. He had returned to England surprisingly calm. The idea of joining up had been in his mind before, but after what had happened in Ireland, he had to change his life. The war was a way to disappear, not from the consequences of his actions, but from himself. He didn't seek out the

Military Police, but they were short of men. Someone looked at his experience as a clerk in the Law Courts and pushed him in that direction. And it suited him. War suited him. He fitted in in a way he never had. He became a sergeant almost immediately. He had a commission before he left for Malta, after his evacuation from Dunkirk. War was all that he had hoped it would be. It was a place in which you could be surrounded by people, and in all the activity no one would ever see your real isolation. No one had to know you. The army and the war were all-enveloping. But that was over. It was all over. And there was nothing to say. They had tried to question him, the Scotland Yard man, Nugent, and the Irish detective, Gillespie. There would be a lot more of that in London. But he had decided to say nothing. Silence. That was all he would give them. He was good at silence. The compartments in his head were full of silences. They did not communicate with one another. He wouldn't let them now. He would stop the seepage. Nothing would come out. No one would know him. He would be no one himself soon enough. He might as well start now. He did not seek death, but he had no real fear of it. In the room inhabited by Lieutenant Yates, CMP, there was a thought of fighting. He knew what they had. He knew most of the evidence was circumstantial. But he couldn't fight without revealing himself in ways that he would not allow. No one could know what was in some of his rooms. And he would make mistakes. He had made some already. The attack on Chief Inspector Nugent had been one. He'd acted out of panic. It was too late to fight. Silence was all he had left. As the hours over the Mediterranean passed, he sat in the seat and closed his eyes. He couldn't sleep but he had a way of shutting down his mind. He was practised at that. The killings did not trouble him. He had come to accept them. They happened. And when they did, they gave him, for a time, a sense of release. He told himself that each one would be the last. He knew better, of course, but he always wanted it to be the last. Yet when the dark came over him, he knew what would happen. The sex and the killing had somehow become indistinguishable for him. He might tell himself that each time was the last time, but he had organised his life so that he could kill again. The men he murdered had no faces. They were never in his head. He encountered them only for minutes. Perhaps they were released from something. He told himself that occasionally, but the words were empty. The first time had been different. He had met James in a bookshop, on a holiday in Ireland. They talked about the books they loved. They walked through Dublin together. They ate and drank and laughed together. They wanted each other in ways that he would not have space for again. There was love; at least he saw it in James. If he felt it too, it was a mistake. The picnic was never meant to end in death. But when they had sex it was as if blood vessels burst in his head. There was darkness and pain and a red, uncontrollable anger. It was over in seconds. He had to destroy what he felt. He had to cleanse himself. Only death was enough. There was too much fury. All he could do was choke and kill, and then strike and strike again, full of despair and shame. The next time, he knew what would happen, what had to happen.

There was a dream that came to him sometimes. He thought he'd dreamt it even before James, but he wasn't sure. Perhaps it had always been there. He had a room for it in his head, shut away with so many shut-away things. In the dream he plunged a knife into himself, over and over, digging out his sex. He stabbed himself, round and round, a circle of blood. He couldn't stop. He had to keep on stabbing, cutting, digging. And as he woke, sweating, trembling, sometimes crying or screaming, the last image the dream left was the smiling face of the old priest, and behind it, framing it, hanging on the sacristy wall from some forgotten Easter pageant, was a black and broken crown of thorns.

242

PART THREE

AN IDEAL HUSBAND

Sir, – While not questioning the truth, the very outspoken truth, contained in your leading article on Irish neutrality, I feel that the writer has not been quite fair, has stated bare facts in the assessment of the rather peculiar character of the people he is dealing with ... Please, Mr Editor, be kind to us Irishmen within your charming island, in spite of all our shortcomings (which alas, are known only too well to us). Was it not the ablest of all Irishmen, Daniel O'Connell himself, 'The Liberator', who uttered the immortal words – 'We are a grand people: Glory be to God!'

Times of Malta, 1941

19

The Salisbury

London

Looking down at Regent Street again, from a window in the Irish High Commission, Stefan Gillespie picked out Hindu Narayan easily enough. The street was not crowded; she stood out anyway, tall, elegant, purposeful. She walked from the Underground at Piccadilly to the small alleyway that led to the entrance of the Veeraswamy restaurant. As she disappeared into the sandbagged passage, he looked across at the windows on the first floor, criss-crossed with tape, like all London's windows, to offer some small resistance to a bomb blast. He watched as if he might see her there.

Stefan had watched Hindu Narayan make the same journey the day before. He wanted to speak to her. But there seemed little point. He had nothing to say, certainly nothing she wanted to hear. He had returned from Malta with a murderer. But however many men Lieutenant John Yates, CMP, had killed, he was not the man who killed Vikram Narayan. Stefan knew that Chief Inspector Nugent would have tried to talk to Vikram's sister. He also knew, without being told, that she would not have seen him. He did not fully understand the gulf between Hindu Narayan and Frank Nugent. At first glance, it was simple. She was an Indian nationalist and he was a member of Indian Political Intelligence, working in London: a spy. It was not difficult to grasp for an Irishman. If Hindu had been an Irish Republican when Britain still ruled Ireland, and Nugent had been a British detective at Dublin Castle, the feelings would have been the same. But there was something deeper in the bitterness Stefan had seen in Hindu's eyes, something far more personal. He had seen how deep it went.

He couldn't guess how much she knew about her brother's relationship with Frank Nugent. She knew something, certainly. She knew that when Vikram was beaten in an Indian jail, if Nugent wasn't there, he wasn't far away. Whether she also understood what Vikram had become – what Frank Nugent and men like him had made her brother: an informer, a traitor – Stefan couldn't know. It was unlikely that Hindu Narayan didn't suspect that, even if she refused to believe it. She wanted to see her brother as a pure, unsullied part of the struggle for independence, as she was, as her family and her friends were, in London as well as India. And she also didn't want to believe he died for nothing, in some squalid, meaningless sexual encounter. She wanted to believe he died for India, in a way she could take home with her, to her parents; in a way she could carry in her heart. That meant Frank Nugent must have played a part in his death, however distantly, however obliquely. It was what Hindu needed to hold on to. It was all she had.

Stefan walked downstairs to the lobby, where the stiff and upright figure of Miss Foye sat pounding at her Remington.

'Is the High Commissioner back yet, Miss Foye?'

'He won't be back today, Mr Gillespie. He has a late meeting and then he's going home. He'll be in first thing. He did leave a message. You're to go to Ireland at the weekend. There will be important papers for the diplomatic bag.'

Stefan nodded, taking out a cigarette. He wanted to get home.

'And there is one more message,' said Miss Foye.

As Stefan lit the cigarette, he sensed a tone of disapproval.

'That man from Scotland Yard, Chief Inspector Nugent . . .'

'Frank,' said Stefan cheerfully.

'Chief Inspector Nugent,' continued Miss Foye, 'said he would be at the Salisbury, in St Martin's Lane. It's a pub, Mr Gillespie. I am sure you know it.'

'I don't, Miss Foye. One of the few! But I'll find it.'

The High Commissioner's secretary resumed typing.

'Nugent's not such a bad feller,' said Stefan, deliberately winding up Miss Foye's Republican prejudices. 'For an English peeler. Harmless enough?'

'I wouldn't have thought harmlessness made for much of a policeman.'

'You may be right, Miss Foye.' Stefan grinned. 'But what about me?'

'How would I know if you're much of a policeman, Mr Gillespie?'

'True.' He gave a shrug. 'I've never been sure about that myself.'

Stefan didn't often get laughter out of Miss Foye; he came close then.

The journey from Malta had been uneventful. A Sunderland flying boat to Gibraltar, an overnight stop, and then on to England. Chief Inspector Nugent had been fit to travel two days after the arrest of Jack Yates. He was walking with a stick, but there was little evidence of the knife wound he'd received from Lieutenant Yates on the way back from the Manoel Theatre. No one had any doubt who did it, though Yates said nothing. He said nothing about anything now. He said nothing in Malta, and he said nothing as he sat in the flying boat.

Frank Nugent had been replaced at Mtarfa Hospital by the last of Yates' victims, Jimmy Gaunt. The gunshot in the house in Triq Marsamxett had done little real damage. Damage elsewhere was less easy to measure. The Provost Marshall's obsession with keeping the investigation of a murder, probably committed by a soldier, relentlessly and secretively in-house, excluding the Malta Police and resisting cooperation with civilian detectives, did not impress his superiors; even though he had been doing exactly what his superiors expected him to do at the time. There was no reason why Colonel Macgregor should not have allowed Lieutenant Yates to figure so prominently in the Military Police investigation, but hindsight didn't make that decision look good. The truth had come despite Macgregor and his Special Investigation Branch officers, not because of them. It came, embarrassingly, from the work of Sergeant Spiteri and his determination to talk to the Maltese men who knew what happened in the Upper Barrakka Gardens after dark. It came from the willingness of Chief Inspector Nugent and an Irishman who shouldn't have been there to listen to Spiteri. There was a net to draw in on Lieutenant Yates, finally, but uncharacteristic panic on his part made him try to dispose of the people who were drawing in that net, in particular Frank Nugent. But he had been careless.

Jimmy Gaunt didn't see his lieutenant try to kill Nugent, but he saw someone in uniform running away. And he saw Jack Yates, in the Military Police Humber Snipe, drive through the Victoria Gate minutes after the ambulance took the chief inspector to Mtarfa. When Lieutenant Yates expressed his shock at what had happened in St Ursula Street, the next day, and told Gaunt he had been in the barracks all evening, the young MP knew something was wrong. He didn't know what. He didn't make a link between his lieutenant and murder, but he was disturbed. He could think no further than what was in front of him, perhaps because he didn't want to. But he had to discover what was happening. He was too loyal, too frightened, to go to the Provost Marshall, but he had to know more. He knew Lieutenant Yates had a room in the town. He had always suspected him of buying and selling contraband, alcohol and cigarettes. It wasn't unusual, even if investigating such crimes was one of the tasks of the Military Police. If that was all it was, he would say nothing to anyone. He'd searched Frank Nugent's room and made his way to Triq Marsamxett to find the truth.

After Jack Yates' arrest, the lieutenant was mute. He would answer no questions. He admitted nothing. He denied nothing. But circumstantial evidence had built up now and there was little doubt it would build further in England. And some evidence was already more than circumstantial. The finger-print that had brought Stefan Gillespie and Frank Nugent to Malta now had a match. Jack Yates' connection to the murder of James Corcoran in Ireland was established beyond doubt. And still he said nothing. He had been handed over to civilian custody with as much speed as possible. The British Army wanted him out of Malta and off their hands. He no longer wore a uniform. But it all washed over him. He seemed to have withdrawn into himself, with a kind of impenetrable finality in everything he did. His face was expressionless. Watching his silence, as Stefan did in Malta and on the hours of the flight to England, he didn't recognise the man he knew as Lieutenant Jack Yates. What he thought he glimpsed, in the strange calmness of the man, was something like relief.

The Salisbury, in St Martin's Lane, was minutes from Piccadilly Circus, and it was still early when Stefan Gillespie arrived there. It was light on customers at that time, but rich in Victorian mahogany and mirrors, in lamps held up by nymphs and long-stemmed flowers. Frank Nugent sat between the nymphs and flowers on the pub's worn leather, closed in by mirrored glass. The barman brought Stefan a bottle of Guinness and a sour, sarcastic expression.

'You here for long, Mr Nugent?'

'A chat with a friend, Kevin, that's all.'

'Any more coppers due? I wasn't expecting a Policeman's Ball.'

'And there's Inspector Gillespie thinking he was incognito.'

'We're born able to spot a copper. If we're not, we soon learn.'

The barman walked away.

'How long are you in London, Stefan?'

'Till the weekend.'

'Good.'

'Good?'

'Unfinished business.'

And what's that?'

'Vikram Narayan.'

'Yours rather than mine, Frank.'

'I wasn't the one his sister asked for help.'

Stefan smiled. Frank Nugent wasn't such a bad policeman after all.

'I'll be heading back to India soon,' said the chief inspector.

'Run out of Indian nationalists to follow round London?'

'Nothing's happening here or at home.'

Stefan had heard Frank Nugent call India home before, but it registered now, in a pub in London's West End. He looked as if he belonged. He didn't.

'Nothing that matters. Games, no more than that. The Congress Party has no interest in cosying up to the Germans. The man who had didn't do himself any favours. You know enough about it. By going to Berlin, my friend Subhas Bose cut himself off from the rest of Congress, especially Gandhi and Nehru. Do they care? It's politics. He's a rival who sidelined himself. Unless Germany wins. But India's not thinking that way. Too far away to see a close-run thing.'

'And what about all these chats with the IRA?' asked Stefan.

'If a few fellers want to cheer on the Boys, why not? It means little enough in London, less in Dublin. And doesn't it keep them off the streets? Between Scotland Yard and Dublin Castle . . . everyone knows who they are.'

'And you've got enough double agents to chase them round in circles.'

'Am I alone in that? Isn't it one of Terry Gregory's specialities? But I'm done here. They want me home. Bigger fish may be coming our way in India.'

Stefan waited for Nugent to continue, but he didn't. He picked up his beer and looked round the Salisbury for a long moment.

'Have you noticed this is a queer pub?'

'Not really,' replied Stefan, looking round too.

'I've taken a leaf out of Sergeant Spiteri's book,' continued the chief inspector. 'Vikram Narayan. The unfinished business. We were pushed in the wrong direction. We took the bait. We didn't look at anything else. We didn't look at his friends . . . at what was going on around him. We looked one way.'

'Yes, someone made sure we looked the wrong way.'

'And that wasn't as hard to do as you might think.'

'No?'

'I'll be handing the Vikram case back to West End Central. Messrs Hardy and Dillon, inspector and sergeant of this parish. Do they fill me with confidence?'

Stefan Gillespie drank and waited. He knew Nugent well enough by now.

'I talked to a couple of people at the club, Billie's, where Vikram met your friend, Mac Liammóir. I didn't get far. But I was reminded of something Hindu Narayan said about one of her brother's friends being frightened. It was the photographer, the one he bought the camera stuff from. Of course, what Hindu was looking for was something to prove Vikram had the police, Special Branch, MI5 and me after him. She wanted to know what he said about that. Only there was nothing to say. But she pressed a trigger somewhere. Without knowing. Someone thought it was worth knocking her down. Don't forget that.'

'I haven't,' said Stefan quietly. 'You still don't buy the accident?'

'No, and I do know it certainly wasn't Lieutenant Yates.'

Chief Inspector Nugent beckoned the barman again.

'Sit down a minute, Kevin.'

The barman did so, wearing the same sour, sarcastic look.

'Tell my friend about how West End Central does business.'

'The Jack the Ripper job?'

Frank Nugent nodded.

'I hear that one's dead in the water now. You got the bastard.'

'Tell the story, Kevin.'

'Well, every so often, the superintendent at West End Central makes a show of clearing off his assorted poofs and pansies. Keep the good citizens onside. Mostly we're left alone, but a copper's got to do what a copper's got to do. So, they make some arrests, clear the cottages and the parks and make themselves unpopular in respectable public houses like this. But last time, Inspector Hardy thought he'd frighten us off with the bogeyman. He told us about the madman out there, waiting to cut us in pieces. He said how he did it. In some detail. Lots of blood. If he wasn't going to cut off your tail with his carving knife, he'd put a fucking frame round it . . . in a striking shade of red.'

'So, no shortage of people who knew about that,' said Stefan.

'Tell us about the blackmail, Kevin,' said Nugent.

'There's always blackmail, Mr Nugent. You know that.'

'This is a bit bigger, isn't it?'

'That's what people say. Been going on for years.'

'Have you been on the end of it?'

'I'm too big a faery, Mr Nugent.' Kevin laughed. 'No point!'

'What I heard,' continued the chief inspector, 'was that it

was well organised. Lots of inside information, photographs, letters, all sorts of evidence bought and sold. With threats of going to people's families, losing them their jobs. Even putting some anonymous tips in the way of the police.'

'They deliver,' said Kevin. 'No money, you're fucked. That's the word.'

Frank Nugent looked at Stefan. 'Something to be frightened of.'

'It would be.' Stefan nodded.

Kevin got up. 'Don't stay too long, gents. You're buggering business.'

The barman walked away. For a moment the two detectives were silent.

'Frightened enough to be worth killing for?' asked Nugent.

'Perhaps,' replied Stefan. 'But can you see Vikram Narayan . . .'

'As a blackmailer? He tried it on with Mac Liammóir, Stefan.'

'That's not the same thing. According to your man Kevin—'

'What about the camera, the telephoto lens? You said it, Stefan. What was it for? If this is a professional set-up . . . there's a lot of collecting and buying information. Vikram needn't have been running it. Maybe he was working for someone.'

Stefan frowned, then another thought struck him.

'No photos, Frank, remember?'

'What?'

'Expensive camera, expensive lenses . . . no photographs anywhere.'

'Except the roll in his pocket,' said the chief inspector.

'And what was on that?' asked Stefan. 'Not much, was there?'

'The funeral he went to, where he saw Mac Liammóir with Noël Coward. He took some pictures of them. The last ones he ever took. There were some pictures he'd taken before, somewhere else. He finished the reel at the funeral. The other pictures were of a woman, probably at a railway buffet, remember? One of the big London stations. A man with her, no clear shot of him. The side of his head, the back of his head. As if Vikram was trying to get a good angle.'

'But he wasn't going to risk getting closer,' said Stefan.

'I suppose so,' replied Nugent. 'There were a couple of photographs of the woman by herself at the station, presumably after the man had left. I'll need to dig them out. As I remember, she was posting letters. Then maybe going to get a train.'

'So, what does all that mean?' said Stefan. 'What's that got to do with blackmailing homosexual men? But if they were taken with the telephoto lens, the photos must mean something. Forget the ones of Micheál and Noël Coward. Vikram had pictures of them on his wall in Greek Street. They're what they seem, aren't they? I'd put money on it, Frank. He was a fan. Yes, he tried to threaten Micheál, maybe out of desperation, but those two were never good candidates for blackmail. Too important. So, it's the other photos we should be looking at. They're the ones that must be telling us something we don't know.'

'But what?' Frank Nugent shook his head.

'And what about the rest?' said Stefan. 'The ones that aren't there. Not a trace. How many photographs did he take? Where did he keep them? Why was he doing it? We know where he bought the camera, the lenses. We know the man he bought them from. His friend with a photography shop in Brixton. And when Hindu Narayan tried to speak to this friend about her brother, all she got was that he was frightened, very frightened. She thought he was scared of the police, even of you. That wasn't it. He was frightened of someone, though.'

'She saw that, and I didn't,' said the chief inspector. 'Jesus!'

'You weren't looking then, were you?' said Stefan. 'Now, we are.'

20

Coldharbour Lane

Driving over Westminster Bridge, through the Elephant and Castle, Kennington, Camberwell, Stefan noticed how the bomb damage drained away, street by street, as they came closer to Brixton. It was still there, in heaps of bricks and mortar and gaps in the Victorian and Edwardian terraces of high streets, but where whole sections of the city had been flattened close to the river – houses, shops, warehouses, factories – further south the damage was intermittent. Mostly high streets were still standing, ordinary, unexceptional, unremarkable.

Frank Nugent turned the black Austin off Brixton Road into Coldharbour Lane. He pulled up outside the shop: Coldharbour Cameras. It was a small, dark shop window; a glass door heavily taped in anticipation of blasts, sandwiched between a greengrocer's and an ironmonger's. There were a few cameras and lenses in the window, looking dusty and uncared-for, backed by bleached black-and-white photographs of the English countryside and a family at the seaside. The shop was open, but it looked as if it might as well be closed. It exuded a mood of failing and indifference. And the bleak interior felt just as weary.

A bell over the door tinkled as the two detectives entered.

The shelves displaying photographic equipment and stacks of film in boxes were half empty. It was difficult to find stock in wartime London, but here it seemed unlikely the proprietor bothered to look hard. He appeared several minutes after Stefan and Frank came into the shop. They heard him walk slowly from upstairs. He was a small, flabby man, grey-haired, in his fifties. He wore a well-pressed suit, a white shirt and a carefully knotted tie. His neatness was at odds with his shop.

'Can I help you, gentlemen?'

'Mr Hopkins, you may remember me. Chief Inspector Nugent.'

Edward Hopkins said nothing, but he did remember.

'This is Inspector Gillespie.'

Nugent had decided that for now Stefan's rank was explanation enough.

'I talked to you about Vikram Narayan, your friend . . . about a camera and some equipment he bought from you. In particular, an expensive telephoto lens.'

The man nodded.

'Friend or boyfriend?' said the English detective.

'There was nothing like that,' said Hopkins, almost indignant.

'Not important, I guess. We are still investigating Mr Narayan's murder.'

'I see. I thought you knew what happened. You said a man who killed—'

'I thought that at the time, Mr Hopkins. I was wrong.'

There was silence in the dark shop. The ticking of a grandfather clock.

'Do you develop photographs, Mr Hopkins?' asked Stefan.

'Yes. I don't do a lot of it now.'

'Did you develop any for Mr Narayan?'

The answer came with a hesitation and awkwardness that told both detectives something was being hidden. The

256

shop-owner saw the need to be careful in what he said. There was also fear.

'I don't remember.' It didn't sound convincing. 'Some, perhaps.'

'Do you remember what sort of pictures he took?' asked Nugent. 'They would have been unusual, with that lens. Close-ups from a distance. A bit odd?'

'I said, some. It was a long time ago.'

'Not that long, surely?' said the chief inspector. 'This sort of thing . . .'

Frank Nugent took several photographs from his pocket and laid them on the counter. They were photographs of a woman at a railway buffet, sitting with a man whose face could only be partly seen; the same woman posting letters, on a station concourse. A picture of a tobacconist's shop and a street name.

'That's all we have. But odd, wouldn't you say?'

'They don't mean anything to me.'

'They were some of the last pictures Vikram Narayan took, before he was killed,' said Stefan. 'Undeveloped, a reel in his pocket. They were the only photographs we found in his flat. That's odd too, I'd say. For a man who was so interested in photography. It's hard to imagine that with a friend like you, he wouldn't have brought his films here to be developed. Especially as they wouldn't be the kind of pictures he'd want just anybody to see. That's what I think. That's what Mr Nugent thinks as well. What do you think, Mr Hopkins?'

'I don't know what you're talking about.'

Hopkins was not a good liar. The sweat on his face told the truth.

'I'll tell you then, shall I?' said Frank Nugent, harder. 'It's about blackmail. I don't know how. I don't know what. Photographs were a part of it. What else do you need a tele-photo lens for, except to spy? I don't know who this woman is

257

or what she has to do with it. I don't know how it got your friend Mr Narayan killed, but maybe that's not difficult to guess. It might give you a good reason to be frightened, though, if you were working with him. What I do know – what is blindingly fucking obvious, Mr Hopkins – is that it involved extorting money out of homosexual men. And you know about it.'

The shop-owner was shaking his head.

'It's not like that. It's not that way, you don't understand . . .'

'Why don't you tell us what it is like, Mr Hopkins?' said Stefan.

It took Edward Hopkins several minutes to pull up a floorboard in the darkroom behind the shop. He levered it up with a claw hammer. He was calmer. He had stopped shaking. But he was still afraid. He took a package from between the joists. It was wrapped in oilcloth. He opened it up and took several paper wallets out. They contained black-and-white photographs. He spread some on the table. Several were versions of what Stefan and Frank had already seen from the reel of film found in Narayan's pocket: the woman, the man, the station, the tobacconist's. But they had been taken at other times. They were clearer.

'It's Waterloo Station,' said Nugent.

'Yes.' Stefan recognised it too.

'And the man,' continued the chief inspector. 'I know who he is. I thought from the profile there was something I recognised. A man called Pettit. He's the maître d' at Billie's, the club where Vikram had his run-in with Mac Liammóir. I talked to him. He knew Vikram, of course. It's his world, isn't it?'

Stefan nodded, looking down at the pictures.

'He'd know a lot of people, Frank. He'd see everything.'

'You know this man?' Nugent turned to Hopkins.

The shop-owner shook his head.

Stefan laid out more photographs. There were several of the woman, getting on a train. There were images of a street – a village street it looked like – and the woman getting into a grey car in the same street. There were photographs of a long, straight stretch of road, somewhere in the countryside. There was a house, old red brick, surrounded by a clump of trees. It was in the country too, somewhere near the long, straight road. It looked dark, isolated.

'Is that it?' Chief Inspector Nugent asked Hopkins.

'Yes.' The shop-owner nodded.

Stefan looked up and shrugged.

'Doesn't look like great shakes on the blackmail front.'

'So, if it isn't blackmail,' said Nugent, 'what the hell is it?'

Hopkins stepped back and sank down on to a chair.

'Those are the people doing it, doing the blackmail, they're the . . .'

Frank Nugent exchanged glances with Stefan. This was unexpected.

'It was when David died . . . Vikram said someone had to do something.'

'And who's David?'

'He was my, he was my very . . . special friend, we . . .'

'Take your time, Mr Hopkins,' said Stefan. 'Don't worry.'

'David was a policeman, you see.' Hopkins looked at them blankly. 'You'd think he could have done something, but he couldn't, not without people finding out. His family was so proud of him . . . only a constable, not like you, but he would have lost his job, you know that, don't you?' Hopkins gazed from Stefan to Frank Nugent, shaking his head. 'So, he paid the money. But he couldn't keep paying. I tried to help. They wanted more, all the time. They had letters he'd sent to a man, when he was hardly out of his teens. They sent them to Scotland Yard. He didn't wait for . . . he hanged himself.'

There was silence in the darkroom. The clock ticked outside.

'I told Vikram, and he said someone had to stop it. We all knew men who were being blackmailed, and no one did anything. Some people did tell the police. They tried. But nothing happened. I don't know if they even looked at it, most of the time they're more interested in putting us inside. Maybe it's easier to do. But Vikram said if there was evidence, if he found out who these people were, the police would have to do something. He said he knew a policeman. Someone important. If he gave him all the evidence he could put together, if he got photos and details . . . then this man would do something.'

There was a different kind of silence now. It came from Frank Nugent. Stefan could feel it. He knew the policeman Vikram Narayan intended to go to.

Stefan waited for Frank Nugent to continue the questioning, but the Englishman said nothing. He picked up one of the photographs. He seemed distant. The silence hung in the air. Even Hopkins was waiting for a question.

'Do you know who these people are,' asked Stefan, 'in the photos?'

'No, Vikram didn't say. He reckoned the less I knew the safer I'd be.'

'Did he tell you where these places are, the village, the house?'

'No. Once he mentioned Guildford, I think. Near Guildford.'

Stefan looked at Frank. The chief inspector nodded, still distracted.

'Could be. I think . . . the village doesn't mean anything . . . but I've maybe been on that main road.' He indicated a picture of a long, empty stretch of tarmac, with trees lining it. 'It looks like somewhere I've seen. I'm not sure.'

'What about the tobacconist's?' Stefan looked back at Hopkins. 'That's in London.'

'I don't know where. I think people sent letters there, money.'

'Well, there's the name of the street,' said Chief Inspector Nugent. He spoke sharply, pointing at another photograph, as if stating the obvious.

Stefan nodded. When Nugent unexpectedly said no more, he was the one who now turned to Hopkins again.

'Did Vikram know if they'd found out what he was doing?'

'I don't know; I think, perhaps. I think he realised . . . he'd been noticed. But he wasn't sure he could prove anything. Not without help. He was full of it at first, then he was . . . afraid suddenly. He said it didn't matter what he found out. No one would help him. That was when he started saying he wanted to get away. I shouldn't have let him do it. Looking into these things . . . it's better to leave it alone. I should have known. But he was determined to do something . . . at the start. Something right. That's what he said. But it changed, and the last time I saw him, he was simply desperate . . . He said he had to leave England.'

'Or what?' said Stefan. 'Did he say he was frightened . . . for his life?'

'No. He didn't . . . He was afraid – of all sorts of things, Mr Gillespie. I don't know what they were. I only know he couldn't see any way out of it.'

Frank Nugent still said nothing. It was as if he hadn't listened to what Hopkins had been saying. He was gazing down at the photographs. He pulled out a packet of cigarettes. He took one and lit it. Stefan looked at the bland photographs again. Pieces of paper. Could they be worth a man's life?

The chief inspector started to gather up the pictures. He seemed almost clumsy, flustered, as if he didn't want to look at anyone, either at Stefan or at the shopkeeper. Stefan couldn't decide whether he was angry or impatient. Finally, with all the photographs bundled together, Nugent turned towards Stefan.

His face was tight and intense. There was none of the calmness Stefan was used to.

'Let's find this fucking tobacconist's. I think I know the street.'

The tobacconist's shop that acted as a letter-drop was easy to find. Along with the photographs of the shop and of Charlie Pettit, the maître d' at Billie's, going in and out, there was a wider shot of the street and its name. It was close to Vauxhall Bridge, a road off Kennington Lane. Frank Nugent drove there from Brixton. It wasn't far. The Englishman was quiet. Stefan was too. They were closer to the Thames; the streets reflected that. The rubble was piled higher. There was more empty space where houses had been. When the car stopped outside the shop, at the corner of a row of terraced houses, half of the other side of the road had gone. It had happened months before, long enough to be unremarked, but only now were the bulldozers clearing the site.

Chief Inspector Nugent looked up at the tobacconist's doorway.

'A Mr Leonard Walshe, licensed to sell tobacco.'

Stefan waited. Frank Nugent gave a wry smile.

'I think this one's less of the softly-softly, more of the heavy hand.'

'You're the boss,' said Stefan. 'I'll follow your lead.'

'I'm sure you didn't get where you are, Stefan, without knowing how to put the screw on. This bastard's probably the sort who's got it coming anyway.'

'Not entirely my philosophy, but close to my superintendent's heart.'

They walked into the shop. The proprietor leant on the counter, a pipe in his mouth, reading a list of runners in the *Sporting Life*. He looked up, smiling.

'Couple of good nights. No bombs this side.'

'Could be worse,' said Nugent.

'It is getting better. Must be tiring the buggers out.'

It was the usual, idle bomb-speak.

'What can I do you for, gents?'

'Let's see, Mr Walshe. Hopefully, you can avoid a few years inside.'

The tobacconist frowned. 'What the fuck's that supposed to mean?'

The chief inspector held up his warrant card.

'It means you're operating a letter-drop. All very discreet, I imagine.'

'Nothing illegal about that.'

'That depends what's in the letters.'

'They're not my bloody letters. People just pay to use the address.'

Stefan smiled at the tobacconist. He let Nugent talk.

'And what if one of your customers was using this address, let's say, for the sake of argument, to collect money they were extorting by blackmail?'

'If I knew that, I'd be shocked. I'd go to the fucking police!' Walshe chuckled. He was pleased with that.

'I'm sure your ignorance goes deep, Mr Walshe. Why would you ask?'

'I assume people are honest,' said the tobacconist. 'Why shouldn't I?'

'Not always wise,' said the chief inspector. 'You'd be surprised what some people get up to.' He looked sideways at Stefan. 'You honest, Inspector?'

'I do my best, sir.'

'We all do,' said Nugent. 'Let's try, shall we?'

He put down photographs of the maître d', Pettit, at Waterloo Station.

'Do you know this man?'

'No, never seen him.'

'Does it ring any bells now?'

Nugent put down pictures of Pettit outside the tobacconist's shop.

'Where did you get these?'

The chief inspector grabbed Walshe by his jacket, pulling him forward across the counter, until his face and the tobacconist's were inches apart.

'Answer the fucking question, you bastard! Tell me about this man.'

'I don't know him. I don't know his name. He comes in now and again.'

'To collect letters?'

'I don't need to answer these bloody questions.'

'You do, you really do, I assure you.'

Nugent's words were softer, but he continued to glare hard into the tobacconist's eyes. Then abruptly he let him go. He turned to Stefan again.

'Why does he have to, Inspector Gillespie?'

Stefan picked up the copy of the *Sporting Life* and scanned it, as if it was of some interest to him. When he spoke, his tone was easy, mild, reasonable.

'Apart from being a law-abiding citizen, he has to do it because if he doesn't we'll plant enough evidence in his private post office, to tie it to so much extortion, robbery, pornography, and whatever else we can think of, it'll put him away for more years than he's had winners on the flat or over the sticks. Got it?'

'Don't you fucking threaten me!'

'It's not a threat, Mr Walshe. But it is a very sure promise,' said Stefan.

'You should trust him,' added Nugent. 'He is a policeman after all.'

The chief inspector picked up another photograph of the maître d'.

264

'So, I still don't know any more about this man, do I?'

'I told you. He collects letters here. He pays and he takes them.'

'And who are these letters for? For him?'

'How the hell do I know? He collects letters in the name of Mr Elliot.'

'That's more like it, Mr Walshe. Any letters for Mr Elliot here now?'

Walshe hesitated, but not for long. He nodded.

'Get them,' snapped Nugent.

The tobacconist went into the room behind the shop. Nugent lifted the counter flap and followed. Stefan Gillespie took the flap and did the same. In a small sitting room was a wooden cabinet full of cubby-holes and letters. Walshe took out a bundle of letters and handed them to Chief Inspector Nugent.

'How often does this man collect?' asked Stefan.

'Usually once a fortnight. On a Friday.'

'When is he due again?'

'This week.'

'The day after tomorrow?'

The tobacconist shrugged.

Frank Nugent flicked through the letters. There were seven. There was nothing to see; the name Elliot, c/o, and the address of the tobacconist's. He handed six of the envelopes back to Walshe and opened the seventh. He took out a ten-pound note and a piece of paper with a four-figure number on it. There was no letter. There was nothing to identify where the letter had come from.

'That's it, cash on delivery,' said Nugent. 'Simple. Neat.'

'The only weakness,' added Stefan, 'is you, Mr Walshe.'

'People can send money, can't they? Sending money means fuck all!'

Chief Inspector Nugent shook his head and tutted.

'I think in this case, Mr Walshe, it means fuck everything . . . So, put the other letters back. Business as usual. When our friend comes to collect on Friday, you hand them over, as always. You say what you always say, the less the better. If all that works, there's a chance we'll leave you to carry on your shitty trade, untroubled by the fact that it would be no bad thing to go through every letter here and see what's what. But if our friend gets even a whiff that anything is wrong, Inspector Gillespie will be back to plant the goods that will send you down for a substantial stretch. Who knows who you might bump into in Brixton or the Scrubs, maybe even the people you just squealed on?'

'That's bollocks! I haven't fucking squealed on no one!'

'The trouble is,' smiled Stefan, 'we'll tell them you fucking have.'

21

Waterloo Station

Charlie Pettit, maître d' of Billie's in Little Denmark Street, had no idea that he was being followed as he left Lennie Walshe's tobacconist's shop and made his way to the river and the Albert Embankment. The Irishman who was following him was unknown to Charlie. He was also good at what he was doing. He had every reason to believe he knew where the maître d' was going, and that meant he could hang back and follow in a leisurely, unobtrusive way. The journey he was making from Vauxhall to Waterloo Station was familiar. It hadn't always been Vauxhall. The letter drops or post restantes changed from time to time. For safety. But nothing else did.

There was something of spring in the morning, and Charlie Pettit felt more content than he usually did at the prospect of an envelope from the woman. There would be good money this time. A fortnight ago he had provided a crop of names and addresses from the club, a list of clients from a male prostitute in Islington, some juicy letters from married men to unmarried men, and a reel of photographs of men at some of the West End's best-known cottages. He had paid through the nose for the photographs, but the photographer was good and that wasn't easy work. There were only two names to go with the pictures, but the people he was giving them to would match more to names and faces they already had. That was their business. Collecting the money was their business. But he would be collecting his today. Tomorrow he would take the train to Stratford and spend the afternoon at the race meeting. A weekend off, out of London. There were shortages everywhere, but money solved most of them. Life was easier than it had been. It was an odd thing to feel in the middle of the war, but Charlie was a survivor; he was surviving well. He was too old for conscription and like everyone else he had learnt to live with bombs. People kept saying it was easing off. They said it when any fool could see it wasn't. They always said it. But he couldn't help feeling it was true now, or truer. He didn't follow the war. He took in what was half heard on the radio and chatted about in the club. He scanned the newspaper headlines, but not much more. He read the papers for the racing pages. But all in all, things weren't so bad. He was more comfortable than he'd been for ages. The money from the man and the woman came regularly. It made a difference. The information they wanted was easy to get. It was business. Business was good.

Stefan anticipated the route the maître d' would take as soon as he reached the Albert Embankment. Waterloo Station would be the destination. The Embankment to Westminster Bridge and then the station. It wasn't difficult to keep the thin, angular figure in view, in his dark suit and trilby. He moved closer only as Pettit moved away from the river into York Road. The station would be full of people and it would be a lot easier to lose him there. He couldn't know what would happen at Waterloo. The assumption was that the maître d' would meet the woman in Vikram Narayan's photographs, but Stefan and Frank Nugent could not be certain. There might be a train journey. Stefan Gillespie needed to be near his quarry. When

Pettit mounted the stone steps that led up to the Victory Arch and the concourse, he was close behind.

A woman's voice echoed around the great, high space beneath the glass roof. Between the announcements of arrivals and departures, music played. The woman's voice was distorted and hard to decipher. No one listened. Instead, people stared up at the high boards that listed trains and stations, waiting for the rattle and click that would bring up information for each platform. They stared and walked and came back to stare again. No one listened to the relentlessly cheerful band music either, as much the sound of the war as the drone of engines overhead at night and the sound of bombs, always, hopefully, somewhere else. The station was not as busy as Stefan expected. The morning trains that brought commuters in from the southern suburbs had long gone. Most of the passengers were soldiers, travelling to army camps and waiting for troop trains to Southampton to ship overseas. They stood in groups round stacked rifles and kitbags. They packed themselves round trolleys with tea urns, drinking tea and eating biscuits. They pushed in and out of station buffets and newspaper kiosks. Over every troop and group and company hung the clouds of smoke that marked what every soldier did when there was nothing else to do.

The line Charlie Pettit took, through the groups of soldiers, brought him to a station buffet at the far end of the concourse. Stefan knew Waterloo, a little. On the right, the platforms, stretching the length of the station; left, the station buildings and buffets and ticket offices and waiting rooms; in the middle the kiosks of W.H. Smith, wooden benches and space to stand and wait.

Outside the buffet were tables and chairs. At one of these sat a woman. Charlie Pettit went to the table and sat down. Stefan watched from beside a newspaper stand. He recognised the woman from the photographs taken by Vikram Narayan. She

269

was probably in her late forties. She was elegant and tall, dressed in a suit that had cost good money; a strong woman, he thought. Her hair was blonde and permed; the colour wasn't hers.

Stefan turned to the newspaper seller and bought an *Evening Standard*. He walked on across the concourse and sat on a bench, close to a row of telephone kiosks. He had clear sight of the woman and the maître d'. The woman poured tea from a pot into a cup in front of Pettit. He didn't drink it. He took a folded manila envelope from his jacket and pushed it across the table. She opened her handbag and put it in. She took out a smaller envelope and gave it to Pettit. He tipped his hat, which he had not taken off. He stood up and left. That was it. Stefan watched as the maître d' walked through the concourse, the way he had come. The transaction had taken no more than five minutes. Hardly any words had been spoken. Stefan assumed that the money from Walshe's had been passed over, perhaps more, perhaps information, names, the stuff of blackmail. In return, another payment had been made, to Charlie Pettit. But whatever it was, it was done. Now Stefan would do what he and Chief Inspector Nugent had decided. They knew where to find Pettit. He would be picked up in due course. It was the woman they needed to know about. She was the one to be followed. That was even clearer to Stefan now. The woman was in charge. The maître d' worked for her.

The woman sat at the table for another few minutes. She smoked a cigarette. She looked about her, but she was at ease. She was confident. Like Charlie Pettit, earlier, she could have no idea that she was being watched, or any sense of why she should be. Stefan felt her calmness. It was helpful for the job he had to do.

When the woman stubbed out her cigarette and stood up, Stefan saw that she picked up two carrier bags: Fortnum &

Mason, Simpsons of Piccadilly. It was a nice touch, he thought. She was an ordinary woman, but well-heeled, shopping in Town. He watched her walk across the station towards the departures board. She stood looking up at it, then turned to walk to one of the platforms. He got up from the bench and followed her. He waited, letting her walk through the barrier. She continued past two dark green carriages, then opened the door and got on the train. Stefan looked at the board over the barrier: Surbiton, Weybridge, Guildford. Frank Nugent hadn't identified the stretch of a rural main road in some of Vikram Narayan's photographs, but he felt the area was right. Somewhere near Guildford, Hopkins had said, and that felt right. It felt more right to Stefan now. The woman was heading that way. He passed through the barrier with several other people. He carried a railway warrant that identified him as a policeman; it gave him the ability to go where she went. He walked the platform and glanced into several carriages unnoticed.

The train was made up of compartment carriages, with no through access. The compartments took up the width of the train, with a door on each side and facing seats. He saw the woman, sitting by the window in a compartment. He couldn't sit with her. It would make him recognisable at some point, however little she noticed him. He got into the first compartment in the carriage behind hers. Sitting by the window, on the same side, he would see her get out. He would need to watch for the platform side. If she went to Guildford it would be easy. The train terminated there.

The journey was little more than an hour. The train had filled up before it left Waterloo, but by Surbiton and Weybridge the passengers were thinning out. The woman had not left the carriage. The train reached Guildford and with a dozen other passengers, the woman got off. Stefan watched her for a minute, still sitting by the window in his compartment.

Getting out of the carriage, Stefan was surprised to see that the woman was still on the platform. She was sitting on a bench by the waiting room. There were other people standing on the platform opposite the one the London train had come in on. She was waiting for another train. Stefan walked to the far end of the platform and leant against the wall, behind a trolley full of postbags. He lit a cigarette. Moments later he heard another train approaching. He walked forward as the train stopped. Doors opened and closed. The woman got into a carriage. Stefan got into a compartment further down the train and waited.

The train had travelled only one stop, to the next station down the line, Wanborough, when the woman got off. Only two other passengers disembarked with her and Stefan walked slowly to the exit of the small station. In a place like this, where everyone would know everyone, he would stand out. He knew that the ticket inspector, peering at his warrant, identified him as a policeman.

Walking out of the station, looking towards the village, Stefan knew where he was. It wasn't the same shot, or the same view. But it was the same village in the photographs he had seen in Coldharbour Cameras.

In the station forecourt, the woman was getting into a grey Riley. There was a man driving. Stefan saw only his outline and the sun on the windscreen, as the car turned and drove away. He read the number. He made a point of not watching the car for more than a few seconds. As he turned away, he saw the ticket inspector, standing in the station entrance, looking at him.

'Are you wanting the police station, then?'

Stefan smiled. It felt like he was back in an Irish village. The village police station wasn't the first place he meant to go. He wanted to find out who the man and the woman were, before he did anything else. But this wasn't an easy place to ask questions. It was like arriving in Baltinglass. Whether he wanted to speak to the local police or not, they would soon know he was there. If he said he didn't want the police station, they would know quicker.

'I suppose I am,' said Stefan reluctantly. 'You'd better point the way.'

Stefan Gillespie's arrival at the police station in Wanborough meant a number of things to Sergeant Ernest Porter; irritation and inconvenience were at the top of the list, but wariness and mistrust were not far behind. Stefan said nothing that dispelled the suspicion that the Guildford train had brought the kind of trouble Wanborough was not used to. The fact that the Irishman offered no indication of what he wanted made matters worse. He didn't elaborate on who he was, except to give his rank, and say that his senior officer was a Special Branch Chief Inspector at Scotland Yard. Irishmen in British police forces, especially the Metropolitan Police, were not so remarkable. It was Scotland Yard, especially Special Branch, that the sergeant didn't like. He left his young constable to make Stefan a cup of tea while he went into his office to phone Guildford. No Metropolitan Police officer should be in Surrey without the permission of the Chief Constable, but when it came to Special Branch, and with the bloody war that turned everything on its head, it was difficult to know what to do. And after several phone calls Sergeant Porter was none the wiser. His superintendent in Guildford came back to the sergeant, finally, to say he should offer Stefan any help he needed, as it was a matter that related to national security.

This took over an hour, by which time the sergeant was in need of a cup of tea too and the constable went off to fill the kettle again. Stefan had spent the hour discussing the war and the Surrey countryside with Constable Harris and learnt that the constable's sister-in-law's father came from Carlow and

273

they still had family there, though he couldn't remember the surname. His sister-in-law's cousin was called Michael. He wondered if Stefan knew him. It was then that a call came from Scotland Yard: Frank Nugent.

Sergeant Porter spoke to Chief Inspector Nugent first. The conversation at the Wanborough end consisted mostly of him saying, 'Yes, sir.' He interspersed it with some asides to both Stefan and Constable Harris.

'Chief Inspector says can we put you up somewhere? . . . He'll be coming down from London tomorrow . . . Any questions you got, Inspector? . . . He'll be driving down, first thing . . . It's all hush-hush . . . you hear, Constable?'

Eventually, Sergeant Porter handed the phone to Stefan.

'You're having a good time, Stefan,' said Nugent, laughing.

'I'm not sure, Frank. Plenty of tea.'

'That's something.'

'We've brought in Charlie Pettit. Picked him up at Billie's.'

'Good, did you get anything?'

'Oh, Charlie's totting up what he might do in the way of stir and putting it in his account book against what he might get off if he sings. He's being extremely tuneful.'

'So, you know who the woman is?'

'No.'

'No?'

'They've been at this a few years. She got hold of Charlie when he was up to his eyes in racing debt. The kind that gets you a couple of broken legs if you don't pay. And that's just for starters. She paid off his debts . . . they went into business. The name he has for her isn't real. It's all done face to face, letter-drops, phone calls. He doesn't know where she lives, just that it's her and her husband. Charlie gives information, they do the rest. Very successfully.'

'And what about the murder?'

'He doesn't know anything about that.'

'Well, he would say that, Frank!'

'I believe him. He still thinks Vikram was killed like the others . . . part of the Yates business. He did know him . . . in Billie's, around Soho. But the rest . . . No, I don't think so. He knows nothing about Vikram's photos. No idea he'd been followed or watched. But that doesn't mean the woman didn't know.'

'So, what do I do now?'

'Find out all you can about these people. But ensure your country sergeant keeps his mouth shut. I'm coming down tomorrow. We want to take them by surprise. As far as anyone there is concerned, it's a security issue so you can't say a fucking thing! You might mention murder, at least to Sergeant Porter. I think he needs to know this is a serious matter. But it's nobody's business but Special Branch's. I'm sure the sergeant has the poster up.' Nugent laughed. 'Walls have ears . . . Point it out to him!'

Stefan Gillespie put the telephone down. He smiled amiably. Sergeant Porter and Constable Harris looked at him with continuing wariness. Stefan took a piece of paper from his pocket. He had written the number of the car on it, from the station.

'Do you recognise this number, Sergeant?'

He handed the piece of paper to Porter.

'Not straight off . . . It's a Surrey number, all right.'

'It's a grey Riley, I think a Kestrel.'

'That's Mr Hollingsworth's car,' said Constable Harris.

'Course it is . . . Mr and Mrs Hollingsworth.'

'Do they live in the village?'

'Up on the Hog's Back, Swithins Barn.'

The sergeant looked at Stefan, frowning.

'Mr and Mrs Hollingsworth?'

'You know them, obviously,' continued Stefan.

'Course I bloody know them, Inspector!' Sergeant Porter was laughing as he spoke the words.

'Course he bloody knows them. Mr H is our ARP Warden!'

The constable echoed his sergeant, starting to laugh now too.

Sergeant Porter stood up, reaching for a packet of Woodbines.

'I think you Special Branch boys have got the wrong end of the stick!'

Stefan shrugged. Not so much a 'maybe' as a 'probably not'.

'That'll make a fucking story and a half . . . Mr and Mrs Hollingsworth!'

The sergeant shook his head, still chuckling.

The constable joined in. 'That'll make a fucking . . .'

His echo faded away at a disapproving look from his sergeant.

'Language, Tim!'

'Not a story you'll be telling anyone tonight, Sergeant . . . Constable.'

Although Stefan was smiling, the seriousness in his voice cut through.

'No, sir,' said Sergeant Porter. 'Whatever you say, Inspector.'

There was still a kind of snigger on Constable Harris's lips.

'The joke's over, Constable,' snapped Stefan.

'Yes, sir.'

'You will be with us tomorrow, gentlemen. We'll be arresting them.'

The two policemen looked bewildered.

'Can I ask what for?' said the sergeant.

'I don't know where it starts,' said Stefan, 'but it ends with murder.'

22

The Hog's Back

Where Surrey meets Hampshire, to the south and west of Guildford, a high, narrow ridge rises out of the gently undulating landscape of neat, square fields, tidy coppices and well-ordered villages. The road that runs along the top of the ridge, long and straight, looks down on all that. It is called the Hog's Back. It was a road of sorts for thousands of years before anything was neat or well ordered, when it was safer and drier than the forests that lay beneath its steep slopes. It marked now the place where the London Road to Portsmouth branched, and the south-westerly route, to Winchester and Southampton, climbed up to follow the ridgeway. Various armies had marched this way in the course of time, and it was busy with military trucks and transports again. Villages clustered along its slopes and there was always traffic, though there was nothing for it to stop for except the view. There was one hotel, a plain, red-brick building, distinguished by a square, central turret that had a lot of windows and no clear purpose. It was here, at the Hog's Back Hotel, that Sergeant Porter found Stefan Gillespie a room for the night, and where, next morning, Chief Inspector Nugent arrived to start the day's work.

The aftermath of Frank Nugent's knife wound from Malta was still there. The drive from London had left him in pain and it was Stefan who drove along the Hog's Back to the house where the couple they now knew as Mr and Mrs Hollingsworth, Ivy and Edgar, lived. Stefan had walked the two miles along the road the evening before to look at the house. Like the road itself, Swithins Barn was solitary. It lay back in a clump of high elms, at the end of a gravel drive, hard to see from the road, behind hedges and rhododendrons. The farm that gave the house its name was long gone. It was a dark, shut-in sort of house, Edwardian, built from the same red brick as the hotel. There was nothing remarkable about it, except its location. It didn't quite fit the ridge. It could have sat more comfortably in a suburban street in the leafier outskirts of London.

They drove from the Hog's Back Hotel to a lay-by near the house, waiting for the two policemen who would be cycling from Wanborough to meet them.

'Edgar and Ivy Hollingsworth,' said Stefan. 'They moved into the house about five years ago. Semi-retired was all Sergeant Porter had to say. Hollingsworth was a civil servant, but that's the limit of what anyone knows. There was talk that he had a nervous breakdown before they came here. They lead a quiet life. Not very sociable. No real friends, but they're liked by the local traders. He grows vegetables and exhibits at the local shows. She plays golf at Farnham but doesn't take part in the club's social activities. They appear at the church in Wanborough on high days and holidays. They travel up to London quite a lot. Shopping and shows . . . that was the sergeant's take on it.'

'Quiet and ordinary, then,' added Nugent.

'Mr Hollingsworth does his bit,' continued Stefan. 'ARP Warden.'

'As I said,' continued the chief inspector, 'our friend Charlie Pettit has no idea where they live. He calls them Mr and Mrs

Elliot, as per the letters. He's met the man, but she's the contact. I spent an hour in records after you called again.'

'Did you get something?'

'Edgar Hollingsworth was arrested in nineteen thirty-seven, for soliciting a man for sex in a public convenience in Carnaby Street. Unfortunately, the man was a police officer. West End Central on one of their missions, I assume. Hollingsworth was tried and got off with a suspended sentence. I think some strings must have been pulled. But he had a senior position in the Treasury. That was the end of that, of course. He lost his job. They moved from a house in Wimbledon . . . and here they are.'

'You still think Pettit doesn't know about the murder?'

'Yes. And I think we should come to that last. Might be better if they don't know we're even aware of it. We don't know what they left behind, once we start looking at fingerprints. My instinct is they didn't set out to kill him. If that's true, they maybe weren't fussy about leaving traces . . . till it was too late.'

"They thought a false trail would do,' said Stefan.

'It nearly did,' nodded Frank Nugent. 'Ah, reinforcements!'

Two weary cyclists in police uniform were approaching the car.

Stefan pulled up in front of Swithins Barn. Sergeant Porter and Constable Harris leant their bicycles against a tree. Frank Nugent walked to the front door. It was opened by the woman Stefan Gillespie had followed from Waterloo.

'Good morning,' she said cheerfully. She saw the Wanborough policemen standing uneasily behind two men she didn't recognise; she had no reason to think anything was wrong. 'You'll want my husband. ARP business?'

'It's not ARP business, Mrs Hollingsworth,' replied Nugent. He took out his warrant card. 'I'm Detective Chief Inspector

Nugent. This is Inspector Gillespie, who is assisting me.' The vagueness covered Stefan's position, just. 'We would like to talk to you and your husband. Mr Hollingsworth is at home?'

The first hint that this related to the part of Ivy Hollingsworth's life that had nothing to do with the solitary house on the Hog's Back stirred in her head.

'I'm sure if you would like to tell me what this is about . . .'

'If we can come in, we'd like to ask you both some questions.'

'About what?' she said, quite sternly.

'Can we come in?'

The woman stared at them. She showed no signs of fear. The expression on her face didn't change. It was hard, but somehow disbelieving. She was struggling with the idea that this had anything to do with the way money came to Swithins Barn. She had been so careful, so very careful.

'Do you have a warrant?' She half laughed, as if this was some banter. But it was a show of nerves. 'Isn't that how these things work, Mr Nugent?'

'I'm a Special Branch officer, Mrs Hollingsworth. I don't need a warrant if I suspect you've been gathering information for reasons I find suspicious.' Frank Nugent smiled. 'The fact that there's a war on covers me for pretty much anything I want, including searching your house. And I will be doing that.'

'Don't be ridiculous!' She looked at Porter. 'Who are these people?'

Sergeant Porter shuffled his feet. 'Scotland Yard, Mrs Hollingsworth.'

'Whoever they are, they can't just walk in here—'

The chief inspector pushed the door hard, and walked in.

Stefan followed.

'Edgar!' Ivy Hollingsworth called out.

'I'm here, dear.'

In an open doorway stood a man in his late fifties. He was

heavy-set, almost jowly. He wore thick, horn-rimmed glasses. He was in his shirtsleeves. There was a faint smile on his face. Stefan saw he had heard the conversation.

'These men, Edgar . . . they say they are police officers.'

'I'm sure they are, if they say they are.'

'I have no idea what they want . . . they seem to think we're spies!'

Again, Ivy Hollingsworth produced a nervous laugh.

'I'd be very doubtful they believe that at all, Ivy.'

She gazed at him uncertainly. He seemed calm.

'We were just having breakfast, gentlemen. Would you like some tea?'

Now all four policemen were in the hall.

'I don't think so, sir,' said Nugent. 'I am Detective Chief—'

Hollingsworth cut him off.

'Yes, I heard. You'll want to make a start. Do come in.'

Edgar Hollingsworth turned back through the doorway he was standing in. A table was laid for breakfast. The linen was crisp and white. There was silverware and there were fresh flowers in a vase. Hollingsworth sat down. He picked up a pipe that lay by a plate of bacon and mushrooms. He lit it slowly.

'Sit down, dear,' he said to his wife. 'You might as well.'

Mrs Hollingsworth glared at him.

Frank Nugent and Stefan Gillespie stood in the dining room.

'We'll take a look round first, Mr Hollingsworth,' said the chief inspector. He glanced at Stefan. Stefan nodded. They walked back to the hall.

'Just keep them where they are, will you, Sergeant Porter?'

The two detectives took their own directions through the house. Nugent went upstairs. Stefan walked through a door into the kitchen. This was not a search, but Stefan understood what the Englishman was doing. There could be obvious things to see, but he wanted a sense of these people before he started talking to them. He had come into this cold. He wanted time to think through his approach: hard or soft, blunt or subtle. If evidence of the blackmail might be easy to establish, the situation with Vikram could prove more difficult. Stefan also knew that keeping the couple waiting, not knowing what the police knew, was putting pressure on them. They would make mistakes.

Stefan walked back into the hall. He glanced into another room, a sitting room, elegant and bright. He saw nothing interesting. There was a baby grand piano in the window. There was a chest of drawers with a vase of flowers. There was a mantelpiece with another vase of flowers. The only thing he noted was that on all the surfaces where you might expect to see photographs, there were none. He moved across the hall and opened another door. It was a study. There were few books. On some of the bookshelves there were small trophies. He read one inscription: *Surrey Show, 1939, Best Mixed Vegetable Basket*. On the desk he saw something he recognised: opened envelopes. They were the envelopes Charlie Pettit had collected from Walshe's shop. Against one wall was a metal filing cabinet, the kind that would normally be in an office. Stefan pulled out the top drawer. Inside were closely packed manila folders, alphabetically ordered, with numbers on tabs. The numbers had four figures. He remembered the piece of paper that accompanied a ten-pound note in the envelope Nugent had opened at the tobacconist's. Four figures, nothing more. It was a simple records system.

He took out one of the folders. There was a sheet of paper with a name and address. There were other names too, with dates. There was a copy of a bill from a hotel in Brighton. There was a letter that started with a declaration of love and a plea from one man to another, asking him to do what he had promised when they were in bed together: to leave his wife and family and come away with him. There were photographs: somewhere dark, blurred, two men kissing; the same men were at a station, one crying, both very identifiable.

Nugent came downstairs as Stefan Gillespie opened the study door.

'You should come and look at this, Frank. It's quite something.'

In the dining room, Ivy and Edgar Hollingsworth sat at the breakfast table, saying nothing. Hollingsworth smoked his pipe. Constable Harris stood in the doorway. Sergeant Porter sat on a chair by the wall, looking uncomfortable, apologetic and confused, all at the same time. He still had no idea why they were there, or what these two ordinary, upright citizens were being accused of.

The two detectives returned.

'I think the best thing we can do is take you both into custody.'

'For what exactly?' said the woman.

'If we take you to Wanborough now,' continued the chief inspector, 'we can organise transport to bring you to London. You'll be questioned fully there.'

'This is ridiculous. What are we supposed to have done?'

'Once we're at the station, Sergeant, if you can keep Mr and Mrs Hollingsworth in separate rooms or cells, whichever is more convenient, and then arrange with your superintendent in Guildford for two cars to take them to Scotland Yard, in custody, again separately. I don't think questioning is necessary at this point. It can wait. However, there is a lot of evidence to look at here . . . right? Inspector Gillespie and I will travel up to London tomorrow.'

'Yes, sir,' said Porter, standing up slowly. 'Can I ask what sort of charges we're talking about? I will need to say something to Superintendent Osborne.'

'Extortion, blackmail . . . that's the bulk of it. The first thing.'

Ivy Hollingsworth stood up, angry, shaking.

'This is madness! What sort of nonsense is this?'

'We'll deal with the nonsense in due course, Mrs Hollingsworth.'

'You have no proof of anything . . . anything at all!'

'Do shut up, Ivy,' said her husband quietly. 'They've been in the study.'

'What does that mean?' she said. 'We don't have to say anything.'

'There is a filing cabinet that speaks louder than words, darling.'

'Thank you, Mr Hollingsworth. Cooperation would be sensible. The details of the people you've been extorting money from speak for themselves.'

'You know who these people are,' said Ivy Hollingsworth angrily.

'I'm afraid that's hardly the point,' said Nugent in a clipped voice.

'Do you think these people should be allowed to do what they do?' Mrs Hollingsworth was looking from Stefan to Frank. 'Do you? Do you think all the disgusting filth they bring with them, the people they corrupt and destroy, the lives they ruin . . . do you think normal people don't have a right to try to stop it? The police don't! They turn a blind eye. Everyone does. They should be locked away; if you won't do that, people have a right to make—'

She stopped, struggling to speak, fighting tears of fear and frustration.

'Make them "pay" is the word you're looking for, Mrs Hollingsworth,' continued Chief Inspector Nugent. 'Well, one way or another, I'd say the two of you have achieved that. And you've lived well off it, too. However, all that can wait. You will find it easier just to tell the truth. If that sounds like the sort of thing a policeman always says, we have already arrested

Mr Pettit. He is finding it easier to speak than to keep his mouth shut. We can hardly stop him. Reflect on that. Reflect on what you'll say about Vikram Narayan.'

Stefan saw the surprise in Mrs Hollingsworth's face. He looked at her husband. He was relighting his pipe. He still seemed unsurprised and unfazed.

'The false trail didn't work. We know someone added the knife wounds to make it look like something else. With all the information you had, you'd heard of the other homosexual murders. We'll find something that puts you in Greek Street.'

Ivy Hollingsworth had run out of words.

Edgar Hollingsworth sucked on his pipe and exhaled the smoke.

'All this was my doing, gentlemen.'

He looked from Frank Nugent to Stefan Gillespie.

'I took it upon myself to put together a little bit of information that might generate some income. I had reasons. Something to be bitter about. I had no job and no prospect of getting one. It worked surprisingly well.'

'Edgar, you don't have to say—'

'Oh, I think I do, Ivy.' Hollingsworth turned back to the two detectives. 'I found ways to get information, more and more. When you start blackmailing people, you can get more than money, you can get even more information. People talk when they're afraid. I'm sure you know that well. It kept growing. I paid people to talk, and to spy, and they just kept on doing it, you see.'

'I have to warn you, Mr Hollingsworth—'

'I know. Anything I might say, and all that, Mr Nugent. Too late. But Ivy was never . . . I dragged her into it. She was the perfect foil. Who would ever suspect my dear wife? She could collect letters and drop letters and do all the secretarial work, while I dug the dirt. That's how it was, but Mr Narayan—'

'Edgar, stop!' Hollingsworth's wife was pleading.

'He started asking questions. He traced us, somehow. We heard that he had an idea who we were. He knew too much, he'd even taken photographs. I had to stop him. Naturally, I did. I didn't mean to kill him. We went to the flat to find out what he had, especially the photographs. I thought we could stop him then, with threats . . . or just money. But we found nothing. We didn't know what he'd done with the evidence. That was worrying. Then he came in. I panicked and hit him from behind. I knocked him out. That was when it seemed there was a simpler way to stop it, a reliable way. I smothered him. Ivy tried to stop me and pull me off. I did it anyway.'

Edgar Hollingsworth put down the pipe.

'Isn't that right, dear?'

Mrs Hollingsworth stared at him.

'And then I had the bright idea of pointing you chaps another way.'

He walked to the far end of the room, and the French windows that looked out on to the garden. 'It is a damn shame about the vegetables.'

'Will you drive, Stefan?' asked Nugent, turning away.

Stefan nodded.

'We'll take them to Wanborough.'

Stefan walked to the door to the hall.

'If you set off to cycle back, Sergeant—'

Suddenly, with unexpected speed, Hollingsworth opened the French windows and was through them, taking the key, locking the windows from outside. Nugent ran to the doors. They were heavy doors. The lock was strong.

'Silly bugger,' said the chief inspector. 'Let's go and get him.'

While Constable Harris stayed with Ivy Hollingsworth, Stefan Gillespie, Frank Nugent and Sergeant Porter raced through the open front door, round to the side of the house. There was no sign of Edgar Hollingsworth.

'Hang on,' said Stefan, listening.

'Can't be far,' snapped Nugent, irritated with himself. 'What's the fucking point!' He turned to the sergeant. 'Phone from the house. If we can't find him, alert all the local stations. Get some cars up here. Damn the man!'

'Listen, Frank!' said Stefan. 'It's a car engine.'

'You're right . . . where . . .?'

They looked towards a wooden garage. The engine revved, roaring now. There was a loud, splintering crash. The grey Riley cut through the door of the garage, out into the drive, racing fast towards the road.

'For fuck's sake! Get on the phone, Sergeant!'

Porter ran back to the house.

Stefan was already in the driving seat of the police Austin.

Frank Nugent slumped in beside him, slamming the door.

'Who's the silly bugger now, Stefan?'

'Could be you, Chief Inspector.'

Stefan sped over the gravel drive, out on to the Hog's Back. He could see the Riley ahead, going flat out. On the long, straight road, speed was easy, and the Riley was a faster car than the Austin. But it wasn't hard to keep it in sight.

'Try and keep on him. Once he's at the end of the Hog's Back, he'll have to slow down. Either he comes off into lanes and villages or he'll hit traffic and bends on the main road. Either way he won't keep that speed up for very long.'

'Well, he's fucking keeping it up now. Jesus!'

The Riley was moving faster than ever.

Stefan had the pedal flat on the floor; the other car was moving away.

'What the hell is he doing now?' said Stefan.

Ahead was a wide verge of grass to one side of the road, and beyond it a clump of huge, ancient elm trees. The Riley swerved off the road, on to the grass. It kept going. The speed didn't slacken. They heard the sound of the crash as

Edgar Hollingsworth's car hit the great trunk of an elm and shattered.

The black Austin crossed the verge of grass, following the tracks left by the Riley. Stefan stopped where the crumpled front of Hollingsworth's car seemed almost embedded in the tree. The two detectives got out and went to the car. They knew what to expect, given the speed of the impact. Edgar Hollingsworth's body had smashed through the windscreen as the car met the immovable elm. He was dead. Frank Nugent shook his head. There could have been no other outcome.

'How did he lose control on a road this straight, even at that speed?'

'He didn't,' said Stefan. 'I imagine he did exactly what he set out to do.'

23

Hungerford Bridge

That evening, Stefan Gillespie sat on a bench outside the bar at the Hog's Back Hotel, gazing out over the fields of the Surrey countryside. It was hard to say what the difference was between this landscape and some of the gentler parts of Ireland he knew, even the view looking from Baltinglass Hill towards Carlow. The English were tidier about the way they gave order to the land they farmed. It wasn't much more than that. He was ready to go home now. In every other area of life he stumbled on, one place was no tidier than another.

He looked up to see Frank Nugent walking towards him.

'Will you have a drink, Frank?'

'I've one more job for you, Stefan.'

'Don't push your luck. My superintendent will be sending Scotland Yard a bill. Not to mention my reputation for collaborating with the bloody English!'

'It's just a bit of babysitting.'

'What?'

'The fucking evidence at Swithins Barn. They want a guard overnight.'

'Wouldn't it be enough to lock the door?' Stefan grinned.

'Orders from on high.' Nugent shrugged. 'Poor old Sergeant

Porter and Constable Harris are stuck on the Hog's Back. I thought we'd do them a favour.'

Stefan finished the beer he was drinking and got up.

'All right, why not? I've got nothing better to do.'

It was getting dark as the two detectives arrived at the house on the Hog's Back. They found the sergeant and his constable sitting in the study, in front of a blazing fire, with several empty bottles of beer in front of them. They had settled in for the night, but they were glad to leave the job to others. They left the remaining beer. Stefan and Frank Nugent replaced them by the fire.

'What's happening with Mrs Hollingsworth?' asked Stefan.

'She's on her way to London now. Full circle. They'll hold her at West End Central. She'll be charged in the morning. And I can exit too, I guess.'

'How's she taking it?'

'Not as troubled as you might expect.'

'No, she seemed . . . phlegmatic enough about her husband's death.'

'She's abandoned the idea that they were on a crusade to save Britain from the depredations of homosexuals. She's turned into a bit of a mouse. Not quite the woman Charlie Pettit knew. He says she was the boss, no question. But that's not Mrs Hollingsworth now. She didn't like what they were doing, she knew it was wrong, that's the story, but Edgar, Edgar had to have his way. I think she'll do well. He said it was all him, didn't he, five minutes before he went out and topped himself? His last words. Next best thing to a death-bed confession. Juries are always impressed by those, judges too. If she sells that story, it'll go down well. He pushed her into it . . . he made all the decisions. And with Vikram Narayan, she can keep coming back to Edgar's last words. She pleaded with him to stop. He wouldn't. She had to look on, helpless!'

'You think that'll stand up?'

'Oh, Mrs H has a lot to be grateful for. A good barrister will make her another victim. A woman who stuck by her husband, loyally, honourably, after he was caught doing unspeakable things in a public convenience. She stuck by him, only to be pulled into his disgusting world when he decided to make money from it. An ordinary, decent woman manipulated by a husband who was a pervert. She was afraid of him. With good reason. And after all, his other victims were perverts too. No jury's going to spend very much time on them.'

'You think she'll get off?' asked Stefan.

'If she doesn't, it won't be much of a sentence.'

'But it's not how it was. You don't think so?'

'I don't. Do you?'

Stefan shook his head.

'I think we saw the real Mrs Hollingsworth briefly in this house. That was the woman Charlie Pettit knew. I guess there'll be others who say the same. People who sold names, stole letters, took photos. That's all Charlie remembers the husband doing, taking pictures. He was a bit of a photographer. There's a darkroom, behind the garage. But how far is this investigation going to go now? Not much further, I think. A trial for her and for Charlie. He won't do so badly either. And that'll be that. Don't turn over any stones that you don't have to.'

'I remember something,' said Stefan, 'from the flat in Greek Street.'

Nugent looked up.

'The pillow that smothered him. There were a couple of hairs. Not that long but bleached and permed. You've looked back at the reports, haven't you?'

'Yes, and I've thought the same thing you're thinking now.'

'She killed him.'

The English detective nodded.

'It's entirely possible. Maybe Hollingsworth hit Vikram, when he came through the door, but did she make the decision to finish him . . . and get rid of him for good? Was Edgar really the one pleading? Who used the knife? We'll never know.'

Stefan Gillespie nodded.

'And a couple of hairs won't prove anything, will they?'

Frank Nugent got up and walked to the filing cabinet.

'I also think she drove the car that hit Hindu Narayan. It had to be one of them. It must have felt as if Hindu was following up on what her brother was doing. I looked at the date and the ARP roster. Hollingsworth was on duty that night. He was nowhere near London. We'll never get near proving anything.'

Nugent opened a filing-cabinet drawer and flicked through files.

'There is a sort of account of the other murders in here – the Yates murders. A note of something Charlie Pettit said about a couple of men being killed. He'd heard rumours. They put that together with something a bit more definite, from people who were selling them material about homosexual men. I'm pretty sure that information came from our chums at West End Central. CID spread it about to put the frighteners on the faeries. Not much more. But that's how some of the details got out, knife wounds and so on. The notes in the Hollingsworths' files are all in her handwriting. Most things are in her hand. In the margin, next to her notes on the murders, she wrote, "This any use to us?"'

'It very nearly was,' said Stefan. 'But not quite useful enough.'

On a table by the filing cabinet, there was a decanter of whiskey. Frank Nugent picked it up, along with two glasses, and walked back to the fire. He set down the glasses and poured two drinks. He sipped at the whiskey, slowly.

'I don't suppose Mr Hollingsworth will begrudge us.'

'So, when are you back to India?' asked Stefan.

'Ten days or so.'

'Then?'

'The usual. Informers and political meetings. Keeping an eye on the politicians who want to kick out the British and take power. An exercise in futility, of course: they will be taking power anyway. As everyone knows.'

'You think so?'

'It depends on the war. Once it's over . . . independence follows, as night follows day.' Nugent smiled. 'Or the other way round . . . as day follows night.'

'And what does that mean for you?'

'Well, if I was an ordinary policeman, I suppose I'd be happy enough in an Indian police force instead of a British one. It won't change overnight. But I've made a different bed . . . I told you, the Great Game isn't for amateurs, and that's what I was. Maybe I didn't look where I was going. When I did, I was already in the snake pit. It was too late. A new India won't have any room for the lads from Indian Political Intelligence. Eventually, I'll end up back here. A country that's not my country, with a pension and a bungalow in Worthing.'

As he finished speaking, Frank Nugent got up and walked to the filing cabinet again. One drawer was still open. Again, he started to flick through it.

'You know what's in here, Stefan?'

'I've seen enough.'

'It's a treasure trove,' said the chief inspector, 'for people like us.'

'How?'

'There are files on close to three hundred people here.'

Nugent moved back to the fire. He took wood from the basket and threw it into the grate, banking it up higher. He stood, looking down at the flames.

'You could divide these files into two sections. In India, my boss would, and I don't doubt your Superintendent Gregory would too. Important people, some very important, and the rest. Mr and Mrs Hollingsworth were clever. They divided them into three. I don't know that they thought that out, but for practical purposes, important people couldn't be blackmailed. You'd think they were the obvious targets, but it's too risky. You've got politicians, major businessmen, a couple of bishops, even a few senior police officers up and down the country. There's a few stars of stage and screen, of course, and assorted artistic types and academics of one kind or another. It's a whole network. But these are men with power, with real influence. They know people who can come after you.'

'So, you leave them alone?'

'You keep your powder dry, anyway,' continued Nugent. 'Who knows? And then there are the ordinary, everyday oiks. Men with no money, so not worth bothering with. Except for getting information. Ten bob could buy some interesting names, even some letters. But it's the middle that mattered to Edgar and Ivy. Bank clerks and managers and shopkeepers and teachers and doctors and civil servants, and maybe a few not-so-senior policemen. They were the people who had lives to ruin and nobody to help them . . . plus a bit of money. Not much, but enough to pay. Of course, I'm sure our friends delivered on their threats of exposure if the money dried up . . . or . . . pour encourager les autres.'

'And if you went to the police, you'd be ruined anyway,' said Stefan.

Chief Inspector Nugent stooped and put another log on the fire, which was now blazing fiercely. Stefan watched him, puzzled. It was hot in the room. Nugent walked back across the study to the filing cabinet. He pulled all the drawers out, slowly, one after another.

'There's a van coming to collect all this tomorrow.'

Stefan nodded. 'It's evidence. No shortage either.'

'They're not coming from Scotland Yard or West End Central.'

'What do you mean?' Stefan could see Frank Nugent's frown.

'It's not about evidence. That's not it at all.'

'Then what is it?'

'It'll be fellers from Intelligence. I'd imagine MI5. Special Branch might get a peep, but this is for the big boys. And what they want is the people at the top. They won't worry too much about the others. Edgar and Ivy have put together information about the predilections of a whole slice of the great and the good that MI5 would take years to collect, even if anyone would let them do it. No one knows what you might need all that for, but there's always going to be a time. It won't be about money, quite a different sort of blackmail, that's why they want it and that's why someone has to sit here all night and keep it safe.'

Stefan nodded. Now it was said, it was obvious enough.

'How's that fire doing, Stefan?'

'I'm starting to sweat like a fucking pig, Frank.'

'Good. Get a bit of fresh air.'

'What?'

'In the back of the car there's a jerry can of petrol. I've still got this bloody pain, courtesy of Mr Yates. I can hardly lift the thing. Will you get it?'

Stefan stood up, frowning, not sure what Nugent was getting at now.

'That's right. There's going to be an accident. What a couple of fools, banking up that fire so high it tumbled out on the carpet! Careless or what?'

'You're going to burn it?' Stefan was looking at the filing cabinet.

'Why not? That'll be the job finished. Finished properly, I mean.'

Stefan Gillespie smiled and nodded. It felt right somehow.

'They will know there was petrol. It won't be hard to work out.'

'Yes.' Frank Nugent was untroubled. 'But what are they going to do about it? It's a secret they're taking the fucking stuff at all. I don't see them making a song and dance out of that. They can't touch you. You're a bystander. You're heading home to Ireland anyway. My boss wants me in India. He's more than capable of telling some arsehole behind a desk in MI5 to fuck himself.'

The two men looked at each other for a long moment.

Stefan laughed. He picked up the bottle of whiskey and poured two more drinks, filling the glasses. He walked to the cabinet and handed one to Nugent.

'Sláinte!' said Chief Inspector Nugent.

'Sláinte mhaith!' said Inspector Gillespie.

It was little more than ten minutes later that Stefan Gillespie and Frank Nugent sat in the black Austin, in the driveway of Swithins Barn, watching the front of the house. The fire was underway in the study, blazing fiercely after the liberal application of petrol to the filing cabinet and the carpet in front of the fireplace. They would wait a little longer, until the fire had taken hold of that part of the house strongly enough to ensure nothing survived. Then they would drive to the Hog's Back Hotel, and the nearest telephone, to call the police and fire brigade. The phone at Swithins Barn being too dangerous to access now. For several minutes neither man spoke. They smoked cigarettes in the darkness.

'Is that a debt paid now?' asked Stefan.

'A debt?' said Frank Nugent.

'To Vikram Narayan. This has always been personal for you, hasn't it? From the start. You didn't have to push investigating his murder, did you?'

'I didn't know what would come up, as far as he was concerned, with the work he was doing for me and Indian Political Intelligence. I couldn't be sure there wasn't a connection. Or that things wouldn't come out . . .'

'That always felt more like an excuse than a reason,' said Stefan.

'You're right. And whatever he was, whatever happened to him, some of that was down to me. A lot of that. It wasn't always about work . . . that took over. There was a time I was close to his family, to Hindu as well. My father brought me up to spend more time with Indians than with the British. He had Indian friends, and not many English ones – another thing my mother never forgave him for. I went to a boarding school with Indians, boys whose fathers worked for the civil service or the railways. I knew Hindu before I knew her brother. She was a lot older. There was a group of us then, all a long time ago . . . what mattered then is gone, long gone . . .' The Englishman let the words fade away.

'That's why she won't speak to you, Frank?'

'Why she hates my guts, you mean?' Nugent laughed.

'All right,' said Stefan. 'You were friends once.'

'As I said, we were close. She thinks I betrayed that. She's right.'

'Why did you?'

'Because I'm weak. Because I do what I'm told. Because I'm the kind of arsehole who runs an empire and doesn't even believe in what I'm doing. But I do it. Hindu Narayan knows. She knows that. Why wouldn't she despise me?'

Stefan could feel there was real pain behind Frank Nugent's words.

'There must have been more,' said Stefan. 'Did you love her?'

The Englishman started the engine. Flames were visible through the house's front windows now. Still the chief inspector gazed at it, unmoving.

'No,' said Frank Nugent, 'it was Vikram. It was Vikram I loved, once.'

Stefan said nothing. He knew he wasn't meant to. The words were a kind of confession, a kind of explanation. They were only addressed to him in part. They had to be said aloud. Even if only one person heard, they had to be heard.

'He did come to me.' Nugent spoke again after a long pause. 'About some people who were blackmailing homosexual men. He told me he was trying to find out who they were. I told him to stop. I started out laughing. Then I lost my temper. He was putting a lot at risk. He was drawing attention to himself. As for the idea I'd help him with this arsing around, that I'd get involved . . . I gave him a real bollocking. What the fuck did he think he was up to? He had a job to do. For me. For my boss in India. And back in Delhi they were already unimpressed with what he was bringing in. He was coming up short. He wasn't getting enough. Or he wasn't giving enough. What were his Indian nationalist friends doing? What were they planning? Who were they talking to in London? What were the instructions from India? No one gave a monkey's about a few queers getting blackmailed. It went with the territory. Queers do get the screw put on them. The sun rises in the east. It's not news. So, I put the fear of God in him. I told him the last thing he needed was to make a spectacle of himself playing the fucking detective. What did he think his friends would do if they found out he was already playing the detective, for real, for me, providing information to Indian Political Intelligence? And that was that.'

The IPI man put the car into gear and turned it round.

'I told him I was protecting him. But I was just another blackmailer.'

Frank Nugent took out a cigarette and lit it. Everything he had said, he had said looking out through the windscreen. He looked round at Stefan.

'You're not much good on the absolution front, Stefan.'

'Do you want absolution?'

'I don't suppose I do.' The man who could have no place in England or India now smiled. 'Who would I be then?'

He drove out from Swithins Barn, into the darkness of the Hog's Back.

The night before Stefan Gillespie left London to return to Ireland, he waited for Hindu Narayan to finish work at the Veeraswamy in Regent Street. He knew she still refused to see Frank Nugent. The past, that Stefan had only some small window into, left no room for any kind of reconciliation between the Indian woman and the Englishman. But he liked Frank Nugent and he liked Hindu Narayan, though he had barely seen her. He assumed Vikram Narayan's sister would want to know what had really happened. He had been a policeman a long time. People wanted to know. It was a need. He recognised it as part of why a death had to be investigated. It wasn't only about justice or revenge; it was the desire to feel the thing had been completed, finished. If it was left unresolved, the gaps and doubts and questions were a continuing pain in people's lives. He felt that Hindu would want to close those gaps, now that they could be closed.

He still wasn't sure how much to say. The truth about how Vikram Narayan died was simple, however complicated the circumstances that led to it. Stefan knew, for instance, from Chief Inspector Nugent, that the Hollingsworths' Riley Kestrel had been fitted with a new wing earlier that year. According to the garage in Wanborough, Ivy Hollingsworth had hit a stone bollard in the blackout, coming out of Guildford. It seemed impossible she hadn't damaged it running into Hindu Narayan in Regent Street. Was it right to tell Hindu that, if she still believed that somehow the British Police or Indian Political Intelligence – or Frank Nugent himself – had something to do with it? Shouldn't she clear her head of that? The facts were what she ought to have. Facts usually helped. And Stefan wanted them to help Hindu. He could have ignored her. But he was trying to do what Frank Nugent would have done himself, if only Vikram's sister would let him. She might not. She must still see him as a proxy for a man she hated.

Stefan Gillespie and Hindu Narayan walked through Piccadilly Circus, down to Trafalgar Square. She lived across the river, not far from Waterloo Station. The route she took, to the Embankment and over Hungerford Bridge, was one Stefan knew from a visit to London years before. The night was overcast and dark. There was no moon. It was the kind of night German bombers avoided, and they had done. The city was quiet, and the night hid the ugly scars of war.

Hindu Narayan was cool and polite. She knew that Stefan's intentions were good. But somewhere in her head she had forced a distinction between the facts of her brother's death, that may or may not have involved a man and a woman he was trying to expose as criminals, and the facts of his life, which would have been utterly different if Nugent had not betrayed his trust in her and her family. If there was one thing Hindu Narayan shared with Frank Nugent it was that personal betrayal lay behind Vikram's death. Surely, without that betrayal, he would still be alive?

She listened as Stefan spoke. She nodded. She heard what he said. But he found himself trailing away as they stepped on to Hungerford Bridge, on to the footpath that ran beside the railway line into Charing Cross. The rattle of trains coming in and out drowned his words. As they did, he realised she preferred not to hear them. He could see that she already had a number of versions of her brother's death, and of his life. All he was doing was giving her another one. He couldn't know what had reached Vikram's mother and father in India, or whether anything he said would be added to it. In that version,

Stefan felt sure, Vikram Narayan was still an Indian nationalist, fighting the good fight until the end. And in that version, too, Vikram Narayan's homosexuality had likely been erased.

Halfway across the bridge, as the rolling thunder of another train passed across the Thames, Hindu Narayan stopped. She smiled, taking Stefan's hand.

'Why don't you walk back, Stefan? I'm fine now.'

'I've said enough, you mean. Or too much.'

'I appreciate what you've done. I know what I need to know.'

The words were both an acceptance and a rejection of what he had said.

'I'm sorry if some of it is . . . not what you want to hear.'

'There's nothing I want to hear . . . unless it could all be undone.'

Stefan nodded. He knew Hindu meant more than her brother's death. There were whole lives – hers, Vikram's, even Frank Nugent's – in that wish.

'I wish it was a different time. And we were here for different reasons.'

The words came unexpectedly, unintentionally into Stefan's mouth.

'There is only one time,' said Hindu.

'I'm sorry.' These seemed the only words Stefan had left.

'Yes, I'm sorry too.'

She leant up and kissed him on the cheek.

'Thank you.'

Stefan watched Hindu walk away until she reached the steps at the other end of the bridge and disappeared. He turned back towards the Embankment. As he reached it and walked down the steps, he looked out along the Thames, west towards Westminster Bridge. He had not thought about the places he had been in over the last few days. He knew some of them, but what he had been doing had pushed that away. Now he had time to look. And something made him look. Perhaps it was no more than the brush of a woman's lips on his cheek. There were some familiar places from years back. Waterloo Station and the train south, through Clapham Junction and Wimbledon; then Hungerford Bridge and the Thames below; the Embankment and the walk into London. They were things that appeared as images in his life. The past was not a great narrative that held together in one piece. Elements of it had seemed that way once, so much so that he had tried to cling on to it. But it had fragmented. There were images, moments, pictures that stayed strong, but they came into his head when they were needed or when it mattered. He had visited London, not long after he and Maeve were married. A honeymoon. They'd had enough money for three days in a hotel in the West End, but that was all. Then they stayed with an aunt of Maeve's near Kingston and travelled in by train. There were images of that now. Leaving a theatre, after a play he couldn't remember, and standing in a street, laughing; a café by the Serpentine and a child feeding ducks. There had been a day they walked from Kingston along the river to Hampton Court. In Hampton Court Park, ambling towards the Long Water that led to the palace, they saw a deer, unlike all the other deer they had seen in the park, startlingly white, only feet away. They saw it for seconds; then it was gone. Now, walking away from Hungerford Bridge, leaving the Thames, heading through the dark into the West End, the images the bridge and the river had brought into his head momentarily were left behind as well. They had come and then, very softly, they had gone.

24

Kilranelagh Graveyard

Dublin

Detective Inspector Stefan Gillespie returned to Ireland with a certain amount of what Sergeant Dessie MacMahon called 'housekeeping' to do. Housekeeping was the tidying up that came with the end of an investigation. There was always something more to provide in terms of a report and there was all the filing away of statements and the consignment of evidence to the bowels of a police station or Garda Headquarters or the cellars of Dublin Castle. In Ireland there had been no day in court where the murder of James Corcoran was concerned. There was, eventually, an account of the trial in London. It was brief, amounting to no more than two typed pages that stated only that a trial had taken place, that evidence had been presented, and that John Eddington Yates had been found guilty of the murder of a number of men, in a number of locations, on a number of dates. Those men included the ones he killed in Ireland and Malta. There was no record of what had been said at the trial, either by the prosecution or by the defence; at least, none of those details crossed the Irish Sea. The trial was held in camera. The reason was a vague resort to the exigencies of war: the defendant was a serving officer, and details of military camps and bases, as well as troop movements, were needed in evidence.

The reality was that the association of such shocking crimes with the British Army was not something anyone wanted to see in the press, in Britain or anywhere else. The image of an army standing alone to save democracy, even civilisation, could not be sullied by John Yates. If no one wanted to open up the secret world of the men Yates had preyed on in Britain and Malta, it was also true that even at the start, when James Corcoran died by a lake in Kildare, no one wanted to look too hard in Ireland either. The account that came from the Home Office in London, to be filed with the details of the seminarian's death, ended with a single paragraph, of one sentence, that gave the date on which John Eddington Yates was hanged at Brixton Prison and buried in an unmarked grave in the prison grounds. The trial had taken place ten days after his return to England from Malta. It lasted two days. Only four more days passed between his trial and his execution.

However, housekeeping, especially where murder was concerned, involved more than paperwork. It took Stefan Gillespie back to Thomastown and the house where James Corcoran had grown up. He gave Mrs Corcoran as much of an explanation as he could of what had happened to her son. It was what he thought she wanted. Mr Corcoran was in Dublin when Stefan went to Kilkenny. He was now a Cabinet minister. Stefan had offered to meet him in Dublin, but Rory Corcoran had been too busy. It didn't surprise Stefan. He arranged to speak to Mr and Mrs Corcoran at home, but Minister Corcoran was too tied up at his ministry to be there. Stefan told James's mother that the man who killed her son had been hanged in England. She wanted few details, but he hoped what he gave her helped bring a kind of end. He knew she would tell her husband almost nothing, except that there had been a hanging. It was enough. They were moving on, as they had to. Mrs Corcoran said that. She said it too many times. Stefan saw that in the garden, the building that was James Corcoran's refuge had been brightly painted. He knew that the debris of his young life would have gone; some few precious things kept, but most of it discarded. He also knew the life had been sucked out of the house in Thomastown. It would be a long time coming back. Probably it never would.

Stefan called at the Gate Theatre. Micheál Mac Liammóir wanted to know what had happened to Vikram Narayan. The shock of what he had found in the flat in Greek Street had not left him, nor had the feeling – he could not shake it off – that a different response to what he now knew to be a desperate cry for help might have meant the difference between life and death for the young Indian. Stefan told him it was unlikely that that was true. The circumstances of Vikram's death had a dynamic that was nothing to do with whether Mac Liammóir could have given him a job in Ireland or helped him in any way.

The actor wanted to hear the details of what had happened, both of Vikram Narayan's murder and of the other killings. These crimes were ultimately unrelated, except for an attempt to disguise one thing as another, but for Micheál Mac Liammóir there were connections. The complexities of Vikram's life had brought him to live on the edge of an ever-growing darkness he couldn't escape from; had made him an informer, a cheat, a liar. Why? Only because of who he was. The things that had put him in a place where his life could be destroyed would not be so different from those that might have marked and marred the secret lives of the men murdered by John Yates. Somewhere, perhaps, those things even touched the black despair that had tortured Yates himself, that had plunged him into a pit of self-loathing almost beyond comprehension. Almost, but not quite. His darkness was so complete that it consumed him, and others with him. Mac Liammóir recognised how lucky he was. He could stand outside the darkness. Only just. He would not forget that.

*

305

When Stefan Gillespie made time for his own life, the first thing he found, grabbing a brief night at home in Baltinglass, was a crisis that was almost refreshing in its parochial simplicity. For the moment, as he arrived at Kilranelagh, it was what occupied everyone in the neighbourhood. It had been abrupt and unlooked for, a shock, and a considerable irritant to many, including the Gillespies. Michael Cashman, the principal at Talbotstown National School, Tom's school, had resigned. One day he was there and the next day he had gone. His house in Kiltegan was shut up. Someone saw him get the train to Dublin. He said he was taking a holiday. He had been away a week when Stefan came home.

Explanations for what had happened were many and varied. There was talk he had inherited money or won the Hospitals' Sweepstake, or that he had been offered a job at an expensive private school in England. None of that made sense of the speed with which he went. There was talk of money going missing from the school, though no one took that seriously. People spoke of a row between Michael Cashman and the parish priest. There had been arguments between the two before. The priest didn't like Cashman and the feeling was mutual. The priest controlled St Joseph's School's Board of Management and everything the principal tried to do that challenged the hold of the Church over school life was knocked back. Increasingly, there had been a feeling that some things were being knocked back out of the priest's bloody-mindedness. But Michael Cashman could be bloody-minded himself. The two men had argued for years without it interfering with the way the school ran. And St Joseph's School was Cashman's life. He gave it everything he had. Even if he had a reason to leave, surely he loved St Joseph's too much not to give good notice.

If the level of crisis Michael Cashman's departure was causing in Baltinglass and Kiltegan made Stefan smile, it annoyed him too. He would not be drawn into the full heat of what was going on, but he was disappointed. It wasn't long ago he had talked to the principal about the extra work he was doing with Tom to help him get a scholarship to secondary school. He had decided, despite the reluctance of his mother and father, to do what Cashman had suggested and make the break with the Catholic Church's demand that Tom go to a Catholic school. It would not be easy. David and Helena, with the Protestant instinct to lie low in Dev's Ireland, were reluctant to face the trouble that would inevitably come. Michael Cashman was an ally. Stefan wondered if Tom was something to do with what had happened. Had Father Brennan got hold of the plan? It seemed unlikely Cashman wouldn't have said something. Tom was unsettled by it too. There was a new teacher and the quiet understanding that had allowed Tom to take his own path while appearing to travel the same one as everyone else was gone. If it all seemed trivial in the world Stefan had just left, he was still pissed off.

While Stefan Gillespie concluded the housekeeping that surrounded the murder of James Corcoran, the usual regime in Special Branch continued. He found himself spending more time collecting information on the Indian community in Dublin. Superintendent Gregory had decided someone needed to specialise in this area of surveillance, and Stefan had drawn that straw. Small as the community was, it could cause friction between Ireland and Britain. There were few Indians actively engaged in the politics of independence who looked to the IRA for support, but there were some. There were fewer who dealt with the German embassy, but it wasn't for lack of trying on the part of the Germans.

Finding out who was pushing the boundaries mattered more than it had when Stefan left for Malta. Three German spies had been picked up while he was away, after landing on the coast of Cork. They had so little idea where they were that their first act was to stop local children and ask. Two of the men were South African, with accents distinctly uncommon in Cork. The other was an Indian, Henry Obed, who wore a white Gandhi cap and offered the children bars of chocolate. The men were, unsurprisingly, arrested. Their suitcases contained incendiary bombs, explosives and large quantities of cash. It was so clumsy that G2 were inclined to think it was a British false-flag operation. But Henry Obed had come from Berlin. He believed he was there to help Ireland fight the British in an imminent war and that somewhere along the line this would free India from British rule. Obed had been interrogated by the time Stefan returned to Special Branch, but he interviewed him himself in Mountjoy Prison, in an attempt to relate names in the Indian community to German espionage. He came to the conclusion that either Obed was a very good liar or he knew hardly any Indians in Ireland. As a spy, he was another incident to file under 'F' for 'farce'.

Farce, however, did not stop there. Stefan Gillespie had watched *The Great Dictator* at the Manoel Theatre in Valletta; indeed, he was one of the few people in Ireland who had seen the banned film. But there was a print in Dublin. Two students from Trinity College had brought it from Belfast. It was due to be shown, secretly, in Trinity. But invitations had been scattered widely around Dublin's student community. On the morning before the showing, Inspector Stefan Gillespie and Sergeant Dessie MacMahon arrived at a staircase in the Courtyard at Trinity College, with two proctors, to seize the film. One student tried to get Stefan to arrest him. A chance to embarrass the censor and the police was too good to miss. Stefan didn't oblige. One farce at a time was enough.

At Dublin Castle, Stefan dumped the film canister on Superintendent Gregory's desk. He knew it had amused his boss to send him to seize it. It was deliberate.

'Right, sir. *The Great Dictator*. A comedy.'

'But a very insidious one, Inspector.'

'We look like fucking eejits,' said Stefan.

'That's the job. As they say, someone has to do it.'

'It's bollocks.'

'You take yourself too seriously, Stevie. You know, I look at this . . .' The superintendent gestured at the canister of film. 'I look at this, and I find myself thinking, I know what's in Inspector Gillespie's head. He's thinking, if this is what it takes to defend the fucking state, is it even worth defending? Now go on, tell me I'm wrong. Tell me this doesn't make you angrier than everything else put together, all the spying, all the arrests . . . even the occasional execution. If we can't even show a fucking Charlie Chaplin film . . . then Jesus Christ!'

'It's not worth arguing about, is it, sir?'

'Not at the moment, no, that's the point. When it is, I'll join you.'

Stefan shrugged.

'Meanwhile, Stevie, if we have to look like a bunch of clowns, we can.'

Stefan smiled.

'I wish we didn't have to do it quite so much.'

Superintendent Gregory's expression changed.

'There's something you should see.'

He pushed aside the film and picked up a newspaper.

'I know this means something to you. I didn't say anything before . . . I heard you talking to Dessie about the teacher at your lad's school. Well, read this now.'

Gregory pointed at a small paragraph, headed 'Tragic Accident'.

Stefan read the article.

The bodies of two men were recovered from the sea off Bray Head yesterday morning, after what appears to have been a tragic swimming accident. The men have been identified as Mr Michael

Cashman, a school principal, of Kiltegan, Co Wicklow, and Mr Kenneth O'Malley, a taxi driver, of Rathmines, Co Dublin. The men drowned after getting out of their depth in a heavy sea. Relatives of the deceased have been informed.

'Jesus,' said Stefan quietly. 'What the hell was he doing?'

'You don't know anything?' asked Gregory.

'I know he resigned from the school . . . it was all very sudden.'

'It wasn't an accident. That's one thing you can be sure of.'

'What do you mean?'

'He was due in court next week.'

'What . . . what for?'

'He was arrested, two weeks ago. In the Phoenix Park. Along with the other feller. Indecency, sodomy, I don't know. There was a sweep on. There'd been complaints about men in the park. You've been in a Dublin station. Some inspector says it's time for a clean-up. Your man was unlucky. I think someone tried to stop the prosecution, but they wanted him. A teacher. As an example.'

'Does anyone know . . .? I mean, do they know in Baltinglass?'

'The Guards will know now. So, the people who matter will know soon enough.'

Stefan stared at the newspaper again. There was nothing to say.

It was two days later that Stefan stood in the bleak graveyard on the slopes of Kilranelagh Hill. It was a bright day, but the wind was stiff as the body of Michael Cashman was lowered into the ground. Stefan held his son's hand. Behind stood David and Helena. There were a lot of people there. A lot of children. And a lot of people who had been children, years ago and not so many years ago. There were those who knew why Michael Cashman was dead. The parish priest who sprinkled

Holy Water over the coffin. The men who were the Board of Management of Michael Cashman's school. The Guards who had turned out in their best uniforms. There would be others, too, who had all the details to hand, though many, perhaps most, would not know anything of the real truth at all.

Stefan had not gone to the funeral service at Talbotstown church. He had no wish to listen to the people who did know talk about what a good teacher the principal had been; people who would have done nothing to help the dead man, who would only have wanted him out of the way. After all, however sad, this was easier than what might have happened, the scandal if Cashman had not chosen to take the course he did. And all the words were true. He was a good man after all, in almost every way. The small community that sent its children to Scoil Naomh Iósaf had recognised that for many years. But Stefan found himself wondering how many there would have been in that community to defend him. Who would have stood beside the principal if the truth had come out? He had always been a solitary man. No one noticed it. They only saw what he gave them. They measured him only by what he did. But when it mattered, when something needed to be given to him, Michael Cashman had no one.

Stefan led Tom home, back through the graveyard. Tom was crying. Stefan, who was not a man to shed tears easily, felt them in his own eyes. Father and son stopped, for a moment, to say a prayer, or something like a prayer, at the grave of Maeve Gillespie. It was not far from where Michael Cashman was being covered by the earth of Kilranelagh Hill.

For part of that evening, Stefan Gillespie sat in the small, dark bar at the pub in Talbotstown. It was busier than it usually was, after the funeral, but he did no more than nod at the people he knew. He sat on his own. He drank more than he intended, but he expected that. He walked home, past the school. It wasn't long ago that he had been talking to Michael Cashman about Tom. He would still do what the principal had believed was the right thing to do. It would be harder. He had not realised how much Michael Cashman's help and conviction meant.

At the farm, David was still up, but Helena had gone to bed.

Stefan went to the kitchen cabinet and took out the whiskey. He found a glass and poured himself another drink. As so often, it was something to do.

'Do you want one, Pa?'

'No, I'm going up.'

Stefan looked at his father.

'When did you know?'

David Gillespie frowned, as if he wasn't sure what his son meant.

'You know what I'm talking about.'

'I heard from the station. I don't think all the Guards knew.'

'Bollocks. They knew well enough, all of them.'

'Yes, you're probably right, Stefan.'

'I've had enough of this, I tell you.'

'Of what?'

'Dead queers, Pa. Dead for no fucking reason anyone can tell you.'

David Gillespie nodded. He didn't understand, but he felt Stefan's anger.

'No one ever knew about him . . . If it could have just stayed that way . . .'

'That's not an answer is it, Pa?'

David could feel that his son was looking for an argument.

'I'm going to bed. I'll see you in the morning.'

'What the fuck does any of it matter, Pa? Does anyone even ask that? Who fucking cares?'

Stefan Gillespie stood in the kitchen as his father went out and climbed the stairs. He drank the whiskey. He picked up the bottle and walked through into the sitting room. The fire was still burning. He knew it had been lit because he was home. They didn't normally use the room. He didn't light the lamp. He sat in the armchair by the fire. The room had a low, warm glow. He looked at the bookshelves, the piano his mother almost never played now. His eyes found a book that was next to him, on the shelf by the mantelpiece. He must have been half looking for it, but even in the low light he recognised the battered brown spine and the faint remnants of some gold lettering: Palgrave's *Golden Treasury*. He had last seen a copy beside the bed where Vikram Narayan died. He took it out and held it. It had been given to him by his parents, as it had been given to Vikram Narayan at school in India. One a present, the other a prize, both recognising an interest in reading, perhaps, what others weren't reading. It was a bridge his own son was crossing now, suddenly, and he hadn't seen it happening until Michael Cashman pointed it out to him.

Stefan couldn't know what else Vikram Narayan had liked in the *Golden Treasury*, but he had been reading one thing Stefan liked too, 'Dover Beach'. It had been bookmarked. He saw it when he picked up the book at the flat in Greek Street. Stefan knew enough to understand that the young Indian was not only reading it because he liked it. Stefan didn't have to strain to guess what the last words of the poem must have meant to him; a statement of the hard, bitter truth of his life. They offered no consolation, no way out. They were honest, maybe, where almost nothing in Vikram Narayan's life had been.

He remembered reading the poem to Maeve once, when they first knew each other; she hadn't liked it. She believed life was better than that. He thought he'd probably told her that wasn't the point. The poem was part of what made life better than that. It was its own refutation. She had laughed at that, of course. It sounded clever, but it didn't mean anything, did it? What made life better than that was simple. It was what was in front of you. It was what you touched. It was the air you breathed. 'Ah, love, let us be true to one another'; everything began with that. It ended with that, too. Those were the words that mattered; the rest was nothing. At the time, it had seemed Maeve was right, and even if the other words of 'Dover Beach' were still in the air Stefan breathed, he picked out the ones she held on to and held on to them as well. There had been times since her death when he had still felt she was right. But there were other times when he knew she was wrong. He did not hear the poem in his head because it was simply a beautiful thing; he heard it because too many times there was nothing else to hear. Because the world that was so various, so beautiful, so new, really did have neither joy, nor love, nor light, nor certitude, nor peace, nor help for pain.

He opened the book and found the poem.

He looked at the all-familiar words. And where was anybody in that world, now more than ever, but on that darkling plain, swept by confused alarms of trouble and flight, where ignorant armies still clashed by night? He sat back in the chair. He drained the glass of whiskey and stared at the dying fire. And he smiled. The image was still there, unbidden, despite everything. The woman and the man, young still, almost not Maeve, not him, and through the trees, with the sun on the Long Water at Hampton Court beyond, the white deer grazing, shining too in the sunlight. And the only movement it seemed, in that bright picture, the only movement in all the world, was his hand as it touched hers.

Notes & Acknowledgements

Island One: Eire

The main action of this story takes place in the early months of 1941. Ireland was still pursuing its course of fierce neutrality; still frustrating the British government, especially over the refusal to let Atlantic convoys use its ports; still letting Germany believe neutrality disguised a non-existent desire for German victory. The show was what mattered. Reality was different. The cooperation between British and Irish Intelligence services was intense. Many records of this were destroyed at the war's end, particularly by the Irish. Even the MI5 history, only declassified in 1999, is selective. It doesn't even mention sharing Garda Special Branch surveillance information about Indian nationalists in Ireland.

Éamon de Valera's government, in 1941, was still haunted by the prospect of war coming to Ireland, even if the threat of Germany invading Britain had receded, along with the chances of Ireland being attacked by the Germans, the British, or both at once. Less pressing, as a result, was the possibility of any IRA uprising. The action of war was shifting elsewhere.

The Emergency, as the war was referred to officially in Ireland, was preoccupied with keeping ordinary life going, hampered by a lack of basic commodities such as coal and oil. But Dublin was still somewhere Britons with the opportunity and the cash could briefly escape the rigours of war. The government continued to frown on its citizens joining the British Armed Forces but did nothing to stop the tens of thousands that did. Even more people left to work in British industries, where their presence made a huge contribution to the war effort.

Germany dispatched a series of laughably incompetent spies to Ireland, most of them believing the country was about to rise up against Britain. What prompted the Abwehr to land an Indian, for instance, dressed as a Jawaharlal Nehru lookalike, is anybody's guess. The idea that the secretly anti-Hitler Abwehr was only ever 'playing' at its espionage in Ireland may well be true.

Island Two: Britain

In Britain, as the chance of German invasion receded, the Blitz took its place as a threat to everyday life. But even this danger would fall away in 1941. German bombing of the United Kingdom, especially London, never reached anything like the scale of the Allied bombing of Germany later in the war. The level of destruction was relatively small in comparison. Though the Blitz did continue in 1941, Hitler's attention was already elsewhere: on the Mediterranean and North Africa, but above all on Russia. That disaster, along with the most brutal manifestation of what Nazi warfare was really about, was waiting in the wings.

Island Three: Malta

War in the Mediterranean and North Africa brought the tiny island of Malta, a British colony since the expulsion of a

Napoleonic army in 1800, into the thick of the conflict. Malta had been a staging post for British shipping since the Suez Canal opened to give faster access to India, the supposed 'jewel' in the Imperial Crown, and to colonies beyond. The island's economy depended on the British naval dockyards, and the presence of British soldiers and sailors, mostly on their way elsewhere, was a part of Maltese life. While Maltese remained the language of the home, English had become the language of everything else.

Maltese history always connected the island to Italy. Before English, Italian had been the language of business and politics. It was a connection Italy's fascist dictator, Mussolini, approved of. His desire to expand Italian territory encompassed Malta. So, when he joined Hitler and declared war on Britain, it was time to grab the island. Italian forces were already attacking the British in North Africa, with the aim of invading Egypt. But Mussolini's war collapsed. His army in North Africa was routed and Malta, weakly defended, with barely any fighter aircraft, at least contained the bombers of the Regia Aeronautica. Hitler had no choice but to prop Mussolini up and intervene.

The Germans changed everything. In North Africa, Rommel's Afrika Corps devastated the British. And though Rommel would eventually be defeated, he came close to taking Egypt and cutting Britain off from India and its colonies. In Malta the Luftwaffe was a different prospect to the Italians for the ill-equipped RAF. The island could be bombed at will. The British could do little to stop it. Italian and German airfields were only a short distance away, in Sicily. The island was now under siege. British convoys could not get through with oil and ammunition or the basic foodstuffs the people of Malta needed.

This was not Malta's first siege. In the sixteenth century a few hundred Knights of St John, along with the people of the island, fought off a massive invasion by the Turkish Ottoman Empire in one of history's most remarkable feats of resistance against overwhelming odds. It was a lot more too. The victory played a crucial role in ending long-running Ottoman plans to conquer Europe.

The new siege could not be resisted by fortresses and bastions. Malta was almost helpless against the Axis bombers. Destruction was everywhere, and civilian deaths ran high. At one point, the island would be the most bombed place on earth. It is a grim statement about the Second World War that it would not hold that distinction for long. But the resilience of the people of Malta is one of the most extraordinary stories of the war. Eventually, Winston Churchill did more to help the island he called an 'unsinkable battleship'. New RAF fighters, including Spitfires to take on the Messerschmitts, did arrive. Convoys got through, often at terrible cost. And Malta's existence as a naval base made all the difference in preventing supplies, especially tank fuel, reaching Rommel. Yet even if things improved, it is still the case that for much of the time the British forces on the island, and the Maltese people, just had to stick it out.

For this reason, the island was awarded the George Cross, the highest British civilian honour for bravery, the equivalent of the Victoria Cross. It is only normally given to individuals. The cross still features on the Maltese flag. Not everyone in Malta feels it sits easily with the symbols of an independent nation, but most Maltese see it as a memorial to their past and to the fact that some wars are fought for ends that matter more than the self-interest that may be there too. We may not always be sure what our civilisation is, but the tiny island of Malta has played a disproportionate part in defending it.

Much of what I have written about in Malta is still there to be seen. The city of Valletta, in particular, small as it is, is one of the most beautiful cities you will see. And at the edge of that city, between Battery Street and St Ursula Street, the British Hotel still looks out over the Grand Harbour, just as it did in 1941.

Island Tongues

There are lines of Irish and Maltese in the story. Both languages look odd if you don't know them, but their alphabets are more regular than English. If you read aloud, this may help. Irish looks like it has too many vowels. Some are there to show how to pronounce adjacent consonants. So, *scoil*, 'school', is like the first part of 'scholar'. If you see *i* following another vowel, for simplicity here, ignore it. Beyond that, pronounce *sh* and *th* as 'h'; *ch* as in Scottish 'loch'; *bh* as 'v'; *c* as 'k'; *ao* as 'ai' in 'wait'. Maltese is a form of Arabic that was transformed and reimagined by absorbing mostly Italian and later English words. The letter *h* is silent; the unique, barred *ħ* is pronounced 'h'. The *q* is a glottal stop, as when we say 'be'er' for 'better'. The airfield at *Luqa* is 'Lu'a', though the British said what they saw: 'Looka'! The word for 'street', *triq*, has no final consonant to English ears; it's 'tri'. For the rest, at its simplest, pronounce *j* is 'y'; *x* as 'sh'; *z* as the 'ts' in 'sports'; *ż* as English 'z'; *għ* is silent at the beginning of a word and also between vowels in the middle of a word. All oversimplified but close enough!

Acknowledgements

Many books, over many years, have contributed to these stories, most of them forgotten. But here I must mention three. Micheál Mac Liammóir's not entirely reliable memoir, *All for Hecuba*; Matt Houlbrook's *Queer London*; Kate O'Malley's *Ireland, India and Empire*. There are many histories of Malta during the Second World War, some focusing on military aspects, others on civilian life. I have only scraped the surface of that story. The best all-round account is James Holland's *Fortress Malta*. I am also grateful to the *Times of Malta*. Its archive pages contain a poignant mix of war's devastation and the ordinary life that went on despite that. Only in those pages could I find that the British Army was giving prizes to soldiers who took an examination in Colloquial Maltese!

Two films should be mentioned. Without *Victim* (1961), the tale of a homosexual blackmail scam in London, I would not have arrived at my story. Several scenes are set in the Salisbury in St Martin's Lane, where a character is played by Micheál Mac Liammóir's partner, Hilton Edwards. Astonishingly, *Victim* contains the first use of the word 'homosexual' in English-speaking cinema. The 1953 film *Malta Story* was close enough to real events to echo their atmosphere. The Lascaris War Rooms sequence is a brief nod to the film.